THE ILLINOIS CONSTITUTION:

AN ANNOTATED and COMPARATIVE ANALYSIS

THE ILLINOIS CONSTITUTION:
AN ANNOTATED and COMPARATIVE ANALYSIS

by George D. Braden
and Rubin G. Cohn

Prepared for ILLINOIS CONSTITUTION STUDY COMMISSION

Thomas G. Lyons, *Chairman*
Terrel E. Clarke, *Co-Chairman*

INSTITUTE OF GOVERNMENT AND PUBLIC AFFAIRS
UNIVERSITY OF ILLINOIS · URBANA

October, 1969

*"What Illinois thinks today the Union
will think tomorrow."*

From an editorial in the London Times,
January 13, 1870, quoted by Delegate
Joseph Medill in the 1870 Constitutional
Convention. (Debates, p. 564.)

STATE OF ILLINOIS

CONSTITUTION STUDY COMMISSION

160 North LaSalle Street
Room 1315
Chicago, Illinois 60601

CHAIRMAN

Thomas G. Lyons
38 South Dearborn Street
Chicago 60603

CO-CHAIRMAN

Terrel E. Clarke
4070 Central Avenue
Western Springs 60558

SECRETARY

Louis Ancel
111 West Washington Street
Chicago 60602

ASSISTANT SECRETARY

Robert G. Day
2601 North Kingston Drive
Peoria 61604

MEMBERS

From the Senate

W. Russell Arrington
Albert E. Bennett
Terrel E. Clarke
Robert Coulson
Alan J. Dixon
James H. Donnewald
Robert J. McCarthy
Cecil A. Partee

From the House

William K. Cavanagh
Eugenia S. Chapman
Robert G. Day
Gene L. Hoffman
James G. Krause
Daniel M. Pierce
Jack E. Walker
Edward A. Warman

Appointed by the Governor

Louis Ancel
David Davis
Jordan Jay Hillman
Alice Ihrig
Thomas G. Lyons
Dawn Clark Netsch
James T. Otis
Elbert S. Smith
William D. Stiehl
Samuel W. Witwer

Staff

Institute of Government
and Public Affairs,
University of Illinois
Samuel K. Gove, Director

Executive Secretary

Mrs. Helen Dennis

September 1969

To the Members
   Illinois Constitutional Convention

   The Illinois Constitution Study Commission was created by
the General Assembly to undertake preparatory work to expedite
the operation and organization of the Illinois Constitutional
Convention.

   One project that the Commission decided to undertake through
its contract with the Institute of Government and Public Affairs
of the University of Illinois, Urbana, was an annotation of the
Illinois Constitution of 1870, somewhat similar to that prepared
for the 1920 Constitutional Convention. The Institute, with
the concurrence of the Commission, engaged George D. Braden of
the New York Bar, and Professor Rubin G. Cohn of the University
of Illinois College of Law, to undertake the project. The
General Electric Company graciously granted Mr. Braden a leave
of absence from his position in New York City. Based on the
experiences in other states, the project was broadened to include
comparative material on constitutions of other states.

   We feel that this impressive and comprehensive manuscript
will be of invaluable help to the members of the Convention.
It should answer most of the questions of the members as they
proceed with their work of preparing a draft of a constitution
for submission to the voters.

   Although this was a Commission project, the two authors take
responsibility for the manuscript. In the Preface, they discuss
the division of responsibility between themselves.

   The Commission is proud to make THE ILLINOIS CONSTITUTION:
AN ANNOTATED AND COMPARATIVE ANALYSIS available to the Convention
members.

                              Thomas G. Lyons, Chairman

                              Terrel E. Clarke, Co-Chairman

PREFACE

The Illinois Constitution: An Annotated and Comparative Analysis, has been prepared to assist the members of the 1969-70 Illinois Constitutional Convention in their most difficult task of drafting a Constitution to be submitted to the voters of Illinois. During the course of the Convention, the members will require a great deal of historical, legal, and comparative information about the present Constitution. The purpose of this volume is to present as much of this information as possible in a readily usable format.

Our approach has been to provide an analysis of each section of the 1870 Constitution. Thus, for each section, there is a history of its development through past Illinois Constitutions; an explanation of its meaning, relying, in particular, on judicial interpretations; a comparison with similar provisions in the constitutions of other states; and, lastly, such comment as each of us has considered appropriate. We sincerely hope that these section analyses will constitute a definitive reference work for the Convention members and research staff.

An annotated Constitution was prepared for the 1920 Illinois Constitutional Convention by the Illinois Legislative Reference Bureau. It was primarily a summary analysis and digest of the decisions interpreting the constitutional provisions. This volume, in contrast, concentrates upon the primary decisions which define the essence of the provisions under analysis. Thus, although it updates the 1920 Annotation, its format and substance give stronger emphasis to the synthesis and understanding of basic principles.

In the process of preparing this work, we reviewed the pertinent literature, and relied heavily on appropriate legal documents and state and federal court decisions. Considerable attention was also given to the published debates and journals of earlier Constitutional Conventions. The principal basis for the comparative analysis was the *Index Digest of State Constitutions* and the *Constitutions of the United States, National and State*, both published by the Legislative Drafting Research Fund of Columbia University. The *Model State Constitution* and other documents by the National Municipal League as part of its State Constitutional Studies Project were valuable research tools.

Since this analysis is keyed to the several sections and articles of the 1870 Constitution as amended, some topics freqently found in other state constitutions either are not discussed or are referred to relatively briefly in an appropriate *Comparative Analysis* or *Comment*. Topics not mentioned at all, such as primary elections and civil service, most students of state constitutions would agree, are not essential constitutional material. Illinois, of course, has its share of nonessential material, such as Article XIII on warehouses, and just as we suggest the desirability of abandoning such material, so we suggest not adding nonessentials that other states, for one reason or another, have adopted.

Abbreviations Used

In order to provide a document that could be readily used by laymen, the normal footnoting of legal and other publications has been omitted. Instead, citations appear in parentheses. Many works thus cited are referred to by abbreviations, as follows:

P.N.C. — State of Illinois, *The Proposed New Constitution of Illinois* (1922).

C.A.M.C. — Citizens Research Council of Michigan, *A Comparative Analysis of the Michigan Constitution* (1961).

I.S.L. — Illinois Commission on the Organization of the General Assembly, *Improving the State Legislature* (1967).

Index — Legislative Drafting Research Fund of Columbia Univ., *Index Digest of State Constitutions* (2d ed. 1959).

Bulletins — Legislative Reference Bureau, *Constitutional Convention Bulletins* (1920).

Annotations — Legislative Reference Bureau, *Constitution of the State of Illinois, Annotated* (1919).

Model State Constitution — National Municipal League, *Model State Constitution* (6th ed. rev. 1968).

Debates — State of Illinois, *Debates and Proceedings of the Constitutional Convention* (1870).

Journal — State of Illinois, *Journal of the Constitutional Convention 1920-1922* (1922).

Proceedings — State of Illinois, *Proceedings of the Constitutional Convention* (1922).

Division of Responsibility

Early in the study, we made this a "joint and several" enterprise. For purposes of research and writing, the Constitution was parceled out article by article, and in a few instances, section by section. Drafts were exchanged for comment and criticism, and each of us takes this occasion to express deep appreciation to the other for such comment and criticism, but in the end, ultimate responsibility for the final product is as follows:

Mr. Braden: Articles I, III, IV, V, VII, and X through XIV in toto; Sections 15, 16, and 20 of Article II; Sections 4 and 5 of Article VIII; Sections 7, 11, and 13 of Article IX; and the Separate Section on Convict Labor.

Mr. Cohn: Article VI in toto; Article II, except for Sections 15, 16, and 20; Article VIII, except for Sections 4 and 5; Article IX, except for Sections 7, 11, and 13; and Separate Sections, except for the Section on Convict Labor.

We included the 1870 Schedule and the Schedules to the 1954 and 1962 Amendments. Schedules are transitional provisions which, if the drafters stick to the rules, soon become obsolete. We would observe that constitution-drafters have a tendency to overwrite a schedule. For example, Sections 1, 2, 3, 5 and 6, and possibly Section 4, of the Schedule to the 1870 Constitution could have been compressed into one short section. It also seems fair to suggest that the extensive details on the procedure for adoption as set forth in Sections 8 through 12 of the 1870 Schedule are not necessary. Notwithstanding the theoretical status of a constitutional convention as a body creating an entirely new government, it seems permissible to rely on all existing laws for purposes of the referendum on adoption. All that a convention has to do is explain what to vote on and when to vote.

The headings of sections used in this volume generally follow those used by the Secretary of State in his publication of the Constitution. In many cases these have been inserted for editorial convenience and are not part of the Constitution. In a few instances the headings have been modified in this volume for the sake of uniformity.

Acknowledgements

As in any study of this magnitude, many persons helped at various stages of its preparation and we should like to acknowledge this assistance. At the outset, we should like to thank the Constitution Study Commission, and its chairman, Thomas G. Lyons, and co-chairman, Senator Terrel E. Clarke, for making the project possible. The commission assisted us in ways too numerous to mention.

Professor Cohn acknowledges the invaluable contributions of Mrs. Susan Wolff. Mrs. Wolff, a member of the Indiana Bar, prepared Sections 1, 2 and 3 of Article VIII; all of

Article IX except Sections 7, 11, and 13; and the Separate Sections on Canals, Municipal Subscriptions, and the Illinois Central Railroad. Her drafts were critiqued, edited and approved by Professor Cohn, but the major credit for their preparation belongs to Mrs. Wolff.

Professor Cohn also acknowledges the fine assistance he had from Mr. Barry R. Miller in the closing phases of the project. Mr. Miller, a senior in the University of Illinois College of Law, provided general research assistance including the indexing of the material. Glenn F. Seidenfeld, then a senior in the College of Law, assisted Professor Cohn in the early stages of the project.

Professor Cohn especially wishes to express his appreciation to Mrs. Rosemary Tucker, of the secretarial staff of the University of Illinois College of Law, whose typing skill miraculously deciphered reams of his undecipherable handwriting.

Mr. Braden acknowledges the assistance of Mr. Robert G. Granda, of the Illinois Legislative Council, who provided valuable historical material concerning the Governor's veto power; the valuable criticism of Mr. William J. D. Boyd, of the National Municipal League, who reviewed the manuscript on Sections 6, 7 and 8 of Article IV; and the most helpful critical review of the manuscript of Article X by Professor Clyde Snider of the University of Illinois.

Mr. Braden wishes particularly to acknowledge the assistance of his secretarial assistant, Mary Jane Van Voast, who performed excellent clerical support.

Together, we wish especially to recognize the assistance of the staff of the Institute of Government and Public Affairs of the University of Illinois. The Institute, the publisher of this volume, through its director, Professor Samuel K. Gove, alternated between wielding a whip to spur us on and holding our hands through difficult periods —

figuratively speaking, that is — in order to bring this study to completion. In particular, we wish to acknowledge the assistance of Assistant Professor Joseph P. Pisciotte and the Institute secretarial staff. We are most grateful to Mr. Anthony Edelblut of the RCS Press for his able technical assistance and for the constant attention he paid to the many details involved in printing a volume of this nature. Ronald Day of the University of Illinois Press rendered valuable technical advice in preparing the manuscript for publication. Mrs. Virginia Speers provided excellent editorial assistance in the concluding work on this project.

In conclusion, we again hope that this volume provides considerable assistance to the members of the 1969 Constitutional Convention. If so, our efforts will be well rewarded.

GEORGE D. BRADEN
RUBIN G. COHN

BIOGRAPHICAL DATA

George D. Braden, a graduate of Swarthmore College and the Yale Law School, was a law clerk for Justice Sherman Minton when he was a judge in the Seventh Circuit and for Judge Charles E. Clark of the United States Court of Appeals for the Second Circuit. After military service, he taught Constitutional Law at the Yale Law School. In 1949-50, he served as Project Director on the Constitution for the Commission on Government Organization of the State of Connecticut. Following a period of private law practice, he joined the General Electric Company. In 1967, on leave from General Electric, he served as Executive Director of the Committee on the Legislature of the New York Constitutional Convention. He is the author of numerous articles on constitutional law, the most significant of which is "The Search for Objectivity in Constitutional Law," 57 Yale Law Journal 571 (1948).

Rubin G. Cohn received both his undergraduate and law degrees from the University of Illinois. From 1935 through 1944, he was employed as a legislative draftsman in the Illinois Legislative Reference Bureau. From January, 1945, until September, 1949, when he joined the faculty of the University of Illinois College of Law, he practiced law in Chicago. Professor Cohn was one of the principal draftsmen of Illinois' new Constitutional Judicial Article. He has served as legislative consultant and draftsman for agencies of state and local governments in Illinois. Professor Cohn's major teaching areas are Legislation and Administrative Law. He has written on Home Rule for Municipal Government, Constitutional Limitations on Taxing in Illinois, The Legislative Process in Illinois, and The Rights of Employees under Public Retirement Systems, as well as other subjects. He has also served, and continues to do so, on a number of state and professional commissions and committees concerned with state and local governmental problems.

TABLE OF CONTENTS

TABLE OF CONTENTS (Continued)

TABLE OF CONTENTS (Continued)

Constitution of the State of Illinois

PREAMBLE

We, the people of the State of Illinois — grateful to Almighty God for the civil, political and religious liberty which He hath so long permitted us to enjoy, and looking to Him for a blessing upon our endeavors to secure and transmit the same unimpaired to succeeding generations — in order to form a more perfect government, establish justice, insure domestic tranquility, provide for the common defense, promote the general welfare, and secure the blessings of liberty to ourselves and our posterity; do ordain and establish this Constitution for the State of Illinois.

History

The Constitution of 1818 contained an untitled introductory paragraph which was essentially a combination of a preamble and a statement of boundaries. The preamble section of the paragraph stated that the "People of the Illinois Territory," through their convention representatives, agreed to form the State of Illinois pursuant to relevant sections in the United States Constitution, the Ordinance of 1787 and the Congressional Enabling Act which authorized such action. Many of the phrases found in the Preamble to the U.S. Constitution ("in Order . . . to establish Justice, . . . promote the general Welfare") were included in this introductory paragraph.

The Constitution of 1848 was the first Illinois Constitution to contain a separate paragraph specifically entitled "Preamble." Unlike the 1818 Constitution, the 1848 Preamble makes explicit reference to God; then it follows with practically the same language as the U.S. Constitution's preamble.

The Preamble in the 1870 Constitution, with a few minor changes in punctuation and spelling, is exactly the same as the 1848 Preamble.

The Preamble in the proposed 1922 Constitution made no significant changes although there were some alterations in wording and punctuation.

Comment

Preambles are now a common feature of written constitutions. All states but two have preambles to their constitutions and most of them follow the general form and wording of the Preamble to the U.S. Constitution. Generally, a preamble is intended to be a broad statement of purpose of the document which follows, and can be a guide to the intention of the constituent assembly which drew up the document. Preambles have never evoked much political controversy and, strictly speaking, are not operative parts of a constitution.

1

Article I

BOUNDARIES

The boundaries and jurisdiction of the State shall be as follows, to-wit: Beginning at the mouth of the Wabash river; thence up the same, and with the line of Indiana, to the northwest corner of said State; thence east, with the line of the same State, to the middle of Lake Michigan; thence north along the middle of said lake, to north latitude forty-two degrees and thirty minutes; thence west to the middle of the Mississippi river, and thence down along the middle of that river to its confluence with the Ohio river, and thence up the latter river, along its northwestern shore, to the place of beginning: *Provided,* that this State shall exercise such jurisdiction upon the Ohio river, as she is now entitled to, or such as may hereafter be agreed upon by this State and the State of Kentucky.

History

The Congressional Enabling Act of April 18, 1818, authorized the "inhabitants of the territory of Illinois . . . to form for themselves a constitution and state government, and to assume such name at they deem proper." (ch. 67, 3 Stat. 428.) The Enabling Act set forth the boundaries of the new state and required the first Constitutional Convention to accept them. The 1818 Convention did this by setting forth and ratifying the boundaries in the Preamble. The 1848 Constitution put the boundaries in a separate Article, added the words "and jurisdiction" at the beginning and added the proviso concerning the Ohio River. The 1870 Convention made no changes. The proposed 1922 Constitution omitted Article I, presumably as a result of the essay by Urban A. Lavery discussed below.

Explanation

Mr. Lavery was the Chief Legislative Draftsman for the 1920-22 Convention. Before the Convention completed its work he wrote an essay (Lavery, "The Boundaries Article of the Illinois Constitution," 16 Ill. L. Rev. 361 (1922)) in which he pointed out that the northern boundary between Illinois and Wisconsin was first officially surveyed between October, 1831, and January, 1833, and that the survey was inaccurate. "In summary it may be said . . . that the line begins on the west about three-quarters of a mile too far north in Wisconsin, and finally comes

3

out on Lake Michigan about the same distance too far south in Illinois." (*Id.* at 365.) In other words, the present line recognized by Illinois and Wisconsin is not in fact "north latitude forty-two degrees and thirty minutes." (There is also a surveyed boundary between Indiana and Illinois north from the point where the Wabash River ceases to be the boundary, but no question appears to have arisen about it.)

In the same article, Lavery pointed out that "and jurisdiction" was added in 1848, and that this turns out to be erroneous. For example, in 1904 in the case of *Wedding v. Meyler* (192 U.S. 573 (1904)), the United States Supreme Court said that Illinois and Kentucky have concurrent jurisdiction over the Ohio River notwithstanding the language of the Enabling Act which placed all of the Ohio River in Kentucky. Lavery also pointed out that in all other cases of a river boundary — with Indiana, Iowa and Missouri — the applicable Act of Congress provided for concurrent jurisdiction over the river. (Lavery, *supra* at 368.)

In *Jewell v. Carpentier* (22 Ill. 2d 445 (1961)), an ingenious argument was offered to the effect that because Article I defined the "boundaries and jurisdiction" of the state, an Illinois driver's license could not be suspended on the basis of an accident occurring in Indiana. The Supreme Court gave the argument short shrift. In fact, the argument could have been made equally well in the absence of the word "jurisdiction" in Article I and equally well in the absence of a Boundaries Article. The problem in the case was whether Illinois could exercise jurisdiction *inside* its own boundaries in the manner in which it acted.

Comparative Analysis

Slightly more than half of the state constitutions contain definitions or descriptions of their territory. Neither the Constitution of the United States nor those of any of the original 13 colonies contains a boundary description or definition.

Comment

In view of the fact that the description of the northern boundary is not the boundary long recognized by Illinois and Wisconsin, it would seem advisable to omit the Boundaries Article. It is questionable in any event whether the Article serves any *constitutional* purpose. Any boundary dispute would involve another state and any resolution of the dispute would have to be by agreement of the states, ratified by Congress, or by litigation. In any such litigation, the controlling documents would be Congressional Enabling Acts and other external sources, not the Illinois Constitution. In the case of the boundary with Wisconsin, the United States Supreme Court would undoubtedly accept the actual boundary as recognized for almost 140 years.

Article II

BILL OF RIGHTS

Introductory and Preliminary Comment

A bill of rights in state constitution, as in the United States Constitution, seeks to define rights and liberties so fundamental to a free society as to remain invulnerable or only partly subject to governmental authority. Mindful of a history of governmental tyranny, unchecked by enforceable restraints, which had trampled rights of conscience, religion, speech, and assembly, and which had denied procedural fairness, primarily to persons accused of crime, the framers of state constitutions deliberately sought to assure a political structure in which governmental power to impair or prejudice these rights would be minimal or nonexistent. The bill of rights is such an effort.

It is an historical fact that ratification of the Federal Constitution by the states was conditioned upon an early submission to and ratification by the states of amendments establishing limitations upon the powers of the newly created national government. These limitations, constituting the first ten amendments to the Federal Constitution, and popularly known as the Bill of Rights, were ratified in 1791, when Virginia became the eleventh state to approve them. In many respects they parallel, sometimes almost in verbatim form, the bill of rights provisions of the several states, a not-surprising fact as some of the states, before the adoption of the Federal Constitution, had adopted their own constitutions and formulated their own bills of rights.

It is of course the accepted generality that the federal Bill of Rights operates as a limitation upon the powers of the federal government and not upon the powers of state government, whereas state bills of rights operate as limitations only upon the powers of state government. This generality, firm and true through most of our constitutional history, has been severely modified by United States Supreme Court decisional law, mostly within the past two decades, which holds that many provisions of the federal Bill of Rights operate as limitations upon the power of state governments as a consequence of their "incorporation" into the due process clause of the Fourteenth Amendment of the Constitution of the United States which expressly prohibits states from enacting laws which deprive any person of life, liberty or property without due process of law. The consequences of this rule of incorporation, without regard to the merits of the constitutional controversies it has provoked, have been momentous.

Action in areas within a state's bill of rights which is held by the state court to be permissible exercises of governmental power may now be invalidated as a violation of the comparable provision in the federal Bill of Rights as incorporated into the Fourteenth Amendment. A ready example is the upholding by the Illinois Supreme Court of the so-called "released time" religious instruction in the public schools against a challenge that it violated the religious freedom guarantees of Article II, Section 3, of the Illinois Constitution and the reversal of this decision by the United States Supreme Court (People *ex rel.* McCollum v. Board of Educ., 396 Ill. 14 (1947), *rev'd* 333 U.S. 203 (1948)) on the ground that it violated the "establishment" clause of the First Amendment of the Constitution of the United States as that clause was now incorporated into the Fourteenth Amendment. The normal effect of the incorporation doctrine, where relevant, is to expand the protective scope of the right or liberty alleged to be infringed by making applicable to the states through the Fourteenth Amendment the frequently greater limitations upon the exercise of federal governmental power encompassed within the federal Bill of Rights. A measure of this effect can be gathered by recalling recent federal decisions involving state criminal prosecutions, including noteworthy decisions dealing with right to counsel, limitations upon powers of arrest, the use of confessions, right to speedy arraignment after arrest, and the application of procedural due process requirements to juvenile court proceedings.

On the other side of the coin is the principle that a state court holding which invalidates governmental action because of a violation of a state bill of rights provision takes precedence over a United States Supreme Court decision that the state action does not violate the due process guarantee of the Fourteenth Amendment. Again, illustratively, the United States Supreme Court sustained a state statute (in fact, in this case, a state constitutional provision) against a Fourteenth Amendment due process challenge which revived a cause of action which had been barred by the running of the statute of limitations. (Chase Sec. Corp. v. Donaldson, 325 U.S. 304 (1945); Campbell v. Holt, 115 U.S. 620 (1885).) The essence of the holding was that a right to a defense arising from the bar of a statute of limitations was not "property" within the meaning of the Fourteenth Amendment. Illinois, however, in *Board of Education v. Blodgett* (155 Ill. 441 (1895)), held that a revival of a barred cause of action did indeed deprive a defendant of property without due process of law in violation of Article II, Section 2, of the Constitution of Illinois. The Illinois decision prevails, since the United States Supreme Court will not normally substitute its judgment for that of the highest state appellate court on issues of interpretation of state constitutional provisions where the effect of the decision is to impose a limitation on the power of state government.

The question may properly be asked whether there is any purpose in retaining provisions in a state bill of rights which have been "pre-empted" by the incorporation doctrine so as to become federally prescribed limitations upon the exercise of state power. The most persuasive case, it is submitted, favors retention in the constitution of the state. Part of the rationale for this conclusion has been developed in the above discussion of the primacy of state court interpretations of state constitutional limitations. Of course, where the incorporation doctrine prevails, state provisions must yield and cannot be given precedence even by state constitutional amendments which offend the federal standards. The customary invalidation of state action, however, involves a state provision which is not, on its face, violative of federal standards but which has been interpreted by the state court in a way which offends the federally protected right. Here the retention of the provision is desirable, not only for the reason already noted, but also because there is nothing immutable about judicial interpretations of the Federal Constitution. The "incorporation" doctrine itself may conceivably be modified or abandoned in all or particular existing applications by judicial re-evaluation. If this occurs, the parallel state provisions take on new vitality. It would appear, therefore, to be the course of good judgment not to discard existing state constitutional guarantees simply because the incorporation doctrine bears heavily upon their meaning and application.

A final preliminary observation is in order. Several of the provisions in the Illinois bill of rights, notably but not exclusively the due process provision in Section 2, have been the subject of "massive" judicial analysis. It would be a futile if not impossible task to analyze all or most of these decisions, nor does such a course of action seem desirable for the purposes of this document. Some of the principles are models of legal abstractions and conceptual generalities which simply defy incisive analysis or definition. "Due process," for example, comprehends a myriad of concepts and subconcepts, pregnant with ambiguity, and extremely difficult of consistent definition and application. The decisions, many of which are not susceptible to rational reconciliation, reflect the accuracy of this assessment. Accordingly, the legal analysis of this Article, perhaps to a degree greater than those of other Articles, will seek to distill the essence of the judicial interpretations, and will deal only with such cases as contribute importantly to an understanding of that essence. Federal decisions arising out of the "incorporation" doctrine will be noted because of their impact upon and relevance to the particular provision under consideration.

Inherent and Inalienable Rights

Sec. 1. All men are by nature free and independent, and have certain inherent and inalienable rights — among these are life, liberty and the pursuit of happiness. To secure these rights and the protection of property, governments are instituted among men, deriving their just powers from the consent of the governed.

History

The 1818 and 1848 Constitutions contained identical provisions to the effect that the great and essential principles of liberty and free government require the recognition and unalterable establishment of the principles that all men are born equally free and independent, and have certain inherent and indefeasible rights, among which are the enjoyment and defense of life and liberty, and of acquiring, possessing and protecting property and reputation, and of pursuing their own happiness; that all power is inherent in the people, and that all free governments are founded on the authority of the people and instituted for their peace, safety and happiness.

The 1922 Convention proposal adopted the 1870 provisions, incorporating, however, the provisions of Section 20 of Article II. (See *History,* Sec. 20, *infra,* p. 97.)

Explanation

The section, a substantially abridged version of the 1818 and 1848 declarations, is an almost verbatim statement of the fundamental principles contained in the second paragraph of the Declaration of Independence. It is not generally considered, of itself, an operative constitutional limitation upon the exercise of governmental powers. Rather, it is considered supplemental to and implicitly within the guarantees of Section 2 which preclude the state from depriving persons of life, liberty and property without due process of law. There is thus little purpose in treating this section as an independent source of constitutional law. Instead the *Explanation* under Section 2 will deal with the relevant concepts under the due process principle.

Comparative Analysis

Approximately three-fifths of the state constitutions contain provisions to the effect that all men are equal, free and independent. Approximately four-fifths of the state constitutions similarly provide that all men have inalienable rights to life, liberty and the pursuit of happiness. All of the state constitutions provide in some form that government derives its just powers from the consent of the governed. The Model State Constitution contains no similar provision. (National Municipal League, Model State Constitution (6th ed. rev. 1968) [hereinafter cited as Model State Constitution].)

Comment

Although the section expresses values of an essentially political nature and of itself has little or no operative legal effect, it comes from constitutional ancestry of unimpeachable and impeccable credentials. It is not easy to suggest that fundamental conceptions expressed in the Declaration of Independence are expendable in the reshaping of constitutional charters. Nor is it necessary to do so. Constitutional tradition justifies the expression of the basic values of a free society as a preface to the more detailed provisions which follow.

It is true that there is considerable argument over the value of provisions like this section and Section 20. (*Infra,* p. 97.) On the one hand, some will argue that the statements are pieties that are not specific enough for courts to use in protecting the rights of the people. On the other hand, some argue that the basic American theory of limited government includes, in addition to the explicit limitations set forth in a bill of rights, a sort of residual limitation that implicitly reserves to the people fundamental rights of freedom not otherwise spelled out. It does not seem necessary to try to resolve this argument. For one thing, both Section 1 and Section 20, as noted, express sentiments that are acceptable to all. Moreover, under our system of judicial review, courts will strike down legislation or administrative action that they believe contrary to fundamental rights, and they will do so in the name of some constitutional provision. Removal of Sections 1 and 20 would not decrease the power of the courts. In sum, this section (and Section 20) may be of value and are certainly not harmful in any respect.

Due Process of Law

Sec. 2. No person shall be deprived of life, liberty or property, without due process of law.

History

The 1818 and 1848 Constitutions contained the historic Magna Charta declaration that "no freeman shall be . . . deprived of his life, liberty, or property, but by the judgment of his peers, or the law of the land." The present provision retains the essence of this principle but substitutes "due process of law" for the last clause.

The 1920 Convention proposal retained the 1870 provision without change. An effort to add clauses in form precisely the same as the privileges and immunities and equal protection clauses of the Fourteenth Amendment of the Constitution of the United States was unsuccessful, presumably because the Fourteenth Amendment secured those precise guarantees to the people of this state.

Explanation

In the *Introductory and Preliminary Comment* on this Article the point was made that due process as a legal concept cannot be defined in incisive and precise terms and that an analysis of the legion of decisions interpreting this fundamental guarantee would be impossible and indeed unnecessary. The breadth of this historic limitation upon governmental power is vast, encompassing almost unlimited areas of governmental impact upon individual (or corporate) rights and privileges.

At the outset, it might be instructive to note that the due process guarantee is not and was not intended to insulate individuals from all forms of governmental action which interfered with or deprived them of their lives, liberty or property. This proposition is, of course, elementary. In a society governed by the rule of law, a society in which governments are the servants and not the masters of men, deriving "their just powers from the consent of the governed," the inherent, inalienable and fundamental rights of individuals must of necessity yield to the paramount interest of society. This notion is obviously implicit in the due process clause. If we recast its language as a grant rather than a limitation of power, it would read "a person may be deprived of his life, liberty or property, but only through the application of due process of law."

The import of this principle, thus phrased, may produce an initial psychological shock, but its truth should be obvious with but a little reflection. The state can and does constitutionally deprive a person of his life if he commits a capital offense, and his liberty, through imprisonment, if he is convicted of a criminal offense. The whole criminal code of the state, and the hundreds of additional statutes which provide sanctions of imprisonment for violation, involves the state precisely in depriving a person of his life or liberty.

The same principle justifies denying to a person the right to use his property as he desires. If Jones wants to build a rendering plant in an area zoned for residential use, he cannot do so. If he maintains his property in a way which creates a nuisance or a threat to public health or safety, the state may compel him to abate the nuisance at a considerable cost to him. The state may condemn one's property for highway or other legitimate governmental purposes. In a host of other ways, the state may legitimately qualify or circumscribe a person's asserted right to own, possess and use his property in accordance with his exclusive aspirations.

Other illustrations readily suggest themselves. One cannot practice medicine or any phase of the healing arts, or engage in business as a plumber, banker, funeral director, common carrier, real estate broker, agent or salesman, and a host of other business activities, without securing a license based on demonstrated competence, frequently conditioned upon successful completion of a prescribed educational curriculum. The state may deny a license, or having granted it, may suspend or revoke it for violation of the regulatory statute, or the rules adopted pursuant thereto. These are extraordinary powers which control or limit one's property or liberty, and the existence of this power is conceded if there is a public interest, paramount to the individual "right," which demands or justifies the exercise of such power, and if such exercise conforms to due process standards. Commonly the power of the state so to act is defined as "police power," a designation which currently may carry other connotations, but which in the traditional context of the due process clause means that none of the rights constitutionally guaranteed to the people may be exercised without regard to the rights of others, and that when it is necessary to protect an important societal interest — e.g., public health, safety, morals or the catchall, common welfare — the rights of individuals must yield to the paramount public interest.

Yet in all of this the critical limitation, due process of law is of the essence, and no exercise of governmental power, admittedly within its competence as an abstraction, will be countenanced if it denies due process to the person affected. In this connection, it is important to note that due process of law was originally conceived of as a procedural guarantee only; that is, before property or liberty or life was taken or impaired, certain procedural steps deemed fundamental as a matter of fair play, and essential as a check upon unfettered, or irresponsible or arbitrary, governmental action, had to be afforded. These procedural requirements normally included notice and right to a fair hearing before an impartial tribunal. The character of the notice and hearing may vary with the nature of the proceeding, e.g., criminal, civil or administrative, but the essential requirement of compliance with due process applies to all agencies and instrumentalities exercising governmental power, whether they be within the legislative, judicial or executive departments of government.

The limited procedural concept of due process gave way, however, to the principle that due process operates as a limitation on the power of government, primarily but not exclusively the legislature, to enact laws which were deemed substantively, and not as a matter of procedure, to be oppressive, arbitrary or unreasonable. It is in this aspect of due process that the awesome power of judicial review, the power of a court to declare an act of the legislature unconstitutional, has had the greatest impact in limiting or prohibiting incursions upon individual rights. For a number of years many state courts, acting perhaps more out of a sense of power than responsibility, declared state enactments to be substantively beyond the legislative power and thus a violation of due process. In more recent times, the courts have become sensitive to the necessity of permitting legislative judgment a greater latitude in meeting the problems besetting society. This attitude, coupled with a keener perception that judicial restraint is essential to the preservation of a proper balance of governmental power, has led to a substantial decrease in the number of laws held unconstitutional by due process standards. This is especially true in matters of economic regulation, and in the licensing of trades, professions and other activities. The protection of "property" against deprivation without due process has become a much less significant concept than in the past. Liberty, however, seems to remain a top-level priority under due process, especially in the administration and enforcement of criminal laws.

As a final general observation, it is not unusual for a court to declare an infringement of a specific constitutional procedural right, such as the right of trial by jury, a violation also of the state's due process guarantee. Frequently the decisions do not designate with the clarity one expects in judicial analysis the particular constitutional grounds relied upon to invalidate a statute. On occasion, more than one constitutional limitation on governmental power may rationally be applied to a judgment of invalidity. In these cases it is not unusual for the court to apply rather indiscriminately the due process clause as the rationale of decision. It is a favorite catchall because its flexibility, ambiguity and adaptability permit a reasonable exercise of judicial discretion.

This analysis thus far has dealt with general principles or so-called "black letter" law. The difficulty with this kind of law is that it is of minimum instructional value. Law unrelated to facts is frequently barren and meaningless. Thus to put some substance into the due process clause, brief reference will now be made to some laws or governmental action which have been declared invalid as a violation of the due process clause by the Illinois supreme and appellate courts. These cases are selected only because they highlight the exceptions to an otherwise general pattern of upholding of laws, and thus, hopefully, provide a sharper insight into the limits of governmental power under the due process clause. No particular pattern of subject matter, or of procedural or substantive issues, is employed in these cases. They are simply illustrative of the principle.

Cox v. Cox (400 Ill. 291 (1948)) invalidated a law which authorized

the confiscation and summary destruction of fish nets not being used for an illegal purpose at the time of confiscation. The inherent lawful nature of the property, unlike "contraband" or other basically dangerous articles, unquestionably swayed the Court against a power summarily to destroy.

In *People v. Weiner* (271 Ill. 74 (1915)), a statute prohibiting the sale of secondhand mattresses was held to be unreasonable, since whatever health hazards they possessed could be removed by sterilization. The state's options of regulation or prohibition will sometimes be assessed in terms of reasonableness.

People v. Doe (334 Ill. 555 (1922)) held invalid a law which in effect required cemeteries to use headstones furnished free by the United States Government, because it unreasonably deprived cemeteries of their right to use their own property as they saw fit. The law had no discernible relation to public welfare, health, safety or morals.

In *City of Chicago v. Drake Hotel Company* (274 Ill. 408 (1916)), an ordinance prohibiting public dancing in restaurants was held invalid as sweeping too broadly in the public morality arena.

In *Figura v. Cummins* (4 Ill. 2d 44 (1954)), the trade of processing metal springs by homeworkers was held not a proper subject for the exercise of the police power absent a showing that such trade endangered the public health, safety, morals or welfare.

In *Marr v. Marr* (43 Ill. App. 2d 25 (1963)), an action by a wife for divorce, defended by the husband on grounds of desertion and adultery, the Court's refusal to permit testimony by children of the marriage, and by a witness who allegedly was living with the wife, was held to be a denial of due process to the husband. (Note — judicial rather than legislative action).

In *People v. Alterie* (356 Ill. 307 (1934)), an amendment to the Vagrancy Act, which declared as a vagabond any person reputed to be an habitual violator of criminal laws, was held invalid under the due process clause because of vagueness and arbitrariness.

In *People v. Savage* (5 Ill. 2d 296 (1955)), a private investigation by the Court in a criminal case was held to violate the defendant's rights to a public and open trial and was, as well, a denial of due process. (Note—judicial action. Note also combined particular grounds and due process.)

In *People v. Thompson* (36 Ill. 2d 332 (1967)), erroneous instruction to the jury which prejudiced the defendant was held to be a denial of due process. (Note — judicial action.)

In *People v. Love* (39 Ill. 2d 436 (1968)), the denial of right to a speedy trial was also held to be a denial of due process. (Note—two constitutional guarantees.)

In *People v. Brown* (39 Ill. 2d 307 (1968)), it was held that the right of appeal in a criminal case was not per se of constitutional dimension but that a dismissal of an appeal was subject to due process and equal protection guarantees of the federal and state constitutions. In this case the dismissal of an appeal from a conviction for pandering was vacated when the dismissal was the result of the defendant's attorney's failure to prosecute the appeal. The rule that a client is bound by the acts or omissions of his attorney is not to be applied in criminal cases when the attorney's failure to act prejudices the subtantive rights of his client.

In *People v. De Simone* (9 Ill. 2d 522 (1956)), it was held that the right of a defendant in a criminal case to counsel is not satisfied by the formality of appointment of an attorney by the court, since the right embraces effective representation; and where the representation is of such low caliber as to amount to no representation or to reduce the trial to a farce, the defendant has been denied due process. (Note—two guarantees: right to counsel—due process.)

It has been noted that the due process guarantee is applicable to administrative as well as judicial proceedings. However, due process of law has frequently been held not necessarily to mean .judicial proceedings, and an administrative proceeding from which may result sanctions administratively imposed will constitute due process if procedural standards of fairness are met. (*E.g.*, Sheldon v. Hoyne, 261 Ill. 222 (1913).)

The due process clause appears to have received judicial treatment substantially comparable to that in other states. Apart from some federal extensions through the incorporation principle (see *Introductory and Preliminary Comment, supra*, p. 5), the course of judicial interpretation and application seems quite normal and unexceptional.

Comparative Analysis

Twenty-seven state constitutions contain the same provision while four others contain similar provisions. The remaining states provide, as in Section 1 above, that all men have inalienable rights to life, liberty, the pursuit of happiness and property. The Model State Constitution contains the same provision but adds that no person shall be "denied the equal protection of the laws, nor be denied the enjoyment of his civil rights or be discriminated against in the exercise thereof because of race, national origin, religion or ancestry." (art. I, § 1.02.)

Comment

Any suggestion that a new Constitution delete or tamper with this section would in all probability be viewed as subversive. It is too fundamental and too deeply embedded in constitutional and political history

to tamper with. A suggestion deserving of serious consideration, however, is that a provision concerning equal protection of laws could be incorporated into this section. (See *Comment*, Art. IV, Sec. 22, *infra*, p. 225.)

Religious Freedom

Sec. 3. The free exercise and enjoyment of religious profession and worship, without discrimination, shall forever be guaranteed; and no person shall be denied any civil or political right, privilege or capacity, on account of his religious opinions; but the liberty of conscience hereby secured shall not be construed to dispense with oaths or affirmations, excuse acts of licentiousness, or justify practices inconsistent with the peace or safety of the State. No person shall be required to attend or support any ministry or place of worship against his consent, nor shall any preference be given by law to any religious denomination or mode of worship.

History

The 1818 and 1848 Constitutions contained identical provisions on religious freedom. They expressed (1) man's natural and indefeasible right to worship God according to his conscience; (2) a limitation on governmental power to the effect that no person could be compelled to attend, erect or support any place of worship or to maintain any ministry against his consent; (3) a denial that human authority can in any case control or interfere with rights of conscience; (4) a principle that no preference shall be given by law to any religious establishments or modes of worship; and (5) a prohibition against the requirement of a religious test as a qualification to any office or public trust.

The religious test prohibition of the prior Constitutions was dropped in 1870 in favor of the broader provision, "no person shall be denied any civil or political right . . . on account of his religious opinions," which was intended to insure also that "no person shall be incompetent to be a witness, on account of his religious opinions." (State of Illinois, Debates and Proceedings of the Constitutional Convention 1563 (1870) [hereinafter cited as Debates]).

The clause in the present Constitution, "but the liberty of conscience hereby secured shall not be construed to dispense with oaths or affirmations, excuse acts of licentiousness, or justify practices inconsistent with the peace or safety of the State," was added to establish that the broad provision substituted for the religious test provision did not prohibit an oath or affirmation and to insure that certain practices (nude religious ceremonies, child sacrifices, and interruption of the Sabbath were examples given) would not be construed as being within the lawful exercise of religious freedom. An additional restriction against polygamy, directed at the Mormons, was not adopted.

The 1922 Convention proposal carried forward the 1870 provisions, including an amendment, adopted after a floor fight, to the effect that the reading in the public schools of selections from the Old or New Testaments, without comment, should never be held to conflict with the Constitution.

Explanation

The length and detail of the current provisions are in marked contrast to the religious freedom guarantee in the First Amendment of the Constitution of the United States which starkly declares that "Congress shall make no law respecting an establishment of religion, or prohibiting the free exercise thereof...." The simplicity of the federal principle has not, however, added to its clarity. What constitutes an "establishment of religion" or a prohibition on the free exercise thereof, as these limitations are applied to state action through incorporation into the Fourteenth Amendment, have proved to be troublesome questions.

It is not likely that any of the specific limitations of this section go beyond the more general First Amendment's proscription on governmental power. That is, it is almost a legal certainty that a denial of a civil or political right on account of religious opinions would be held an unpermissible infringement under the Fourteenth Amendment if sought to be applied by a state which did not have the specific Illinois limitation. Nor is it likely that the provisions of this section which preserve the state's power to require oaths or affirmations, and which do not, in the name of religious freedom, excuse acts of licentiousness or justify practices inconsistent with the peace or safety of the state, would be held to conflict with First and Fourteenth Amendment limitations on state power. One can hardly suppose that human sacrifice or sexual debauchery would be sanctioned by federal doctrine. Indeed, in *Cleveland v. United States* (329 U.S. 14 (1946)), a criminal conviction of Mormons under the federal Mann Act for transporting plural wives across state lines was sustained by the United States Supreme Court, notwithstanding that polygamy, as pointed out in the minority opinion, was a cultural institution deeply rooted in the religious beliefs of the societies in which it appears. The point is that though the state seems to have spelled out areas of permissible governmental interference with religious practices and rights of conscience which on the surface appear to be proscribed by the categorical First Amendment denial of any legislative power, the kinds of interferences which would be held valid under state law would in all probability be held valid under federal interpretations of the Fourteenth Amendment, and conversely, the kinds of infringements held to be beyond state power under Section 3 would in all probability be held invalid under the Fourteenth Amendment.

In recent years, the most significant decisions respecting religious freedom have concerned laws and practices in the public schools. Since the

Explanation and Analysis of Article VIII, Section 3 (*infra,* pp. 405-8) deal with the relationship between education and religion *in extenso,* involving the same decisional law as is applicable here, no effort will be made to duplicate that discussion.

In areas other than education, some of the state decisional law is instructive but some of it may, under present theory, be deemed questionable. Religious freedom, like all other constitutional liberties and rights, is relative and may have to yield to state action which can be justified as within permissible concepts of police power. In *People* ex rel. *Wallace v. Labrenz* (411 Ill. 618 (1952)), the Illinois Supreme Court held valid a law which interfered with the religious beliefs and practices of parents who sought to prevent blood transfusions believed medically necessary to save their child's life. To be compared with this, however, is In re *Estate of Brooks* (32 Ill. 2d 361 (1965)), a more recent Illinois Supreme Court decision, in which the Court held that the appointment of a conservator for an adult woman, and authorization for him to consent to transfusions for her, without notice to her and her husband who had religious scruples against such transfusions, violated their constitutional rights of religious freedom where they had notified their doctor and hospital of their beliefs and had executed documents releasing the doctor and hospital from civil liability. The *Labrenz* case was distinguished on the grounds that a minor was there involved, whereas in *Estate of Brooks* an adult insisted upon a religious belief under circumstances (no minor children) in which the state's abridgement of her religious beliefs served no legitimate state interest.

Of perhaps questionable validity today is *Reichwald v. Catholic Bishop of Chicago* (258 Ill. 44 (1913)) which held that the building of chapels on county poor farms was not a violation of the prohibition relating to compulsory support of a place of worship.

People ex rel. *Bernat v. Bicek* (405 Ill. 510 (1950)) involved a statutory provision authorizing a judicial officer in divorce proceedings to invite representatives of religious denominations of the contending parties to a conference for the purpose of effecting a reconciliation. This was held to be a denial of religious freedom and due process of law. And in *Hronek v. People* (134 Ill. 139 (1890)) the Court quite predictably held that any civil or political right, privilege or capacity enjoyed by citizens generally could not be denied because of religious belief.

Comparative Analysis

All state constitutions provide substantially similar provisions for free exercise of religion and religious worship. Eight states similarly provide that no preference shall be given by law to any religious denomination and the remaining states provide that the states may neither establish nor support religious denominations. The Model State Constitution adopts the First Amendment formulation that "No law shall be enacted respecting an establishment of religion, or prohibiting the free exercise thereof . . . ." (art. I, § 1.01.)

Comment

It is a question of judgment whether the detailed statement of limitations and power respecting religious freedom is to be preferred over the First Amendment or the suggested provision of the Model State Constitution. As noted, despite the categorical nature of the First Amendment provision, a measure of reserved governmental power has been recognized. On the other hand, the present formulation in Section 3 does have the merit of defining with a fair degree of certainty the essential principles of religious freedom while expressing the principle of a reserved governmental power to protect the public interest. A judgment of preference for the Illinois statement is certainly supportable in principle. It is noted, however, that the Commentary in the Model State Constitution quite bluntly rejects the necessity of a provision prohibiting denial of the enjoyment of civil rights, because the "protection of 'civil rights' has been subsumed in both federal and state courts under due process and equal protection . . . ." (Model State Constitution 30.)

Perhaps the correct assessment is that it is dangerous to meddle, even with good intentions, with traditional bill of rights guarantees of religious freedom. The effort usually generates passionate and conflicting reactions. It may therefore be the better part of wisdom to retain the existing language unless the making of a substantial change is deemed essential.

Freedom of Speech

Sec. 4.   Every person may freely speak, write and publish on all subjects, being responsible for the abuse of that liberty; and in all trials for libel, both civil and criminal, the truth, when published with good motives and for justifiable ends, shall be a sufficient defense.

History

With the exception of several minor and insignificant style changes, the 1818 and 1848 Constitutions contained identical provisions. They provided that (1) the printing presses shall be free to every person who examines the proceedings of the General Assembly or any branch of government, and that no law may ever restrain this right; (2) the free communication of thoughts and opinions is one of the invaluable rights of man, and that every citizen may freely speak, write or print on every subject, being reponsible for the abuse of that liberty; and (3) in prosecutions for the publication of papers investigating the official conduct

of officers or of men acting in a public capacity, or where the matter published is proper for public information, the truth thereof may be given in evidence; and (4) in all indictments for libels, the jury shall have the right of determining both the law and the fact, under the direction of the court as in other cases.

The 1870 section eliminated the printing press provision; adopted without substantive change and almost verbatim the provision respecting the rights of citizens to speak, write and publish freely; broadened the provisions respecting libels to cover all trials, civil and criminal, without limitation to public officials; retained truth as a defense in libel actions, but added significantly "when published with good motives and for justifiable ends"; and deleted the provision giving the jury the right to determine issues of law and fact in libel cases. This section was reported out of the Bill of Rights Committee in substantially its present form. It was adopted with little debate or discussion and with no explanation for the changes effected in the 1848 provisions.

The 1922 Convention proposal retained the 1870 provisions, making only stylistic nonsubstantive changes.

Explanation

It is somewhat absurd to suggest priorities among the fundamental rights and liberties protected against impairment by a bill of rights; yet among these rights a strong case can be made for freedom of speech and press as the most basic of all rights, without which there could be no truly free society. The decisions, federal and state, frequently reflect this view, though like all other rights, freedom of speech and press is not absolute. Because of its absolutely central role, speech or press cannot be punished or censored unless utterance or publication presents a clear and present danger to society (the classic Holmesian principle) or unless it is "shown likely to produce a clear and present danger of serious substantive evil that rises far above public inconvenience, annoyance, or unrest." (Terminiello v. Chicago, 337 U.S. 1, 4 (1949).)

Freedom is the rule and restraint is the exception. So the courts have said or implied in many cases. But the exceptions which allow governmental sanctions are by no means minimal. Speech which incites to violence or crime, or which slanders or libels, or which is coupled with unlawful conduct, or which is obscene, is subject to punishment or other governmental sanctions.

Press is not limited to newspapers, but includes periodicals, pamphlets, and every other sort of publication that affords a vehicle of information (Montgomery Ward & Co. v. United Employees, 330 Ill. App. 49 (1946)); it embraces published matter whether circulated with or without charge (City of Blue Island v. Kozul, 379 Ill. 511 (1942)); and it guarantees the right to publish, circulate, distribute and make known, and not merely the right to speak and write (Village of South Holland v. Stein, 373 Ill. 472 (1940)).

Curiously, motion pictures were not recognized as speech or press within the protection of the First and Fourteenth Amendments (the doctrine of incorporation applies the restraints of the First Amendment of the Constitution of the United States to the states through the Fourteenth Amendment) until 1952 when the United States Supreme Court so held in *Joseph Burstyn, Inc. v. Wilson* (343 U.S. 495 (1952)). A 1915 decision, reflecting the novelty of the medium, had held motion pictures a business pure and simple, having no communicative values within the protection of the First Amendment. (Mutual Film Corp. v. Industrial Comm'n, 236 U.S. 230 (1915).)

The nature of the governmental power exerted in respect to speech or press is an all-important factor in determining the validity of the power. As a general proposition, criminal punishment by fine or imprisonment for nonprotected speech or press is acceptable. This may be called after-the-fact punishment, whereby the actor is not initially censored by prior restraints, but, as in other cases of criminal offenses, is prosecuted for speech deemed unlawful. The critical inquiry, of course, is whether the speech is indeed constitutionally protected against any form of punishment. Speech which simply stirs people to anger, or invites public dispute or brings about a condition of unrest, absent the factors previously noted, is not subject to any form of governmental sanction. (Terminiello v. Chicago, 337 U.S. 1 (1949).) In *Pickering v. Board of Education* (391 U.S. 563 (1968)), a decision of the Illinois Supreme Court which sustained the administrative dismissal of a school teacher for publishing letters in newspapers critical of the Board of Education was reversed as a violation of the free speech and press guarantee.*

On the other hand, speech or press which may be subjected to after-the-fact criminal punishment may not, except in the area of obscenity in motion pictures, be made the subject of a prior restraint which classically involves governmental consent as a precondition to publication, normally through administrative licensing. This form of sanction is censorship in its most suspect form in a free society, and its current limitation to obscenity in motion pictures is understandable. A form of prior restraint applied to newspapers — injunction to suppress as a nuisance the publication of newspapers devoted to defamatory, scandalous and scurrilous attacks upon public officials — was stricken as an infringement upon freedom of the press in the landmark case of *Near v. Minnesota* ex rel. *Olson* (283 U.S. 697 (1931)). Not until 1961, in *Times*

Film Corp v. City of Chicago (365 U.S. 43 (1961)), did the United States Supreme Court concede the constitutional validity of prior restraint in its purest form, when it upheld the Chicago motion picture censorship ordinance against a broadside attack which asserted a total absence of governmental power to require administrative approval as a condition to publication. Earlier, in 1957, the same Court converted prior dicta into law by holding for the first time that obscenity was not protected expression within the First and Fourteenth Amendments, and sustained both state and federal criminal after-the-fact punishment for the publication of obscene printed materials. (Roth v. United States, 354 U.S. 476 (1957).) Also in 1957, the Court in *Kingsley Books, Inc. v. Brown* (354 U.S. 436 (1957)) had sustained a form of prior restraint by injunction similar to that outlawed in *Near v. Minnesota* as applied to obscene publications. Distingushing *Near v. Minnesota,* the Court held in *Kingsley* that it was dealing with constitutionally unprotected obscenity and with a limited restraint on publication of a particular book pending judicial determination of obscenity, as contrasted with the *Near* restraint on future publications of the newspaper.

Illinois, of course, under its own constitutional guarantee of free speech and press, could outlaw prior restraints on the publication of motion pictures if it so desired. As a matter of history, however, Illinois anticipated *Roth, Kingsley* and *Times Film* by holding (1) that obscenity was not protected expression within Section 4 of Article II of the state Constitution or the First and Fourteenth Amendments of the Federal Constitution, and (2) that an administrative licensing scheme for motion pictures was a permissible constitutional restraint on liberty of press. (ACLU v. City of Chicago, 3 Ill. 2d 334 (1954).)

Notwithstanding the federal validation of an administrative licensing scheme for motion pictures, the United States Supreme Court, sensitive to this extraordinary and potentially dangerous governmental power, has severely circumscribed this power by insistence upon procedural safeguards which require an expedited administrative and judicial process and which keeps to a minimum the degree of prior restraint. Thus in *Freedman v. Maryland* (380 U.S. 51 (1965)), the Court prescribed the standards for a valid prior restraint on the publication of motion pictures which (1) imposed upon the administrative censor the burden of proving that the film is obscene, (2) limited administrative restraint prior to judicial determination to an undefined brief and minimum period, and (3) assured a prompt and final judicial determination.

The City of Chicago rewrote its censorship ordinance to meet the *Freedman* standards and in *Cusack v. Teitel Film Corporation* (38 Ill.

2d 53 (1967)) the state Supreme Court sustained the ordinance which permitted a 50- to 57-day period for the administrative determination and required an expedited judicial procedure. The United States Supreme Court reversed on the ground that the ordinance failed to meet the *Freedman* standards for an expedited administrative and judicial process which would assure a minimum of prior restraint. (Teitel Film Corp. v. Cusack, 390 U.S. 139 (1968).)

Prior restraints through the administrative licensing mechanism in areas other than motion pictures, and on grounds other than obscenity, have not been attempted in Illinois, nor is it likely that if attempted they will be sustained. On the other hand, there is a significant developing law which recognizes governmental power to curb speech associated with demonstrations and the use of public places which interferes with the rights of others. In *City of Chicago v. Gregory* (39 Ill. 2d 47 (1968)), a conviction under a disorderly conduct statute was sustained against civil rights marchers whose peaceful conduct aroused potentially dangerous adverse reaction by a hostile crowd of onlookers. The civil rights marchers had refused police suggestions to leave the area, based on the police judgment that violence would otherwise be unavoidable. The United States Supreme Court reversed in a decision which did not find it necessary to reach the constitutional issue concerning the marchers' rights to free speech and to assemble. (Gregory v. City of Chicago, 394 U.S. 111 (1969).)

In *City of Chicago v. Joyce* (38 Ill. 2d 368 (1967)), a conviction for disorderly conduct was upheld against a First Amendment challenge, the Court holding that the defendant's conduct in sitting on sidewalks, blocking entrance to the city hall, and obstructing pedestrian traffic, had no connection with any constitutionally protected freedoms.

These Illinois decisions appear to be more than amply supported in recent federal decisional law. Of particular importance are *Cameron v. Johnson* (390 U.S. 611 (1968)) sustaining a Mississippi statute prohibiting picketing or parading which obstructs or unreasonably interferes with ingress or egress to or from the courthouse; *Cox v. Louisiana* (379 U.S. 536 (1965)) which upheld convictions of civil rights marchers for "obstructing public passages," where the demonstrators, in peaceful fashion, marched from the state capitol to the courthouse grounds where they prayed, sang and listened to speeches; and *Adderly v. Florida* (385 U.S. 39 (1966)) sustaining a state conviction for trespass, against a First Amendment challenge, as to a group of student demonstrators who entered jail grounds to protest arrests based on segregation ordinances and who, without violence or disorder, temporarily blocked a driveway to the jail entrance not normally used by the public.

Illinois has followed the prevailing rule that speech which is an integral part of unlawful conduct is not constitutionally protected expression. (Chicago Real Estate Bd. v. City of Chicago, 36 Ill. 2d 530 (1967) sustaining an ordinance proscribing the distribution by real estate brokers of printed matter which was aimed at block-busting and panic selling.) In the important area of picketing as a form of speech, Illinois has held that picketing cannot be dogmatically equated with constitutionally protected speech and may be curtailed where it is conducted for purposes unlawful under state laws or policies. (Board of Educ. v. Redding, 32 Ill. 2d 567 (1965).)

In contrast, note should be taken of *Food Employees Local 590 v. Logan Valley Plaza, Inc.* (391 U.S. 308 (1968)) which validated as a First Amendment freedom peaceful picketing of a shopping center located on wholly owned private grounds, the Court equating the center, under the conditions of its operation, to a business area located within the city. The Court relied principally on a comparable holding relating to a "company town" (private property), holding that the streets and other public places in the company town were proper places for the exercise of speech under the aegis of the First and Fourteenth Amendments. (Marsh v. Alabama, 326 U.S. 501 (1946).)

In summation it must again be stressed that this analysis is not exhaustive. Its purpose is to inform of the basic meaning and application of the constitutional provision under discussion by reference to and description of the more important federal and state decisional law.

Comparative Analysis

All the states guarantee freedom of speech but four do not have a constitutional provision guaranteeing freedom of press. Thirty-five other states have a provision regarding libel. Of these, 21 provide similarly that truth, when published with good motives, is a defense; 13 establish that truth "may be given in evidence" without specifying its effect; and one provides simply that truth is a justification. The Model State Constitution adopts the federal First Amendment language that "no law shall be enacted . . . abridging the freedom of speech or of the press . . . ." (art. I, §1.01.)

Comment

That portion of Section 4 which deals with speech and press is fundamental to a state constitution which seeks to preserve these indispensable liberties. The last clause which deals with trials for libel and truth as a defense, when published with good motives and for justifiable ends, is somewhat more difficult to assess as a constitutional principle. It was not discussed in the *Explanation* because it has not been productive of litigation or law which varies from its plain meaning. Perhaps truth alone, without regard to the difficult burden of establishing good motives and justifiable ends, should be sufficient for defense in civil or criminal libel suits. An important consideration may be that many states do not consider the provision, or variations thereof, worthy of constitutional status.

Trial by Jury

Sec. 5. The right of trial by jury as heretofore enjoyed, shall remain inviolate; but the trial of civil cases before justices of the peace by a jury of less than twelve men, may be authorized by law.

History

The 1818 Constitution stated only that the right of trial by jury shall remain inviolate. To this provision the 1848 Constitution added that the right extends to all cases at law, without regard to the amount in controversy. The present constitutional provision introduced the phrase "as heretofore enjoyed" as well as the clause permitting the legislature to authorize a jury of fewer than 12 men in civil cases before justices of the peace. Deleted as unnecessary was the 1848 provision making the right to a jury trial applicable to all cases, without regard to the amount in controversy.

The 1922 Convention proposal suggested a radical revision of the 1870 provision. It retained the opening phrase but removed the words "as heretofore enjoyed," the debates noting this to be necessary to the remainder of the proposal which (1) authorized waiver of a jury trial except in capital cases, (2) expressly qualified women to serve as jurors, and (3) authorized the General Assembly to provide by law for juries of fewer than 12 men and nonunanimous verdicts in all civil cases.

Explanation

Although this section applies to civil and criminal proceedings, the discussion here is limited to civil cases. For the discussion of jury trials in criminal cases see Section 9 of this Article. (*Infra,* pp. 41-2.)

The trial by jury guarantee is, in common understanding, a fundamental and incontestable political policy in free society. The public consensus that one has the inalienable right to be tried by a jury of his peers in civil as well as criminal cases probably remains quite firm. In other democratic societies, however, and in England particularly, the right to trial by jury has virtually gone by the boards in all but criminal cases.

As a practical matter, however, the sweeping nature of this guarantee, modified by the ambiguous phrase "as heretofore enjoyed" (a phrase which has resulted in a welter of confusing and irreconcilable interpretations by the Illinois Supreme Court) has not prevented the legislature from devising and the courts from sustaining legal mechanisms for the trial and determination of facts by agencies other than juries. Perhaps the most striking example is the Workmen's Compensation Act which established an administrative mechanism for the determination of compensation claims. Initially the law, which substituted a statutory claim for employment-related injuries for the common law action available to employees, was effective only as to employers and employees who elected to accept its provisions. This elective feature saved the act from a serious constitutional challenge that it deprived employers of the right to a trial by jury "as heretofore enjoyed." (Chicago Rys. v. Industrial Bd., 276 Ill. 112 (1916); Deibeikis v. Link-Belt Co., 261 Ill. 454 (1914).) A few years later, however, the law was made mandatorily applicable, without election, to certain defined hazardous employments. Employers claimed this deprived them of their common law right to a jury trial. The Court disagreed and employed an ingenious rationale to sustain the new administrative scheme. It held that the right to a trial by jury was guaranteed only in those causes of action recognized by law. Since the original cause of action was destroyed or merged into a new statutory remedy, the "incidental" right of trial by jury had nothing left upon which to operate. (Grand Trunk Ry. v. Industial Comm'n, 291 Ill. 167 (1919).) Lost somewhere in this analysis was a right "as heretofore enjoyed" which was to remain inviolate. The realistic analysis is that common law principles of tort liability in the master-servant relationship were no longer appropriate in an industrial society in which the incidence of employment injuries and deaths was soaring to unprecedented heights, and that a process, more adaptable and sympathetic to the new concepts of liability, was essential as a substitute for judicial determinations. The Court rose to the occasion by finding a constitutional rationale.

In like manner the administrative process which licenses and regulates professions and business activities, and denies or grants licenses, and suspends, revokes or refuses to renew licenses, all without a jury, has been sustained because the right to a jury in these kinds of cases was not "heretofore enjoyed." The rationale makes much more sense than in the Workmen's Compensation case, but even here the administrative determination of fact, a function supposedly peculiarly within the province of a jury, can have devastating consequences to the person aggrieved by the administrative judgment.

Numerous other exceptions are also recognized. Thus the constitutional guarantee does not apply to cases in equity as distinguished from cases in law, as, for example, mortgage foreclosure, specific performance of contracts, and injunction cases. Nor does it apply to special statutory proceedings such as a proceeding to commit for mental illness. (People v. Niesman, 356 Ill. 322 (1934).) Of course a jury trial may be provided by statute in these and other types of cases in which the constitutional guarantee is inapplicable, but this would be simply a matter of legislative grace.

It should again be noted that the phrase "as heretofore enjoyed" has caused some trouble but the law is fairly well crystallized now to the effect that it means both the right as it existed at common law and as it had come to be at the time of the adoption of the Constitution.

A special problem arises in respect to the provision concerning juries of fewer than 12 persons in civil actions before justices of the peace. Under the new Judicial Article (Article VI) there are no justices of the peace. The magistrates of the circuit courts are not the lineal or constitutional descendants of the justices of the peace. Although the magistrates by law have been assigned substantially the same kinds of civil and quasi-criminal cases previously handled by justices of the peace, they are full-fledged judicial officers of the circuit court. The provision authorizing a jury of fewer than 12 men has not been construed judicially. Its constitutional status is quite uncertain, although the General Assembly has authorized a jury of six, unless either party requests a jury of 12, in all cases where the damage claim does not exceed $10,000. (Ill. Rev. Stat. ch. 110, §64 (2) (Supp. 1968).)

There appears to be no particular purpose in analyzing the hundreds of judicial decisions which deal with collateral aspects of the right, such as waiver of jury, selection of jury, the functions of the jury, the role of appellate courts in reviewing fact determinations, and numerous other aspects incident to the application and meaning of the right. The central point is that these principles must for the most part be left to judicial determination in the interpretation of the basic constitutional guarantee. There is no basis for any judgment that these decisions have seriously misconceived the essential purpose of the guarantee.

Comparative Analysis

All state constitutions provide that the right of trial by jury is to remain inviolate, but only seven provide that the right is to remain inviolate "as heretofore enjoyed." Approximately one-fifth of the states authorize juries of fewer than 12 in courts not of record such as the justices of the peace courts. The present Illinois Judicial Article (VI) has abolished all courts not of record. The Model State Constitution provides that "[i]n prosecutions for felony, the accused shall enjoy the right of trial by an impartial jury of the county [or other appropriate political subdivision of the state] wherein the crime shall have been committed, or of another county, if a change of venue has been granted." (art. I, §1.06.)

Comment

The guarantee of this section, as applied to civil cases, may perhaps be less compelling in principle than when last adopted in 1870. Given its evolutionary development, particularly in England where jury trials in civil cases are virtually a thing of the past, and the probability that the administrative process may in some additional instances be an appropriate substitute for the judicial process, the need for a hard look at this section may be indicated. The principle is, however, too important to be lightly treated, and no modification should be accepted which dilutes its political and psychological value. In short, there are difficult policy choices here which cannot be resolved easily. For the reasons noted, the provision for juries of fewer than 12 must also be evaluated in terms of its utility or need under the new Judicial Article.

Searches and Seizures

Sec. 6.   The right of the people to be secure in their persons, houses, papers and effects, against unreasonable searches and seizures, shall not be violated; and no warrant shall issue without probable cause, supported by affidavit, particularly describing the place to be searched, and the persons or things to be seized.

History

The 1818 Constitutional provision, re-adopted without change in 1848, provided that (1) people shall be secure in their persons, houses, papers and possessions, from unreasonable searches and seizures, and (2) general warrants authorizing search of suspected places without evidence of the fact committed, or seizure of any person not named whose offenses are not particularly described and supported by evidence, are dangerous to liberty and "ought not to be granted." The 1870 provision substituted "effects" for "possessions," introduced specifically the probable cause and affidavit requirements for issuance of warrants, and mandated that warrants particularly describe the place to be searched, and the person or things to be seized, eliminating the somewhat innocuous and ambiguous phrase that general warrants "ought not to be granted."

The present section was drafted almost entirely in committee. No explanation, then, is recorded in the Debates for the changes made in the section as it existed in the 1818 and 1848 Constitutions.

The Convention as a whole added to the committee recommendation only that a warrant must be "supported by affidavit" — reflecting concern about the practice of permitting the issuance of a warrant on the basis of oral evidence alone. Several delegates noted that a permanent record of the evidence should be made, and apparently the Convention agreed.

The 1870 provision is almost an exact statement of the Fourth Amendment of the Constitution of the United States, the only difference in fact being the word "affidavit" in lieu of the federal requirement of "oath or affirmation" to support the warrant. The difference is not substantive.

The 1922 Convention proposal retained the 1870 provision unchanged.

Explanation

This great bulwark against governmental abuse of power had its origin in the practice which prevailed in the American colonies and in England of issuing so-called "writs of assistance" to revenue officers, empowering them in their discretion, to search suspected places for smuggled goods, and a similar practice of issuance of general warrants for searching private houses for the discovery and seizure of books and papers that might be used to convict their owner of libel. The issuance of general warrants for indiscriminate search and seizure originated in the Star Chamber. To the colonists these practices were an abhorrent and indefensible invasion of privacy, and a tyrannous exercise of governmental power totally incompatible with fundamental principles of individual liberty.

The history is quite clear that the Fourth Amendment to the United States Constitution, the direct lineal ancestor of Section 6 of Article II of the Constitution of Illinois, was designed to prevent these feared and hated governmental infringements upon freedom. The framers of the Constitution of the United States recognized, however, that the protection of individual rights, as in other instances, must yield to a superior public interest. In the just administration and enforcement of criminal laws, governmental seizure of papers and effects, or of persons, if controlled by reasonable safeguards, is an indispensable need in a civilized and ordered society.

The apprehension, prosecution and punishment of criminals require a governmental power to seize and search. The problem again is one of balance. The amendment sought to secure that balance by a categorical denunciation of unreasonable searches and seizures, and by recognizing the legitimacy of searches and seizures authorized by warrants (1) based on probable cause and supported by affidavit, and (2) particularly describing the place to be searched and the persons or things to be seized. In this way the evils of the open-ended, indiscriminate writs of assistance and general warrants were to be ended, while preserving the public interest in the administration and enforcement of its criminal laws.

The first and perhaps most important point of emphasis, therefore, is that the constitutional principle prohibits only unreasonable searches and seizures, and that a reasonable search or seizure, based upon a proper warrant, is constitutionally permissible. In addition, this provision has been construed in most states, including Illinois, as not abridging the common law power of search and seizure without warrant in cases where (1) voluntary consent to a search of the person or premises is secured, and (2) where the search and seizure are incident to a valid arrest.

The second important point is that warrants must be issued by a judicial officer, the interposition between the government and the individual of an impartial magistrate being central to a reasonable search and seizure, and that the warrant may not issue except upon probable cause being established. Probable cause is not proof of guilt but more approximately a showing that a reasonable ground for suspicion, sufficiently strong to warrant a cautious man to believe that the accused is guilty of the offense, exists. (People v. York, 29 Ill. 2d 68 (1963); People v. Dolgin, 415 Ill. 434 (1953).)

The decisions interpreting this section are legion. Quite understandably, defendants in criminal actions are quick to insist upon one or more violations of the standards. Among the most common are the insufficiency of the complaint and the absence of probable cause for the issuance of a warrant, the insufficiency of the affidavit, the insufficiency of the warrant (failure to describe with particularity the place to be searched and the persons or things to be seized), the search and seizure not being incident to a valid arrest, the invalidity of the search, and the inadmissibility of evidence unlawfully seized. Most of these questions raise issues of law which, however, are critically dependent upon the facts. A review of the cases dealing with the reasonableness or unreasonableness of search and seizure, with or without warrant, and the myriad of other issues generated by searches and seizures and the proceedings incident thereto, would not be sufficiently instructive to justify the enormous effort necessary to a detailed treatment. Suffice it to say at this point, however, that the Illinois judicial interpretations of this provision are markedly similar for the most part to the federal and state decisional law which interpret similar or identical constitutional provisions.

This *Explanation* would be deficient, however, if it did not deal with several recent federal decisions which have a direct and important bearing upon the meaning and application of the Illinois provision. *Mapp v. Ohio* (367 U.S. 643 (1961)) held that the Fourth Amendment rights to be free from unreasonable searches and seizures and to have excluded from criminal trials any evidence illegally seized were applicable to state criminal trials under the due process clause of the Fourteenth Amendment. (Herewith our old friend — the incorporation doctrine.) The decision reversed *Wolf v. Colorado* (338 U.S. 25 (1949)). The central though not exclusive importance of the *Mapp* reversal of *Wolf* was

its effect upon the issue of the admissibility of evidence which had been
illegally seized. The federal rule, established in *Weeks v. United States*
(232 U.S. 383 (1914)), was that evidence seized in violation of the
Fourth Amendment was inadmissible in federal court criminal prosecutions. Most states interpreting their own constitutional search and
seizure provisions refused to accept the *Weeks* principle in state prosecution for a state crime. Illinois was among the minority of states that
followed the *Weeks* rule. (*See* City of Chicago v. Lord, 7 Ill. 2d 379
(1956); People v. Touhy, 361 Ill. 332 (1935).) Illinois prior to *Mapp*
could have reversed its decisional law to make unlawfully seized evidence
admissible in state prosecutions, and indeed might have done so in the
light of current and aggravated tensions which have substantially increased the problems of law enforcement. It can not do so so long as
Mapp remains the definitive law.

The total implications of the *Mapp* rule on other aspects of the Fourth
Amendment are not certain. Whether federal law will take precedence
over state law in the many procedural and substantive issues which
derive from probable cause, arrest, reasonable and unreasonable searches
and seizures, and related issues, is not certain, but in the critical area
of admissibility of evidence unlawfully seized, and its crucial relationship to proof of guilt or innocence of the defendant, the rule is now
Mapp.

The effect of *Mapp* on state and municipal efforts to control and
prevent health and safety hazards may be devastating. In *Frank v.
Maryland* (359 U.S. 360 (1959)), a Baltimore City Code provision authorized municipal health inspectors, without a warrant, to demand entry
to any house, cellar or enclosure if they had cause to suspect that a
nuisance existed. A refusal subjected the owner or occupant to a $20 fine
or penalty for each refusal. The ordinance, in a 5-4 decision was sustained against a Fourteenth Amendment due process challenge (*Mapp's*
incorporation doctrine re Fourth Amendment was two years distant),
but Fourth Amendment policy considerations were uppermost in both
the majority and minority opinions as they weighed the interest of
privacy of the home against a strong governmental argument that protection of the public health in modern urban conditions simply made
unrealistic and unreasonable a warrant requirement for inspection.

One year later the Court, by an equally divided vote, sustained a
warrantless municipal health inspection ordinance applicable to private
homes which did not require "cause to suspect that a nuisance exists"
(the Frank ordinance). (Ohio *ex rel.* Eaton v. Price, 364 U.S. 263 (1960).)
But in *Camara v. Municipal Court* (387 U.S. 523 (1967)), the Court, in

a 6-3 decision, reversed *Frank,* holding that warrantless periodic routine area health inspections of homes violated Fourth and Fourteenth Amendment proscriptions against unreasonable searches and seizures. In a companion case, *See v. City of Seattle* (387 U.S. 541 (1967)), a fire inspection ordinance authorizing the same kind of inspection for commercial and industrial buildings was invalidated on the grounds relied upon in *Camara.*

In both *Camara* and *See,* the Court recognized the grave nature of the public health problem in densely populated urban areas and, in an effort to partially alleviate the anguish of municipal health officials who claimed that protection of the public health was impossible under standard Fourth Amendment procedures, suggested that a warrant procedure could be devised in which the probable cause criteria need not be the same as was required for the issuance of warrants in criminal cases.

The effect of *Camara* and *See,* based as it now is upon the *Mapp* incorporation doctrine, is to impose substantial curbs upon municipal health protection measures which had become fairly regularized. And, as in the *Mapp* case, the states are powerless to adopt a different rule.

It is not to be inferred that *Mapp, Camara, See* and other decisions imposing federally determined limitations upon states are arbitrary, irrational or even unreasonable federal intrusions upon state powers. This may be and indeed is a hotly debated issue, even within the Court itself. The important point is that such decisions, for as long as they are not themselves overruled or modified by the United States Supreme Court, or by amendment of the United States Constitution, provide new dimensions in the philosophy of federalism and state powers.

Comparative Analysis

A similar provision is contained in all state constitutions. As noted, the federal provision is also the same. The Model State Constitution contains the same provision but adds the following:

"The right of the people to be secure against unreasonable interception of of telephone, telegraph and other electronic means of communication . . . shall not be violated, and no orders and warrants for such interceptions shall issue but upon cause . . . that evidence of crime may be thus obtained, and particularly identifying the means of communication and the person or persons whose communications are to be intercepted.

"Evidence obtained in violation of this section shall not be admissible in any court against any person." (art. I, § 1.03.)

Comment

Every consideration of policy suggests that this principle be retained in the Illinois Constitution. A contrary conclusion is certainly not compelled simply because the *Mapp* decision applies the federal Fourth Amendment guarantees to the states through the Fourteenth Amendment. (See *Preliminary and Introductory Comment* to this article, *supra,* p. 5.) Such frustrations as may be caused in some parts of the body politic by *Mapp, Camara* and other decisions imposing new limitations upon state owners are surely not shared by other segments who view the decisions as great milestones in the continuing struggle of people against governmental power. In any event, there is nothing that can be done in a convention to change the new constitutional interpretations.

As to whether the state should add limitations beyond those which presently are embraced within the state and federal amendments, such as the proposal in the Model State Constitution, this issue presents subtle and difficult policy problems. The genius of generalized constitutional principles is that they protect fundamental individual rights in respect to which a broad public consensus exists, while permitting flexibility and adaptation as the dynamics of a changing society may require. The moment specifics are added to the great general principles, a whole host of new or related issues will command the support of different constituencies hoping to enshrine their particular ideals into constitutional concepts. This is not to say that new particular limitations upon state governmental power are unnecessary. The problem is to define those which are worthy of constitutional status, and to prevent the inclusion of new limitations which time will prove to be impractical or unwise.

Bail and Habeas Corpus

Sec. 7. All persons shall be bailable by sufficient sureties, except for capital offenses, where the proof is evident or the presumption great; and the privilege of the writ of *habeas corpus* shall not be suspended, unless when in cases of rebellion or invasion the public safety may require it.

History

This section, except for minor grammatical changes, is the same as the provisions of the 1818 and 1848 Constitutions.

The 1922 Convention proposal suggested that the section read as follows:

"Excessive bail shall not be required. The privilege of the writ of habeas corpus shall not be suspended unless in case of rebellion or invasion the public safety may require it."

Curiously, the proposal when first offered was withdrawn, partly because of opposition to the principle that bail was to be discretionary with the court in all cases, and partly because it permitted bail for persons charged with capital offenses on grounds more liberal than the existing provision. It was revived and adopted after the rejection of another amendment which retained the existing language of the present Constitution, but added a discretionary power of the court to refuse bail to a person previously convicted of a crime.

Explanation

The section is self-explanatory and has been productive of little litigation. It reflects the humane philosophy that persons accused of crime should not be made to languish in the dungeon pending trial. Bail is a matter of right except for capital offenses, where the proof is evident or the presumption great. Of course if the accused cannot meet the bail as set by the court, he must make the best of it. The amount of the bail, though discretionary with the court, must be reasonable. In a preposterous abuse of judicial discretion, the setting of $50,000 bail on a vagrancy charge, the trial judge was reversed despite his insistence that his discretion was properly exercised in view of the defendant's past criminal record. (People *ex rel.* Sammons v. Snow, 340 Ill. 464 (1930).)

Judicial discretion in fixing bail must take into account the state's interest in assuring the defendant's appearance for trial. (People *ex rel.* Gendron v. Ingram, 34 Ill. 2d 623 (1966).) In this case, the "sufficient sureties" provision of this section was held not to be violated by a statute which liberalized procedures for release on bail. The statute (Ill. Rev. Stat. ch. 38, §§ 110-2, 110-7, 110-8 (1967)) destroyed the harsh and frequently odious bail bondsman's racket by providing the following options: (1) the execution of a personal bond without security, the condition of performance being the promise to appear at the date set for trial; (2) the execution of a personal bail bond in a fixed amount coupled with a cash deposit of 10 per cent of the bail set by the court; (3) the execution of a personal bond in a fixed amount and the deposit of cash or securities equal to the amount so set, or the transfer as security of unencumbered real estate equal to twice the amount of the bail.

The guarantee that the writ of habeas corpus shall not be suspended except in the extraordinary instances noted has produced no problems of interpretation or application.

Comparative Analysis

Twenty-three state constitutions contain the same provision relating to bail while those of the remaining states contain variations thereon. Every other state provides that "excessive" bail is prohibited. The United States Constitution provides that "[e]xcessive bail shall not be required . . . ." (U.S. Const. amend. VIII.) All the state constitutions contain similar provisions relating to habeas corpus. The United States Constitution in Article 1, Section 9 (not in Bill of Rights), is precisely the same as the Illinois provision on habeas corpus. The Model State Constitution contains similar provisions relating to bail and habeas corpus.

Comment

A number of states leave the matter of bail in all cases to the discretion of the court rather than mandating it as a constitutional right available to a person accused of crime. The current concern with "lawlessness" has prompted some discussion that the right to bail be re-evaluated as a constitutional principle. It should be noted that the United States has not transferred the federal provision into the Fourteenth Amendment through the incorporation doctrine. Since denial of bail will work, as it has in the past, to the disadvantage of the poor, often with rank injustice, it would be well to consider most cautiously any proposal which would diminish the existing right.

The habeas corpus provision is standard state and federal constitutional doctrine. No reasons are suggested which justify its repeal or modification.

Indictment

Sec. 8. No person shall be held to answer for a criminal offense, unless on indictment of a grand jury, except in cases in which the punishment is by fine, or imprisonment otherwise than in the penitentiary, in cases of impeachment, and in cases arising in the army and navy, or in the militia when in actual service in time of war or public danger: *Provided,* that the grand jury may be abolished by law in all cases.

History

The 1818 Constitution made no express reference to grand juries but clearly implied their constitutional necessity by providing that no person "for any indictable offense" shall be proceeded against criminally by information. The term "indictable offense" was not defined. Presumably the common law had established the general distinctions between crimes of a serious nature punishable by death or imprisonment in the penitentiary, *e.g.*, felonies, and criminal offenses of lesser gravity, *e.g.*, misdemeanors for which the punishment was either by fine only, or fine and imprisonment in penal institutions other than the penitentiary, *e.g.*, county jails, workhouses, etc., for a term generally less than one year, or by both such fine and imprisonment. In a curious, almost unintelligible form, the 1818 provision excepted from the "indictable offense" category "cases arising in the land or naval forces, or the militia when in actual service, in time of war or public danger, by leave of the courts for oppression or misdemeanor in office." Whether the phrase "by leave of the courts" was tied to the antecedent or succeeding clauses, or stood by itself as a grant of unlimited discretionary power to foreclose grand jury action for indictable offenses was only one of the interpretive difficulties raised by this language. Fortunately the occasion to test these ambiguities does not seem to have arisen, or if it did, it apparently did not reach the Supreme Court.

The 1848 Constitution was somewhat of an improvement in clarity, though it seemed substantially to change the 1818 philosophy of permitting a wide range of nonindictable offenses. Introducing the first express constitutional reference to "grand jury," it mandated a general application of the grand jury indictment for any "criminal offense," excepting impeachment, the military and militia cases designated in 1818, and "in cases cognizable by justices of the peace." A proviso prohibited such justices from trying any person, except as a court of inquiry, for any offense punishable with "imprisonment or death, or fine above $100." The scope of this alteration of the 1818 provision was also uncertain. It seemed to exclude grand jury involvement in misdemeanors by the general exception of "cases cognizable by justices of the peace," but whether in fact this was so was made uncertain by the reference to misdemeanors punishable by a fine of more than $100. Again the ambiguities apparently caused no complications.

The 1870 provision is a marked improvement in the elimination of the ambiguities of the 1818 and 1848 provisions, but its major substantive contribution was in its authorization of the General Assembly to abolish the grand jury "in all cases." A great deal of criticism directed at the grand jury system was voiced during the Convention, causing extensive debate. It was argued on the one hand that the grand jury system was outmoded, overly expensive, secretive, irresponsible, cruel, and unjust, and on the other hand that the system was necessary, traditional, and effective. In the end, after considering several compromises, it was decided to defer the decision to the legislature which could provide substitute systems, test them, and replace them, if necessary.

The 1870 provision retained the exceptions for impeachment and the military and militia cases. In excluding the indictment requirement for criminal offenses in which the punishment was by fine only, or nonpenitentiary imprisonment, the framers were drawing for the first time a fairly clear distinction between felonies and misdemeanors as established by law.

The 1922 Convention proposal offered several innovations. It read as follows:

"No person shall be held to answer for a capital offense unless on indictment of a grand jury. Offenses which may be punished by imprisonment in the penitentiary may be prosecuted by indictment or on information filed by the attorney general or by a state's attorney. No such information shall be filed by a state's attorney except by leave granted, either in term time or in vacation, by a judge of a court of record having jurisdiction of the offense, after a showing of probable cause. All other offenses may be prosecuted as provided by law."

As drafted by the Committee on the Bill of Rights, this section in the 1922 Convention proposal apparently froze the grand jury system into the Constitution. It provided no authority in the General Assembly to abolish it. An attempt to grant this authority failed in part because it was felt that abolition might endanger the liberties of accused persons. It was pointed out, as well, that the legislature had not seen fit to act on the existing authorization, and that this could reflect a legislative judgment of the value of the grand jury. One delegate, however, expressed the thought that legislative inaction was due to an attorney general's opinion that "the legislature had no right to abolish the grand jury in any case unless it abolished it in all . . . ."

Explanation

The grand jury indictment procedure derives from the Magna Charta, as do most of the limitations upon governmental power expressed in the Bill of Rights. In construing a comparable provision of the Massachusetts Constitution, Chief Justice Shaw, in *Jones v. Robbins* (74 Mass. (8 Gray) 329, 344 (1857)), expressed the most frequently cited rationale for this provision.

"The right of individual citizens to be secure from an open and public accusation of crime, and from the trouble, expense and anxiety of a public trial, before a probable cause is established by the presentment and indictment of a grand jury, in cases of high offenses [sic], is justly regarded as one of the securities to the innocent against hasty, malicious and oppressive public prosecutions, and as one of the ancient immunities and privileges of English liberty."

Among the more important of its related objectives was to limit a person's jeopardy to offenses charged by a group of his fellow citizens acting independently of either the prosecuting attorney or judge (Stirone v. United States, 361 U.S. 212 (1960)), and to give a citizen the opportunity to have the benefit of a charge specifying with reasonable certainty the statute violated and wherein it was violated. (Conklin v. Cozart, 158 F. 2d 676 (1946), *cert. denied,* 332 U.S. 801 (1947).)

The federal Bill of Rights grand jury requirement appears as the first clause of the Fifth Amendment of the Constitution of the United States (applicable to "capital, or otherwise infamous crime"). However, unlike other procedural rights in criminal cases secured to the accused by that section, the grand jury guarantee has not been incorporated into the due process clause of the Fourteenth Amendment as a federal limitation upon state power. *Hurtado v. California* (110 U.S. 516 (1884)) established the nonapplication of the Fourteenth Amendment and no subsequent United States Supreme Court decision has disturbed it. (*See* Morford v. Hocker, 394 F.2d 169 (9th Cir. 1968).) State decisional law, therefore, remains supreme in its area.

The Constitution of Illinois does not define a grand jury. Its composition and procedure are left to statute and the common law. (People *ex rel.* Ferrill v. Graydon, 333 Ill. 429 (1928).) Important decisional law establishes that this section draws the line between felonies punishable by imprisonment in the penitentiary which must be prosecuted by indictment, and misdemeanors, by information (Brewster v. People, 183 Ill. 143 (1899)); and that if any offense is punishable by fine only, or imprisonment other than in a penitentiary only, or by both such fine and imprisonment, it requires only complaint by information to prosecute. It is not at all clear whether the legislature may expand the grand jury indictment process to include misdemeanors. Given customary rules of constitutional and statutory interpretation, there appears to be nothing in this section which operates as a limitation upon legislative power to do so. The legislature has not seen fit to pursue this policy; thus there is no decisional law on this subject.

The fact that a criminal offense provides for fine or imprisonment in other than the penitentiary (thus establishing it as a misdemeanor) does not, however, empower the legislature to authorize prosecution by the information route where a conviction called for the additional punishment of loss of civil rights. (People v. Russell, 245 Ill. 268 (1910).) However, where a conviction for drunken driving, then a misdemeanor, was prosecuted by information, the fact that a conviction authorized revocation of the license, in addition to fine or imprisonment, did not convert the offense into an indictable one, revocation being considered an incident of the regulatory power and not a punishment. (People v. Kobylak, 383 Ill. 432 (1943).)

In respect to the constitutional grant to abolish the grand jury "in all cases," the Supreme Court has held that the power can be exercised in a selective class of cases and that abolition of the grand jury in less than all criminal offenses is not a violation of this provision. (People *ex. rel.* Latimer v. Randolph, 13 Ill. 2d 552 (1958).)

Finally it is important to note that the institution of criminal prosecution by the "information" route involves the formal presentation of a charge by the state's attorney or other appropriate prosecuting official to a court. The secrecy, confidentiality, and other procedural incidents of grand jury deliberation which results either in a "true bill," in effect a determination that probable cause has been established upon which prosecution may follow, or a "no true bill," are not applicable to the information process. The difference derives from the presumed distinction in the gravity of felonies and misdemeanors and the consequent need of assuring greater secrecy in the felony-grand jury cases.

Comparative Analysis

Only 25 states have constitutional provisions for indictment by grand jury and in nine of these authorization is given to the legislature to dispense with the requirement or to limit the offenses to which it is applicable. Prosecution by information is permitted in the other states. Only Texas provides similarly that an indictment must be returned for all criminal cases, subject to the exceptions in the Illinois Constitution. The Fifth Amendment to the United States Constitution provides: "No person shall be held to answer for a capital, or otherwise infamous crime, unless on a presentment or indictment of a Grand Jury, except in cases arising in the land or naval forces, or in the Militia, when in actual service in time of War or public danger . . . ."

The Model State Constitution contains no comparable provision.

Comment

There appears to be something basically contradictory in the inclusion of a grand jury indictment procedure in specified cases as a fundamental liberty deserving of constitutional status in a Bill of Rights, and the coupling of this requirement with legislative authority to abolish the grand jury in all cases. Given its historical context and the reasons customarily given in support of its status as a fundamental liberty, the power of legislative abolition seems to be "a most ingenious paradox."

On the other hand, the fact that the legislature has not moved to dispense with this requirement in any significant way suggests that the guarantee is firmly fixed in political consciousness as a basic protection against abuse of governmental power. It is not possible to gauge its relationship to proper and effective law enforcement, but if it makes more difficult a casual or arbitrary approach to the administration of criminal justice, this very fact may justify its constitutional status. The assessment of the guarantee and the legislative power to abolish it is indeed most difficult. It is not likely that any rationale behind any change in the existing provision will secure a substantial consensus. This is, of course, a most speculative judgment.

Rights after Indictment

Sec. 9. In all criminal prosecutions, the accused shall have the right to appear and defend in person and by counsel; to demand the nature and cause of the accusation, and to have a copy thereof; to meet the witnesses face to face, and to have process to compel the attendance of witnesses in his behalf, and a speedy public trial by an impartial jury of the county or district in which the offense is alleged to have been committed.

History

The 1818 Constitution provided that in all criminal prosecutions the accused had a right to be heard by himself and counsel; to demand the nature and cause of the accusation; to meet the witnesses face to face; to have compulsory process to compel the attendance of witnesses in his favor; and to have a speedy public trial by an impartial jury of the vicinage. The final provision was to the effect that the accused shall not be compelled to give evidence against himself.

The 1848 Constitution changed the 1818 provisions only in respect to the locale of the jury. Instead of an impartial jury of the vicinage, the new provision required a jury "of the county or district wherein the offense shall have been committed, which county or district shall have been previously ascertained by law."

The current provisions of the 1870 Constitution, nonsubstantive style changes aside, retained the 1848 section intact except (1) in respect to the locale of the jury wherein the jury was required to be drawn from the county or district in which the offense "is alleged to have been" (instead of "was") committed, and the deletion of the last clause pertaining to the county or district having previously been ascertained by law, and (2) in removing the self-incrimination provision and transferring it to Article II, Section 10.

The 1922 Convention proposal retained the 1870 provisions intact after defeating an amendment which would have added, as a final sentence, an authorization to the legislature to provide for the taking of depositions of nonresident witnesses, other than in homicide cases, by the state or the accused, to be used for or against the accused.

Explanation

The critical relevance of federal decisional law in respect to the often-mentioned incorporation doctrine requires at the outset that it be noted that the following comparable guarantees of the Sixth Amendment of the Constitution of the United States have been applied to the states through the Fourteenth Amendment: (1) the right to counsel (Gideon v. Wainwright, 372 U.S. 335 (1963)); (2) the right to a speedy trial (Klopfer v. North Carolina, 386 U.S. 213 (1967)); (3) the right to a public trial (*In re* Oliver, 333 U.S. 257 (1948)); (4) the right to confrontation of opposing witnesses (Pointer v. Texas, 380 U.S. 400 (1965)); (5) the right to compulsory process for obtaining witnesses (Washington v. Texas, 388 U.S. 14, (1967)); and (6) the right to an impartial jury (Witherspoon v. State of Illinois, 391 U.S. 391 U.S. 510 · (1968)).

To the extent that these federal decisions circumscribe state power beyond the limitations adjudged by the state courts to be within the scope of the state guarantees, the state is powerless to react. What remains of state power in these areas of incorporation of specific federal Bill of Rights provisions into the Fourteenth Amendment is essentially the discretion to impose additional limitations upon governmental power. This it may do by constitutional amendment, by legislation or by judicial interpretation of the existing state constitutional provisions.

These considerations are of course important to the Convention. Reduced to its essence, it means that a constitutional change cannot be proposed which negates the *Gideon v. Wainwright* principle of right to counsel in criminal cases, but that the constitutional right to counsel may be extended to civil or administrative proceedings.

As in other general guarantees in Article II, the state decisions interpreting the complex of rights of an accused after indictment or information are legion. Many of these, in whole or in part, have been superseded or modified by the application of the new federal law. Many others already approximated the standards imported by federal decisions into the comparable federal Sixth Amendment provisions. To attempt a substantial collation, synthesis or analysis of hundreds of state and federal decisions in these areas seems pointless. Guideline principles can be offered simply to sharpen understanding. Beyond this, a review of several of the recent decisions establishing new conceptions of some of the guarantees will be helpful.

Taking the specific rights in the order of statement in this section, the *right to appear* embraces the right to be present at every stage of the trial (People v. Smith, 6 Ill. 2d 414 (1955)), but does not extend to the right to be present for argument in a post-trial motion People v. Berry, 37 Ill. 2d 329 (1967)).

The *right to defend in person* permits a defendant to conduct his own case if he so desires, and waives the otherwise available right to counsel. (People v. Robinson, 27 Ill. 2d 289 (1963).) The *right to counsel* extends to all critical stages in the criminal prosecution, beginning with the "accusatory stage," including the interrogation phase, and extending into the trial phases. The definitive rules are expressed primarily in *Escobedo v. Illinois* (378 U.S. 478 (1964)) and *Miranda v. Arizona* (384 U.S. 436 (1966)).

The *right to demand the nature and cause of the accusation* runs to the critical issue of notice. The offense and the salient factors associating the accused with it must be described with that particularity which enables him to prepare his defense. (People v. Williams, 30 Ill. 2d 125 (1963).)

The *right to meet the witnesses face to face* is designed to assure the critical right of cross examination without which the guarantee of a fair trial could be a mockery. (People v. Ferguson, 410 Ill. 87 (1951).) In *Smith v. Illinois* (390 U.S. 129 (1968)), there is a strong hint that the right of confrontation may be violated where the prosecution fails to disclose the identity of an informer who testifies under an assumed name with the consequence that it deprives the defendant of testimony which could have been significant on the issue of the informer's credibility.

The *right to compel the attendance of witnesses in behalf of the accused,* if denied or substantially impaired, will deny the accused the fair trial to which he is entitled. (People v. Wilson, 24 Ill. 2d 425 (1962).)

The *right to a speedy, public trial* means a trial without undue delay. The period may be relative and delays occasioned by the defendant's conduct cannot be asserted as a violation of the right. (People v. Jones, 33 Ill. 2d 357 (1965); People v. Bryarly, 23 Ill. 2d 313 (1961); People v. Utterback, 385 Ill. 239 (1944).) The public trial requirement is violated only by a blanket exclusion of members of the public. (People v. Dronso, 83 Ill. App. 2d 59 (1967).)

The *right to an impartial jury trial* means generally a jury made up of persons prepared to exercise their personal judgment, favoring neither the prosecution nor the accused, standing indifferent to both, and guided only by the law and the evidence. (People v. Hobbs, 35 Ill. 2d 263 (1966).)

The *right to be tried in the county or district in which the offense is alleged to have been committed* incorporates the common law right to be tried by jurors familiar with the locale and the accused. (Buckrice v. People, 110 Ill. 29 (1884).) The right includes the right to seek a change of venue, a recognition of the accused's privilege of waiver.

Numerous subtleties, modifications, exceptions, variations and circumlocutions surround these basic general interpretations. We leave them untouched as unnecessary to this explanation.

Several recent decisions must be noted, however. *Witherspoon v. Illinois* (391 U.S. 510 (1968)) establishes the important principle that a statute authorizing unlimited challenges for cause for jurors who express general conscientious scruples against the death penalty substantially affects the fairness and impartiality of the jury by virtually assuring a psychologically attuned "hanging jury" in violation of the Sixth and Fourteenth Amendments of the Constitution of the United States.

In *Duncan v. Louisiana* (391 U.S. 145 (1968)), the Sixth and Fourteenth Amendments were held to require a jury trial for "serious offenses," and a state statute defining a simple battery as a misdemeanor for which a two-year sentence of imprisonment was authorized, without trial by jury, was a violation of these guarantees. And in *Bloom v. Illinois* (391 U.S. 194 (1968)), the Court, reversing hallowed precedent, applied the jury trial requirement and "'serious offense" concept of *Duncan* to a conviction for criminal contempt of a court. In *United States v. Jackson* (390 U.S. 570 (1968)), the provision of the Federal Kidnapping Act, interpreted to subject the accused to a death sentence only if he demanded a jury, a risk not assumed if he pleaded guilty or waived a jury trial, was held to impair the Sixth Amendment guarantee of a jury trial. This holding would apply, of course, to state statutes similarly construed, through application of the incorporation doctrine.

Comparative Analysis

All state constitutions provide for right to counsel in criminal prosecutions. Forty-four states provide a right to know the charge, while 21 provide also that the accused be given a copy of the charge. Forty-four states provide that the accused has the right to be confronted by witnesses against him. Forty states provide that the accused has the right to compulsory process to obtain witnesses in his favor. Forty-four states also provide a right to a speedy and public trial. (In relation to the requirement of jury trial, see *Comparative Analysis* under Sec. 5 of this article.) The Sixth Amendment of the Constitution of the United States contains provisions virtually identical with this Section 9. The Model State Constitution makes comparable provisions for rights of accused persons.

Comment

No attempt has been made to explain the political and legal philosophy behind the fundamental post-indictment rights guaranteed by this amendment. The rights are so basic, so well known, so intuitively understood as indispensable to a free society, that any explanation of their supporting rationale would be an affront to the Convention delegates.

What then does an analyst suggest as to the merit of such provisions? The only sensible response that this analyst can suggest is that the amendment should be left untouched, with its meaning and application subject to the normal process of judicial interpretation, leaving to the wisdom of that department the responsibility of assuring that these limitations on governmental power are not abused. It is confidently suggested that this judicial responsibility has thus far been exercised in a manner which vindicates this delegation to the judicial department. Any attempt to enlarge or diminish these familiar and time-honored guarantees could be productive of harm and confusion. Again the cautionary observation is made that this conclusion is subjective. Others may reasonably disagree with it.

Self-Incrimination and Double Jeopardy

Sec. 10. No person shall be compelled in any criminal case to give evidence against himself, or be twice put in jeopardy for the same offense.

History

The 1818 and 1848 Constitutions included the prohibition against self-incrimination in the sections dealing with post-indictment rights of the accused in criminal trials. (See *History,* Sec. 9, *supra,* p. 39.) Each Contution carried an identical double jeopardy prohibition in a separate section. The 1870 Constitution combined these two provisions with minor and nonsubstantive language changes. The 1922 Convention proposal recommended the 1870 provision without change.

Explanation

Self-Incrimination

Again as a preliminary observation, it is important to note that the federal Sixth Amendment right to be free of compelled self-incrimination has been incorporated into the Fourteenth Amendment's due process guarantee as a specific limitation upon state power. (Malloy v. Hogan, 378 U.S. 1 (1964).) To this extent the Convention's power to dilute the guarantee as interpreted by federal standards is abridged. Of course, the state's authority to expand upon these limitations, beyond the federal standards, should it so desire, remains inviolate.

The right against forced self-incrimination has its origins in Twelfth Century efforts of the Church to seek incriminating evidence concerning secular and religious misconduct, thus provoking the concern and hostility of the kings. The practice of that and succeeding centuries, both religious and secular, however, sanctioned the use of torture to make suspected persons give evidence against themselves, upon the basis of which conviction and punishment would follow. The infamous Star Chamber, and its use of corporal punishment to compel a person to establish his guilt, extended well into the Seventeenth Century, when in a celebrated case, the House of Commons ruled illegal a Star Chamber sentence which had severely punished a person for refusing to incriminate himself. Thus was born the rule, first phrased in terms of "no one should be required to accuse himself," that a person may not be compelled in any criminal case to give evidence against himself. The principle became a part of the common law and constitutional tradition in the colonies and their successor original states, and by their insistence was incorporated into the federal Bill of Rights as well as in the state constitutional provisions.

The history and initial objectives of the provision seemed fairly clear. As important as society's interest was in convicting and punishing persons accused of crime, that interest could not, in the light of history, justify compelled self-accusation of crime. The protection against self-incrimination came to be viewed as a truly fundamental liberty.

In the course of litigation, subtleties, nuances and shadings of meaning were developed which went far beyond the initial simplistic Star Chamber-torture-self-accusation syndrome. The abiding conviction that the rule was an indispensable attribute of freedom led to a rejection of what seemed to be the plain and unambiguous limitation of the privilege to criminal cases. Because any governmental inquiries, investigations or proceedings could lead to the disclosure of evidence which might thereafter be used in a criminal prosecution, the privilege was extended to legislative investigations (Watkins v. United States, 354 U.S. 178 (1957)) and in fact to any proceedings, criminal, civil, administrative, judicial, investigative, or adjudicatory, whenever an answer to an inquiry might tend to subject the person to criminal responsibility (Brown v. United States, 356 U.S. 148 (1958); United States v. Goldsmith, 272 F. Supp. 924 (E.D. N.Y. 1967)). Moreover, the privilege is not limited to the defendant in a criminal or civil case or the principal subject of an administrative or legislative investigation; it may, as well, be claimed by any witness to any such proceeding. The normal connotation of the phrase "to be a witness against himself" reasonably suggests a privilege to refuse to give a truthful answer the substance of which would support a conviction under a criminal statute. It has been interpreted far beyond that meaning, however, so as to permit a person to refuse to answer any question which might furnish "a link in the chain of evidence" required to sustain a criminal prosecution. (Blau v. United States, 340 U.S. 159 (1950).)

So complex has the law of self-incrimination become, that in the words of one very competent observer: "[T]he law and the lawyers despite endless litigation over the privilege have never made up their minds just what it is supposed to do or just whom it is intended to protect." (Kalven, "Invoking the Fifth Amendment: Some Legal and Impractical Considerations," 9 Bull. Atom. Sciences 181, 182 (1953).)

Despite this devastating professional appraisal, it may still be desirable to suggest some of the more important applications and nonapplications of the rule. *Escobedo v. Illinois* (378 U.S. 478 (1964)) relied upon the privilege against self-incrimination as the constitutional foundation of a person to have counsel during the post-arrest police interrogation stage. That decision, and the guidelines which followed in *Miranda v. Arizona* (384 U.S. 436 (1966)), have left many law enforcement officers in a state of shock from which they are just beginning to emerge. If the mandated *Miranda* advice and warnings are not given to the person in custody, *e.g.,* that he has a right to remain silent, and that any statement he makes may be used as evidence against him, the clear impact of the decision is that no statement, even if voluntarily offered, may be used against the accused by the prosecution.

In a less liberal vein the Supreme Court has held that the privilege concerns only evidence given by a person which is testimonial or communicative in nature, and that it does not apply to a withdrawal of blood from the accused and the admission in evidence of the analysis thereof (Schmerber v. California, 384 U.S. 757 (1966)); to a compelled post-indictment police lineup inspection (United States v. Wade, 388 U.S. 218 (1967)); to the taking and use of a handwriting sample of the accused (Gilbert v. California, 388 U.S. 263 (1967)); or to the taking of fingerprints (United States v. Braverman, 376 F. 2d 249 (2d Cir. 1967), *cert. denied,* 389 U.S. 885 (1967).)

In a remarkable denial of the privilege, *Shapiro v. United States* (335 U.S. 1 (1948)) applied the "required records" doctrine to a businessman who produced his records, after claiming the privilege, and was thereafter convicted on the basis of his own evidence. The relevant statutory immunity provision under these circumstances was held not to apply to business records required by law to be kept, which records were held not to be within the scope of the privilege against self-incrimination. However, in *Marchetti v. United States* (390 U.S. 39 (1968)) and in *Haynes v. United States* (390 U.S. 85 (1968)), some of the sting may have been taken out of *Shapiro,* which was distinguished but not overruled. In those cases the registration provisions of the federal wagering tax statutes and the National Firearms Act, respectively, were held to violate the privilege against self-incrimination. These latter decisions were almost predictable after *Albertson v. Subversive Activities Control Board* (382 U.S. 70 (1965)) which held invalid, under the privilege, orders of the board requiring named individuals, found by the board to be members of the Communist Party, to file registration statements acknowledging such membership, the effect of which could be to subject them to criminal prosecution under federal statutes.

Of particular interest is *Griffin v. California* (380 U.S. 609 (1965)) which held that a prosecutor's comment on the accused's refusal to testify, or an instruction that the jury may consider the defendant's silence in weighing the evidence, violated the defendant's privilege against self-incrimination. The Illinois posture on this issue under the state constitutional provision appears to be the same as the federal rule. Indeed, in most issues arising out of the state and federal constitutional guarantees, prior to *Malloy v. Hogan* (378 U.S. 1 (1964)) applying the federal self-incrimination provision to the states, the holdings were more parallel than disparate. Thus, both state and federal decisions generally agreed that in the absence of claim of privilege it is waived; that the privilege is personal and does not apply to corporate records which may incriminate corporate officers; that physical examinations of the person, including other evidence of a nontestimonial nature, are not within the privilege; and that statutes granting immunity for compelled testimony do not violate the guarantee if the scope of the immunity is as broad as the protective umbrella of the privilege. These examples do not exhaust the areas of concurrence.

The relationship of the guarantees against unreasonable search and seizure and self-incrimination is immediately apparent. Evidence unlawfully seized, if permitted to be used, can obviously involve self-incrimination. The decisions suggest that the two guarantees, though not identical, have an area of overlap. (*See* People v. Kalpak, 10 Ill. 2d 411 (1957); People v. Perry, 1 Ill. 2d 482 (1953).)

Again as in the explanations under other sections of the Article, the purpose has been to inform generally, and not in an exhaustive and critical way, of the meaning, scope and application of the provision in its more common and important contexts. Many of the procedural complexities with which the decisions abound, primarily in respect to when the privilege may be claimed and the scope of judicial power or discretion in assessing the legitimacy of the claim of privilege, have not been dealt with. Though important, they are essentially collateral to an analysis of the principal objectives of the provision.

Double Jeopardy

In *Palko v. Connecticut* (302 U.S. 319 (1937)), the United States Supreme Court held that the state could appeal and secure a new trial of an accused it had charged with first degree murder, but convicted, in a jury trial, of second degree murder. Against the defendant's claim that the Fourteenth Amendment of the Constitution of the United States incorporated the federal Fifth Amendment requirement that no person "be subject for the same offense to be twice put in jeopardy of life or limb," the response was negative. The decision further held that the due process guarantee of the Fourteenth Amendment would be applied in state cases involving jeopardy only when the jeopardy subjected a defendant to "a hardship so acute and shocking that our polity will not endure it." (*Id.* at 328.)

On June 23, 1969, in *Benton v. Maryland* (395 U.S. 784 (1969)), the Supreme Court overruled *Palko* and applied the incorporation doctrine to a situation in which the state was successful in securing a conviction on a burglary count after the accused was acquitted of larceny. The conviction was subsequently set aside on appeal on a wholly different constitutional principle and the accused was thereupon retried on both the burglary and larceny counts. His constitutional challenge of a retrial, on due process grounds, of the larceny charge was rejected by the trial court and conviction followed on both the burglary and larceny charges. The Supreme Court of the United States could have ruled that a subsequent retrial and conviction of an offense which had earlier resulted in an acquittal subjected the defendant, on due process grounds, to "a hardship so acute and shocking that out polity will not endure it." In a clear rejection of this obvious approach to the resolution of jeopardy issues under the Fourteenth Amendment, it chose instead to follow the trend of its own decisional expansion of the incorporation doctrine.

The double jeopardy principle, on its face, seems disarmingly clear and simple. In fact it is quite complex and abstract, and has given rise to conflicting and troublesome issues of law and policy. The meaning of "jeopardy" and the "same offense" is hardly crystal clear. The facts of the *Benton* case present the issue in its most simplistic form, a retrial after an acquittal for what is clearly the same offense. The problem is rarely posed, however, in such obvious terms. Some of the most difficult problems arise out of the dual sovereignty concept of federalism, wherein the federal and state governments seek and secure convictions against the same person for separately defined state and federal offenses, involving the same facts and conduct. Other serious problems arise where multiple prosecutions ensue for what is essentially the same criminal act, *e.g.,* robbing five persons, prosecution related to three of the victims resulting in acquittal, followed by a prosecution based on robbery of the fourth victim. In this not too uncommon instance of selective and multiple prosecutions arising out of the same criminal offense, the United States Supreme Court, in *Hoag v. New Jersey* (356 U.S. 464 (1958)), sustained the conviction as within the permissible latitude of the states' power to administer their own systems of justice. An even more dramatic illustration of this latitude is *Ciucci v. Illinois* (356 U.S. 571 (1958)) where the defendant, charged with the killing of his wife and three children, was prosecuted in separate trials involving different victims, the state seeking most earnestly to secure the death penalty. In the first two trials the defendant was convicted but received sentences of imprisonment. In the third trial the state finally secured the death penalty. The same evidence involving all four deaths was introduced in each of the trials. The United States Supreme Court, in a 5-4 decision, upheld the murder conviction, holding that the state could proceed either by a multiple-count indictment in a single trial, or by separate trials. *Hoag* and *Ciucci* antedated *Benton's* incorporation rule and were decided only on due process grounds. Whether *Benton* will have a significant effect on this and other issues of double jeopardy is, of course, questionable at this point.

On the federalism matter, the issue is even more sensitive. The dual sovereignty concept and the reluctance of the federal courts to impede, except on the most compelling of grounds, the right of a state to prosecute for an offense for which a prosecution has already occurred under a federal criminal statute, suggests that *Benton* will not be applied to such cases.

The dual sovereignty concept received its first recognition in *Moore v. Illinois* (55 U.S. (14 How.) 13 (1852)), wherein the Court said:

"Every citizen of the United States is also a citizen of a State or territory. He may .be said to owe allegiance to two sovereigns, and may be liable to punishment for an infraction of the laws of either. The same act may be an offense or transgression of the laws of both. . . . That either or both may (if they see fit) punish such offender, cannot be doubted. Yet it cannot truly be averred that the offender has been twice punished for the same offense; but only that by one act he has committed two offenses, for each of which he is justly punishable." (*Id.* at 20.)

This principle was reaffirmed in two major decisions, both involving Illinois. The first was *Bartkus v. Illinois* (355 U.S. 281 (1958)). The facts were as follows: defendant was tried for robbery in the federal district court under the Federal Bank Robbery Statute and acquitted. Shortly thereafter Illinois indicted and tried the defendant for the same offense under the state robbery statute. He was convicted and the conviction was affirmed by the Illinois Supreme Court, with the Court relying heavily on the *Moore* rationale of dual sovereignty. (People v. Bartkus, 7 Ill. 2d 138 (1955).) The United States Supreme Court affirmed the conviction.

The second case is *Abbate v. United States* (359 U.S. 187 (1959)), decided at the same term as *Bartkus*. The facts were different; Abbate was separately tried and convicted first in the federal district court and then in the state court for defined federal and state criminal offenses arising out of the same conduct, whereas in *Bartkus* a state conviction followed a federal acquittal. The Supreme Court sustained the state conviction in an 8-1 decision, refusing to yield on either due process or double jeopardy grounds from its prior holdings. It may be that the argument most persuasive to the Court was the government's contention that a reversal of the dual sovereignty principle could lead to a race by the defendant (or the state) to the state courts for a conviction with a nomial punishment which would then immunize the defendant from federal prosecution and a potentially more severe punishment.

Whatever the merits of these decisions, the dual sovereignty rule seems firmly entrenched at the moment and, as indicated, is probably not endangered by the *Benton* rule of incorporation of the federal jeopardy provision into the Fourteenth Amendment. In Illinois, the principle of dual sovereignty is applied to multiple prosecutions under state statutes and local ordinances. In *Robbins v. People* (95 Ill. 175 (1880)), it was held in a decision which seems valid today that the same act may be an offense against the state and a municipality and may be punished under both.

In the more mundane areas of conflict, lIIinois has held, among other decisions, that a statute which provides increased penalties for second or subsequent criminal offenses does not violate the state's double jeopardy guarantee (People v. Manning, 397 Ill. 358 (1947)); that aquittal of an offense operates as an acquittal and as a bar as to all lesser included offenses on which a conviction could have been secured on the indictment charging the higher offense (People v. Harrison, 395 Ill. 463 (1946)); that the right is a personal privilege which may be waived (People v. Scales, 18 Ill. 2d 283 (1960)); and that acquittal bars any appeal (People v. Miner, 144 Ill. 308 (1893)).

Illinois decisions dealing with collateral issues such as the time when jeopardy attaches, the stage at which in a criminal proceeding the procedure establishes a bar to further prosecution, problems of waiver, and others, need not be analyzed in this already too lengthy explanation. Suffice it to say, in conclusion, that the areas of uncertainty are many, and that the *Benton* decision will in all probability increase the uncertainty.

Comparative Analysis

All state constitutions contain comparable provisions relating to the right against self-incrimination. Seven states have no constitutional provision on double jeopardy. The Model State Constitution contains similar provisions. The Fifth Amendment of the Constitution of the United States provides, "nor shall any person be subject for the same offense to be twice put in jeopardy of life or limb; nor shall be compelled in any criminal case to be a witness against himself . . . ."

Comment

Self-Incrimination

It may come as a surprise that much respectable authority exists for the proposition that this provision, as interpreted, goes far beyond appropriate notions of its proper meaning, and that legitimate state interests in arriving at the truth in criminal and other proceedings are being thwarted in ill-conceived efforts to protect individual freedoms. Jeremy Bentham, an acknowledged giant among legal philosophers, asserted that not only was there no justification for the privilege, but that it also operated as an illogical and indefensible obstruction to justice. The pre-eminent Dean Wigmore in his famous treatise on evidence (J. Wigmore, VIII Wigmore on Evidence §§ 2250-2284 (1961)) denigrated the reasons most frequently offered in defense of the rule and believed firmly that it was too frequently abused to the detriment of the administration of justice and the public. He concluded, however, that on balance the retention of the rule was probably more desirable than its abolition. Justice Walter V. Schaefer of the Illinois Supreme Court, one of the nation's most distinguished jurists, has severely criticized the moral and ethical foundations of the privilege and particularly its application to police interrogation procedures as defined in the *Escobedo* and *Miranda* decisions, and to virtually total prohibitions upon the right of a prosecutor in a criminal case to comment upon the failure of a defendant to take the stand. (Schaefer, "Police Interrogation and the Privilege Against Self-Incrimination," 61 Nw. L. Rev. 506 (1966).)

There is, however, no lack of defenders of the privilege in its total or partial meanings and applications. The mere statement of the privilege seems to evoke a most passionate defense that it is a fundamental and inviolate freedom against the threat of arbitrary governmental power. Given the psychological consensus that it commands, it would seem almost heretical to suggest that it be tampered with in any form. In the last analysis it seems well to agree with Dean Wigmore that its retention will be less harmful than its abolition. Rather than suggest constitutional amendment, it would appear preferable to leave to the courts and the legislature the further development and evolution of the principle, in the hope, perhaps well founded, that by this approach the appropriate accommodation of public and private rights will eventually be achieved.

Double Jeopardy

As with the privilege against self-incrimination, the double jeopardy rule is deeply embedded in constitutional doctrine. It enjoys in its doctrinal meaning a greater acceptance in principle among legal scholars than does the privilege against self-incrimination. Despite its many uncertainties it surely deserves constitutional status, again with the thought that the normal evolutionary processes of the law will better assure its effective implementation than any effort to engraft particular emphasis or limitations upon the existing constitutional language.

Limitation of Penalties after Conviction

Sec. 11. All penalties shall be proportioned to the nature of the offense; and no conviction shall work corruption of blood or forfeiture of estate; nor shall any person be transported out of the State for any offense committed within the same.

History

Each of the three clauses of this section were parts of separate sections, identically worded, in the 1818 and 1848 Constitutions. The section providing for proportioning penalties to the offense added the benevolent thought that it is "the true design of all punishment . . . to reform, not to exterminate mankind." The 1818 and 1848 provisions, absent the philosophical observation, were consolidated into the present section. The 1922 Convention proposal retained the present version except for minor stylistic language changes.

Explanation

Penalties to be proportioned to the nature of the offense

This provision, it has been plausibly suggested, is the lineal descendant of that clause of the Eighth Amendment of the Constitution of the United States which forbids cruel and unusual punishment. In terms, it is quite clear that the whole of the Eighth Amendment dealing with excessive bail, fines and cruel and unusual punishment is based precisely on the tenth Section of the historic English Bill of Rights of 1689 which established the decisive victory of the people, through Parliament, over the monarchy.

In *O'Neil v. Vermont* (144 U.S. 323 (1892)), the Supreme Court refused to apply this clause of the Eighth Amendment, through the principle of incorporation into the Fourteenth Amendment, as a limitation upon state power, leaving undisturbed an unusually severe state sentence. In *Louisiana* ex rel. *Francis v. Resweber* (329 U.S. 459 (1947)), the Court assumed without deciding that the Eighth Amendment was applicable to the states through the due process clause of the Fourteenth Amendment, but denied that a second try at electrocution of the accused (the first having gone awry) was cruel and unusual punishment. In *Robinson v. California* (370 U.S. 660 (1962)), however, the Supreme Court invalidated that portion of a California statute which made it a criminal offense to "be addicted to the use of narcotics" as a denial of due process under the Fourteenth Amendment, but in another reference clearly implied that the Eighth Amendment prohibition was applicable to the states. Addiction was distinguished from use as being a nonpunishable status offense, comparable to an illness. The Court refused to extend the *Robinson* principle in *Powell v. Texas* (392 U.S. 514 (1968)) where a state criminal offense of "public intoxication" was held to apply to use and not to status.

State decisional law views the clause as directed to the law-making body. Judicial self-restraint in second-guessing the legislature has led the Illinois Supreme Court to the general position that an objection to a penalty established by the lawmakers will not be sustained unless it is cruel and degrading punishment unknown to the common law, or so wholly disproportionate as to shock the moral sense. (People v. Elliott, 272 Ill. 592 (1916).)

Whether this general proposition would today sustain a punishment imposing some of the extreme physical tortures known to the common law is highly doubtful, but in terms of capital punishment or imprisonment the authority of the state is most expansively construed. Illustratively, the following punishments have been held not to violate this clause of the state Constitution: the death sentence for murder, including such sentence on a plea of guilty (People v. Chesnas, 325 Ill. 361 (1927)); a sentence of one year to life for armed robbery where the fruits of the crime were but twenty-five cents (People v. Williams, 4 Ill. 2d 440 (1954)); a sentence of 199 years for murder which effectively precluded the possibility of parole (People v. Grant, 385 Ill. 61 (1943); life imprisonment for aiding in rape (People v. Mundro, 326 Ill. 324 (1927)); a sentence of five to 14 years for forgery where the defendant obtained but $45 (People v. Haynes, 73 Ill. App. 2d 85 (1966)); sentences within the indeterminate limits fixed by law (People v. Calcaterra, 33 Ill. 2d 541 (1965)); and increased penalties for subsequent offenses under the Habitual Criminal Act (Kelly v. People, 115 Ill. 583 (1886)).

In contrast, the Court has invalidated an act which made it a criminal offense to be under the influence of or addicted to the use of narcotic drugs. (People v. Davis, 27 Ill. 2d 57 (1963).) The Illinois Supreme Court relied on the drug addiction decision in *Robinson v. California* (*supra*, p. 51) but curiously made no mention of the relevance of this section of the state Constitution. Earlier and somewhat surprisingly the Court held that a statute prohibiting freight rate discriminations and providing for the forfeiture of all franchises as a penalty for violation offended this clause, as the penalty would in some cases amount to a fine of millions of dollars. (Chicago & A. R.R. v. People *ex rel.* Koerner, 67 Ill. 11 (1873).) The "somewhat surprisingly" reference is used because the revocation of licenses which frequently involves the death of a professional career and the loss of great investments and potential earnings is uniformly sustained as not involving "punishment" in a constitutional sense. In *Hayes Freight Lines, Inc. v. Castle* (2 Ill. 2d 58 (1954)), the Court sustained authorized suspensions of operating privileges of certificated motor carriers for repeated violations of weight and load limitations. (See the extended treatment of the *Chicago & A. R.R. Co.* case, *infra*, pp. 367-8.)

Corruption of blood and forfeiture of estate

This clause of the section has no verbatim counterpart in the United States Constitution. Article 3, Section 3, clause 2, of that Constitution which provides that no attainder of treason shall work corruption of blood, or forfeiture, except during the life of the person attainted, is obviously much more limited in scope. Illinois decisional law is sparse but illuminating. In *Wall v. Pfanschmidt* (265 Ill. 180 (1914)), the Court held that an heir who murdered the intestate did not lose his rights of inheritance under the laws of intestacy and strongly suggested that a contrary holding might involve an unconstitutional forfeiture of estate under this section. *Welsh v. James* (408 Ill. 18 (1950)) reached the same result with the same hint in sustaining the common law right of survivorship of a joint tenant who murdered his co-tenant. Both decisions in respect to the forfeiture issue were rejected and reversed, however, in *Bradley v. Fox* (7 Ill. 2d 106 (1955)), involving the survivorship rights of a murderer of his joint tenant. The forfeiture provision was also held inapplicable in *Collins v. Metropolitan Life Insurance Co.* (232 Ill. 37 (1907)), where on public policy grounds the Court adopted the prevailing view that a beneficiary who murders his insured loses his claim to insurance benefits.

Transportation out of the state for any offense committed within the state

Historically, banishment or exile from the realm was an accepted form of punishment. The legislature has heeded the admonition against the imposition of this particularly cruel form of punishment, thus obviating any decisional law.

Comparative Analysis

Approximately half the states provide that penalties shall be proportioned to the nature of the offense. Twenty-one states also provide that no conviction shall work corruption of blood or forfeiture of estate. Fifteen other states provide that no person shall be transported out of the state for any offense committed within the same. The Model State Constitution makes no similar provision. The Eighth Amendment of the United States Constitution forbids cruel and unusual punishments; the Article 3, Section 3, clause 2, reference in the Constitution of the United States to forfeiture and corruption is not relevant, and there is no provision comparable to the prohibition on banishment.

Comment

The "punishment shall fit the crime" provision, despite the wide latitude it reserves to the legislature, appears, nevertheless to be worthy of retention. It is at least a reminder to the legislative body that it is not completely uninhibited in defining punishment. In all probability, in view of the widespread and generally successful state efforts to abolish capital punishment, efforts will be made to establish a constitutional ban on the death penalty. The issue has been extremely sensitive in recent Illinois legislative sessions and efforts to provide experimental moratoriums on capital punishment, though receiving substantial support, have failed of passage. Whether the issue should be left to legislative judgment rather than being raised to constitutional status depends initially on the resolution of the basic policy issue. It is not possible to provide purely objective guidelines on this important issue.

As to corruption of blood and forfeiture of estate, these provisions appear to be anachronistic. It is difficult to envision a legislative body providing now for either of these ancient sanctions. If such a law were to be enacted, the reasonable probability is that it would be stricken under the state and federal due process guarantees. The same observations apply to the banishment clause. The Convention may well wish to consider seriously the abolition of these clauses.

Imprisonment for Debt

Sec. 12. No person shall be imprisoned for debt, unless upon refusal to deliver up his estate for the benefit of his creditors, in such manner as shall be prescribed by law; or in cases where there is strong presumption of fraud.

History

The current section is a verbatim restatement of the identical provisions in the 1818 and 1848 Constitutions. The 1922 Convention proposal retained this provision in essentially the same language.

Explanation

Imprisonment for debt arising from contract, where the failure of payment was untainted by fraud or concealment of assets and was due simply to economic inability, was one of the horrors of the common law. This section was designed to remedy the injustice by making wrongful refusal or fraud, instead of mere inability to pay the debt, the standard for imprisonment. To imprison for debt it is necessary to establish that the debtor is wrongfully refusing to deliver up his estate in satisfaction of the debt, or that he was guilty of fraud in contracting the debt or in avoiding the payment of it. (Huntington v. Metzger, 158 Ill. 272 (1895).)

The term "debt" means an obligation in the proper and popular sense, involving a debtor-creditor relationship, and, with few exceptions, debts which arise out of contract. (Cox v. Rice, 375 Ill. 357 (1940); *In re* Blacklidge, 359 Ill. 482 (1935); People v. Zito, 237 Ill. 434 (1908).) Accordingly, the ban on imprisonment does not apply to imprisonments incident to and arising from the commission of an intentional or malicious tort. (Lipman v. Goebel, 357 Ill. 315 (1934); Shatz v. Paul, 7 Ill.

App. 2d 223 (1935).) Nor is imprisonment barred where the "debt" is in the nature of a penalty imposed for violation of a penal law of the state (People v. Zito, 237 Ill. 434 (1908)) or for penalties for violations of municipal ordinances or for fines and costs in criminal proceedings (City of Chicago v. Morell, 247 Ill. 383 (1910)).

Continuing the logic, the failure to pay alimony and a consequent commitment for contempt is not imprisonment for a debt; the rationale is that the imprisonment is for disobeying a binding command of the court. (Mesirow v. Mesirow, 346 Ill. 219 (1931); Barclay v. Barclay, 184 Ill. 375 (1900).) The distinction which justifies imprisonment for failure to abide by decrees for the payment of money in alimony decrees has been applied to other orders classified as equitable in nature (Tudor v. Firebaugh, 364 Ill. 283 (1936); First Nat'l Bank & Trust Co. v. Desaro, 43 Ill. App. 2d 153 (1963)); but other decisions have evidenced a judicial reluctance to enforce contempt orders by imprisonment unless the failure to pay money is based on fraud or a willful defiance of the court (Blake v. People, 80 Ill. 11 (1875); LaRue v. LaRue, 341 Ill. App. 411 (1950); Meaden v. W. J. Anderson Corp. 301 Ill. App. 390 (1939)).

Federal decisional law is sparse on this issue. This section has no counterpart in the Constitution of the United States. Any issue of unconstitutional imprisonment for debt would surely invoke the due process guarantee of the Fifth Amendment or the cruel and unusual punishment provision of the Eighth Amendment.

Comparative Analysis

Thirteen states prohibit imprisonment for debt in all cases. Three other states make an exception where the debtor refuses to deliver his estate for the benefit of his creditors as required by law, and 24 others except cases where there is fraud or a strong presumption thereof. There is no similar provision in the Model State Constitution, nor is there any comparable provision in the Constitution of the United States.

Comment

The section has not been the subject of much critical professional analysis nor, for that matter, has it engendered much litigation. In its basic policy of barring imprisonment for honest failure to pay contractual debts, the section expresses a desirable limitation upon state power. Some question may exist as to a policy which permits imprisonment for nonpayment of alimony or other types of equitable decrees. Whether it is possible to single out particular additional areas deserving of constitutional protection for nonpayment of debts or other obligations is most speculative. It is difficult to suggest whether this section is worthy of retention or in what manner this section should be amended.

In all likelihood the due process guarantee of the state Constitution or the state requirement that punishment shall be proportional to the offense would today invalidate imprisonment for debt where no fraud or evasion was present. The variation in state constitutional provisions and the absence of a comparable provision in the Model State Constitution strongly suggest that the section may no longer be necessary as a distinct constitutional principle.

Right of Eminent Domain

Sec. 13. Private property shall not be taken or damaged for public use without just compensation. Such compensation, when not made by the State, shall be ascertained by a jury, as shall be prescribed by law. The fee of land taken for railroad tracks, without consent of the owners thereof, shall remain in such owners, subject to the use for which it is taken.

History

The 1818 and 1848 antecedent provisions were identical. They stated "nor shall any man's property be taken or applied to public use without the consent of his representatives in the General Assembly, nor without just compensation being made to him." The 1870 revision (1) substituted the words "or damaged" for "or applied"; (2) deleted the provision requiring the consent of the person's representatives in the General Assembly; (3) added the provision requiring jury determination of the compensation where compensation was to be paid by someone other than the state; and (4) added the final sentence preserving the fee of land taken for railroad tracks in the landowner.

It is clear that the words "or damaged" were inserted to overcome decisions under the 1818 and 1848 Constitutions interpreting "taken or applied" provisions to the effect that compensation was allowed only when property was physically taken. Mere damage to property as a result of state action which did not involve a physical taking was not compensable under the just compensation provision.

The deletion of the provision "without the consent of his representatives in the General Assembly" was without explanation in the 1870 proceedings. The addition of the provision requiring jury determination of compensation in nonstate action was apparently intended to eliminate administrative abuse of discretion in determining "just compensation." The provision for retention of the fee in land taken for railroad tracks was also designed to prevent takings for railroad purposes, abandonment of the original purpose, and subsequent use for a different purpose.

The proposed 1922 Constitution deleted the provision concerning the fee and provided simply that: "Private property shall not be taken or damaged for public use without just compensation which, when not made by the state, shall be ascertained by a jury."

Explanation

Eminent domain is the power of the state to take private property for public use. The power is normally exercised through a so-called condemnation action. The power is said to be inherent in all sovereignties, existing independently of constitutions or statutes. (Sanitary Dist. v. Manasse, 380 Ill. 27 (1942).) One commentator has gone so far as to suggest, without supporting authority, that "[w]ithout constitutional or statutory restriction, each of us holds his property subject to the right of the state to take it without any compensation." (Righeimer, "The Law of Eminent Domain," 43 Ill. Bar J. 206 (1954).) The point is probably overstated. Agreed that many decisions hold or suggest that the power of eminent domain is an inherent power of sovereignty, and that its existence does not depend on constitutional or statutory grant, it is at least very questionable that the power is as unlimited as suggested. Due process guarantees, as well as limits upon the exercise of the police power, would surely be adequate today, without express limitations upon the power of eminent domain, to foreclose the state from taking private property for a public use without payment of just compensation. However, the question is basically academic, since all state constitutions and the United States Constitution (Amendment V) forbid such taking. Indeed, the Fifth Amendment prohibition has been held to apply to the states through incorporation into the Fourteenth Amendment due process guarantee. (Chicago B. & Q R.R. v. Chicago, 166 U.S. 226 (1897).)

Perhaps the first point to be made is that there is an interrelationship, possibly even a conflict in realistic if not legal terms, between eminent domain and the police power of the state. A taking or damaging of property which is an incident of and referable to a governmental purpose to protect the public health, safety, morals or welfare is not within the terms of the constitutional eminent domain provision which mandates just compensation. (State Bank & Trust Co. v. Village of Wilmette, 358 Ill. 311 (1934).) The distinction between compensable takings for a public use and noncompensable takings or damages which are a consequence of the police power have been recognized and applied in many cases. As good an elucidation of this distinction as any is expressed in *Chicago & Northwestern Railway v. Illinois Commerce Commission* (326 Ill. 625 (1927)), wherein it is noted that regulations under the police power to promote and safeguard the health, safety, morals or general welfare of the public which govern and restrict the use of property do not constitute a taking or damaging for which compensation is required; that police regulations of this nature may destroy the use and value of

property and, in cases of necessity, may even destroy the property itself
when its continued existence constitutes a menace to the public; that
police legislation is directed against property and the uses of property
which are considered harmful to society and that it operates by prohibiting the use, or by destroying the property; and that no such elements
enter into a taking under the power of eminent domain which is simply
the appropriation of property or the use of property for public purposes.

Most of what is stated in that case is dicta, but it does reflect with fair
accuracy the general status of the law. Zoning laws restrict the uses to
which an owner may wish to devote his property. Building codes impose construction requirements which effect substantial economic bur-.
dens, as do laws which restrict the height of buildings or set lot line
dimensions. Property which is a nuisance and a threat to public health
or safety may be taken or destroyed. These and other instances of noncompensable police power takings illustrate the point.

On the other hand, it has been held that the police power is itself subject to the constitutional restraints of due process and just compensation.
(Forbes v. Hubbard, 348 Ill. 166 (1932) (zoning ordinance restriction
held an unconstitutional taking); City of Chicago v. Lederer, 247 Ill. 584
(1916) (ordinance purporting to be a police measure restricting the right
to erect a driveway across a public sidewalk subject to just compensation
requirement); Klever Shampay Karpet Kleaners v. City of Chicago, 238
Ill. App. 291 (1925) (invalidating an ordinance requiring a dry cleaner's
benzine room to be located at least 50 feet from any other building).)

The courts are obviously torn between competing constitutional values
and the decisions reflect the dilemma. The limits of police power cannot be defined or applied with logical precision. What are the criteria,
beyond the instinctive or visceral predilections of judges, which determine that an enactment, purporting to be an exercise of the police
power, is or is not reasonably designed to remedy the evils which the
legislature has determined to be a threat to an important public interest?
When, in short, does a taking or damaging transcend police power limitations and become a taking of private property for public use without
compensation or a deprivation of property in violation of due process?
These are difficult questions which pose the interrelationship (and conflict) between the power of eminent domain and the police power. Nor
are they answered by the generalities above detailed which purport to
define the difference between these powers. For despite the grandiose
judicial pronouncements covering the scope of noncompensable police
power takings or damagings, the decisions, as we shall see, tend rather
substantially to favor the property owner over the state, and to assert
the eminent domain-just compensation principle as the paramount value.

The issue is not novel. It was discussed in sharply divergent views by Justices Holmes and Brandeis in *Pennsylvania Coal Company v. Mahon* (260 U.S. 393 (1922)), in which a statute making it unlawful to conduct coal-mining operations in such a way "as to cause the caving in, collapse or subsidence" of public and private buildings was held to exceed the police power and to impair the company's conceded contract right to mine for coal beneath the complainant's home, free from liability for any damage which might be occasioned thereby. It was evident that Justice Holmes, speaking for himself and seven of his colleagues, was sorely tried. "Government hardly could go on if to some extent values incident to property could not be diminished without paying for every such change . . . ." (*Id.* at 413.) Some values must yield to the police power "[b]ut obviously the implied limitation must have its limits, or the contract and due process clauses are gone." (*Id.* at 413.) "When it [the police power] reaches a certain magnitude, in most if not in all cases there must be an exercise of eminent domain and compensation to sustain the act." (*Id.* at 413.) The resolution of the issue depends upon the particular facts. No general rule is determinative; one of the critical factors is the extent of the diminution; another is the extent of the public interest which the act seeks to protect. "The protection of private property in the Fifth Amendment presupposes that it is wanted for public use, but provides that it shall not be taken for such use without compensation. A similar assumption is made in the decisions under the Fourteenth Amendment. . . . When this seemingly absolute protection is found to be qualified by the police power, the natural tendency of human nature is to extend the qualification more and more until at last private property disappears. But this cannot be accomplished this way under the Constitution of the United States." (*Id.* at 415.)

The general rule, said Justice Holmes, is that while property may be regulated to a certain extent, if regulation goes too far it will be recognized as a taking. This to him was such a case: "We are in danger of forgetting that a strong public desire to improve the public condition is not enough to warrant achieving the desire by a shorter cut than the constitutional way of paying for the change." (*Id.* at 416.)

Justice Brandeis in dissent reacted with vigor.

"Every restriction upon the use of property imposed in the exercise of the police power deprives the owner of some right theretofore enjoyed, and is, in that sense, an abridgment by the State of rights in property without making compensation. But restriction imposed to protect the public health, safety or morals from dangers threatened is not a taking. The restriction here imposed is merely the prohibition of a noxious use. The property so restricted remains in the possession of the owner. The State does not appropriate it or make any

use of it. The State merely prevents the owner from making a use which interferes with the paramount rights of the public." (*Id.* at 417.)

As to Justice Holmes' position that condemnation is available and
appropriate, Justice Brandeis replied:

"Nor is a restriction imposed through exercise of the police power inappropriate as a means, merely because the same might be effected through exercise
of the power of eminent domain, or otherwise at public expense. Every restriction
upon the height of buildings might be secured through acquiring by eminent
domain the right of each owner to build above the limiting height; but it is
settled that the State need not resort to that power." (*Id.* at 418.)

The purpose — protection of public safety — being legitimate, it need
not be purchased on the market.

"If by mining anthracite coal the owner would necessarily unloose poisonous
gases, I suppose no one would doubt the power of the State to prevent the
mining, without buying his coal fields. And why may not the State, likewise,
without paying compensation, prohibit one from digging so deep or excavating
so near the surface, as to expose the community to like dangers? In the latter
case, as in the former, carrying on the business would be a public nuisance."
(*Id.* at 418-19.)

References to this case have been extensive because the issue is sharply
illumined and the respective protagonists so pre-eminent. Yet, in the
final analysis, what do these conflicting decisions establish other than that
each position is persuasive and logically compelling, and supported on
strong legal and public policy grounds? To Justice Holmes, the police
power must yield to private property and contractual rights when the
occasion or necessity for a taking without compensation is not convinc-
ingly evident. Conceding the existence of a valid public purpose, if
government has the option of taking without compensation under the
police power or taking with compensation under its power of eminent
domain, the equities demand that the property owner be compensated.
Justice Brandeis "zeroes in" instead on the governmental interest to protect the public health, safety, morals and general welfare. Fearing that
this inherent and essential power will be diluted to the detriment of
society if encumbered by a compensation requirement whenever property
rights are taken, damaged or impaired, he opts for the supremacy of the
police power.

The decisions, federal and state, reflect one or the other of these major
premises, but without any observable synthesis which establishes clear-
cut guidelines of application. In fact, there is sometimes a bewildering
confusion even on the basic premises. How does one evaluate the sweeping pronouncement in *Dube v. City of Chicago* (7 Ill. 2d 313 (1955))
that constitutional declarations that private property shall not be taken

for public use without just compensation or due process are always subordinated to interests of public welfare as expressed through the exercise of the police power, with the statement in *Heimgaertner v. Benjamin Electric Manufacturing Company* (6 Ill. 2d 152 (1955)) that the police power, while paramount to the rights of the individual, is still restrained by the fundamental principles of justice connoted by the phrase, due process of law, and that it cannot override the natural demands of justice, nor disregard the constitutional guarantees in respect to the taking of private property, due process and equal protection of laws? There may be consistency in these views based on implicit or unexpressed premises, but it requires an act of faith to find that harmony.

Among the decisions supporting the police power supremacy thesis are *Mugler v. Kansas* (123 U.S. 623 (1887)), denying compensation for the greatly diminished value of a brewery business by a state law imposing prohibition, and *Village of Euclid v. Ambler Realty Company* (272 U.S. 365 (1926)), sustaining a building restriction alleged to reduce the value of the complainant's property. (*See also* Welch v. Swasey 214 U.S. 91 (1909); Hadacheck v. Sebastian, 239 U.S. 394 (1915); Reinman v. City of Little Rock, 237 U.S. 171 (1915); and Thomas Cusack Co. v. City of Chicago, 242 U.S. 526 (1917), for comparable holdings on building construction and open-area requirements in building and zoning laws.) *St. Regis Paper Company v. United States* (110 Ct. Cl. 271 (1948), *cert. denied*, 335 U.S. 815 (1948)) sustained as a noncompensable act, under the war powers, an order requiring the closing of a mine, and *Omnia Commercial Company v. United States* (261 U.S. 502 (1923)) sustained the government's requisition of a steel company's entire production for 1918, the effect of which was, in each case, to nullify contractual rights. (*See generally,* United States *ex rel.* TVA v. Powelson, 319 U.S. 266 (1943); Oro Fino Consol. Mine Inc. v. United States, 118 Ct. Cl. 18 (1950).)

Takings under war powers are not, however, authorized constitutional exceptions to the Fifth Amendment Just Compensation Clause, and other decisions require the payment of compensation where the effect of the governmental exercise of power is characterized as a taking instead of a regulation. (Russian Volunteer Fleet v. United States, 282 U.S. 481 (1931).) Again the reconciliation of the decisions is frequently nothing more than an exercise in futility. One gets the uneasy feeling that the Court is applying preconceived labels, *e.g.,* "police power," "taking," "regulation," from which the inevitable conclusion follows. The results may be just or equitable in the given case, depending upon how one views the original label; the compelling logic and unity of legal concept which the analyst hopes to find, however, are frequently missing.

The decisions which support the compensable compensation doctrine are legion. A rather dramatic holding is *United States v. Causby* (328 U.S. 256 (1946)), in which flights of military aircraft over private property at such low altitudes as to substantially interfere with the owner's use and enjoyment was held to be a taking requiring compensation. (*Cf.* Town & Country Motor Hotel, Inc. v. United States, 180 Ct. Cl. 563 (1967).) In a more mundane setting, property rights affected by land acquisitions for highway purposes have been held to be within the protection of the eminent domain provision. Typically illustrative is *Creasy v. Stevens* (160 F. Supp. 404) (W.D. Pa. 1958), *rev'd on other grounds* sub nom Martin v. Creasy, 360 U.S. 219 (1959)), holding that the right of access to a public highway is a protected property right for which compensation must be paid. (*See also* United States v. Gossler, 60 F. Supp. 971 (Ore. 1945), holding that an easement in land, the fee simple of which was condemned, was also a compensable right.)

Beyond the generalities and the philosophy, certain broad principles do emerge. Since a taking must be for a public use, the courts do have the ultimate review of whether a public use is in fact involved, but the legislative determination is accorded great deference and is rarely upset. (United States *ex rel.* TVA v. Welch, 327 U.S. 546 (1946); Poole v. City of Kankakee, 406 Ill. 521 (1950).) Property which is subject to condemnation and the taking of which is compensable extends to every kind of property, tangible and intangible, and all rights and interests therein. (City of Edwardsville v. County of Madison, 251 Ill. 265 (1911); United States v. Finn, 127 F. Supp. 158 (S.D. Cal. 1954).)

The United States may condemn private lands in the states (Fort Leavenworth R.R. v. Lowe, 114 U.S. 525 (1885)) as well as property owned by the state (United States v. South Dakota, 212 F. 2d 14 (8th Cir. 1954)). Similarly, the state may condemn property already devoted to a public use. (People v. Illinois Toll Highway Comm'n, 3 Ill. 2d 218 (1954).) The power may be delegated to municipalities, political subdivisions, governmental instrumentalities, and to private corporations operating as public utilities, subject of course to the public use standard and compensation requirement. (Central Ill. Pub. Serv. Co. v. Vollentine, 319 Ill. 66 (1925); Village of Depue v. Banschbach, 273 Ill. 574 (1916).)

What constitutes "just compensation" is in particular cases a difficult problem. The general rule that just compensation is to be measured by the property's fair cash market value for its highest and best use at the time the condemnation petition is filed (Illinois Cities Water Co. v. City of Mt. Vernon, 11 Ill. 2d 547 (1957)) may be adequate for tangible property, but where the determination of value concerns the taking or damage of intangible interests, or consequential damages, the problem is most complex. Decisional principles in this area are not very helpful. (Useful readings include G. Schmutz, Condemnation Appraisal Handbook (1963); Dolan, "Consequential Damages in Federal Condemnation," 35 Va. L. Rev. 1059 (1949); "Methods of Establishing 'Just Compensation' in Eminent Domain Proceedings in Illinois: A Symposium," 1957 U. Ill. L.F. 289.)

In this connection, the rule that just compensation is that which places the owner of property in as good a position financially after the property is taken and improvement made as he was prior thereto (Department of Pub. Works & Bldgs. v. Oberlaender, 92 Ill. App. 2d 174 (1968)) is a comforting assurance but hardly a principle of meaningful certainty.

A "taking" for which compensation must be paid offers few conceptual difficulties. What constitutes compensable "damage" is quite another story. Again the decisions are legion, confusing and sometimes seemingly contradictory. Structural damage to a building caused by removal of lateral support resulting from the construction of a public improvement in an adjoining street was held compensable damage. (Kane v. City of Chicago, 392 Ill. 172 (1945).) Obstruction of light and air and interference with free access to the street and view occasioned by the construction of elevated railways and other structures have also been held to be damage in a constitutional sense. (Aldis v. Union Elev. R.R., 203 Ill. 567 (1903); Field v. Barling, 149 Ill. 556 (1894).) Noise, smoke, cinders and vibrations caused by the operation of trains were held to be compensable damages in *Calumet & Chicago Canal & Dock Company v. Morawetz* (195 Ill. 398 (1902)), *Illinois Central Railroad v. Turner* (194 Ill. 575 (1902)), and *Chicago North Shore Street Railway v. Payne* (192 Ill. 239 (1901)), but were held noncompensable in the absence of a showing that the damage was special to the claimants as distinguished from a damage suffered by the public generally (Illinois Central R.R. v. Trustees of Schools, 212 Ill. 406 (1904); Aldrich v. Metropolitan West Side Elev. R.R., 195 Ill. 456 (1902)).

In several cases it has been said that a claim for inconvenience, expense or loss of business occasioned to property owners by the temporary obstruction of a street and interference with rights of access because of the construction of a public improvement does not involve damage in a constitutional sense. (Chicago Flour Co. v. City of Chicago, 243 Ill. 268 (1909); Lefkovitz v. City of Chicago, 258 Ill. 23 (1908).) But in *Barnard v. City of Chicago* (270 Ill. 27 (1915)), it was held that an owner of property whose rights of access and egress were obstructed by improvements in a street was entitled to compensation for damages. No mention was made of the *Chicago Flour* case, the holding being quite categorical that such temporary obstructions constituted damage within the meaning of this section. Yet in *Department of Public Works & Buildings v. Maddox* (21 Ill. 2d 489 (1961)), the *Chicago Flour* rule of noncompensability was reaffirmed.

The requirement that compensation be determined by a jury does not apply to a taking by the state, but statutory provisions have made jury trial applicable to the state upon request of either party. (Ill. Rev. Stat. ch. 47, §1 (1967).) In nonstate proceedings the jury trial requirement was held violated by a statute which authorized commissioners in lieu of a jury, in the sense recognized by the Constitution, to determine compensation. (Juvinall v. Jamesburg Drainage Dist., 204 Ill. 106 (1903).) Notwithstanding what appears to be words of mandate in the constitutional provision, it has been held that the language imports only a privilege which may be waived by the parties. (Chicago, M. & St. P. Ry. v. Hock, 118 Ill. 587 (1886).) Indeed in the *Juvinall* case above, it was stated that a waiver of the right to a jury trial will be implied if a specific objection to trial without jury is not raised.

Illinois, for highway acquisitions and for land acquisitions for the Weston, Illinois, Atomic facilities, has enacted the so-called "quick taking" procedure. (*See* Ill. Rev. Stat. ch. 47, §2.1 (Supp. 1968).) Under this statute the taking, possession and use of private property by the state, prior to the fixing and payment of compensation, a procedure condemned in earlier decisions, has been sustained against eminent domain, due process and other challenges. (Department of Pub. Works & Bldgs. v. Butler Co., 13 Ill. 2d 520 (1958).)

Comparative Analysis

Nearly all states have some form of constitutional provision for the exercise of eminent domain. Only 20 states other than Illinois require compensation for both "taking" and "damaging." All others cover only a "taking." Some 37 states require the payment of a "just" amount, all others requiring "adequate," "reasonable" or a similar standard. Only 16 other states, however, provide for a jury determination of the amount of compensation, and four of these provide a commission determination as an alternative. Only two other states establish that the fee in lands taken for railroad tracks remains in the owner.

The Fifth Amendment of the United States Constitution provides: "[n]or shall private property be taken for public use, without just compensation." The Model State Constitution contains no eminent domain provision.

Comment

The long explanation is not an indication that the section requires change. The importance of the subject and its relationship to the due process clause and to the police power concept were deemed to justify extended treatment in order to achieve a proper understanding of this provision. The many uncertainties, ambiguities and contradictions in the decisional law reflect only the extremely difficult task of reconciling competing constitutional values. Whatever may be one's feelings about particular applications of this section, there is little or no basis for disturbing the general principle concerning just compensation for taking or damaging of property. Caution should be the watchword in respect to any proposals which may seek to change the present language. It is not likely that new principles of constitutional significance can be defined in this area. Suggested changes are more likely to reflect attitudes concerning particular decisions in respect to which there may be some unhappiness. To tamper with the traditional language of this section may be productive of much harm.

On the jury trial requirement, given the nature of the issue that the jury must determine, one could reasonably argue that a jury is frequently less qualified than the court to evaluate economic data and to arrive at a proper determination of just compensation. This conclusion seems borne out by the absence of a jury requirement when the state is the condemnor. Nevertheless, the tradition of a jury trial is so deeply rooted that its retention may be deemed politically, if not practically, necessary.

The provision concerning railroad tracks seems at this point in history to be unnecessary. It is not likely that new railroads or additions to existing railroads are the wave of the future. If indeed a problem should arise, no reason exists why this provision, if deemed important, cannot be legislatively prescribed.

Ex Post Facto Laws and Impairing Contracts

Sec. 14. No *ex post facto* law, or law impairing the obligation of contracts, or making any irrevocable grant of special privileges or immunities, shall be passed.

History

The 1818 Constitution provided that "No *ex post facto* law, nor any other law impairing the validity of contracts, shall ever be made, and no conviction shall work corruption of blood or forfeiture of estate." The 1848 Constitutional provision deleted the word "other" in the first clause, because of the inapt connotation that an *ex post facto* law meant exclusively or substantially a law which impaired contracts. In other respects the 1848 provision was precisely the same as its 1818 source. The 1870 constitutional provision retained the 1848 *ex post facto* and contract impairment clauses with only a minor nonsubstantive language change but made two major alterations: it deleted the clause pertaining to corruption of blood and forfeiture of estate and transferred it into Section 11 of this Article, and added the present final clause imposing a limitation on the passage of any law making any irrevocable grant of special privileges or immunities. This clause appears to parallel in purpose, ·if not in scope, the prohibition in Article IV, Section 22, against the passage of special and local laws "granting to any corporation, association or individual any special or exclusive privilege, immunity or franchise whatever." The 1870 Debates disclose no explanation of the relationsip between this provision and the provision in Article IV, Section 22. Section 14 was adopted as reported from committee without any debate. After extensive debate, with no reference to Article II, Section 14, Section 22, of Article IV was adopted.

The 1922 Convention proposal offered the 1870 provision without change.

The United States Constitution in Article I, Section 10 (not in Bill of Rights), imposes a number of limitations upon states, including a denial of power to "pass any . . . *ex post facto* Law, or Law impairing the Obligation of Contracts . . . ." Article I, Section 9, of the Constitution of the United States prohibits Congress from enacting an *ex post facto* law. There is no reference in the Constitution of the United States relative to the power of Congress to enact laws impairing the obligation of contracts.

Explanation

This section deals with three distinct though not necessarily disparate limitations on legislative power, namely, (1) *ex post facto* laws, (2) laws which impair the obligation of contracts, and (3) laws which make irrevocable grants of special privileges and immunities. As noted, the United States Constitutional provision (art. I, §10) imposes upon states the *ex post facto* and contract impairment limitations, thus making it unnecessary for the federal courts to apply these limitations to states through the Fourteenth Amendment due process clause. Each of the three limitations of this section of the Constitution of Illinois will be treated separately.

Ex Post Facto Laws

In *Calder v. Bull* (3 U.S. (3 Dall.) 386 (1798)), Justice Chase defined *ex post facto* as limited to legislation which (1) makes criminal and punishable an act innocent when done; (2) aggravates a crime, or makes it greater than it was when committed; (3) increases the punishment for a crime and applies the increase to crimes committed before the enactment of the law; and (4) alters the legal rules of evidence so that testimony insufficient to convict for the offense when committed would be sufficient as to that particular offense and accused person.

With but minor and infrequent modifications, these rules have formed the basis for the construction and application of the federal and state constitutional provisions forbidding *ex post facto* laws. The principle applies only to criminal laws. Thus, in *Harisiades v. Shaughnessy,* 342 U.S. 580 (1952), it was held that deportation, though a severe sanction, is a civil proceeding to which the *ex post facto* ban is inapplicable, and in *Jewell v. Carpenter,* 22 Ill. 2d 445 (1961), it was held that the provision has no applicability to civil financial responsibility requirements of the Motor Vehicle Law. Occasionally the principle is blurred by nondis-criminating rejection of the *ex post facto* principle on grounds unrelated to the noncriminal nature of the law. (*See* People *ex rel.* Nabstedt v. Barger, 3 Ill. 2d 511 (1954), upholding a law permitting the adoption of children of parents who had prior to the law been adjudged mentally ill. The clear inference of the decision is that the law is not *ex post facto* because a parent's right or interest in his children is not an absolute vested property right. *See also* Trustees of Schools v. Batdorf, 6 Ill. 2d 486 (1955), sustaining a law terminating certain interests in land after 50 years, in which it appears that an *ex post facto* challenge was rejected, not because the law was noncriminal in nature, but because the rights affected were mere expectancies of a nonvested character.)

The *Barger* and *Batdorf* cases suggest an important corollary to the principle that *ex post facto* applies only to criminal laws, namely that retroactive noncriminal laws may be valid though affecting property rights, if such rights are not deemed vested. In addition to *Batdorf,* see *McNeer v. McNeer* (142 Ill. 388 (1892)), right of dower; *Wood v. Chase* (327 Ill. 9 (1927)) and *Jennings v. Capen* (321 Ill. 291 (1926)), terminating right of life tenant and remainderman to destroy contingent remainders; and *Butterfield v. Sawyer* (187 Ill. 598 (1900)), enlarging contingent remainder class of heirs by statute defining adopted children as heirs. (*See also* J. Scurlock, Retroactive Legislation Affecting Interests in Land (1954).) What constitutes a "vested right," however, is a most vexatious legal problem. It is not an incorrect assessment, viewing the contradictory and irreconcilable decisions across the nation, or even within a single state, to suggest that "vested" right is simply indefinable in meaningful conceptual terms. (*See* Smith, "Retroactive Laws and Vested Rights," 5 Tex. L. Rev. 231 (1927).) The problem of retroactivity, however, apart from the *ex post facto* context, is not within the scope of this section. Insofar as retroactivity is relevant to the contract clause of this section, it will be considered under that heading.

There have been relatively few decisions involving a classic *ex post facto* law. It is not very likely that legislatures today would enact statutes making criminal and punishable conduct which was innocent when committed. This kind of raw power passed from the realm of reasonable legislative possibility years ago. Even without a specific *ex post facto* ban, such a law today would most likely be held to violate state and federal due process guarantees. Such *ex post facto* issues as do occasionally arise involve tangential aspects of the problem. For example, habitual criminal laws which punish an offense more severely if the offender has previously been convicted of the same or other criminal offenses have frequently been challengd as *ex post facto* in that the punishment is related to the prior criminal offense. The general holding is that such laws do not violate the *ex post facto* prohibition, it being within the power of the state to provide increased punishment for recidivists. In *People v. Turner* (396 Ill. 221 (1947)), the statute was sustained even though the prior conviction was for an offense not mentioned in the Habitual Criminal Act initially. (*See also* People v. Manning, 397 Ill. 358 (1947), sustaining habitual criminal statutes where proof of prior convictions was given to the jury before a determination of guilt or innocence on the offense being prosecuted.)

Where the criminal offense occurred prior to the enactment of the statute defining the conduct as an offense or increasing the punishment therefor, the statutes will not be considered *ex post facto* if the offense is continuing in nature. Thus in *Leyvas v. United States* (371 F. 2d 714 (9th Cir. 1967)), a statute increasing the penalty with respect to a criminal conspiracy which began prior to but continued beyond the effective date of the statute was held not *ex post facto*. (*See also* People v. Jones, 329 Hl. App. 503 (1946), sustaining an act providing a penalty for permitting an abandoned oil well to remain unplugged as applied to an abandonment prior to the passage of the statute, since the gravamen of the offense was permitting the well to remain unplugged.)

Although there are no Illinois decisions on the point, it has long been held that the clause applies only to legislative and not judicial acts which might otherwise be deemed to have *ex post facto* attributes. (Frank v. Mangum, 237 U.S. 309 (1915).) Thus in a specific application it was held in *United States* ex rel. *Almeida v. Rundle* (255 F. Supp. 936 (E.D. Pa. 1966)) that if an aspect of the felony murder rule under which the defendant was convicted was the result of a judicial construction of the murder statute made for the first time in that case, such judicial action would not involve the application of the *ex post facto* principle. However, in *Bouie v. City of Columbia* (378 U.S. 347 (1964)), the Court stated that the fundamental principle that the criminal statute must have existed when the conduct in issue occurred must apply to bar retroactive criminal prohibitions emanating from courts as well as from legislatures. In that case the state court applied a 1961 construction of a criminal statute to conduct taking place in 1960 and at that time not within the statute. Due process was the ground of invalidation, but the Court equated the *ex post facto* ban on legislative action to judicial action having the same retroactive consequences as a statute.

Impairment of Contracts

As in the case of *ex post facto,* legislative action challenged as an impairment of the obligation of contracts must run the gauntlet, not only of this state constitutional limitation, but also of the specific limitation on state power contained in Article I, Section 10, of the Constitution of the United States. Because of this, a brief treatment of the history and of several decisions defining the limitations of the federal clause may be helpful.

Chief Justice Marshall, in *Ogden v. Saunders* (25 U.S. (12 Wheat.) 212 (1827)), best expressed the historical origin of the clause and its purpose:

"The power of changing the relative situation of debtor and creditor, of interfering with contracts, a power which comes home to every man, touches the interest of all, and controls the conduct of every individual in those things which he supposes to be proper for his own exclusive management, had been used to such an excess by the state legislatures, as to break in upon the ordinary intercourse of society, and destroy all confidence between man and man. This mischief had become so great, so alarming, as not only to impair commercial intercourse, and threaten the existence of credit, but to sap the morals of the people, and destroy the sanctity of private faith. To guard against the continuance of the evil, was an object of deep interest with all the truly wise, as well as the virtuous, of this great community, and was one of the important benefits expected from a reform of government." (*Id.* at 354-55.)

The evil against which the great Chief Justice was inveighing was the practice in some states in the period following the Revolution and prior to the adoption of the Constitution of granting relief to debtors who had incurred contractual obligations during this period of economic dislocation and hardship, and who were hard pressed to meet their debts. The state laws took several forms but most common were measures suspending the collection of debts, remitting or suspending the collection of taxes, and providing for delays in legal enforcement proceedings.

As is almost predictable, the reasons which had occasioned the constitutional principle were soon expanded to embrace state legislative action within the generic scope of the language. The first United States Supreme Court invalidation of a state law for impairment of the obligation of contracts was *Fletcher v. Peck* (10 U.S. (6 Cranch) 87

(1810)). This decision, ironically, held invalid a 1796 Georgia law repealing an unconscionable 1795 statute which had conveyed millions of acres of land, for what turned out to be a price of less than two cents per acre, to a group of land speculators. The 1795 grant was held to be a contract, the obligation of which could not, as against subsequent innocent purchasers not implicated in the original state conveyance, be impaired. Given the 1796 repeal, it is not likely that subsequent grantees could meet bona fide purchaser-for-value standards. There had been, however, a great number of conveyances since 1795 and 15 years had elapsed when the Supreme Court rendered its decision. A contrary holding would surely have thrown many land titles in doubt, generating extended litigation and great uncertainty in the ownership of property interests.

The famous *Dartmouth College* case (Trustees of Dartmouth College v. Woodward, 17 U.S. (4 Wheat.) 518 (1819)) established the contractual inviolability of Dartmouth's original royal charter against a New Hampshire statutory attempt to provide what it believed to be a more democratic charter. In the same year came *Sturges v. Crowninshield* (17 U.S. (4 Wheat.) 122 (1819)) invalidating a New York statute which apparently had the effect of discharging some classes of insolvent debtors from their debts. In 1843, a period of serious economic depression, Illinois enacted a mortgage relief law, extending the period for redemption from foreclosure, and prohibiting foreclosure sales unless two-thirds of the value of the property, as determined by an appraisal, was bid. The act was held invalid under the federal contract impairment clause. (Bronson v. Kinzie, 42 U.S. (1 How.) 311 (1843).)

These and other early landmark decisions established the central core of the great principle which they were expounding. As in other constitutional areas, however, great principles are rarely immunized from exceptions which carry their own constitutional justification. Thus, in time, the relative, nonabsolute nature of the right against impairment began to emerge in the federal and state decisional law. Among the identifiable exceptions is the exercise of the right of eminent domain. This right, inherent in the concept of political sovereignty, needing no constitutional grant to authorize its exercise and subject only to constitutionally expressed limits on its exercise, is not restrained by the existence of a contract. (City of Cincinnati v. Louisville & N.R.R., 222 U.S. 390 (1912).) Contract rights, holds Illinois, like all property rights, are subject to eminent domain and the state may, for public use and by making compensation therefor, impair and destroy rights granted by charter from the state. (Metropolitan City Ry. v. Chicago West Division Ry., 87 Ill. 317 (1877).)

Another recognized exception concerns the ever present, formidable police power concept. Generally phrased in terms of the inability of the legislature to bargain away the public health, morals or safety, the principle has permitted the exercise of legislative power which clearly interfered with, abridged or in some cases abolished contract rights. Thus in *Chicago Life Insurance Company v. Auditor of Public Accounts* (101 Ill. 82 (1881), *aff'd*, 113 U.S. 574 (1885)), the state was held to have power to provide for the dissolution of an insurance company where its financial condition made its continued acceptance of risks improper. (*See also* Yates v. People *ex rel.* Anderson, 207 Ill. 316 (1904) (termination of legal existence of insurance company if it fails to transact business for one year).) A number of Illinois decisions recognize the contractual nature of special railroad charters validly issued prior to the 1870 Constitution but sustain safety regulations affecting such rights. (City of Chicago v. Illinois Commerce Comm'n *ex rel.* Chicago & W. Ind. R.R., 356 Ill. 501 (1934); State Public Util. Comm'n *ex rel.* Quincy R.R. v. City of Quincy, 290 Ill. 360 (1919); Venner v. Chicago City R.R., 246 Ill. 170 (1910).) Perhaps the best general summation of the relationship of police power to contract rights in the railroad cases is contained in *City of Chicago v. O'Connell* (278 Ill. 591 (1917)). In that case the state regulatory commission's order for the improvement of a street railway service was held validly to supersede part of the contract between the city and the railroad. The court drew a distinction between contractual provisions relating to matters other than those affecting the public safety, welfare, comfort and convenience, such as the division of net receipts and an option of purchase in the city, which were immunized from impairment, and legitimate police measures to which contractual provisions must yield. The rule is broadly applicable to all contract rights, and the character of the contracting parties — whether individual, corporate, governmental, or a combination of these — is immaterial.

A number of "impairments" have been legitimized by what the Supreme Court of the United States has characterized as the "continuing and dominant protective power" of the state in respect to its economic interests. (Home Bldg. & Loan Ass'n v. Blaisdell, 290 U.S. 398 (1934).) Conceptually distinguishable from the police power, though at times the distinction seems quite fuzzy, this category of permissible impairments reflects the balancing concept which underlies so much of constitutional interpretation, pursuant to which individual rights are measured against the public interest, and governmental action is sustained or invalidated by a judgment which defines the superior value.

One of the earliest and most important decisions in this area was *Proprietors of the Charles River Bridge v. Proprietors of the Warren*

Bridge (36 U.S. (11 Pet.) 420 (1837)) in which the United States Supreme Court sustained, against a challenge of contract impairment, a state enactment establishing a toll-free bridge (after a short period of authorized toll charges) which would substantially diminish the value of a toll bridge authorized by a prior charter. The basic holding was that the first charter did not create an exclusive privilege, but the broader implications of a reserved state power to control its economic destiny were the important constitutional legacy. Earlier than *Charles River Bridge*, in 1827, the United States Supreme Court, which in 1819 had invalidated the New York Insolvent Debtors Law in *Sturges v. Crowinshield (supra,* p. 70), took another look at the issue and sustained a state insolvency law discharging contract obligations as to contracts executed *after* the passage of the law. (Odgen v. Saunders, 25 U.S. (12 Wheat.) 213 (1827).) Therein was born the important principle that a law in effect at the time the contract is made becomes an implied condition of the obligation. Under these circumstances, the contract clause has no application. The principle has been widely adopted in the states. In Illinois, an illustrative case is *Bossert v. Granary Creek Union Drainage District* (307 Ill. 425 (1923)) holding invalid an amendment authorizing the abolition of drainage districts on petition as applied to districts with contract obligations, but valid as to districts organized after the effective date of the law. (*See also* Schewe v. Glenn, 302 Ill. 462 (1922); Deneen v. Deneen, 293 Ill. 454 (1920); Burdick v. People, 149 Ill. 600 (1894).) Of more than passing interest is *Home Building & Loan Association v. Blaisdell* (290 U.S. 398 (1934)) in which a Minnesota law providing temporary relief from mortgage obligations was sustained as a valid emergency economic measure. It will be recalled that in *Bronson v. Kinzie (supra,* p. 70), a similar Illinois statute, also the progeny of an economic depression, was invalidated. Although the Court in *Home Building & Loan Association* strove mightily to distinguish the cases, the fact is that the distinctions were insubstantial and that new conceptions of the state's powers to protect vital economic interests had evolved.

Rate regulatory laws are another instance of permissible "impairment" of contract rights, though here the decisions are not always clear as to whether the police power or the power to protect the state's vital economic interests is the controlling rationale. In any event, it has been held that rates of public utilities can be changed as an integral part of the regulatory scheme and that such changes do not violate the prohibition on impairment of the obligation of contracts. (*See Hoyne v.* Chicago & O.P. Elev. R.R., 294 Ill. 413 (1920); State Pub. Util. Comm'n *ex rel.* Quincy Ry. v. City of Quincy, 290 Ill. 360 (1919); Railroad Comm'n Cases, 116 U.S. 331 (1886).) Of course rates established by law may be confiscatory and a violation of due process, but that issue is not the same as the contract impairment clause under consideration.

The state's power of taxation is another illustration of reserved state power, the exercise of which may validly impair contract rights. Thus, in *Wabash Eastern Railway v. Commissioners of East Lake Fork Special Drainage District* (134 Ill. 384 (1890)), a lien for property assessments which was given statutory precedence over liens of existing encumbrances was valid though it had a clear effect on existing contract rights between individuals. A word of caution is necessary, however. Tax laws normally need not take account of their effect on contract rights. It would be intolerable if private contracts could delimit or proscribe the governmental taxing power. But there may be instances where rights arising under state or municipal contracts may be invalidly impaired under the contract clause by subsequent governmental action. Such a case, apparently, is *People* ex rel. *Browne v. Chicago & Eastern Illinois Railroad* (300 Ill. 467 (1921)), which held that the legislature may not reduce a tax rate to a point where the revenues produced will be inadequate to meet the obligations of bonds issued under a statute authorizing the extension of a tax to pay the principal and interest on the bonds.

This explanation has emphasized the exceptions to the state's power to impair the obligation of contracts. This should not be taken to mean that the clause has no vitality. Quite to the contrary, contract impairments not involving the state's police power, the exercise of eminent domain, or the regulation of economic interests superior on a balancing test to individual rights, are stricken, if not frequently, at least not uncommonly. Illustrative are *Murray v. Village of Skokie* (379 Ill. 112 (1942)), invalidating an ordinance which impaired the obligation to holders of special assessment bonds; *Bardens v. Board of Trustees* (22 Ill. 2d 56 (1961)), invalidating an amendment affecting rights to a public annuity; and *Jensen v. Wilcox Lumber Co.* (295 Ill. 294 (1920)), giving preference to a lien under the Garagekeeper's Lien Law over a chattel mortgage of prior origin.

Interlaced with the problem of contract impairments are sub-issues of vested rights, retroactivity of application, and differences between laws affecting remedies only and those which affect the obligation of the contract to which the remedy relates. It is simply not possible, within the limits of this analysis, to deal with these as separate phases of the problem. Nor is it necessary to do so, as they would add little to the basic principles which have been discussed. We leave this subject noting an important rule of general application that the contract clause is a limitation on action of a legislative nature only and has no relevance to judicial decisions which may affect contract rights. (Prall v. Burckhartt, 299 Ill. 19 (1921); Thomson v. Thomson, 293 Ill. 584 (1920).)

Irrevocable Grants of Special Privileges and Immunities

In the *History* of this section (*supra*, p. 66) it was suggested that this clause of Section 14 seems to parallel in purpose, if not in scope, the prohibition in Article IV, Section 22, against the passage of special or local laws "granting to any corporation, association or individual any special or exclusive privilege, immunity or franchise whatever." The Debates of the 1870 Convention throw no light upon the relationship of these provisions to each other. One proposed amendment sought to limit the prohibition in this Section 14 to special laws. The argument was directed almost exclusively to the point that corporate investment capital, especially in the railroad field, would wither away unless the limitation on the making of irrevocable grants of special privileges or immunities was limited to special laws. The logic and persuasiveness of the argument were apparently lost on the members. Nothing was said as to the provision in Article IV, Section 22, nor indeed as to the provisions of Article XI, particularly Section 1 thereof, which prohibited the creation of corporations or the extension or change of corporate charters by special laws.

Insofar as the provisions of this section do so interrelate, a reading of the *History* and *Explanation* of the designated provisions in Article IV, Section 22 (*infra*, pp. 153-4), and Article XI (*infra*, pp. 515-6) is desirable.

The annotations under this section are few and in some instances erroneous or irrelevant. The decisions of importance establish, not always with precision and clarity, that the creation of municipal corporations to perform a special public service, the effect of which may be to create a monopoly, does not necessarily violate the ban on the making of an irrevocable grant of special privileges or immunities. (People *ex rel.* Gutknecht v. Chicago Regional Port Dist., 4 Ill. 2d 363 (1954); People v. Chicago Transit Authority, 392 Ill. 77 (1945).) There are limitations in these cases that municipal corporations are not within the excluded class of grantees since they must of necessity, in the exercise of governmental power, be granted monopolistic privileges or immunities. (For further discussion of this problem, see Art. IV, Sec. 20, *infra*, p. 197.) They also intimate that in fact the grants are not exclusive or monopolistic since the use of the public streets or other facilities, which are the subject of the grant, is not restricted to the particular grantee.

Grants to a private corporation in the nature of privileges and immunities have been sustained on grounds that the grants are not exclusive or monopolistic since other corporations may under the challenged law qualify for a similar grant (People *ex rel.* Shallberg v. Central Union Tel.

Co., 232 Ill. 260 (1908)), or that the grant is not irrevocable since the grantee's legal tenure is limited or the grant itself is terminable (People v. City of Chicago, 349 Ill. 304 (1932)). Indeed in *People v. City of Chicago,* the Supreme Court embraced a broad concept of permissible grants to private corporations under this section, stating:

"[E]ven if the act [statute amending general corporation act authorizing municipalities over 500,000 population to create local transportation companies] could be said to foster a monopoly in one company doing a local transportation business in a given metropolitan area, it would not necessarily be invalid. While the public policy of this State formerly encouraged competition among public utility companies and forbade monopolies, it is now recognized by the State that under proper regulations a monopoly in this field is preferable to unrestricted competition, and an act which permits such a monopoly is free from constitutional objections." (*Id.* at 326.)

Whether this pronouncement is based on the reserved power of the state to protect its vital economic interests (see *supra,* p. 54, impairment of contracts) or on a police power concept, is not clear. The statement does suggest qualifying limits but the sweep of the rule seems materially to negate, at least in the public utility field, the unqualified ban in this section on the power of the legislature to pass laws making irrevocable grants of privileges or immunities.

Comparative Analysis

Thirty-seven other state constitutions expressly prohibit *ex post facto* laws. Thirty-six other states prohibit the making of laws impairing the obligation of contracts. Some 21 other states prohibit irrevocable grants of special privileges or immunities. Article I, Section 10, of the Constitution of the United States prohibits states from enacting *ex post facto* laws and laws impairing the obligation of contracts. Article I, Section 9, imposes the *ex post facto* ban upon the Congress. The Model State Constitution has no similar provisions.

Comment

The *ex post facto* and contract impairment clauses are considered among the more important limitations upon state power. The presence in the United States Constitution of an identical ban has not persuaded very many states to omit these limitations in their constitutions. (See *Comparative Analysis.*) Although federal limitations may be urged as making comparable state provisions superfluous, there may nevertheless be a substantial residual legal utility in the coexistence of such provisions. For political and psychological reasons as well, it may be inapt to propose the elimination of these clauses. Assurances of equivalent protection against abuse of power under the federal clauses, or under the state due process provisions, may not be sufficiently persuasive to many people. The retention of these clauses may, therefore, be wise, though an argument can be made to the contrary.

The clause prohibiting the grant of irrevocable privileges or immunities is somewhat more difficult to assess. The relationship of this clause to the Article IV, Section 22, ban on special or local laws granting special privileges, franchises or immunities, and to the Article XI limitation on the creation of corporations by special law, as noted, is obscure, and the decisions do not add much clarity. The clause generally expresses an appropriate constitutional limitation which seems worthy of retention. If retained, it should be integrated with the related provisions which have been noted. In this connection, the suggestion in the *Comment* to Article IV, Section 22 (*infra,* pp. 225-6), appears to be an appropriate solution.

Subordination of Military Power

Sec. 15. The military shall be in strict subordination to the civil power.

History

This section, as well as Section 16 concerning quartering of soldiers, first appeared in the 1848 Constitution. The proposed 1922 Constitution combined this section with the section on quartering soldiers.

Explanation

This self-evident proposition is a fundamental principle of American democratic government.

Comparative Analysis

The fundamental nature of this principle of subordination of military power is demonstrated by the fact that every one of the 50 states except New York has a comparable provision. The United States Constitution does not have one, but the principle underlies the provisions that the President is Commander in Chief of the armed forces and that Congress shall not appropriate money to support an army for a period longer than two years. The Model State Constitution is silent on the subject.

Comment

See *Comment* under Article XII. (*Infra,* pp. 538-9.)

Quartering of Soldiers

Sec. 16. No soldier shall, in time of peace, be quartered in any house without the consent of the owner; nor in time of war except in the manner prescribed by law.

History

As noted above, this section and Section 15 first appeared in the

1848 Constitution. Also, as noted, the proposed 1922 Constitution combined the two sections. The combined section differed in one substantive respect from the 1870 Constitution. The words "in any house without the consent of the owner" were changed to "on a householder without his consent." The official explanation stated that the revision was "to require the consent of the occupant of a house, the word 'householder' being substituted for the word 'owner.'" (State of Illinois, The Proposed New Constitution of Illinois 24 (1922) [hereinafter cited as P.N.C.].)

Explanation

This section is not only self-explanatory; it is so rooted in our traditions that there appears never to have been any litigation in Illinois invoking the provision. With one irrelevant exception, this is also true of the equivalent Third Amendment of the United States Constitution.

Comparative Analysis

Section 16 is almost an exact duplicate of the Third Amendment of the United States Constitution. Most of the states have a similar provision, and one state, Kansas, has a provision similar to the change recommended in the proposed 1922 Constitution. Four states, including the two newest, Alaska and Hawaii, call for the consent of the owner *or* occupant. The Model State Constitution is silent on the subject.

Comment

It is instructive to speculate on the significance of the change from "owner" to "householder" proposed in 1922 and the formulation "owner or occupant" used in the recent constitutions of Alaska and Hawaii. It is reasonable to assume that there was no special significance in the use of the word "owner" in the constitutions adopted at the end of the Eighteenth Century. It is doubtful that the drafters were consciously deciding that in nonowner-occupied houses, the power of consent to quartering rested with the landlord and not the tenant. The evil to be prohibited was involuntary and presumably unpaid-for billeting of soldiers in private residences. If a lawsuit had arisen about 1800 in which a tenant sued military personnel for trespass, it seems likely that by one means or another a court would have held that permission of the owner was no defense.

If, however, a situation arose under the 1922 proposal where a tenant had consented to quartering but the owner objected, it would be difficult for a court to get around the constitutional language. The language in the Alaskan and Hawaiian provisions seems even more questionable, for it permits either the landlord or the tenant to consent, notwithstanding the other's objection. From all this, some might argue that the language should be changed to require consent of the owner *and* the occupant.

The point of this speculation is to suggest two rules of constitution-drafting. One is that, when adopting a provision embodying a fundamental principle, it is advisable to use simple language that can easily be construed to cover all situations that fall within the spirit of the principle. The second rule is that it is not advisable to tamper with the historic language of fundamental provisions. For example, the foregoing discussion concerning different language in the Twentieth Century could be the basis for an argument that the changed quartering provision did not cover apartment buildings. The argument would build on the theory that drafters who covered "occupants" in place of or in addition to "owners" in recognition of the realities of the Twentieth Century but did not change the word "house" must have meant to exclude the equally important Twentieth Century reality of apartment buildings.

It is also instructive to consider the comment made concerning the Michigan quartering provision in the comparative analysis of the Michigan Constitution: "Because of the provision in the United States Constitution, the necessity for this provision within the state constitution is questionable." (Citizens Research Council of Michigan, A Comparative Analysis of the Michigan Constitution at 11-17 (1961) [hereinafter cited as C.A.M.C.].) The premise of this comment is probably correct even though there has been no pronouncement by the United States Supreme Court making the Third Amendment applicable to the states. But even assuming such applicability, it does not follow that the substantially identical provision in the Illinois Constitution is superfluous. It is true that if the United States Supreme Court forbids state action as unconstitutional under the United States Constitution, no Illinois court can uphold such action. But it is equally true that if the Illinois courts forbid state action as unconstitutional under the Illinois Constitution, such action remains unconstitutional in Illinois notwithstanding any number of pronouncements by the United States Supreme Court that such action would not be unconstitutional under the United States Constitution. (Such a pronouncement would not be made in a case arising out of Illinois, for the United States Supreme Court will not review a case decided on an adequate state ground. The situation would have to arise from another state with a state constitutional provision identical with the Illinois and United States provisions where the courts of that state upheld the state action and the United States Supreme Court agreed with the state interpretation of the Third Amendment.) In short, the people of Illinois may reinforce their liberties for themselves by preserving constitutional restrictions that also appear in the United States Constitution against the day when the United States courts might be less solicitous of those liberties than the courts of Illinois.

Right to Assemble and Petition

Sec. 17. The people have the right to assemble in a peaceable manner to consult for the common good, to make known their opinions to their representatives, and to apply for redress of grievances.

History

The 1818 and 1848 Constitutions stated "[t]hat the people have a right to assemble together in a peaceable manner to consult for their common good, to instruct their Representatives, and to apply to the General Assembly for redress of grievances." The 1870 proposal was in the form ultimately adopted. Without debate the earlier provision referring to application to the General Assembly for redress of grievances was changed to delete entirely the reference to the General Assembly. One can only speculate that the Convention believed the right to be too narrowly stated or that the reference to the General Assembly was redundant. Whatever the reason, the 1870 provision is clearly more expansive than the earlier provisions in defining the right to petition for redress of grievances.

The 1922 Convention proposal retained the 1870 provision unchanged.

Explanation

The *Annotated Constitution of the State of Illinois,* prepared by the Legislative Reference Bureau for the guidance of the Constitutional Convention which convened in 1919 (hereinafter cited as Annotations), contained not a single judicial citation under this section. Perhaps this was an editorial lapse. If so, it was not a serious one, for the fact probably was that litigants and courts alike were not attuned as they are today to the issues implicit in these liberties. The great and continuing social convulsions in recent years have generated governmental restraints which have jarred the sensitivities of many civil libertarians, resulting in the invocation of the Bill of Rights to a degree undreamed of in past generations. The process has been substantially aided by the United States Supreme Court's establishment and steady expansion of the "incorporation" doctrine. The comparable guarantees of the First Amendment of the Constitution of the United States, applied to the states through the Fourteenth Amendment due process clause, and the states' own constitutional pronouncements of protected liberties, have been the subject of much litigation in recent years. Because the rights of peaceable assembly and petition are frequently intermeshed with rights of speech, it is not always feasible or possible to establish distinct categories in the decisions. Thus, the explanation of the free speech guarantee of Section 4 of this Article provides analysis of some decisions which are as relevant to the guarantees of assembly and petition for the redress of grievances. (*Supra,* pp. 19-23.) Nonetheless, some additional analysis is appropriate here, as the Supreme Court of the United States continues to draw distinctions between "pure speech" and "speech plus" which involves the communication of ideas by conduct such as patrolling, marching and picketing on streets and highways, or assembling in public places for purposes of protest against governmental action.

Hague v. CIO (307 U.S. 496 (1939)), though recognizing that the privilege of persons to use the streets and parks for communication of views was not absolute, registered in strongest terms the predominance of the privilege and the narrow and limited areas of permissible governmental restraint. *Edwards v. South Carolina* (372 U.S. 229 (1963)) was the first case which raised the broad *Hague* principle in the context of a civil rights demonstration. In that case, a group of Negroes marched to the statehouse and walked through the capitol carrying placards protesting segregation. When ordered by the police to leave, they refused. In peaceful fashion they sang, clapped hands, stamped their feet, and one person made a speech. Although a group of several hundred white persons gathered and showed signs of hostility, there was no violence or disorder. The Negroes were arrested and charged with breach of peace. The state convictions were reversed by the United States Supreme Court. Justice Stewart, who wrote the Court's opinion, did not deal directly with the issue of whether the persons had a constitutional right to use the capitol grounds for a demonstration. But in the course of the opinion which invalidated the convictions on Fourteenth Amendment due process grounds of vagueness of the statute, he said that the demonstration was a clear exercise of "petitioners' constitutionally protected rights of free speech, free assembly, and freedom to petition for the redress of their grievances." (*Id.* at 235.) This pronouncement was generally construed to mean that the *Hague* principle, assumed to express a constitutional right to use public open places for public assemblies, was being reaffirmed. Shortly thereafter, in *Cox v. Louisiana* (379 U.S. 536 (1965)), involving another peaceful student demonstration and a march from the state capitol to the courthouse, the Court, though reversing convictions of an ordinance for "obstructing public passages" because of unequal application, sustained the ordinance and for the first time indicated a deviation from the assumed *Hague* and *Edwards* principle of a constitutional right to peaceful use of open public places. Justice Black, however, tackled the constitutional issue directly. Viewing the First and Fourteenth Amendments as removing from the federal and state governments "all power to restrict freedom of speech, press and assembly *where people have a right to be for such purposes*" (emphasis added), he went on to say that this "does not mean, however, that these amendments also grant a constitutional right to engage in the conduct of picketing or patrolling, whether on publicly owned streets or on privately owned property." (*Id.* at 578.) This he followed with a categorical statement that government could impose a ban on most forms of assembly in public open places provided it did so without discrimination.

The impact of violence in the streets was beginning to show in the decisions. In *Adderly v. Florida* (385 U.S. 39 (1966)), Justice Black's doctrine prevailed, the Court sustaining convictions, under a trespass statute, of a group of student demonstrators who entered jail grounds to protest prior arrests and municipal segregation practices. There was no violence or disorder; only some evidence that a driveway, not normally used by the public, had been temporarily blocked to vehicular traffic. The holding was clear: the arrest and conviction under the statute did not violate First Amendment rights of speech, press, assembly or petition. (*See also* Cameron v. Johnson, 390 U.S. 611 (1968), validating a state law punishing unlawful obstruction of public facilities.)

The course of federal decision is hardly a total retreat, however. In *Shuttlesworth v. City of Birmingham* (394 U.S. 147 (1969)), a conviction for a peaceful march conducted without securing a permit from the local authorities was reversed on grounds that First Amendment rights of assembly and speech could not be curtailed by a prior restraint exercisable by an open-ended delegation of discretionary power to grant or deny a permit for reasons related to the city's needs to regulate the flow of traffic. The government's right, indeed duty, to keep the streets open and available for movement, was conceded, but the exercise of the power could be justified only on narrowly drawn criteria. In this decision, the Court was asserting principles established in other cases which generally condemned state action authorizing prior restraints or too broadly and prematurely applying state power to curtail speech and assembly.

Federal law invalidating state action in First Amendment cases is of course binding upon the states. Federal decisions, however, which sustain state restraints upon First Amendment freedoms do not prevent the states from taking a contrary view. The state courts or legislatures may recognize the need for limitations upon governmental power beyond those which federal rules have defined. It is not a common occurrence, however, for states to impose shackles upon their powers beyond those clearly mandated by federal decisions or their own constitutions. More often than not in this age the states seek to impose restraints upon speech, assembly, and petition for redress of grievances where the conduct is deemed inimical or dangerous to public safety. Such a case was *City of Chicago v. Gregory* (39 Ill. 2d 41 (1968)) where the Supreme Court sustained a conviction, under a disorderly conduct ordinance, of a group of demonstrators who were marching in peaceable and orderly fashion around the Mayor's home protesting the retention of the city's Superintendent of Schools. When the marchers were surrounded by a crowd of counter demonstrators, the police, fearing violence, requested the marchers to leave, offering to provide an escort. The demonstrators refused and the arrests followed. The state court construction of the disorderly conduct ordinance did not include refusal to obey a police order to disperse. A unanimous state court distinguished federal decisions reversing state or local convictions of peaceful demonstrators on factual grounds establishing the existence or nonexistence of violence or disorder, or the imminence of such conditions. The United States Supreme Court reversed, avoiding the sensitive constitutional issue of whether disorder created or threatened by other persons can justify a restraint upon otherwise constitutionally protected conduct. The prevailing opinion was based simply on the premise that there was no evidence in the record that the defendants' conduct was disorderly. Since the conviction was for disorderly conduct, an offense neither defined nor interpreted to include refusal to obey a police order, the conviction could not stand. In the course of its brief decision the Court stated that "[p]etitioners' march, if peaceful and orderly, falls well within the sphere of conduct protected by the First Amendment." (Gregory v. City of Chicago, 394 U.S. Ill. 112 (1969), citing *Shuttleworth* and other cases.)

In another conviction for disorderly conduct and obstructing a sidewalk, the Supreme Court of Illinois saw no unconstitutional interference with rights of assembly and petition where the defendant, with others, sat or knelt before the city hall entrance. (City of Chicago v. Joyce, 38 Ill. 2d 368 (1967).) The Court was quite blunt:

"These rights do not mean that everybody wanting to express an opinion may plant themselves [sic] in any public place at any time and engage in exhortations and protest without regard to the inconvenience and harm it causes to the public." (*Id.* at 371.)

The decision is probably sustainable on federal criteria. In an uncommon application of the guarantee of speech and peaceful assembly, it was held in *Centennial Laundry Company v. West Side Organization* (34 Ill. 2d 257 (1966)) that a temporary injunction, directed against peaceful picketing in protest of allegedly discriminatory hiring practices, was so broad in scope as to offend the constitutional guarantees in question.

In *Landry v. Daley* (280 F. Supp. 938 (N.D. Ill. 1968)), a state criminal statute defining "mob action" as the assembly of two or more persons to do an "unlawful act'" was invalidated on First Amendment grounds of suppression of peaceful assembly and on Fourteenth Amendment due process grounds of vagueness. Section 17 of Article II of the Constitution of Illinois was not mentioned.

The provisions of this section were considered in a civil tort action in *Arlington Heights National Bank v. Arlington Heights Federal Savings & Loan Association* (37 Ill. 2d 546 (1967)). The gravamen of the offense was that defendant had unlawfully induced the governing authorities of a village to breach its contract with plaintiff for the vacation of a street. Defendant had appeared before the Village Board to urge that the street not be vacated. Its defense was based on its constitutional right to petition government for a redress of grievances under the state and federal guarantees. The Court held that the right asserted was not absolute, but that its conditional nature nevertheless required a showing of actual malice to sustain a tort action, a burden which was not sustained by the plaintiff.

An earlier decision under this section is probably valid on federal standards. It held that a statutory prohibition against soliciting campaign contributions from employees in the city civil service did not violate the right of assembly guaranteed by this section. (People v. Murray, 307 Ill. 349 (1923).) Comparable federal provisions have been sustained. Perhaps less likely to meet federal standards of permissible governmental restraint is *Coughlin v. Chicago Park District* (364 Ill. 90 (1936)), which too broadly suggests a constitutional power in a municipal corporation to deny a park facility for a political gathering. Few of the later pronouncements of even-handed nondiscriminatory treatment under narrowly drawn standards seem to be implicit in this decision.

Comparative Analysis

All other state constitutions make similar provisions for the right to assemble and petition. The Constitution of the United States carries a comparable provision in the First Amendment. The Model State Constitution has a similar provision.

Comment

As so frequently said before, the existence of a comparable limitation in the United States Constitution should not be deemed a justification for the elimination of the state guarantee. They are not parallel in scope, since the state may establish limitations upon its powers that federal courts may justify under federal standards. The fundamental nature of the rights expressed in this section would seem to mandate its retention.

Free Elections

Sec. 18. All elections shall be free and equal.

History

This section appeared in both the 1818 and 1848 Constitutions. A resolution submitted to the 1870 Convention provided that "all elections, whether by the people or the legislature, shall be free and voluntary," followed by a lengthy series of prohibitions in the nature of a Corrupt Practices Act. The Committee on the Bill of Rights, however, without comment, submitted the section in its present form. It was adopted by the Convention, without debate or explanation, after a bit of whimsy by a delegate who inquired whether the section meant that the number of votes on each side had to be equal.

The 1922 Convention proposal retained the 1870 provision unchanged.

Explanation

The section received its first significant construction in *People* ex rel. *Grinnell v. Hoffman* (116 Ill. 587 (1886)). Its definition of free and equal elections has been frequently cited:

"Elections are free, where the voters are subjected to no intimidation or improper influence, and where every voter is allowed to cast his ballot as his own judgment and conscience dictate. Elections are equal, when the vote of every elector is equal, in its influence upon the result, to the vote of every other elector, — when each ballot is as effective as every other ballot." (*Id.* at 599.)

This definition of "equal" elections is remarkably similar to the "one man-one vote" principle pronounced some three-quarters of a century later by the United States Supreme Court. The fact that the shock of the federal decision is still felt in many states attests only to the gap between the pretension and the reality. The above-quoted definition of free and equal elections was reiterated most recently in *Thompson v. Conti* (39 Ill. 2d 160 (1968)) where it was used to invalidate a township election under this section and the Fourteenth Amendment of the Constitution of the United States, the election being conducted in a town meeting under conditions approximating a controlled election in a totalitarian state.

The section has had several other commendable applications in voiding state action limiting the freedom and equality of elections. Thus in *People* ex rel. *Breckon v. Board of Election Commissioners* (221 Ill. 9 (1906)), a provision of the 1905 Primary Election Law requiring candidates for a certain office to pay a filing fee was held to be an unwarranted restriction upon the right to seek elective office. Although the decision speaks in terms of an arbitrary fee bearing no relation to the services for filing the petition or to the expenses of the election, the import is clear that the right to run for office cannot be conditioned upon monetary exactions. The same decision invalidated other provisions of the Primary Act on Article IV, Section 22, grounds of special or local laws, an approach which not too uncommonly overlaps into the free and equal election provisions of this Section 18.

In a more pedestrian context, *Emery v. Hennessy* (331 Ill. 296 (1928)) condemned an election as violating the free and equal guarantees where the true electors were not separated from the false, where the safety of the ballots was not secured and where other gross irregularities and frauds were committed in the conduct of the election. Although this section was not expressly mentioned, the decision referred generally to the violation of the free and equal election guarantees.

People ex rel. *Phillips v. Strassheim* (240 Ill. 279 (1909)) invalidated the Primary Election Law of 1908 because of several provisions which were construed to deny to qualified voters in one part of the state the right to vote in primary elections, while voters with the same residence qualifications were permitted to vote in the remainder of the state. A specific ground of decision was Article VII, Section 1, of the Constitution of Illinois, but the Court also relied upon and adopted language from *Rouse v. Thompson* (228 Ill. 522 (1907)) which, in invalidating the 1906 Primary Election Law on somewhat similar grounds of discrimination, referred to the destruction of the freedom and equality of elections guarantees secured to the people by their fundamental law, an obvious reference to Article II, Section 18.

Primary Election Laws were still fair game for the constitutional axe when in *McAlpine v. Dimick* (326 Ill. 240 (1927)) and in *People v. Fox* (294 Ill. 263 (1920)) the 1910 and 1919 Primary Election Laws, respectively, were invalidated as denying free and equal elections because the party nomination machinery gave disproportionate voting strength in the selection of candidates to the voters in small wards and districts.

Free and equal elections may be denied in proceedings antecedent to elections. Thus in *Larvenette v. Elliott* (412 Ill. 523 (1952)), an election statute which limited a circulator of a nominating petition for a candidate for state office to the county in which the circulator resided, but authorized circulators of petitions for other offices comprising more than one county to solicit signatures in all such counties, was invalidated on Article IV, Section 22, grounds of special legislation arising from an unreasonable classification. The act had been challenged on the free and equal grounds of Article II, Section 18, but the decision was silent as to that issue, though it appears to be as relevant as, if not more so than, the Article IV, Section 22, challenge.

Article IV, Section 22, was also the basis for the invalidation of the Hospital Authorities Act of 1947, although again the free and equal guarantee of Article II, Section 18, seems more appropriate. (Grennan v. Sheldon, 401 Ill. 351 (1948).) In this case a provision which required a separate affirmative majority of the votes cast within the corporate limits of a municipality and within the area of the proposed Hospital Authority

District outside the city was held to be an unreasonable classification. However, in *People v. Francis* (40 Ill. 2d 204 (1968)), a similar provision applicable to a referendum on the establishment of a Public Junior College District was sustained. The Court strained mightily to distinguish *Grennan* but in the end simply overruled the broad holding that the requirement of separate city-rural majorities violated either this section or the equal protection guarantee of the Fourteenth Amendment of the Constitution of the United States.

Francis may have been mortally stricken, however, by *Moore v. Ogilvie* (394 U.S. 814 (1969)) which invalidated a section of the Illinois Election Law that required petitions for the nominations of candidates for a new political party to be signed by at least 25,000 qualified voters, including 200 qualified voters from each of at least 50 counties. The law was held to violate the due process and equal protection clauses of the Fourteenth Amendment. Given the uneven population distribution in Illinois, namely 93.4 per cent of the state's registered voters resident in the 49 most populous counties, the statutory requirement of 200 voters from each of at least 50 counties gave to the electors in the 53 counties having 6.6 per cent of the state's registered voters a disproportionate voting strength in violation of the "one man-one vote" principle. The decision overruled *MacDougall v. Green* (335 U.S. 281 (1948)) involving the same statute. The free and equal guarantee of this section was not mentioned in *Moore*.

The great early decisions under this section, as may already have become evident, dealt with the Primary Election Laws. Political parties, striving both for statutory recognition as a legal entity, and for control of the nomination process through the party machinery, were inclined to embody procedures which gave precedence to party control over the electoral rights of their members. This raised the critical issue of whether primary elections, a mechanism unknown at the time of the 1870 Convention, were elections within the meaning of the free and equal guarantees of this section. The issue was settled in *People* ex rel. *Breckon v. Election Commissioners* (221 Ill. 9 (1906)), which held without reservation that a primary election was an election within the meaning of Article II, Section 18, of the Constitution of Illinois, and that the rights of electors at primary elections were the same as those constitutionally granted to electors at regular (or general) elections. This principle was reaffirmed in *Rouse v. Thompson* (228 Ill. 522 (1907)), *People* ex rel. *Phillips v. Strassheim* (240 Ill. 279 (1909)), *People v. Fox* (294 Ill. 263 (1920)), and *McAlpine v. Dimick* (326 Ill. 240 (1927)). In the course of these decisions the Primary Election Laws of 1905, 1906, 1910, 1912 and 1919 were invalidated for infringements of the free election guarantee in primary elections. Some of the outlawed provisions have already been noted, but the most perverse issue involved the statutory authority delegated to party committees to limit the number of candidates for the office of representative in the General Assembly. This authority was related directly to the minority representation provision (Article IV, Sections 7 and 8, prior to 1954 amendments), the purpose of which was to assure to the minority political party, through the cumulative voting authorization, the election in each senatorial district of at least one of the three representatives to be elected. If a party member could be limited in a primary election to voting for fewer than three candidates of his party for that office, his rights would not be equivalent to those of an elector at a general election to vote for three candidates. The issue had been directly and indirectly raised in several of the early cases cited, and resolved against the authority of a party, or its committee, to so limit the rights of its members. Finally, in *People* ex rel. *Lindstrand v. Emmerson* (333 Ill. 606 (1929)) the issue was again raised in a challenge to the 1927 Primary Election Law. The provision authorizing the senatorial committee to fix and determine the number of candidates to be nominated by its party at the primary election for representative in the General Assembly had resulted in a committee designation of two candidates. The petitioner in a mandamus action to compel certification of his nomination had received the third-highest number of votes for the office. In rejecting the petitioner's challenge, the Court was forced to rethink the long-standing rule that primary elections were elections within the meaning of the free and equal guarantees. Recognizing that minority representation simply could not be guaranteed if party electors at a primary election had the constitutional right to vote for three candidates for the office, the Court overruled its prior decisions and held that a primary "is an election only in a qualified sense." (*Id.* at 622.) In that sense the statutory provision permitting the party committee to determine the number of such candidates, and the action of the committee limiting the number of party nominees to two, though three candidates would ultimately be elected to office, did not offend the free and equal guarantees of this section.

The *Emmerson* decision gave the political parties the flexibility needed to insure minority representation. In no other way does it affect or reverse prior holdings respecting concepts of freedom and equality for party members in respect to party structure, organization and administration of elections. In this connection, however, it should be noted again that uniformity in the administering of the election machinery is not mandated under the "equal" requirement of this section if the system is not discriminatory in respect to basic electoral rights. This principle, first stated in *People* ex rel. *Grinnell v. Hoffman* (166 Ill. 587 (1886)) to sustain an election law applicable only to such cities, villages and towns as adopted it by referendum, has been reaffirmed in *People* ex rel. *Mayes v. Wanek* (241 Ill. 529 (1909)) and does not appear to be subject to serious constitutional challenge today.

This explanation would be incomplete if it did not treat the extraordinary at-large election of members of the Illinois General Assembly in 1964, an election occasioned by the failure of the constitutional processes to produce a required redistricting bill. The legislation establishing the procedures for this election provided for party convention nomination of not more than two-thirds of the total number of seats in the House of Representatives, and suspension of cumulative voting rights for this election. The legislation *in toto* was sustained in *People* ex rel. *Daniels v. Carpentier* (30 Ill. 2d 590 (1964)). The cumulative voting provision was held to be applicable, by constitutional intendment, only to regular district elections, and the at-large state-wide election was held consistent with the "one man-one vote" concept. In fact, the Court stated: "In our view, it would be difficult to envision a system of nomination and election that is in closer harmony with the Federal 'one man-one vote' concept." (*Id.* at 596.) The act was sustained as establishing a free and equal election under this section and as conformable as well to the Fourteenth Amendment requirements.

One other problem should be noted. Legislation frequently authorizes submission of proposals to the people for their approval or rejection. Article II, Section 18, has been construed to prohibit the General Assembly or other governmental units from prescribing a form of ballot which combines two or more separate unrelated propositions into a single question. A voter under these circumstances has no true freedom of choice. Although a number of elections based on allegedly unlawful combination ballots have been challenged, the Illinois Supreme Court has been generous in validating the elections. Customarily the Court has found that the propositions, though appearing to be separate and unrelated, were in fact single and germane. Illustrative is *Voss v. Chicago Park District* (392 Ill. 429 (1946)) where a ballot for a $24,000,000 bond issue for the acquisition, improvement, completing, ornamenting and protecting of land and buildings, and for rebuilding all types of permanent improvements and construction necessary to render park property usable for enjoyment as a public park, was held valid against a challenge that it joined in one proposition a number of distinct, separate and unrelated purposes. Only occasionally is a contrary result reached. (*See, e.g.,* O'Connor v. High School Bd. of Educ., 288 Ill. 240 (1919).)

Comparative Analysis

All other state constitutions have comparable provisions for free elections. Only 13 other states, however, require "equal" elections. Three states provide that voters shall have equal rights. The Model State Constitution by implication calls for free elections in its Suffrage Article, quoted elsewhere. (See *infra*, p. 388.) There is no comparable provision in the United States Constitution.

Comment

In all probability the equal protection clause of the Fourteenth Amendment of the Constitution of the United States would guarantee all the rights protected against state impairment under this section. The state guarantees, however, have a long and honored tradition. They have been recognized and protected specifically in a number of decisions. The specifics of the guarantees will probably commend themselves more readily to voter acceptance than the more vague protections of due process and equal protection. All states carry similar provisions for free elections. The Convention must weigh the benefits of a simply stated and generally understood constitutional right against the cold logic which may argue for a change. To this analyst, retention of the present section seems preferable.

Right to Remedy and Justice

Sec. 19. Every person ought to find a certain remedy in the laws for all injuries and wrongs which he may receive in his person, property or reputation: he ought to obtain, by law, right and justice freely and without being obliged to purchase it, completely and without denial, promptly and without delay.

History

Except for minor and nonsubstantive language variations, this section appeared in identical form in the 1818 and 1848 Constitutions. In that form it was offered to the 1870 Convention with an accompanying statement by its sponsor that it was a fundamental and abiding constitutional principle, expressing indisputable objectives which sorely needed implementation. Noting that many people, especially the poor, were victims of unconscionable delays in securing remedies in the courts for their wrongs, and implying that justice indeed could be purchased by the affluent, the sponsor virtually accused the legal profession of being the malefactors in this sorry drama of democracy subverted. Noting also that there were some 50-60 lawyers who were convention delegates, he added, "I am not saying anything against lawyers. They are just as good as laboring men, if they behave as well, if they are honest." Nothing further appears until the vote on adoption when a delegate stated: "This section is also in the present Constitution. It is declaratory of rights, not of powers." After the defeat of a proposed amendment which would have substituted "shall" for the words "ought to," the section in its present form was adopted. The record contains nothing to indicate that the 50-60 lawyers reacted to the slur upon their profession and the administration of justice.

Explanation

The Illinois courts have never been quite sure what to do with this section. The 1870 Convention member's explanation that the section "is declaratory of rights, not of powers" is hardly a source of inspiration as to its meaning. The uncertainty is evident in the judicial pronouncements. The Fourth District Appellate Court in 1950 stated that "this reference to the Constitution [Article II, Section 19] is more of a statement of philosophy than a rule which can be used to solve cases . . . ." (Welch v. Davis, 342 Ill. App. 69, 77 (1950).) One year earlier the First District Appellate Court categorically stated that this section "is a clear mandate to the courts, that wherever the legislature has failed to provide a remedy, the courts must." (Skelly Oil Co. v. Universal Oil Prod. Co., 338 Ill. App. 79, 84 (1949).) Yet in 1963 another division of the First District Appellate Court denied relief on both contract and tort theories to an infant illegitimate child who sought recovery against his alleged father, deferring to the legislature in this novel case the determination of whether a cause of action should be created for "wrongful life." (Zepeda v. Zepeda, 41 Ill. App. 2d 240 (1963).) The constitutional sting had been taken out of this case when the Supreme Court of Illinois transferred the appeal to the appellate court, refusing to accept the case on the constitutional challenges based on this section and the Fourteenth Amendment of the Constitution of the United States. Lastly (though hardly the only remaining judicial observation on the point) the Supreme Court, in *Heckendorn v. First National Bank* (19 Ill. 2d 190 (1960)), in sustaining a statute which barred husbands and wives from suing each other for a tort to the person committed during coverture (the statute was an immediate legislative response to and rejection of the decision in *Brandt v. Keller* (413 Ill. 503 (1952)) interpreting the statute as repealing the common law immunity), held that Article II, Section 19, was not violated since that section "enunciates a basic policy of jurisprudence that serves both to preserve the rights recognized by the common law and to permit the fashioning of new remedies to meet changing conditions." (Heckendorn v. First Nat'l Bank, 19 Ill. 2d 190, 194 (1960).) The decision continues, "However, this policy expression does not authorize us to create a cause of action unknown to the common law in the face of an express statutory prohibition." (*Id.* at 194.) It is difficult to reconcile the language in this case. If the provision permits the fashioning of new remedies, the withdrawal therefrom of discretion to establish a cause of action unknown to the common law leaves little room for judicial creativeness. A statutory bar to a particular remedy should be critically measured against the constitutional policy of this section and the due process guarantees of the state and federal constitutions, rather than being casually accepted as a reasonable exercise of police power and a rational determination of the public policy of the state.

One contrasts the analysis in the *Heckendorn* case, affirmed in *Wartell v. Formusa* (34 Ill. 2d 57 (1966)), with *Molitor v. Kaneland Community Unit District* (18 Ill. 2d 11 (1959)), wherein the Court reversed a long-settled judicial rule of school district immunity from tort liability. Although the case involved no statutory bar as in *Heckendorn,* and though the grounds of reversal were solely "public policy" unrelated to constitutional guarantees, the Court fashioned a remedy where none existed at common law. Indeed, in a series of decisions which followed *Molitor,* the Court held invalid under the Article IV, Section 22, prohibition against a grant of special privilege and immunities by special or local law, several laws, enacted in direct response to *Molitor,* which granted total or partial immunity from tort liability to certain types of municipal corporations. (Haymes v. Catholic Bishop, 41 Ill. 2d 336 (1968) (limited liability of nonprofit private schools); Treece v. Shawnee Community Unit School Dist., 39 Ill. 2d 136 (1968) (limited liability for *public* school districts); Hutchings v. Kraject, 34 Ill. 2d 379 (1966) (total immunity of counties); Harvey v. Clyde Park Dist., 32 Ill. 2d 60 (1964) (total immunity of park districts).) Although Article II, Section 19, was urged in *Harvey,* the first of these challenges, that section was not, in that case nor in any of the subsequent cases, the constitutional basis of invalidation, the Court preferring to go the route of unreasonable classification creating a local or special law in violation of Article IV, Section 22. This approach was in fact dictated by the Court's analysis in *Harvey* which virtually invited the legislature to preserve the principle of sovereign immunity for municipal government by classifications based on functions rather than the type of the municipal government. The legislature obliged in 1965 by enacting the Local Governmental and Governmental Employees Tort Immunity Act. (Ill. Rev. Stat. ch. 85, §§1-101 to 10-101 (1967).) The net effect may be a substantial diminution of the ringing policy declaration of Article II, Section 19, that "every person ought to find a certain remedy in the laws for all injuries and wrongs which he may receive in his person, property or reputation." To this may be added the state's constitutionally established sovereign immunity (Art. IV, Sec. 26) which also diminishes the force of Article II, Section 19, though the creation of the Court of Claims mechanism for defined claims against the state and certain other state instrumentalities has to some extent alleviated the harshness of the immunity principle. (See *Explanation,* Art. IV, Sec. 26, *infra,* pp. 232-3.)

This section has had its moments of constitutional significance and they have not been of a minor character. Notwithstanding general judicial pronouncements that "no person has any vested right in any rule of law entitling him to insist that it shall remain unchanged for his benefit; . . . that no constitutional right is necessarily violated by changing or abolishing a remedy available at common law. . . ." (Grasse v. Dealer's Transp. Co., 412 Ill. 179, 190 (1952)), some legislative attempts to change or abolish common law remedies have outraged the judicial conscience and have been invalidated under this section. Thus in *Heck v. Schupp* (394 Ill. 296 (1946)), a 1935 statute (Law of May 4, 1935, ch. 38 [1935], Illinois Laws 716) which sought to outlaw civil causes of action for alienation of affections, criminal conversation and breach of contract to marry, based on an expressed policy that such actions were conducive to extortion and blackmail, was held to violate this section. The Court said:

"It requires no more than a cursory examination to discover that the act under consideration here tends to put a premium on the violation of the moral law, making those who violate the law a privileged class, free to pursue a course of conduct without fear of punishment even to the extent of a suit for damages. The contract of marriage has always been known in the law as a contract involving civil rights just as other contracts involve such rights, and no reason appears why, under section 19 of article II of our constitution, such rights should not have their day in court." (*Id.* at 299-300.)

The decision then held that members of a family and the state have a right to protect the family relationship and that to tie the hands of injured members of the family who seek to vindicate that right by pursuing actions of criminal conversation or alienation of affections would be "not only clearly in conflict with section 19 of article II of our State constitution, but . . . contrary to all sense of justice." (*Id.* at 300.) The state's interest in outlawing such actions was summarily dismissed as inadequate, a somewhat remarkable substitution of judicial wisdom for legislative judgment in an area of public policy.

A few months earlier, in *Daily v. Parker* (61 F. Supp. 701 (N.D. Ill. 1945)), the same Illinois statute was also declared in violation of Section 19 of Article II of the Constitution of Illinois, thus constituting no bar to the filing of an action in a federal district court for alienation of affections.

It is of more than passing interest that in 1947 the Illinois General Assembly, presumably in response to the *Heck* and *Daily* decisions, enacted several statutes limiting recovery in civil actions for breach of contract to marry (Ill. Rev. Stat. ch. 89, §26 (1967)), alienation of affections

(Ill. Rev. Stat. ch. 68, §35 (1967)), and criminal conversation (Ill. Rev. Stat. ch. 68, §§42-44 (1967)) to actual damages (outlawing recovery of punitive, exemplary, vindictive or aggravated damages). The statutes expressly forbade the consideration of the wealth or position of defendant, the plaintiff's mental anguish, any injury to plaintiff's feelings, shame, humiliation, sorrow or mortification suffered by plaintiff, defamation or injury to the good name of the plaintiff or his spouse, or dishonor to the plaintiff's family resulting from the tort, as elements of damage. Blackmail and extortion were the expressed public policy premises underlying these statutes. In *Smith v. Hill* (12 Ill. 2d 588 (1958)) the statute was sustained as to actions for breach of promise to marry, and in *Siegall v. Solomon* (19 Ill. 2d 145 (1960)) as to alienation of affections. In both cases it was urged that a holding of validity would clearly circumvent *Heck* and *Daily* and Section 19 of Article II. The Court sustained the laws, drawing a distinction between abolition of a common law remedy and limitation of damages recoverable. In *Siegall,* the Court held further that a marriage contract was not a contract within the meaning of the contract impairment clause of the federal and state constitutions. Somewhere between *Heck v. Schupp* and the *Smith* and *Siegall* cases, the Court's sense of outrage was mollified by a statute which virtually, though not technically, served the same "immoral" objectives as the invalid 1935 statute.

A somewhat similar legislative-judicial conflict involving legislation seeking to curb the alarming increase in divorce and separate maintenance cases occurred in 1953 and 1955. The 1953 law required as a condition precedent to the filing of an action in divorce, separate maintenance or annulment of marriage, the filing by the plaintiff of a "statement of intention" to institute the action. It precluded the institution of the actual suit for a period of 60 days after the filing of the statement of intention. During this "waiting period," voluntary informal conferences were to be held between the parties, with the judge participating, for the purpose of trying to effect a reconciliation of the parties. In *People* ex rel. *Christiansen v. Connell* (2 Ill. 2d 332 (1954)), the act was declared invalid under this section of the Constitution of Illinois as denying the plaintiff a right of access to the courts.

In 1955, the legislature reacted by passing a law which provided that actions for divorce should be commenced by filing a *praecipe* for summons "but prohibiting the filing of the complaint and entry of a decree for a period of 60 days from the date the summons was served or the last day of publication of notice." The purpose of the 60-day period was to provide a mechanism for reconciliation of the parties, but the 1955 statute omitted all references to conciliation conferences involving judges, since provisions of that nature in the 1953 statute had also been invalidated as imposing nonjudicial duties upon the courts. In *People* ex rel. *Doty v.*

Connell (9 Ill. 2d 390 (1956)), the 1955 statute was sustained since immediate access to the courts was secured by the filing of the *praecipe.* The 60-day waiting period was not discussed in terms of the Article II, Section 19, provision that the remedy shall be available "promptly and without delay." Instead it was analyzed against a due process challenge and sustained as a reasonable exercise of the police power.

This section has generated some additional liberal conceptions of wrongs for which there should be remedies. In one of the most far-reaching applications of this section, the Second District Appellate Court in *Johnson v. Luhman* (330 Ill. App. 598 (1947)) sustained a cause of action by minor children against a woman who had alienated the affections of their father, depriving them of his support and society. Recognizing that the existence of such an action at common law was extremely doubtful, the Court, relying upon *Daily v. Parker* (152 F. 2d 174 (7th Cir. 1945)), followed the principle of that decision which expressed the conviction that "because such rights have not heretofore been recognized, is not a conclusive reason for denying them." (*Id.* at 177.) The Second District Appellate Court stated:

"It is the opinion of this court, however, that the frank recognition by the circuit court of appeals that the cause was without precedent, but that, nevertheless, the common law was sufficiently flexible tô protect what are presently regarded as family rights under our social standards and conceptions of the family unit, is more conducive to the development of unambiguous legal precepts, than if the court had invoked some legal fiction to accomplish what it deemed to be a desirable result." (Johnson v. Luhman, 330 Ill. App. 598, 603 (1947).)

Great reliance was placed upon "the doctrine of justice embodied in the Illinois constitution." (*Id.* at 607.) Although not clear cut, the decision verges upon a holding that Section 19 of Article II permits or requires courts, in the discharge of their responsibility, to fashion remedies for wrongs for which the common law provided no redress. This bold approach, however, was not applied in *Wallace v. Wallace* (60 Ill. App. 2d 300 (1965)), wherein the Second Division of the First District Appellate Court refused to invoke this section in behalf of an illegitimate child seeking rights of visitation for his putative father so that the child's rights of companionship would be protected. Denying the existence of a common law cause of action, the Court cited *Heckendorn v. First National Bank* (19 Ill. 2d 190 (1960)) for the proposition that Section 19 of Article II "enunciates a basic policy of jurisprudence that serves both to preserve the rights recognized by the common law and to permit the fashioning of new remedies to meet changing conditions." The Court failed to explain why the objective of "fashioning new remedies" was inapropos to this case other than in its reference to the action not being recognized at common law, an obvious non-sequitur if the quoted reference meant what it seems to say.

Challenges to statutory remedies for wrongs or injuries not recognized by the common law have not been successful on the ground that the denial of a concurrent law remedy violates this section. The ground of challenge customarily is that the statutory remedy, in limiting the amount of recovery, or in other ways establishing conditions for recovery more restrictive than those normally applicable to a common law remedy, fails to provide the "certain remedy" that this section mandates. Thus in *Zostautas v. St. Anthony De Padua Hospital* (23 Ill. 2d 326 (1961)), the parents of a child, whose death allegedly occurred because of the negligence of a doctor and his attendants, sought to recover on a common law claim of breach of contract which, they insisted, was not barred, merged in or superseded by the Wrongful Death statutory remedy limiting the maximum monetary recovery. The knotty issue was whether the contract claim survived the death of the patient. In this issue the law was in a state of utter confusion and conflict in other jurisdictions, there being no precedent in Illinois. Against the parents' claim that a denial of a common law action would violate Section 19 of Article II, the Court held to the contrary, stating that since there was no common law remedy (in Illinois) and since the Wrongful Death Act provides, rather than abrogates such remedy, there was no violation of the constitutional provision. Relying on *Knierim v. Izzo* (22 Ill. 2d 73 (1961)), the Court stated; "we are not required by Section 19 of Article II of our constitution to recognize a remedy where the legislature has already created one, even though the statutory remedy be limited as to recoverable damages." (Zostautas v. St. Anthony De Padua Hosp., 23 Ill. 2d 326, 336 (1961).) To the same effect concerning this section is *Cunningham v. Brown* (22 Ill. 2d 23 (1961)) involving the statutory Dram Shop Act remedy, and *Hall v. Gillins* (13 Ill. 2d 26 (1958)) sustaining the limited monetary recovery under the Wrongful Death Act. In all these cases the critical holding is that a statutory remedy which fills the void of a nonexistent common law remedy supports rather than violates the constitutional provision in question.

In *McDaniel v. Bullard* (34 Ill. 2d 487 (1966)) and *Welch v. Davis* (410 Ill. 130 (1951)), the Court was able to avoid similar constitutional challenges by a liberal construction of the Wrongful Death Act, establishing in *Welch* a cause of action under that act for a beneficiary not literally within its terms, and in *McDaniel* preserving the action after the death of the statutory beneficiary.

The provision of this section to the effect that a person ought to obtain right and justice freely and without being obliged to purchase it has been productive of several decisions of interest. In *Griffin v. Illinois* (351 U. S. 12 (1956)), the United States Supreme Court held that a defendant could not be denied an appellate review of his conviction where his inability to secure the necessary transcript of proceedings was due to his destitute condition. Though the specific grounds of decision are the due process and equal protection clauses of the Fourteenth Amendment of the Constitution of the United States, the Court noted the relevance of Section 19 of Article II of the Illinois Constitution.

Wilson v. McKenna (52 Ill. 43 (1869)) held invalid under the 1848 Constitution predecessor section, a statute requiring payment of taxes as a condition to questioning a tax title on the land in question, its effect being to require a person to purchase justice. To the same effect in respect to a statute requiring the payment of redemption money and interest as a condition to questioning the validity of a tax deed are *Reed v. Tyler* (56 Ill. 288 (1870)) and *Senichka v. Lowe* (74 Ill. 274 (1874)).

On the other hand, *City of Chicago v. Collin* (302 Ill. 270 (1922)) sustained a statute which prohibited entry of a judgment involving title or interest in land until the party holding the tax deed was fully reimbursed for his outlay, the Court distinguishing *Wilson v. McKenna* and *Reed v. Tyler* on the ground that the statutes in those cases *prohibited* a resort to the courts to determine rights unless payment was made *before* the right was determined.

In *Williams v. Gottschalk* (231 Ill. 175 (1907)), a statutory provision requiring the payment of a prescribed jury fee as a condition to a trial by jury was held not to violate the right to trial by jury guaranteed by Aritcle II, Section 5, of the Constitution of Illinois. The "purchase" provision of Section 19 of Article II was not mentioned. Of more relevance, however, is *People* ex rel. *Flanagan v. McDonough* (24 Ill. 2d 178 (1962)) where a Chicago ordinance increasing the jury demand fee from $12 to $100 for a twelve-man jury, and from $6 to $50 for a six-man jury, was sustained against a number of constitutional challenges, including the "admonition of section 19 of article II . . . concerning the purchase of justice." (*Id.* at 181.)

The standard practice of requiring the payment of taxes under protest as a condition to a suit seeking recovery of such taxes is sometimes challenged but invariably dismissed as without merit. (Lakefront Realty Corp. v. Lorenz, 19 Ill. 2d 415 (1960).)

Comparative Analysis

Only the constitutions of Louisiana, Maine and Arizona contain comparable provisions. The Constitution of the United States has no such provision nor does the Model State Constitution.

Comment

The section in style and tone appears to be a pious, homiletic pronouncement of incontestable verities. Yet, as shown, it has played an important role in several instances. In all likelihood, statutory provisions held invalid under this section could have been stricken under state or federal due process and equal protection guarantees. As noted in the *Comparative Analysis,* only three other states have a comparable provision. It would indeed be astonishing to find that persons in states lacking this constitutional provision have suffered deprivations of rights as a consequence. Notwithstanding, the section does have historic, political and psychological significance. Since its abolition or change may be misconstrued, it may be good constitutional policy to preserve it.

Fundamental Principles

Sec. 20. A frequent recurrence to the fundamental principles of civil government is absolutely necessary to preserve the blessings of liberty.

History

This section appeared in the 1818 Constitution and was unchanged in the 1848 Constitution. The proposed 1922 Constitution combined this section with Section 1.

Explanation

One commentator has included this section among several from different state constitutions as examples of "Constitutional Sermons." (*See* R. Dishman, State Constitutions: The Shape of the Document 47-48 (1968).) He notes that in several states the constitution calls for countenance of or adherence to justice, moderation, temperance, industry, frugality, honesty, punctuality, and sincerity in some combination and, in addition, calls for frequent recurrence to fundamental principles. Four states, including Illinois, he notes, "are content merely to urge a 'frequent recurrence to fundamental principles' without specifying what these may be." (*Id.*) It is not surprising to find that the courts have not found this section particularly significant as a restriction on governmental action. In only two reported cases successfully attacking governmental action, *Commissioners of Union Drainage District v. Smith* (233 Ill. 417 (1908)) and *Wice v. Chicago & Northwestern Railway* (193 Ill. 351 (1901)), does it appear that the Supreme Court referred to Section 20, but in neither case did the section control the decision.

Comparative Analysis

Four states — Arizona, North Carolina, Utah, and Washington — have substantially identical provisions. (Dishman apparently overlooked Utah.)

Seven other states have similar but more extensive provisions. Neither the United States Constitution nor the Model State Contitution contains such a provision.

Comment

It is difficult to see what "right" is reserved by the people through this section of the bill of rights; it is equally difficult to see any harm in preserving the section. If it is preserved, it could appropriately be combined with Section 1 as was proposed by the 1922 Convention. As pointed out in the *Comment* on Section 1 (*supra,* p. 9), there is respectable constitutional theory for a provision making it clear that under our system of limited government, the enumeration of specific rights reserved by the people does not exhaust their reserved rights. Section 20, if it serves any purpose, reinforces the social compact theory embodied in Section 1.

Frequent reference has been made to the relationship between the Illinois bill of rights and the Bill of Rights in the Constitution of the United States. In addition, it has been noted that a number of provisions in the Illinois bill of rights are not included in the Model State Constitution. It will be instructive and of interest to the delegates to examine the Commentary to the Bill of Rights Article of the Model State Constitution which deals with these matters. (Model State Constitution 25.)

Article III

DISTRIBUTION OF POWERS

The powers of the government of this State are divided into three distinct departments — the legislative, executive and judicial; and no person, or collection of persons, being one of these departments, shall exercise any power properly belonging to either of the others, except as hereinafter expressly directed or permitted.

History

This Article, in two sections and with somewhat more flowery language, first appeared in the 1818 Constitution. It was carried over into the 1848 Constitution with the addition of the following concluding words: "and all acts in contravention of this section shall be void." (The "section" was the part of the present Article following the semicolon.) The Committee on the Bill of Rights of the 1870 Convention reported the Article as it now appears, but offered no explanation for the deletion of the words that had been added in 1848. The Article was accepted without debate or change. The proposed 1922 Constitution further shortened the provision to read:

"The legislative, executive and judicial departments shall be separate and no one of them shall exercise powers properly belonging to another."

Explanation

This Article is the Illinois version of the principle of the separation of powers. One of the earliest, and best, explanations of the principle was given by Chief Justice Wilson in the early case of *Field v. People ex rel. McClernand:*

"This is a declaration of a fundamental principle; and although one of vital importance, it is to be understood in a limited and qualified sense. It does not mean that the legislative, executive, and judicial power should be kept so entirely separate and distinct as to have no connection or dependence, the one upon the other; but its true meaning, both in theory and practice, is, that the whole power of two or more of these departments shall not be lodged in the same hands, whether of one or many. That this is the sense in which this maxim was understood by the authors of our government, and those of the general and State governments, is evidenced by the constitutions of all. In every one there is a theoretical or practical recognition of this maxim, and at the same time a blending and admixture of different powers. This admixture in practice, so far as to give each department a constitutional control over the other, is considered, by the wisest statesmen, as essential in a free government, as a separation. This clause, then, is the broad theoretical line of demarcation, between the great departments of government." (3 Ill. 79, 83-84 (1839).)

Although there have been a great many instances of invocation of Article III in litigation and a great many judicial opinions concerning the Article, its absence probably would not have changed the course of litigation. Once a written constitution is adopted wherein there are created legislative, executive and judicial branches, the stage is set for the delineation of the power of each and the interrelationships among them, and for the interdiction of encroachments of one upon another. An explicit statement of the principle of separation of powers adds little, if anything, to the process of delineation and interdiction.

The statement of the attributes of the three great powers of government is deceptively simple. The legislative power is simply the power to make laws, to set down the rules governing the society. The executive power is simply the power to administer, to enforce, to execute those laws. The judicial power is simply the power to determine how a particular fact situation fits within the laws or rules of the society. In the Anglo-Saxon world, the judicial power also includes the administration of the great body of rules of private relationships known as the common law, a body of law that can be changed by either the judiciary or the legislature. In the United States, operating under written constitutions, the judicial power also includes the power to determine the legitimacy of the exercise of legislative and executive power.

Although each of the three branches of government can be described in a manner that makes each appear completely different from the others, there is in fact a great deal of overlapping. The Supreme Court once put it this way:

"The legislative, executive and judicial powers are not to be kept so entirely separate and distinct as to have no connection or interdependence. In every constitution there is a blending and admixture of different powers. 'This admixture, in practice, so far as to give each department a constitutional control over the others, is considered by the wisest statesmen as essential in a free government as a separation.' (*Field v. People,* 2 Scam. 79; *Sherman v. People,* 210 Ill. 552.) In Cooley on Torts that author says (p. 375): 'Official duties are supposed to be susceptible of classification under the three heads of legislative, executive and judicial, corresponding to the three departments of government bearing the same designations; but the classification cannot be very exact and there are many officers whose duties cannot properly, or at least exclusively, be arranged under either of these heads.' Certain administrative officers are frequently charged with duties that partake of the character of all three of the departments but which cannot be classed as belonging essentially to either. Administrative and executive officers are frequently called upon, in the performance of their duties, to exercise judgment and discretion, to investigate, deliberate and decide, and yet it has been held that they do not exercise judicial power, within the meaning of the constitutional provision." (Illinois v. Illinois Cent. R.R., 246 Ill. 188, 230-31 (1910).)

A great many of the cases that appear to be matters of violation of the principle of separation of powers are equally susceptible of invalidation under another constitutional principle. For example, the legislature may declare that a given fact is *prima facie* evidence of something (People v. Beck, 305 Ill. 593 (1922)) but may not declare that a given fact is conclusive evidence of something, because that is an invasion of the judicial power. (Carolene Prods. Co. v. McLaughlin, 365 Ill. 62 (1936).) The United States Supreme Court would say that such a conclusive presumption is a denial of due process of law. (*See* Tot v. United States, 319 U.S. 463 (1943).) For purposes of an analysis of Article III, therefore, the discussion which follows will deal only with those instances that are solely matters of separation of powers.

Legislative Encroachment: There have been relatively few instances of judicial findings of true legislative encroachment on either of the other two branches of government. This may be in part because of the unusual constitutional theory expounded by Chief Justice Wilson in the *Field* case quoted from at the beginning of this discussion. He said that the "constitution is a limitation upon the powers of the legislative department of the government; but it is to be regarded as a grant of powers to the other department[s]. Neither the executive nor the judiciary, therefore, can exercise any authority or power, except such as is clearly granted by the Constitution." (Field v. People *ex rel.* McClernand, 3 Ill. 79, 81 (1839).) This is not the occasion for indulging in a discussion of political theory; suffice it to say that the *Field* theory increases the likelihood that legislative action will not be found to be an encroachment on the powers of the executive and judicial departments. (See *Explanation* of Sec. 1, Art. V, *infra*, pp. 254-7, for discussion of *Field* case.)

The courts have protected their own power in several areas. They have made it clear that, although the legislature may generally prescribe the qualifications to practice professions and callings, only the judiciary may prescribe the qualifications for engaging in the practice of law. (*In re* Day, 181 Ill. 73 (1899).) The courts also assert the inherent power to define the practice of law, and any legislation making the unauthorized practice of law illegal and punishable is solely in aid of the judicial power. (People *ex rel.* Chicago Bar Ass'n v. Goodman, 366 Ill. 346 (1937).)

The extent to which the legislature may control practice and procedure in the judicial system is not clear. Neither the Judicial Article as adopted in 1870 nor the current Article makes any reference to general judicial rule-making power, and if anyone were to take the *Field* theory seriously, it could be argued that the absence of any such reference means that there is no judicial rule-making power. (As to how seriously the *Field* theory should be taken, see the *Explanation* of Sec. 1, Art. V, *infra,* pp. 254-7.) Moreover, one of the enumerated cases of forbidden special legislation under Section 22 of Article IV is "regulating the practice in courts of justice," which implies that the legislature has the power so to regulate by general law. Whatever the basis in theory, the practice has been for the legislature to adopt comprehensive rules of practice and procedure. The Supreme Court has generally accepted this legislative practice, stating, however, that there could be no infringement of the judiciary's inherent powers. (Agran v. Checker Taxi Co., 412 Ill. 145 (1952).) But until very recently, the only infringement that the courts found and stopped were attempts by the legislature to control the essence of the judicial process — the rendering of judgments. (See the *Agran* case, *supra;* People *ex rel.* Sprague v. Clark, 300 Ill. 583 (1921); People *ex rel.* Lafferty v. Owen, 286 Ill. 638 (1919).)

In 1968, the Supreme Court held that its rule on admission to bail pending appeal from a sentence of imprisonment overrode a subsequent legislative amendment to the Code of Criminal Procedure that forbade bail in the case of conviction for felonies involving the use or threat of the use of force or violence. (People *ex rel.* Stamos v. Jones, 40 Ill. 2d 62 (1968).) The Court indicated, however, that it did not consider the various references to limited rule-making power in the new Judicial Article to represent any general revision of the relationship between the legislature and the judiciary as it existed under the old Judicial Article. Moreover, it is significant that serious constitutional issues of the right to bail would have had to be met if the Court had not been able to rely on a specific rule-making power granted to it under the new Article VI. (For a general discussion of judicial rule-making power, see *infra,* p. 327.)

People v. Bruner (343 Ill. 146 (1931)) is primarily a case involving the nature of trial by jury under Section 5 of Article II (*supra,* pp. 24-7), but the case has a separation of powers side that should be mentioned. In a criminal trial, the defendant's attorney asked for an instruction to the jury that it was the judge of both the law and the facts. The instruction was refused. On appeal following conviction, error was charged because a statute dating from 1827 stated that juries in criminal cases were judges of both the law and the facts. The Supreme Court first decided that trial by jury as guaranteed in the bill of rights was limited to permitting the jury to determine the facts. That disposed of the case, but the Court went further, perhaps because of the nagging fact that the statute had been around over 40 years when the Constitution was adopted in 1870. The Court said that interpreting the law was an inherently judicial function that the legislature could not exercise. This, the Court apparently thought, would be the case if the 1827 statute were valid. An accurate characterization would seem to be that the statute was an invalid attempt to delegate judicial power. But with such a characterization, the Court might have puzzled over who was receiving the delegation. The jury is part of the judicial process. Presumably, the Court meant that the legislature was trying to interfere with judicial power by denying to judges the exclusive right to interpret the law. All in all, the *Bruner* case is more confusing than enlightening on separation of powers.

Legislative encroachment on the executive department, in the eyes of the judiciary at least, has been minor. Again, this may be in part the result of the *Field* case discussed earlier. (*Supra,* p. 101.) It may also result in part from the fact that, by virtue of the long ballot, executive power is widely dispersed. (See discussion of Art. V, Sec. 1, *infra,* p. 256.) In any event, whatever the reason, there appear to have been only two areas of serious judicial concern over legislative encroachment on the executive department. One area dealt with the extent to which the civil service system could cover executive employees. In the case of *People* ex rel. *Gullett v. McCullough* (245 Ill. 9 (1912)), it was argued that the Civil Service Law was invalid in that it limited the power of the elected state officers to choose their own employees and thus constituted legislative encroachment on the executive department. Three judges agreed with this argument and three did not. The seventh judge agreed with the argument in so far as the constitutional duties of the elected officers were concerned but not as to those duties which were imposed by statute. Four years later, a divided Court found that the Civil Service Law could cover employees of the elected clerk of the Supreme Court. No distinction was made between constitutional and statutory duties of the clerk. (People *ex rel.* Vanderburg v. Brady, 275 Ill. 261 (1916).) This later case probably killed the peculiar distinction made by the "swing" judge in the earlier case. In any event, the current Personnel Code exempts from civil service all positions under the elected state officers other than the Governor, all employees of the Governor at the Executive Mansion and on his immediate personal staff, all positions under the Clerk of the Supreme Court, and all officers and employees of the courts. (Ill. Rev. Stat. ch. 127, §63b104c (Supp. 1968).) The head of any of the exempted offices can, however, request extension of civil service to his employees. (§63b104b (1967).) Thus, the present statutory scheme is consistent with the argument unsuccessfully advanced in the *McCullough* case.

An even stranger judicial finding of legislative encroachment on the executive department was the case of *Fergus v. Russel* (270 Ill. 304

(1915)), in which the Court ruled that an appropriation to the Insurance Superintendent for legal purposes could not be used to employ attorneys. The ground was that the Attorney General constitutionally possessed the powers which the English Attorney General had had at common law, that under English common law the Attorney General was *the* law officer of the Crown, and that, therefore, the separation of powers doctrine forbade any legislative shift of any of those powers to any other executive department. (For further discussion of this strange case, see *infra,* pp. 256-7.) As recently as 1956, the Supreme Court adhered to the position taken in the *Russel* case. (People *ex rel.* Castle v. Daniels, 8 Ill. 2d 43 (1956).) The characterization of the *Russel* case as "strange" is based solely upon the Court's unusual interpretation of Section 1 of Article V (see *infra,* pp. 256-7) and not on any theory that the legislature should be free to move executive powers around willy-nilly. The Auditor of Public Accounts, for example, has specific duties carefully spelled out in the Constitution and the Court has rightly said that there can be no legislative encroachment on those duties. (See People *ex rel.* State Bd. of Agr. v. Brady, 277 Ill. 124 (1917).)

Executive Encroachment: So far as has appeared, there has been no executive encroachment on any other department except pursuant to a statute. If the statute purports to give legislative power to the executive, the question is one of whether or not the delegation is valid and not whether the executive is "encroaching" on the legislature. The problem of delegation of legislative power is discussed in connection with Section 1 of Article IV. (See *infra,* pp. 114-15.) A problem of vicarious encroachment does arise when the legislature attempts to give the executive adjudicatory powers, for this can result in executive encroachment on the judicial power. It is not appropriate, however, to attempt to analyze the constitutional intricacies of this form of delegation at this time. For one thing, such an analysis would embody much of the stuff of which administrative law is made. For another thing, the delineation of the limits of administrative adjudicatory power is as much a matter of procedural due process of law as it is of separation of powers.

As a general rule, delegation to administrators or agencies of the quasi-judicial power to adjudicate rights or to revoke privileges such as licenses is not invalid so long as there is an opportunity for judicial review of the administrative action. Such judicial review normally permits an aggrieved party to contest the fairness of the procedure used, the constitutionality of the substance of the regulatory statute and implementing rules and regulations, the correctness of the administrator's interpretation of the statute under which he operates, and whether or not his decision was arbitrary. In short, if the judiciary is given an adequate opportunity to review what has been done, the principle of separation of powers — or due process of law, if you will — is generally satisfied. There are, of course, some judicial utterances at variance with this generalization, but this is inevitable, particularly in an area of law that was once novel and has grown in importance rather rapidly. For example, the Supreme Court once said that it would violate Article III and due process to require the judiciary to let an administrative adjudication stand if there were substantial evidence to support it, for such a requirement would preclude an independent judicial weighing of the evidence. (Commerce Comm'n *ex rel.* City of Bloomington v. Cleveland, C. C. & St. L. Ry., 309 Ill 165 (1923); Otis Elevator Co. v. Industrial Comm'n, 302 Ill. 90 (1922).) Shortly thereafter, the Court said that all it had really meant in the earlier cases was that the legislature could not tell courts *how* to weigh the evidence *if* it gave the courts power to weigh evidence. (Nega v. Chicago Rys., 317 Ill. 482 (1925).) Moreover, statutory language objected to in the *City of Bloomington* case is still on the statute books and the courts are following the legislative command to accept the administrative findings if they have substantial foundation in the evidence. (*See* Champaign County Tel. Co. v. Illinois Commerce Comm'n, 37 Ill. 2d 312 (1967).)

Judicial Encroachment: In the nature of things, judicial "encroachment" on the legislative and executive branches is almost impossible. (This is not to deny that people make speeches and write articles, editorials and letters alleging that the judiciary is usurping the law-making function or unduly interfering with the executive function.) Since the judiciary has the last word in interpreting the Constitution, the form in which "judicial encroachment" normally manifests itself is a refusal by the judiciary to do something on the ground that to act would be an encroachment. For example, the Supreme Court invalidated a provision of the divorce law that, in effect, required the judge to be a marriage counselor, a nonjudicial function imposed on the judge. (People *ex rel.* Christiansen v. Connell, 2 Ill. 2d 332 (1954).) The Supreme Court will determine whether a public utility rate imposed directly by legislation or through the administrative process is confiscatory, but it will not determine what the rate should be, for that would be encroaching on the legislative function. (*See* Chicago, M. & St. P. Ry. v. State Pub. Util. Comm'n, 268 Ill. 49 (1915).) On at least two occasions when the legislature, instead of limiting judicial review of administrative action, tried to give an aggrieved party the right to a trial de novo, the Court refused to accept the power because to do so would encroach on the executive branch. (West End Sav. & Loan Ass'n v. Smith, 16 Ill. 2d 523 (1959); Borreson v. Department of Pub. Welfare, 368 Ill. 425 (1938).)

There is, however, a form of indirect judicial encroachment on the executive function. This occurs whenever the courts accept a legislative delegation to them of the power to appoint executive officials to political subdivisions. (See *e.g.,* People *ex rel.* Lowe v. Marquette Nat'l Fire Ins. Co., 351 Ill. 516 (1933).) This indirect encroachment is a fairly flexible matter, for the courts can turn it on and off like a spigot, so to speak. The 1919 Annotation observed that the Supreme Court had made distinctions between permissible and not permissible delegations of powers of appointment that the annotators found difficult to understand. (Annotations 70.)

The courts recognize the significance of the principle of separation of powers by their consistent refusal to issue a writ of mandamus, a writ that commands action, directed to the Governor (People *ex rel.* Billings v. Bissell, 19 Ill. 229 1857)), to a board or commission of which the Governor is a member (People *ex rel.* Bruce v. Dunne, 258 Ill. 441 (1913)), or to a department which can act in the circumstances only with the Governor's approval (MacGregor v. Miller, 324 Ill. 113 (1926)). The courts will, however, issue such writs against executive officers, including constitutional officers, such as the Secretary of State, the Treasurer, and the Auditor of Public Accounts. (People *ex rel.* Sellers v. Brady, 262 Ill. 578 (1914); People *ex rel.* Akin v. Rose, 167 Ill. 147 (1897).) The rationale for this distinction appears to be that all duties of the Governor are executive, that is, discretionary, whereas other officers have ministerial duties, and mandamus will lie to compel a ministerial, that is, a nondiscretionary, act.

The courts will not issue writs of mandamus against the legislature, but, separation of powers apart, the reason therefor is simply impossibility. In a civilized society, at least, there is no conceivable way to command the legislature to act, in general or in a specific manner. For a long time, this was part of the rationale by which the courts refused to meddle in the problem of redistricting legislative seats, notwithstanding a constitutional command to redistrict. (*See* Fergus v. Kinney, 333 Ill. 437· (1928); Fergus v. Marks, 321 Ill. 510 (1926).) Once the United States Supreme Court forced the issue (Baker v. Carr, 369 US 186 (1962)), the courts had to act, and since they still could not effectively mandamus the legislature, their only recourse was to do the job themselves, which was, of course, a nonjudicial act. (See discussion of Sec. 8, Art. IV, *infra,* pp. 142-3.)

Permitted Encroachment: Article III ends with the words "except as hereinafter expressly directed or permitted." This clause is an unnecessary but cautious recognition that other parts of the Constitution make exceptions to the strict separation of powers. The most notable of these are the Governor's veto power over legislation and the Senate's veto power over gubernatorial appointments. (Art. V, Sec. 16 and 10.) Lesser examples are the judicial power of each house to punish for contempt in its presence and of the Senate to try impeached officers. (Art. IV, Sec. 9 and 24). Many of these exceptions add to the system of checks and balances that is part of the purpose of separation of powers.

The most interesting exception is one that is now explicitly a dead letter and probably was implicitly dead from the day the 1870 Constitution went into effect. Section 21 of Article V directs the Governor biennially to transmit various reports to the General Assembly, including "the reports of the Judges of the Supreme Court of defects in the Constitution and laws." Section 31 of Article VI, as it existed prior to the adoption of the new Judicial Article in 1962, provided that all judges of courts of record were to report in writing each year "to the judges of the Supreme Court, such defects and omissions in the law as their experience may suggest; and the judges of the Supreme Court shall . . . report in writing to the Governor such defects and omissions in the Constition and laws as they may find to exist, together with appropriate forms of bills to cure such defects and omissions in the laws." (See *History* of Sec. 21, Art. V, *infra,* pp. 315-16, for the origin of this unusual provision.) These provisions go far beyond the system of advisory opinions obtaining in a few states. Since the courts are the final interpreters of the laws, their advice to the Governor and General Assembly on the "defects and omissions in the laws" would carry great weight and would constitute a serious encroachment on the legislative branch.

In 1909, Governor Charles S. Deneen sought to rely on these sections in obtaining advice from the Supreme Court, but the Court declined to give the requested advice. The problem arose out of the difficulty encountered by the legislature and the Governor in obtaining a valid primary law. A statute passed in 1905 was invalidated in 1906. (People *ex rel.* Breckon v. Board of Election Comm'rs, 221 Ill. 9 (1906).) At a special session in 1906, another act was passed which was promptly invalidated. (Rouse v. Thompson, 228 Ill. 522 (1907).) At a special session in 1908, a third primary law was enacted, but this too was invalidated. (People *ex rel.* Phillips v. Strassheim, 240 Ill. 279 (1909).) Presumably in despair at having struck out, Governor Deneen wrote to the Supreme Court on July 14, 1909, reviewing the foregoing chronology and, on the authority of the quoted portion of Section 31, requesting the Supreme Court to draft a primary law that would be constitutional. On August 23, 1909, the Court politely declined to act. It observed that it was not set up in such a way that it could appropriately render advisory opinions. Notwithstanding the language of Section 31, the Court stated that its duty was limited to pointing out omissions and defects in the ordinary course of litigation. Thus ended a novel constitutional experiment in judicial "encroachment" on the legislative branch. (The correspondence is set out in 143 Ill. 9-41. It is reported that in March, 1919, "Justice James H. Cartwright of the Supreme Court sent two communications, one his own, and the other that of Judge Charles M. Thomson, of the Circuit Court of Cook County, to the Governor, indicating defects in the real estate and divorce statutes, together with bills embodying suggested remedies. These the Governor forwarded to the General Assembly." *See* Annotations 180.)

Dual Office Holding: Section 3 of Article IV, (*infra,* p. 120) prohibits dual office holding under two circumstances: where one of the offices is that of legislator and where one of the offices is of honor or profit under the United States or a foreign country. On several occasions, the Attorney General has relied on Article III to extend the prohibition to dual offices not covered by Section 3. His reasoning was that it is a violation of separation of powers to hold two offices, one of which is in one of the three departments and the other in another department. For example, a mayor of a city could not also be a county judge. (1912 Ill. Att'y Gen. Rep. 1343.) The Attorney General also said that a justice of the peace could not also serve as an alderman, village trustee, or town clerk. (1916 Ill. Att'y Gen. Rep. 788; 1914 Ill. Att'y Gen. Rep. 1157; 1915 Ill. Att'y Gen. Rep. 789. He also ruled out combining justice of the peace and circuit clerk (1915 Ill. Att'y Gen. Rep. 782), but the separation of powers argument is not particularly convincing in this instance.) On at least one occasion, the courts have used the same separation of powers argument. (People v. Bott, 261 Ill. App. 261 (1931) (police magistrate and town clerk imcompatible offices).)

Article III has also been used as an additional argument in dual office holding situations that may fall afoul of Section 3 of Article IV. For example, the Attorney General ruled that a legislator could not be a probation officer. (1916 Ill. Att'y Gen. Rep. 931.) In the case of *Saxby v. Sonnemann* (318 Ill. 600 (1925)), the Supreme Court used Article III to prohibit a member of the General Assembly from serving as deputy or assistant to the Attorney General and from receiving any compensation therefor if his services involved exercise of executive powers. It may be that the Court did not rely on Section 3 of Article IV because of problems arising from the meaning of the word "office." (See discussion of People v. Capuzi, 20 Ill. 2d 486 (1960), *infra,* pp. 122-3.)

Comparative Analysis

Four-fifths of the states specifically spell out the principle of separation of powers, and approximately 30 of them also recognize the principle of checks and balances by an "except" clause similar to the one in Article III. Separation of powers with checks and balances obtains in all the other states, of course, even without a specific provision therefor. The same is true of the United States Constitution and the Model State Constitution, neither of which has an explicit provision comparable to Article III.

Comment

As noted at the beginning of the *Explanation* (*supra*, p. 99), Article III really is nothing more than an explicit statement of what is implicit in all American constitutions. Article III could easily be dropped without significant effect, but by the same token, it could be preserved without significant effect. If preserved, it ought to be simplified in language. The 1922 proposed language (quoted, *supra*, p. 99) is as good as any concise formulation. (See also *Comment* under Sec. 1, Art. V, *infra*, pp. 258-9.)

Article IV

LEGISLATIVE DEPARTMENT

General Assembly

Sec. 1. The legislative power shall be vested in a General Assembly, which shall consist of a Senate and House of Representatives, both to be elected by the people.

History

The 1818 and 1848 Constitutions used the words "authority of this State" in place of the word "power," but otherwise the section was the same as the present one. The section as proposed by the Committee on the Legislature of the 1870 Convention was unchanged. A delegate proposed to substitute "power" for "authority" in order to be consistent with Article III, and the applicable sections of the Executive and Judicial Articles. The Committee Chairman indicated that he preferred not to change existing language unless there was some overriding necessity for change and that he saw none. An extensive debate ensued on the relative merits of using "authority" or "power." In the end, the decision was to retain "authority." (Debates 497-500.) The change was apparently made by the Committee on Revision and Adjustment, evidently without objection. The proposed 1922 Constitution retained the section substantially unchanged. The words "both to be elected by the people" were dropped, but this is hardly a change of substance. Indeed, the deletion was proposed in 1870 and although the proposal was defeated, no strong arguments for retention were advanced. (*Id.*)

Explanation

The Legislative Power: Under traditional constitutional theory, the basic "sovereign" power of the state resides in the legislature. From this it follows, again in theory, that there is no need to grant any power to the legislature. All that need be done is to place such limitations as are desired on the legislature's otherwise unlimited power. This is normally done by a bill of rights, which is the ultimate "sovereign" people's reservation of governmental power, and by distributing powers among the three branches of government with accompanying checks and balances. The 1818 Constitution was written in the traditional form. (The current

Constitution of Connecticut essentially dates also from 1818 and is likewise in the traditional form.) In the last half of the Nineteenth Century, however, two lines of constitutional development altered the traditional forms of constitutions. One was the addition of further limitations on legislative powers. Examples in Illinois are Section 22 of this Article, prohibiting local and special legislation; Section 18, limiting the incurring of debt; provisions in Article XI concerning street railways, banks, and railroads; and some of the restrictions in Article IX on revenue. In general, these limitations were the direct result of abuse of the relatively unlimited legislative power under the early constitutions. It is important to note, however, that these additional limitations are not inconsistent with traditional constitutional theory. Rather, the people simply withdrew more power from the legislature than is normally withdrawn by a bill of rights.

The other line of development in the late Nineteenth Century and well into the Twentieth Century was the great expansion of judicial invalidation of substantive legislation as in violation of bill of rights' limitations, particularly the prohibition against depriving any person of "life, liberty or property, without due process of law." (See Art. II, Sec. 2, *supra,* p. 9.) This is a long and complicated story in the political and judicial history of the United States which cannot be set forth at this point. Suffice it to say that, although in theory the courts were simply interpreting the limitations on the legislature imposed by the people in a bill of rights, the fact was that the course of decision tended to turn the legislature into a branch of government with only those powers that, so to speak, the courts graciously consented to recognize as having been granted. (See discussion of police power below.) The result in many states, including Illinois, was a tendency to place specific grants of power in the constitutions. Examples are Sections 29, 30 and 31 of this Article, two of which, Section 30 and Section 31 as amended in 1878, were the results of limiting court decisions. (See *infra,* pp. 239 and 241.)

The Police Power: By virtue of the judicial expansion of due process referred to above, there developed a theory that the legislature's power was, in effect, limited to legislating for the protection of the public health, safety, morals and welfare. This is commonly called the "police power." In a sense, the courts are dealing with two sides of a coin: If a matter is within the police power, it is not a deprivation of life, liberty or property without due process of law; or, if it is a deprivation, then it is not within the police power. This way of looking at the matter could be considered simply a matter of semantics, but the history of the development included a tendency on the part of the courts to require the state to demonstrate that a given statute was in fact for the protection of the public health, safety, morals or welfare. For a good many years, the burden of proof tended to be on the goverment, a burden hardly consistent with the theory that the legislature has all power not withdrawn from it. Moreover, judges who were unsympathetic to government meddling in the affairs of men might find it more difficult to be convinced that a given regulation was within the police power than would a judge who was sympathetic to government action.

If courts found legislative regulation outside the police power, the only remedy, short of inducing the courts to change their minds, was to amend the constitution by granting the legislature the power to act. This was done in many states in such fields as workmen's compensation, minimum wages, public housing, and the like. That it was not done so frequently in Illinois may have been because of the difficulty of amending the Constitution or because of a somewhat less restrictive judicial attitude. This is fortunate for Illinois, for there is a built-in danger in the indiscriminate spelling out of affirmative legislative powers. The very fact of detailed powers reinforces the tendency to develop a theory of granted power, and even when the courts adhere to the traditional theory that the legislature has all power not withheld, there is a tendency to limit a specific grant by inferring that what was not granted was meant to be withheld. (For example, a court might infer that a grant of power to set maximum hours of labor for women and children denied legislative power to set maximum hours of labor for men.)

Over the past thirty years or so, state courts, led by the United States Supreme Court, which drastically changed its interpretation of the due process clause of the Fourteenth Amendment, have substantially reversed their overall approach and today tend to uphold regulatory legislation as within the police power if there is any reasonable basis for regulation. The courts, in many instances, have not changed the language used in older cases, but they have in fact upheld regulatory legislation that would have been struck down half a century or so ago. The constitutional theory that the legislature has all power not withheld from it may never have been abandoned, but the course of judicial interpretation was inconsistent with the traditional theory. The courts have moved so far in the recent past that, today, theory and practice tend to coincide. (For the significance of the foregoing, see *Comment, infra,* p. 116.)

Classification: There are two technical meanings to "classification" in the delineation of legislative power: one is related to the problem of general versus special or local legislation, the other to due process and equal protection of the laws. There is, of course, no provision in the Illinois bill of rights comparable to the Fourteenth Amendment's equal protection clause which provides that no state shall "deny to any person within its jurisdiction the equal protection of the laws." This created no difficulty in the days of expansive reading of the due process provision of Section 2 of Article II, and creates no difficulty today, for the requirement for general legislation under Section 22 of Article IV affords a court an adequate basis for striking down arbitrary classification. The fact is that, with the exceptions of classifications for local government purposes and for tax purposes under the uniformity requirement of Section 1 of Article IX (*infra,* pp. 413), problems of classification in relation to the prohibition of special legislation and to the bill of rights' protection are essentially the same. For example, if the legislature restricts drivers' licenses to persons 18 years of age and over, an attack on the law as "special" fails because the classification is reasonable and a claim of denial of due process or, in the name of the Fourteenth Amendment, of equal protection fails, also because the classification is reasonable; but if the legislature were to deny drivers' licenses to bald-headed men, the legislation could be successfully attacked as special legislation since it would arbitrarily single out one group of the population or it could be attacked as a denial of due process or equal protection because the classification would be unreasonable.

For purposes of determining the extent of the legislative power to classify, the key word is "reasonable." In any but the simplest of societies, it is inevitable that groups will be treated differently, and if there is to be a constitutional limitation on different treatment, the only criterion for judging the validity of differentiation is whether it is reasonable. In general, the history of judicial review of the legislature's power to classify is the same as the history of the police power. When courts were unsympathetic to legislative regulation of private affairs, it was more difficult to find "reasonable" classifications than it is today. (See *Explanation* of Sec. 22, *infra,* p. 206, for further discussion of the problem of reasonable classifications.)

Delegation of Power: The legislative power may be vested in the General Assembly, but the facts of life in this complex industrial society demand a flexibility of adjustment to different situations that is not available to a legislature meeting for limited periods. The result has been the growth of what has sometimes been referred to as a "fourth" branch of government — the administrative agency. Whether independent, or quasi-independent, of the executive, or simply an administrator responsible to the executive, the administrative agency has been granted the legislative power to issue rules and regulations in furtherance of a policy determined by the legislature. This delegation of legislative power is limited by the separation of powers doctrine embodied in Article III. The courts are realistic enough to concede the need for some delegation of legislative power to administrators, but they recognize that the principle of separation of powers and, for that matter, common sense, prohibit unlimited delegation.

There are various ways in which the courts express the limits of permissible delegation of legislative power. A court sometimes observes that, while the legislature may not delegate its general legislative authority, it may delegate to an administrative agency some legislative power so long as it does not invest the agency with arbitrary powers. (*See* Department of Pub. Works & Bldgs. v. Chicago Title & Trust Co., 408 Ill. 41 (1950).) Or a court may say that, while the legislature cannot delegate the power to make a law, it can delegate the power to determine the state of facts which makes the law operative. (*See* People *ex rel.* Adamowski v. Chicago Land Clearance Comm'n, 14 Ill. 2d 74 (1958).) Perhaps the best formulation of the rule of delegation is that the legislature must so express the limits of its delegation that a court can tell whether the executive has acted within those limits. Thus, a court will invalidate a delegation that is so vague that it is subject to arbitrary and capricious interpretation and application. (*See* People *ex rel.* Schoon v. Carpentier, 2 Ill. 2d 468 (1954).)

There is also a general rule that legislative power may not be delegated to private groups. There appear to be only two Illinois cases that clearly follow this general rule. One case invalidated a statutory provision authorizing owners of 60 per cent of street frontage to change the name of a street. (People *ex rel.* Chicago Dryer Co. v. City of Chicago, 413 Ill. 315 (1952).) The other case was one of the ill-fated trio of primary cases discussed under Article III. (*Supra,* p. 107.) In *Rouse v. Thompson* (228 Ill. 522 (1907)), the Supreme Court found, in addition to other defects, an invalid delegation to political party central committees. In some instances, an invalid delegation may become swallowed up in a broad invalidation under the due process clause or as "special" legislation under Section 22 of Article IV. (*See* Schroeder v. Binks, 415 Ill. 192 (1953) (statute giving master plumbers right to determine who may learn the plumbing trade held invalid).) In other instances, it may be that a judicial determination that a statute is not contrary to due process or "special" legislation may cause a court to brush off a delegation to private parties. (*See* Kinsey Distilling Sales Co. v. Foremost Liquor Stores, Inc., 15 Ill. 2d 182 (1958) (Fair Trade Act under which manufacturer can make law applicable to all by signing a contract with only one retailer held valid).)

Referendum: A referendum is a limited form of delegation of legislative power, since it gives to someone else the determination of whether or not the law shall be operative. The Supreme Court has held that, except when required by the Constitution, the legislature may not submit general legislation to referendum by the voters. (People *ex rel.* Thomson v. Barnett, 344 Ill. 62 (1931).) It is permissible, however, to provide for local option whereby a law dealing with local matters does not become operative in a given community unless accepted by the voters of the community. (*Id.*)

Bicameralism: Section 1 lodges the legislative power of the state in a General Assembly consisting of two houses, a Senate and a House of Representatives. Thus, Section 1 commits the state to bicameralism.

Comparative Analysis

All states explicitly vest the legislative power in a legislature. In all states except Nebraska, the legislature consists of two houses, one of which is invariably called the senate, the other of which is usually called either the house of representatives or the assembly. The single house in Nebraska is called the senate. The Model State Constitution recommends a unicameral legislature.

Comment

Bicameralism: An essay on the pros and cons of unicameral and bicameral legislatures is not an appropriate part of this analysis, but it is appropriate to note that this is a subject which the Convention will want to consider.

Grants of Power: In the *Explanation* (*supra,* p. 111), it was pointed out that, today, the courts really do accept the fact that legislatures have all power not denied to them by the Constitution. The importance of this to constitution-drafting is twofold. First, it is clear today that there is no need to make any grant of power to the legislature to deal with substantive police power matters. (It can also be asserted with confidence that the courts will not revert to the limited view of the police power that once prevailed.) Since there are dangers in unnecessarily granting unnecessary powers to the legislature, every effort should be made to keep out any new grants and, if politically possible, to remove those presently in the Constitution. The foregoing applies equally to commands to the legislature to act on substantive matters. Apart from the fact that there is no way to force the legislature to carry out a command to legislate, the American tradition has been to limit the statement of the positive duties of government to the preamble. (There is one major exception to this tradition: a majority of the states make the provision of free public education a positive duty of government. See Art. VIII, Sec. 1, *infra,* pp. 399-402.) If constitution-drafters leave the legislature free to cope with society's problems, people will see that the legislature acts. A constitutional command adds precious little to the voter's persuasivenesss, but such a command may encourage unnecessary litigation after the legislature acts.

If the decision is made to forgo unnecessary grants of power and commands to legislate on substantive matters, it will be appropriate to point out to everyone, and particularly to the courts, what that decision means. This should be done by a provision much like that of the Model State Constitution:

"The enumeration in this constitution of specified powers and functions shall be construed neither as a grant nor as a limitation of the powers of state government but the state government shall have all of the powers not denied by this constitution or by or under the Constitution of the United States." (art. II, § 2.01.)

Election — Vacancies

Sec. 2. An election for members of the General Assembly shall be held on the Tuesday next after the first Monday in November, in the year of our Lord one thousand eight hundred and seventy, and every two years thereafter, in each county, at such places therein as may be provided by law. When vacancies occur in either house, the Governor, or person exercising the powers of Governor, shall issue writs of election to fill such vacancies.

History

This section is a combination without substantive change of two sections in the 1848 Constitution. Except for holding elections in a different month, the 1818 Constitution sections were in substance the same as those of 1848. The proposed 1922 Constitution transferred the rules for staggered terms for senators from Section 6 of the 1870 Constitution to the second sentence to read: "Vacancies shall be filled by special elections equivalent of Section 2. The proposed Constitution also simplified the called by the governor." (art. III, §26.)

Explanation

This section serves two purposes. It provides that elections for senators and representatives shall be held on the customary general election day in even-numbered years and provides that vacancies shall be filled at special elections called by the Governor. Notwithstanding the simple, straightforward nature of this section, two serious questions have arisen. One concerns whether or not the Governor may declare a vacancy when a legislator enters upon the duties of another office which, by virtue of Section 3 (*infra,* p. 120), he is forbidden to hold. An appellate court in 1908 said that the courts could determine the existence of such a vacancy (People *ex rel.* Myers v. Haas, 145 Ill. App. 283 (1908)), notwithstanding Section 9 (*infra,* p. 145), which provides that each house shall be the judge of the qualifications of its members; but in 1916, the Attorney General expressed doubt that the Governor could declare such a vacancy. (1916 Ill. Att'y Gen. Rep. 135.)

The second question concerned the discretion of the Governor in setting the day for an election to fill a vacancy. In 1923, sometime after adjournment of the General Assembly, a senator resigned his seat. Nothing was done about filling the vacancy because the General Election Law provided that no special election should be held unless the General Assembly was in session or unless there would be a session before the next general election. There were three general elections — November, 1923; June, 1924; and November, 1924 — before the next regular session. At the first of those elections, two votes for a W. G. Anderson were written in, and Anderson sought a writ of mandamus directing certification of election. In affirming a denial of the writ of mandamus, the Supreme Court held that, although only the Governor could issue a writ of election, a statute could prohibit him from calling an unnecessary special election. The Court further construed the statute to leave with the Governor the discretion to choose which general election to use for filling the vacancy. (People *ex rel.* Anderson v. Czarnecki, 312 Ill. 271 (1924). See *Comment* below concerning the Governor's discretion.)

Comparative Analysis

Time of Election: A fairly large number of states set the specific day for election of members of the legislature, a few states set the day but permit the legislature to change it, and two states simply provide that the date shall be set by law. About a third of the states evidently cover the matter in a general provision on elections, for the Index Digest has entries for time of election for the legislature for only 32 states. (Legislative Drafting Research Fund of Columbia University, Index Digest of State Constitutions 639·(2d ed. 1959) [hereinafter cited as Index].) The United States Constitution leaves the time of election to the several states but reserves to Congress power to act. The traditional first Tuesday after the first Monday in November was first adopted by Congress in 1845 as the day for presidential elections. (This presumably explains the adoption of that date in the 1848 Constitution.) Congress in 1872 set the same day for Congressional elections, effective in 1876. The Model State Constitution provides that the legislature shall be elected "at the regular election." This term is not defined. Presumably, it is covered in the Suffrage and Elections Article by the command to the legislature to "provide for . . . the administration of elections . . . ."

Vacancies: Almost half the states provide for a special election to fill vacancies. In most of these instances the Governor has the power to choose the time of election. In several states the manner of filling vacancies is to be fixed by law. In a few states the vacancy is filled by appointment, usually by the Governor. In many of the appointment provisions, the appointing power is required to preserve the party alignment either by the terms of the provision or by accepting the recommendation of an appropriate party committee. The United States Constitution requires special elections to fill vacancies, but in the case of Senators permits a "temporary" appointment by the Governor pending an election. The Model State Constitution simply says that vacancies "shall be filled as provided by law." (art. IV, §4.06.)

Comment

The method of filling vacancies highlights one of the problems of constitution-drafting — the balancing of principle and flexibility. On the one hand, it can be argued that the people through their constitutional convention or by constitutional amendment should decide as a matter of constitutional principle whether vacancies in the legislature should be filled only by the same people who normally choose the senator or representative or should be filled in some other manner. On the other hand, it can be argued that the method should be left to the legislature in order to avoid the detail required to cover all contingencies — for example, a vacancy occurring within three months of the regular election for the office. The *Czarnecki* case, discussed above, is a case in point. The Court had no difficulty in accepting some statutory regulation of filling vacancies. The new Constitution of Michigan explicitly provides for such regulation. It states that the Governor shall issue writs of election to fill vacancies but also provides that "any such election shall be held in a manner prescribed by law." (art. V, §13.)

The Illinois Commission on the Organization of the General Assembly recommended a constitutional change similar to the Michigan change just referred to. (Commission on the Organization of the General Assembly, Improving the State Legislature 9 (1967) [hereinafter cited as I.S.L.].) The commission noted that it is important to fill vacancies because of the constitutional requirement for passage of bills by a majority of those elected. The custom in Illinois has been to leave house seats vacant and to leave a senate seat vacant if the remainder of the term is less than two years. In 1969, however, there was a partial departure from custom in that special elections were called for one house and one senate vacancy. This whole business can be taken out of the realm of custom by the addition of the words "as provided by law" at the end of the last sentence. (See also *Comment* on Sec. 12, *infra,* p. 160.)

It was noted above that the proposed 1922 Constitution simplified the language of Section 2. One of the changes proposed was the elimination of the phrase "or person exercising the powers of Governor." This change exemplifies two important drafting principles: consistency in usage and avoidance of unnecessary wordage by a single definitive statement. The latter principle is presumably covered in the sections dealing with succession in power to act as Governor. (See Secs. 17 and 19 of Art. V, *infra*, pp. 303 and 310.) If this is correct, then the phrase is unnecessary. If it is unnecessary but is in fact used in one place and not in another, it can be argued that where not used only the Governor can exercise whatever power is involved. It follows that if the phrase is used any place, it must be used every place where a successor to the Governor may act. Presumably, the drafters of the proposed 1922 Constitution had these two principles in mind in simplifying the vacancies provision.

One further comment concerning the 1922 proposal is in order for those who are tempted to read too quickly. The proposed provision said that vacancies should be filled in "special elections." One quickly assumes that a "special" election is held at a time other than a "regular" or "general" election. Upon reflection, it is obvious that the inclusion on the ballot at a general election of candidates for an office that is not ordinarily voted upon at that election is something "special." "Every election called to fill a vacancy is a special election, and the fact that it is held on the same day as the general election does not change its character." (People *ex rel*. Anderson v. Czarnecki 312 Ill. 271, 274 (1924).) Notwithstanding this sentence, the Court used the term "special election" throughout the rest of its opinion to mean an election held on a day other than a regular election day.

Eligibility and Oath

Sec. 3. No person shall be a Senator who shall not have attained the age of twenty-five years, or a Representative who shall not have attained the age of twenty-one years. No person shall be a Senator or a Representative who shall not be a citizen of the United States, and who shall not have been for five years a resident of this State, and for two years next preceding his election a resident within the territory forming the district from which he is elected. No judge or clerk of any court, Secretary of State, Attorney General, State's Attorney, recorder, sheriff, or collector of public revenue, member of either House of Congress, or person holding any lucrative office under the United States or this State, or any foreign government, shall have a seat in the General Assembly: *Provided*, that appointments in the militia, and the offices of notary public and justice of the peace, shall not be considered lucrative. Nor shall any person holding any office of honor or profit under any foreign government, or under the government of the United States, (except postmasters whose annual compensation does not exceed the sum of three hundred dollars) hold any office of honor or profit under the authority of this State.

History

Age, Residence and Citizenship: The 1818 Constitution required United States citizenship, one year's residence in the county or district, payment of a state or county tax, and a minimum age of 25 for senators and 21 for representatives. In the 1848 Constitution, state residence of three years was added and the minimum ages were raised to 30 and 25, respectively.

The section — *i.e.,* the first two sentences of Section 3 — as proposed in the 1870 Convention changed the minimum ages back to 25 and 21, respectively, and increased residence requirements to five years in the state and two years in the district. There was an extended debate on the subject of age, some delegates favoring 30 and 25 and some favoring 21 across the board. There was also a proposal to reduce the minimum state residence to three years. None of the several proposed amendments was accepted. The proposed 1922 Constitution retained the age, residence and citizenship requirements unchanged.

Dual Office Holding: It is to be noted, first, that this part of the section covers dual office holding by members of the General Assembly and also generally covers dual office holding "under the authority of this State" where the second office is federal or foreign. Second, it is to be noted that, as to members of the General Assembly, there is a prohibition against dual office holding as to named offices and also in general. For purposes of clarity, the history of this part of the section will be traced separately as to each element.

Named Offices: The long list of named offices which a legislator can- not also hold first appeared in the 1818 Constitution. The list differed from the current Constitution only by reference to an "attorney for the state" instead of "state's attorney" and by reference to a "register" instead of a "recorder." The latter was the only change made in the 1848 Con- stitution and the former, the only further change in 1870. The proposed 1922 Constitution dropped the list of named offices.

Legislative Dual Office Holding: The 1818 prohibition against lucra- tive office holders also serving in the legislature did not mention foreign government office holders and, in addition to the militia and justices of the peace, excluded all postmasters from the definition of lucrative posi- tions, but did not exclude notaries public. The 1848 Constitution struck out the exception for postmasters but made no other change. The 1870 Convention added the foreign government office holder and the excep- tion for notaries public. The proposed 1922 Constitution prohibited a legislator from holding "any other lucrative public office or employment (except as a militia officer or justice of the peace)." (It is worth noting that the 1922 draftsmen were the first to put "other" in front of "lucra- tive.") The proposed 1922 language was the broadest legislative dual office holding prohibition in any of the. Constitutions. (Presumably, notaries public were not mentioned on the theory that they are not lucrative offices.) The office of justice of the peace was abolished by the new Article VI adopted in 1962. (See Secs. 12 and 16 of Art. VI, *infra,* pp. 361 and 368.)

General Dual Office Holding: The 1818 and 1848 Constitutions differed from the present provisions only in omitting the $300-a-year postmaster exception and in not mentioning offices in foreign governments. In the proposed 1922 Constitution this provision was moved quite properly from the Legislative Article to an article on Public Servants. In the course of re-drafting, the words "of honor or profit" were dropped, but there is no indication that any change in substance was intended.

Explanation

Age, Residence and Citizenship: These qualifications are straightforward and have created no problems of interpretation. The qualifications are exclusive, however, and the legislature cannot add to them. The 1905 Primary Election Act attempted to limit the number of candidates from a single county in a multiple-county district. This, the Supreme Court said, was an invalid extension of the residence qualification contained in Section 3. (People *ex rel.* Breckon v. Board of Election Comm'rs, 221 Ill. 9 (1906).) It may be noted in passing that this section does not require a legislator to be a registered voter and that Section 6 of Article VII (*infra,* p. 394) also requires him to be a United States citizen.

Legislative Dual Office Holding: Until quite recently, the Supreme Court had never addressed itself to the dual office holding limitation on legislators. In 1960, in the case of *People v. Capuzi* (20 Ill. 2d 486 (1960)), the Court considered several instances of local government officials who also served in the legislature. The most difficult was the case of the president of the Village of Elmwood Park who received a salary and participated in the municipal retirement fund. During legislative sessions he took a leave of absence but continued to receive retirement credit. The other legislators were all in appointive positions, namely: deputy county coroner, and chief deputy clerk, deputy clerk, and deputy bailiff of the Municipal Court of Chicago. All took oaths of office, posted bonds, participated in a retirement system, and took leaves of absence during legislative sessions, but, unlike the village president, received no retirement credit. None of these in appointive positions had civil service status or any specified term of "office."

The Court held that none of the legislators held another "office." The Court's approach was to distinguish "offices" from other jobs, not so much in terms of the distinctions attempted in Section 24 of Article V (*infra,* p. 322), as in terms of the class deduced from the offices listed in Section 3. In other words, a position not listed is an "office" only if the position is of the same general nature as a judge, clerk of court, and so on through member of Congress. On this theory, the Court disposed of the cases by noting that the defendants held relatively minor local ministerial positions. The village presidency was held not to be an "office" because the executive power in the town was in the hands of the town manager and the presidency was largely honorary. The Court did not rule on whether any of the positions were "lucrative," but did note that no one drew double salaries and that only the village president earned double retirement credits.

Prior to the *Capuzi* case, there had been a great many Attorney General opinions on this issue, but in the light of that case, it seems inadvisable to rely on those opinions. In one lower court case it was held that a member of the legislature could not also serve as a clerk of the Municipal Court of Chicago, a decision consistent with *Capuzi*. (People *ex rel.* Myers v. Haas, 145 Ill. App. 283 (1908).) In *Saxby v. Sonnemann* (318 Ill. 600 (1925), discussed *supra*, p. 108), the Supreme Court held incompatible under Article III the offices of legislator and deputy to the Attorney General. In the *Capuzi* case, the Court distinguished *Saxby* on the ground that as deputy, the legislator exercised executive functions and observed that the Court in *Saxby* had implied that the result might have been different had the duties been ministerial only.

General Dual Office Holding: As noted above in discussing the proposed 1922 Constitution, this part of Section 3 has nothing to do with the legislature and should be somewhere else in the Constitution. Indeed, the juxtaposition of these two provisions has probably created difficulties. A police magistrate who accepted a commission in the army argued that a magistrate was the same as a justice of the peace and that since a justice of the peace was not a "lucrative" office forbidden to legislators, so a position of "honor or profit" in the United States Army should not be inconsistent with the office of police magistrate. The Supreme Court would not accept the argument. (People *ex rel.* Cromer v. Village of Maywood, 381 Ill. 337 (1942). *See also* Fekete v. City of East St. Louis, 315 Ill. 58 (1924) (U. S. Army commission and city attorney positions incompatible).) This juxtaposition has also created confusion. In the case upholding the constitutionality of the Enabling Act for the 1970 Convention, the Supreme Court lumped the two types of dual office holding together, leading, in the eyes of the dissenting judges, at least, to an erroneous analysis. (*See* Livingston v. Ogilvie, — Ill. 2d — (1969). The case is discussed in detail under Sec. 1 of Art. XIV, *infra*, pp. 559-61.)

Once it is determined that two offices are incompatible, there is the question of precedence of offices. The general rule is that acceptance of the second office automatically vacates the first office. Illinois follows the general rule. (Livingston v. Ogilvie, — Ill. 2d — (1969); People *ex rel.* Myers v. Haas, 145 Ill. App. 283 (1908).)

Comparative Analysis

Age: The minimum ages for legislators, as of May, 1967, can be summarized thus:

| | Number of States | |
Minimum Age	Senate	House
21*	13	38
22	1	1
24	1	3
25	23	5
26	1	—
27	1	—
30	7	—
No minimum	2	2

*Nebraska's unicameral legislature has a minimum of 21.

The United States Constitution sets a minimum of 25 for the House of Representatives and 30 for the Senate. The Model State Constitution leaves a blank space for age, but does recommend in its alternative provision for a bicameral legislature that the minimum age requirement be the same for both houses. At least 18 states have the same minimum age for both houses. These are the 13 with a minimum of 21 for the Senate, Idaho (22), and four of the states with a 25-year minimum for the House.

Citizenship: There appear to be only 26 states, including Illinois, that explicitly require legislators to be United States citizens. It is likely that most of the other states in fact require United States citizenship. In some states, for example, a legislator must be a voter and a voter must be a citizen. In some states, a legislator must be a citizen of the state and presumably it is assumed that that means citizen of the United States. (See *Comment* on Sec. 1 of Art. XII concerning the Fourteenth Amendment citizenship fallacy, *infra,* p. 538.) The United States Constitution requires nine years' citizenship for Senators and seven for Representatives. The Model State Constitution requires legislators to be voters and requires voters to be "citizens."

Residency: All states have a residency requirement, but not all constitutions spell it out in the section on qualifications of legislators. Connecticut, for example, requires a legislator to be an elector (voter) residing in his district, but to be an elector he must have resided in a town (township) for at least six months. The following summary is limited to states with constitutional provisions on qualifications of legislators where the residency requirement is specified.

Residency in State

Number of Years	Number of States
One	5
Two	4 (5)*
Three	7 (1)*
Four	1 (1)*
Five	(1)*
Six	(1)*
Seven	(1)*

*In five states the residency requirement is two years for the lower house and longer for the upper house as indicated by the figures in parentheses. In North Carolina, a senator must have resided in the state two years, a representative one year.

Residency in District

Period	Number of States
60 days	1
3 months	1
6 months	1
1 year	22
2 years	2 (1)*
4 years	(1)*

*In New Jersey — two years for lower house, four years for senate. In one state, New Hampshire, residency in the district is not required prior to time of election. The same is true in Massachusetts and Vermont as to the upper house only.

Under the United States Constitution, as is well known from the case of the late Senator Robert F. Kennedy, residency is required only as of the time of election. The Model State Constitution requires a legislator to be a voter and a voter must have a minimum of three months' residence in the state and can be required by law to have a local residency of not exceeding three months.

Dual Office Holding (Legislators): The variations in dual office holding restrictions in the state constitutions are almost infinite. For example, no other state appears to single out a "recorder" as does Illinois, but Tennessee does single out a "register." Other singular dual offices noted are "receiver-general" in Massachusetts, and "sergeant" and "tax collector" in Virginia. For comparative purposes, a generalized tabulation by the Citizens Conference on State Legislatures will be used with the understanding that, as exemplified above in connection with the *Capuzi* case (*supra,* p. 122), the precise constitutional language in each state may provide significant exceptions. The Citizens Conference summarizes dual office holding thus:

Foreign Employment: "12 prohibit legislators to hold a job with a foreign country."

Federal Employment: "43 forbid legislators to hold a job with the national government."

State Employment: "38 state that legislators shall hold no position under the state government."

County Employment: "3 forbid legislators to hold a position with a county government."

Municipal Employment: "3 ban legislators from employment by municipalities."

(State Constitutional Provisions Affecting Legislatures 19-20 (May 1967))

In the Citizens Conference tabulation, Illinois is included under the first three categories but not under the last two.

The United States Constitution provides:

"No Senator or Representative shall, during the Time for which he was elected, be appointed to any civil Office under the Authority of the United States, which shall have been created, or the Emoluments whereof shall have been increased during such time; and no Person holding any Office under the United States, shall be a Member of either House during his Continuance in Office." (art. I, § 6.)

The Model State Constitution is silent on dual office holding.

Dual Office Holding (General): About a dozen states prohibit state officers from holding offices, usually of trust or profit, under any foreign government. In several of these states, the prohibition also runs to any other state government. Approximately 18 states extend the same prohibition to United States offices, frequently with exceptions. The most common is for service in the National Guard. A few states exclude postmasters, but usually only those above a maximum compensation. Some 15 states prohibit, in greater or lesser degree, dual office holding within the state.

The United States Constitution prohibits any office holder from accepting any "present, emolument, office, or title, of any kind whatever, from any king, prince, or foreign state" without the consent of Congress. The Constitution also prohibits the President from receiving any emolument from any state. The Model State Constitution is silent on the subject.

Comment

Age, Residency, Citizenship: In view of the fact that, under the United States Supreme Court's "one man-one vote" rule, regular redistricting will have to take place, consideration should be given to the problem of the legislator who finds that, after redistricting, his residence has been separated from the geographical area which he used to represent. If such a legislator wishes to run for re-election, he has at least one problem and possibly two. He has to run in a new district where he may not be well known and he may be faced with running against a legislator who has always been in the new district and is well known. In the proposed 1967 New York Constitution this eventuality was covered, though it must be conceded that the drafting problem was most complex. The proposed provision read as follows:

"Every member of the legislature shall be at least twenty-one years old and eligible to vote in this state. He shall have been domiciled in the state for the three years preceding his election and for the twelve months preceding his election in his legislative district. If, however, any redistricting plan for senate or assembly has been certified pursuant to section two of this article since the last general election for the legislature, he shall have been domiciled for the twelve months preceding his election in a county in which all or part of the new district is located or in a county contiguous to such district if such district be composed of a whole county and all or parts of another county or counties."

Dual Office Holding: This subject, as well as the related problem of conflict of interest, was strong in the minds of the delegates to the 1870 Convention. One of the results of this concern was a proliferation of different provisions. (In addition to Sec. 3, see Secs. 15 and 25 of this Art., *infra,* pp. 176 and 230; Sec. 5 of Art. V and Sec. 4 of Art. VIII, *infra,* pp. 267 and 409.) Consideration should be given to consolidating such provisions as are to be retained in one section or, if legislators are to be treated differently from other government officials, then in two sections. (For some policy considerations on this subject, see the *Comment* on Sec. 15, *infra,* p. 177-8.)

Disqualification for Crimes

Sec. 4. No person who has been, or hereafter shall be convicted of bribery, perjury or other infamous crime, nor any person who has been or may be a collector or holder of public moneys, who shall not have accounted for and paid over, according to law, all such moneys due from him, shall be eligible to the General Assembly, or to any office of profit or trust in this State.

History

The 1818 and 1848 Constitutions contained comparable provisions concerning paying over public moneys due, and contained provisions giving the legislature "full power to exclude from the privilege of . . . being elected any person convicted of bribery, perjury or any other infamous crime." (The word "any" before "other" was omitted in 1848.) In the 1870 Convention, the proposal as originally offered changed the part concerning convicted persons from power to exclude by law to a command to the legislature to exclude. A delegate suggested that the Convention ought to make the decision and be done with it. Accordingly, an amendment was offered embodying the suggestion. (Debates 572.) The amendment was accepted and the Committee on Revision and Adjustment combined it with the proposed section on accounting for public moneys. The drafters of the proposed 1922 Constitution created a new article called "Public Servants," one of the sections of which consisted of a simplified version of Section 4, the prohibition against dual office holding in Section 3 (supra, p. 119), and the moneys-in-default part of Section 11 of Article IX (infra, p. 474).

Explanation

This straightforward section is designed to keep criminals out of government and, apparently, to use the obtaining of a government position as a collection device. The latter characterization may appear inappropriate, but any broader characterization would imply some sort of criminal behavior and that would presumably be encompassed by the other half of the section. The Supreme Court has held, however, that there must be a proper determination, by a court or other competent authority, that the moneys are in fact in default. (Cawley v. People, 95 Ill. 249 (1880).)

The Supreme Court has added two important glosses to this section. It has held that the courts, not the legislature, ultimately decide what is an "infamous crime" for purposes of this section. (People ex rel. Keenan v. McGuane, 13 Ill. 2d 520 (1958). See also People ex rel. Ward v. Tomek, 54 Ill. App. 2d 197 (1964), where the crime was a misdemeanor, but, significantly, was a conspiracy to defraud a township.) In the Keenan case, the Supreme Court did not, of course, purport to have the legislative power of definition; the judicial decision is to be made "in the light of the common law as it existed when the Constitution was adopted in 1870." (Id. at 533.) In the same case, the Supreme Court added its second gloss by construing "conviction" to mean after trial and before disposition of any appeals. If this construction were to be applied literally, the disqualification upon conviction would remain, notwithstanding subsequent reversal. It can be argued, however, that a reversal — on the merits and not for a new trial — wipes out the conviction as if it never existed. In any event, this question is an open one. (See also the Explanation of Sec. 9, infra, p. 147, concerning judicial review of a decision by the legislature to seat a person alleged to be ineligible.)

Comparative Analysis

Conviction of Crime: Approximately 30 of the states have some constitutional disqualification for holding public office upon conviction of stated crimes. Only a half dozen or so have one as sweeping as in Illinois. In those states which limit the range of disqualifying crimes, the one most commonly included is bribery. A few states simply authorize the legislature to provide for disqualifications by law. In at least five states it is possible to have the disqualification removed either by pardon or by restoration of civil rights. Neither the United States Constitution nor the Model State Constitution contains any provision on this subject.

Moneys in Default: About a third of the states have comparable provisions. Most of them cover all public offices, but a few are limited to eligibility to serve in the legislature. Neither the United States Constitution nor the Model State Constitution contains any provision on this subject.

Comment

It seems appropriate to note the permanence of the disqualification for infamous criminal behavior. There is no room for the concept of a single "payment of a debt to society" or for the concept of rehabilitation. In this connection, it is interesting that the comparable section as revised in the 1964 Michigan Constitution provides that the disqualification is limited to convictions "within the preceding 20 years."

Oath of Office

Sec. 5. Members of the General Assembly, before they enter upon their official duties, shall take and subscribe the following oath or affirmation:

"I do solemnly swear (or affirm) that I will support the Constitution of the United States and the Constitution of the State of Illinois, and will faithfully discharge the duties of Senator (or Representative) according to the best of my ability; and that I have not, knowingly or intentionally, paid or contributed anything, or made any promise in the nature of a bribe, to directly or indirectly influence any vote at the election at which I was chosen to fill the said office, and have not accepted, nor will I accept or receive, directly or indirectly, any money or other valuable thing, from any corporation, company or person, for any vote or influence I may give or withold on any bill, resolution or appropriation, or for any other official act."

This oath shall be administered by a judge of the supreme or circuit court in the hall of the house to which the member is elected, and the Secretary of State shall record and file the oath subscribed by each member. Any member who shall refuse to take the oath herein prescribed shall forfeit his office, and every member who shall be convicted of having sworn falsely to, or of violating, his said oath, shall forfeit his office and be disqualified thereafter from holding any office of profit or trust in this State.

History

The 1818 Constitution simply required that all public officers take an oath to support the United States and Illinois Constitutions and an oath of office. The Schedule of that Constitution provided that justices of the peace could administer oaths until the legislature otherwise directed. Both provisions were repeated in the 1848 Constitution and a new oath was added: against dueling. In the 1870 Convention, debate on this section was extensive. The argument was over whether to strike from the proposed oath the words following "ability." The vehemence with which the longer oath was defended is some indication of the low repute in which legislators were then held. There were three different attempts to strike, but they all failed. The proposed 1922 Constitution left this section unchanged.

Explanation

In addition to providing for the customary oath of office, this section utilizes the oath-taking process to get at improper lobbying, special interest influences, bribery and other means of corrupting the legislative process. There has been no judicial interpretation of this section except to note that the word "forfeit" in the first part of the last sentence of the section means that an elected legislator has title to the office before taking the oath. (People *ex rel.* Douglas v. Barrett, 370 Ill. 464 (1939).)

Comparative Analysis

There are, of course, a great many minor variations in the oath requirements of the several states. The important point to note is that in only a few states does the oath include detailed disclaimers of improper influences. There appear to be three states — Nebraska, South Dakota and Wyoming — that cover both pre-election and in-office improper influences and provide for disqualification from office. Two states — Missouri and West Virginia — speak only to improper influences in office and disqualification therefor. Three states — Montana, Oklahoma and Pennsylvania — cover both pre-election and in-office improper influences but omit disqualification. Texas prohibits only pre-election chicanery. Of these nine states, all except Missouri, South Dakota and West Virginia include the detailed disclaimer in the general oath of office. (For further comparison of oaths of office see discussion of Sec. 25 of Art. V, *infra,* p. 323.)

Comment

It is traditional to require an oath of office. Oath-taking is a ritual of great solemnity and dignity, but it is debatable whether an oath serves any purpose other than ritual. It is not traditional to utilize an oath of office as either a device to ferret out previous wrong-doing or to exact a promise against future wrong-doing. Nor is it traditional to use violation of an oath as the device for punishment of the wrong-doing. It was noted above that there is no reported judicial review of this section. Since it seems doubtful that no legislator has ever violated this oath of office, one can speculate as to the usefulness of this detailed disclaimer.

SENATORIAL APPORTIONMENT
State Senators

Sec. 6. The General Assembly in 1955 shall redistrict the state for the purpose of electing state senators. There shall be fifty-eight senatorial districts. Cook county shall have twenty-four of the districts. These twenty-four districts shall be located as follows: Eighteen in the territory that is within the present corporate limits of the city of Chicago; and six in the territory that is in Cook county outside such corporate limits. The remaining one hundred and one counties of the state shall have thirty-four of the senatorial districts.

All senatorial districts shall be formed of contiguous and compact territory. In their formation, area shall be the prime consideration.

The senatorial districts shall be numbered one, two, three, and so forth, including fifty-eight. Each such district shall elect one senator, whose term of office shall be four years. Senators elected in districts bearing even numbers shall be elected in 1956 and every four years thereafter; and senators elected in districts bearing odd numbers shall be elected in 1958 and every four years thereafter.

History

The 1818 Constitution called for four-year staggered terms for senators from districts fixed by the General Assembly and apportioned "according to the number of white inhabitants." The number of senators was "never to be less than one-third nor more than one-half of the number of representatives."

The 1848 Constitution continued four-year staggered terms, but fixed the number of senators at 25. Districts were to be "composed of contiguous territory bounded by county lines; . . . *Provided,* that cities and towns containing the requisite population [could] be erected into separate districts." Districts were to be "apportioned among the several counties according to the number of white inhabitants." A state census in 1855 and every tenth year thereafter was provided for, and redistricting was to take place every five years following each state and federal census. There was also a technical direction for distribution of population in the case of an excess in a single county.

The 1870 Convention included the classic debate over representation — whether representation should be solely on the basis of people, whether every county should have its own representation, whether the downstate areas needed protection against Cook County, and so on. A special twist was given to this problem by Joseph Medill, Chairman of the Committee on Electoral and Representative Reform, when he offered his plan for cumulative voting. Most of the debate centered on representation in the lower house, however, and will be discussed in the *History* of Section 7. (*Infra,* p. 136.)

The proposal for the Senate as originally offered was in substance much as Section 6 in the 1870 Constitution prior to adoption of the 1954 Amendment. There were to be 51 senators, elected for staggered four-year terms, from districts "formed of contiguous and compact territory, bounded by county lines," and containing, "as nearly as practicable, an equal number of inhabitants." A certain amount of population flexibility was provided for in a technical exception. (In the light of the one man-one vote requirement promulgated by the United States Supreme Court, it seems pointless to explain these technical provisions.) The General Assembly was to redistrict the state after each Federal Census.

The only debate of significance was over a proposal to cut the size of the Senate from 51 to 37. (There is no indication in the Convention debates where these magic numbers of 37 and 51 came from. For cumulative voting in the House, Mr. Medill, of course, had to have a number divisible by three, and the delegate who proposed 37 indicated that he was thinking of a lower house of 100 or 101. Whether he also thought that 37 times 3 equals 101 is not known.) It should be noted that Mr. Medill's committee originally proposed cumulative voting for senators, which would have meant 17 districts electing three senators each. The decision to limit cumulative voting to the House of Representatives was made by Mr. Medill and his committee long after the original proposal had been filed with the Convention. It is fairly clear from the debates that a great many decisions on the representation problem were made off the floor, and the decision to leave the Senate with single-member districts may have been one of them.

The senatorial districting provision of the proposed 1922 Constitution was one of several controversial products of the 1920-22 Convention. The number of senators was set at 57, of which 19 were allotted to Cook County and 38 to the rest of the state. Periodic districting was to be on the basis, not of population, but of persons voting for governor. The districting would be confined to realignment of the 19 districts inside Cook County and of the 38 districts outside.

The last redistricting of the Senate called for under the original Section 6 took place in 1901. As the years passed, the under-representation of Cook County became more and more pronounced. And since representatives were elected from senatorial districts, under-representation was the same in both houses. After the 1922 Constitution was rejected, many proposed constitutional amendments on legislative apportionment and districting were offered in the General Assembly, but none passed. The first effort to succeed was the compromise proposal in 1953 that became Sections 6, 7 and 8 following approval in November, 1954. The compromise was, of course, to make senatorial representation geographical and to limit population representation to the lower house. The United States Supreme Court changed all that and there is today no valid constitutional provision for senatorial districting.

Explanation

In *Germano v. Kerner* (378 U.S. 560 (1964)), the United States Supreme Court made it clear that Section 6 is unconstitutional. After the 74th General Assembly adjourned without redistricting the Senate, the United States District Court for the Northern District of Illinois, where the *Germano* case had been instituted, and the Supreme Court of Illinois, which had retained jurisdiction over a like case in the state courts, co-operated in the development of a districting plan. In *People* ex rel. *Engle v. Kerner* (33 Ill. 2d 11 (1965)), this plan was promulgated with the instruction that all 58 senators were to be elected for four years in 1966 and in 1970.

One of the things that fell by the wayside as a result of the one man-one vote requirement was the interesting argument that since Section 6 provides for a "one-shot" districting plan, the 1955 Act which created the senatorial districts became, in effect, a permanent part of the Constitution without following the amendment procedure. (See the majority and dissenting opinions in People *ex rel* Engle v. Kerner, 32 Ill. 2d 212 (1965).)

Comparative Analysis

Size: It may come as a surprise to many to learn that only Minnesota (67) and Iowa (61) have more members in their Senates than has Illinois. Ten states, including Illinois, have between 50 and 59 members; 12 between 40 and 49; 20 between 30 and 39; and six under 30. The foregoing refers to actual members as of May, 1967. Only 19 states, including Illinois, specify constitutionally the exact number of senators. The other states set maximums and minimums, or have other criteria for size. Minnesota, for example, ties size of Senate to total population. Moreover, the one man-one vote rule is a monkey-wrench thrown into the districting system across the country and there may be instances where, with judicial sanction, the actual size of a Senate may not conform to the constitutional provision.

Terms: Illinois is one of a large majority of 38 states setting four-year terms for the Senate. This includes unicameral Nebraska. The remaining 12 have two-year terms. Most of the four-year-term states stagger the elections as Illinois normally does. A few states have four-year terms for both houses.

Apportionment: There is not much point in reviewing the constitutional methods of apportionment in the several states. Not only have the United States Supreme Court's rulings invalidated many provisions; states which, as formerly the case in Illinois, required districting on the basis of population frequently failed to redistrict after a decennial census. It may be noted, however, that in theory some states provided that apportionment of both houses was to be by population, and that in states apportioning only one house by population, it was frequently the Senate that was to be so apportioned. As of the middle of 1967, 25 states chose their Senates from single-member districts. Of the remaining 25, only two, Florida and West Virginia, chose all senators from multi-member districts. The other 23 had a mixture of single- and multi-member districts, ranging from states where most members of the Senate are chosen from single-member districts to states where most are from multi-member districts.

United States Constitution: The United States Constitution provides for two senators from each state, elected for six-year terms. Approximately one-third of the Senate is elected every two years, and, of course, in each state the terms are staggered. (Thus, districts are multi-member, but, except on some occasions involving an unexpired term, elections are as if from single-member districts.) Article V further provides that no state may be deprived of its representation in the Senate without its consent. It is worth mentioning, perhaps, that the United States Senate has been used as an argument against the concept that both houses of a state legislature should be apportioned on a population basis. There is a theoretical and a practical answer to the argument. The theoretical answer is that the several states, as, in effect, sovereign nations following dissociation from England, banded together in a federation under their own terms. No local government within a state — county, city or town — can stand on any such theory. The practical answer is that in most states, tradition divides the two senators between the urban and rural areas, or between the "big city" and the rest of the state, or on some other geographic basis, and this has produced a senatorial cross-section that is much more complex than the urban/rural division that would normally obtain in a single state with geographic districting.

Model State Constitution: The Model State Constitution recommends a unicameral legislature consisting of senators elected for two-year terms from single-member districts, with a constitutional maximum and minimum number of districts, but with the numbers left blank. An alternative recommendation for a bicameral legislature provides for a number of senators not exceeding one-third the number of assemblymen, elected from single-member districts for six-year staggered terms.

The Model's recommendation for districting is that each "district shall consist of compact and contiguous territory. All districts shall be so nearly equal in population that the population of the largest district shall not exceed that of the smallest district by more than ---- per cent. In determining the population of each district, inmates of such public or private institutions as prisons or other places of correction, hospitals for the insane or other institutions housing persons who are disqualified from voting by law shall not be counted." (art. IV, §4.04.)

Comment

At the present time, apportionment and districting are so tightly controlled by the United States Supreme Court that there is little leeway in constructing constitutional rules for the guidance of those charged with reapportionment and redistricting following an official census. In the light of the United States Supreme Court's *Kirkpatrick* and *Wells* decisions, discussed under Section 7 (*infra*, p. 139), even the percentage variance in the Model State Constitution's provision quoted is not acceptable. (The next edition of the Model will undoubtedly reflect this latest constitutional command.)

Nevertheless, there are two possibilities from recent constitutional convention experience which are worthy of consideration. One is the ingenious open-ended provision adopted by Connecticut in 1965. After specifying the maximum and minimum allowable number of senatorial and assembly districts, all of which shall be contiguous, and with no other specification except that a town (township or city in Illinois) shall not be divided other than to make two or more assembly districts wholly within the town, the Connecticut Constitution states: "The establishment of districts in the general assembly shall be consistent with federal constitutional standards." Thus, if the United States Supreme Court modifies its one man-one vote rule or if the United States Constitution is amended in some fashion that alters the rule, Connecticut, after the next decennial census following such modification or alteration, can take advantage thereof without an amendment of its constitution. In the same year, Tennessee adopted an amendment achieving the same end as in Connecticut but spelling out in some detail alternative criteria for districting.

The other possibility worth considering is the proposed solution to the problem of gerrymandering offered in the unsuccessful 1967 New York Constitution. The rubric, "compact, contiguous and as nearly equal in population as is practicable," has not prevented gerrymandering. Suggestions for inhibiting partisan gerrymandering have, in general, followed two lines: one is to use additional criteria, such as following natural geographic, political and social boundaries; the other is to provide for a wholly independent commission to do the redistricting. The New York proposed solution was to include among the criteria for districting the flat statement: "Gerrymandering for any purpose is prohibited." This would have provided for judicial review of a districting plan where the claim was that, even though the districts were compact,

contiguous, and almost equal in population, the plan was in fact the result of partisan gerrymandering. (Up to now the United States Supreme
Court has not extended the equal protection rule to include gerrymandering as such, except in the case of *Gomillion v. Lightfoot,* 364 U.S. 339
(1960), which involved gerrymandering for strictly racial purposes.)

Representatives

Sec. 7. The General Assembly in 1955 and in 1963, and every ten years thereafter, shall redistrict the state for the purpose of electing state representatives.
There shall be fifty-nine representative districts. In the 1955 redistricting Cook
County shall have thirty of the districts. These thirty districts shall be located
as follows: Twenty-three in the territory that is within the present corporate
limits of the City of Chicago; and seven in the territory that is in Cook County
outside such corporate limits. In the 1955 redistricting, the remaining one hundred and one counties of the state shall have twenty-nine of the representative
districts. In redistricting subsequent to the 1960 census, and thereafter, the fifty-
nine representative districts shall be divided among (1) that part of Cook County
that is within the present corporate limits of the City of Chicago, (2) that part of
Cook County that is outside such corporate limits, and (3) the remaining one
hundred and one counties of the state, as nearly as may be, as the population
of each of these three divisions bears to the total population of the state.

Representative districts shall be formed of contiguous and compact territory,
and shall contain, as nearly as practicable, a population equal to the representative ratio; outside of Cook county, such districts 'shall be bounded by county
lines unless the population of any county entitles it to more than one representative district. The representative ratio for the entire state shall be the quotient
obtained by dividing the population of the state by fifty-nine. No representative
district may contain less population than four-fifths of the representative ratio.

Three representatives shall be elected in each representative district in 1956
and every two years thereafter. The term of office shall be two years. In all
elections of representatives aforesaid, each qualified voter may cast as many
votes for one candidate as there are representatives to be elected, or may distribute the same, or equal parts thereof, among the candidates as he shall see fit;
and the candidates highest in votes shall be declared elected.

History

The 1818 Constitution called for two-year terms for representatives
from districts fixed by the General Assembly and apportioned "according to the number of white inhabitants." The number of representatives
was to be not "less than twenty-seven, nor more than thirty-six, until the
number of inhabitants shall amount to 100,000." It was not stated what
was to happen after the population passed 100,000.

The 1848 Constitution continued two-year terms, but fixed the number of representatives at 75, "until the population of the state shall
amount to 1,000,000 souls, when five members may be added to the house.
and five additional members for every 500,000 inhabitants thereafter,
until the whole number of representatives shall amount to 100; after

which the number shall neither be increased nor diminished." Districts were to be "composed of contiguous territory bounded by county lines; . . . *Provided,* that cities and towns containing the requisite population may be erected into separate districts." Districts were to be "apportioned among the several counties according to the number of white inhabitants." It was further provided that not more than three representatives could be elected from a single district and that if more than one county comprised a district, all representatives for that district were to be elected by the entire district. The five-year redistricting requirement and the technical direction for distribution of excess population applicable to senators (see *History* of Sec. 6, *supra,* p. 131) also applied to representative districts.

One of the most extensive debates in the 1870 Convention concerned Sections 7 and 8 governing representative districts. The irony of it all was that the voters were given the alternative of accepting Mr. Medill's cumulative voting provision, described below, and they took it in preference to the carefully worked out Sections 7 and 8. The debate over Sections 7 and 8 was complex, partly because the sections themselves were complex, so much so that at one point the Convention recessed for several hours to permit the Committee on the Legislative Department to redraft one of the sections. The members of the committee had demonstrated on the floor that they themselves did not agree on the meaning of what they had drafted. But behind the debate lay the classic rural-urban, downstate-Cook County problem. Since the sections never went into effect, it suffices to note that most counties would have been entitled to representation and that population increases and shifts were partly to be compensated for by increasing the size of the House every ten years. (Under the formula, there would be at least 219 representatives today.)

Joseph Medill was Chairman of the Committee on Electoral and Representative Reform and a member of the Committee on the Legislative Department. He addressed himself to the problem of minority representation. His primary concern was not with rural-urban or downstate-Cook County problems, but with the peculiar historical accident that the northern half of the state was overwhelmingly Republican and the southern half was overwhelmingly Democratic. Mr. Medill's theory was that people who voted for the losing candidate ended up being unrepresented, and that this was inconsistent with the democratic process as manifested in a traditional town meeting. His solution was the three-member district with the privilege of cumulative voting. (*See* Debates 560-64.)

For reasons that do not appear in the Debates, the Committee Report was not acted upon by the Convention sitting in Committee of the Whole.

It was taken up by the Convention proper late in the session, at which time Mr. Medill offered a substitute that omitted the Senate from the minority representation plan. There was a minimum of debate and the substitute was accepted and referred to the Committee on Revision and Adjustment. (Debates 1729.) It is reasonably clear that acceptance was on the assumption that minority representation would be referred to the voters as an alternative mode of representation in the lower house. (*Id.*) In the special election on the Constitution, there were nine separate votes, including one for or against the whole Constitution. The vote on minority representation was much closer than on any other question. The alternative Sections 7 and 8 provided that three representatives would be elected every two years in each senatorial district. Each voter had three votes which he could distribute as he wished.

The proposed 1922 Constitution abolished multi-member districts and, perforce, cumulative voting. There were to be 153 representative districts, compact and contiguous but following county lines. Districts were to contain, as nearly as practicable, the same number of people who had voted for governor in the last preceding gubernatorial election, but there was a technical rule of distribution that gave a slight advantage to counties of lesser population.

The compromise set of amendments proposed in 1953 and approved in November, 1954, preserved the principle of representation by population in the House of Representatives and multi-member districts with cumulative voting. Since the new basis of representation for the Senate was geographical, house districts could no longer be co-extensive with senate districts. The number of house districts was increased to 59 and the size of the House perforce became 177.

Explanation

Following the adoption of the 1954 Amendment, the 69th General Assembly adopted a districting plan of 59 three-member districts, 23 in Chicago, seven in the rest of Cook County, and 29 in the balance of the state. This apportionment among the three areas of the state was as directed in the amendment itself. After the 1960 Federal Census, the 73rd General Assembly attempted a new apportionment and districting plan as directed by Section 7, but the Governor vetoed it. In accordance with the requirements of Section 8 (*infra,* p. 141), a commission was appointed, but it failed to act within the time specified and the House of Representatives of the 74th General Assembly was elected at large. At a Special Session held in 1964 prior to the election, the legislature abandoned cumulative voting for the election at large, but preserved minority representation by providing that no party could list more candidates than a number equal to two-thirds of the total membership of the House. (Ill. Rev. Stat. ch. 46, §8A-8 (1967).) The Supreme Court upheld the arrangement. (People *ex rel*. Daniels v. Carpentier, 30 Ill. 2d 590 (1964).)

In 1965, the 74th General Assembly failed to apportion and district the lower house, but the commission appointed pursuant to Section 8 was successful. Under the plan now in operation, there are 21 Chicago districts, nine Cook County "ex-Chicago" districts, and 29 for the balance of the state. For the Chicago and Cook County districts, the commission used the senatorial district boundaries promulgated by the Supreme Court. (See Sec. 6, *supra,* p. 131.) The 1965 districting plan has not been challenged in the courts.

The latest United States Supreme Court decisions on the one man-one vote requirement create two questions about the wording of Section 7. In *Kirkpatrick v. Preisler* (394 U.S. 526 (1969)), decided April 7, 1969, the Court clearly stated that the requirement of equality of population, "as nearly as practicable," from district to district is not met by adherence to some minimum plus or minus variance from what in Section 7 is called the "representative ratio." A good faith effort to attain mathematical equality is required, and this would not likely be attainable if the command to follow county lines outside of Cook County were to be followed. On the same day, the United States Supreme Court handed down *Wells v. Rockefeller* (394 U.S. 542 (1969)), in which it upset a Congressional redistricting plan principally because the legislature first carved seven "homogeneous" sections out of the state and then produced districts of almost identical population in each section, but ending up with substantial deviation among all the districts, including the ten (out of a state total of 41) which were not included in any of the seven "homogeneous" sections. In the light of the *Wells* case, it seems unlikely that Illinois can continue to follow the two-step process of first apportioning 177 seats among Chicago, the balance of Cook County and the rest of the state, and then districting on a population basis in each area either according to the representative ratio, which is computed on a state-wide basis, or according to a representative ratio for each of the three segments.

With reference to cumulative voting, it should be noted that in practice the need for cumulating one's votes is frequently obviated because the majority party nominates only two candidates and the minority party one. (Compare the statutory scheme for the at-large election of 1964 referred to above.) Since the purpose of cumulative voting is to assure minority representation, such party nominating practice guarantees the minority representation originally envisioned by Mr. Medill. Unfortunately, such a practice effectively destroys the franchise of independent and *minor* minority party members and partially destroys the franchise of the two major party members who cannot exercise any power except in their own party's primary. The practice was approved by the Supreme Court in *People* ex rel. *Lindstrand v. Emmerson* (333 Ill. 606 (1929)).

The principle of minority representation requires multi-member districts, and presumably that is the only reason Illinois has them. But, as noted·in the *Comparative Analysis* below, many states have them, usually in a mix of single-member and multi-member districts. On July 28, 1969, a three-judge Federal District Court held unconstitutional the present multi-member districting scheme in Indiana. The Court said that multi-member districts are valid only if all districts have the same number of members. (Chavis v. Whitcomb, — F. Supp. — (S.D. Ind. 1969). *See also* Banzhaf, "Multi-Member Electoral Districts — Do They Violate the 'One Man, One Vote' Principle?" 75 Yale L.J. 1309 (1966).)

Comparative Analysis

Size: There are four states with a larger lower house than that of Illinois, and one state, Connecticut, which also has 177 members. Seven states have precisely 100 representatives, 19 states have fewer than 100, and 17 states have more than 100 but fewer than 177.

Terms: All states except Alabama, Louisiana, Maryland, and Mississippi have two-year terms for representatives. Those four states have four-year terms for members of both houses. (Nebraska, of course, has no lower house.)

Apportionment: For the reasons discussed under Section 6 (*supra,* p. 131), there is no reason to review apportionment among the several states. It should be noted, however, that 34 states have multi-member districts in the lower house. In three of those states, including Illinois, all districts are multi-member. In the other 31 states the lower house has both single- and multi-member districts, in varying arrangements from mostly single-member districts to mostly multi-member. No other state has cumulative voting. It should be noted, moreover, that in some states, the seats in a multi-member district are numbered so that Carp runs against Bass and Doe runs against Buck and a voter cannot "vote for two," but must choose between each pair. (This also obtains in some of the states with multi-member districts in the upper house.)

United States Constitution: Representatives are apportioned among the several states on the basis of population with the provision that every state is entitled to at least one representative. (There are five states with only one representative.) Until the 1920 Census, Congress regularly increased the size of the House of Representatives as the country's population increased. Since then, the practice has been to retain the size of the House at 435 and to reapportion after each Census. Since 1930, reapportionment has been automatic under a permanent formula. Congress can, of course, change the present method at any time.

Model State Constitution: The Model recommends a unicameral legislature, but provides alternative sections for a bicameral legislature. The bicameral recommendation is for a lower house of single-member districts with a constitutional maximum and minimum size, but without insertion of maximum and minimum numbers. Terms are set at two years. The requirement for districting is the same as for the unicameral senate. (See quotation, *supra,* p. 134.)

Comment

If the Convention decides to preserve cumulative voting, districts will presumably continue to have three members each. If cumulative voting is abandoned, it would be tempting Fate to go to a system of mixed single- and multi-member districts or all multi-member districts of unequal numbers. United States Supreme Court watchers are not likely to offer attractive odds that the *Chavis* case would be reversed. (See also *Comment* for Sec. 6, *supra,* p. 135.)

Redistricting

Sec. 8. In performing its duties under Sections 6 and 7 of this amendment, the General Assembly shall redistrict and reapportion in a single legislative enactment. If, however, the regular session of the General Assembly in 1955 as to both senatorial and representative districts or in 1963, or any ten years thereafter as to representative districts, fails by the first day of July to redistrict the state into such districts, then the redistricting shall be accomplished by a commission. Within thirty days after such first day of July, the state central committee of each of the two political parties, casting the highest votes for governor at the last preceding gubernatorial election, shall submit to the governor of the state a list of ten persons. Within thirty days thereafter, the governor shall appoint the commission of ten members, five from each list. If either of the state central committees fails to submit the list within the specified time, the governor, within the specified time, shall appoint five members of his own choice from the party of such committee. Each member of the committee shall receive $25.00 a day, but not more than $2,000 for his service.

This commission shall redistrict the state into senatorial districts and into representative districts in the manner specified above. This commission shall file with the secretary of state a full statement of the numbers of the senatorial and representative districts and their boundaries. No such statement shall be valid unless approved by seven members of such commission.

After such statement is filed, senators and representatives shall be elected according to the statement and the districts therein determined, until a redistricting and reapportionment are thereafter made by the General Assembly as provided in this amendment. If, however, the statement is not filed within four months after the commission is appointed it shall stand discharged. Thereupon, all senators, scheduled for election at the next election for state senators, and all state representatives shall be nominated and elected at the next election from the state at large. Following such an election at large, the General Assembly at its next regular session shall perform the duties specified in this amendment.

But if such a General Assembly fails to perform these duties, then another commission, as specified in this Section 8, shall be appointed in like manner, with like duties, and power, and with like effect; and so forth until a valid senatorial and representative redistricting and reapportionment are secured in this 1950 decade and each decade thereafter. But there can be only one valid senatorial and representative redistricting and reapportionment during a particular decade.

History

This section was part of the amendment adopted in 1954. There was nothing comparable in any of the earlier Constitutions. The proposed 1922 Constitution did have a provision for action in case the General Assembly failed to redistrict, as follows:

"If the general assembly fails to make any such apportionment it shall be the duty of the secretary of state, the attorney general and the auditor of public accounts to meet at the office of the governor within ninety days after the adjournment of the regular session of the year designated for that purpose and make an apportionment as provided in section twenty-three of this constitution." (art. III, § 24.)

Explanation

With one exception, nothing in Section 8 is affected by the one man-one vote requirement. The exception is that Section 8 does not include senatorial redistricting after initial creation of senatorial districts. (*See* People *ex rel.* Giannis v. Carpentier, 30 Ill. 2d 24 (1964).) Under the one man-one vote requirement, periodic redistricting of both houses will be necessary.

In *Williams v. Kerner* (30 Ill. 2d 11 (1963)), the Supreme Court held that the Governor's power of veto was part of the legislative process involved in redistricting under Section 8.

Comparative Analysis

Traditionally, redistricting was confined to the legislature, and, traditionally, the job did not get done. Even before the United States Supreme Court opened the door to judicial enforcement of redistricting, some states had begun to experiment with ways of accomplishing redistricting in the face of obvious legislative reluctance to act. Indeed, Section 8 was adopted a good many years before the breakthrough in *Baker v. Carr* (369 U.S. 186 (1962)). Now, of course, as state after state undertakes the task of adopting new provisions to take the place of invalid ones, attention is given to including some method for carrying redistricting forward if the legislature fails to act. There are at least seven states besides Illinois which provide for an alternative procedure for redistricting. Another state, Colorado, used the sanction route of providing no compensation to legislators and ineligibility for reelection after a given period and until redistricting was accomplished. No other state appears to have an "election at large" sanction.

The United States Supreme Court's redistricting rulings have also probably caused more states to take the route of by-passing the legislature and providing for initial redistricting by some nonlegislative agency. There are at least ten states that by-pass the legislature, several of which antedate the Supreme Court's rulings. In some states, the Governor is given the task, usually with an advisory group. In other states, there is a redistricting commission of designated elected officials, and in some states the commission is appointed, normally from lists submitted to the Governor. A goodly number of states specifically include a constitutional authorization for judicial review of any redistricting plan.

The United States Constitution is silent as to the process of apportionment of seats in the House of Representatives. The current system, as noted earlier (*supra,* p. 140), is to redistribute the 435 seats automatically by statutory formula following the decennial census. The Model State Constitution recommends the appointment by the Governor of a board of qualified voters to make redistricting recommendations which the Governor must publish but may change with appropriate explanations of the reasons for such changes. Original jurisdiction is conferred on the highest court for judicial review, including power to promulgate a revised plan, or an original plan if the Governor fails to act.

Comment

There are two key problems in considering who should redistrict. The first is whether the legislature should have a bite at the cherry at all. The second is whether the bite, first or second, should be antiseptic — *i.e.,* nonpolitical and nonpartisan.

The arguments in favor of by-passing the legislature are fairly persuasive. Leaving aside for the moment the question of whether redistricting is essentially political, the special problem facing a legislature undertaking redistricting is the personal vested interest of the sitting members. One of the conclusions drawn from an analysis of the Illinois experience in 1955 was expressed as follows:

"Redistricting proposals that dislodge a minimum number of sitting members, irrespective of party, will be favored over proposals that do not take into account the sitting members. There is no evidence that in the 1955 redistricting either party persisted in an attempt to improve the existing legislative strength of the party by a favorable redistricting scheme. On the other hand, neither party showed any disposition to give up any of its safe seats or sacrifice any of its sitting members. In short, if it had been possible to achieve a redistricting that would have satisfied the constitutional mandate without imperiling the seat of any member, such a plan would have had virtually unanimous support in the General Assembly. To the extent that future redistricting plans can approach this goal, they will meet a minimum of opposition. Neither party nor principle nor region is more important than a legislator's colleagues." (G. Steiner and S. Gove, Legislative Politics in Illinois 117 (1960).)

But districting is part of the political process and it is arguable whether it is appropriate to attempt to insulate districting from that process. One possibility is the use of computers. This is a tricky business because, as everyone familiar with computers knows, the result produced is no better than the programmed instructions. (In computer lingo, it's GIGO — garbage in, garbage out.) An abstract plan based on compactness, contiguity, equality of population and nothing more could be fed to a computer, but the result, outside of Chicago, could be statewide slices from border to border, east and west or north and south.

It follows that a great deal of thought must go into the preparation of the program that is to be given to the computer. Such thought should be political, not in any narrow, partisan sense, but in the sense that the end sought is a system of fair representation in the political process of law-making. Some balance must be struck between the use of knowledgeable people who are likely to be highly partisan and nonpartisan people who are not likely to be knowledgeable in practical, political realities.

It may very well be that the use of a computer could be the vehicle for striking the balance. If the districting plan is prepared by hand, so to speak, by a bipartisan group, there is a danger that it will engage in all sorts of trade-offs on the basis of assumed short-range partisan advantages. If the plan is prepared by hand by a nonpartisan group, there is a danger that the result may reflect hidden prejudices that may or may not be appropriate to the political process, or may produce a short-range chaotic situation because too many delicate political balances are upset. But if the group charged with producing a districting plan has no more to do than prepare the rules that guide a computer, a bipartisan board or commission might be preferable.

It is arguable, of course, that even the rules that guide a computer can be "rigged," so to speak. One rule, for example, could be that the maximum number of incumbents should be protected. But it is equally arguable that a nonpartisan group might adopt a rule that the maximum number of incumbents should have their seats put in jeopardy.

In sum, there are three propositions that can be set down for the guidance of those who must decide who is to do the redistricting. First, for the reasons set out earlier, the legislature is not the appropriate agency. Second, there are many pros and cons for either bipartisan or nonpartisan boards or commissions, and the choice may approach a toss-up. Third, in any event, no one need wander around with a lantern looking for perfection in the world of politics.

Organization Procedure

Sec. 9. The sessions of the General Assembly shall commence at twelve o'clock noon, on the Wednesday next after the first Monday in January, in the year next ensuing the election of members thereof, and at no other time, unless as provided by this Constitution.

A majority of the members elected to each house shall constitute a quorum. Each house shall determine the rules of its proceedings,. and be the judge of the election, returns and qualifications of its members; shall choose its own officers; and the Senate shall choose a temporary President to preside when the Lieutenant Governor shall not attend as President or shall act as governor. The Secretary of State shall call the House of Representatives to order at the opening of each new Assembly, and preside over it until a temporary presiding officer thereof shall have been chosen and shall have taken his seat. No member shall be expelled by either house, except by a vote of two-thirds of all the members elected to that house, and no member shall be twice expelled for the same offense. Each house may punish by imprisonment any person, not a member, who shall be guilty of disrespect to the house by disorderly or contemptuous behavior in its presence. But no such imprisonment shall extend beyond twenty-four hours at one time, unless the person shall persist in such disorderly or contemptuous behavior.

History

Sessions: The 1818 Constitution provided for biennial sessions in much the same language as in the first paragraph of Section 9. The only difference was the beginning date of the first Monday in December. (The election for senators and representatives was on the first Monday in August.) The 1848 Constitution changed the meeting date to the first Monday in January. (Election Day became the first Tuesday after the first Monday in November under the 1848 Constitution.)

The first paragraph of Section 9, offered to the 1870 Convention as a separate section, made the change to Wednesday after the first Monday and specified noon as the magic hour. A proposal was offered to strike the words following "thereof" and substitute the words "unless otherwise provided by law or by this Constitution." This was actually an amendment to a proposal to specify annual sessions which the proponent of annual sessions accepted at the end of the debate on the subject. The debate was spirited, but the final vote was only 16 for the amendment with 33 against. (Debates 511-22.) The proposed 1922 Constitution made no change of substance.

In 1963, by joint resolution, the General Assembly proposed an amendment to Section 9, providing for annual sessions, one of which was to be limited to budget matters. The first paragraph of the proposed amendment read:

"The regular sessions of the General Assembly shall commence at 12 o'clock noon, on the Wednesday next after the first Monday in January, in each odd-numbered year; and on the first Monday in May of each even-numbered year.

At its regular session in each even-numbered year, the General Assembly shall consider only appropriation bills for existing functions of the State for the succeeding fiscal year, revenue bills directly pertaining and restricted thereto, and bills, motions and resolutions pertaining to the functions of the General Assembly during such session; and shall consider no other matter."

The balance of the proposed amendment was unchanged from the balance of Section 9 except for a technical adjustment to make it clear that the Secretary of State's duty to call the House of Representatives to order was limited to the sessions in odd-numbered years. The amendment was defeated at the general election in 1964. The amendment was favored by 63.1 per cent of those voting on the amendment, but the vote was a little over 108,000 short of a majority of those voting in the election.

The provision for the Secretary of State to call the House of Representatives to order was added by the Committee on the Legislative Department. The debate on a motion to strike the provision reveals that the committee had two precedents in mind: One was the confusion that attended the organization of the 1870 Convention itself; the other was an occurrence in 1857 when, according to one delegate, "there was actually a fight between the officers of the late house of representatives and the new members." (Debates 525-27.) The proposed 1922 Constitution made one change in the organizational rubric. It was spelled out that the temporary presiding officer was to preside until a speaker was chosen.

Quorum, Rules and Officers: The 1818 and 1848 Constitutions set a quorum at two-thirds of the members of each house, but provided that a smaller number could adjourn from day to day and could compel the attendance of absent members. In the 1870 Convention, the Committee on the Legislative Department proposed to set the quorum at a specific number of senators and a specific number of representatives, the number in each house being approximately one-half of the membership. In the course of debate, it became clear that the proposed change was in part designed to avoid a situation that had arisen the year before in Indiana. There, to avoid ratification of the Fifteenth Amendment, all of the Democratic members of the legislature resigned and the remaining Republican members construed the quorum requirement to be two-thirds of the remaining members. It was argued in the Convention that the words "a majority of the members elected" would avoid the Indiana example and the proposal was so amended. The change from two-thirds to a majority was based on previous experience in Illinois when members absented themselves to defeat a quorum. There was apparently no sentiment for retaining the higher requirement. No question was raised about the omission of the words authorizing a smaller number to adjourn and to compel attendance. The proposed 1922 Constitution made no substantive change in the quorum requirement.

All three Constitutions and the proposed 1922 Constitution provided that each house should determine the rules of its own proceedings and all provided that each house should judge the qualifications and elections of its members. The 1870 Committee on the Legislative Department added "returns" to "qualifications and elections" and in the 1920-22 Convention, the Committee on Phraseology and Style took out "returns." In neither case was there an explanation for the change.

All four documents provided that each house should choose its own officers, excepting, of course, the presiding officer of the Senate. The 1870 Convention neglected to state that the presiding officer of the House of Representatives is called the "Speaker," an omission noted in 1921 by the Committee on Phraseology and Style which put the Speaker back into the proposed 1922 Constitution. (There are, of course, references to the Speaker in the 1870 Constitution. See Sec. 13 of this Art. and Sec. 19 of Art. V, *infra,* p. 160 and p. 310.)

Sanctions: The 1818 Constitution provided that either house could "punish its members for disorderly behavior," including expulsion by a two-thirds' vote, but only once for the same offense. The 1848 Constitution contained the foregoing and added "the reason for such expulsion shall be entered upon the journal, with the names of the members voting on the question." The provision as proposed to the 1870 Convention omitted both the reference to disorderly behavior and to a journal entry and changed the required vote from two-thirds to a "majority of all the members elected to that house." (In neither the 1818 nor the 1848 Constitution was it clear what the two-thirds' vote was measured by, though the 1848 journal entry language quoted above would imply that the measure was of those present and voting.) A delegate pointed out that the deletion of the journal entry requirement removed one of the two previous safeguards against abuse and moved that the required vote be made two-thirds. The amendment was accepted without debate. The proposed 1922 Constitution made no substantive change.

Both the 1818 and 1848 Constitutions provided for sanctions against nonmembers, but limited their punishment to 24 hours. The proposed change now in Section 9 was objected to in the 1870 Convention. In reply, two delegates pointed out that without the change any uncooperative witness could spend his 24 hours in jail and avoid ever having to testify. The proposed 1922 Constitution made no substantive change.

Explanation

Few questions have arisen in connection with this section. In 1935, the legislature appropriated an amount equal to a biennial salary to the widow of a veteran legislator who had died after the election but before the legislature met. The Supreme Court stated that the act of appropriating money was by implication a determination that the deceased had been duly elected. (People *ex rel.* Douglas v. Barrett, 370 Ill. 464 (1939).)

In *Reif v. Barrett* (355 Ill. 104 (1933)), the Supreme Court upheld the finality of legislative determination of the "election, returns and qualifications of its members." It was alleged that a man in default to the state had run for the House of Representatives, had been elected, had taken his seat, and had voted for the bill under attack in the litigation, and that the bill passed by precisely the minimum majority required. It was further alleged that the person in question was ineligible to serve by virtue of Section 4 (*supra,* p. 127), that his vote for the bill should not be counted, and that the bill did not pass since without his vote there was no constitutional majority. This case was a traditional test case — in this instance, to determine the constitutionality of the "sales tax" — and as is customary, all alleged facts were admitted. Notwithstanding all these admissions, the Court refused to invalidate the vote by which the bill passed. The representative in question "regularly received his certificate of election and qualified as a member of the house, and the House of Representatives seated him as a member of that body. We are constrained to hold that at the time he voted he was a member of the General Assembly." (*Id.* at 129.) "No court has the right to review the decision of the house . . . . When the house once acts upon the qualifications of its membership the matter is beyond further controversy." (*Id.* at 127.)

The United States Supreme Court has ended any such blanket judicial refusal to review legislative decisions on seating members. In *Bond v. Floyd* (385 U.S. 116 (1966)), the Court overturned the refusal of the Georgia House of Representatives to seat Julian Bond. The Court held that it had jurisdiction to review the state legislative determination that Bond was not qualified, and further held that such determination in the circumstances actually represented a denial of Bond's right of free speech. (*See also* Powell v. McCormack, 395 U.S. 486 (1969), where the Court held that the United States House of Representatives could not refuse to seat Adam Clayton Powell, Jr., in view of the fact that he was not ineligible under any provision of the United States Constitution.)

On several occasions the Attorney General has issued rulings concerning this section. He has stated that the decision by either house on seating or not seating a member may be made by a majority of those present and voting, provided, of course, that a quorum is present. (1915 Ill. Att'y Gen. Rep. 455.) He has also stated that only a member of the House of Representatives is eligible to election as Speaker. (1915 Ill. Att's Gen. Rep. 144.)

Section 9 provides for biennial sessions, but does not literally prohibit more frequent sessions by the parliamentary device of not adjourning *sine die.* The first two legislatures to meet after adoption of the 1870 Constitution each met twice, as did the 45th General Assembly in 1907 and 1908. The device was not utilized again until 1967, when the General Assembly adjourned to a day certain on several occasions through 1967 and 1968, adjourning *sine die* in January, 1969, just before the 76th General Assembly convened. In 1966, the Attorney General had rendered an opinion to the effect that the procedure subsequently followed would be constitutional. (*See* I.S.L. 133-38, app. D.) He also ruled that the state could switch from a biennial to an annual budget. (*Id.* See *Explanation* of Sec. 18, *infra,* p. 185.)

Comparative Analysis

Sessions: As a result of amendments adopted in 1968, a majority of the states for the first time in this century have constitutional provisions for annual sessions. There are now 27 states with such a provision. Three states, Ohio, Tennessee and Vermont, joined Illinois in using the adjournment device to stay active during the 1967-68 biennium. Of the 27 states with annual sessions, ten have general sessions with no limitation on length, eleven have limitations, and six alternate general sessions with sessions limited to adoption of a budget, but in all six the lengths of both the general and the budget sessions are limited. A majority of the states with biennial sessions also have limitations on their length. In Illinois, June 30th is, of course, a traditional "required" adjournment date. (See Sec. 13, *infra,* p. 160.) It is worth noting that in the many states with limitations on session length, only one has a required adjournment date later than June 30th. Both the Model State Constitution and the United States Constitution call for annual sessions and permit them to be unlimited in length.

Approximately three-fourths of the states specify in their constitutions the date of convening of the session, usually a day early in January. Only about a dozen include a specific hour, usually noon, but in a couple of states 10 A.M. is the magic hour. Another half dozen states or so set the time of convening but permit the time to be changed by law. Three states appear to leave the whole business up to the legislature. The Model State Constitution does the same. The United States Constitution calls for Congress to convene at noon on the third day of January, "unless they shall by law appoint a different day."

Quorum: Forty-four states set the quorum at a majority of all the members and four states set it at two-thirds. Vermont requires a majority except on bills raising taxes, in which case two-thirds of the members of the lower house must be present. New Hampshire requires a majority for a quorum, but if fewer than two-thirds of the members are present, then a measure must receive a two-thirds vote to pass. A majority is the quorum in Congress and under the Model State Constitution.

Forty-three states provide that a smaller number of members than a quorum may adjourn from day to day and may compel attendance of absent members. Illinois is, of course, one of the seven states without such a provision. Both the United States Constitution and the Model State Constitution contain the provision.

Rules: Strangely enough, two states, Georgia and North Carolina, do not have a provision stating that each house shall determine its own rules. The United States Constitution and Model State Constitution contain the customary provision.

Qualification and Election of Members: Again, strangely, there are two states, Connecticut and Missouri, that do not empower each house to determine the qualifications of its members. Likewise, there are two states, Missouri and Wyoming, that do not empower each house to determine the election of its members. As noted in the *History* above, the word "returns" was added in 1870 and proposed to be dropped in 1922. Among the 48 states having a provision on determination of elections, there are several variations. Thirty-two states join Illinois in giving each house the power to judge the elections and returns of its members. (In Arkansas it is "sole judge" and in Connecticut, "final judge.") Twelve states speak only to elections, and three states refer to "election returns." (See the *Comment* below concerning these variations in wording.) The United States Constitution uses the traditional language while the Model State Constitution drops the word "returns."

Officers: Most state constitutions provide, as in Illinois, that each house shall choose its own officers. In two states, the provision is drafted with precision by stating that such officers shall be so chosen except as otherwise provided in the constitution. This takes care of the fact that normally a senate does not choose its presiding officer. Some states specify what officers shall be chosen. In one state, Minnesota, it is provided that each house shall choose its own officers as prescribed by law, a formulation that theoretically permits the governor to participate in the process of determining what offices shall exist. The United States Constitution states that the House of Representatives shall choose "their Speaker and other officers"; and that the Senate shall choose "their other officers, and also a President pro tempore." The Model State Constitution states that the unicameral legislature shall choose "its presiding officers from among its members and it shall employ a secretary to serve for an indefinite term. . . . The secretary of the legislature shall be its chief fiscal, administrative and personnel officer and shall perform such duties as the legislature may prescribe." The Commentary on the foregoing states:

"The only novel feature of section 4.09 is the reference to a 'secretary of the legislature' who is to be employed for an indefinite term to manage fiscal and personnel matters. The purpose is to fill the need for better housekeeping in the legislative branch with its increased career staffs in legislative reference, bill-drafting and other services. The need for improved personnel and fiscal administration has become evident. It might be added that reference to the secretary of the legislature is not a constitutional necessity, for such an office could be established by a legislature entirely without such express authorization. Its inclusion, however, may prove useful." (Model State Constitution 53.)

Comment

Sessions: From the recent practice in Illinois and the close vote on the 1964 proposed amendment, it would appear that a proposal to switch to annual sessions will be high on the agenda in the Convention. Of all the proposals for modernizing, streamlining, if you will, the legislative process, the annual session proposal has had the most dramatic acceptance in the last three decades. The change is shown by the following table:

Annual Sessions

Year	Number of States
1941	4
1950	10
1960	18
1969	31*

* Including the four biennial session states which used the adjournment device.

If the decision is made to go to annual sessions, consideration should be given to the addition of words to make it clear that unfinished business carries over from the first to the second session of a single two-year legislature. Such a provision is not essential, of course, for Congress operates by such a rule, but since the tradition in state legislatures has been otherwise, specific coverage might be appropriate. Michigan adopted the following in its new Constitution:

"Any business, bill or joint resolution pending at the final adjournment of a regular session held in an odd numbered year shall carry over with the same status to the next regular session." (art. IV, § 13.)

It should be noted, however, that the previous Michigan provision stated explicitly that bills were not to be carried over from one session to another.

The Model State Constitution provides that the legislature "shall be a continuous body during the term for which its members are elected." But as the Commentary to the Model makes clear, the purpose of this provision is to permit the utmost flexibility. An accompanying provision permits the legislature to meet in "regular sessions annually as provided by law." The commentary states:

"Under these provisions it is not at all necessary that every session be a miniature of the prevalent annual or biennial session. Priority could be given to those measures requiring consideration during the period the legislature happens to be convened. Action on local matters could be timed in accordance with the fiscal year, tax-levying, budget-making or bond-issuing requirements of localities. The state budget could receive ample consideration at one session without crowding other measures on the calendar which could be taken up subsequently. Committees could plan their work with preliminary hearings and specific arrangements for further hearings at the next session or between sessions. An orderly process of distributing the work over the 24-month term would provide greater opportunity for adequate consideration and would quiet the public's fear of hasty or ill-considered action." (Model State Constitution 51.)

Quorum: Presumably, no problem has arisen because of the absence of the traditional authorization for a smaller number than a quorum to adjourn and to compel attendance, but it would be worth considering whether it ought to be put back in.

Officers: In connection with the Model State Constitution's recommendation for a career secretary of each house of the legislature, it is to be noted that the drafters concede that the position could be established by legislation. Immediately following this concession, the Commentary notes that the Model used to contain a constitutional requirement for a legislative council. The Commentary then observes:

"Omission of the legislative council from the *Model* merely marks recognition of the fact that the battle for legislative councils has largely been won, that legislative councils may — and do — function well under authority of legislation or legislative rules and may function even better given the flexibility of legislative rather than constitutional authorization. Finally, the omission signifies recognition that the creation and operation of legislative councils is essentially a matter of legislative procedure which, particularly in the case of a continuous legislature, ought to be left to the legislature itself." (*Id.* at 54.)

Returns, Elections and Qualifications: Notwithstanding the fact that there are variations among the states in the use of "returns and elections," "elections," and "election returns," the variations are probably of no great significance. But it would probably be a mistake to drop "returns" as was proposed in the 1922 Constitution. Presumably, the drafters considered "returns" to be unnecessary because they are included in "elections." This seems a fair conclusion, but there is the usual difficulty that a change in wording always opens the door to the argument that the drafters of the change meant something thereby. It should also be noted that the *Bond* case, discussed earlier, in no way justifies dropping, or qualifying, the traditional statement of legislative control over seating members.

Open Sessions — Adjournments — Journals

Sec. 10. The doors of each house and of committees of the whole shall be kept open, except in such cases as, in the opinion of the house, require secrecy. Neither house shall, without consent of the other, adjourn for more than two days, or to any other place than that in which the two houses shall be sitting. Each house shall keep a journal of its proceedings, which shall be published. In the Senate at the request of two members, and in the House at the request of five members, the yeas and nays shall be taken on any question, and entered upon the journal. Any two members of either house shall have liberty to dissent from and protest, in respectful language, against any act or resolution which they think injurious to the public or to any individual, and have the reasons of their dissent entered upon the journals.

History

The provision for open meetings, but with secrecy permitted, first appeared in 1818, was continued in 1848, and was not changed in substance in the proposed 1922 Constitution. The limitation on adjournment appears in all Constitutions, but the proposed 1922 Constitution increased the period of non-agreed-upon adjournment from two days to three. Likewise, the requirement for publication of the journal appears in all four Constitutions. In the 1818 and 1848 Constitutions, any two members in either house could call for the yeas and nays. The requirement for five in the House of Representatives was added in 1870 and continued in the proposed 1922 Constitution. Permission for any two members to have their dissenting views entered upon the journal was given in 1818 and continued in 1848, but in 1870 the requirement to use respectful language was added. The proposed 1922 Constitution continued the permission and the respectful language requirements.

Explanation

In connection with serious problems that arise under Sections 12 and 13 (*infra*, pp. 156 and 160), the journal is an important document. So far as Section 10 itself is concerned, not many problems of interpretation have arisen. The Supreme Court long ago announced that the officers of the legislature did not have to sign the journal and that there was no requirement that the journal clerk certify as to the accuracy of the journal. (Miller v. Goodwin, 70 Ill. 659 (1873).) Indeed, even though Illinois is a "journal entry rule" state (*see* Neiberger v. McCullough, 253 Ill. 312 (1912)), that is, a state that permits the use of the journal to show that the constitutional requirements for passage of a bill were not met, as opposed to an "enrolled bill rule" state, which does not permit such evidence, there is no way to impeach the accuracy of the journal. In *Sangamon County Fair & Agricultural Association v. Stanard* (9 Ill. 2d 267 (1956)), the House Journal stated that the bill in litigation had been read at large, but two members exercised their privilege to dissent to the effect that the journal was in error, that in fact the bill had been read by title only. Thus, there were contradictory statements in the journal. The Court refused to accept the dissent as proof that the formal journal entry was in error. Presumably, the Court was aware that "[b]y common acquiescence and by fraud upon the journals of both houses this constitutional requirement is avoided. Bills are read by title only but the journal shows the bills are read at large." (Elson, "Constitutional Revision and Reorganization of the General Assembly," 33 Ill. L. Rev. 15, 26 (1938).)

Although the Court will accept journal entries as written, it will also draw inferences from the absence of entries. In a famous case arising under the 1848 Constitution concerning the Governor's power to adjourn the legislature (see *History* of Sec. 9, Art. V, *infra*, p. 278), the Court avoided the political thicket involved by relying on the journal. There were no entries for a ten-day stretch and since the 1848 Constitution also prohibited adjournment of either house for more than two days without the consent of the other, the Court concluded that the legislature had adjourned *sine die*. (People *ex rel.* Harless v. Hatch, 33 Ill. 9 (1863). See also discussions of Secs. 12 and 13, *infra*, pp. 156 and 160. For a comprehensive review of the journal entry problem, see Cohn, "The Process of Legislation," 1963 U. Ill. L.F. 27.)

Comparative Analysis

Public Sessions: Approximately three-fourths of the states call for open sessions of the legislature, but almost all of them also contain an appropriate exception for secrecy. Neither the United States Constitution nor the Model State Constitution specifies public sessions.

Adjournment of One House: Of the 49 states with a bicameral legislature, all except two limit the power of one house to adjourn without the consent of the other. Most of the states limit such power to three days. About 40 states also require consent to adjourn to another place. The United States Constitution has the usual requirement for consent to adjourn for more than three days or to another place. The Model State Constitution has no comparable provision. This is obvious for its recommended unicameral provisions, but not so obvious for its alternative provisions for a bicameral legislature.

Journal: All of the states except Massachusetts appear to require that a journal be kept and almost all require that it be published. A good many states have a secrecy exception. The United States Constitution requires that a journal be kept and that it be published from time to time, except such parts as may require secrecy. The Model State Constitution calls for a journal which shall be published "from day to day."

Yeas and Nays: All except four of the states have a requirement for entering the yeas and nays in the journal upon demand. There is, however, wide variation in the number required to make the demand. In a few states any one member can call for the vote. Louisiana has the highest minimum required, one-fifth of the members elected. In ten states one-fifth of those present is required. The next-largest number of states with identical requirements is eight — at the desire of any two members in either house. The United States Constitution requires one-fifth of those present. The Model State Constitution has the same requirement.

Protest and Dissent: There appear to be some 13 other states which guarantee the privilege of entering a protest or dissent in the journal, but only Minnesota joins Illinois in requiring two members to exercise the privilege. No other state conditions the privilege on the use of respectful language. Neither the United States Constitution nor the Model State Constitution extends the privilege of entering a dissent in the journal. All dissents in Congress are preserved, of course, because the debates are published.

Comment

All of the requirements of this section are normal and could very well be preserved unchanged. What should be guarded against is a proposal to add further requirements because of a past reluctance of the legislature to adopt them in its rules. For example, some people advocate a state equivalent of the Congressional Record, in part so that legislative "intent" can be more easily determined and in part so that the news media can report legislative activities more accurately. In the proposed 1967 New York Constitution, the issue was compromised. Each house was to be required to keep a journal and a transcript of its debates, the former to be published, the latter to be available to the public. It is certainly sound to advocate that verbatim transcripts of debates be made and, at the very least, that they be available to the public, but it should not be necessary to put the requirement into the Constitution.

Enacting Clause

Sec. 11. The style of the laws of this State shall be: *"Be it enacted by the People of the State of Illinois, represented in the General Assembly."*

History

The identical provision appears in both the 1818 and 1848 Constitutions. The proposed 1922 Constitution changed the beginning to read: "The enacting clause of laws shall be:" In another section the proposed Constitution included the statement: "No law shall be passed except by bill." (See *History* of Sec. 12 *infra*, p. 157.)

Explanation

In almost half the states there is a provision that laws may be enacted only by a bill. In 1887 the Supreme Court relied on Section 11 to produce the same effect by holding that a joint resolution cannot have the force of law because it does not have an enacting clause. (Burritt v. Commissioners of State Contracts, 120 Ill. 322 (1887).) Because the section is a simple and explicit statement of form, it is not surprising that the Attorney General made a cautious but hypertechnical ruling that an act was unconstitutional if the enacting clause varied in any respect from the specified form. (1910 Ill. Att'y Gen. Rep. 77.)

Comparative Analysis

An enacting clause section is found in 45 of the state constitutions. Most of the clauses speak only in the name of the legislature, a few include the people as does Illinois, and a few enact in the name of the people only. Three of the five states which have no enacting clause section — California, Pennsylvania, and Virginia — do have a requirement that laws be enacted only by bills. The other two states — Delaware and Georgia — have no such requirement. The United States Constitution has neither an enacting clause section nor a requirement for enacting laws by bill only. The Model State Constitution has no enacting clause section but does have a "law by bill only" provision.

Comment

Notwithstanding the nearly universal practice of setting forth the style of enactment, it is obvious that such a provision is not indispensable. It is important, however, to provide clear rules governing what the legislature can do alone and what requires the participation of the Governor. A "law by bill only" provision nails down the distinction. (In this respect the United States Constitution is not clear. Although it spells out the procedure for "bills," it also states that "[e]very Order, Resolution, or Vote to which the Concurrence of the Senate and the House of Representatives may be necessary . . . shall be presented to the President . . . ." (art. I, § 7.) Since Section 1 vests all legislative powers in Congress, it can be deduced that any exercise of legislative power must include the President.) By virtue of the *Burritt* case discussed above, Section 11 serves as the vehicle for guaranteeing that a law can be enacted only by bill and only by including the Governor in the process. This was reinforced recently when the Supreme Court held that the Governor has the power of veto over a redistricting act enacted pursuant to Section 8. (Williams v. Kerner, 30 Ill. 2d 11 (1963).)

Origin of Bills

Sec. 12. Bills may originate in either house, but may be altered, amended or rejected by the other; and on the final passage of all bills, the vote shall be by yeas and nays, upon each bill separately, and shall be entered upon the journal; and no bill shall become a law without the concurrence of a majority of the members elected to each house.

History

The first clause of this section appeared in the 1818 Constitution, but a separate section required revenue bills to originate in the House of Representatives. The 1848 Constitution omitted the revenue bill section, and except for the words "upon each bill separately," added the second and third clauses as they now appear. These additional words were proposed to the 1870 Convention and accepted by it without explanation or debate. The proposed 1922 Constitution put the substance of the first clause in a separate section and added the sentence "No law shall be passed except by bill." The substance of the balance of the section was combined with elements of Section 13.

Explanation

Since Illinois has adopted the "journal entry rule" (see *Explanation* of Sec. 10, *supra,* p. 153), constitutional procedural provisions such as Section 12 are more than instructions to the legislature about how to enact laws. They are also quasi-substantive provisions which litigants may rely upon in attacking the validity of legislation. (For an extended discussion, see *Comment* below.)

In general, judicial interpretations of a provision like Section 12 fall into one of two categories: one is the nature of the proof required to upset an enactment, the other is a matter of definition of terms used in the provision. Even though Section 12 says that the yeas and nays shall be entered on the journal, a recording of the yeas only will be accepted if the number constitutes a required constitutional majority. (People *ex rel.* Wies v. Bowman, 247 Ill. 276 (1910).) But if the journals indicate that a bill passed one house with an emergency clause, passed the other without the clause, and neither journal exhibits a concurrence in the other version, then the Court will invalidate the statute as not having had the concurrence of a majority of both houses. (People *ex rel.* Oliver v. Knopf, 198 Ill. 340 (1902).) Or, if the journal entries show passage of a bill from the other house but with amendment followed by a recorded yea or nay vote to rescind the amendment, this is adequate evidence of conformance with the constitutional requirements for passage (People *ex rel.* City of Springfield v. Edmands, 252 Ill. 108 (1911); but the rescinding vote would have to be by a constitutional majority (People *ex rel.* Reitz v. DeWolf, 62 Ill. 253 (1871)). In any of these evidentiary journal questions, the burden of proof is upon him who would upset the law. Thus, if the journal is ambiguous in the description of amendments as a bill moved back and forth from one house to the other, the Court will presume that both houses were adopting the same amendments. (People *ex rel.* Badger v. Loewenthal, 93 Ill. 191 (1879).)

On the matter of definition of terms, the principal problem has concerned the requirement of a yea and nay vote "upon each bill separately." Although the purpose of this phrase seems to be to guard against voting on a batch of bills at once, the Court has had to beat down the claim that the phrase requires separate votes on separate parts of a single bill. (*See* Hagler v. Small, 307 Ill. 460 (1923); Mitchell v. Lowden, 288 Ill. 327 (1919).) A more reasonable argument can be made if separate parts of a single bill are amendments of separate laws, but it does not appear that the argument will prevail. (*See* Routt v. Barrett, 396 Ill. 322 (1947).) Of course, such arguments are almost automatically also claims that the act violates the one-subject requirement of Section 13. (*Infra,* p. 160.)

The Court has also determined that the title of an act is not an essential part of the legislation, at least to the extent that infirmities in the voting on the title do not invalidate the act. (Johnson v. People, 83 Ill. 431 (1876) (constitutional majority did not vote on title); Larrison v. Peoria, A & D R.R., 77 Ill. 11 (1875) (two houses did not concur on title); Plummer v. People, 74 Ill. 361 (1874) (same).)

Comparative Analysis

Origination of Bills: All states, except unicameral Nebraska, of course, permit bills to originate in either house and to be amended in either house, but only about half of the states so specify in their constitutions. In 21 states, revenue bills may originate only in the lower house, and in Georgia appropriation bills also must originate in that house. The United States Constitution requires revenue bills to be introduced in the House of Representatives. The Model State Constitution's alternative provisions for a bicameral legislature are silent on origin of bills. Eleven states have some kind of prohibition on the introduction of bills toward the end of the session.

Yeas and Nays: Thirty-one other states require the entry of the yeas and nays upon final passage, and 13 of these specifically require that the name of each member and his vote be entered. It was noted in the *Comparative Analysis* of Section 10 (*supra,* p. 154) that in all except four states, a demand could be made for the yeas and nays on any question. Three of those four exceptions are included in the 31 that require entry upon final passage, so that it either is mandated or is possible, with a demand by the requisite number of members, to obtain entry of a yea and nay vote on final passage in the journal in 49 states. (The exception is, of course, Massachusetts, which has no requirement that a journal be kept.) The United States Constitution provides for entry of any vote upon demand of one-fifth of those present and requires the entry, with the names of those voting, on any vote to override a veto. The Model

State Constitution has no provision for yeas and nays upon final passage, but does provide for a record vote on any question if demanded by one-fifth of the members present.

Required Majority: The vote required for passage of a bill in the several states is summarized in the following table:

Vote Required	*Number of States*
Majority of members elected	26*
Majority of members to which each house is entitled	2
Majority of those present but not less than a stipulated minimum	3
Majority of each house	3
Majority of those present	5
No majority requirement specified	11**

* Includes Illinois. The Model State Constitution requires a majority of "all the members." (See *Comment* below.)

** The United States Constitution is also silent on the vote required to pass a bill.

Comment

Serious consideration should be given to the problems that arise in Illinois because the courts have followed the "journal entry rule." By virtue of this rule, anyone wishing to attack the validity of a statute, in addition to arguing the merits of the constitutionality of the legislation, can search the journals of the two houses to see if there is any procedural error in the legislative process upon which to make a claim that the act was not validly passed. All of this increases both the likelihood and the complexity of litigation. The first question to ask is whether or not the protection afforded by the journal entry rule is worth the cost. It must be noted that the journal entry rule serves a real purpose only in a case of either fraudulent or inadvertent signing of a bill by either the Speaker of the House or the Lieutenant Governor, or other presiding officer. It must be further noted that even a fraudulent or inadvertent signing of a bill will survive if the journal has all the proper entries. As the *Sangamon County Fair* case, discussed under Section 10 (*supra,* p. 153), and other cases discussed above demonstrate, the courts do not question the accuracy of the journal entries. Thus, so long as the journal clerks make all the "correct" entries, a bill is "home safe." It follows that the journal entry rule does not protect people against fraudulent or inadvertent signing by the presiding officer, but against "sloppy" journal-keeping. Assuming that the foregoing is a convincing argument against the journal entry rule, the question becomes one of how to rewrite the section to insulate bill-passing from invalidation for procedural defects; in other words, how to shift Illinois to an "enrolled bill rule" state, under which the signing of a bill by the presiding officers of the two houses would be conclusive proof that constitutional procedures had been properly followed. One possibility would be to use the language proposed in the Model State Constitution as part of its section on confining bills to a single subject. The sentence reads: "Legislative compliance with the requirements of this section is, a constitutional responsibility not subject to judicial review." Another possibility is to make a minor change some place which, while not conclusive on its face, can be explained in Convention debates to be for the purpose of ending the Illinois rule. An example would be the addition of the following words to the requirement, now in Section 13, that bills be signed by the presiding officers: "which signing shall constitute a certificate that all procedural requirements for passage have been complied with."

A word is also in order concerning the constitutional requirement that bills pass by a majority of the members elected to each house. It was noted earlier in connection with filling vacancies (see *Comment* on Sec. 2, *supra,* p. 119) that the Commission on the Organization of the General Assembly recommended a constitutional change to force the calling of special elections. The principal reason for the recommendation was the need for an absolute majority to pass a bill. The commission noted that it had considered but rejected a recommendation to eliminate the absolute majority requirement. (I.S.L. 9.) Notwithstanding the desirability of requiring special elections, the constitutional majority problem could be met by using the wording of the Model State Constitution — "all the members" — instead of "all the members elected." It would, of course, be advisable to explain in the official record of the Convention that the word "elected" was dropped in order to make the constitutional requirement a majority of the sitting members, excluding vacancies, and not a majority of the total number to which each house is entitled.

Passage of Bills

Sec. 13. Every bill shall be read at large on three different days, in each house; and the bill and all amendments thereto shall be printed before the vote is taken on its final passage; and every bill, having passed both houses, shall be signed by the Speakers thereof. No act hereafter passed shall embrace more than one subject, and that shall be expressed in the title. But if any subject shall be embraced in an act which shall not be expressed in the title, such act shall be void only as to so much thereof as shall not be so expressed; and no law shall be revived or amended by reference to its title only, but the law revived, or the section amended, shall be inserted at length in the new act. And no act of the General Assembly shall take effect until the first day of July next after its passage, unless, in case of emergency, (which emergency shall be expressed in the preamble or body of the act), the General Assembly shall, by a vote of two-thirds of all the members elected to each house, otherwise direct.

History

The 1818 Constitution contained only the requirement that every bill be read (but not "at large") on three different days, and the requirement that the speakers sign every bill that passed. Three-fourths of a house could vote to dispense with a reading "in case of urgency."

The 1848 Constitution preserved the foregoing and made two additions: a requirement that a private or local law embrace only one subject, to be expressed in the title; and a requirement that no public act take effect until 60 days after adjournment, "unless in case of emergency the General Assembly shall otherwise direct."

Perhaps the most interesting thing about this section in the 1870 Constitution is that it was accepted by the Convention as proposed. There was an effort to strike out the printing requirement on the ground that it was an unnecessary, mandatory expense and there were several efforts to amend the "one subject only" requirement. The debate on these efforts was fairly confused and it is difficult to say whether the efforts to amend were designed to strengthen or weaken the provision. In the end, all efforts at amendment were beaten down. The Committee on Revision and Adjustment made several stylistic changes and one substantive change that is rather interesting. The section as presented to the Convention — or at least as printed in the debates — read in part "and no law shall be revised or amended . . . , but the act revised or the section amended . . . ." It appears thus at least five times in the Debates. (Debates 291, 393, 533, 916, 952.) When Article IV came back from the Committee on Revision and Adjustment, the word "revised" had become "revived" and remained so.

The proposed 1922 Constitution split Section 13 into several sections and made several changes. The bill-reading requirement was changed to provide for reading by title on three different days but with a proviso that the rules of either house could require reading "at greater length on second and third reading." The printing requirement was retained, but with a proviso that an amendment striking out an emergency clause need not be printed. The requirement that after passage a bill be signed by the presiding officers was retained and the following was tacked on: "and the facts of printing, placing on the desks of members, signing and presentation to the governor and the date of such presentation shall be entered upon the journals." (art. III, § 41.) The single-subject requirement was retained unchanged. The amendment-by-reference requirement was modified to "overrule" the line of cases, discussed below, that held that a completely independent act could fall afoul of the prohibition. The wording was:

"No act shall be revived by reference to its title only. An act *expressly* amending an act shall set forth at length the section or sections as amended." (art. III, § 36. Emphasis added.)

The provision concerning the effective date of legislation was changed to provide that appropriation acts were to take effect on July 1 but all other acts were to take effect 60 days after adjournment. The emergency exception was retained unchanged in substance.

Explanation

Bill Reading: The requirement that every bill be read at large three times is as simple and clear a rule as could be drafted. It is hopelessly unrealistic and, as noted earlier (*supra,* p. 154), such reading does not take place, but the journals say it does and this satisfies the courts. The only additional point that has arisen is whether or not amendments have to be read at large on three different days. The answer is that they do not. (People v. Lewis, 5 Ill. 2d 117 (1955).) Such unread amendments must, however, be germane to the subject matter of the original bill. (Giebelhausen v. Daley, 407 Ill. 25 (1950) (appropriation act invalidated where unread amendment struck out everything after the enacting clause and substituted appropriation for wholly different purpose).)

Bill Printing: Again, this is a requirement that is clear and specific. Moreover, the requirement includes "all amendments thereto." It was this requirement that was the cause of the most extreme Supreme Court ruling under the journal entry rule. In *Neiberger v. McCullough* (253 Ill. 312 (1912)), the question was raised whether journal entries of yea and nay votes in both houses to adopt a conference committee report that included amendments was adequate evidence that the amendments had been printed. The Court held that unless the journal affirmatively stated that the amendments had been printed, it would be presumed that they had not been and that the statute was invalid for not having been passed in accordance with the constitutional requirement. Three years later the Court retreated from the *Neiberger* ruling and held that if there was something in the journal that would permit an inference of printing, such as an entry after second reading that the amendments "were ordered printed and engrossed," printing would be presumed. (Dragovich v. Iroquois Iron Co., 269 Ill. 478 (1915).)

In the relatively recent case of *Peoples Gas Light & Coke Company v. City of Chicago* (9 Ill. 2d 348 (1956)), the Supreme Court found another means of mitigating the harshness of the *Neiberger* rule. In *Peoples,* there was nothing in the journal of one house from which to draw an inference of the printing of amendments adopted by a conference committee. Instead of invalidating the statute as in *Neiberger,* the Court examined the amendments and concluded that it could not conclude that the legislature would not have passed the act without the amendments. By means of this "double negative" inference, the Court upheld the act and invalidated only the amendments. This, in a way, is a rewriting of the section, for it calls for the printing of the bill *and* amendments. Moreover, there is conceptual confusion confounded, for Section 16 of Article V *(infra,* p. 293) requires a bill to be presented to the Governor. What was presented to him in the *Peoples* case was not the act which the Court declared to be valid. The Court must have concluded, if it thought about the Governor at all, that he would have signed the bill if presented to him without the amendments. (*Cf.* People *ex rel.* Dezettel v. Lueders, 283 Ill. 287 (1918), where an act was invalidated because, through an engrossing error, the bill presented to the Governor omitted amendments that had been adopted. *See generally* Cohn, "The Process of Legislation," 1963 U. Ill. L.F. 27, 44-46.)

Bill Signing: Aside from noting that the drafters of the 1870 Constitution were in error in using the word "Speakers," there is little to explain about the requirement. It can be suggested, however, that once the courts decide to follow the journal entry rule, the principal reason for having the bills signed has vanished. In a state following the enrolled bill rule, the signature of the presiding officers is accepted as conclusive certification that constitutional requirements have been met.

Title and Subject: Two flat assertions may be made about this requirement. One is that it is clear, simple, and unambiguous. The other is that it has been involved in a bewildering and enormous amount of litigation which cannot be intelligently analyzed. The long and short of it is that almost any act can be demonstrated either to consist of only one subject or to consist of two or more subjects. One could, for example, argue with a straight face that some outlandish combination of regulations dealt with one subject: relationships among people. Likewise, one could argue that an act prohibiting gambling and making it a crime to gamble embraced two subjects: gambling and criminal behavior. The foregoing may be sophistical, but the fact is that most of the litigation involving multiple-subject legislation consists of each side making whatever argument it can. The case of multiple subjects which no one would disagree with — *e.g.,* an act to regulate roller coasters and to establish a state-wide system of junior colleges — just does not arise.

Lest it appear that the foregoing is far-fetched, the following two cases may be noted. In *Sutter v. People's Gas Light & Coke Company* (284 Ill. 634 (1918)), a statute which gave the City of Chicago the power to sell surplus electricity and to regulate private utility gas and electric rates was held to embrace two subjects. In *People v. Sargent* (254 Ill. 514 (1912)), "An act defining motor vehicles and providing for the registration of the same and of motor bicycles, and uniform rules regulating the use and speed thereof; prohibiting the use of motor vehicles without the consent of the owner and the offer or acceptance of any bonus or discount or other consideration for the purchase of supplies or parts for any such motor vehicle or for work or repairs done thereon by others, and defining chauffeurs and providing for the examination and licensing thereof, and to repeal certain acts therein named" was held to embrace only one subject.

The problem of expressing the one permitted subject in the title embraces all of the foregoing confusion and a bit more. Obviously, there are two extremes in title-drafting. At one end, the title could simply repeat everything contained in the statute. At the other end, some totally general expression could be used, as for example, "An Act concerning motor vehicles." The first extreme is far-fetched, to be sure, but for the other extreme, consider *Larned v. Tiernan* (110 Ill. 173 (1884)). The statute in question permitted a person who lost money by gambling to sue for recovery of his money. This was held to be embraced in the title "An Act to revise the law in relation to criminal jurisprudence." The additional wrinkle comes if the title-drafters slip up and make the title a bit too narrow. In *Rouse v. Thompson* (228 Ill. 522 (1907)), the Court held that the title, "An act to provide for the holding and the regulation of primary elections of delegates to nominating conventions, for the holding of such conventions, filling vacancies and fixing penalties for the violation of the provisions thereof," was not broad enough because the act also covered nomination of candidates directly. The Court gave a little lecture on the subject, noting that an "Act to define larceny" could not include burglary, but that an "Act to revise the law in relation to criminal jurisprudence" could cover both. (And a civil remedy for gambling losses, too, for that matter.)

Section 13 includes the instruction to the courts to invalidate only the part of an act not included in the title. This is a sensible instruction, but its usefulness is limited. One of the purposes of a single-subject requirement is to prevent the tacking on of a rider not germane to the principal legislation. The rule of limited invalidation would protect the principal legislation in such a case. But, as noted earlier, this is not the type of legislation that shows up in courts because it does not get passed in the first place. What gets passed is legislation that the legislature thinks, and hopes the courts will think, is embraced in one subject. When the courts decide otherwise, they are likely to conclude either that they do not know which of the two subjects that the legislature thought was one subject is embraced in the title, or that both subjects are embraced in the title. The statute is, accordingly, invalidated in toto. (*See* Sutter v. People's Gas Light & Coke Co., 284 Ill. 634 (1918).)

On one point, at least, it is possible to be specific about the judicial interpretation of the one title and subject requirement. It applies only to acts of the General Assembly and not to municipal ordinances. (Chicago Cosmetic Co. v. City of Chicago, 374 Ill. 384 (1940).) Indeed, an ordinance need not even have a title. (City of Metropolis v. Gibbons, 334 Ill. 431 (1929).)

Revival and Amendment: The problem of *revival* can be disposed of rather quickly. There is no problem because the legislature does not revive a law by the simple device of reference to it. (Compare the historical note, *supra,* p. 161, concerning "revised" and "revived.") This is the case, in part, because violation of the constitutional command would be so obvious. It is probably also partly because the legislature would be unlikely to revive an old law without change. It should be noted, however, that if Statute B repeals Statute A and Statute B is subsequently declared unconstitutional, Statute A is "revived," but this is a matter of traditional constitutional theory and not related to the presence or absence of a revival provision. (*See* People v. Fox, 294 Ill. 263 (1920).) It can also be noted that the policy expressed in this section is carried over as a public policy to municipal ordinances, and an ordinance that attempted to revive a repealed ordinance by reference to section numbers only was declared void. (City of Chicago v. Degitis, 383 Ill. 171 (1943). But, as noted above, the policy does not carry over so far as title and subject are concerned.)

There really was no serious problem about *amendment* by reference until after 1900. The prohibition against amendment by reference was designed to prevent the enactment of a statute that might read somewhat as follows: "Section 11 of 'An Act to do thus and so' is amended by inserting the word 'not' before the word 'prescribe" and Section 12 thereof is amended by deleting the word 'not' from the second sentence." Whatever the merits of a constitutional provision to prevent this sort of nonsense, amendatory legislation can easily be drafted so that he who reads knows what is being undertaken. But in 1900, the Supreme Court threw a monkey wrench into the legislative process by stating that if the purpose of an independent bill is in fact to amend an existing law or to add to it, then insertion at length of the amended act is required. (People *ex rel.* Stuckart v. Knopf, 183 Ill. 410 (1900).) This, naturally, produces a guessing contest between the legislature and the courts, and the courts always have the last guess.

In 1913, the Supreme Court attempted to set forth the guiding principles:

"(1)   An act which is complete within itself and does not purport, either in
its title or in the body thereof, to amend or revive any other act, is valid even
though it may by implication modify or repeal prior existing statutes....

"(2)   An act, though otherwise complete within itself, which purports to
amend or revive a prior statute by reference to its title only, and does not
set out at length the statute amended or revived, is invalid, regardless of all
other questions....

"(3)   An act which is incomplete in itself and in which new provisions are
commingled with old ones, so that it is necessary to read the two acts together
in order to determine what the law is, is an amendatory act and invalid under
the constitution, and it is unimportant, in such case, that the act does not
purport to amend or revive any other statute." (People *ex rel.* Cant v. Crossly,
261 Ill. 78, 98.)

One commentator recently quoted the foregoing and then observed:

"These principles are so difficult of application that it is often impossible to
predict with any degree of certainty whether or not an act will be held to offend
in this manner." (Nichols, "Legislative Bill-Drafting in Illinois," 41 Ill. B. J.
136, 138 (1952).)

There are a great many cases involving the amendment by reference
rules, but it seems useless to review them. As long ago as 1919, it was
noted that with the "large mass of statutes in force at any given time, it
is possible to hold that practically any new piece of legislation is amendatory of earlier legislation . . . ." (Legislative Reference Bureau, Constitutional Convention Bulletins 558 (1920) [hereinafter cited as Bulle-
tins].) That observation is much more apt 50 years later. Suffice it to say
that sometimes the courts find a statute void, sometimes not, and that
no amount of analysis of the cases advances one beyond the observation
of Mr. Nichols quoted above.

There is one minor aspect of amendment by reference that should be
mentioned. It has been pointed out that the prohibition "means that it
is frequently necessary to have several 'companion' bills to accomplish a
single purpose. For example, it took 70 separate bills at the 1961 session
to try to make 55 percent of full, fair cash value of property the assessed
valuation for property tax purposes." (Gove, "The Business of the Legislature," 1963 U. Ill. L.F. 52, 68.)

Into this lugubrious tale of the difficulties with amendment by reference, there are a couple of cheerful observations that can be inserted.
This prohibition does not extend either to explicit repeal of an existing
law, or to repeal by implication. (*See* People v. Borgeson, 335 Ill. 136
(1929).) Nor is Illinois saddled with a prohibition against incorporating
parts of other laws by reference. (New York has such a prohibition. In
order to allow New York taxpayers to use their federal income tax com-

putations for purposes of computing their state income tax, it was necessary to amend the Constitution. Otherwise, large chunks of the Internal Revenue Code would have had to be inserted at length in the New York income tax laws. Indeed, when the legislature subsequently adopted an act enabling the City of New York to levy an income tax, the foregoing amendment was found not to be applicable. The enabling act includes an appendix of over 400 pages of provisions from the Internal Revenue Code.)

Effective Date: The most important effect of the provision that, except for emergency legislation, legislation goes into effect on the first day of July following enactment, is that it puts a practical limit on the length of the regular biennial session. This naturally produces a jam of legislative activity towards the end of June. On occasion, the legislature has a "stop-the-clock" session in order to complete action "prior" to July 1, but actually after midnight on June 30. Fortunately, courts will not look beyond the journal and an affidavit by a legislator that the clock was so stopped will be ignored. (Gouker v. Winnebago County Bd. of Supervisors, 37 Ill. 2d 473 (1967).) The requirement is that passage take place before July 1, and this has been construed to refer to the time of legislative action and not to the date when the Governor signs the bill. (People *ex rel.* Kell v. Kramer, 328 Ill. 512 (1928).) In those cases of signature after July 1, the act takes effect immediately. (*Id.*) The legislature can, however, provide that an act become effective on a date later than July 1. (People *ex rel.* Thomson v. Barnett, 344 Ill. 62 (1931).)

Section 13 allows immediate effectiveness of an act if there is an emergency and if the bill passes both houses by a two-thirds vote. In *Graham v. Dye* (308 Ill. 283 (1923)), the Supreme Court made it clear that a simple statement that there is an emergency is insufficient, that the legislature must include words sufficient to spell out the nature of the emergency. Although the Court implied that the existence of an emergency is an objective fact from which one might infer that the Court could "second guess" the legislature, it seems more likely that the courts will be satisfied with a recital describing the emergency. For example, the Court has held that it was sufficient to state that a substantial amount of money would be saved for the taxpayers if the statute went into effect immediately. (People *ex rel.* Tuohy v. City of Chicago, 394 Ill. 477 (1946); People v. Chicago Transit Authority, 392 Ill. 77 (1945).) In neither case is there any hint that evidence would be received to refute the legislative finding of an emergency. (See *Comment* below for further discussion.)

Comparative Analysis

Bill Reading: Thirty-four states, including Illinois, require three readings before passage, three states require two readings, and 13 states have no requirement. In six states, including Illinois, such reading must be at large on all three occasions. Two states say it must be at large twice. Seven states say once, usually on third reading. A few states call for reading by sections on various numbers of occasions. Of those states (37) requiring readings, 33 require them to be on various days, but eight of these either permit two of the readings on the same day or empower the legislature to waive the different-day requirement by a specified majority vote. A dozen or so states have provisions for totally dispensing with a reading, such as in case of actual insurrection, upon unanimous consent, or upon an extraordinary vote of two-thirds, three-fourths or four-fifths. Neither the United States Constitution nor the Model State Constitution mentions bill reading.

Bill Printing: Approximately a half dozen states specifically cover printing of both bills and amendments before final passage, and another half dozen require printing of a bill before final passage under circumstances that would require printing of amendments. New York requires bills to be printed and on members' desks in final form at least three calendar legislative days prior to passage, but the governor may certify an emergency requiring an immediate vote, and even then the bill in final form must be on every member's desk before the vote is taken. Michigan's new Constitution contains one small change in the bill-printing requirement — the words "or reproduced" have been inserted after the word "printed." The United States Constitution has no printing requirement. The Model State Constitution's provision is substantially the same as New York's, but without the governor's power of waiver.

Bill Signing: Twenty-nine other states specify that the presiding officers of each house shall sign a bill after passage, and in 20 of the states the signing is to take place in the presence of the house. Two states require the additional signatures of the clerks of the houses. Sixteen states require that the fact of signing be entered in the journal. Minnesota even covers the contingency of a refusal by the presiding officer to sign a bill after passage. Neither the United States Constitution nor the Model State Constitution speaks of bill signing.

Subject and Title: Some 40 other states limit a bill to one subject, and almost all of them also specify that that subject be expressed in the title. Fifteen states permit exceptions, generally either for appropriation bills or statutory revisions, or both. Six of the nine states with no "one subject" requirement are the New England states. The United States Constitution has no such requirement. The Model State Constitution has a "one subject" provision with the two exceptions just mentioned, but also the following sentence:

"Legislative compliance with the requirements of this section is a constitutional responsibility not subject to judicial review." (art. IV, § 4.14.)

Revival and Amendment: Some 31 other states prohibit amendment by reference and, in most cases, specify that the section amended be set out in full. Some 15 other states have much the same prohibition on revival of a statute, and some 13 states prohibit revision of a statute by reference. Interestingly, none of the states prohibiting *revision* by reference prohibits *revival* by reference, but all except two of the states prohibiting amendment by reference also prohibit either revival or revision but, of course, not both. (See the history of this word change, *supra,* p. 161.) There appear to be three states prohibiting incorporation of part of another statute by reference. Only one of these states, New York, is not included among the amendment and revival/revision by reference states. Neither the United States Constitution nor the Model State Constitution has any kind of prohibition on legislative action by reference.

Effective Date: Twenty-eight states, including Illinois, specify when a law is to become effective; four specify that a law becomes effective either when published (2), or as provided in the act (1) or both (1); and 18 states have no provision concerning an effective date. The 28 states have specifications as follows:

Effective Date	Number of States
90 days after end of session	13
60 days after end of session	3
20 days after end of session	1
3 months after end of session	1
90 days after passage	4
60 days after passage	1
40 days after passage	1
July 1 after passage	2
July 1 after end of session	1
June 1 after end of session	1

All of the 28 states have a provision for an exception to the specified date of effectiveness. (The other 22 states have no need for an exception.)

Exception for Emergency	Number of States
Four-fifths of members voting	1
Two-thirds of members elected	16*
Two-thirds of members voting	1
Three-fifths of members elected	1
Majority of members elected	1
By declaration in statute	7
By governor's certification to the legislature	1
Not applicable to appropriation and/or money bills	12**

* In one of these states the governor may declare an act an emergency measure.
** These are included in the 28.

The United States Constitution has no provision concerning an effective date. The Model State Constitution provides that "no act shall become effective until published as provided by law."

Comment

Bill Reading: Since the original reasons for this requirement — the absence of printing and, on occasion, legislators who could not read — are gone, the provision could easily be dispensed with. If this seems too great a break with tradition, or if there is a wish to insure that the legislature acts with all *deliberate* speed, then it would suffice to delete the words "at large" and substitute "by title." This, at least, would make the Constitution conform to reality. (This is the recommendation of the Commission on the Organization of the General Assembly. I.S.L., p. 13.)

Bill Printing: In any well-run legislature, bills will be printed — or "reproduced" as Michigan now also permits — and it is highly unlikely that removal of a requirement for printing would have any effect on the practice of printing. By the same token, there is no reason for removing a requirement that will in practice be followed — except, unfortunately, for the journal entry rule and the consequence that a statute may be invalidated through the inadvertence of not reprinting after a minor final change or the even less crucial inadvertence of failing to make the appropriate entry in the journal. Unless some such solution for ending the journal entry rule as suggested in the *Comment* on Section 12 (*supra,* p. 159) is adopted, it would be advisable to consider dropping the printing requirement as a means of eliminating the possibility of a technical journal entry error that can invalidate a statute.

Bill Signing: It would appear that this requirement either ought to be rewritten in a manner that would serve to end the journal entry rule as suggested in the *Comment* on Section 12 (*supra,* p. 159) or it ought to be dropped, for unless the signatures of the presiding officers serve the purpose of certification of procedural conformance, they are an empty ritual.

Title and Subject: There is certainly nothing objectionable about the principle of one bill-one subject-one title. (Even so, life goes on where the principle is not followed, as in the United States Congress. Students of federal jurisdiction know that the Urgent Deficiencies Act of 1913 provided for certain types of three-judge court litigation, notwithstanding the fact that the title describes an appropriation act.) What is objectionable is the mischief wrought by litigants. There are two groups of people for whom the rule is written. One is the legislators themselves; the other is the general public or, to be more realistic, the legal profession. The litigants who seek to invalidate legislation on the basis of violation of the one subject-one title rule are surely not legislators. They are, obviously, members of the general public. But there probably has never been a case where the litigation arose because the plaintiff or defendant, as a member of the public, or, realistically, his lawyer, behaved as he did because he was misled by the title of the act or because he missed a statutory requirement that was in an act principally dealing with another subject. Without exhausive research, it is safe to assert that almost every case involving the one subject-one title rule has been either a case to test the constitutionality of a new law or a case in which the litigant was really interested only in the substance of the legislation. In both instances, one subject-one rule was thrown in for good measure.

There is, of course, the argument that the rule is designed to protect the general public vicariously. This is the argument that the legislature would never have passed the act in the first place if they had not been misled by the title. Or it is argued that the general public must be protected from the log-rolling and other devices by which "bad" legislation can be pushed through if there is no enforceable one subject-one title rule. This is not unlike the United States Supreme Court's efforts through exclusion of evidence to get police to change their methods. In many instances, the police quickly find ways to get around the Court decisions. Similarly, legislators can find ways of engaging in log-rolling and achieving other questionable results even if the multiple-subject-bill road is forbidden to them.

The Model State Constitution has solved the problem of preserving the principle of one-subject bills without the accompanying misuse of the principle by litigants. As noted above in the *Comparative Analysis,* the following sentence is added to the one-subject bill section: "Legislative compliance with the requirements of this section is a constitutional responsibility not subject to judicial review."

In explanation and justification for the recommendation, the following commentary is provided by the drafters of the Model State Constitution:

"The main provision is common to most state constitutions. It requires that all laws be enacted by bill, i.e., in a manner which gives notice to all legislators and to the people that the legislature is not merely expressing a sentiment or an opinion but is in fact passing a law in the prescribed and approved manner. The section further provides that all bills, except the appropriation bills and codified revisions and rearrangements of existing law, be confined to a single subject. This has been considered a beneficial rule to avoid such abuses as log-rolling, the attachment of special interest riders to bills to which they are not germane and other devices whereby legislatures and the people may have to accept an undesirable piece of legislation in order to get a useful and necessary one or to avoid a situation in which the content of a particular piece of legislation may be completely obscured or may be rendered incomprehensible by the coupling of unrelated matter.

"While there is little disagreement over the desirability of limiting each bill to a single subject, a great body of highly technical decisional law has grown up explaining what is a 'single subject.' (Footnote: Millard H. Ruud, 'No Law Shall Embrace More Than One Subject,' *Minnesota Law Review*, 42 (January 1958), 389-452.] In its most restrictive applications, the so-called single subject rule has resulted in the invalidation on essentially extraneous if not frivolous grounds of perfectly sound legislation which misled neither the legislators nor the people. In order to create what appears to be a desirable balance between the necessity of affirming the value of the single subject rule and the undesirability of having the rule operate as a basis for the invalidation of sound legislation on merely technical grounds, the last sentence has been added. It is not part of any state constitution. It provides that legislative compliance with the technical requirements of this section is not subject to judicial review, though it remains a constitutional responsibility of the legislature. In effect, this means that the legislature will have to police the single subject rule in the first instance and, if abuses should occur, then the governor's veto might be the proper remedy in response to public pressure or on the basis of information received from the state legislature itself. The unavailability of judicial review may encourage mischief which would then have as its sole corrective the normal political processes and a prompt governor's veto. On balance this appears to be wiser than to permit the courts, as has been the case under existing rules, to invalidate a law, often many years after it has been passed, merely on the basis of a technical infirmity where, in fact, no one had been misled. It might be noted that similar considerations were persuasive in omitting the 'subject title' rule which required not only that bills be confined to a single subject but that the single subject be expressed in the title. The past history of the single title rule leads to the conclusion that it is more creative of the mischief of highly technical invalidations than beneficial to the achievement of its purposes." (Model State Constitution 59-60.)

Revival and Amendment: As in the case of the one-subject bill provision, a prohibition on amendment by reference is a perfectly good principle. (But again, it may be noted that Congress does not follow the rule.) The explanation of this provision (*supra,* p. 169) demonstrates that the arguments set forth above in discussing the "one subject" rule are even more apt in the case of amendment by reference. Moreover, with the existence of a Legislative Reference Bureau, the increasing acceptance of legislative staff assistance and the practice of preparation of digests of bills, both official and unofficial, the need for a prohibition on amendment by reference to protect legislators against acting in ignorance is hardly necessary. So far as the general public, and their lawyers, are concerned, the existence of an up-to-date compilation of statutes with annotations decreases, if it does not eliminate, the need for covering a library table with many volumes in order to put together a single statute. The revival and amendment requirement could be dropped without harm.

If, however, it is desired to preserve the requirement, one of two things should be done. Either the Model State Constitution's approach, discussed above, should be followed, or the provision should be changed, as recommended in 1922, to cover only an act *expressly* amending another act. This should eliminate substantially all judicial review and should leave the legislature under an injunction that would be easy to obey.

Effective Date: It would appear advisable to make some change in the effective date provision. If the decision is made to go to annual sessions, some of the end-of-session log jam will be alleviated but hardly enough to justify preservation of the July 1 effective date. The 1922 proposal to change to 60 days after adjournment on all bills except appropriations would end the forced June 30 adjournment, but it is worth considering whether any provision is required, whether a requirement that the effective date be no earlier than publication would suffice, or whether a stated period of delay—30, 60, 90 days—should be computed from passage rather than from adjournment.

If the decision is to preserve a constitutionally delayed effective date, then, of course, there must be an exception for "emergencies." It would seem advisable to obviate the possibility of judicial second-guessing of the "emergency" by simply deleting the words "in case of emergency, (which emergency shall be expressed in the preamble or body of the act)."

Privileges of Members

Sec. 14. Senators and Representatives shall, in all cases, except treason, felony or breach of the peace, be privileged from arrest during the session of the General Assembly, and in going to and returning from the same; and for any speech or debate in either house, they shall not be questioned in any other place.

History

Except for variations in punctuation, this section is identical with provisions in the 1818 and 1848 Constitutions. The section was reworded in the proposed 1922 Constitution. The official explanation said that "[t]his section is the same . . . . "(P.N.C. 32), but this is arguable. (See *Comment* below.)

Explanation

This section serves two purposes — to protect legislators from harassment and to protect freedom of debate from threats of libel actions. Freedom of debate offers no difficulty. Indeed, the apparent absence of reported cases probably indicates a general understanding that the privilege is absolute.

Freedom from arrest is a different matter. Again, there are apparently no cases on this but one can doubt that the matter is clear. A natural assumption is that the exception to freedom from arrest for "treason, felony or breach of the peace" leaves legislators with some protection from criminal process. For example, in Section 4 of Article XII (*infra*, p. 541), the same phrase appears as an exception to the freedom from arrest of a militiaman under comparable circumstances. In an opinion in 1915, the Attorney General ruled that militiamen arrested for assault and drunkenness were under the "breach of the peace" exception. (1915 Ill. Att'y Gen. Rep. 229.) The implication of his opinion is that militiamen would be free from arrest for misdemeanors that do not constitute "breach of the peace."

The question is whether the Illinois courts would ultimately follow the United States Supreme Court's interpretation of the same exception in the United States Constitution. That Court held that the words "treason, felony or breach of the peace" were well understood in 1787 to limit the privilege from arrest to the same privilege granted to members of Parliament — namely, freedom from civil arrest. (Williamson v. United States, 207 U.S. 425 (1908).) In other words, "breach of the peace" was used in the sense of "any crime not a felony," rather than in the sense of the common law offense of breach of the peace. Civil arrest is relatively rare today but it was still common in the colonies at the time of the adoption of the Constitution.

As noted below, some states include protection from civil process. The Illinois Supreme Court has held that Section 14 does not deprive the legislature of the power to provide such protection, but it effectively destroyed the power by holding that an exemption from civil process for legislators only was a prohibited special act under Section 22 of this Article. (Phillips v. Browne, 270 Ill. 450 (1915).) Either the delegates to the 1920 Convention were unaware of the *Phillips* case or did not care to provide protection from civil process. In any event, there was no debate on the matter.

Comparative Analysis

Privilege Against Arrest: Some 40 states besides Illinois provide some protection against arrest, the vast majority of the provisions closely resembling Section 14. Some 13 states also include protection against civil process and four states protect only against civil process. The new Michigan Constitution has a unique provision protecting against "civil arrest and civil process." This presumably was done to conform to In re *Wilkowski* (270 Mich. 687 (1935)), which construed "treason, felony or breach of the peace" to exclude criminal process just as the United States Supreme Court had done in the *Williamson* case. The language of the United States Constitution is in substance the same as Section 14. The Model State Constitution has no comparable provision.

Protection of Speech: Some 42 states besides Illinois protect legislative speech, almost two-thirds of them using substantially the same language as in Section 14. The two new states, Alaska and Hawaii, have adopted modern language to cut back the breadth of "questioned in any other place." Obviously, constituents and others can very well "question" remarks made on the floor. These two states provide that legislators are "not to be held to answer before any other tribunal." (Alas. Const. art. II, §6; Hawaii Const. art. III, §8.)

Comment

In the *Comment* on Article II, Section 16, it was suggested as a principle of constitution-drafting that traditional language ought to be left alone. The equivalent of Section 14 in the proposed 1922 Constitution is an example of the significance of this principle. That equivalent read:

"Except for treason, felony or breach of the peace senators and representatives shall be privileged from arrest while going to, attending or returning from sessions of the general assembly. They shall not be questioned elsewehere for any speech in either house. (art. III, § 53.)

First, it is to be noted that in the first sentence the provision was changed from "during the session" to "attending . . . sessions." If one assumes that constitution-drafters choose their words carefully and further assumes that a change in wording is made for good reason, then one searches for the significance of the change. In the example here, it would be logical to conclude that the protection against arrest is removed during periods when a member is not in attendance — for example, during a long recess, or while ill, and the like. To be sure, the official explanation stated that the section is the "same" as Section 14, and this would weigh heavily in litigation. The point is that an unnecessary change is simply an invitation to litigation. The litigation may be doomed to failure, but if no change is made, there probably will be no litigation at all.

The second sentence of the proposed provision had two changes — "in any other place" became "elsewhere" and "speech or debate" became simply "speech." The "elsewhere" change seems harmless enough, but the dropping of "debate" clearly raises a question. Legislators make what are customarily denominated "speeches"; they also engage in "debate." Obviously, spontaneous debate needs more protection than a carefully prepared speech and thus any distinction deduced from the proposed change would have been at cross purposes with the spirit of the protection. Nevertheless, the proposed change could have given rise to litigation.

Section 14 is an excellent example of the obverse of the foregoing. A failure to change wording which has acquired a technical meaning will frequently be construed to mean that the drafters accepted the technical meaning. For example, it is doubtful that the delegates to the 1920 Convention were aware of the civil arrest interpretation of the "treason, felony or breach of the peace" exception. It may be that a discussion of the matter would have resulted in preservation of the interpretation, perhaps by such wording as Michigan used (see above), or would have resulted in a change in wording in order to protect legislators against certain limited criminal process.

Restrictions of Members

Sec. 15. No person elected to the General Assembly shall receive any civil appointment within this State from the Governor, the Governor and Senate, or from the General Assembly, during the term for which he shall have been elected; and all such appointments, and all votes given for any such members for any such office or appointment, shall be void; nor shall any member of the General Assembly be interested, either directly or indirectly, in any contract with the State, or any county thereof, authorized by any law passed during the term for which he shall have been elected, or within one year after the expiration thereof.

History

The 1818 Constitution simply prohibited the appointment of a legislator, during his elected term, to any civil office under the state which had been created or the emoluments increased during such term. The 1848 Constitution substituted a section that differs in only one respect from the present Section 15. The 1848 provision included a prohibition against appointing a member of the legislature to the United States Senate. The present Section 15 was accepted by the 1870 Convention without change, but only after an extended debate over a proposal to add a prohibition on railroad employees also holding public office and on any legislator or other public officer holding a free railroad pass. The proposed 1922 Constitution extended the civil appointment coverage to include county and local "lucrative" positions and the contract coverage to include local governments as well as the state and counties.

Explanation

The first part of this section duplicates Section 3 (*supra,* p. 120) to some extent, but in two respects goes beyond it. That section, it will be recalled, covers named offices and other "lucrative" offices. This section covers "civil appointments." Indeed, because of the potential breadth of "civil appointments," it was necessary for the Supreme Court to devise an intrepretation that would permit legislators to serve, without salary, on commissions such as the Gettysburg Memorial Commission, Golden Gate Exposition Commission, and New York World's Fair Commission. The Court said that the prohibition was aimed at appointments that are of a permanent nature and that lend themselves to personal aggrandizement with opportunity for private gain, pecuniary or otherwise. (Gillespie v. Barrett, 368 Ill. 612 (1938).)

The second respect in which this section goes beyond dual office holding is the formulation that prevents a legislator from accepting a civil appointment by resigning his legislative seat. (*See* 1921 Ill. Att'y Gen. Rep. 167.) The purpose of this formulation is to prevent the Governor from "bribing" a legislator for a favorable vote or for a legislator to "extort" a job from the Governor in return for a favorable vote.

The second half of the section is a straightforward prohibition of a particular form of conflict of interest.

Comparative Analysis

Dual Office Holding: (See the *Comparative Analysis* of Sec. 3, *supra,* p. 125.)

Contracts: Seven states have a comparable provision. Twelve states, one of which is included among the seven, have a provision requiring a legislator who has a personal interest in a measure to disclose that fact and to refrain from voting on the measure. Neither the United States Constitution nor the Model State Constitution has a comparable conflict-of-interest provision.

Comment

Paradoxically, there are two important principles, somewhat contradictory, which should govern the drafting of a comprehensive dual office holding provision. One is that careful consideration should be given to precisely what purposes are served by the prohibition against dual office holding, what types of positions should be covered, and how the prohibition is to operate. (That is, for example, whether a legislator can vacate one office to take another, as under Section 3, or can not, as under Section 15.) The second principle is that the constitutional provision embodying the precise purpose and coverage should *not* be too precise. There are two reasons for this. One is that precision, entailing, as it must, considerable detail, may soon be out of date. (Consider, for example, the anachronism involved in distinguishing between postmasters on the basis of annual compensation above and below $300, as in Section 3.) The other is that precision either decreases judicial flexibility in developing a body of law designed to carry out the provision's purposes, or results in an unsatisfactory body of law because the judiciary engages in strained reasoning in order to preserve flexibility. The paradox can be handled by a simple statement in the draft to be considered by the delegates, accompanied by a comprehensive report that spells out the purposes of the provision, the types of positions that are covered, the types that are not covered, and the like. This becomes a "legislative record" that the courts can use in carrying out the purpose of the provision through time and notwithstanding changes in job content and job titles.

Conflict of interest is an equally vexing problem, but it is doubtful that it can be solved in the manner suggested above. The difficulty is that the entire subject is murky and any enforceable statement of general principle is likely to produce as many injustices as it prevents wrongdoing. A provision such as now appears in Section 15 is safe enough, but it obviously is only a segment of the conflict-of-interest problem. The real question is whether it is better to leave the entire problem on the statutory level than to place only a partial solution in the Constitution.

There is, however, a special problem concerning conflict of interest and the legislature. Experience has shown, most notably in the case of Congress, that there is a natural reluctance on the part of legislators to enact as strict conflict-of-interest rules applicable to themselves as they enact for the executive department. Moreover, if the Constitution contains conflict-of-interest restrictions on the legislature, there is little doubt that it will see to it that the rest of the government is equally restricted, and this obviates any need for sprinkling conflict-of-interest provisions throughout the Constitution. A neat balancing act between excessive detail and the need to prod the legislature to police itself is called for.

Appropriations

Sec. 16. The General Assembly shall make no appropriation of money out of the treasury in any private law. Bills making appropriations for the pay of members and officers of the General Assembly, and for the salaries of the officers of the government, shall contain no provision on any other subject.

History

The second sentence of this section first appeared in substance in the 1848 Constitution. The first sentence was added in 1870. According to the Chairman of the Committee on the Legislative Department of the 1870 Convention, the sentence was requested by the Auditor of Public Accounts who had found that sometimes amendments appropriating money had been tacked onto private bills. The proposed 1922 Constitution omitted the first sentence. The second sentence was changed in two respects. The General Assembly portion of the sentence was made to cover the pay of legislative employees in addition to members and officers. So far as officers of the government were concerned, the proposed section required that appropriations for the office of each of the seven elective state officers be in separate bills.

Explanation

Private Bills: As noted above, the primary purpose of the first sentence of this section was to stop an earlier practice of tacking appropriation amendments onto private bills. Since Section 13 (*supra,* p. 160) prohibits multiple-subject bills and Section 22 (*infra,* p. 203) greatly cuts down the passage of private acts, the appropriation prohibition has not been of great significance. The only litigation invoking this sentence appears to have been in the nature of a make-weight argument, usually in a test case involving a general law. (*See, e.g.,* Cremer v. Peoria Housing Authority, 399 Ill. 579 (1948); Hagler v. Small, 307 Ill. 460 (1923).)

Pay: This sentence, analogous to the one subject-one bill rule of Section 13 (*supra,* p. 160), has brought forth considerable litigation, including some of the cases brought by the famous litigating taxpayer, J. B. Fergus. In the first *Fergus v. Russel* case (270 Ill. 304 (1915)), the Supreme Court dealt with what was called the "Omnibus Bill." It made a number of appropriations for a number of different purposes. Included were sums of money for the compensation of various people in various positions. The claim was made that these appropriations violated the second sentence of Section 16. The Court first had to dispose of a matter of principle — namely, whether the concluding words "any other subject" really meant "any other subject than appropriations." All earlier cases construing this sentence had involved appropriations mixed with substantive legislation. The Court was unwilling to accept the proffered distinction and ruled that the concluding words meant "any other subject than pay of members and officers." The Court then went through each of the items of appropriation for pay and decided on the basis of the definition of officer in Section 24 of Article V (*infra,* p. 322) whether the position was that of officer or employee. (There were a great many other constitutional problems involved in this landmark case, but they are discussed in connection with other sections of this and other Articles.) The third *Fergus v. Russel* case (277 Ill. 20 (1917)) involved the first sentence of this section and held that appropriations to pay claims against the state were not "appropriations in a private law."

In one of the cases distinguished by the Court in the first *Fergus* case, the Court had in fact construed appropriation language not to be an appropriation but only a provision for the amount to be paid to an officer from an appropriation. (People v. Joyce, 246 Ill. 124 (1910).) Some years later, in a case which did not refer to the *Joyce* case, the Court quite consistently held that such a provision did not entitle an attorney to payment of his salary where the Governor struck the item therefor from the "members and officers" appropriations bill. (People *ex rel.* Millner v. Russel, 311 Ill. 96 (1924).)

The recent case of *People* ex rel. *Coons v. Howlett* (33 Ill. 2d 304 (1965)) involved this section, at least in the eyes of the dissenting judge. It appears that the legislature passed an amendment to the regular compensation of legislators provision increasing salaries from $6,000 to $7,500 per annum. The Governor vetoed the bill. The appropriation act, passed after the compensation amendment and on the assumption that it would not be vetoed, provided a sum for legislators' salaries at the rate of $7,500 per annum. The Supreme Court refused to issue a writ prohibiting payment of the larger salary. "The later law constitutes an amendment by implication and its provisions must prevail." (*Id.* at 308.) What happened to amendment by reference? Neither the opinion of the Court nor the dissent discusses the matter. (See discussion of Sec. 13, *supra,* p. 160.) The dissenting judge argued that to allow an amendment by implication in an appropriation act was a violation of the second sentence of Section 16. He also argued that an appropriation act, covering, as it does, only two fiscal years, can hardly be a "law" under the rubric of Section 21 — "compensation as shall be prescribed by law." (*Infra,* p. 200.)

Comparative Analysis

Private Bills: No other state appears to have a comparable provision. Two states forbid appropriations for private purposes, a prohibition found by the courts in Illinois to be the thrust of Section 20. (See *Comment* on Sec. 20, *infra,* p. 199.) The absence of such a specific prohibition in other state constitutions does not mean that appropriations for private purposes are permitted. Most state courts would invalidate an appropriation for a purely private purpose. Four states permit appropriations for private or local purposes but only by a two-thirds' vote of the membership of each house. But here again, such permission is probably of a limited nature. In New York, for example, a two-thirds' vote is required for state grants to local governments, but another provision comparable to Section 20 effectively prohibits truly private appropriations. The United States Constitution has no comparable prohibition. The Model State Constitution has a limited prohibition on private laws. (See *Comparative Analysis* of Sec. 22, *infra,* p. 223.)

Pay: The Nebraska Constitution (1875) and the West Virginia Constitution (1872) have a limitation in almost the same wording as the second sentence of Section 16. Two states include in the limitation both salaries and other current expenses of the state. Three states simply specify that appropriation bills should not have extraneous riders attached. The United States Constitution does not prohibit riders and, in fact, Congress frequently includes substantive legislation in appropriation acts, sometimes germane to the appropriation, sometimes totally irrelevant. The Model State Constitution limits appropriation bills to appropriations, but states that the requirement is not subject to judicial review. (See *Comment* on Sec. 13, *supra,* p. 170.)

Comment

As noted in the *Explanation* above, there is some question whether the first sentence of this section serves any purpose. The only purpose served by the second sentence presumably was to prevent the legislature from forcing an unwanted appropriation on the Governor who would have had to deny pay to himself and all other state officers if he were to veto the bill. But this eventuality was obviated by the item veto amendment to Section 16 of Article V. (*Infra,* p. 293.) Any legislative matter other than an appropriation could as easily be stricken under the one-subject rule of Section 13 (*supra,* p. 160) as by this sentence in Section 16. In this connection, it should be noted that the Model State Constitution exempts appropriation bills from the one-subject rule but provides that appropriation bills must be limited to appropriations.

Treasury Warrants — Duty of Auditor

Sec. 17. No money shall be drawn from the treasury except in pursuance of an appropriation made by law, and on the presentation of a warrant issued by the Auditor thereon; and no money shall be diverted from any appropriation made for any purpose, or taken from any fund whatever, either by joint or separate resolution. The Auditor shall, within sixty days after the adjournment of each session of the General Assembly, prepare and publish a full statement of all money expended at such session, specifying the amount of each item, and to whom and for what paid.

History

The 1818 Constitution provided that no money should be drawn from the treasury except in consequence of an appropriation made by law. That Constitution also provided that "[a]n accurate statement of the receipts and expenditures of the public money shall be attached to and published with the laws, at the rising of each session of the General Assembly." The 1848 Constitution made no substantive change in the foregoing. The present version of Section 17 was accepted by the 1870 Convention without explanation or debate. The proposed 1922 Constitution retained the first half of the first sentence and the substance of the second sentence. The second half of the first sentence was omitted as a repetition, in effect, of the first half. (*See* State of Illinois, Journal of the Constitutional Convention 1920-1922 at 363-64 (1922) [hereinafter cited as Journal].)

Explanation

The first half of the first sentence is a peculiar combination of two distinct propositions. One is the universal principle that money that flows into the treasury gets paid out only pursuant to appropriations. The second makes the Auditor of Public Accounts, not the Treasurer, the state's chief disbursing officer, and thereby indirectly adopts the principle of an independent pre-audit of public expenditures. The second half of the sentence is, as the 1920-22 Convention recognized, simply repetitious. This is so because by virtue of Section 11 (*supra,* p. 155), a law requires an enactment clause and separate and joint resolutions do not have one.

There have been a number of cases and opinions of the Attorney General under the appropriation portion of the first sentence of this section. With one exception, the cases and opinions all say that the sentence means what it says. (*See, e.g.,* People *ex rel.* Board of Trustees v. Barrett, 382 Ill. 321 (1943); Burritt v. Commissioners of State Contracts, 120 Ill. 322 (1887); 1917 Ill. Att'y Gen. Rep. 40; 1914 Ill. Att'y Gen Rep. 194.) The one exception is *Antle v. Tuchbreiter* (414 Ill. 571 (1953)) where the Supreme Court quite sensibly held that social security taxes withheld from state employees pursuant to an Enabling Act could be paid over to the United States without the necessity of an appropriation.

There are two other recent cases which, if read too hastily, appear to permit disbursements without an appropriation, but which, when read carefully, are revealed to have subtle rationales. In *People* ex rel. *Conn v. Randolph* (35 Ill. 24 (1966)), attorneys representing indigent defendants in murder trials ran up expenses and provided legal services far in excess of a statutory maximum for indigent representations. The Court pointed out that the indigents were constitutionally entitled to representation at the expense of the state, and that the state could hardly defeat this constitutional requirement by failing to provide adequate funds to meet the requirement. Under some circumstances, the result might have been that the lawyers had a just claim against the state which they would have had to prosecute. In the *Conn* case, however, the Court was able to find the money. The accused were prisoners and the murders had occurred in the course of a prison riot. The Court noted that the Department of Public Safety was responsible for the prosecution of crimes committed in prison, and that such prosecution could not take place unless the accused were provided with counsel. The Department had a fund for contingencies, and the Court simply stated that payment should be made from that fund. The other case involved the not uncommon situation of having to decide whether or not a specific proposed expenditure could be brought under one of the more general line items in an appropriation. Here taxpayers sought to enjoin the construction by the University of Illinois of a television station. The University appropriation for ordinary and contingent expenses consisted of a small number of general items under classifications established by law, and the Court had no difficulty in finding that that appropriation included a television station. (Turkovich v. Board of Trustees, 11 Ill. 2d 460 (1957).)

It should also be noted that it is possible under certain circumstances to operate without an appropriation if the required funds are obtained directly and do not have to be paid into the treasury. (*See* Elliott v. University of Ill, 365 Ill. 338 (1936).)

As noted above, the first sentence also sets forth the constitutional duty of the Auditor of Public Accounts to be the state's disbursing officer and by implication to conduct a pre-audit of every expenditure from state funds in the treasury. This pre-audit duty of the Auditor of Public Accounts indirectly expressed in the first sentence is the only constitutional auditing duty spelled out in the Constitution. (To be sure, Secs. 7 and 20, Art. V, *infra*, pp. 273 and 313, require executive accounting, but accounting is not auditing.) Over the years, many nonauditing and nondisbursing duties were given to the Auditor of Public Accounts, and other agencies were given pre-audit powers which were, of course, in addition to the Auditor's constitutional power. Following the notorious scandal involving the Auditor of Public Accounts in the period 1953-56, a number of statutory changes were made. The situation today, in brief, is that the Auditor of Public Accounts retains his disbursing function, his pre-auditing function, and general supervision of some municipal and county auditing, but almost none of his nonauditing functions. As of January 1, 1958, a Department of Audits under the command of an Auditor General took over all of the post-audit activities formerly handled by the Auditor of Public Accounts.

The second sentence of Section 17 refers only to money expended by the General Assembly in the course of operating the legislative session. During the 1920-22 Convention, the Committee on Phraseology and Style inquired of the Auditor of Public Accounts concerning the ambiguous wording of the sentence. He replied to the effect that, from the beginning, the Auditor had construed the sentence to cover only the legislature's expenditures for its own purposes and not all money expended as a result of the session. (Journal 364.)

Comparative Analysis

Most states either provide specifically that no money shall be drawn from the treasury except pursuant to an appropriation made by law, or provide by some indirect language for an equivalent restriction. A few states permit interest on the state debt to be paid without a specific appropriation therefor. About a third of the states have a provision calling for warrants. Nebraska and West Virginia follow Illinois in having the Auditor issue the warrant. In three states the issuing officer is the Comptroller. In Missouri, the Comptroller must certify for payment and the State Auditor must certitfy that the expenditure is within an appropriation and that there is an adequate unexpended balance thereof. Some half dozen states require that the warrant be drawn by the "proper officer." Both the United States Constitution and the Model State Constitution contain the traditional restriction on withdrawal of money from the treasury, but neither has any language covering the issuance of warrants.

Mississippi and Nebraska appear to have copied the Illinois requirement that the Auditor prepare a statement of the expenses of the legislative session. No other state has a comparable provision. The United States Constitution and the Model State Constitution have no comparable provision. (But see the quotation from the Model concerning the secretary of the legislature, *supra*, p. 150.)

Comment

The second sentence of this section seems to be a minor matter hardly of constitutional significance. The repetitious part of the first sentence could easily be dropped. The point has been made from time to time in the *Comments* that care must be taken not to give rise to the inference that some substantive change is intended by an omission. In this case the addition of the words "No law shall be passed except by bill" in an appropriate section as recommended elsewhere (see *Comment* to Sec. 11, *supra*, p. 156) would justify the dropping of the repetitious language.

Considerable thought should be given to financial controls, particularly the extent to which a particular pattern of control should be frozen into the Constitution by virtue of detailed language. It is also important to analyze the effect on the distribution of power of different formulations of financial controls. As a rough generalization, a system of controls that virtually guarantees that no money will ever be illegally, improperly or foolishly spent is incompatible with effective and prompt administration. This is so because the paperwork and the double-checking slow everything down, and speed in taking action is frequently the effective and sometimes even the less expensive alternative. In devising a constitutional framework for financial controls, a balance must be struck between these incompatible objectives. In striking the balance, consideration should be given to the degree of flexibility that the Constitution should permit. In other words, consideration should be given to the extent to which the legislature should be left free to alter the control system from time to time.

It is clear that an audit after the fact, a post-audit, does not inhibit efficient administration. It is also clear that the agency charged with such an audit should be independent of the agencies whose books are to be audited. The United States, by statute, achieves this result by making the General Accounting Office an arm of the Congress and by setting the term of office of the Comptroller General at 15 years. The Model State Constitution recommends that the auditor be appointed by the legislature to serve at its pleasure. He would conduct post-audits as prescribed by law. The two newest states, Alaska and Hawaii, have adopted this recommendation, except that Hawaii gives the auditor an eight-year term, subject to removal for cause by a two-thirds' vote of the legislature. Another dozen or so states provide for legislative appointment of the auditor, but in most cases the auditor is not a constitutional officer.

Appropriations for State Expenditures

Sec. 18. Each General Assembly shall provide for all the appropriations necessary for the ordinary and contingent expenses of the government until the expiration of the first fiscal quarter after the adjournment of the next regular session, the aggregate amount of which shall not be increased without a vote of two-thirds of the members elected to each house, nor exceed the amount of revenue authorized by law to be raised in such time; and all appropriations, general or special, requiring money to be paid out of the State treasury, from funds belonging to the State, shall end with such fiscal quarter: *Provided,* the State may, to meet casual deficits or failures in revenues, contracts debts, never to exceed in the aggregate two hundred and fifty thousand dollars; and moneys thus borrowed shall be applied to the purpose for which they were obtained, or to pay the debt thus created, and to no other purpose; and no other debt, except for the purpose of repelling invasion, suppressing insurrection, or defending the State in war, (for payment of which the faith of the State shall be pledged), shall be contracted, unless the law authorizing the same shall, at a general election, have been submitted to the people, and have received a majority of the votes cast for members of the General Assembly at such election. The General Assembly shall provide for the publication of said law for three months, at least, before the vote of the people shall be taken upon the same; and provision shall be made, at the time, for the payment of the interest annually, as it shall accrue, by a tax levied for the purpose, or from other sources of revenue; which law, providing for the payment of such interest by such tax, shall be irrepealable until such debt be paid: *And provided, further,* that the law levying the tax shall be submitted to the people with the law authorizing the debt to be contracted.

History

The 1818 Constitution contained no restrictions on either the appropriations process or the incurring of debt. Under the 1818 Constitutiton, the legislature incurred considerable indebtedness in furtherance of such internal improvements as the Illinois-Michigan Canal and the laying down of railroads. In the great depression years of the middle 1830's the state was threatened with bankruptcy. (*See* Debates 298-300.) The 1848 Constitution reflected this experience. A section was inserted in the Legislative Article that differs from the present Section 18 in only three respects: (1) appropriations were for the period ending with adjournment of the next legislature instead of at the end of a fiscal quarter following adjournment; (2) the lapsing of appropriations was not covered; and (3) the temporary deficit debt limit was only $50,000. Section 18 does not differ in substance from the section as proposed to the 1870 Convention. There was extensive debate, and several amendments were offered, mostly designed to restrict the legislature further, but all were defeated.

The proposed 1922 Constitution contained a number of technical and simplifying changes in the appropriations and debt provision, but only two changes of substance: the temporary deficit limit was increased to $1,000,000 and bonds for the Illinois Waterway were exempted from the referendum requirement. This latter change was solely for the purpose of consistency, since the proposed canal section authorized a bond issue of $10,000,000 for the waterway. (The technical changes are discussed below in the course of the *Explanation.*)

Explanation

Appropriations: The provision for appropriations is fuzzy and indefinite, but if the unexpressed assumptions of the drafters of the 1848 and 1870 Constitutions are considered, it is reasonably clear what was intended. In 1848, it was assumed that the General Assembly would appropriate enough money to run the government until the next General Assembly could again appropriate money to run the government. The drafters of the 1870 Constitution modified the earlier provision on the assumption that appropriations for running the government would be for a two-year period beginning July 1. This came about because Section 13 (*supra*, p. 160) made legislation effective July 1, and the delegates assumed that the General Assembly would normally finish its regular session prior to April 1. (*See* Debates 540.) The extra fiscal quarter was designed to provide a two-year "budget." (It has been noted elsewhere (see *Explanation* of Sec. 7, Art. V, *infra*, p. 273) that the delegates to the 1870 Convention anticipated, perhaps unwittingly, modern budgeting.)

Over the years, regular sessions got longer and June 30 became the normal adjournment target. Thus, the "expiration of the first fiscal quarter" after adjournment became an "overlapping" quarter in which the previous biennium's appropriations and the new biennium's appropriations were available. The proposed 1922 Constitution sought to clear up this confusion by provididng that appropriations were for a two-year period from July 1 to June 30, but that money obligated before June 30 could be paid up to September 30.

The fuzzy language of Section 18 made it possible recently for the Attorney General to advise the Chairman of the Commission on the Organization of the General Assembly that not only could the legislature turn itself into an "annual session" body (see Sec. 9, *supra*, p. 145), it could adopt annual appropriation acts. (*See* I.S.L. 133-38, app. D.) In his opinion dated October 19, 1966, the Attorney General discussed the ambiguity of the appropriations language of Section 18 and noted that the legislature had long since specified that appropriations expire on June 30 of the second year of the biennium. (Section 25 of the State Finance Act, Ill. Rev. Stat. ch. 127, §161 (1967). Section 27 of the State Finance Act authorizes payment, not until September 30, but "until the expiration of the first fiscal quarter after the adjournment of the General Assembly held next after that at which the appropriation was made." Ill. Rev. Stat. ch. 127, §163 (1967). This would seem to mean that, since the 75th General Assembly did not adjourn until January, 1969, payments could be made until June 30, 1969, on obligations incurred prior to June 30, 1967, under appropriations made by the 74th General Assembly.) The Attorney General concluded that this long-standing statutory resolution of the ambiguity of the length of the overall appropriation period would be accepted by the courts.

It is not clear why the Attorney General discussed the ambiguity of the length of the appropriation period. It may be that he wanted to stress the literal absurdity of the indefinite appropriation period in justification of steps to regularize the appropriation process. Or it may be that he wanted to nail down the validity of the specific 24-month period before deciding that it could be divided into two equal twelve-month periods. In any event, after discussing the ambiguity of the appropriation period, the Attorney General addresseed himself to the principal question, thus:

"Although the General Assembly must make appropriations for the biennial period as set forth in Section 18 of Article IV, the Constitution does not state that the General Assembly might not make annual appropriations in order to discharge its duty.

"A state constitution is not a grant of power but is a limitation on legislative power, and the legislature may enact any law not expressly or inferentially prohibited by the state or national constitution....

"I can find nothing in the Constitution which expressly or inferentially prohibits the making of annual appropriations. Although the General Assembly must make appropriations for a certain period, there is no requirement that such appropriations cannot be made one year at a time." (I.S.L. 136.)

The foregoing leaves open the question of whether or not the second annual appropriation bill must be passed by a two-thirds' vote. The Attorney General, after quoting the operative words from Section 18 — "the aggregate amount of which shall not be increased" — said:

"The word 'aggregate' means the entire number, sum, mass, or quantity of anything. (*Bauer v. Rusetos & Co.*, 306 Ill. 602, 609). The words 'of which,' which follow the words 'aggregate amount,' can mean nothing except the *entire* amount of the appropriations made for the period for which the General Assembly is under a duty to make appropriations, i.e., for the two-year period from July 1st of an odd-numbered year to and including June 30th of the next odd-numbered year. Appropriations made for this period would not be subject to the two-thirds rule if increased by the same General Assembly which made the original appropriation. However, if the increase were made by the new successor General Assembly, a two-thirds vote would clearly be required, since there would be an increase in the aggregate amount of the appropriations provided by the previous General Assembly which was responsible primarily for making appropriations for the period in question." (*Id* at 138.)

There are three things to be said about the appropriations portion of the Attorney General's opinion. One is that his conclusions are difficult to square with the debates of the delegates to the 1870 Constitution. The changes in the proposed 1922 Constitution appear to represent a formulation of the way the appropriation process was originally supposed to operate. The second thing to be said is that, fortunately, the 1870 drafters used ambiguous language that permits a shift to annual budgeting. Finally, there is only a limited area for judicial review of this question. Certainly, the courts could hardly invalidate the first-year appropriation acts. The only question which could arise over second-year appropriation acts is whether a two-thirds' vote is required. It seems most unlikely that the courts would disagree with the Attorney General's opinion, considering the chaos which would ensue if such acts were invalidated and in view of the fact that to require a two-third's vote would be a technical matter, since a second one-year appropriation is not the second-guessing at which the restriction on increases in aggregate amounts is aimed. In any event, for the first time, the budget presented on April 1, 1969, was for one fiscal year, beginning July 1, 1969.

Section 18 provides that the aggregate amount appropriated shall not exceed the amount of revenue authorized. This provision is unenforceable, and for this reason it was omitted from the proposed 1922 Constitution. It is unenforceable because, as discussed above, the period of time covered by appropriations is not definite, and because it is literally impossible to know until long after the event whether revenues are adequate to cover appropriations. An argument was once made that "revenue" should be construed to cover only amounts raised by direct taxation, but the Supreme Court rejected the argument in favor of the ordinary meaning of total income from whatever source. (Fergus v. Brady, 277 Ill. 272 (1917).) Notwithstanding unenforceability, the Supreme Court has relied on the provision to invalidate indefinite appropriations, on the ground that otherwise it would not be possible to know whether or not appropriations exceeded revenues. Thus, an appropriation of "such sums as may be necessary" for a stated purpose was held void. (Fergus v. Russel, 270 Ill. 304 (1915) (but also held void under Art. V, Sec. 16, requiring "amounts in distinct items," *infra*, p. 293).)

It was noted earlier that the requirement that appropriations lapse at the end of "such fiscal quarter" has been implemented by statute to provide that the power to use an appropriation lapses on June 30 of the biennium, but authority to pay continues to the end of "such fiscal quarter." This precludes continuing appropriations. (People *ex rel.* Millner v. Russel, 311 Ill. 96 (1924).) And, of course, payments after the end of the "fiscal quarter" are absolutely prohibited. (People *ex rel.* Polen v. Hoehler, 405 Ill. 322 (1950).) Nevertheless, if an appropriation lapses and a person through no fault of his own fails to get paid, a valid claim exists that will be recognized by the Court of Claims. (*See, e.g.,* King v. State, 11 Ill. Ct. Cl. 577 (1941); Riefler v. State, 11 Ill. Ct. Cl. 381 (1941).)

Debts: In contrast to the fuzzy appropriation language, the restrictions on incurring debt are precise and definite. (The concept of "debt" is another matter. See discussion of revenue bonds below.) There has been litigation, of course, but usually these have been test cases to settle the constitutionality of a bond issue, an important adjunct to the successful marketing of bonds. As is customary in such test cases, every conceivable argument is offered and the result is a series of cases that, in a way, simply underscore the obvious. Thus, the requirement that the legislature provide for publication of the law to be voted upon can be met by a provision in the law itself, by a separate law, or by resolution. (Mitchell v. Lowden, 288 Ill. 327 (1919).) Likewise, there is no need for separate laws, one to create the debt and one to provide a tax for repayment of interest. One law can cover both and one vote can be submitted to the people. (*Id.* But, of course, Sec. 18 does not require a special tax; "other sources of revenue" may be used.) And when the matter is submitted to the voters, a simple proposition suffices, notwithstanding the wording of Section 18 calling for submission of "the law" to the voters. (Routt v. Barrett, 396 Ill. 322 (1947).) Perhaps the most incredible argument made in any of the test cases was the claim that the requirement that a bond issue receive "a majority of the votes cast for members of the General Assembly" was to be read literally. Since every voter normally votes for three representatives and half of the voters normally vote for a senator, a majority of all those votes would be more than the total number of voters who could vote for the bond issue and a bond referendum could never pass. Needless to say, the Supreme Court said the majority required is of those *persons* voting for members of the General Assembly. (Mitchell v. Lowden, 288 Ill. 327 (1919).)

The determination by the United States Supreme Court that the Fourteenth Amendment requires equality of voting — the "one man-one vote" rule — has raised questions about the constitutionality of the majority required to approve a bond issue. The argument, in brief, is that a person casts a vote against the bond issue if he votes for members of the General Assembly even though he does not vote on the bond issue at all; that a person can cast "two votes" against a bond issue by voting for members of the General Assembly and against the bond issue; and that a person can cast "two votes" for a bond issue by refraining from voting for members of the General Assembly while voting for the bond issue.

This question is in litigation in Illinois in an action in the Circuit Court of Cook County contesting the announced result of the referendum on the Natural Resources Development Bond Act at the November, 1968, election. The State Electoral Board found that 1,656,000 favorable votes and 1,216,814 unfavorable votes were cast on the bond issue, but that, under the requirement of Section 18, the issue failed because 4,267,956 votes were cast for members of the General Assembly, and the required majority would have been 2,133,979.

In Illinois, as in many other states, a simple but expensive device has been used to get around bond limitations. This is the device of creating a public authority to issue revenue bonds which do not involve the faith and credit of the state, but, consequently, carry a higher interest rate. The first use of state public authorities for this purpose was the Illinois Armory Board, created in 1935. The board was empowered to obtain land and construct or purchase buildings to be used as National Guard Armories. It would issue bonds, the payment of principal and interest for which was obtained from rentals to the state. Apparently, no attack on this operation was made until after the *Greening* case, discussed below, was decided. In *Loomis v. Keehn* (400 Ill. 337 (1948)), the Supreme Court held that Section 18 was not violated by the Armory Board Act because there was no irrevocable obligation on the state to use the buildings and pay rent therefor and provision was made for the board to lease to others if the state failed to pay its rent.

In 1941, the Illinois State Public Building Authority was created to perform a similar function for state buildings generally, but in 1943 the Supreme Court invalidated this Authority in *People* ex rel. *Greening v. Green.* (382 Ill. 577 (1943).) The principal difficulty was that the members of the Authority consisted of all of the elected state executives plus a member of the Supreme Court, and this was simply too transparent to support a claim that the Authority was not the state. Not until 1961 was a new Illinois Building Authority created with a membership of seven, none of whom could be an elected official. With this change, and others that met technical objections raised in the *Greening* case, the new Authority was upheld. (Berger v. Howlett, 25 Ill. 2d 128 (1962).)

There are, of course, other public authorities engaged in making capital expenditures financed by revenue bonds for such purposes as toll highways, college dormitories, and recreational facilities in state parks. These are much easier to defend than the State Building Authority, for the money received is from third persons utilizing the facilities rather than from the general taxpayer through appropriations for rent.

In summary, it may be noted that the debt limitation applies only to debt for which the state pledges its credit. Revenue bonds are outside the limitation because the state's credit is not pledged. In the case of state office buildings, the arrangement approaches a fiction because, whatever the technicalities involved, the real source for payment of the "debt" is the taxing power to raise the rent which the state pays to the authority, and as a practical matter the state's credit is involved. Since the state's credit is not legally pledged, the interest rate on the bonds is higher.

Comparative Analysis

Appropriations: There is a vast range of constitutional provisions concerning the appropriations process. There are a few states which have adopted an executive budget system which gives the governor consider-able control over the appropriations process through restricting the power of the legislature to make changes in the executive budget. In most of the other states, constitutional provisions generally consist of specific limitations designed, principally, to preserve the integrity of the appropriations process. Some of these limitations appear in other sec-tons in the Illinois Constitution and the appropriate comparisons ap-pear elsewhere. (*See* Secs. 13, 16 and 17, *supra,* pp. 160, 178, and 181; and Art. V, Sec. 16, *infra,* p. 293.)

Approximately a fifth of the states have a provision that, in one way or another, specifically prohibits deficit financing. Many other states in-directly prevent deficit financing through limitations on the incurring of debt. Several states, including states with a formal executive budget, prohibit the passage of supplementary or special appropriations until after the general appropriation act is passed. About a dozen states limit the life of appropriations, but at least two states have specific provisions permitting certain continuing appropriations. A few states specifically provide that payment may be made during a period, usually two years, after the oblgation has been incurred and the appropriation has lapsed.

The United States Constitution has only one limitation on appropria-tions, the restriction on appropriating money to "raise and support" armies for more than two years. (Three states have copied this limitation for their state militia.) The purpose of this limitation is to prevent the creation of a standing army, and in the light of that purpose the two-year limitation actually covers only such items as pay and other current ex-penses. Congress regularly makes "no-year" appropriations which are available until spent, "one-year" appropriations which must be obligated, that is, committed, before the end of the fiscal year, and appropriations for a specific period beyond one year. In all cases, a distinction is made between "obligation" and "payment." Limitations on the life of ap-propriations are related to obligation, or commitment, of funds. Payment can be made at any time.

The Model State Constitution provides:

"The governor shall submit to the legislature, at a time fixed by law, a budget estimate for the next fiscal year setting forth all proposed expenditures and anticipated income of all departments and agencies of the state, as well as a general appropriation bill to authorize the proposed expenditures and a bill or bills covering recommendations in the budget for new or additional revenues." (art. VII, § 7.02.)

Debt: States can be divided into roughly four groups in regard to power to incur debt: (1) states with no significant constitutional limitations; (2) states with absolute limitations; (3) states with no limitations but requiring voter approval by referendum; and (4) states requiring referendum approval but still retaining a maximum debt limit. There appear to be only six states in the first category, four of which are in New England. One of the six, Delaware, requires a three-fourths' vote in each house to create any debt other than to meet casual deficits or defense needs, or to refund existing debt. A seventh state, Maryland, has no limitation, but does require the enactment of a special tax to cover interest and repayment of the debt within 15 years. Approximately 23 states fall in the second category of absolute limitations. Most of these states have exceptions of one sort or another, but the most common exceptions — to meet casual deficits, repel invasion, or suppress insurrection — are not significant. The most common form of limitation is a percentage, frequently one percent, of the assessed value of taxable property. There are about 17 states in the third category of states with no limitation, but requiring approval by referendum. Three states join Illinois in requiring a majority of those voting in the election. South Carolina requires a two-thirds' majority of those voting on the question. In the fourth category, there are four states requiring a referendum on incurring debt within the stated limitation.

The United States Constitution simply empowers Congress to "borrow money on the credit of the United States." The Model State Constitution simply states:

"No debt shall be contracted by or in behalf of this state unless such debt shall be authorized by law for projects or objects distinctly specified therein." (art. VII, § 7.01.)

Comment

Appropriations: There are a great many signs pointing to annual sessions of the legislature and, naturally, annual budgets and annual appropriations. Even if the decision is not to require annual sessions, it seems unlikely that they will be prohibited. In either event, redrafting of the first part of Section 18 will be appropriate, particularly to remove the present fuzzy language. Before new language is drafted, however, there are several crucial decisions to be made. The budgeting and appropriations process is an intricate business, and thought should be given to the advisability of limiting the constitutional language to a simple and flexible provision. But if the decision is to introduce details of control, care must still be taken that the desired control does not have an undesirable consequence in some other area of the budgeting process. For example, the requirement in Section 16 (*supra,* p. 178) that appropriations for pay for officers of the government be in a separate bill, whatever its supposed value, certainly increases the legislative task of relating appropriations to the budget. It would also be appropriate to weigh the pros and cons of such matters as continuing appropriations, longer-than-one-year appropriations, and the federal rule that all that expires with an appropriation is the authority to obligate, not the authority to pay. It is not necessary, of course, to put decisions on all these matters into the Constitution. It may be acceptable to leave some or all of them to legislative decision. But if that is the decision, care must be taken not to draft language that will lead courts to impose unintended restrictions on the budgeting and appropriations process.

Debt: There is much respectable argument for the proposition that debt limits are both ineffective and expensive and for the proposition that participatory democracy in the complicated business of rational financing of government is not particularly rewarding. (*See, e.g.,* the Model State Constitution's Commentary, especially the explanation for dropping the referendum requirement of previous Models. Model State Constitution 91-92.) The political realities are such, however, that the wholesale abandonment of debt limits is probably not a practical proposal. Instead, consideration will probably have to be limited to (a) whether to keep the casual deficit limit and if so, at what sum in place of the unrealistic $250,000; (b) whether to liberalize the referendum voting requirement for debt above the casual deficit limit; or (c) whether to substitute a maximum debt limit for casual deficit and the referendum. It should be noted, however, that the more difficult full faith and credit borrowing is made, the more expensive borrowing becomes. By one means or another, methods of essential financing will be found, all more expensive than regular state bonds. It should also be noted that the most common form of debt limitation is a percentage of assessed valuation of property. In today's world, this is a poor measure of wealth or financial capacity. A novel, but economically sound, measure would be a percentage of the Illinois Gross "National" Product.

Two minor points of style and arrangement should be made. Appropriation procedure and debt rules should be in separate sections and both should be in an article on finance that would replace the article on revenue.

Unauthorized Compensation and Payments Prohibited

Sec. 19. The General Assembly shall never grant or authorize extra compensation, fee or allowances to any public officer, agent, servant or contractor, after service has been rendered or a contract made, nor authorize the payment of any claim, or part thereof, hereafter created against the State under any agreement or contract made without express authority of law; and all such unauthorized agreements or contracts shall be null and void: *Provided,* the General Assembly may make appropriations for expenditures incurred in suppressing insurrection or repelling invasion.

History

The first part of this section, down to the words "nor authorize," first appeared in the 1848 Constitution. The balance of the section was added in 1870. There was no debate or explanation for the addition. The proposed 1922 Constitution retained the substance of the section.

Explanation

This section serves two distinct purposes: the first part states the traditional rule against payments of money without consideration, and the second states the traditional rule that agents of the government must have express authority in order to bind the government. Since they are traditional rules, they would probably have developed in the absence of Section 19 in somewhat the same manner as the courts have construed the section. This is to say, in general, that the courts have ruled that an employee or contractor who has struck his bargain cannot later get more for his services, and that he who contracts with the state must ascertain at his peril that the agent of the state has the authority to act and that there is an appropriation therefor. (*See e.g.,* Gholson v. State, 12 Ill. Ct. Cl. 26 (1941); Amick v. State, 11 Ill. Ct. Cl. 625 (1941); and Mandel Bros. v. State, 10 Ill. Ct. Cl. 448 (1939). For the latter, see the leading case of Fergus v. Brady, 277 Ill. 272 (1917).)

In relatively recent times, the courts have had problems with this section in connection with pension plans. Almost any politically feasible pension plan has elements of retroactivity in it, and against an argument that pension payments will be made in part for past service, the courts have had to find an answer. The answer, taken from J. Dillon, Municipal Corporations, Section 430 (5th ed. 1911), has been that pensions

" 'are in the nature of compensation for services previously rendered for which full and adequate compensation was not received at the time of the rendition of the services. It is, in effect, pay withheld to induce long-continued and faithful service, and the public benefit accrues in two ways:' By encouraging competent employees to remain in the service, and by retiring from the public service those who have become incapacitated from performing the duties as well as they might be performed by younger or more vigorous men." (People *ex rel.* Kroner v. Abbott, 274 Ill. 380, 384-85 (1916).)

The foregoing somewhat ingenuous argument suffices to get around giving credit for past service, but it is of no value in the case of an effort to increase the pensions of those already retired. Such efforts have been invalidated under Section 19 in the case of noncontributory pensions and compulsory contributory pensions. (*See* Raines v. Board of Trustees, 365 Ill. 610 (1937); Porter v. Loehr, 332 Ill. 353 (1928).) The rule is different, however, in the case of a voluntary contributory pension plan. There, the courts argue, a contractual relationship is created and the legislature can amend the contract for retired persons. Thus, a retired teacher was allowed to pay a small additional contribution to the pension fund and have his annual pension increased from $400 to $600. (Raines v. Board of Trustees, 365 Ill. 610 (1937).)

A related problem in compensation for services already rendered arose in the case of the soldiers' bonus after World War I. The Supreme Court said that Section 19 did not stand in the way since soldiers and sailors were not, in the words of the section, officers, agents, servants or contractors. (Hagler v. Small, 307 Ill. 460 (1923).) Interestingly enough, the same argument was used on behalf of a pension increase for the widow of a retired fireman, but the Court would not accept the argument. (People *ex rel*. Schmidt v. Yerger, 21 Ill. 2d 338 (1961). See also *Comment* below.)

Comparative Analysis

Approximately half of the states have a restriction on extra payments for services rendered by officers and employees, or for contractors and agents after performance or service rendered. Four states permit overriding the restriction by a two-thirds' vote of the legislature. Two states make an exception for increases in pension payments, but in one of them a three-fourths' vote is required.

Only about a third of the states specify the necessity for express authority to obligate the state. Four of these states permit overriding the restriction by a two-thirds' vote of the legislature, and three states join Illinois in providing an exception for insurrections.

The United States Constitution has no comparable provision, but the standard rule against implied authority to obligate the government is followed. There are also strict criminal statutory rules against over-obligating appropriated funds. The Model State Constitution provides that no "obligation for the payment of money [may] be incurred except as authorized by law."

Comment

It seems likely that the delegates to the 1870 Convention would have been astounded if some one had argued that Section 19 would prevent the state from increasing the pensions of retired employees. The delegates probably would have been unable to conceive of the state's having an obligation to provide for pensions at all. It is even possible that around the turn of the century the courts, in the absence of a Section 19, would have held a proposed increase in pensions of retired employees to be the "application of tax money for other than public purposes" and, therefore, "a deprivation of property without due process of law." (See quotation from the *Schuler* case, *infra,* p. 199.) By 1961, a dissenting judge argued in the *Yerger* case, cited earlier, that since widows of retired employees do not come within the express terms of Section 19, the section ought not to stand in the way of helping widows faced with a "decreasing" pension relative to the increase of the cost of living. (It is only fair to note that public pension plans involve more legal problems than those arising out of Section 19. *See* Cohn, "Public Employee Retirement Plans — The Nature of the Employees' Rights," 1968 U. Ill. L.F. 32.)

There are two morals in this story of pensions. One is that it is difficult to foresee the effects of rigid constitutional restrictions in a changing society. A second is that it is difficult to find words to prohibit outrageous "giveaways" without also prohibiting justifiable "giveaways."

Assumption of Debts Prohibited

Sec. 20. The State shall never pay, assume or become responsible for the debts or liabilities of, or in any manner give, loan or extend its credit to, or in aid of any public or other corporation, association or individual.

History

The 1848 Constitution forbade the state to give its credit "to or in aid of any individual, association or corporation." There were two similar proposals that wound their way through the 1870 Convention to the last week of the Convention when the Chairman of the Committee on Revision and Adjustment obtained unanimous consent to eliminate one of them. The eliminated section forbade the legislature to pay or assume any debt of "any county, town or township, or of any corporation whatever." The section which was substituted, now Section 20, had been proposed by the Committee on State, County and Municipal Indebtedness. The Chairman urged the substitution on the grounds that one section was a little broader than the other and that two sections would be repetitive. The only debate over either section concerned whether or not it was necessary to specify "public or other" corporations. One or two of the lawyers argued that courts usually ruled that the generic term "corporations" did not include municipal corporations and on the strength of these arguments, the section was revised to specify "public" as well as all other corporations. The proposed 1922 Constitution retained the substance of Section 20, but included the introductory words "Except as otherwise provided in this constitution." The "otherwise provided" referred to such things as a new section authorizing loans to farmers, and a provision authorizing the state to share the cost of some of the activities of drainage districts.

Explanation

It would appear that this section was aimed at two mid-Nineteenth Century problems arising from the drive for internal improvements —

particularly, railroads and canals. One was the use of state credit or funds to assist private entrepreneurs engaged in building such improvements. The other was fear that the state might be induced to bail out local governments that had gotten deeply into debt, usually in connection with internal improvements. As noted in the *History* above, there was an extensive debate in 1870 over the wording necessary to insure coverage of municipal corporations. Mr. Medill, whose proposed substitute language was essentially the language of the present Section 20, noted that local indebtedness in 1870 aggregated $40,000,000, and went on to say:

"I can see, like a creeping shadow on the wall, the time approaching when a log-rolling scheme will be brought into some near future Legislature, to saddle on the State of Illinois the assumption of that $40,000,000, perhaps twice, aye! thrice told." (Debates 220).

Over the years there have been a great many court cases in which someone has invoked Section 20, but, by and large, none have been situations approaching either of the original purposes of the section. Indeed, there appear to have been only three successful invocations of Section 20, and two of them are rather indirect. The only straightforward case is that of *Schuler v. Board of Education* (370 Ill. 107 (1938)), where the Supreme Court upset an agreement between a school board and a private junior college for joint use of a library and laboratory equipment to be paid for with public funds. The two indirect uses of Section 20 were in *Chicago Motor Club v. Kinney* (329 Ill. 120 (1928)), where the Court said that to permit a refund for a tax paid indirectly would be a payment for a private purpose, and *Fergus v. Russel* (270 Ill. 304 (1915)), where the Court said that to pay the expenses of a legislative committee for work done' after adjournment *sine die* would be to make payments to private individuals.

Over the years, government has entered many new areas and has adopted new ways of utilizing private and local organizations to carry out its functions. As noted above, except in the *Schuler* case, Section 20 has not stood in the way. For example, the state has been permitted to aid a private college as a means of assuring an adequate supply of public school teachers (Boehm v. Hertz, 182 Ill. 154 (1899) (the institution in question was technically "private" but in reality "public")); to assist a public housing authority (Cremer v. Peoria Housing Authority, (399 Ill. 579 (1948)); to assist the Chicago Regional Port District (People *ex rel.* Gutknecht v. Chicago Regional Port Dist., 4 Ill. 2d 363 (1954)); and to assist local governments in road construction (Martens v. Brady, 264 Ill. 178 (1914)). In short, if the money is spent for a public purpose, the utilization of a public or other corporation is not likely to be forbidden through a rigid reading of Section 20.

Comparative Analysis

Most states have restrictions on the extension of state credit to private groups. Almost a majority of the states have some sort of restriction on gifts or grants for private purposes. Section 20 does not in specific terms prohibit such gifts or grants, but the section has been so construed by the courts. (See *Comment* below.) Only about ten states refer to assumption of debts. In many of the states with one or more of the foregoing restrictions, there are exceptions which, in many cases, were undoubtedly designed, either in advance or after the fact, to avoid overly restrictive judicial interpretations of the restrictions. For example, several states prohibit grants and loans except to assist the poor; or to the sick and the poor; or to institutions for support of orphans, dependent children, and aged poor; or to orphans, dependent children, the blind, the physically handicapped, and veterans. Georgia has an exception to permit the legislature to provide $250,000 to the first person or company to bring in a commercial oil well. Neither the United States Constitution nor the Model State Constitution has any comparable restriction.

Comment

There are two observations to be made about this section. The first is that it is aimed at a specific problem of a bygone era, but the restrictions are so broadly expressed that they can create difficulties in coping with completely different problems today. The Nineteenth Century problem was that of free-wheeling entrepreneurs financing grandiose schemes with public money. In today's complex society, it appears inevitable that there will be an increase in the use of public subsidies to private groups to help solve public problems. If Section 20 were followed literally, such public subsidies would not be permissible.

The second observation is that the courts have effectively rewritten Section 20. In short, the courts look not to whom money or credit goes, but to the purpose for which the money or credit is to be used. In the *Cremer* case, cited above, the Court said:

"The fundamental principle of the unconstitutionality of appropriating public funds for a private purpose is stated in a more forthright manner in section 20 of article IV...." (399 Ill. 579, 586-87 (1948).)

Another formulation of the principle appears in the *Schuler* case, also cited above:

"We have expressly decided that the application of tax money for other than public purposes is a deprivation of property without due process of law." (370 Ill. 107, 109 (1938).)

From the foregoing it may be argued that if Section 20 were deleted, the courts could continue, as they do now, to distinguish between the use of public funds for private purposes and for public purposes, striking down the former and upholding the latter. There would be no loss of protection of the public fisc. The gain would be in the elimination of a sternly worded command that of necessity cannot be followed literally.

Compensation of Members

Sec. 21. The members of the General Assembly shall receive for their services the sum of five dollars per day, during the first session held under this Constitution, and ten cents for each mile necessarily traveled in going to and returning from the seat of government, to be computed by the Auditor of Public Accounts; and thereafter such compensation as shall be prescribed by law, and no other allowance or emolument, directly or indirectly, for any purpose whatever; except the sum of fifty dollars per session to each member, which shall be in full for postage, stationery, newspapers, and all other incidental expenses and perquisites; but no change shall be made in the compensation of members of the General Assembly during the term for which they may have been elected. The pay and mileage allowed to each member of the General Assembly shall be certified by the Speakers of their respective houses, and entered on the journals, and published at the close of each session.

History

The 1818 Constitution had no provision of any kind covering legislative salaries and expenses. The 1848 Constitution set members' pay at two dollars per day for the first 42 days' attendance and one dollar per day thereafter, plus a travel allowance of ten cents a mile. The Speaker of the House of Representatives received an additional dollar a day. The 1848 Constitution contained substantially the same language concerning certification as now appears in the last sentence of Section 21.

The subject of compensation for legislators evoked considerable debate in the 1870 Convention. There was unanimity only on the necessity for forbidding any indirect means of increasing compensation. Thus, all versions considered by the Convention included the flat $50 expense allowance and the requirement that the Auditor of Public Accounts compute mileage allowances. There were two views on the means of computing compensation: one argument was that a flat sum for a biennium might tempt the legislature to do a hasty job and adjourn quickly; the other argument was that per diem compensation would tempt the legislature to stretch out the session in order to increase their pay. On the fundamental principle of legislative compensation, there were three points of view. One delegate, who may very well have been a minority of one, argued that the 1818 Constitution, which was silent on the subject, had worked well, and that the best solution was to leave compensation up to the legislature. The opposite view was that nobody else in government fixed his own salary and that only the people speaking through their Constitution should fix legislators' compensation. The middle ground was the proposal that a legislature could determine the compensation to be enjoyed by the next legislature. This was the view which prevailed by a vote of 35 to 24. (See Debates 540-55.)

The proposed 1922 Constitution went the full route of allowing the legislature to set both compensation and allowances, but provided that an increase could take effect only after the *second* regular session following enactment. The requirement of certification and entry in the journal of each member's pay and allowances was retained.

Explanation

This section has three significant operative provisions concerning compensation: It allows (1) the legislature to set its own compensation; (2) but only for future legislatures; and (3) prohibits indirect increases through the device of allowances for expenses. Two of the famous *Fergus v. Russel* cases struck down efforts to get around the section's restrictions. In the first case (270 Ill. 304 (1915)), an appropriation of $2,500 to the Secretary of State "for telephone toll for members of the General Assembly" was held invalid under the $50 expense allowance limitation. In the second case (270 Ill. 626 (1915)), a joint resolution allowed reimbursement at the rate of two cents per mile for 21 round trips between home and Springfield for each member from the contingent expense funds of the legislature. The Court held that if this were considered an expense reimbursement, it ran afoul of the $50 limitation, and if it were not so considered, then it was an increase in compensation for sitting members and ran afoul of the restriction on an increase "during the term for which they may have been elected."

At the 1870 Convention, on the occasion of the final vote on Article IV, the following exchange took place:

"Mr. CHURCH. . . .

"It occurs to me here, without stopping for much reflection, that at all times, if a law shall have been proposed either to decrease or increase the pay, there will be under this Constitution, a portion of one house of the General Assembly in being, whose term will not have expired, and that the inconsistency may result of there being one portion of the General Assembly drawing one kind of pay, and another portion drawing another kind of pay. . . .

"Mr. UNDERWOOD. Mr. President: I understand that the law will not take effect for two years after its passage.

"Mr. CODY. Mr. President: This matter was fully discussed in the Convention upon that very view of it, and it was understood that no provision made by the General Assembly with regard to the pay of members, should apply to the members of either the house of representatives or the senate, until after the expiration of their terms of office — that it shall apply to their successors." (Debates 1780.)

The language of Section 21 does not literally require a two-year delay in the effective date of a salary change and the custom has been otherwise. For example, the 75th General Assembly increased legislative compensation to $12,000 per year and fifteen cents per mile. By virtue of the redistricting case (People *ex rel.* Engle v. Kerner, 33 Ill. 2d 11 (1965)), all Senate seats were filled at the 1966 election for four-year terms. For the 76th General Assembly, all Representatives were elected in 1968 and are receiving $12,000 per year in 1969 and 1970, but all Senators are receiving only $9,000 per year. (See also the discussion of the *Coons* case under Sec. 16, *supra,* p. 180.)

Comparative Analysis

There appear to be 14 states which set legislative salaries in their constitutions and another five states which set maximum salaries. With three exceptions, all other states permit the legislature to determine their own pay. The three exceptions, Massachusetts, Vermont and Wisconsin, have no salary provision of any kind. Within the past three years, eight of the 19 states with constitutional salary provisions appear to have amended their constitutions to increase salaries. There appear to be 23 states, including Illinois, which prohibit an increase in salary during the term for which a legislator is elected. All except one of these states are among the states which authorize legislative determination of salary. The exception is a "maximum salary" state.

Approximately 38 states have a constitutional provision concerning legislators' expenses. Seven states leave it up to the legislature to provide for "compensation" without distinguishing between salary and expenses, and five have no provision of any kind. There appear to be only four states with restrictions comparable to the Section 21 limit of $50. Delaware has a limit of $25 per regular session and $10 per special session for stationery and other supplies; Nevada has a limit of $60 per regular or special session for express charges, newspapers and stationery; Maryland forbids purchase of any book or other printed matter not pertinent to the business of the session; and West Virginia has prohibitive language much like that of Section 21 without even a permissible $50.

Whether by constitutional provision or by statute, all states directly or indirectly reimburse legislators for travel expenses, usually on a flat mileage rate, but in some 20 states only for one round trip per session. Almost three-fourths of the states provide a per diem living allowance, and a few additional states provide a flat allowance large enough to cover living expenses.

The United States Constitution provides that compensation shall be "ascertained by law." It is of interest to note that the original batch of amendments to the Constitution, which resulted in the first ten commonly known as the Bill of Rights, actually included two that were not ratified. One of the two that failed provided that no law changing compensation "shall take effect, until an election of Representatives shall have intervened." The Model State Constitution provides that the legislature determine its own salaries and allowances, "but any increase or decrease in the amount thereof shall not apply to the legislature which enacted the same."

Comment

It seems fairly obvious that the 1870 Convention made a sound decision when Section 21 was so drafted that legislators' salaries could be increased by statute. At first blush it would appear that to have limited reimbursement of expenses so severely was inconsistent. But at the time there was no income tax, and it was reasonable to prevent legislatures from hiding their pay increases by increasing their expense perquisites. For example, if the amount normally required for postage, telegrams, and the like were $50 a session per legislator and the allowance were $500, this would be a hidden pay increase. Today, many decisions are vitally affected by income tax rules, and in the light of those rules it is illogical to compensate a legislator for deductible expenses by an increase in salary. To use the same example, if today the amount normally required for postage, telegrams and the like is $500 and the $50 limitation stands, a salary increase must exceed $450, for a legislator must pay an income tax on the salary and he ends up with less than enough to cover his expenses. (See also the *Comment* on Sec. 11 of Art. IX, *infra*, p. 476, concerning the general problem of salary changes.)

Special Legislation Prohibited *

Sec. 22. The General Assembly shall not pass local or special laws in any of the following enumerated cases, that is to say: For —
 (1) Granting divorces;
 (2) Changing the names of persons or places;
 (3) Laying out, opening, altering and working roads or highways;
 (4) Vacating roads, town plats, streets, alleys and public grounds;
 (5) Locating or changing county seats;
 (6) Regulating county and township affairs;
 (7) Regulating the practice in courts of justice;
 (8) Regulating the jurisdiction and duties of justices of the peace, police magistrates, and constables;
 (9) Providing for changes of venue in civil and criminal cases;
 (10) Incorporating cities, towns, or villages, or changing or amending the charter of any town, city or village;
 (11) Providing for the election of members of the board of supervisors in townships, incorporated towns or cities;
 (12) Summoning and impaneling grand or petit juries;
 (13) Providing for the management of common schools;
 (14) Regulating the rate of interest on money;
 (15) The opening and conducting of any election, or designating the place of voting;

(16) The sale or mortgage of real estate belonging to minors or others under disability;
(17) The protection of game or fish;
(18) Chartering or licensing ferries or toll bridges;
(19) Remitting fines, penalties or forfeitures;
(20) Creating, increasing, or decreasing fees, percentage or allowances of public officers, during the term for which said officers are elected or appointed;
(21) Changing the law of descent;
(22) Granting to any corporation, association or individual the right to lay down railroad tracks, or amending existing charters for such purposes.
(23) Granting to any corporation, association or individual any special or exclusive privilege, immunity or franchise whatever.

In all other cases where a general law can be made applicable, no special law shall be enacted.

*Note: For purposes of discussion, item numbers have been given to the enumerated cases. These numbers are not official.

History

The 1818 Constitution had no prohibition on special legislation. The 1848 Constitution nibbled at the edges of the problem. There was a specific prohibition against legislative divorces and against the "sale of any lands or real estate belonging in whole or in part to any individual or individuals." That Constitution also recommended creating private, but not municipal, corporations by general law, but did not actually prohibit private corporate charters. (See *History* of Sec. 1 of Art. XI, *infra*, p. 515.) By negative implication, the 1848 Constitution prohibited local legislation creating a township organization in a county. (See *History* of Sec. 5 of Art. X, *infra*, p. 496.)

By the time the 1870 Convention met, the problem of local and special legislation had become alarming. Some indication of the magnitude of the problem is given in the Municipal Home Rule Bulletin prepared for the 1920 Convention:

"The total mass of special legislation is indicated in the increasing volume of state laws. In 1857 the private laws formed a volume of 1,550 pages. By 1867, the private laws were published in three volumes of more than 2,500 pages, of which 1,050 related to cities, towns and schools. In 1869 there was a further increase to four volumes of 3,350 pages, of which 1,850 pages related to cities, towns and schools." (Bulletins 384.)

It is small wonder that the Committee on the Legislative Department of the 1870 Convention presented a section not differing too much from what became Section 22. The debate on the section opened with a proposal to substitute an absolute prohibition on passing "any local or special law in any case whatever." Several delegates supported this blanket prohibition, including one who observed that some of the itemized prohibitions covered subjects on which he had never known any private or special legislation to be passed. The principal argument for the "laundry list" approach was made by Mr. Medill of Chicago, a member of the committee. He said, in part:

"The members of the committee considered in detail all the objects of special legislation of which the people have complained for a quarter of a century or more, and we carefully provided against every instance of that kind. We went through the similar provisions in the Constitutions of other States, and copied all the best things we could find therein.

". . . It would be probably unsafe and imprudent to foreclose every contingency that might arise in the future, requiring some special act to be passed. There are some things that no Legislature can provide for, by general laws, in advance of the event or necessity. There are contingencies that may arise requiring a particular act for a local and particular purpose. . . . No human wisdom can foresee all the necessities and contingencies of the future." (Debates 583.)

Some delegates supported Mr. Medill's opposition to the blanket prohibition while other delegates indicated that they favored more freedom for the legislature than was provided by the committee proposal. Presumably, these two groups joined hands in voting. In any event, the blanket prohibition was voted down by voice vote and the Convention, sitting in Committee of the Whole, turned to a consideration of each clause of the section.

One and a half days were devoted to consideration of Section 22, about a third of which time concerned the foregoing effort to prohibit all special and local legislation. The balance of the debate, a full day, was mostly devoted to one enumerated case — "Incorporating cities, towns or villages, or changing or amending the charter of any town, city or village." Here the Cook County delegates were the principal opponents of the prohibition. (For their arguments, see *History* of Sec. 34, *infra*, p. 247.) At the end of the debate on the charter prohibition, all efforts at amendment were defeated by voice vote.

Most of the other enumerated cases proposed by the Committee on the Legislative Department were accepted as written or with a slight change, and in either case without extended debates. Two or three enumerated cases were offered from the floor and accepted, again without extended debate. There were one or two proposals to weaken prohibitions, but all were turned away. At the very end of the debate, the concluding "In all other cases" sentence was offered from the floor and accepted. When the section was considered by the Convention proper, the work of the Committee of the Whole was accepted without change. The Committee on Revision and Adjustment made some style changes, moved one prohibition to the article on corporations (Sec. 1 of Art. XI, *infra*, p. 515), and dropped a prohibition on extending a term of office by special act, since Section 28 of Article IV *(infra,* p. 236) is a total prohibition on such extensions.

The proposed 1922 Constitution preserved the "laundry list" format of this section with several changes, one of which is particularly instructive. To the enumerated "protection of game or fish" were added the words "unless by reasonable classification of waters." (See discussion below, p. 220, concerning the necessity for this exception.) Several items were omitted because they were adequately covered by other provisions. For example, at the time of adoption in 1870, the "county seat" removal enumeration was unnecessary by virtue of Section 4 of Article X. *(Infra,* p. 494.) Presumably, the 1922 drafters thought that locating a county seat for a new county would not arise. In any event, they omitted the prohibition. The other omissions were rules of practice in courts, changes of venue, and jurisdiction of justices' courts; elections of members of boards of supervisors; and the prohibition on increasing or decreasing fees and allowances. All of these were covered elsewhere. The prohibition on creating private corporations by special act was taken out of the article on corporations and placed in the "laundry list" section. The catch-all sentence at the end of Section 22 was made a separate section.

Explanation

Introduction: In general, it has been possible in preparing this analysis of the Illinois Constitution to include references to those court cases that have contributed significantly to the meaning or understanding of the section. In a way, a rather stripped-down annotation has been provided. It is not feasible to do this with Section 22. There are too many cases involved and, for reasons spelled out below, the cases cover almost the entire range of government activity, so that a comprehensive discussion of the cases would approach a discussion of the constitutionality of almost everything other than levying taxes that the legislature has attempted to do in the last hundred years. In what follows, there is a general discussion of local and special legislation and the problem of classification; a reference, as appropriate, to cases concerning each of the 23 enumerated cases; and a discussion of the catch-all prohibition on special legislation.

In General: Any discussion of this complicated subject of special and local legislation requires a primer-like exposition. To begin with, there is a clear-cut distinction between "local" and "special" legislation, but, unfortunately, the terms are used loosely and, as is so often the case, situations arise which do not fit the distinction neatly. A local law is one which applies only to the government of a portion of the territory of the state, and a special law is one which applies only to a portion of the state — its people, its institutions, its economy — in some sense other than geographical. A general law is one which applies universally. Local and special laws are known as "private laws" and general laws as "public laws." It must be pointed out that, in addition to the imprecise use of these terms, the accepted practice of classification, discussed below, results in "universal" laws which in fact have only a "local" application; and that, by use of Section 22 as the equivalent of an equal protection clause, general laws that are invalidated are said to be "local or special laws." Moreover, even an effort at precision in the use of the terms is difficult. For example, a general law may provide for local government charters under the mayor-council, the commission, or the city manager system. If one of the three forms of government is permitted to do something denied to the others, and a court invalidates the permission under Section 22, it is a neat question whether the problem is one of a "local law" or a "special law." In one sense, the matter deals with a limited geographical area, but in another sense, the distinctions are state-wide, and the problem hinges on the special way in which one of three groups is treated. (In another context, a recent case involving this very distinction is discussed below, pp. 211-12.)

Normally, in the law as elsewhere, the obvious violation of a rule not only creates no problems, it rarely occurs. This is true of local and special legislation. An obvious example of local legislation would be a statute proposing to permit the city of Onetown to have five dog-catchers, notwithstanding a general law that limited all cities to four dog-catchers. Another example would be a law which permitted Onetown to annex North Onetown, whether or not there was a general law setting forth a procedure for annexation. An obvious example of special legislation would be a bill granting a divorce to John Doe from his wife, Dosie. Another example would be a law granting a corporate charter to Tom, Dick and Harry for the business of operating an employment service.

In order to keep the problem of local and special legislation in perspective, it is appropriate to mention briefly the reasons for prohibiting it. The major reason, at least in the middle of the Twentieth Century, is that, if it is permitted, an inordinate amount of legislative time is taken up with local and special legislation. Connecticut, for example, until the adoption of a new constitution in 1965, permitted local and special legislation, and the common practice, particularly in the area of local legislation, was to solve any local problem by getting the local legislator to introduuce a private bill. Under such a system, legislators are normally interested only in their own private bills, and passage is relatively easy. Moreover, many legislators can achieve high status as easily by their attention to

the support of local and special legislation as by their qualities as legislators concerned with the problems of the state as a whole.

In the case of special legislation, there are two significant dangers. One
is that the influence of special interests is greatly increased and the likelihood of corruption, "honest and dishonest,". is accordingly increased. If
there is public concern, as there usually is, over the influence of special
interests in protecting themselves from the effect of general legislation,
such concern would be much greater if special legislation were freely
permitted. The other danger is that some special legislation, particularly
in the case of corporate charters, can create vested rights that cannot be
taken away easily. Much of the Nineteenth Century crusade against special legislation was directed at the effective "sale" of permanent privileges and the corruption that "greased" the way for such "sales."

One final point in the story of the history of local and special legislation
is that, by and large, legislators under a system permitting such legislation dislike it. But for obvious reasons, they find it most difficult to
resist the requests of their constituents. It borders on irony that those
students of constitutional theory who oppose restrictions on the power
of the legislature generally support a prohibition on special and local
legislation. (See the Model State Constitution's provision in the *Comparative Analysis* below.) It also borders on irony that legislators probably do not object to such a constitutional restriction on them, for there
is surely no easier way to turn away an insistent constituent than to point
to a prohibition in the Constitution. Perhaps two ironies make a right.

The reasons for prohibiting local and special legislation may be
exemplary, the examples of the evils may be delineated in blacks and
whites, and yet the realities of a complex society quickly introduce exceptions and circumlocutions that produce borders of gray. And the
controversies, the litigation, naturally fall in the gray area. The gray-area
problems of local legislation differ, however, from the problems of special legislation. Moreover, in the case of special legislation, for reasons
discussed below, rules have been imported into the gray area that are
actually irrelevant to the real evil of special legislation. The portman-
teau word that carries within it all these grays is "classification."

In the case of local legislation, a simple black and white example of
five dog-catchers for Onetown was given above. But suppose that Onetown were the only city in the state which bordered on an uninhabited
wilderness in which there were packs of wild dogs. It would make great
sense to permit Onetown to have more dog-catchers than other cities in
the state. (If it is asked why the state concerns itself with the number of
dog-catchers anyway, it can be assumed that experience has taught that
the job of dog-catcher is a traditional sinecure for faithful party workers

and that without a state limit, many cities would end up with dozens of dog-catchers who drew pay but did no work.) This assumed example demonstrates the means by which general legislation can be constructed which is applicable only to one locality. Instead of passing a bill allowing Onetown to have five dog-catchers, the legislature amends the general law by including an exception for any city bordered by an uninhabited wilderness. The exception purports to be general, but in fact applies only to Onetown. (There is a special problem in drafting, discussed below in connection with Professor Kales' article, which would make it advisable to include after the word "wilderness" such words as "conducive to the harboring of packs of wild dogs which prey on such bordering city.")

From the foregoing analogy, it is easy to see that there are innumerable matters of justifiable state concern, even with acceptance of maximum home rule, in which the impact of legislation on Chicago should be different from the impact on any other city in the state. In most instances, the reason for this is that Chicago is different because it is so large. The classification solution is simply to pass a general law applicable to cities with a population in excess of 500,000. Again, the assumption must be that the classification is reasonable in relation to the purpose of the legislation. It would be difficult to support a classification applicable to cities in excess of 500,000 if there were three large cities with populations of 468,000, 493,000, and 531,000, respectively. But if the third city was the only one on a lake and if the purpose of the statute was related in some way to the presence of a lake, then a classification of coverage of cities over 500,000 bordering on a lake would be a rational one. There have been occasions in some states when the legislature goes to the other extreme. Instead of passing what is a legitimate general law tailored to a special local problem, the legislature tries to pass a purely local law by the device of an artificial classification. For example, a bill applicable to cities over 95,000 but under 100,000 in population would be suspect, for there can hardly be a legitimate purpose for singling out such a narrow population spread. (For an Illinois example of a classification by description found to be too narrow, see Pettibone v. West Chicago Park Comm'rs, 215 Ill. 304 (1905).)

In 1906, Albert M. Kales, a noted legal scholar, wrote an article in the *Illinois Law Review,* now the *Northwestern Law Review,* under the title "Special Legislation as Defined in the Illinois Cases." (1 Ill. L. Rev. 63.) Professor Kales was an authority in a completely different field of law, and the explanation for his article appears to be simply that he was rather annoyed with a broadside attack on constitutional prohibitions against local legislation which had appeared the previous year. (*See* Hubbard, "Special Legislation for Municipalities," 18 Harv. L. Rev. 588 (1905).) In any event, Kales carefully analyzed the Illinois cases, mostly involving local legislation, or more accurately, local problems treated on a selective basis by the classification device. Kales pointed out at the beginning of his article that he was not in any way concerned with general regulatory legislation that was called special legislation because the courts disagreed with the legislative basis for determination of whom or what to regulate. (See discussion of special legislation below.)

After analyzing the local legislation cases in Illinois to the date of his article, Kales extracted three principles, as follows:

"First: If there is a rational ground for legislating in behalf of the objects to which the Act applies and not for others of the same general sort, and if the rationale of the distinction is embodied in the Act's description of the objects themselves to which it applies, then the Act is not 'local or special' law. (Kales, "Special Legislation as Defined in the Illinois Cases," 1 Ill. L. Rev. 63, 66-67 (1906).)

"Second: If there be no rational ground of distinction, on any view of the facts, upon which some objects are legislated for and others of the same general sort are not, the Act is a 'local or special' law. (*Id.* at 70.)

"Third: Even if there be one or more rational grounds for legislating in behalf of the objects to which the Act applies and not for others of the same general sort, yet *if no rational ground is embodied in the Act's description of the objects to which it applies* then the Act is held to be 'local or special.' " (*Id.* at. 76.)

There are three comments to be made about these three principles. The first comment is that the first two principles are neither startling nor earth-shaking. They represent the careful, scholarly formulation of the two sides of the obvious proposition that a good reason is required to support "general" legislation that is not universally applicable. It is Kales' third principle that is a key to acceptable classification. Kales is saying, in effect, that if the legislature has a reason for classification, it must state what the reason is and the courts will judge the rationality of the classification by the stated reasons, not by any conceivable basis that someone might dream up. The importance of this formulation is that it may explain the invalidation of legislation which appears to have a rational basis for classification. It is this type of invalidation that causes people to throw up their hands in despair at understanding the theory of classification.

In order to put some meat on the Kales' skeleton, it is appropriate to review the examples that he used to demonstrate his third principle. His principal one is *People* ex rel. *Gleeson v. Meech* (101 Ill. 200 (1881)), where the Supreme Court invalidated an act which said that justices of the peace should have county-wide jurisdiction except in Cook County which was to be divided into two districts, one consisting of Chicago and the other of the balance of the county. Suppose, Kales suggested, the act had said that every county should have one district except a county containing a city with a population in excess of 100,000, in which case there should be two districts. The point Kales made was that the actual statute singled out Cook County, whereas his suggestion separated counties into two classes on a basis that on its face was rational.

He drove his point home by contrasting two cases that involved statutes passed as a result of the Chicago fire. One case involved the Burnt Records Act which dealt with establishing land titles in any county whose land records had been destroyed by fire. The act was upheld. (Bertrand v. Taylor, 87 Ill. 235 (1877).) The other case involved a statute of limited duration authorizing a county with a population in excess of 100,000 to issue bonds for the construction of a courthouse on a site "heretofore used for that purpose." The act was held invalid. (Devine v. Board of Comm'rs, 84 Ill. 590 (1877).) Kales noted that the first statute applied only to Cook County but by its terms would apply to any other county which ever lost its land records by fire, whereas the second statute in fact simply permitted Cook County to issue bonds for a new courthouse. Presumably, though Kales was not this explicit, if the legislature had authorized any county which lost its courthouse by fire to issue bonds for a new courthouse, the statute would have been upheld. It might even have been possible to qualify the fire as one causing a specified amount of destruction in the county seat in order to limit the authority to a situation where special power to issue bonds would be essential. Kales concluded his article by conceding that the distinctions made were a matter of form, but he maintained that form is important if the courts are to be able to determine that there is a reasonable basis for classification.

The second comment to be made about the Kales' principles is that with all their precision, they had an accordion word throughout — "rational." One man's "rational" is another man's "irrational," and judges are men. It is likely that any group of lawyers could sit around a table reviewing all the local legislation cases of Illinois and agree on the controlling principles of decision while disagreeing on whether the courts followed the principles.

The third comment is a corollary to the foregoing. The process of deciding whether a given classification is or is not rational is sufficiently subjective that the milieu in which the problem arises may influence the course of decision. For example, in the recent case of In re *Struck* (41 Ill. 2d 574 (1969)), the Supreme Court decided that the provision of the Municipal Code that permits the recall of elective officials under the commission form of government is invalid under Section 22 because "there is no reasonable relation between the objectives sought to be accomplished by the recall procedure and the differences in the various forms of municipal government. Either the recall procedure should apply to none, or all forms of municipal government should be free to adopt it." (*Id.* at 579.) The interesting point about the facts of that case is that the alleged ground for wanting the officials removed was that they had voted for ordinances that they knew the voters opposed. The ordinances were the Uniform Housing Code and Uniform Building Code Short Form, the State Plumbing Code, a national Fire Prevention Code, and the National Electrical Code. Although simply disagreeing with policy decisions is an acceptable reason for recall, one can speculate whether the Court would have read the problem of classification differently in a case where the petition alleged bribery, corruption and embezzlement rather than opposition to ordinances of a type generally believed worthwhile. In any event, it is certain that the judicial process of determining when a classification is acceptably rational is one in which the governing principles may be crystal clear but the prediction of decisions under the principles is difficult. (Compare the discussion of "Revival and Amendment" under Sec. 13, *supra,* p. 160.)

This discussion of local legislation may be summarized thus: (1) The purpose of a ban on local legislation is to prevent the state legislature from concerning itself with a purely local problem. (2) But, a state problem does not affect all parts of the state in the same way, and the legislature is entitled to classify parts of the state in order to produce a reasonable solution to a state problem. (3) In steering a course between (1) and (2), a court should demand that the legislature so draft its statutes that the rationality of the classification is explicit. (4) Notwithstanding the clarity of the principles involved, there is such latitude in applying them that the courts have considerable freedom, and there is little assurance that accurate predictions can be made — by legislature or litigants.

The story of special legislation is quite different. As noted earlier, there is little difficulty in recognizing a blatant bit of special legislation, and, in fact, legislatures do not pass that kind of bill. The difficulty arises because it is almost impossible to legislate on a truly universal basis. Any statute, explicitly or implicitly, excludes somebody or something. Even the fundamental proposition that anyone born in the United States is a citizen has an explicit exception. The Fourteenth Amendment to the United States Constitution includes the phrase, "and subject to the jurisdiction thereof," thereby excepting, for example, children born of parents who have diplomatic immunity. Thus, courts enforcing a prohibition on special legislation are constantly faced with an argument that the general law before the court is really a special law because of some exclusion from coverage.

Out of all this grows the body of rules of classification. The short statement is that a law remains general so long as the basis for inclusion and exclusion under the law is reasonable. But, as in the case of reasonable classification for local laws discussed above, the statement of principle is of limited value, for reasonable men frequently disagree about what is reasonable. Moreover, as discussed earlier in connection with Section 1 of this Article (*supra*, p. 111), reasonableness of classification has been used by the courts in the same manner as they use the due process and equal protection clauses. That is, .the determination of reasonableness becomes, to some extent, an expression of opinion on the soundness of the legislature's action.

One fairly recent case, *Monmouth v. Lorenz* (30 Ill. 2d 60 (1963)), will suffice to demonstrate the complexity of classification as an element in the judicial process. The case involved the Prevailing Wage Law (Ill. Rev. Stat. ch. 48, §§ 39s-1 to 39s-12 (1967)), which requires the payment of wages at the prevailing area rate to craft workers on public works construction projects. One of the specific issues in the case was the validity of the requirement that such prevailing wages had to be paid to construction employees of government bodies as well as to construction workers employed by private contractors building public works. The law "in effect made a single classification of all employers of laborers, workmen and mechanics engaged in the construction of public works whether the employer be a contractor or a public body." (City of Monmouth v. Lorenz, 30 Ill. 2d 60, 65-66 (1963).)

The Court continued:

"It is well established that equal protection of the law is not violated as long as the selection of objects for inclusion and exclusion within the class, upon which the legislation acts, rests upon a rational basis. ... Here the legislation has put into a single class public bodies and construction contractors which are for most purposes two entirely different classes. It is true that each class may employ laborers, workmen and mechanics for the construction of public works and that the legislation in question deals only with this common characteristic of the two classes. Labels may be deceptive, however, and labeling the two classes as employers of workmen for the construction of public works does not cover the vital and real differences between the two classes of employers and their respective employment relationships with their employees. Government employment is generally of a steady nature and entails fringe benefits, whereas employment by a private contractor is unusually seasonal and does not carry like fringe benefits. These disadvantages of seasonal employment and lack of fringe benefits are compensated, of course, by the payment of higher wages. The workmen employed by the public body may do as well as or better in the long run than the workmen employed by a private contractor although his *rate* of pay be not as high. The object of the legislation in question is to insure that workmen on public projects receive the same economic benefits as workmen on projects of a similar nature by regulating the rate of pay they are to receive but rate of pay is just one factor in determining the economic benefits to be derived from employment, and where, as here, the two classes of employers are by their very nature in such a position that they cannot and do not confer similar economic benefits on their employees exclusive of the rate of pay, an act requiring both classes to pay their employees on construction at the same rate violates the equal protection clause of both the fourteenth amendment to the Federal constitution and section 22 of article IV of the Illinois constitution." (*Id.* at 67-68.)

The foregoing quoted excerpt from the *Monmouth* case serves as a demonstration of the somewhat subjective nature of the determination of the reasonableness of a given classification, as a demonstration of the complexity of the concept of classification, and as an example of the difficulty of trying to cover in this *Explanation* the entire range of constitutional decisions on reasonableness of classification.

The words "somewhat subjective" are used because, following the initial sentence setting forth the general principle of classification, the Court's opinion is simply a well-reasoned argument for not requiring the payment of prevailing construction wages to government employees. It is a wise argument that should have been made to the legislature and one that many people would think should have prevailed. But wisdom aside, it is not easy to see how a legislature can be labeled irrational for deciding that all people who work on public construction should be paid the prevailing wage.

The *Monmouth* case also demonstrates the complexity of classification. Consider, first, the initial sentence of the quoted portion of the opinion. It speaks of "equal protection," not of "general legislation." It speaks of "objects for inclusion and exclusion within the class," not of "exclusion" only. Thus, the sentence prepares the ground for invalidating the legislation under Section 22 on the ground that two things that are different are treated alike. Conceptually, this is understandable in the context of equal protection of the laws, but it is most difficult to conceive of a law as "special" because it is universal rather than limited in its application.

Once it is recognized that the prohibition on special legislation has been used by the courts for purposes far beyond the particular evils which the drafters of the 1870 Constitution had in mind, it is clear that no comprehensive annotation can be undertaken here. In the Annotation to Section 22 by Smith-Hurd there are over 180 headings, of which approximately 85 deal with the 23 enumerated cases. Most of the rest of the headings deal either with the general principles of classification or with different businesses, occupations, and other specific subjects. One heading, "Classification for legislative purposes—In general," (Smith-Hurd, Illinois Annotated Statutes, Constitution, arts. I-V at 643 (1964)), includes two paragraphs simply listing cases, in the one instance of those in which the classification was held void, and in the other of those in which the classification was sustained. A third paragraph cites a couple of cases for the proposition:

"The classification of objects of legislation is not required to be scientific, logical or consistent, if it is reasonably adapted to secure purpose for which it is intended, and is not purely arbitrary." (*Id.*)

The general principle is clear; the application, case by case, is not.

The Specified Prohibitions:

(1) *Granting Divorces*: Apparently, the legislature has never tried to violate this prohibition. Two court cases have, however, referred to it. In one case, a rather far-fetched attack was made on a statute permitting waivers of a 60-day waiting requirement in divorce actions under which individual judges could differ in deciding what facts justified a waiver. The Supreme Court gave short shrift to the claim that a special law granting divorces was involved. (People *ex rel.* Doty v. Connell, 9 Ill. 2d 390 (1956).) In the other case, a statutory effort to provide different procedures for divorce actions in counties of over 500,000 population was invalidated under the local law rule discussed earlier, but was held not to be a special law under this specific prohibition. (Hunt v. County of Cook, 398 Ill. 412 (1947).)

(2) *Changing Names*: No cases and, presumably, no special laws. Obviously, it is necessary on occasion to change the name of a place. This prohibition simply forces the legislature to delegate the power to make changes. (*See, e.g.,* Ill. Rev. Stat. ch. 105, § 8-9 (1967), giving the governing board of a park district the power to change the name of a park.)

(3) *Laying Out Roads*: An act attempting to validate an administrative selection of a road route appears to be the only truly special act invalidated under this prohibition. (Watts v. Department of Pub. Works & Bldgs., 328 Ill. 587 (1928).) Other cases involving roads have been cases of local versus general legislation. For example, it was held not permissible to make highway commissioners in nontownship counties personally liable for negligence in not keeping roads repaired while leaving commissioners in township counties not liable. (Kennedy v. McGovern, 246 Ill. 497 (1910).) (See also discussion on *Vacating Roads* below.)

(4) *Vacating Roads*: In a few instances of these specific prohibitions, it is evident that in fact action can be taken only on a case-by-case basis and that the legislature has to adopt a general law that delegates to someone the power to act. In 1870 there was no state highway system, and presumably the prohibition was aimed at preventing the legislature from superseding local governments. But somebody must have the power to vacate a single road, and the courts have recognized that a general law which delegates such power to a subordinate agency is no violation

of the prohibition. (*See* People *ex rel.* Hill v. Eakin, 383 Ill. 383 (1943); People *ex rel.* Franchere v. City of Chicago, 321 Ill. 466 (1926).)

(5) *County Seats*: No cases and undoubtedly no special acts. Indeed, so far as changing county seats is concerned, this prohibition was redundant from the beginning by virtue of Section 4 of Article X, covering removal of county seats. See *infra*, p. 494.)

(6) *Regulating County Affairs*: There are many cases involving statutes regulating county and township affairs, but they all appear to deal with validity of the classification under a general law. As a matter of fact, any local or special law purporting to be a general law within the coverage of any of the 23 specific prohibitions falls as a specifically prohibited act once the classification is found to be unreasonable. To put it another way, in one sense there are no local laws under this specific prohibition because there have been no laws regulating the affairs of County A by name or Township B by name; but in another sense, there have been such laws because the courts have refused to accept the purported classification.

(7) *Practice in Courts*: It is not clear whether this prohibition was aimed primarily at preventing a special act giving John Doe a one-shot procedural favor — *e.g.*, a cause of action notwithstanding the running of the statute of limitation — or at preventing a special act covering practice in one specific court — *e.g.*, the time to answer is extended from 20 days to 30 days in a particular circuit court. It seems doubtful that the prohibition was aimed at any of the types of legislation that have fallen afoul of it. For example, the Supreme Court once said that a statute setting forth the weight to be given to an administrative adjudication under workmen's compensation was a special law regulating the practice of courts. (Otis Elevator Co. v. Industrial Comm'n, 302 Ill. 90 (1922). The Court also said that the provision was in violation of separation of powers under Article III and contrary to due process. See discussion of Art. III, *supra,* p. 99.) Relatively recently, the Supreme Court struck down a provision under the school code which allowed only ten days in which to appeal one type of administrative decision while other types could be appealed within 35 days. (Board of Educ. v. County Bd. of School Trustees, 28 Ill. 2d 15 (1963).) Statutes such as are involved in cases like these purport to be general laws, and the question raised is the reasonableness of the "classification," normally in the sense of due process or equal protection of the law.

There are other cases involving court practice in which the classification problem is the traditional geographical local law situation discussed earlier. For example, a requirement for the payment of a jury fee is reasonable, even if in fact applicable only to Cook County. (Hunt

v. Rosènbaum Grain Corp., 355 Ill. 504 (1934). The Court also said that "juries" were not included under "practice in courts.") But a population classification of counties for the purpose of appointment of administrators of estates of nonresidents was held not reasonable. (Strong v. Dignan, 207 Ill. 385 (1904). As to the question of general legislative power over rules of practice, see *Explanation* of Art. III, *supra,* p. 99.)

(8) *Jurisdiction of Justices*: One of the cases on classification, *People* ex rel. *Gleeson v. Meech* (101 Ill. 200 (1881)), discussed earlier in connection with Professor Kales' article (*supra,* p. 210), was invalidated as a local law regulating the jurisdiction of justices of the peace. In view of the abolition of justices of the peace and police magistrates under the new Article VI, this specific prohibition is now presumably a dead letter.

(9) *Changes of Venue*: As in the case of other specific prohibitions, the original purpose of this change of venue restriction was probably to stop the legislature from passing private legislation such as shifting John Doe's suit to a different county notwithstanding the general venue statute. The only cases that appear to have arisen involved general venue matters. In one instance, special venue rules were proposed for the municipal courts of Chicago, but the statute fell because venue was not considered to be within the scope of permitted local legislation under Section 34 (*infra,* p. 246), and, paradoxically, part of a law which had been tailored to Chicago's special court system could not stand because Section 34 did not authorize a venue variation. (Feigen v. Shaeffer, 256 Ill. 493 (1912).) In the other instance, the Supreme Court gave short shrift to an argument that a venue differential between town courts and circuit courts was prohibited by Section 22. (People *ex rel.* Norwegian-American Hospital, Inc. v. Sandusky, 21 Ill. 2d 296 (1961).)

(10) *Special Municipal Charters:* This prohibition was one upon which the delegates in 1870 were most insistent. The speediest way to induce proliferation of local legislation is to allow special municipal charters, because subsequent amendments will also be by local law. But, as noted earlier (*supra,* p. 207), genuinely universal general laws are not practicable, and classification of one sort and another becomes a common practice. The earlier extended discussion on classification is applicable here.

Nevertheless, it is important to note that the prohibition is limited to "town, city or village." It is possible, therefore, to create a "municipal corporation" by special act. (*See* People *ex rel.* Coutrakon v. Lohr, 9 Ill. 2d 539 (1956).) Of course, such a "municipal corporation" would not be available to regulate county and township affairs ((6) above), or management of common schools ((13) below). (See also discussion of final sentence of Sec. 22, *infra*, p. 222.)

It has been noted from time to time in this discussion, that courts use "special legislation" as a way to get at general laws that, in the eyes of the court, violate concepts of due process and equal protection. The same judicial manipulation of the concept of "local legislation" has been indulged in. In *Kremers v. City of West Chicago* (406 Ill. 546 (1950)), the Supreme Court was faced with a statute which set a state-wide maximum rate for a library tax for cities, towns and villages. The computation of the maximum was tied to a figure for an earlier year in such a manner that the maximum possible levy would vary "irrationally" from town to town. The Court held the statute invalid. Such a statute does not appear on its face to be a local law "changing or amending the charter." But the Court said that if a statute purporting to be a "general law is to establish dissimilarity in the powers and modes of different municipalities in the levy and collection of taxes, then, since the laws conferring such powers and prescribing such modes become a part of the charters of the municipalities, it will be regarded as within the prohibition of [this section prohibiting local or special laws for incorporating municipalities or changing or amending municipal charters]." (*Id.* at 552.) It is also noteworthy that the statute in question was as "general" as it could be — one formula universally applicable. Unfortunately, it was a bad formula. (Compare the discussion of the *Monmouth* case, *supra*, p. 213.)

(11) *Election of Supervisors*: No cases and presumably no questionable statutes.

(12) *Summoning Juries*: There have been a few cases that referred to this prohibition, but none dealt with the literal meaning of it, which would seem to be designed to cover special acts which summoned and impaneled specific grand and petit juries out of the ordinary course of judicial administration. The cases that have arisen generally appear to have involved statutes classifying counties according to population so that Cook County had different rules for juries. In one case, a section providing a lower maximum age for jury service in Cook County was held invalid, but all other parts of the statute were upheld. (People v. Bain, 358 Ill. 177 (1934). Incidentally, the jury commissioners in Cook County had ignored the age differential and no one had been "injured" by the law.)

(13) *Management of Schools*: The key word in this prohibition is "management." Local laws concerning schools are prohibited only if they deal with "management." Two early cases stated that this referred only to conduct of the schools in imparting instruction. (Fuller v. Heath,

89 Ill. 296 (1878); Speight v. People *ex rel.* County Collector, 87 Ill. 595 (1877).) Both of these early cases concluded that laws concerning raising revenue for schools were not within the specified prohibition. Likewise, a law concerning the filling of vacancies on certain types of school boards does not come under the prohibition. (People *ex rel.* Peterson v. Pollock, 306 Ill. 358 (1922).) It follows that many local laws concerning education may be passed. (*See, e.g.,* Land Comm'rs of the Commons v. President & Trustees of the Commons, 249 Ill. 578 (1911).)

Nevertheless there are a great many cases involving school legislation, and some of them invalidate legislation which purports to be general. In almost all cases, invalidity was based on the "exclusive privilege" prohibition. (*See, e.g.,* People *ex rel.* Board of Educ. v. Read, 344 Ill. 397 (1931). See (23), *infra,* p. 221.)

(14) *Interest*: A handful of cases involved attacks on legislation dealing with interest, but in all instances the legislation survived. The ground was either that the classification was reasonable (*e.g.,* Meier v. Hilton, 257 Ill. 174 (1912)), or that the "interest" was actually a penalty, as in delinquency in payment of taxes (*e.g.,* People *ex rel.* Johnson v. Peacock, 98 Ill. 172 (1881)).

(15) *Elections*: It is sometimes unclear what evil produced one of these specific prohibitions, but, presumably, the evil was one of special ad hoc legislation. In the case of elections, the presumption would be that the type of act to be prohibited would be one changing the general law for one specific election for some specific political advantage. If this presumption is correct, it can be said that the legislature does not appear to have passed any such law. The reported cases have concerned general laws under attack on some argument of improper classification. (*See, e.g.,* Heimgaertner v. Benjamin Elec. Mfg. Co., 6 Ill. 2d 152 (1955); Larvenette v. Elliott, 412 Ill. 523 (1952).)

(16) *Realty of Minors*: The purpose of this prohibition is obvious. Many instances arise when land cannot be conveyed because someone with an interest therein is under a disability. It would be tempting, if permissible, to get the land transferred by legislative fiat. As the *History* above notes, this sort of legislation was forbidden under the 1848 Constitution. Except for two cases prior to 1890, neither of which seems particularly relevant today, no question appears to have arisen under this specific prohibition.

(17) *Fish and Game*: Whatever the original reason for inserting this prohibition, the principal result was a disastrous judicial holding that caused the drafters of the 1922 Constitution to modify the prohibition. (*Supra,* p. 206.) An act required a license for fishing with a hoop net or

seine in any state waters except Lake Michigan. The exclusion of Lake Michigan was held to make it a special act void under this prohibition. (People v. Wilcox, 237 Ill. 421 (1908).) Three judges dissented on the grounds of reasonableness of the classification, and it appears probable that the Court would now follow the dissenters. (*See* People v. Diekmann, 285 Ill. 97 (1918).)

(18) *Ferries and Toll Bridges*: No charters or licenses for ferries or toll bridges appear to have been granted by special act, or if they were, no one appears to have objected by way of a lawsuit.

(19) *Remittance of Fines*: The Supreme Court once pointed out that the purpose of this prohibition was to prevent the legislature from remitting a particular fine or penalty. (Compare the *History* of Sec. 23, *infra*, p. 226.) The court went on to note that the legislature could authorize courts to remit fines. (People v. Heise, 257 Ill. 443 (1913).) Notwithstanding a judicial explanation of the purpose of the provision, the Supreme Court some years later invalidated a law, limited by classification to Cook County, under which delinquent taxes could be paid in installments. The Court said it was a local law remitting fines, penalties and forfeitures. (People *ex rel.* Clarke v. Jarecki, 363 Ill. 180 (1936).) The Court could have said that the act was a local law regulating county affairs ((6) above), or even a special law granting an exclusive privilege ((23) below), on the theory that only Cook County taxpayers had the exclusive privilege of paying delinquent taxes on the installment plan. Apparently, litigants and courts are not overly fastidious about which local and special law slot they use. (See also discussion below concerning exclusive privileges.)

(20) *Changing Compensation:* This prohibition was probably redundant when adopted in 1870 and is certainly so under judicial interpretation of other sections of the Constitution. It would appear that anyone who could be covered by a local or special law would be covered by one of the other sections prohibiting compensation changes by general law. (See the discussion of Sec. 11 of Art. IX, *infra*, pp. 473-7.)

(21) *Changing Law of Descent:* This is a prohibition, like granting divorces, changing names, selling real estate, and remitting fines, aimed at private bills that are designed to allow a John Doe to inherit property contrary to the general rules of descent. Only two cases appear to have referred to the prohibition and both of them dealt with general laws. (*See* Jahnke v. Selle, 368 Ill. 268 (1938); Wunderle v. Wunderle, 114 Ill. 40 (1893).) The *Wunderle* case is noteworthy, however, because the situation is conceptually comparable to the *Kremers* case discussed under (10) above. In *Wunderle,* the general law prohibited any nonresident alien from acquiring real estate by descent, but certain treaties of the United States

permitted such acquisition. The Supreme Court would not go beyond the general law to consider its actual operation.

(22) *Railroad Tracks:* This prohibition was aimed at one aspect of the internal improvement abuses of the middle of the Nineteenth Century. The whole business is substantially dead today. Indeed, except for an early case in 1874, only one case appears to have referred to this prohibition, and that was a traditional action to determine the constitutionality of a new authority. (*See* People v. Chicago Transit Authority, 392 Ill. 77 (1945).) Resort to the railroad track prohibition was a makeweight and so treated by the Court.

(23) *Special Privileges:* It has been noted in several instances above that the original purpose of an enumerated prohibition was lost sight of long ago. This is particularly true of this last specific prohibition. The evil of special legislation which the 1870 delegates had in mind was the act that gave John Doe or the John Doe Corporation an exclusive franchise or privilege of some sort. In some manner that cannot be traced here — if it can be traced at all — the special privileges prohibition became a constitutional vehicle for attacking discriminatory legislation. The prohibition is, in effect, Illinois' version of the Fourteenth Amendment's equal protection clause. Indeed, the Supreme Court has said as much:

"This provision supplements the equal-protection clause of the fourteenth amendment to the federal constitution and prevents the enlargement of the rights of one or more persons in discrimination against the rights of others." (Schuman v. Chicago Transit Authority, 704 Ill. 313, 317 (1950).)

For the reasons set forth at the beginning of this *Explanation,* it is not feasible to cover all of the many examples of discrimination in legislative treatment of individuals, associations or corporations — those found valid and those found invalid. Nor is there any need to discuss the general principles involved, for they are set out in the introductory discussion of special legislation. (*Supra,* pp. 212-15.) There is, however, one technical interpretation of the prohibition that should be noted. The word "corporation" is limited to private corporations. Exclusive privileges not otherwise invalid may be granted to public corporations. (*See* People *ex rel.* Greening v. Green, 382 Ill. 577 (1943).)

From the discussion up to now, particularly the relatively detailed analysis of several cases, it should be clear that there is almost no limit to the way in which an argument of discrimination can be turned into one of exclusive privilege. For example, if a law classifies counties or cities on a basis which the courts do not deem reasonable, and if the subject matter cannot be pushed under one of the first 22 prohibitions, it probably can be called an exclusive privilege. If the law is burdensome, the counties or cities not covered have a privilege denied others; if the law confers a benefit, the counties or cities covered have a privilege, denied the others. If a "general" law affects some people and not others, and if courts consider the differentiation unreasonable, one group or the other has an exclusive privilege, depending on whether the law is beneficial or burdensome. Even in cases where the law treats all alike and the courts think that it is unreasonable not to differentiate, it may be possible to argue that some part of "all" gets a privilege denied to the rest of "all."

There may be occasions when it is not possible to find an exclusive privilege, but this need not stop the courts. Consider the *Monmouth* case discussed above. *(Supra,* p. 213.) That case, it will be recalled, struck down a requirement that both public bodies and private contractors pay prevailing wages to construction workers on public works. It is difficult to find an exclusive privlege here or any other specific prohibition that fits. But then the Court apparently did not either. It simply said that the act violated Section 22.

It is probably safe to say that by now the equal protection/special legislation rule is so firmly established that there is no longer a need to be precise in relating an alleged local or special act to one of the specific prohibitions. If the relation is obvious, that is all to the good. But of it is not obvious, a demonstration of unreasonable classification or discrimination will undoubtedly suffice.

In All Other Cases: In the light of the preceding paragraph, it is paradoxical to mention two flat statements that the courts consistently make. One is that there is no absolute prohibition against a local or special law on any subject not included in the 23 enumerated cases. *(See* Foutch v. Zempel, 332 Ill. 192 (1928).) The other statement is that the admonition to act by general law whenever applicable is addressed to the legislature and not to the courts. If the legislature passes a local or special law not otherwise prohibited, the courts consider such passage a conclusive and unreviewable finding by the legislature that a general law cannot be made applicable. (Wilson v. Board of Trustees, 133 Ill. 443 (1890).)

Paradoxical or not, there is good reason for the first of these rules. There are a great many occasions when a local or special act is the proper, perhaps the only, way to solve a legislative problem. The way must be cleared by a judicial affirmation that the last sentence of Section 22 means that sometimes local and special laws are permissible. (The word "local" does not appear in the last sentence, but there is no reason to believe that the 1870 Convention meant anything by this omission. In any event, the courts do not appear to have considered the omission significant). If some local and special laws are permissible, the only logical way to accept them is to say that they may cover any subject not excluded by the 23 enumerated cases. Indeed, the last sentence begins "In all other cases . . . ."

Once the courts have come to this conclusion, it is easy for them to embrace the second rule. The assumption is that the Constitution has covered all the serious local and special legislation evils. Why then, the courts might ask themselves, should we "knock ourselves out" trying to determine "in all other cases" whether or not the legislature could have handled some problem by a general law? Moreover, the courts might sense that once they agree to review such acts, the legislature will start dressing them up in tortured language of generality. (See further discussion in *Comment* below.)

Perhaps the best way to explain the paradoxes of Section 22 is to reclassify the types of laws which may be involved. Using "local" in the geographical sense and "special" in the nongeographical sense, there are the following types of laws that can get involved with Section 22:

  (a) A local law which is prohibited by one of the enumerated cases.
  (b) An artificial general law which is actually a local law in a prohibited area.
  (c) A local law which is not prohibited.
  (d) A special law which is prohibited by one of the enumerated cases.
  (e) A special law which is not prohibited.
  (f) A general law which the courts find unconstitutionally discriminatory and therefore call "special."

(Note that there is no artificial general law which is actually special. So long as the courts use Section 22 to strike at discriminatory general laws, an artificial general law would fall in that category.)

Comparative Analysis

Approximately 36 states have some general prohibition against the enactment of local and special laws. Fourteen states, including most of the New England states, do not. Some of these 14 states may, however, have limited local or special law prohibitions. For example, two of the 14, Delaware and New York, prohibit legislative divorces. The new Connecticut Constitution for the first time contains an article on home rule. The local law prohibition reads:

"After July 1, 1969, the general assembly shall enact no special legislation relative to the powers, organization, terms of elective offices or form of government of any single town, city or borough, except as to (a) borrowing power, (b) validating acts, and (c) formation, consolidation or dissolution of any town, city or borough, unless in the delegation of legislative authority by general law the general assembly shall have failed to prescribe the powers necessary to effect the purpose of such special legislation." (Conn. Const. art. X, § 1.)

(The Constitution was effective at the end of 1965. The July 1, 1969, effective date for prohibiting local legislation was necessary to give the General Assembly adequate time to adopt the necessary general laws.)

It is not essential to compare every one of the 23 enumerated cases with other states, but a significant sampling seems appropriate:

Changing names (2)	31 states
County seats (5)	24 states
County affairs (6)	19 states
Change of venue (9)	25 states
Municipal charters (10)	20 states
Juries (12)	22 states
Interest rates (14)	23 states
Property of minors (16)	27 states
Law of descent (21)	24 states
Exclusive privileges (23)	31 states

(Citizens Conference on State Legislatures, State Constitutional Provisions Affecting Legislatures (May 1967).)

The United States Constitution has no comparable restriction and Congress regularly passes special acts. The equal protection clause in the Fourteenth Amendment applies only to the states, but the United States Supreme Court has made the due process clause of the Fifth Amendment, which is applicable to Congressional action, serve as an equal protection clause. Thus, the United States Supreme Court has found a substitute, just as the Illinois Supreme Court found a substitute in Section 22.

The Model State Constitution has the following recommended provision:

"*Special Legislation.* The legislature shall pass no special or local act when a general act is or can be made applicable, and whether a general act is or can be made applicable shall be a matter for judicial determination." (art. IV, § 4.11.)

(See also the home rule provisions of the Model quoted in the *Comparative Analysis* of Sec. 34 of this Article and Sec. 5 of Art. X, *infra*, pp. 251 and 498.)

The Commentary to the Model states, in part:

"The distinction between general and special laws may be far from clear in any given case.

"But, even though the question as to what is a special law may not be capable of a categorical answer, it is not the major question under the common constitutional provison that no special law be passed when a general one is or can be made applicable. Rather, the problem has been when *is* a general law applicable and who is to determine, finally, whether or not such a general act is or can be made applicable.

"In the absence of specific constitutional directions, state courts have divided on the issue as to which branch of government is to make this determination. Some have held that this is not open to judicial review but can be decided only by the legislature, while others have held that the question is initially for the legislature but that the courts may set aside the legislative judgment when the determination of the legislature is arbitrary, unreasonable or clearly an abuse of discretion. Still others hold the question to be a purely judicial one. In any event, it has been troublesome in some jurisdictions where the courts have wavered in the holdings from case to case." (Model State Constitution 56.)

It should be noted that the observations above (*supra*, p. 222) concerning the Illinois Supreme Court's rule that legislative determinations "In all other cases" are not reviewable is not necessarily inconsistent with the foregoing Commentary. In the absence of a large number of enumerated prohibitions, the Model's approach is the only one that assures some control over a legislature bent on evading the constitutional restriction.

Comment

It seems fair to begin by observing that Section 22, with its hundreds of judicial offspring, is a "mess." Unfortunately, in this imperfect world, it is a lot easier to criticize than it is to offer a blueprint for perfection. The way to proceed is not at all clear, and suggestions can only be tentative.

First, it seems feasible to abandon the "laundry list" approach. A constitution is supposed to be a fundamental document, and if a limitation on legislative power is appropriate, it ought to be possible to express the limitation in the form of a statement of principle. Moreover, some of the 23 enumerated cases probably were not necessary in 1870, and even more are probably so unlikely today that it would no longer occur to a legislator to propose legislation on the subject. (The Commission on the Organization of the General Assembly made the same recommendation. I.S.L., p. 13.)

Second, it seems appropriate to try to entice the courts away from using Section 22 as a substitute for or supplement to equal protection and due process. These are two fundamental rights that belong in the bill of rights. If the words "No person shall be denied the equal protection of the laws" are added to the bill of rights, either as a separate section or as an addition to Section 2 thereof (*supra*, p. 9), a first step will have been taken.

Third, it would be advisable to keep "local" and "special" legislation separated to the maximum extent possible. If an article on local government is to be prepared, combining county government and new material on other local governments, all with an eye to greater home rule, then a prohibitory section on "local" legislation, using that word and not "special," would be appropriate. Such a prohibitory section could take any of many forms — there are a number of "models" around. The only suggestion to be made here is to keep it simple. It should be either a flat prohibition with a minimum of exceptions as in the Connecticut example quoted above, or a general statement as in the Model provision concerning "special" legislation quoted above, or as in a flat prohibition with a proviso that the legislature may provide for different treatment on the basis of reasonable classification of local governments.

Finally, there remains the problem of real special legislation. One would like to believe that this sort of legislation would not be revived if there were no prohibition, but it probably is not safe, or in any event not worth the gamble, to experiment with this sort of legislative freedom. (The point here is that real special legislation has not been a problem since 1870, whereas local legislation in artificial classification disguises has. If there were no restraints on the latter, the legislature might stop struggling with classifications and simply pass local legislation from time to time, but they might not do the same in such areas as granting divorces, changing names, changing the law of descent, and transferring real property—cases of real special legislation.) The cautious solution is a provision like that of the Model quoted above, including the words of subjecting applicability of general laws to judicial determination. There is, of course, no assurance that the courts would not gallop through such a hole, dragging the old pseudo-special legislation rules with them. (One can rest assured that litigants would try to get the courts to do just that.) But if the problem of local and special legislation is handled in a comprehensive fashion as suggested here, with a well-documented explanation of the four interrelated steps — (1) abandonment of enumerated cases, (2) substitution of equal protection, (3) coverage of local legislation in the local government article, and (4) the limited general prohibition on special legislation — the courts might go along.

Release of Nonstate Debts Prohibited

Sec. 23. The General Assembly shall have no power to release or extinguish, in whole or in part, the indebtedness, liability, or obligation of any corporation or individual to this State or to any municipal corporation therein.

History

This section dates from 1870. Notwithstanding the breadth of the section, the debate on it in the Convention revealed that the section was aimed at one specific abuse. It was argued that tax collectors, instead of remitting collections promptly, would retain the money and use it improperly. If through such use it was lost, the collectors would fraudulently establish a robbery and then seek relief for themselves and their sureties by private bill. Several delegates protested that the proposed section was too harsh, for, it was argued, there would be no relief for the collector who was in fact robbed through no fault of his own. These arguments were to no avail and all proposals to provide for exceptions were defeated. It should be noted, however, that the delegates were aware that the section was broader than the abuse at which it was aimed. (*See* Debates 634.)

The proposed 1922 Constitution retained this section in a much simplified form. In the article on Public Servants of the proposed Constitution, a provision was included stating that no statute of limitation could begin to run in favor of a public officer until an audit of his accounts had been made.

Explanation

The principal problem with this section is that it prevents the adoption of a statute of limitation that runs against the state or any municipal corporation. It was this problem that presumably led the 1920-22 Convention to narrow the provision so that it approached in coverage the matter about which the 1870 delegates were worried.

Over the years, a great many attempts have been made to rely upon this section in litigation, but in only two cases does it appear to have been effective. In 1931, a taxpayer sent in his check for fuel tax collected, but the bank failed before the state could deposit the check. The state filed a claim with the bank receiver and then, it was alleged, the Director of Finance canceled the taxpayer's surety bond. In a subsequent action on the bond, the taxpayer's defense of cancellation was turned aside on the ground that state officials had no power to release the obligation. (People *ex rel.* Ames v. Marx, 370 Ill 264 (1938).) In 1949, the Supreme Court relied on the *Marx* case to hold that one Attorney General's consent to settlement of an action for refund of taxes paid under protest without a judicial determination of liability was no bar to his successor's reviving the issue. (Massell v. Daley, 404 Ill. 479 (1949).)

Notwithstanding the foregoing cases, it appears fairly clear that the courts are not anxious to push Section 23 to its literal extreme. In *People v. Evanuk* (320 Ill. 336 (1926)), the claim was made that the legislature did not have the power to permit a judge to set aside a bail bond forfeiture after judgment where the surety subsequently produced the defendant. The Supreme Court held that all the statute did was to change the circumstances under which the obligation finally became an obligation. Another section of the same statute permitted the County Commissioners or Board of Supervisors to compromise such a judgment. In an action attacking a compromise of $100 on a $5,000 bond forfeiture, the Supreme Court had a more difficult time with the statute, but concluded that since such fines went into a fund to pay the state's attorney's salary with any surplus going into the school fund, the obligation was not really an obligation of the state and, therefore, the legislature could permit a settlement for a smaller sum. (People *ex rel.* Marcus v. Swanson, 340 Ill. 188 (1930).) It should also be noted that a compromise of a doubtful claim is not prohibited by Section 23. (Burr v. City of Carbondale, 76 Ill. 455 (1875).) Nor is the section a bar to the release of a claim for a consideration believed to be of equal or greater value. (City of Chicago v. Pittsburgh, C., C. & St. L. Ry., 244 Ill. 220 (1910).)

Comparative Analysis

Nine states appear to have a comparable section. Three other states with a comparable provision exempt taxes delinquent for a specified period: ten years in two cases, the period of prescriptive rights in the third case. Two states are content with an extraordinary vote for any bill releasing a state claim. Eleven states simply prohibit release by private or local act. Neither the United States Constitution nor the Model State Constitution has a comparable provision.

Comment

It would seem appropriate to take a leaf from the 1920-22 Convention and then go a little further and drop this section entirely. The need for flexibility in providing general statutes of limitation and means of compromise and settlement of state claims far outweighs the danger that on some occasion the legislature may propose the release of a good claim and the Governor may not veto it.

Impeachment

Sec. 24. The House of Representatives shall have the sole power of impeachment; but a majority of all the members elected must concur therein. All impeachments shall be tried by the Senate; and when sitting for that purpose, the Senators shall be upon oath, or affirmation, to do justice according to law and evidence. When the Governor of the State is tried, the Chief Justice shall preside. No person shall be convicted without the concurrence of two-thirds of the Senators elected. But judgment, in such cases, shall not extend further than removal from office, and disqualification to hold any office of honor, profit or trust under the government of this State. The party, whether convicted or acquitted, shall, nevertheless, be liable to prosecution, trial, judgment and punishment according to law.

History

The impeachment provisions in the Legislative Articles of the 1818 and 1848 Constitutions included, in substance, most of what is now in Section 24 and the sentence now appearing as Section 15 of Article V. Neither Constitution provided for the Chief Justice to preside at a trial of the Governor. In the 1818 Constitution, a simple majority of the members present was required to impeach, and a two-thirds' vote of senators present was required to convict. The change to votes of the members elected was made in 1848. In all other respects the substance of Section 24 is the same. The proposed 1922 Constitution combined Section 15 of Article V and Section 24. No changes were made except in punctuation.

Explanation

The impeachment process is an historic means of removing someone from office. In some cases, such as state-wide elected officers, it is the only means of removal unless, of course, another constitutional provision provides for removal. Under Section 30 of the original Judiciary Article, for example, judges could be removed by a three-fourths' vote of all elected members of each house of the legislature. The present Article VI provides a method for the judiciary itself to remove a judge for cause. (Sec. 18, *infra*, p. 372.)

Impeachment is a rare event and it is not at all clear what its limits are. It seems likely, however, that the legislature can remove any state official through the impeachment process, notwithstanding any other method of removal provided by constitution or law. In addition to removal of judges by the impeachment process, it seems clear that the House of Representatives could impeach and the Senate try an officer appointed by the Governor, notwithstanding the Governor's removal power. (*See* Sec. 12 of Art. V, *infra*, p. 285.)

The one exception to impeachment is legislators themselves. Section 9 (*supra*, p. 145) gives each house the power to expel members. It seems most unlikely that the Senate would try one of its own members following a purported impeachment by the House of Representatives, or that the House would impeach one of its own members for trial by the Senate. (For definitional purposes, it is to be noted that "impeachment" is analogous to an indictment.)

Comparative Analysis

There are a great many variations in impeachment procedures among the several states. Only Oregon has no provision for impeachment. (See *Comment* below.) In Alaska, the senate impeaches and the lower house tries. In all other states, except unicameral Nebraska, the lower house impeaches and in most states the senate tries. In Nebraska and Missouri the highest court tries, except when one of its own members is impeached, in which case a different group of judges is used. In New York, the judges of the highest court join the senate for the trial.

About a third of the states require a majority of all members of the house to impeach, a few require a two-thirds' vote, and a large number of the states are silent on the required vote. Almost all of the states require a two-thirds' vote to convict, and a majority of them require that the two-thirds be of all the members of the senate. It is customary to have the Chief Justice preside when the Governor is on trial, in a few states also when the Lieutenant-Governor is on trial, and in some states in all cases, except, of course, when he himself is on trial. Equally customary are the limitation on the judgment that can be rendered and the liability for trial for any crimes alleged to have been committed. Most states and the United States except impeachment convictions from pardons, and a majority of the states except such convictions from commutation. Illinois is silent on this point. (*See* Sec. 13, Art. V, *infra*, p. 287.) The United States Constitution provides for impeachment in much the same manner as Illinois except that no specific vote is called for in the House of Representatives and the two-thirds vote in the Senate is of the members present. The Model State Constitution calls for a two-thirds vote of all members to impeach and provides that trials shall be as provided for by law.

Comment

Impeachments are relatively rare, but it is a matter of important constitutional principle either to preserve the impeachment process — at least for constitutional officers — or to provide, as Oregon does, that "incompetency, corruption, malfeasance or delinquency in office may be tried in the same manner as criminal offenses, and judgment may be given of dismissal from office...." (Ore. Const., art. VII, § 6.)

State Contracts

Sec. 25. The General Assembly shall provide, by law, that the fuel, stationery, and printing paper furnished for the use of the State; the copying, printing, binding and distributing the laws and journals, and all other printing ordered by the General Assembly, shall be let by contract to the lowest responsible bidder; but the General Assembly shall fix a maximum price; and no member thereof, or other officer of the State, shall be interested, directly or indirectly, in such contract. But all such contracts shall be subject to the approval of the Governor, and if he disapproves the same there shall be a re-letting of the contract, in such manner as shall be prescribed by law.

History

The first sentence of this section first appeared in the 1848 Constitution, but without the words "printing paper." Those words were included in the proposed section as submitted to the 1870 Convention. The section sailed through without discussion or debate until the day when the section was to be enrolled in the Constitution. At that time a motion was made to suspend the rules for the addition of what is now the second sentence of Section 25. The Chairman of the Committee on Revenue supported the motion, observing:

"I am satisfied such a provision is necessary to the operation of this clause with any benefit to the State. It would have saved thousands of dollars heretofore, and will save thousands of dollars in the future to the State." (Debates 1780.)

The rules were suspended and the sentence added. The section was omitted from the proposed 1922 Constitution.

Explanation

This is the most limited in coverage of the several conflict-of-interest provisions. (See Sec. 15, *supra*, p. 176, and Sec. 4 of Art. VIII, *infra*, p. 409.) Only two cases appear to have arisen under this section. In *Dement v. Rokker* (126 Ill. 174 (1888)), the Supreme Court held that a contract that was the result of collusion among printers would be void. In *Callaghan & Co. v. Smith* (304 Ill. 532 (1922)), the Supreme Court invalidated an act authorizing a named concern to compile and publish the statutes of the state. The act was also held to be special legislation invalid under Sec. 22. (*Supra*, p. 203.)

Comparative Analysis

There appear to be 15 states with comparable provisions. Some are more limited in coverage, such as printing only or stationery only, and some are broader, such as covering lights in addition to fuel. West Virginia's provision is the same in substance and so close in language to Section 25 that it must have been copied by the drafters of the 1872 West Virginia Constitution. Michigan deleted a comparable provision in its recent revision. The United States Constitution and Model State Constitution are silent on the subject.

Comment

Even though 15 states have comparable provisions, it seems obvious that this is a minor matter of no constitutional significance. To be sure, corruption in government contracting, for printing or anything else, is important, but there is a limit to how far the people can go in trying to prevent corruption by constitutional fiat. Moreover, there is a danger in trying to put too many controls into a constitution. The legislature, for example, takes a dim view of the executive control over legislative printing that has been facilitated by Section 25. The Commission on the Organization of the General Assembly recommended that Section 25 be deleted so that the legislature can control its own printing. (I.S.L. 11-12.)

Suit Against State Prohibited

Sec. 26. The State of Illinois shall never be made defendant in any court of law or equity.

History

The 1848 Constitution stated that the "General Assembly shall direct, by law, in what manner suits may be brought against the State." The

Committee on the Legislative Department proposed the following to the 1870 Convention:

"The State of Illinois never shall be made defendant in any court of law or equity; but the General Assembly may provide, in any case that they may deem it advisable, for commissioners or arbitrators to investigate and report any claims against the State, subject to review of the General Assembly; and the General Assembly shall provide means for the payment of all just claims against the State."

When the section was brought up in the Committee of the Whole, a delegate immediately moved to strike everything after the word "equity" on the ground that the "General Assembly have all the power that is attempted to be conferred upon them by this provision." (Debates 612.) Without debate and by a vote of 25 to 21, the motion was passed. (It was also agreed to transpose "never shall" to "shall never." *Id.*)

At a subsequent session an effort was made to put the stricken material back in. The principal argument was that the Constitution ought to spell out how creditors of the State "may seek their remedy." (*Id.* at 961.) Many delegates appeared to be afraid that any invitation to set up something like a court of claims would be abused. (There was a great deal of concern about the "Macalister and Stebbins bonds" and, apparently, a fear that anything except a prohibition against suing the state might open the door to another such situation. A brief description of the Macalister and Stebbins bonds will be found in Bulletin No. 10, Bulletins 865.) In the end, the original decision was sustained. The proposed 1922 Constitution omitted the section.

Explanation

The doctrine of sovereign immunity is traditional and would be applicable in Illinois in the absence of Section 26. (In Molitor v. Kaneland Community Unit District, 18 Ill. 2d 11 (1959), the Supreme Court on its own abandoned common law immunity as to tort actions involving political subdivisions of the state. The legislature can, of course, grant sovereign immunity to such subdivisions, totally or under certain limitations.) The only significance of the section, therefore, is that it prohibits the state from legislating permission to be sued. (*See* People el rel. Greening v. Green, 382 Ill. 577 (1943).) The state is not prohibited, however, from paying just claims against it (Fergus v. Russel, 277 Ill. 20 (1917)) or creating an "advisory" agency, a court of claims, to determine the justness of claims against the state. (*See* Dinwiddie v. Siefkin, 299 Ill. App. 316 (1939).)

Notwithstanding sovereign immunity, there are several ways in which, in effect, the state can be sued. A suit against a state official is not a suit against the state if the allegation is that the official is operating outside his authority or that the authority conferred is unconstitutional.

(*See* People *ex rel.* Freeman v. Department of Pub. Welfare, 368 Ill. 505 (1938).) Likewise, one can sue an official to compel him to carry out a mandatory duty. (*See* People *ex rel.* First Nat'l Bank v. Kingery, 369 Ill. 289 (1938).) The state may also create instrumentalities that act on behalf of the state but that have shed enough attributes of the sovereign to permit suit. (*See* People v. Illinois Toll Highway Comm'n, 3 Ill. 2d 218 (1954).)

It should also be noted that the legislature grants a right of judicial review of many administrative determinations and adjudications. Indeed, in many situations, the courts have required such right as a matter of due process of law. (See *Explanation* of Art. III, *supra,* p. 99.) In such cases of judicial review, the state is the defendant, whether the action is viewed as at law or equity — in theory, it has to be one or the other — but the courts do not consider these cases as precluded by Section 26. Here, as in some other areas of the law, there is a semantic fog and the courts are sometimes no better than the rest of us in describing the course taken.

To complete the judicial circle, it must be noted that although illegal and unconstitutional acts of the state can usually be stopped by suit against an official, it is not possible to sue the state by purporting to sue an individual who is legally acting for the state. (*See* Schwing v. Miles, 367 Ill. 436 (1937).) There are also technical problems that arise in involved litigation. For example, on one occasion the Attorney General was not permitted to intervene in a condemnation proceeding under circumstances that would make the state a "defendant" (People v. Sanitary Dist., 210 Ill. 171 (1904)), but on another occasion a person sued by the state was permitted to file a cross-bill against the state. (Brundage v. Knox, 279 Ill. 450 (1917).)

Comparative Analysis

There appear to be only two states, Alabama and Arkansas, that join Illinois in prohibiting all suits against the state. West Virginia prohibits all suits against the state except where the state or a subdivision is made defendant in garnishment or attachment proceedings. Some ten state constitutions provide that the legislature may prescribe the manner in which suits may be brought against the state, and another four say that the legislature shall do so. Three states cover the problem by permitting suit, but not permitting the entry of enforceable judgments. The United States Constitution has no comparable restriction, and the United States has waived sovereign immunity by statute in certain areas. The Model State Constitution has no comparable provision.

Comment

As noted in the *History* above, Section 26 was inserted in 1870 in an abundance of caution as the result of a specific state bond dispute that had arisen earlier. It would seem appropriate to drop the section as unnecessary. Indeed, in view of the steady increase in the impingement of government on the daily activities of people, it is more likely that some will argue that a provision should be inserted guaranteeing the right to sue the state.

Lotteries Prohibited

Sec. 27. The General Assembly shall have no power to authorize lotteries or gift enterprises, for any purpose, and shall pass laws to prohibit the sale of lottery or gift enterprise tickets in this State.

History

This denial of legislative power was first introduced in the 1848 Constitution in a provision that, curiously, included in the middle of the sentence a denial of power to charter certain banks. (See discussion of Sec. 5, Art. XI, *infra,* p. 520.) In 1870 the words "or gift enterprises" were added by motion on the floor of the Convention. There was no explanation of the phrase, no debate, and adoption, apparently, was by voice vote. (Debates 612.) Presumably, the delegates knew the generally accepted meaning of the phrase — a scheme whereby a merchant sells wares at the market value but by way of inducement gives the purchaser a ticket for a prize-drawing. The proposed 1922 Constitution changed the section to read: "Lotteries and gift enterprises are forbidden." The official explanation said the proposed section was the same as Section 27, indicating, presumably, a belief that an unenforceable command to the legislature to pass laws is a meaningless constitutional provision. (P.N.C. 31. See the *Comment* on Sec. 32 of Art. IV, *infra,* p. 245.)

Explanation

It should be noted first that this section prohibits only lotteries, not all gambling. A lottery is understood to have three controlling ingredients: a consideration, or price, to participate; a prize; and a determination of the winner by pure chance. (In the current wave of contests through the mail, in gasoline service stations, and elsewhere, the "no purchase necessary" part is the means of trying to avoid a lottery.) Prior to 1932, there apparently had been no judicial construction of Section 27. In that year, the Supreme Court decided that pari-mutuel betting in horse races is not a lottery. (People v. Monroe, 349 Ill. 270 (1932). [Could the legislature authorize bookmaking?]) Since then there has been litigation concerning how close one can get to making the distribution of tickets "free" while still keeping some strings on the distribution. There has been no interpretation of "gift enterprises." Generally, a gift enterprise is considered covered by a statute prohibiting lotteries.

Comparative Analysis

Over 35 states have constitutional prohibitions of lotteries and approximately 14 of them add a prohibition of "gift enterprises." A few states prohibit gambling, but in most of these, exceptions have been added by amendment. New York, for example, has a strict gambling provision to which an exception for pari-mutuel horse racing was added in 1939, an exception for nonprofit bingo in 1957, and an exception for a state lottery for education in 1966. (Thus, the gambling provision has grown from approximately 45 words to approximately 450 words.) With the exception of Rhode Island, no New England state has a gambling or lottery provision in its constitution. Neither the United States Constitution nor the Model State Constitution has a gambling or lottery provision.

Comment

Gambling has been one of the frailties of men that has plagued societies for centuries. Probably the greatest efforts to suppress gambling have been carried on in countries with a strong Protestant, Puritan tradition. In the middle of the Nineteenth Century there was a nation-wide movement against lotteries culminating in widespread adoption of provisions like Section 27. It is obvious, however, that such constitutional provisions and accompanying statutory prohibitions have not been particularly successful in stopping lotteries. "Policies" or "numbers" games are widespread and because of their illegality constitute one of the main supports for organized crime. Presumably, it is partly the recognition of the pervasiveness of the weakness for gambling that has caused states to make exceptions to gambling prohibitions and two states, New Hampshire and New York, to sponsor state lotteries.

Notwithstanding the ineffectiveness of a constitutional gambling prohibition, it is one of the more controversial provisions in a state constitution and one that a convention is not likely to remove. Cogent arguments can be adduced to demonstrate that protection of the people against the temptation of gambling is hardly one of the fundamental principles of limited government for which constitutional protection is necessary. Nevertheless, delegates to a convention are not likely to wish to appear to be in favor of sin and a decision to delete Section 27 could be so characterized. (Ironically, a more accurate characterization would be that Section 27 must be preserved because of a fear that the legislature might some day be in favor of "sin" — *i.e.*, gambling.) Fortunately, the limited nature of the restriction of Section 27 preserves Illinois from the difficulties encountered in states such as New York which have had to amend their constitutions from time to time to permit exceptions to a prohibition against all gambling.

Extension of Term of Office Prohibited

Sec. 28. No law shall be passed which shall operate to extend the term of any public officer after his election or appointment.

History

This section first appeared in the 1870 Constitution. It was explained on the floor of the Convention that the section "was intended to meet such a case as happened in 1865, when the Legislature extended the term of the school commissioners for two years beyond the time for which they were elected." (Debates 744.) The proposed 1922 Constitution rearranged the words to read thus: "No public officer shall have his term extended by law after his election or appointment." The section was moved to a new article called "Public Servants."

Explanation

This straightforward prohibition, especially in the improved language of the 1922 proposal, is self-explanatory. Its purpose is equally obvious: to prevent a partisan protection of incumbents likely to be ousted at the next election. There has been some litigation involving this section, but in general it has simply confirmed that the section means what it says. (*See, e.g.,* People *ex rel.* Bua v. Powell, 39 Ill. 2d 202 (1968).)

Comparative Analysis

Only a handful of states — eight besides Illinois — have a comparable provision. Georgia, for completeness, has a provision prohibiting lengthening *or* shortening terms except under certain circumstances. Neither the United States Constitution nor the Model State Constitution has a comparable provision.

Comment

As indicated above, this is the sort of prohibition that gets into a constitution because of some specific prior abuse. The relative rarity of the provision among the states indicates that it is not a necessary or traditional limitation of legislative power. As is frequently the case with a prohibition of legislative abuse of power, the ability to act properly is also prohibited. One can think of any number of circumstances in which an extension of term of office would be salutary, would solve some problem, or would simply be a minor aspect of some far-reaching change.

(*Compare* People *ex rel.* Bua v. Powell, 39 Ill. 2d 202 (1968).) In the heat of outrage at some legislative abuse, there is frequently a failure to consider the consequences of withholding all power to act.

Protection of Miners

Sec. 29. It shall be the duty of the General Assembly to pass such laws as may be necessary for the protection of operative miners, by providing for ventilation, where the same may be required, and the construction of escapement shafts, or such other appliances as may secure safety in all coal mines, and to provide for the enforcement of said laws by such penalties and punishments as may be deemed proper.

History

This bit of legislative material was reported early to the 1870 Convention and apparently was the first substantive provision adopted by the delegates. It may be for this reason that the debate was so extensive. In the end, the section was adopted with only one dissenting vote. The dissenter had indicated earlier that he believed the Convention was acting too hastily. (*See* Debates 264 - 276, esp. 275.) The proposed 1922 Constitution retained this section. The official explanation stated that the section was unchanged (P.N.C. 33), but this is questionable. From the 1870 debates, it is clear that the delegates meant to require legislation for ventilation of all mines, but "escapement shafts" for coal mines only. The 1922 language omitted the word "coal."

Explanation

This section is, in effect, a dead letter. There appears to have been only one judicial reference to the section since 1920. In 1967, it was stated that mine safey legislation must be liberally construed in order to comply with the constitutional mandate of Section 29. (Freeman Coal Mining Corp. v. Ruff, 85 Ill. App. 2d 145 (1967).) The case concerned only alternative constructions of an ambiguous statutory provision. No constitutional issue was considered.

The current insignificance of Section 29 can be demonstrated by the history of the problem of providing washrooms for coal miners. In 1906, the Supreme Court held unconstitutional a requirement that coal mine operators provide washrooms. The Court said that Section 29 could not be relied upon because the section mandated legislation for the "safety" of miners, not for their "health and safety." (The Court refused to consider the 1870 Convention debates on the ground that Section 29 was unambiguous. The debates make it clear that the delegates were concerned about both health and safety. (*See* Debates 264-276.) Once Section 29 was disposed of, the legislation fell under the special legislation prohibition of Section 22, on the ground that the health of miners who would have to trudge home in wet clothes was no different from the health of other workmen who would have to trudge home in wet clothes but whose employers were not required to supply washrooms. (Starne v. People, 222 Ill. 189 (1906).) In 1913, an act was passed requiring washrooms in every "coal mine, steel mill, foundry, machine shop, or other like business in which employees become covered with grease, smoke, dust, grime and perspiration to such an extent that to remain in such condition . . . will endanger their health . . . ." The Court upheld the act. (People v. Solomon, 265 Ill. 28 (1914).) In 1919, the Court held that the act did not cover railroad roundhouses. (People v. Cleveland, C., C., & St. L. Ry., 288 Ill. 523 (1919).) In 1931, "railroad" was inserted after "machine shop," and so far it appears that no railroad has questioned the amendment. (Ill. Rev. Stat. ch. 48, § 98 (1967).)

If the foregoing demonstrates the failure of the 1870 mandate to go far enough, the case of *Fowler v. Johnston City & Big Muddy Coal & Mining Company* (292 Ill. 440 (1920)) demonstrates the futility of mandating legislation. In that case, the claim was made that there should be an escapement shaft to match every main shaft, even though the legislature had permitted a connecting passageway between two mines to suffice where one mine had such an escapement shaft. The Court refused to rewrite the statute and thrust aside the argument that the statute was unconstitutional because it did not properly carry out the constitutional mandate. (But see *Comment* on Sec. 32, *infra*, p. 245.)

Comparative Analysis

There appear to be four states besides Illinois that specifically mandate legislation for the protection of miners. All except one of them cover both "health" and "safety" of miners. Another five states have such a mandatory provision but include one or more additional industries, such as railroads, smelters and "factories." Again, all except one of the five cover both health and safety. Three states have negative statements: that is, declarations that nothing else in the constitution shall be deemed to deny the legislature the power to protect the health and safety of employees. Neither the United States Constitution nor the Model State Constitution has a comparable provision.

Comment

If, as noted above, this section is, in effect, a dead letter, one would assume that the section could easily be removed. But there is always the interest of those who feel, rightly or wrongly, that they may lose something if the section is dropped. At the least, an effort should be made, in this case as well as in others, to convince those directly interested that in the long run the ability of the legislature to solve the day-to-day problems of Illinois is facilitated if the Constitution does not appear to set priorities on problem-solving.

Establishing Roads and Cartways

Sec. 30. The General Assembly may provide for establishing and opening roads and cartways, connected with a public road, for private and public use.

History

In 1866 the Supreme Court in two cases, *Nesbitt v. Trumbo* (39 Ill. 110 (1866)) and *Crear v. Crossley* (40 Ill. 175 (1866)), held that the due process clause of the 1848 Constitution prohibited the state from condemning an easement over one man's property in order that another man might have access to a highway. The purpose of Section 30 was to get around these two decisions. There was an extended debate in the 1870 Convention revolving principally around two important questions: (1) who should pay for the easement — the man who needed access to the highway, the public, or both? and (2) if the state exercised its power of condemnation, could the resulting easement remain a private road? (The practical significance of the second question is whether the man for whose benefit the easement existed could put up a gate at the junction with the highway or only at his own property line at the opposite end of the easement.) The consensus of the delegates appears to have been that if the state were to exercise its power it must do so for the benefit of the public and that, therefore, the easement must be public; and if this were so, that the cost of condemnation should not be borne wholly by the owner who needed access to the highway. This consensus was developed by abandoning a majority committee report after many floor amendments and substituting therefor a minority committee report containing the language of Section 30.

In the proposed 1922 Constitution, Sections 30 and 31 were combined and new matter related to Section 31 was added. The operative words for purposes of Section 30 were that the legislature could provide for "opening private roads to communicate with public roads."

Explanation

In 1924, the Supreme Court confirmed the understanding of the delegates to the 1870 Convention. (Road District No. 4 v. Frailey, 313 Ill. 568 (1924).) The Court said in effect that the state cannot condemn the land of "A" for the sole use of "B," but that it can do so if the public also participates in the use. Since the stretch of road in question in that case was less than 300 feet, it is fairly clear that the public-use aspect was more theoretical than real. Moreover, the condemnation award was

$140.00 of which $115.00 was to be paid by the property owner and only $25.00 by the road district. In short, one must always use the rubric "private and public use" and be sure that some small part of the condemnation award is assessed against the public. (Actually, the award was set aside for a procedural error not pertinent to this discussion.)

The clarity of the foregoing paragraph is smudged a bit by the case of·*Libbee v. Imhoff.* (11 Ill. App. 2d 344 (1956).) Unfortunately, only an unofficial abstract of the case is published and nothing is known of the facts except that the county superintendent of highways refused to lay out a road. The abstract says:

"The Appellate Court held that a roadway to provide access to land isolated from any public road would be solely for the benefit of owner of such land and those having business with him and that hence such road could not be laid out under statute authorizing public authorities to lay out roads for private and public use, since to do so would amount to the taking of private property for private use in violation of Constitution." (Libbee v. Imhoff, 137 N.E. 2d 85, 85-86 (1956).)

The only relevant speculation about this abstract is what kind of business the landowner was in that "those having business with him" were not the "public." It is relevant, however, to observe that the court might not have ruled the same if the superintendent of highways had laid out the road.

Comparative Analysis

No other state appears to have a provision precisely like Section 30. A dozen or so states specifically permit the opening of a private road provided that there is a necessity therefor. In some of these cases, it is made clear that the cost of condemnation is to be borne by the landowner who benefits. Neither the United States Constitution nor the Model State Constitution has a comparable provision.

Comment

Section 30 is an example of a constitutional provision made necessary by a bad judicial decision. As the *Frailey* case discussed above demonstrates, the problem is more theoretical than real. It would seem obvious today that a property owner who cannot reach the highway and cannot purchase an easement therefor at a reasonable price should be able to enlist the aid of the state to exercise the right of eminent domain to enable him to have access to the highway and the public to have access to him. It may be that the 1866 cases that created the problem in Illinois were badly handled or that something lay behind the disputes that does not appear in the opinions. If this is not the case, one can only conclude that the judges comprising the majority in those cases read "public use" in much too narrow a sense.

The problem arises, however, whether it is advisable to remove what should be an unnecessary provision. In many instances (see the discussions of Sec. 29, *supra,* p. 237, and Sec. 31, below, of this article and of Art. XIII, *infra* pp. 545), the removal of a grant of powers creates no problem, for the legislature has all the powers of government not denied to it. Unfortunately, the grant of power in Section 30 was made necessary by a judicial ruling based on a traditional denial of power. If Section 30 were omitted, someone some day could argue that the power to condemn land for a connection to a highway had been lost. But if the essence of Section 30 is to be retained, it probably ought to be included as part of the eminent domain section.

Drains and Ditches

Sec. 31. The General Assembly may pass laws permitting the owners of lands to construct drains, ditches and levees for Agricultural, Sanitary or mining purposes, across the lands of others, and provide for the organization of drainage districts, and vest the corporate authorities thereof, with power to construct and maintain levees, drains and ditches, and to keep in repair all drains, ditches and levees heretofore constructed under the laws of this State, by special assessments upon the property benefited thereby.

History

Section 31 dates from 1870 and originally read as follows:

"The General Assembly may pass laws permitting the owners or occupants of lands to construct drains and ditches for agricultural and sanitary purposes, across the lands of others."

It was proposed as a section of the Bill of Rights Article by a delegate who argued that the *Nesbitt* and *Crear* cases, which had been the occasion for adopting Section 30 (*supra,* p. 239), would also invalidate existing drainage laws. The Committee on Revision and Adjustment moved the section to Article IV.

The present Section 31 was adopted in 1878 as the first amendment to the Constitution. In 1876, the Supreme Court had held that since Section 31 did not mention "levees," the state could not authorize a drainage district to condemn land for a levee, and had also held that no drainage district could be authorized to finance itself by special assessment since Section 9 of Article IX (*infra,* p. 460) limited special assessment powers to "cities, towns and villages." (Updike v. Wright, 81 Ill. 49 (1876).) The amendment was designed both to cover the problem of levees and to overcome the restriction of Section 9 of Article IX. Interestingly enough, one delegate in 1870 had suggested that perhaps some language covering levees ought to be included and expressed

hope that more time would be given to the examination of the problem.
He was followed by a delegate who doubted the necessity of *any* provision granting power to the legislature but conceded that if others
thought such a provision was necessary, it was perhaps advisable to
accept it. He moved the previous question, the section was adopted as
written, and the problem of including levees was apparently forgotten.
(Debates 1589.) The proposed 1922 Constitution retained this section
in a simplified version, but with some substantive changes. The principal
changes were to make it explicit that drainage districts had the power
of eminent domain and that the state could give them financial aid.
In addition to clearing up the ambiguity of whether a grant of one
power negates other powers, it was further provided that the proposed
section should not be construed as a limitation on the powers of the
legislature.

Explanation

In one of the Bulletins prepared by the Legislative Reference Bureau
for the 1920-22 Convention, the subject of drainage districts was introduced by the statement: "The drainage laws of Illinois present a highly
complex and confusing body of legislation." (Bulletins 1030.) That
statement continued to hold until the Drainage Code was adopted in
1955. In some measure, the complexity and confusion were the result of
constitutional limitations, but not particularly limitations in Section 31
itself. Presumably, the codification of the many drainage acts has ended
the confusion. Since 1947, at least, the courts have apparently had no
constitutional question involving Section 31.

Roughly speaking, there are two types of drainage districts, using
the term as a catchall. One is a district formed at the instance of landowners for their own benefit. The other is a governmental agency formed
at the instance of voters for the benefit of the public. The first type
is organized pursuant to a statute enacted in conformance with Section
31, and the second type is organized pursuant to a statute enacted under
the general police power.

Section 31 districts are quasi-municipal corporations. They can raise
money only by assessments against the land benefited and only to the
extent of the benefit to the land. For example, in *North Wichert Drainage District v. Chamberlain* (340 Ill. 644 (1930)), Drainage District "A"
engaged in drainage work of benefit to District "B" and pursuant to
statute obtained a judgment against "B" for the cost of such work.
Objection was raised that an assessment against all of the landowners
of "B" would be unconstitutional because not every landowner necessarily benefited from the work done. The Supreme Court construed the

statute to require the Commissioners of District "B" to allocate the amount of the judgment by assessment against landowners in "B" according to the benefit received. Another case which exemplified this fundamental limitation on the fiscal powers of a Section 31 district was *Marshall v. Commissioners of Upper Cache Drainage District* (313 Ill. 11 (1924)), where the Court invalidated a statutory provision that authorized the county court, in the course of dissolving a district, to assess the costs of the unsuccessful attempt against the landowners. Since the project failed, there were no benefits, and without benefits there could be no assessment.

Section 31, it should be noted, goes further than simply to permit the formation of a drainage or levee district. The legislature is empowered to provide for a method whereby a property owner can run a drain through the property of another. (Ill. Rev. Stat. ch. 42, §§ 2-2 to 2-7 (1967).) Landowners may also mutually establish drains or levees by agreement. (Ill. Rev. Stat. ch. 42, §§ 2-8 to 2-11 (1967).)

When a district is created, in the words of Section 31, there is a "corporate authority" which has the power to levy assessments. In the early days under the amended Section 31, the courts apparently were not concerned about the significance of the fact that, normally, "corporate authorities" are persons selected by the people affected or by a method to which they assented. When faced with districts created by special act, the analogy to municipal corporations was relied upon to require some form of consent by affected landowners in order to have a valid district whose commissioners could levy assessments. (*See* Funkhouser v. Randolph, 287 Ill. 94 (1919); Herschbach v. Kaskaskia Island Sanitary & Levee Dist., 265 Ill. 388 (1914). See also discussion of corporate authorities under Art. IX, Sec. 9, *infra,* p. 460.)

Districts which are for the benefit of the general public are not Section 31 districts. This means that they may raise necessary funds by taxation rather than assessment. This important principle was settled in the landmark case of *Wilson v. Board of Trustees of Sanitary District* (133 Ill. 443 (1890)). Such districts are not covered by the Illinois Drainage Code, but are part of the chapter on drainage under the head of "Sanitary and Other Districts." Sanitary districts may be organized for purposes of flood control or sewage disposal or both. Other types of districts provided for are river conservancy districts and surface water protection districts.

Comparative Analysis

Only about ten states have a comparable drainage district authorization. Michigan deleted one in its recent constitutional revision. In most cases, the provision appears to have been designed either to meet an asserted lack of eminent domain power or lack of special assessment power, or both, as was the case in Illinois. The Model State Constitution has no comparable provision.

Comment

It would appear safe to delete this section. There is no inherent restriction on the power of the legislature to create appropriate districts except as courts narrowly construe the power of eminent domain or except as a presumably inadvertent restriction on taxing power gets into the Constitution. The former is unlikely these days, and the Convention can avoid the latter.

Homstead and Exemption Laws

Sec. 32. The General Assembly shall pass liberal Homestead and Exemption laws.

History

This section was first added to the Constitution in 1870. It was first proposed to the Convention, sitting in Committee of the Whole, as a detailed article which "made very few modifications of our present statute law." (Debates 895.) Over four hours of debate ensued, including a great many proposed amendments. When the article came before the Convention proper, the amending process started all over again. Some delegates became alarmed at the rigidity of the article, and efforts were made to insert 'some flexibility by giving the legislature power to act. What is now Section 32 was offered on the floor as a flexible substitute that raised no problem of any kind. The section was quickly adopted. (Debates 1689-92.) The proposed 1922 Constitution preserved it unchanged.

Explanation

This is a simple, straightforward, unenforceable command to the legislature to pass homestead and exemption laws — laws to preserve one's home and, sometimes, other defined property, from being taken in satisfaction of one's debts. Homestead and Exemption laws have been passed pursuant to this command. Whether they are liberal is another question. Since any exemption law is more "liberal" than none, it is difficult to see how a court could judge compliance with the constitutional command. An appellate court has, however, stated that such laws should be "liberally" construed. (Perkins v. Perkins, 122 Ill. App. 370 (1905).)

Comparative Analysis

Two states, Colorado and Montana, have provisions substantially identical with Section 32. Some 25 other states have actual exemptions written into the constitution. (It is of interest to note that no state east of Indiana and Michigan and north of the Mason and Dixon line has any provision concernng homestead and exemption laws.) In many states there are provisions of great detail, including, for example, the maximum allowable value of a homestead to be exempted. Michigan is a case in point. In 1943 the amount was increased by amendment from $1,500 to $2,500. In the 1963 revision the applicable provision was changed to read: "A homestead in the amount of not less than $3,500 . . . as defined by law, shall be exempt from forced sale on execution or other process of any court." (Mich. Const. art. X, § 3.) Neither the United States Constitution nor the Model State Constitution mentions the subject.

Comment

So long as courts accept the theory that the legislature has the power to pass laws covering any subject in any manner unless the power is denied in the Constitution, a provision like Section 32 is an unnecessary grant of power. The command to the legislature to pass "good" laws adds nothing because, as noted above, there is no way to force the legislature to act and no likely way to eliminate a law on the grounds that it is not "good" enough. The most that can be said is that if the legislature repealed an existing homestead exemption law and did not replace it with any exemption, an argument could be made that Section 32 implicitly denies to the legislature the power to take away an exemption once given. An intriguing question is whether such an argument could be made against any change in the law that reputedly decreased the homesteader's rights. Nevertheless, if one believes that there should be something in the Constitution concerning homestead and exemption laws, then a provision like Section 32 is to be preferred to a provision that establishes the substance of the homesteader's rights.

State House Expenditures

Sec. 33. The General Assembly shall not appropriate out of the State treasury, or expend on account of the new capitol grounds, and construction, completion, and furnishing of the State House, a sum exceeding, in the aggregate, three and a half millions of dollars, inclusive of all appropriations heretofore made, without first submitting the proposition for an additional expenditure to the legal voters of the State at a general election; nor unless a majority of all the votes cast at such election shall be for the proposed additional expenditure.

History

This section was first added to the Constitution in 1870. On the floor of the Convention the proposal was offered with a ceiling of $4,000,000. The leading elder statesman in the Convention announced that he had made a study of the cost of the state house and found that it would be less than $3,000,000. After discussion, the matter was referred to committee. (Debates 1320.) In the end, the Convention split the difference. The proposed 1922 Constitution deleted the section.

Explanation

This quaint section puts a ceiling on the expenditures for the state house and surrounding grounds under the normal appropriations process, but permits additional expenditures if approved at a referendum. Notwithstanding an 1880 case that held that new grounds added to the capitol grounds after 1870 were covered by this section (People v. Stuart, 97 Ill. 123 (1880)), it seems likely that Section 33 is now a dead letter. In 1948, the Supreme Court made it clear that the limitation applies only to the capitol at Springfield and not to other state office buildings. (Owens v. Green, 400 Ill. 380 (1848).) Presumably, anything done at the state house today would be construed as repair, replacement, maintenance, or something other than "construction, completion and furnishing."

Comparative Analysis

There is no comparable state provision. Three states — Colorado, Montana, and Washington — forbid expenditures prior to the determination by the people of the permanent capital city, but those provisions serve a different purpose. Indiana has a provision forbidding the sale or lease of certain capitol grounds. There are, of course, many constitutional requirements for referenda in connection with the expenditure of money, both in general and for specific purposes.

Comment

In the light of some of the famous scandals connected with the building of state capitols and other public building, this section may very well have been prudent in 1870. It could surely be dropped now without fear.

Special Laws for City of Chicago

Sec. 34. The General Assembly shall have power, subject to the conditions and limitations hereinafter contained, to pass any law (local, special or general) providing a scheme or charter of local municipal government for the territory now or hereafter embraced within the limits of the city of Chicago. The law or laws so passed may provide for consolidating (in whole or in part) in the municipal government of the city of Chicago, the powers now vested in the city, board of education, township, park and other local governments and authorities having jurisdiction confined to or within said territory, or any part thereof, and for the assumption by the city of Chicago of the debts and liabilities (in whole or in part) of the governments or corporate authorities whose functions within its territory shall be vested in said city of Chicago, and may authorize said city, in the event of its becoming liable for the indebtedness of two or more of the existing municipal corporations lying wholly within said city of Chicago, to become indebted to an amount (including its existing indebtedness and the indebtedness of all municipal corporations lying wholly within the limits of said city, and said city's proportionate share of the indebtedness of said county and sanitary district which share shall be determined in such manner as the General Assembly shall prescribe) in the aggregate not exceeding five per centum of the full value of the taxable property within its limits, as ascertained by the last assessment either for State or municipal purposes previous to the incurring of such indebtedness (but no new bonded indebtedness, other than for refunding purposes, shall be incurred until the proposition therefor shall be consented to by a majority of the legal voters of said city voting on the question at any election, general, municipal or special); and may provide for the assessment of property and the levy and collection of taxes within said city for corporate purposes in accordance with the principles of equality and uniformity prescribed by this Constitution; and may abolish all offices, the functions of which shall be otherwise provided for; and may provide for the annexation of territory to or disconnection of territory from said city of Chicago by the consent of a majority of the legal voters (voting on the question at any election, general, municipal or special) of the said city and of a majority of the voters of such territory, voting on the question at any election, general, municipal or special; and in case the General Assembly shall create municipal courts in the city of Chicago it may abolish the offices of justices of the peace, police magistrates and constables in and for the territory within said city, and may limit the jurisdiction of justices of the peace in the territory of said county of Cook outside of said city to that territory, and in such case the jurisdiction and practice of said municipal courts shall be such as the General Assembly shall prescribe; and the General Assembly may pass all laws which it may deem requisite to effectually provide a complete system of local municipal government in and for the city of Chicago.

No law based upon this amendment to the Constitution, affecting the municipal government of the city of Chicago, shall take effect until such law shall be consented to by a majority of the legal voters of said city voting on the question at any election, general, municipal or special; and no local or special law based upon this amendment affecting specially any part of the city of Chicago shall take effect until consented to by a majority of the legal voters of such part of said city voting on the question at any election, general, municipal or special. Nothing in this section contained shall be construed to repeal, amend or affect section four (4) of Article XI of the Constitution of this State.

History

Chicago was first organized as a town under a general act for incorporation of towns. It received a special town charter in 1835 and a special city charter in 1837. A second special charter was enacted in 1851 and a

third in 1863. In between enactment of these charters there were numerous amendments by special act.

At the 1870 Convention, as noted above in connection with Section 22
(*supra*, p. 203), some of the delegates from Chicago argued that it would
not be practicable to handle all municipal charter problems, particularly
of large cities, by means of general legislation. The Chicago delegates
were also worried about charter changes not to the liking of the citizens
of the city. A Cook County delegate offered a proposal which, he said
he believed, had the approval of all other Cook County delegates. The
proposal would have permitted special legislation concerning original
municipal charters but, in the case of changes or amendments, only if
the voters of the community had the power of veto by referendum. There
was an extended and rather discursive debate which, among other things,
showed that the delegates generally did not have much of a theory
about home rule. In the end, the strong bias against special legislation
evidently won out, for the delegates retained the prohibition on any
special legislation incorporating cities, towns or villages, or changing
or amending such charters.

In 1872, a general act was passed to cover municipal incorporation.
Chicago adopted the new law in 1875. (With the prohibition on special
legislation, it was not possible, of course, to obtain amendments to an
existing special charter.) The Cook County delegates had been right,
however, and it soon became evident that Chicago could not operate
satisfactorily under the general act. Section 34, the sixth amendment to
the Constitution, adopted in 1904, was the proposed answer to Chicago's
problem.

The 1920-1922 Convention made another stab at the special problem
of Chicago. In place of Section 34, it produced 16 sections in a 34-section
article on Local Governments. The first of these sections opened with the
following expansive expression of home rule:

"Except as expressly prohibited by law the city of Chicago is hereby declared
to possess for all municipal purposes full and complete power of local self-
government and corporate action. This grant of power shall be liberally construed and no power of local self-government or corporate action shall be denied
the city by reason of not being specified herein." (art. VIII, § 178.)

There followed in that section and in many of the succeeding 15
sections various withholdings of power, reservations of control in the
hands of the legislature, requirements for referendum approval of certain actions, and detailed instructions for consolidation of overlapping
governmental units. The several sections as a whole added up, however,
to more home rule than that afforded by Section 34. For present purposes
only some of the more important sections need be summarized. The most
important limitation on Chicago was in the sentence immediately fol-

lowing the grant of power quoted above. The sentence read: "The city however may impose taxes and borrow money only as authorized by the general assembly or by this article." Since "this article" did not authorize any taxes, the legislature retained all power for the authorization of taxes. (The legislature's power was, of course, circumscribed by the revenue article.) The article did provide, however, that no municipal corporation (other than a county) exercising taxing power inside the city could be created or have its taxing power enlarged without the city's consent. Borrowing power was to be limited to 7 per cent of the value of taxable real property. (This was not an increase over the 5 per cent in Section 34, for that limitation included personal property.) Approval by referendum was required.

Chicago was given power to create its own city charter but only by an "elective convention." The voters had to approve the calling of a convention and to approve any charter adopted by the convention. Likewise, amendments had to be approved by the voters. One interesting proviso was that the charter and any ordinances passed under it would "prevail over state laws so far as the organization of the city government, the distribution of powers among its official agencies and the tenure and compensation of its officers and employees are concerned." But there followed another proviso stating that compensation, employment and promotion "in the classified civil service" should be in accordance with a general plan recognizing "merit and fitness as controlling principles." The legislature was authorized to pass special legislation for Chicago, but only with the city's consent.

One of the more ingenious proposals in the 1922 Constitution was an authorization to issue unlimited bonds on the city's faith and credit for transportation or water purposes provided that a tax for repayment of principal and interest was to be levied but not collected if enough money was set aside from revenues to make the necessary repayment. This device would have allowed bonds to be floated at a lower rate of interest than would be required for revenue bonds.

A final portion of the Chicago home rule proposal worth discussing is the authorization for consolidation of all other local governments or other authorities wholly within the city *and* that part of any town within the city. (The latter authorization went beyond Section 34.) The city was also authorized to take over the Sanitary District and the Forest Preserve District, or either of them, but only with the approval of a majority vote "both in the district and the city." The authorization further provided that, after consolidation, no taxing power would exist outside the city limits and that the city would not make any charge outside the city for sewage service in existence at the time of the take-over.

It should be noted that in the Cook County portion of the proposed 1922 article on local government, there was an authorization for the legislature to propose consolidation of the city and that part of the county within the city limits, but only with the approval by referendum of the voters in the city and the voters in the county outside Chicago.

Explanation

The need that was considered most pressing at the time Section 34 was adopted was a reorganization of the local court system. For this reason, in part, Section 34 contains detailed authorization for legislative alteration of the then-existing judicial system. In part, however, this detail was necessary because, in effect, Section 34 had to "amend" Article VI as it then existed. Shortly after adoption of Section 34, the Supreme Court had to rule on whether Section 34 was validly adopted in the light of the then-existing restriction on amending more than one article of the Constitution at a time. Section 34 was upheld. (City of Chicago v. Reeves, 220 Ill. 274 (1906).)

Shortly after adoption, a municipal court system was established by statute and the required approval by referendum was obtained. Over the years there was extensive litigation concerning the municipal courts, but since, with the adoption of the new Article VI, the municipal court system has been superseded, there is no need to discuss the judicial interpretations of that part of Section 34.

For the most part, Section 34 has not been used as a home rule authorization for Chicago. Shortly after the section was adopted, Chicago proposed a new charter, but after it was amended by the legislature, Chicago rejected it. A second charter passed the General Assembly but was vetoed by the Governor. A third effort was rejected by Chicago. (See Bulletins 940-41.) In the meantime, the legislature adopted the practice of enacting general legislation applicable to cities over a given population so that the law would apply only to Chicago. (The figure now used is 500,000 but in earlier days was smaller.) The courts have held that Section 34 is in no way exclusive and that general legislation affecting Chicago but not "based upon this amendment" is not subject to the referendum requirement of Section 34. (See Alexander v. City of Chicago, 14 Ill. 2d 261 (1958).) Normally, the courts determine that an act is not based upon Section 34 by the absence of a provision for a referendum. (Id.) In 1941, an optional act under Section 34 was passed and in November, 1947, Chicago by referendum opted to operate under the act. (Ill. Rev. Stat. ch. 24, §§ 21-1 to 21-49 (1967).) No changes under that act can be made, of course, without referendum approval by Chicago voters.

Section 34 has a parenthetical clause to the effect that new bonded indebtedness is subject to a referendum. The Supreme Court has observed that this "provision becomes operative only in the event that the legislature provides a consolidated government for the city of Chicago." (People *ex rel.* Gutknecht v. City of Chicago, 414 Ill 600, 623 (1953).) The legislature can, of course, require a referendum on a bond issue. (*See* Ill. Rev. Stat. ch. 24, § 8-4-1 (Supp. 1968).) It is worth nothing that the proposed 1922 Constitution made a referendum on any new bond issues mandatory. (art. VIII, § 191.)

Comparative Analysis

No other state constitution has a single section dealing with a single city in the combination of powers and restrictions contained in Section 34. Several states have provisions dealing with the principal large city in the state. Examples are St. Louis, Denver, New Orleans, Baltimore, and, in Pennsylvania, two large cities, Philadelphia and Pittsburgh. These may be grants of power to adopt local charters or power to consolidate city and county, or both. In each case, the provision is, as in Illinois, tailored to the specific problem of the municipality.

The varations in municipal home rule provisions in the various state constitutions are too great for a detailed comparative analysis. Not quite half of the states prohibit special acts of incorporation. Many, but not all, of those states specifically state that the legislature shall provide by general law for the incorporation of municipalities. In some states, this takes the form of a limitation on the powers of the legislature; in other states, the language is that of a grant of power to the legislature to provide for home rule which, of course, is no guarantee of home rule.

The Model State Constitution provides for the organization of local governments as set forth in the *Comparative Analysis* of Section 5 of Article X. (*Infra,* p. 498.) This is followed by a "limitation of powers" section as follows:

"*Powers of Counties and Cities.* A county or city may exercise any legislative power or perform any function which is not denied to it by its charter, is not denied to counties or cities generally, or to counties or cities of its class, and is within such limitations as the legislature may establish by general law. This grant of home rule powers shall not include the power to enact private or civil law governing civil relationships except as incident to an exercise of an independent county or city power, nor shall it include power to define and provide for the punishment of a felony." (art. VIII, § 8.02.)

Comment

It is obvious that Section 34 should be dropped. What should take its place is a complicated matter. It would appear inadvisable to adopt the approach of the 1920-22 Convention of a detailed local government article with some 16 sections devoted to Chicago alone. It may be appropriate to say something about Chicago, but in general, a minimum of

·substantive detail is the goal. It is important to spell out *who* has power to make decisions in what areas — the people through denial of power to any government, the state through denial of power to local government, local voters through reservation of referendum rights, or the local government. It is equally important to avoid making substantive decisions in the Constitution.

Article V

EXECUTIVE DEPARTMENT
Officers — Terms

Sec. 1. The executive department shall consist of a governor, lieutenant governor, secretary of state, auditor of public accounts, treasurer, superintendent of public instruction and attorney general, who shall each hold his office for the term of four years from the second Monday of January next after his election and until his successor is elected and qualified. They shall, except the lieutenant governor, reside at the seat of government during their term of office, and keep the public records, books and papers there, and shall perform such duties as may be prescribed by law.

History

This section dates from 1870. In the earlier constitutions, the various elective officials were covered in different sections of the article on the executive department. Thus, the first half of the first sentence of Section 1 simply makes explicit what was implicit before. Likewise, in the 1848 Constitution, the designation of the time of beginning and ending of the terms of Governor and Lieutenant Governor was explicit, but partially implicit as to other elected officers. (For the length of terms of office, see *History* of Secs. 2 and 3, *infra*, pp. 260 and 262.) The second sentence, as an all-inclusive statement, also dates from 1870. In the 1848 Constitution, only the Governor was required to reside at the seat of government and only the Secretary of State, the Auditor of Public Accounts and the Treasurer were to have duties as prescribed by law. (It is to be noted, however, that the Superintendent of Public Instruction was first added in 1870, and that the Attorney General who had been provided for in 1818 was omitted from the 1848 Constitution.)

The proposed 1922 Constitution preserved the substance of Section 1 in the course of splitting it into several sections. One substantive change was made. The executive department was stated to consist of the named elected officers "and such other officers as provided by law." In a section concerning performance of duties as prescribed by law, all officers of the executive department, not just constitutional officers, were covered.

There was a technical amendment to Section 1 in 1954 as part of the proposal to increase the term of the Treasurer to four years. The change was simply the deletion of words that had excepted the Treasurer from the clause prescribing the length of term of the executive officers.

Explanation

Executive Power: In the beginning, one might say, there was *Field v. People* ex rel. *McClernand.* (3 Ill. 79 (1839).) This monumental case — in length, 105 pages, if nothing else — is of such historical importance in the development of constitutional theory in Illinois that a fairly full statement of the case is warranted. Under the 1818 Constitution, the Governor appointed the Secretary of State, subject to Senate confirmation. There was no stated length of term. A. P. Field was appointed Secretary of State in 1829 by Governor Ninian Edwards, following the resignation of the incumbent Secretary. Secretary Field served under two succeeding Governors and was still in office when Thomas Carlin was elected in 1838. Governor Carlin nominated John A. McClernand to be Secretary of State, but the Senate rejected the nomination and, by a vote of 22 to 18, adopted a resolution to the effect that consent was not given because there was no vacancy in the office of Secretary of State. (*Id.* at 154.) After the legislature adjourned, the Governor removed Field and appointed McClernand to fill the vacancy. The lawsuit followed.

It is clear from the opinions that the case was a political hot potato. (Each of the three sitting justices wrote an opinion, one of which was a dissent. The fourth member, a relative of McClernand, declined to sit.) The decision was that the Governor had no power to remove the Secretary of State, a decision that the 1870 Convention subsequently "overruled" by the addition of Section 12. (See *infra,* p. 285.) Moreover, the *Field* decision was ignored. At the next session in 1840, Governor Carlin nominated Stephen A. Douglas, who had been one of the principal counsel for McClernand. A Senate motion not to consent on the ground that no vacancy existed was defeated. A motion to advise and consent to Douglas' nomination was then adopted. Apparently, Field accepted this, for Douglas took office the same day.

The importance of the *Field* case lies in the broad constitutional doctrine enunciated by Chief Justice Wilson. (In passing, it is interesting that the Chief Justice was speaking only for himself. Neither the dissenting nor the concurring justice agreed with the Chief Justice's constitutional theory. Yet, presumably because his opinion was printed first, the theory therein expressed became the theory of the "Court.") The doctrine is:

"The constitution is a limitation upon the powers of the legislative department of the government; but it is to be regarded as a grant of powers to the other
department[s]. Neither the executive nor the judiciary, therefore, can exercise
any authority or power, except such as is clearly granted by the Constitution."
(*Id.* at 81.)

It is difficult to point out how Chief Justice Wilson's sweeping statement affected the course of constitutional development in Illinois. The
case has been cited for this theory many times. (For the most recent,
see *In re* Estate of Quick, 333 Ill. App. 573, 579 (1948).) But because
of its fundamental nature, the theory is influential in a general, unexpressed way. To put this rather difficult thought another way, if the
concurring opinion of Mr. Justice Lockwood had been the opinion of
the Court, one assumes that the concept of executive power would have
developed differently because he carefully limited his remarks to the
question of whether or not removal of a constitutional officer at will
was an inherent part of the executive power. Under his theory, there
was some inherent executive power, and if he had spoken for the Court,
no one could have cited the *Field* case for the proposition that the
executive and the judiciary have only powers "clearly granted by the
Constitution." It is simply not possible to point to any particular decision and state categorically that the decision would have gone the other
way under Mr. Justice Lockwood's theory. The most that a student
of the subject can say is that some aspects of constitutional development
in Illinois appear to have been influenced by Chief Justice Wilson's
pronouncement. (See, *e.g., Explanation* of Art. III, *supra,* p. 99.)

There have, of course, been cases in which the argument was made
that the legislature was unconstitutionally interfering with executive
powers. These cases are discussed in connection with the separation of
powers doctrine embodied in Article III. (See *supra,* p. 101.) The important point about those cases is that the courts were not concerned
with alleged interference with inherent executive power, but interference
with the executive power as "granted" by the Constitution. Those cases
are in no way inconsistent with the *Field* theory. Indeed, aside from the
power of removal, now amply covered by Section 12 (*infra,* p. 285), there
are very few ways in which the question of an inherent executive
power over and above specific constitutional grants can arise. In the
case of the United States, the President has asserted, and the courts have
recognized, inherent executive power in the conduct of foreign affairs.
(*See* United States v. Curtiss-Wright Export Corporation, 299 U.S. 304
(1936).) Other presidential attempts at action in the absence of statutory authority have not fared so well. (*See* Youngstown Sheet & Tube
Co. v. Sawyer, 343 U.S. 579 (1952). For a discussion of the power of

removal, see *Explanation* of Art. III, *supra,* p. 99. See also *Comment* below.)

Executive offices: Illinois has what is called the "long ballot." The problems connected with this are discussed in the *Comment* below. For present purposes, it is sufficient to note that the courts have said that the legislature may not take away any constitutional powers or duties of a constitutional executive officer. (*See* American Legion Post No. 279 v. Barrett, 371 Ill. 78 (1939); People *ex rel.* State Bd. of Agr. v. Brady, 277 Ill. 124 (1917).) The rule that constitutional powers and duties may not be taken away from constitutional officers is in itself unobjectionable. There are, however, very few specific constitutional powers and duties set forth in the Constitution for officers other than the Governor. (For the Auditor of Public Accounts, see Secs. 17 and 21 of Art. IV, *supra,* pp. 181 and 200; and for the Secretary of State, see Sec. 9 of Art. IV, *supra,* p. 145, and Secs. 16 and 22 of Art. V, *infra,* pp. 293 and 318. The Lieutenant Governor is really an executive officer only when he is acting as Governor.) In the case of the Treasurer, Attorney General, and Superintendent of Public Instruction, constitutional powers and duties can be only such as necessarily flow from the title of the office. Moreover, Section 1 specifically states that the officers of the executive department "shall perform such duties as may be prescribed by law."

From the foregoing, one would normally assume that the legislature is relatively free to parcel out powers and duties in the executive department. Such an assumption is clearly wrong in the case of the Attorney General. In *Fergus v. Russel* (270 Ill. 304 (1915), also see *supra,* p. 103), the Supreme Court decided that the Attorney General had all the powers that the English Attorney General had at common law. Since there was no Attorney General provided for in the 1848 Constitution, and in the Schedule to the 1818 Constitution, only an authorization to the legislature to appoint an Attorney General whose duties could "be regulated by law," it is difficult to believe that the drafters of the 1870 Constitution had any such understanding of the title "Attorney General." But the really strange thing about the case is that the Court used the words "such duties as may be prescribed by law" to back up its argument that the 1870 drafters meant to clothe the Attorney General with the powers of the English common law Attorney General. In a feat of masterful legerdemain, the Court took words that appear to allow the legislature to take away common law powers, assuming such an original meaning, and converted them into words that establish the "original" meaning. It should be conceded that the Supreme Court has taken the same approach to legislative efforts to curtail the power of the sheriff (see *Explanation* of Secs. 7 and 8 of Art. X, *infra,* pp. 501, 505), but at least in that instance there is no reference to "duties as may be prescribed by law." It might also occur to someone that the legislature's lack of power over the Attorney General and his duties is a little inconsistent with the *Field* theory. The *Fergus* Court had a ready answer to that. *Field,* it seems, was different because the Governor was not an official known to the common law! (See also *Comment* below.)

Comparative Analysis

Executive Power: There does not appear to be any state constitution that expresses a theory of executive power such as that of Chief Justice Wilson discussed above. Whether any other state Supreme Court adopted such a theory is rather difficult to ascertain. The traditional expression of executive power in a state constitution is in a provision comparable to Section 6, and the *Comparative Analysis* of that section, together with the *Comparative Analysis* of Section 12 on removal power, will serve as a comparison with other states. (*Infra,* pp. 271 and 286.)

Executive Offices: Three states — Idaho, Kansas, and Montana — list precisely the same seven elected constitutional officers as those comprising the executive department. Approximately 17 other states have an "executive department" provision, listing anywhere from five to 12 officers, most of whom are elected constitutional officers.

The presence or absence of an "executive department" provision is not, however, a guide to the presence or absence of a long ballot, which is a matter of the number of elected executive officials, whether or not grouped together under the title of the "executive department." The following is a summary tabulation of elective constitutional executive offices with any elective statutory offices included in parentheses. (Not included are multimember boards and commissions. For example, Illinois elects nine statutory university trustees. In Michigan, there are three different constitutional governing boards, each consisting of eight elected members.)

Number of Elective Offices	Number of States
2	2
3	2
4	4
4 (1)	2
5	4
5 (1)	3
6	7
6 (1)	3
6 (2)	1
6 (6)	1
7	8
7 (1)	1

Number of Elective Offices	Number of States
8	3
8 (1)	2
8 (3)	1
8 (4)	1
9 (1)	1
11	3
12	1

(Council of State Governments, The Book of the States, 1968-1969 at 134-5 (1968).)

In some cases, the official, constitutional or statutory, is elected by the legislature, but insofar as the executive power of the governor is concerned, the difference is slight. In most states, one of the elected officials is either a comptroller or an auditor. Any auditor whose duties are limited to post-audit is not really an executive officer.

A few states have a constitutional provision designed to force a rational administrative arrangement on the executive branch. The customary statement is that there shall be no more than 20 executive departments.

The United States Constitution provides for the election of one executive official, the President, and his potential successor, the Vice President. The Model State Constitution recommends only one elected executive official, the Governor. The Model State Constitution has a "20 department" provision reading as follow:

"Administrative Departments. All executive and administrative offices, agencies and instrumentalities of the state government, and their respective funcions, powers and duties, shall be allocated by law among and within not more than twenty principal departments, so as to group them as far as practicable according to major purposes. Regulatory, quasi-judicial and temporary agencies established by law may, but need not, be allocated within a principal department. The legislature shall by law prescribe the functions, powers and duties of the principal departments and of all other agencies of the state and may from time to time reallocate offices, agencies and instrumentalities among the principal departments, may increase, modify, diminish or change their functions, powers and duties and may assign new functions, powers and duties to them; but the governor may make such changes in the allocation of offices, agencies and instrumentalities, and in the allocation of such functions, powers and duties, as he considers necessary for efficient administration. If such changes affect existing law, they shall be set forth in executive orders, which shall be submitted to the legislature while it is in session, and shall become effective, and shall have the force of law, sixty days after submission, or at the close of the session, whichever is sooner, unless specifically modified or disapproved by a resolution concurred in by a majority of all the members." (art. V, § 5.06.)

Comment

Executive Power: It was pointed out above that Chief Justice Wilson's theory of executive and judicial power is, to say the least, unusual, but is was also conceded that it is difficult to point to specific, concrete effects of his theory. It follows that there is no way that the Convention could safely draft anything designed explicitly to eliminate the *Field* theory. Any formulation of a theory of government beyond the separation of powers expressed in Article III (*supra*, p. 99) would probably usher in a new period of constitutional confusion. The fact is that there is a theory of constitutional government in the United States, a sort of "brooding omnipresence in the sky," that in a general way runs throughout the country. Chief Justice Wilson represents an aberration, a man out of step, and as time passes, citation of his theory probably means less and less. The Illinois courts will undoubtedly move along the same road that constitutional decisions across the country take.

Nevertheless, it would be advantageous if the Illinois courts would forget Mr. Chief Justice Wilson's theory. For one thing, aberrations in the law are of no value except when they are the first step in a shift in the law, which is certainly not the case with *Field*. For another thing, the political process is a matter of balancing interests, of effecting compromises among forces. The process is a delicate one, and a categorical theory that the legislature is "top dog" except to the extent that the Constitution says otherwise, is not a delicate theory of balancing interests. Having said all of this, there are only two suggestions that seem appropriate. One is that in the course of considering Article III and its relationship to Articles IV, V, and VI, the Convention could make a legislative record to the effect that the Convention adheres to the traditional constitutional theory of separation of inherent powers and not to the *Field* theory. The other suggestion is that a scholarly article developing more fully the presentation made here might convince the Illinois courts to drop the *Field* theory.

Executive Offices: In any constitutional convention, the long versus the short ballot is an important policy question. It is not appropriate here to spell out the whole range of policy considerations relevant to reaching an informed decision. It should be noted, however, that the "long ballot-short ballot" controversy has two facets, only one of which is particularly relevant to Section 1. It is argued that voters cannot exercise their choices intelligently if they are confronted with too many elective offices to fill. In the case of Section 1, this side of the problem becomes a matter of five people, not seven, since the Treasurer and Superintendent of Public Instruction are elected in the "off" even-numbered year. (See Sec. 3, *infra*, p. 262.) If the Convention were to join the current trend of having voters vote for Governor and Lieutenant Governor as a team (see *infra*, p. 263), the number of state-wide executive offices to be filled could drop to four in one election. Moreover, by a judicious arrangement of elections and by small decreases in elective offices at various levels of government, the ballot could be shortened considerably.

The facet of the "long ballot-short ballot" controversy that is relevant here is exemplified by the sign President Truman had on his desk: "The buck stops here." The "short ballot" proponents would argue that a similar sign cannot be put on the desk of the Governor of Illinois. The proponents add, obviously, that such a sign belongs on the Governor's desk. The argument of the proponents of the long ballot is simply that it avoids giving one man too much power. (See also *Comments* on Secs. 6 and 21, *infra*, pp. 272 and 318.)

If the Convention decides to keep some or all of these elective officers, it would seem appropriate, and, it is to be hoped, not too controversial, to do something about the *Fergus v. Russel* determination concerning the Attorney General. There is a simple drafting change that will introduce adequate flexibility in allocating legal work within the Executive Department. The change is to use the words of the 1818 Schedule — "whose duties may be regulated by law" — in place of "perform such duties as may be prescribed by law." Such a change would require a recasting of the second sentence of the section, but it is such a hodgepodge as it is that recasting is necessary anyway.

Whether the Convention should adopt some version of a "20 department" section depends on whether it is believed that the legislature cannot be expected to permit rational ordering of the executive departments or that the legislature cannot be trusted to leave a rational ordering alone, or both. There is no reason in constitutional theory for a "20 department" provision. Anyone who is champing at the bit to force a good organization chart on the Executive Department might well pause to consider who else is champing at the bit to put in his pet project. All good men will not agree on what is essential in a constitution, but all good men ought to agree that once the door is opened to "good" nonessentials, "bad" nonessentials will slip in, too. A "20 department" provision is a good nonessential.

Treasurer

Sec. 2. The treasurer shall hold his office for the term of four years, and until his successor is elected and qualified, and shall be ineligible to said office for four years next after the end of the term for which he was elected. He may be required by the governor to give reasonable additional security, and in default of so doing his office shall be deemed vacant.

History

The 1818 Constitution provided for the appointment of a treasurer every two years by the joint vote of the two houses of the legislature.

The 1848 Constitution continued the two-year term but made the office elective. The 1870 Constitution added the prohibition against a treasurer succeeding himself and the requirement that he give "reasonable additional security" if so required by the governor. By Amendment in 1954 the term was extended to four years. Through a Schedule accompanying the amendment, the first four-year term began with the election of the treasurer in 1958. The proposed 1922 Constitution increased the term of office to four years, but otherwise retained the substance of the section.

Explanation

A separate provision for the treasurer was originally required because of his two-year term, all other constitutional executive officers having four-year terms. A separate section was and is still required to cover the treasurer's ineligibility to succeed himself and the requirement for "additional security." As to the latter, see *Comment* below. As to the former, it was observed by a delegate to the 1870 Convention: "Now, there is a good reason why the Treasurer of the State should not be eligible to a second term. There ought to be, with reference to the custodian of the public treasury, a change, in order that we may have an actual account — an actual, as distinguished from a constructive accountability — with regard to the funds in the treasury . . . ." (Debates 762.) There has been only one case construing this section, *Fairbank v. Stratton* (14 Ill. 2d 307 (1958)), and that simply made the obvious point that the legislature cannot deprive the treasurer of his constitutional powers.

Comparative Analysis

The treasurer is elected by the voters in 40 states. In four states the treasurer is elected by the legislature and in three states, he is appointed by the governor. Three states have no treasurer. The states are approximately equally divided between two- and four-year terms. About 13 states limit immediate succession as treasurer and another seven or so have a less stringent restriction on length of service as treasurer. Some seven state constitutions specify some requirement for bonding, but no other state has a provision for "additional security." The treasurer is not a constitutional officer under the United States Constitution or the Model State Constitution.

Comment

The last sentence of Section 2 is one of the more curious provisions in the Illinois Constitution. There is an assumption that the treasurer gives a bond upon taking office, but there is no constitutional requirement for the initial bond. In the debates of the 1870 Convention, it was noted that existing statutes required an initial bond and additional security "[b]ut before the committee there was a doubt whether the Legislature would have the power to confer such a discretion upon the Governor without a constitutional provision . . . ." (Debates 809.) What the doubt really was was whether the legislature could enforce the requirement for additional security by declaring the office vacant upon default.

Election and Terms of Office

Sec. 3. An election for governor, lieutenant governor, secretary of state, auditor of public accounts, and attorney general, shall be held on the Tuesday next after the first Monday of November, in the year of our Lord 1872, and every four years thereafter; for superintendent of public instruction, and treasurer, on the Tuesday next after the first Monday of November, in the year 1958, and every four years thereafter at such places and in such manner as may be prescribed by law.

History

This section, a composite statement of terms of office and times of election, first appeared in 1870. Under the 1818 Constitution the Governor and Lieutenant Governor were elected by the voters for four-year terms. The Secretary of State was appointed by the Governor subject to Senate confirmation. The Treasurer was chosen by joint vote of the two houses of the General Assembly for a two-year term. In the Schedule of the 1818 Constitution it was provided that the General Assembly could appoint an Auditor, Attorney General, and "such other officers for the State as may be necessary." (§ 10.) It is said that the original plan of the 1818 Convention was to have the appointing power in the Governor but that when the members of the Convention learned that the man who was expected to be elected Governor was not going to appoint as Auditor a man favored by the members, the original plan was abandoned and the section quoted from was inserted in the Schedule. (See E. Anthony, The Constitutional History of Illinois 39-40 (1891).) In the 1848 Constitution, the Secretary of State and Auditor of Public Accounts were made elective with four-year terms corresponding to the terms of Governor and Lieutenant Governor. The Treasurer was made elective but the two-year term was continued. In. 1870, the Attorney General and Superintendent of Public Instruction were made elective with four-year terms, but the Superintendent's election was to be in the non-gubernatorial even-numbered year. By amendment adopted in 1954, the Treasurer's term was extended to four years, effective in 1958, so that his term coincides with that of the Superintendent. The proposed 1922 Constitution preserved the election of the Superintendent of Public

Instruction in the off even-numbered year but included the Treasurer with the other four-year-term offices.

Explanation

This section is self-explanatory. The only judicial comment appears to have been the observation that the election day referred to does not necessarily govern any election for offices not named in the section. (Bilek v. City of Chicago, 396 Ill. 445 (1947).)

Comparative Analysis

In 39 states, including Illinois, the governor is elected for four years. In 11 of those states, he cannot succeed himself and in another 12 he is limited to two consecutive terms. Pennsylvania is in transition. The present governor cannot succeed himself, but future governors will be eligible for one additional term. Two states have an absolute limit of two terms, consecutive or otherwise. One of the 11 states with two-year terms limits consecutive terms to two and another by statute prohibits nomination for a third consecutive term. Wisconsin switches from two to four years in 1971.

Of the 39 four-year states, 11, including Illinois, hold gubernatorial elections in presidential years. Twenty-four hold their elections in the other even-numbered year. Five states hold their elections in an odd-numbered year. All two-year states elect governors in even-numbered years. The Model State Constitution calls for four-year terms, election in an odd-numbered year, and has no limitation on re-election.

One of the more popular changes in recent years has been the adoption of the President-Vice President team system. In at least nine states, voters cast one vote for a governor-lieutenant governor team (secretary of state in Alaska), so that succession will be within the same political party. A little over a decade ago, New York was the only state with a team system.

In general, in states electing treasurers and state school superintendents, election takes place at the same general election at which the governor and other state officers are chosen. In no state does it appear that the treasurer is elected in an off-year. In Wisconsin the superintendent is elected for four years at the election for members of the Supreme Court, which must be on a day other than, and not within 30 days of, the election for any other state or county office.

Comment

If the State School Superintendent is to be elected, it may make sense to elect him apart from the other state-wide offices on the theory that education ought to be nonpartisan. It is difficult to justify the election of the Treasurer, if he is to be elected, in an off-year.

Canvass of Election Returns — Contests

Sec. 4. The returns of every election for the above named officers shall be sealed up and transmitted, by the returning officers, to the Secretary of State, directed to "The Speaker of the House of Representatives," who shall, immediately after the organization of the House, and before proceeding to other business, open and publish the same in the presence of a majority of each House of the General Assembly, who shall, for that purpose, assemble in the hall of the House of Representatives. The person having the highest number of votes for either of said offices shall be declared duly elected; but if two or more have an equal, and the highest, number of votes, the General Assembly shall, by joint ballot, choose one of such persons for said office. Contested elections for all of said offices shall be determined by both houses of the General Assembly, by joint ballot, in such manner as may be prescribed by law.

History

The 1818 Constitution contained the substance of the foregoing in the section providing for the election of a Governor. (Except for a Lieutenant Governor, no other state official was elected. In the section providing for a Lieutenant Governor, it was stated that he should be chosen at "every election for governor" and "in the same manner.") No change was made in 1848. (Although the Secretary of State, Auditor and Treasurer were made elective in 1848, returns for their election were handled according to the law concerning election of United States Representatives. (Schedule, § 17).) In 1870, the Secretary of State was named as recipient of the returns, the hall of the House of Representatives was designated as the meeting place, and the timing — "immediately after the organization of the House, and before proceeding to other business" — for the canvass was spelled out. The 1870 Constitution also added the words "by joint ballot" to the last sentence of the section.

The proposed 1922 Constitution had a considerably rephrased section but did not change the substance. In the course of such rephrasing the rare use of "either" as one of more than two was abandoned and the word "up" was omitted. It is interesting to recall from the 1870 Convention that on the occasion of the adoption of the Executive Article in its final form, the following took place:

"Mr. PEIRCE. Mr. President: I move to strike out the word 'up' in the first line. I consider that if the returns are sealed, they will be sealed up. The expression is unnecessary and inelegant.

"A division was ordered. The Convention divided, when, there being twenty-four in the affirmative, and twenty-five in the negative, the motion of Mr. Peirce to strike out was not agreed to." (Debates 1781.)

Explanation

This section serves three purposes: It provides (1) a method for canvassing the election returns and determining who has been elected; (2) a means for breaking a tie; and (3) a system for settling election contests. These purposes are served, however, only as to the offices named in Section 3. Canvassing, breaking ties, and settling contests for elections of other officials are governed wholly by statute.

In the applicable chapter of the Election Code there is a section on procedure to be followed in contesting the election of any of the named officials. The section follows the language of the Constitution and thus leaves the entire issue in the hands of the legislature. (Ill. Rev. Stat. ch. 46, § 23-1 (1967).) One can speculate whether this was done to keep control in legislative hands or in the belief that the Constitution so requires. It is to be noted that the Chairman of the Committee on the Executive Department stated to the delegates of the 1870 Convention that the provision concerning contests "is substantially the law of the State at the present time; and while a mode is pointed out here, it does not take away the right of contesting elections in the courts of law, which would also have jurisdiction of such cases." (Debates 747.) The Chairman presumably represented the intent of the Convention, but the language used is difficult to square with such intent. There do not appear to have been any reported cases or other pronouncements on election contests.

In 1913, the outgoing Governor wrote to the Attorney General on January 15th inquiring whether he, the Governor, should continue in office in view of the fact that the House of Representatives had not yet organized and so the General Assembly had not been able to announce the election of his successor. The Attorney General assured the Governor that he remained in office until his successor qualified and that this could not occur until the General Assembly followed the procedure called for in Section 4. (1912 Ill. Att'y Gen. Rep. 1237.) On January 22nd of the same year the Secretary of the Senate inquired whether it could conduct business while waiting for the House to organize. The Attorney General replied that the restriction on proceeding to other business applied only to the House of Representatives. (1912 Ill. Att'y Gen. Rep. 1240.)

Comparative Analysis

Just under half of the states provide that the determination of the election for governor shall be handled by the legislature. In seven states the canvassing procedure is specified but the group named is not the legislature. Eight states leave canvassing to be determined by law and, presumably, the same obtains in the states that have no provision for canvassing the votes for governor. About 20 states direct the legislature to deal with contests for election of governor, four specify that the method be prescribed by law, and one state specifies that the highest court settle contests. Presumably, in the other states, the matter is handled by legislation. About three-quarters of the states direct the legislature to break a tie in the election of governor. Kentucky directs choice by lot. In general, each state applies the same rules to canvassing, contests and ties for other state offices. But there are exceptions as, for example, in Maryland where the Governor breaks the tie in the case of the election for attorney general and in Connecticut where the canvass is done by the Secretary of State, Treasurer, and Comptroller except that in the canvass of each of those three the other two do it. The United States Constitution covers the matter through the Electoral College. In the absence of a majority vote for one person, the election shifts to the House of Representatives. This would cover a tie, of course, as was the case in 1800, though that was a tie vote between Thomas Jefferson and Aaron Burr of the same party. The Twelfth Amendment eliminated this particular tie-vote problem by requiring that the elector designate which person was to be President and which to be Vice President. The Constitution is silent as to election contests. The Model State Constitution simply provides that the legislature shall provide for the administration of elections.

Comment

It is obvious that detailed provisions for canvassing votes, breaking ties, and determining contests are traditional and that placing control in the hands of the legislature is also traditional. But it is questionable whether there is any value in retaining such an anachronism. With modern equipment and rapid communications, election results are known within a short time after the polls close. It seems unnecessary to hold all official action in abeyance for almost two months. This is particularly a problem in Illinois, where the official ritual may be delayed by the inability of the House of Representatives to organize. It is also questionable whether the handling of contests should be left to the legislature. The contest is essentially legal and evidentiary, and courts are best equipped to handle that kind of dispute. Moreover, the stakes are political and the legislature, a political body by definition, is more likely to make a political decision than a judicial one. Furthermore, the contest cannot be handled by the legislature until after the results are known and this, under Section 4, is after publication in the House of Representatives. Under a normal procedure, the contest could be started in the courts soon after Election Day.

Nevertheless, traditional rituals have tenacious life and it may be better to concentrate on changes more crucial to the operation of the state. After all, the occasions when the existing ritual is likely to create an inconvenience are rare indeed. In any event, it is advisable to preserve the right of the legislature to break a tie. It is certainly not appropriate to choose a Governor by tossing a coin.

Elective State Officers — Eligibility

Sec. 5. No person shall be eligible to the office of Governor, or Lieutenant Governor, who shall not have attained the age of 30 years, and been, for five years next preceding his election, a citizen of the United States and of this State. Neither the Governor, Lieutenant Governor, Auditor of Public Accounts, Secretary of State, Superintendent of Public Instruction nor Attorney General shall be eligible to any other office during the period for which he shall have been elected.

History

The 1818 Constitution required the Governor to be at least 30 years of age, a United States citizen for at least 30 years, and to have resided in the state for two years "next preceding his election." In the 1818 Schedule, Section 14, the requirement of 30-year citizenship for Lieutenant Governor was removed, notwithstanding the section in the Executive Article which said that the Lieutenant Governor should have "the same qualifications" as the Governor. There was no reference to eligibility to any other office, but the Governor could serve for only four years out of any eight-year period. In the 1848 Constitution the minimum age was raised to 35, the citizenship requirement was reduced to 14 years, and the residency requirement was increased to ten years, but with no words of "next preceding his election" accompanying residency. The Lieutenant Governor was now required to meet the same qualifications as the Governor. (It is not clear, but it was probably intended that the "four in eight year" limitation applied to the Lieutenant Governor.) The 1848 Constitution also provided that the Governor was not eligible "to any other office until after the expiration of the term for which he was elected." (It is not clear, but it would seem that the "any other office" limitation did not apply to the Lieutenant Governor.) In 1870, age was dropped back to 30, United States citizenship to five years, and residency to five years, but "next preceding his election" came back in. The limitation on successive terms was dropped. Everybody except the Treasurer came under the "any other office" ban. In 1922, it was proposed to increase the age requirement back to 35 and the residency back to ten years but to retain "next preceding his election." (Actually, the 1922 provision changed "preceding" to "before.") In the official explanation the foregoing age changes were pointed out. It was not noted that the Treasurer now came under the "any other office" ban. (P.N.C. 35.)

Explanation

The first sentence of this section is self-explanatory. The second sentence is not. There was an extended debate in the 1870 Convention on this sentence, but the debate turned principally on whether to limit the named elected officers to one four-year term in every eight. In the course of the debate it was indicated that none of the named officers could run for any other office while serving, including, though this is not crystal clear from the debates, another office at the general election just preceding the end of his term of office. (Debates 773.) One delegate moved to change "shall be eligible to" to "shall hold" but the motion was not agreed to. Thus, the thrust of the sentence was clearly aimed at using one office as a stepping stone to another office and not at dual office holding. Dual office holding is, however, prevented by the "eligible to" formulation.

At no point in the debates was there an explanation for the omission of the Treasurer from the list of those who could not run for another office. The most plausible explanation is that the drafters overlooked him because he is covered by a different section. The drafters apparently also overlooked the fact that Section 6 of Article VII (*infra,* p. 394) requires United States citizenship for any elective office, thus making part of the first sentence superfluous.

There have been several reported cases involving a claim of dual office holding. The cases uniformly held that Section 5 does not prohibit additional duties to one of the named officers. (Baro v. Murphy, 32 Ill. 2d 453 (1965) (Governor *ex officio* member of State Parks Revenue Bond Commission); People v. Illinois Toll Highway Comm'n, 3 Ill. 2d 218 (1954) (Governor *ex officio* member thereof); People *ex rel.* Graham v. Inglis, 161 Ill. 256 (1896) (Superintendent of Public Instruction *ex officio* trustee of state normal school).)

By virtue of the definition of "office" in Section 24 (*infra,* p. 322), it is clear that any of the named officers can run for federal office during the term for which he is elected. By virtue of the last sentence of Section 3 of Article IV (*supra,* p. 120), he would be prohibited from retaining his state office if elected to federal office.

Comparative Analysis

Qualifications: In some 35 states besides Illinois, the minimum age for governor is 30. A couple of states have a higher (31 and 35) and four states have a lower minimum (25). Eight states have no minimum. About 40 states specify that the governor must be a citizen of the United States. Almost half of these specify no minimum number of years. Of the others, the number of years ranges from two to 20. More states (seven including Illinois) choose five as the appropriate minimum than any other number of years. Residency (or state citizenship) requirements also vary widely from no minimum up to ten years. The most common minimum is five years (18 states, including Illinois). Not all states combine the governor and lieutenant governor in the same qualification sentence as does Illinois. Generally speaking, the requirements are much the same for the two offices. The United States Constitution requires that the President be native born, 35 years old and 14 years a resident. By implication the same requirements must be met by the Vice President. The Model State Constitution requires only that the governor be a qualified voter of the state but includes a minimum age requirement with the number of years left blank.

Dual Office Holding: Only about half of the states have dual office holding restrictions on executive officers set forth in connection with qualifications for their office. In most of those states, the limitation appears to run only against the governor, and most of them prohibit "holding" another office. Only a handful of states, principally Arkansas, Delaware, Montana, Nebraska and West Virginia, follow the Illinois provision of declaring most elective executive officers ineligible for any other office. It does not appear that any of those states specifically omit a constitutional officer as the treasurer is omitted in Illinois. Nebraska, it is interesting to note, amended its constitution in 1962 to provide an exception to allow the lieutenant governor to be a candidate for governor. Neither the United States Constitution nor the Model State Constitution has any comparable restriction.

Comment

There are good reasons for prohibiting dual office holding, but the formulation of a policy needs to be thought through carefully. The most important restrictions are those concerning legislators and judges as discussed elsewhere. (*Supra,* p. 120, and *infra,* p. 368.) Insofar as constitutional executive officers are concerned, it seems appropriate to prohibit dual office holding even though in a large industrial state it probably is not necessary. In such a state, any of the constitutional offices, except perhaps that of lieutenant governor, is so obviously a full-time position that as a practical matter it seems unlikely that anyone would attempt to hold down a second job, public or private. Moreover, in the absence of a constitutional prohibition, litigation of the type set out above (p. 268) would be avoided. But if a prohibition is to be retained, careful consideration should be given to the distinction between "ineligibility for" and "holding" any other office. The underlying policy against dual office holding is quite different from the underlying policy against permitting a person holding one office to run for another office.

Governor — Supreme Executive Power

Sec. 6. The Supreme executive power shall be vested in the Governor, who shall take care that the laws be faithfully executed.

History

The substance of this section appeared in two sections of the 1818 Constitution which were continued unchanged, except for punctuation, in the 1848 Constitution. In the course of creating this section, the 1870 Convention added the word "Supreme" and dropped the words "of the state" after "power." The proposed 1922 Constitution left this section unchanged in substance.

Explanation

The most important point to be made in explanation of this section is that it is not accurate. Leaving aside for the moment the significance of the word "Supreme," it is obvious that the executive power of the state is not vested in the Governor. There are, according to Section 1 of this Article (supra, p. 253), six other elected officers in the executive department, five of whom have executive duties. The Lieutenant Governor presumably has no executive duties except when acting as Governor pursuant to Section 17. (Infra, p. 303.) The other elected officers have both express and implied executive duties. The Secretary of State is specifically given custody of the state seal by Section 22 (infra, p. 318), and the Auditor is specifically given power to control every state expenditure by Section 17 of Article IV. (Supra, p. 181.) The other three elected officers, Treasurer, Superintendent of Public Instruction, and Attorney General, and the Secretary and Auditor as well, have implied executive powers by virtue of their titles. Thus, the executive power is divided up and vested in a half dozen people, all independent of each other. Moreover, the Supreme Court, as mentioned earlier (supra, pp. 103 and 256), has held that the Attorney General's implied powers are so solid that the legislature cannot pry any of them loose for transfer elsewhere in the Executive Department. So far, the Court has not frozen any powers of the other named officers.

It is possible that the word "Supreme" was added on the theory that some special recognition should be given to the Governor as the one who had all the executive power not parceled out to the other elected executives. (The more likely reason is that it is traditional. See Comparative Analysis below. But also see the quotation from the 1870 Debates in the History of Sec. 21, infra, p. 315.) There have been judicial opinions that refer to this section, but in general the point of the litigation has in fact been the theory of separation of powers enunciated in Article III. It is clear that the courts will not issue a writ of mandamus to compel the Governor to act (People *ex rel.* Bruce v. Dunne, 258 Ill. 441 (1913)), but will issue the writ to compel other constitutional executive officers to act. (People *ex rel.* Mosby v. Stevenson, 272 Ill. 215 (1916); People *ex rel.* Sellers v. Brady, 262 Ill. 578 (1914); People *ex rel.* Akin v. Rose, 167 Ill. 147 (1897).) This distinction lies in part in the fact that in this section the Governor is singled out for the vesting in him of executive power. (See also the *Explanation* of Art. III, *supra,* p. 99.)

The second part of the section commanding the Governor to take care that the laws are faithfully executed is a truism taken, directly or indirectly, from the United States Constitution.

Comparative Analysis

Executive Power: All states except Arizona, Minnesota and Utah explicitly state that the executive power is vested in the governor. Thirteen of them are without a qualifying adjective, six make it the "chief" executive power, and 27 join Illinois in using the adjective "supreme." Michigan, it is interesting to note, had "supreme" in its first (1835) constitution, removed it from the second (1850) constitution, put "chief" in the third (1908) constitution, and removed it from the fourth (1963) constitution. (Citizens Research Council of Michigan, A Comparative Analysis of the Michigan Constitution, at vi-9 to vi-10 (1961) [hereinafter cited as C.A.M.C.]; Mich. Const. art. V, § 1.) It is also to be noted that the three states that really do vest executive power in their governor by virtue of having no other elected executive officers — Alaska, Hawaii and New Jersey — are among the states that have no qualifying adjective. (Strictly speaking, Alaska has left a loophole in executive power by providing for the election of a secretary of state who has such duties as are delegated to him by the governor or "as may be prescribed by law." There is no lieutenant governor in Alaska, voting for governor and secretary of state is by joint ballot, and the secretary of state acts for the governor in his absence and succeeds him for the balance of his term when necessary. The election of a potential successor to the elected governor is, of course, most appropriate. The Alaskan practice may develop so that the secretary of state remains a minor official comparable to the lieutenant governor in most states, but the language quoted above permits a diffusion of executive power.) The United States Constitution vests executive power in the President, and the Model State Constitution vests it in the governor.

Execution of the Laws: Almost all of the states enjoin the governor to take care that the laws be faithfully executed. The two new states, Alaska and Hawaii, state that he is *responsible* for their faithful execution. Massachusetts and New Hampshire are silent on the subject. South Carolina rather endearingly enjoins him to take care that the laws are "faithfully executed in mercy." (S.C. Const. art. IV, § 12.) The United States Constitution uses the traditional language and the Model State Constitution uses the same language as in Alaska and Hawaii. (See also *Comment* below.)

Comment

See the *Comment* for Section 1 of this Article for a general discussion of executive power. (*Supra,* p. 253.) It is to be noted here only that if executive power is to be diffused as it now is by virtue of Section 1, it is appropriate to put in a qualifying adjective such as "chief" or "supreme" if it is made clear in convention debate or committee report that the adjective is designed to enhance the executive power of the Governor.

If a decision is made to go the route of the short ballot, consideration might be given to the Model State Constitution's implementation of gubernatorial power to see that the laws are faithfully executed. The Model provides:

"The governor shall be responsible for the faithful execution of the laws. He may, by appropriate action or proceeding brought in the name of the state, enforce compliance with any constitutional or legislative mandate, or restrain violation of any constitutional or legislative power, duty or right by an officer, department or agency of the state or any of its civil divisions. This authority shall not authorize any action or proceeding against the legislature." (art. V, § 5.04 (a).)

The Commentary on the foregoing provision explains it as follows:

"As a further device for enhancing the governor's powers, the section authorizes him to take appropriate action in the name of the state to enforce compliance with constitutional or legislative mandates and to restrain violations of constitutional or legislative powers and duties by state officers or instrumentalities. This provision, derived from an earlier edition of the *Model State Constitution,* has been incorporated into the recent constitutions of Alaska and New Jersey. Its effect is to enable the governor to initiate proceedings or to intervene in proceedings on behalf of the people of the state or on behalf of any individual, even in situations where the interest of the state is not directly involved. It gives the governor "standing to sue" even in cases where he might previously not have had it by reason of the fact that, either as a matter of procedure or substance, the state itself had nothing to lose or gain in consequence of such litigation. The provision makes the governor, the only statewide elected official, a spokesman for all of the people." (Model State Constitution 69.)

If the decision is to preserve the long ballot with executive power diffused, such a provision would be inappropriate, for it would allow the Governor to interfere with his constitutional equals.

Governor — Powers and Duties

Sec. 7. The Governor shall, at the commencement of each session, and at the close of his term of office, give to the General Assembly information, by message, of the condition of the State, and shall recommend such measures as he shall deem expedient. He shall account to the General Assembly, and accompany his message with a statement of all moneys received and paid out by him from any funds subject to his order, with vouchers, and, at the commencement of each regular session present estimates of the amount of money required to be raised by taxation for all purposes.

History

The 1818 Constitution simply enjoined the Governor to give the legislature information on the state of the government, from time to time, and to recommend such measures as he deemed expedient. The 1848 Constitution made no changes in the section. The 1870 Constitution added the specified times for messages, including a farewell message. The details about accounting for funds and the hint of an executive budget were added at the same time. The proposed 1922 Constitution preserved the message requirements, greatly shortened the accounting requirement and deleted the hint of an executive budget.

Explanation

It is traditional to expect the Governor to send a "state of the state" message to the legislature at the beginning of the session. It is not so common to require a farewell message. Although the present Constitution specifies the times of message as contrasted with the 1818 and 1848 Constitutions which simply said "from time to time," presumably no one has argued that the Governor is stopped from sending up messages whenever he wishes.

In the light of the requirement that no money be drawn from the treasury except on a warrant issued by the Auditor, a requirement also added in 1870, it is difficult to see the significance of the detailed accounting called for from the Governor. It appears from the 1870 debates that the accounting was of the Governor's own expenditures and not of all of the executive departments. "Heretofore, the method has been to make appropriations to the Governor for his use and benefit. . . . The people have a right to know what becomes of all moneys appropriated, and the uses to which they are applied." (Debates 747.) This is borne out by the Governor's biennial messages. For example, in 1927, Governor Small's message included the following:

"For a statement of the expenditures made by me for this department from funds subject to my order, your attention is directed to the Biennial Report of the Auditor of Public Accounts for the period ending September 30, 1926. Vouchers for all such expenditures have been filed in the Auditor's office."

Precisely the same wording appeared in Governor Deneen's message in 1911. (See also the discussion of Sec. 20, *infra,* p. 313. It may be that the Governor was supposed to account for his expenditures under Section 7 and not under Section 20.)

Since deficit financing is in theory prohibited by virtue of Section 18 of Article IV (*supra,* p. 185), an estimate by the Governor at the beginning of a regular session of the moneys required to be raised by taxes is tantamount to an operating budget for the biennium. Only by the preparation of such a budget can the Governor make a realistic estimate of revenues required. Today, this is not a startling thought, but in 1870 this indirect approach to a single executive budget for the whole state was not so common. Indeed, it was not until 1921 that the Federal Government adopted an executive budget. In all fairness, it must be noted that for a long time Illinois governors did not in fact carry out this implied requirement for an executive budget. The first such formal presentation of an executive budget was made in 1913, not much earlier that the Federal Government's adoption of an executive budget. Prior to 1913, each executive officer sent up his own estimates. (*See* N. Garvey, The Government and Administration of Illinois 182-83 (1958).)

Comparative Analysis

Almost every state constitution calls for messages and recommendations from the governor to the legislature. The only exceptions are Alabama, which calls for a message and no recommendation; Vermont, which calls for recommendations but no message; and Massachusetts, New Hampshire, New Mexico and Rhode Island, which say nothing about messages. Many states make it clear that the governor can send up a message whenever he wants to, sometimes in addition to the requirement of a message at the beginning of the session, sometimes with no mention of timing. Only five states besides Illinois call for a message at the end of the governor's term of office. Seven states besides Illinois call for an accounting of monies paid out, and five require estimates of revenues required. Several state constitutions require the governor to send up a budget message. The United States Constitution commands the President "from time to time" to give Congress "Information on the State of the Union," and to recommend "such Measures as he shall judge necessary and expedient . . . ." (art. II, § 3.) The Model State Constitution commands the governor to give information and recommendations to the legislature at the beginning of each session and permits him to give information at other times. The Model State Constitution also provides for a budget message as follows:

"*The Budget.* The governor shall submit to the legislature, at a time fixed by law, a budget estimate for the next fiscal year setting forth all proposed expenditures and anticipated income of all departments and agencies of the state, as well as a general appropriation bill to authorize the proposed expenditures and a bill or bills covering recommendations in the budget for new or additional revenues." (art. VII, § 7.02.)

Comment

In any large industrial state the vast majority of significant government policies are fiscal matters. The level of government expenditures, the extent of services to the populace, the formulas for state aid to local governments, grants from the Federal Government, the distribution of tax burdens among the population and between state and local taxing units — all these have a greater impact on the life of inhabitants than the regulatory activities of state government. It would seem more important to provide for a comprehensive budget message along the lines called for in the Model State Constitution than to call for "state of the state" messages. There is no reason to drop the traditional message requirement, but it would seem appropriate to simplify it and to substitute a comprehensive budget message. In any event, it seems appropriate to drop the requirement that the Governor account specially for his own expenditures. The quotation from Governor Small's message shows how meaningless the requirement is.

Special Sessions

Sec. 8. The Governor may, on extraordinary occasions, convene the General Assembly, by proclamation, stating therein the purpose for which they are convened; and the General Assembly shall enter upon no business except that for which they were called together.

History

The 1818 Constitution gave the Governor power to call special sessions and instructed him to tell the legislature, when assembled, why he had called them together. In the 1848 Constitution, he was required to give the reason for the call in his proclamation and for the first time the legislature was forbidden to transact any other legislative business. No substantive change was made in 1870 except to excise the word "legislative" from in front of "business." The proposed 1922 Constitution transferred this section from the Executive to the Legislative Article. It preserved the substance of Section 8 but gave the Governor the power to add to the business to be considered "in one additional message . . . during the session."

Explanation

The courts, governors and attorneys general have all agreed that this section means what it says. The Supreme Court has said that the Governor's decision that an "extraordinary occasion" exists is final. (Herzberger v. Kelly, 366 Ill. 126 (1937).) The Governor has vetoed as unconstitutional legislation on a subject not mentioned in his proclamation but passed at the special session. (Veto Messages 1911 at 31, 33.) The Attorney General has ruled that the Governor can add to the subject matter for a special session, but only by issuing a new proclamation for another special session and not by amending the proclamation for the special session already called. (1912 Att'y Gen. Rep. 964.) According to the Attorney General, if the second proclamation arrives while the legislature is in session pursuant to the first proclamation, the two sessions should run along concurrently with all entries made in a single legislative journal. (*Id.* at 966.)

Comparative Analysis

In all states the governor has the power to call special sessions. In North Carolina he does so "by and with the advice of the Council of State," consisting of named constitutional elected executive officers. In Louisiana, he has to have the consent of three-fourths of the members of each house of the legislature to call a special session within 30 days of the beginning of a budget session or within 30 days after adjournment *sine die*. In approximately nine states, the legislature, sometimes by simple majority, sometimes by an extraordinary vote, can call itself into session or require the governor to issue a call. A dozen or so states authorize the governor to call the senate into session alone. In Alaska he may convene either house.

Approximately 19 states limit the special session to the subject matter specified by the governor. With one exception, these are states in which no one else can call for a special session. In that one exception, Arizona, the governor may convene the legislature specifying the subject matter, but two-thirds of the members of each house can force a special session with no limitation on subject matter. The President of the United States may "convene both houses, or either of them," but he has no power to limit the subject matter to be discussed. Under the Model State Constitution, a special session may be called by the governor or by the presiding officer upon the written request of a majority of the members.

Comment

There are three important policy decisions to be made in considering special sessions of the legislature. One concerns an automatic or semiautomatic return after adjournment to act on vetoes. (See discussion under Section 16, *infra,* p. 293.) The second is whether to permit the Governor to control the agenda absolutely as in Illinois, with some qualifications such as allowing an extraordinary majority of the legislators to broaden the agenda, or not at all as in many states. The third is whether to give the legislature any power to convene itself. (The Commission on the Organization of the General Assembly recommended that the presiding officers of the two houses be empowered to call a special session upon the written request of two-thirds of the members of both houses. I.S.L. 8.) The second and third policy decisions involve intricate practical political considerations. For example, if the Governor controls the subject matter, he need not hesitate to meet any emergency; but if he has no such control, he must weigh the emergency against the Pandora's Box that he opens. In this connection an exchange during the 1870 Convention is instructive:

"Mr. TINCHER. ...

The beauty about this is, that these gentlemen come around and get information a little before hand as to when the Governor is going to call an extra session, so that they can all come down and get everything they want embraced in the subject of the call.

Mr. SKINNER. Mr. Chairman: The gentleman may have been nearer the throne than myself. I never knew the session was to be called till it was all fixed up.

Mr. TINCHER. Then, Mr. Chairman, all I have to say is, that the gentleman should get nearer the throne. [Laughter.]

I saw it announced that there was to be an extra session called a year or two ago. A correspondent got the news weeks ahead; and I think these correspondents, sir, are a valuable part of this government, for they will give notice of such things. I came down to see the Governor, sir, and got some little railroad matters I was interested in included in the- call." (Debates 775-76.)

It is also appropriate to give some thought to the change proposed in 1922. It is obvious that the change was designed to eliminate the artificial device of issuing additional proclamations. It is not so obvious that the proposed language would have prevented the Governor from issuing a new proclamation once he had exhausted his one additional message privilege. In any event, the proposed language demonstrates two interrelated unsatisfactory practices of constitutional conventions. One is to look at a problem narrowly instead of broadly. The other is to provide a precise and limited solution to a problem created by a precise and limited provision. It would seem more appropriate to consider the basic policy question of whether the Governor is or is not to control the agenda. If the decision is to give the Governor control, then the drafter should use language that creates no other problem. For example, "The Governor may, on extraordinary occasions, convene the

General Assembly; but the General Assembly shall enter upon no business except such as the Governor recommends for consideration." Two further thoughts are in order. In a convention debate, it is likely that some one will observe that under the foregoing "loose" language, a governor could keep the legislature in session indefinitely. So he could. But this is an example of the "parade of horribles" debating technique and should be countered with the argument that a constitution is a document for all men for all seasons, and that an attempt to limit possible but unlikely abuse will inevitably restrict probable and proper action. Finally, it must be conceded that the political process — and a constitutional convention is a proper part of the political process — is oiled by compromise. On occasion only by compromise can a consensus be reached. Sometimes, this produces a bad constitutional provision. The most that one can ask for is that all concerned strive to keep their eye on the fundamental issue and compromise on that level, rather than to get entangled in details and compromise on that level.

Adjournment of Houses in Case of Disagreement

Sec. 9. In case of a disagreement between the houses with respect to the time of adjournment, the Governor may, on the same being certified to him by the house first moving the adjournment, adjourn the General Assembly to such time as he thinks proper, not beyond the first day of the next regular session.

History

In the 1818 and 1848 Constitutions the substance of Section 9 was the same except for the certification requirement. It appears that, during the regular session in 1863, a disagreement on adjournment arose between the two houses and before the disagreement could be worked out, the Governor exercised his power to declare the legislature adjourned. Apparently this was not what the legislature, or at least one of the political parties, wanted and litigation ensued. The Supreme Court found that the legislature acquiesced in the action of the Governor and avoided a decision on the correctness of the Governor's action. (People ex rel. Harless v. Hatch, 33 Ill. 9 (1863).) The certification language was added to meet the defect. (See *Explanation* below.) In the proposed 1922 Constitution, the section was moved to the Legislative Article and changed to permit the Governor to act upon a certificate from either house rather than only from the house first moving the adjournment. (Such a change was suggested during the debates in the 1870 Convention, but no one so moved. Debates 778.)

Explanation

In reporting to the 1870 Convention, the Chairman of the Committee on the Executive Department explained that "disagreement" is an accepted term of parliamentary usage with a precise technical meaning, to wit: after a motion by one house to adjourn to a set time and an amendment by the other house, if (1) the first house non-concurs, (2) the amending house insists, (3) the first house insists, (4) the amending house adheres, and (5) the first house adheres, then there is disagreement. (Debates 748.) During debate it was noted that, in the litigation that followed the 1863 mix-up, the Court did not use the parliamentary meaning of "disagreement." (Debates 778.) Presumably, it was for this reason that the drafters introduced the certification concept, thereby permitting the legislature to follow technical steps to "disagreement" before the Governor could act.

In 1911, the Governor requested an opinion from the Attorney General on what he should do with a certificate of disagreement. It appeared that the Senate on October 26 moved to adjourn *sine die* on November 9. The House did nothing until November 9, when it moved to adjourn to November 14. Upon receipt of the House proposal, the Senate voted not to concur and instructed its officers to prepare a certificate of disagreement. The Attorney General assured the Governor that he had the power to adjourn the legislature, that his action would not be reviewable in the courts, but declined to say whether the Governor should act. (1912 Ill. Att'y Gen. Rep. 73.) The Attorney General quoted from the 1870 Convention debates, including the five technical parliamentary steps, and then observed: "I have referred to, and quoted, the debates in the constitutional convention, not for the purpose of indicating the construction which should be adopted, but solely for the purpose of affording information which may be of assistance to your Excellency in reaching a conclusion as to whether or not, as a matter of fact, there is a disagreement within the meaning of the constitution." (*Id.* at 79.) In the same opinion he told the Governor that if he set the day before the next regular session as the adjournment day he could still call a special session if need be.

In 1963, the Governor adjourned the legislature following receipt of a certificate of disagreement. On June 28 the House adopted a joint resolution to adjourn that day *sine die* and a resolution stating that it was ready to adjourn and asking the Senate if it had anything more for the House to consider. The House heard nothing from the Senate. A second joint resolution was adopted proposing to adjourn *sine die* no later than 9:00 P.M. This was delivered to the Senate at 8:56 P.M., but the Secretary of the Senate refused to accept it. The House then adopted a resolution at 9:30 P.M. reciting a disagreement and directing the Speaker so to certify to the Governor. At 10:45 P.M. the Speaker read to the House a proclamation from the Governor adjourning the legislature. The House adjourned *sine die*. The Senate recessed and reconvened the next day and purported to conduct business.

In *People* ex rel. *Myers v. Lewis* (32 Ill. 2d 506 (1965)), the Supreme Court confirmed the effectiveness of the Governor's proclamation of adjournment. No reference was made to the technical meaning of "disagreement," and from the nature of the Court's discussion it would not appear that the issue was even raised. Apparently, the principal argument against effectiveness was that the Senate Journal did not recite receipt of the Governor's proclamation on June 28 and that therefore the proclamation was not effective. The Court gave the argument short shrift.

Comparative Analysis

Twenty-two states besides Illinois authorize the governor to adjourn the legislature in case of disagreement. Five states besides Illinois require a certificate of disagreement, but only Oklahoma calls for a certificate from the house first moving adjournment. In Colorado, it is the house last moving adjournment; in Alaska and Rhode Island, either house; and in Arkansas, both houses. In most of the 22 states the governor is limited only by the requirement to adjourn not beyond the next regular session, but in a few states there are specific limitations such as not exceeding four months. The President of the United States, in the case of a disagreement, may adjourn Congress "to such time as he shall think proper." There is no comparable provision in the Model State Constitution.

Comment

Although it is obvious that a gubernatorial power to adjourn the legislature is not absolutely essential, it is not inappropriate to provide for the rare contingency of disagreement. It seems appropriate also to provide for a certificate of disagreement. The proposal in the 1922 Constitution that either house could make the certification seems preferable to the present language which gives one house a tactical advantage over the other.

Appointments

Sec. 10. The Governor shall nominate and, by and with the advice and consent of the Senate, (a majority of all the Senators elected concurring, by yeas and nays), appoint all officers whose offices are established by this constitution, or which may be created by law, and whose appointment or election is not otherwise provided for; and no such officer shall be appointed or elected by the General Assembly.

History

The 1818 Constitution contained a comparable provision, differing only in the absence of a specified majority vote for confirmation and in the absence of the prohibition on appointment of officers by the General Assembly. In fact, the 1818 Constitution provided for the appointment by the General Assembly of a treasurer and public printers and authorized the legislature to appoint an auditor, attorney general and "such other officers for the state as may be necessary." The 1848 Constitution added, in substance, the majority of elected senators requirement and the appointment prohibition. In the 1870 Convention, the only debate over the section concerned the breadth of the concluding prohibition. As noted in the *History* of Section 24 (*infra*, p. 322), that definitional section was drafted in lieu of amending Section 10. The proposed 1922 Constitution put the substance of the concluding prohibition into the article on the legislature and combined the substance of the balance of the section with Section 11. (See *infra*, p. 283.)

Explanation

This rather convoluted section really has only two constitutionally operative provisions: (1) the legislature may not appoint any officers; and (2) consent of the Senate, when called for, must be by yeas and nays and a majority of those elected must concur. (Even (1) is not strictly true, for Sec. 9 of Art. IV (*supra*, p. 145) allows each house to choose its own officers.) Beyond this, the section does not settle any matters of gubernatorial power of appointment. First, there are no offices "established by this constitution" except ones whose election is "otherwise provided for." Even if "established" is stretched to include filling the vacancies under Section 20 (*infra*, p. 313), "appointment" is otherwise provided for, since Section 20 says the Governor shall fill the vacancy. Thus, Section 10 is operative only as statutes are passed which establish offices and which provide for nomination by the Governor and appointment by and with the consent of the Senate. But by the very language of Section 10, it is clear that offices may also be created by statutes which provide for appointment by the Governor without Senate confirmation, or which provide for appointment by someone else. (*See, e.g.*, People v. Chicago Transit Authority, 392 Ill. 77 (1945); People v. Evans, 247 Ill. 547 (1910).) It should also be noted that "officers" in this section refers only to state officers and not local officers. (*See* Ramsay v. Van Meter, 300 Ill. 193 (1921); People v. Evans, 247 Ill. 547 (1910).)

Comparative Analysis

As an easy generalization, it can be said that the usual rule among the states is the same as in Illinois — appointments are made by the

governor by and with the advice and consent of the senate. But there are
so many qualifications to the generalization that it is relatively meaningless. To begin with, many states have much the same provision as in
Section 10 to the effect that the section is operative only to the extent not
otherwise provided for by constitution or law. In a great many states there
are constitutional officers, from adjutant general to wildlife and fish-
eries commissioners, whose appointments are covered by specific reference
in the constitution. In most of these cases the governor makes the appointment, sometimes with confirmation required, sometimes without.
In a couple of states the chief administrative officer of an operation is
chosen by the policy-making board or commission, and in one of those
states, New Jersey, the power of approval may be given to the governor.
In one state, Connecticut, there is no constitutional provision of any
kind concerning appointments. Moreover, the important point is the
extent to which the governor has the power to appoint the chief administrative officers in the executive department, and this need not be
a constitutional matter. Apart from elective offices, which are discussed
elsewhere (*Comparative Analysis* of Sec. 1, *supra,* p. 257), there are a
great many variations among the states.. Some states follow Illinois' practice of requiring senate confirmation of most department heads. Some
states, notably neighboring Indiana and Iowa, do not require legislative
confirmation of the governor's appointments. Most states have one or
more departments headed by a board or commission that in turn appoints
an administrative head, subject, in some cases, to gubernatorial approval.
In the new Michigan Constitution there is a unique provision on senate
confirmation, as follows:

"Appointment by and with the advice and consent of the senate when used in
this constitution or laws in effect or hereafter enacted means appointment subject to disapproval by a majority vote of the members elected to and serving
in the senate if such action is taken within 60 session days after the date of such
appointment. Any appointment not disapproved within such period shall stand
confirmed." (art. V, § 6.)

The Model State Constitution provides:

"The governor shall appoint and may remove the heads of all administrative
departments. All other officers in the administrative service of the state shall be
appointed and may be removed as provided by law." (art. V, § 5.07.)

The second sentence of the model provision is based on the assumption
that most such officers will be under the civil service system that the
Model State Constitution mandates.

The United States Constitution provision on presidential appointments is, of course, the model for the many states that call for legislative confirmation. The second clause of Section 2 of Article II reads
in part:

"[A]nd he shall nominate, and by and with the Advice and Consent of the Senate, shall appoint Ambassadors, other public Ministers and Consuls, Judges of the supreme Court, and all other Officers of the United States, whose Appointments are not herein otherwise provided for, and which shall be established by Law: but the Congress may by Law vest the Appointment of such inferior Officers, as they think proper, in the President alone, in the Courts of Law, or in the Heads of Departments."

Comment

Once in a while — one is tempted to say once in a lifetime — a really new idea enters the world of constitution-drafting. The Michigan provision on advice and consent quoted above is an ingenious new idea. It is analogous to the device of permitting the President (or Governor) to reorganize executive departments subject to veto by the legislature within a specified period of time. Whatever its origin, the Michigan provision is an interesting solution to one of the criticisms of senatorial confirmations. The stated purpose of advice and consent is to make sure that incompetent people are not appointed. This purpose is met by the Michigan provision. The potential evil in the traditional provision is that the necessity for affirmative action may compel the executive to make trades in order to obtain confirmation. Moreover, the power of appointment can almost be nullified by a tradition of senatorial courtesy such as is followed in the United States Senate, whereby a nomination is killed by a Senator's statement that a nominee from the Senator's state is personally obnoxious to him. The Michigan provision does not wholly preclude any such misuse of the confirmation process, but it certainly makes misuse more difficult.

Vacancies — Temporary Appointments

Sec. 11. In case of a vacancy, during the recess of the Senate, in any office which is not elective, the Governor shall make a temporary appointment until the next meeting of the Senate, when he shall nominate some person to fill such office; and any person so nominated, who is confirmed by the Senate (a majority of all the Senators elected concurring by yeas and nays), shall hold his office during the remainder of the term, and until his successor shall be appointed and qualified. No person, after being rejected by the Senate, shall be again nominated for the same office at the same session, unless at the request of the Senate, or be appointed to the same office during the recess of the General Assembly.

History

The 1818 Constitution had a simple provision permitting the Governor to fill appointive vacancies occurring during a recess of the General Assembly, such recess appointment to expire at the end of the next session. This included those offices for which the power of appointment was vested in the legislature. The 1848 Constitution provided, in the Judiciary Article for some strange reason, that all vacancies of elective (except the Secretary of State) and appointive offices should be filled as provided by law. The Governor was empowered to fill a vacancy in the office of Secretary of State without the advice and consent of the Senate.

In the 1870 Convention, the Chairman of the Committee on the Executive Department stated that the first sentence, offered as a separate section, was "as in the present Constitution." (Debates 748.) This is curious, for, as noted above, the 1848 Constitution left the method of filling vacancies to be prescribed by law. He noted that the second sentence, also offered as a separate section, was new. (*Id.*) The two sections were adopted by the Convention without change and subsequently combined into one section by the Committee on Revision and Adjustment.

The proposed 1922 Constitution combined the first part of Section 10 (*supra,* p. 280) with Section 11. In the course of revision by the Committee on Phraseology and Style, the words "in any office which is not elective," were changed to "where the appointing power is vested in the governor subject to the consent of the senate." In all other respects the substance remained unchanged.

Explanation

The change in the proposed 1922 Constitution, referred to above, made explicit what is only implicit in Section 11; namely, that the section is operative only in the case of a vacancy in an office which is filled by an appointment subject to confirmation by the Senate. So limited, the section is substantially self-explanatory. It is, in short, simply a means of preventing the Governor from getting around the requirement for confirmation of his appointees. The only questions that appear to have arisen are (1) What about an office that has never been filled? (2) What about an office with a term that expires during a recess but with the usual provision that the incumbent holds over until his successor is appointed and qualified? and (3) What about the failure of the Senate to act as opposed to rejection? As to (2), the Attorney General has said there is no vacancy (1910 Ill. Att'y Gen. Rep. 172); and as to (3), he has said that Section 11 permits a reappointment after adjournment of the Senate. (1925 Ill. Att'y Gen. Rep. 331.) As to (1), a case under the 1818 Constitution held that a position could not be filled initially during a recess of the Senate. (People *ex rel.* Ewing v. Forquer, 1 Ill. 104 (1825).) It has been pointed out, however, that the 1818 wording was sufficiently different from Section 11 to raise doubts that the *Forquer* case would be followed today. (Annotations 138.) It was also pointed out that the legislature customarily provides in the appropriate case that if the Senate is not in session when an act takes effect, the Governor is to make a temporary appointment as in the case of a vacancy. (*Id. See, e.g.*, Ill. Rev. Stat. ch. 144, § 182 (1967).)

Comparative Analysis

Approximately ten states appear to have no constitutional provision for the filling of vacancies in appointive positions. Of the remaining states, approximately 17 have provisions generally comparable to Section 11 in that they are designed in one way or another to back up the requirement for legislative confirmation of appointees. The rest of the states require that vacancies not otherwise provided for in the constitution shall be filled by the governor, shall be filled as provided by law, or shall be filled by the governor unless otherwise provided by law.

The United States Constitution provides that the President "shall have power to fill up all vacancies that may happen during the recess of the senate, by granting commissions which shall expire at the end of their next session." Since the Model State Constitution gives the governor unrestricted power to appoint and remove officers, he obviously has the power to fill vacancies. (The applicable section is quoted in the *Comparative Analysis* of Sec. 10, *supra*, p. 281.)

Comment

It is worth emphasizing that Section 11 precludes reappointment of a nominee only if the Senate *rejects* him. Compare this with the Michigan advice and consent definition discussed in the *Comment* on Section 10. (*Supra*, p. 283.)

There is no question but that Sections 10 and 11 could be greatly shortened and combined somewhat along the lines of the proposed 1922 Constitution.

Removal from Office by Governor

Sec. 12. The Governor shall have power to remove any officer whom he may appoint, in case of incompetency, neglect of duty, or malfeasance in office; and he may declare his office vacant, and fill the same as is herein provided in other cases of vacancy.

History

In the course of presenting Article V to the 1870 Convention, the Chairman of the Committee on the Executive Department said, with reference to this section:

"The [twelfth] section is a new section, and gives power to the Governor to remove any officer he may appoint, in case of incompetency, neglect of duty, or malfeasance of office.... Under the present Constitution the Governor may appoint a person to an important office, and when appointed he has no power whatever to remove him, though he may be incompetent. ... The executive should have some power as well as responsibility, and he should have power enough, at least, to execute the laws; and if he is first to appoint men and be held responsible for his appointments, and then, in case they should prove failures, not have the power to remove then [sic], what a ridiculous spectacle would be presented. This power of removal is for the benefit of the people and for their security, and not for the glory of the executive." (Debates 748.)

The section was accepted without debate and without change. The proposed 1922 Constitution preserved the substance of the first half of the section but dropped the second half as unnecessary.

Explanation

Although the 1870 delegates may have considered the quoted reasons adequate justification for Section 12, the pressing need for the section was to "overrule" *Field v. People* ex rel. *McClernand.* (3 Ill. 79 (1839).) In that case, Chief Justice Wilson held that, under the 1818 Constitution, the Governor, with the advice and consent of the Senate, appointed a Secretary of State but had no power to remove him. Moreover, under the rather novel constitutional theory enunciated by the Chief Justice (see *Explanation* of Sec. 1, *supra,* pp. 254-5), it would be necessary to provide for the power of removal in the Constitution, at least for any constitutional officers appointed by the Governor. The irony of the matter is that Section 12 goes much further than the *Field* theory required, for under the section the Governor has the power to remove any officer whom he appoints, including, naturally, statutory officers. (This means that the removal power may be greater than the President's power under the United States Constitution. See *Comment* below.) Moreover, the Supreme Court, in what may have been an act of expiation for the *Field* case, construed Section 12 in just about as broad a manner as is possible. In *Wilcox v. People* ex rel. *Lipe* (90 Ill. 186 (1878)), the Court held that (1) Section 12 covered any officer appointed by the Governor and not just those who were subject to senatorial confirmation; (2) that no notice or hearing was required; and (3) that the Governor's discretion was not reviewable in the courts. Although the power of removal under Section 12 is limited to appointed officers, the legislature has some inherent power to provide by statute for the removal of elected officers. Thus, the Supreme Court upheld a statute giving the Governor the power to remove a sheriff who permitted a mob to take a prisoner from him. (People ex rel.Davis v. Nellis, 249 Ill. 12 (1911).) Whether this inherent power covers any *state* constitutional officers has apparently never been raised.

Comparative Analysis

About a dozen states have provisions giving the governor power to remove state officials, but, of course, there are many variations in both the stated reasons for removal and the offices covered under the power. A somewhat larger number of states provide that removal from office shall be as prescribed by law, but in almost half of those states such legislative power is limited to officers not subject to impeachment. (Without extended analysis of individual constitutions, it is not possible to state whether such an impeachment exception is the means of distinguishing between elective and appointive offices, the means of covering causes beyond those specified for impeachment, or something else.)

The United States Constitution has no provision, other than the impeachment section, for removal. In *Myers v. United States* (272 U.S. 52 (1926)), the United States Supreme Court held unconstitutional an Act of Congress that required the consent of the Senate for the removal of postmasters. The argument was that the doctrine of separation of powers required leaving the President with a free hand in administering the government. But in *Humphrey's Executor v. United States* (295 U.S. 602 (1935)), the Court held otherwise in the case of a member of the Federal Trade Commission. The argument this time was that the Commission was a quasi-legislative and quasi-judicial body and that the members of such an "independent" agency could be protected by statute from arbitrary removal without cause. (*See also* Wiener v. United States, 357 U.S. 349 (1958).)

The Model State Constitution gives the governor an unrestricted power to remove heads of departments and empowers the legislature to prescribe by law for the removal of other executive department officials. (The applicable section is quoted in the *Comparative Analysis* of Sec. 10, *supra,* p. 282.)

Comment

As noted above, Section 12 is unusually broad. It would appear difficult, for example, for the Illinois courts to follow the *Humphrey's Executor* case in the face of such broad language. Nevertheless, it may be better to leave the section alone than to attempt to narrow it. Any such attempt is likely to produce too much detail. Nor is it advisable to use any "as prescribed by law" language to avoid detail, for that would revive the *Field* doctrine and permit the "ridiculous spectacle" deplored by the Committee Chairman in 1870.

It is clear that the 1922 drafters were justified in dropping the second half of the sentence as unnecessary.

Pardons

Sec. 13. The Governor shall have power to grant reprieves, commutations and pardons, after conviction, for all offenses, subject to such regulations as may be provided in law relative to the manner of applying therefor.

History

The 1818 Constitution contained a simple statement of power to "grant reprieves and pardons after conviction, except in cases of impeachment." The 1848 Constitution went to the opposite extreme with a complex provision that included special rules for conviction for treason, a prohibition on pardons for convictions on impeachment, power to condition pardons, an authorization to the legislature to regulate the manner of applying for pardons, and a requirement for a detailed biennial report to the legislature on every reprieve, pardon or commutation granted.

In the 1870 Convention, the section as proposed was substantially as it now appears, but without the concluding words "relative to the manner of applying therefor." An extensive debate ensued between those who felt that, notwithstanding the restrictions added in 1848, the power of pardon had continued to be abused, and those who feared that the proposed language would permit the legislature to destroy the Governor's traditional power. A compromise was reached by the addition of the words quoted above which thus limited the legislature's power of regulation to only one of the alleged areas of abuse — failure to notify interested parties, such as judge and prosecutor, that an application for a pardon was under consideration.

The proposed 1922 Constitution made one substantive change in the section. It was provided that the Governor's grant could be "on such terms as he thinks proper." This was designed to permit the grant of conditional pardons.

Explanation

It is perhaps appropriate to begin by defining terms that are used in this section.. A "reprieve" is a suspension of the sentence that has been imposed. The popular understanding of the word is in connection with a death sentence where the Governor or a court grants a reprieve pending further consideration of some claim of error. But a reprieve can be any suspension of execution of any sentence. A "commutation" is a shortening or lessening of a sentence. A "pardon" is, in effect, a complete exoneration of the convicted person. A "conditional pardon," proposed in effect in 1922, is the equivalent of a release on parole.

The courts have consistently supported the gubernatorial power which the 1870 delegates preserved from legislative regulation. For example, the legislature is specifically given the power to regulate the manner of applying for a pardon, but the courts have refused to set aside a pardon where the Governor acted without having before him the written statements of the judge and prosecutor called for by statute. (People ex rel. Smith v. Jenkins, 325 Ill. 372 (1927).) Moreover, the courts have denied to themselves any general power of reprieve (People *ex rel.* Smith v. Allen, 155 Ill. 61 (1895)), and have denied to the legislature any power to authorize the courts to commute sentences. (People *ex rel.* Brundage v. La Buy, 285 Ill. 141 (1918).)

There are, however, definite limits on the Governor's power. For one thing, he cannot pardon someone sentenced for civil contempt of court. (People *ex rel.* Brundage v. Peters, 305 Ill. 223 (1922). For present purposes, it is sufficient to note that a civil contempt order is in furtherance of effective judicial power; criminal contempt is punishment for disrespect of the court, or interference with the judicial process. A pardon would be appropriate in a case of criminal contempt.) For another, the Governor has to go all the way; he cannot "commute" a conviction for murder to a conviction for manslaughter so that a "lifer" would become eligible for parole. (People *ex rel.* Fullenwider v. Jenkins, 322 Ill 33 (1926).) The change in the proposed 1922 Constitution would not have permitted such a "commutation" but would have authorized a conditional pardon which is what the Governor presumably was trying to do in the *Fullenwider* case.

It is important to note that, absent a proviso authorizing conditional pardons, there is a clear distinction between commutation and pardon on the one hand and parole on the other. The former is, under Section 13, wholly and exclusively in the hands of the Governor, and the latter is wholly and exclusively subject to legislative control. A parole board may be empowered pursuant to legislative direction to act in the case of parole but empowered only to advise and recommend in the case of commutations and pardons. (*See generally* People *ex rel.* Abner v. Kinney, 30 Ill. 2d 201 (1964).)

Comparative Analysis

Almost all states give the governor power to grant pardons. A majority of the states deny the power to grant pardons in cases of treason and impeachment. Approximately a third of the states leave the governor's power relatively unrestricted, another third permit legislative regulation in general, and about a third require the governor to share his power with a parole board. In the case of commutations, approximately a third of the states have a grant of power comparable to Section 13, about a quarter of the states do not grant any power of commutation to the governor, and in the rest of the states the power is either shared or subject to statutory regulation. As for reprieves, about half the states leave the governor relatively unrestricted, in most of the rest the power is shared or subject to statutory regulation, and in a few no power is granted to the governor. In all but a handful of states, whatever the grant of power, it is a grant "after conviction."

The United States Constitution gives the President power to grant reprieves and pardons except in the case of impeachment. The Model State Constitution states that the "governor shall have power to grant reprieves, commutations and pardons, after conviction, for all offenses and may delegate such powers, subject to such procedures as may be prescribed by law." (art. 5, § 5.05. See *Comment* below concerning an ambiguity in the foregoing.)

Comment

It would appear appropriate to consider whether to go back to the original language proposed in 1870 and thus permit the legislature to regulate the entire pardoning process. There are cogent arguments on both sides of the issue and the choice is a relatively balanced one. But if the decision is in favor of retention of the Governor's power, it would seem desirable to give him the power to grant conditional pardons as was proposed in 1922.

One of the easiest drafting ambiguities to create is that of a modifying clause that is so placed that it is unclear whether it is designed to modify only the last of a series of statements. The pardon provision of the Model State Constitution quoted above has just such an ambiguous modifying clause. The question there is: Does the legislature have power to prescribe procedures only in the case of delegation or can the legislature also prescribe procedures for the exercise of the power to grant reprieves, commutations and pardons? The natural reading of the sentence leads one to believe that the clause refers only to delegation and, indeed, the Commentary to the Model makes this clear. (Model State Constitution 70.) But the point is that either of two minor changes in the wording would erase the ambiguity completely. One change is to make a separate sentence on the power to delegate. The other is to move the clause from the end of the sentence and place it between "and" and "may." The alternatives would read thus:

"The governor shall have power to grant reprieves, commutations and pardons, after conviction, for all offenses. He may delegate such powers, subject to such procedures as may be prescribed by law."

"The governor shall have power to grant reprieves, commutations and pardons, after conviction, for all offenses and, subject to such procedures as may be prescribed by law, he may delegate such powers."

Governor — Commander-in-Chief of Militia

Sec. 14. The Governor shall be commander-in-chief of the military and naval forces of the State (except when they shall be called into the service of the United States); and may call out the same to execute the laws, suppress insurrection, and repel invasion.

History

The first half of Section 14 appeared in substance in both the 1818 and 1848 Constitutions. The second half was added in 1870. The Chairman of the Committee on the Executive Department reported to the 1870 Convention that Section 14 "is the same as in the (1848] Constitution . . . ." (Debates 748.) At no time during the deliberations was any explanation offered for the added words. The proposed 1922 Constitution changed "military and naval forces" to "armed forces" and revised the last half to read: "and may call them out to execute the law, protect life or property, suppress insurrection or repel invasion."

Explanation

This traditional statement is in support of the fundamental subordination of military power to civilian power. (See Art. II, Sec. 15, *supra*, p. 76.) The only reported case construing this section observed that military activities are under the control of the state and cannot be delegated to city or other local authorities. (City of Chicago v. Chicago League Ball Club, 196 Ill. 54 (1902).)

In 1906, the Attorney General ruled that the Governor's power to call out the militia "to execute the laws" did not include the power to do so just because local officials were failing to enforce the Sunday Closing and Dram Shop Laws. The Attorney General suggested that citizens who were concerned about saloons that were open on Sunday could file complaints themselves. (1906 Ill. Att'y Gen. Rep. 54.) In 1915, the Attorney General ruled that the Governor could not use the militia to aid a judge who was unable to get his orders carried out by the sheriff in another county. (1915 Ill. Att'y Gen. Rep. 78.) Both of these instances, it can be seen by reading between the lines, were simply efforts to dramatize a situation by calling on the Governor to call out the militia. In both instances, the Attorney General politely refused to distort the meaning of "execute the laws."

The official explanation of the proposed 1922 Constitution stated that Section 14 was revised because "the power of the governor to call out the militia to protect life or property at times of great public disaster, danger or catastrophe was questioned." (P.N.C. 37.)

Comparative Analysis

Every state except Connecticut makes the governor the commander-in-chief of the state's military forces. In Connecticut the governor is the Captain-general of the militia. The title used for the military forces varies from state to state. The two new states of Alaska and Hawaii use the contemporary term "armed forces." The 1964 Michigan Constitution adopted the same term. Thirty states join Illinois in acknowledging that the governor's supreme command is not applicable when the armed forces are under United States control. Three states are careful to warn the governor not to take personal command of his forces without legislative consent.

Approximately 20 states use substantially the same language as Illinois in setting forth the exigencies for calling out the armed forces — execute laws, suppress insurrection, repel invasion. A couple of states add "suppress riots," a couple add "preserve public peace," and Oklahoma adds "protect public health." The United States Constitution states that the President shall be "Commander in Chief of the Army and Navy of the United States, and of the Militia of the several States, when called into the actual Service of the United States . . . ." The Constitution also grants power to Congress to "provide for calling forth the Militia to execute the Laws of the Union, suppress Insurrections and repel Invasions . . . ." The Model State Constitution makes the governor "commander-in-chief of the armed forces of the states," and authorizes him to call them out "to execute the laws, to preserve order, to suppress insurrection or to repel invasion."

Comment

It would seem appropriate to change the term to "armed forces" if this section is to be revised. It would also be appropriate as a matter of accurate grammar and felicitous phrasing to change the authority to read "and may call them out to execute the laws, to suppress insurrection, or to repel invasion." It would seem that the caution expressed in 1922 was undue and that the power to call out the armed forces to execute the laws is adequate to cover preservation of peace, suppression of riots, protection of public health and to "protect life or property."

Impeachment of Officers

Sec. 15. The Governor, and all civil officers of this State, shall be liable to impeachment for any misdemeanor in office.

History

See *History* of Section 24 of Article IV. (*Supra,* p. 228.)

Explanation

The purpose of this section is to designate what class of people is subject to impeachment. In the case of *Donahue v. County of Will* (100 Ill. 94, (1881)), the Supreme Court held that the constitutional county officers provided for by Section 8 of Article X are not "civil officers of this State" and are, therefore, not subject to impeachment. This did not, however, result in an inability to provide for removal of county officers.

In *People* ex rel. *Davis v. Nellis* (249 Ill. 12 (1911)), the Supreme Court upheld a statute authorizing the Governor to remove a sheriff who was derelict in prescribed duties. It is fair, therefore, to assume that the legislature has the power to provide for the removal of any elected officials whom it cannot remove via the impeachment process.

Comparative Analysis

Almost every state has a different formulation of coverage for impeachment purposes. Only Mississippi has an exact duplicate of Illinois' coverage. Delaware covers the governor and civil officers *under* the state. Only a few states appear to include constitutional local officials, but in a small number of states the coverage is subject to increase by law. The United States Constitution covers the "President, Vice-President and all civil Officers of the United States." The Model State Constitution covers the "governor, the heads of principal departments, judicial officers and such other officers of the state as may be made subject to impeachment by law." (The Model State Constitution provides for no constitutional elective offices other than the governor and members of the legislature.)

Comment

This section requires no change.

Approval or Veto of Bills

Sec. 16. Every bill passed by the General Assembly shall, before it becomes a law, be presented to the Governor. If he approve, he shall sign it, and thereupon it shall become a law; but if he do not approve, he shall return it with his objections, to the House in which it shall have originated, which house shall enter the objections at large upon its journal and proceed to reconsider the bill. If then two-thirds of the members elected agree to pass the same, it shall be sent, together with the objections, to the other house, by which it shall likewise be reconsidered; and if approved by two-thirds of the members elected to that house, it shall become a law notwithstanding the objections of the Governor; but in all such cases the vote of each house shall be determined by yeas and nays to be entered upon the journal.

Bills making appropriations of money out of the Treasury shall specify the objects and purposes for which the same are made, and appropriate to them respectively their several amounts in distinct items and sections, and if the Governor shall not approve any one or more of the items or sections contained in any bill, but shall approve the residue thereof, it shall become a law as to the residue in like manner as if he had signed it. The Governor shall then return the bill, with his objections to the items or sections of the same not approved by him, to the house in which the bill shall have originated, which house shall enter the objections at large upon its journal, and proceed to reconsider so much of said bill as is not approved by the Governor. The same proceedings shall be had in both houses in reconsidering the same as is hereinbefore provided in case of an entire bill returned by the Governor with his objections; and if any item or section of said bill not approved by the Governor shall be passed by two-thirds of the members elected to each of the two houses of the General Assembly, it shall become part of said law notwithstanding the objections of the Governor. Any bill which shall not be returned by the Governor within ten days (Sundays excepted) after it shall have been presented to him shall become a law in like manner as if he had signed it, unless the General Assembly shall, by their adjournment prevent its return, in which case it shall be filed with his objections, in the office of the Secretary of State, within ten days after such adjournment, or become a law.

History

The 1818 Constitution created a Council of Revision, consisting of the Governor and the justices of the Supreme Court of which there were four during the life of that Constitution. A majority of the Council could reject a bill. A majority of all the elected members of each house could override the "veto." There was the customary ten-day provision, but with an unusual twist. In the case of adjournment within ten days, the "bill shall be returned on the first day of the meeting of the General Assembly, after the expiration of the said 10 days, or be a law." The 1848 Constitution dropped the Council of Revision and vested the veto power in the Governor alone. No other changes were made except to provide that Sunday was not to be counted as one of the ten days, and to require a recorded yea and nay vote in each house.

In the 1870 Convention, the veto section proposed by the Committee on the Executive Department purported to differ in substance from the 1848 section only in changing the required vote to override to two-thirds. Both in Committee of the Whole and in the Convention proper, an effort was made to go back to the majority vote requirement, but in each case the effort was defeated by a wide margin. The item veto portion of the section was added by amendment in 1884. The proposed 1922 Constitution made one substantive change. The period within which the Governor had to act after adjournment intervened was extended to 30 days. The section was moved to the Legislative Article and the portion dealing with the form of appropriation bills was made into a separate section. (See *Comment* below concerning this change.)

Explanation

General Veto: A routine procedural provision in the nature of rules of the game ought to be clear enough that no judicial gloss is required. This is certainly the case with so important a matter as the Governor's power to veto. Unfortunately, the drafters in 1870 created ambiguities, one of which showed up almost immediately and the second of which showed up many decades later as the result of an informal practice designed to cope with the mass of bills passed on the last days of a session.

The 27th General Assembly, the first to meet under the 1870 Constitution, adjourned on April 17, 1871, under an adjournment resolution calling for reconvening on November 15, 1871. Prior to that date, the Governor called a special session which convened on May 24, 1871. The Governor's call included a number of items, the last of which was:

"Thirteenth — The reconsideration of bills passed by both branches of the General Assembly and laid before the Governor, and by him filed in the office of the Secretary of State, with his reasons for withholding his signature therefrom." (1871 Ill. H.R. Jour. 3 (1st Spec. Sess.).)

In his message to the Special Session, Governor Palmer listed the five bills which he had vetoed after adjournment and then said:

"And these several bills were, within ten days after the adjournment of the session, filed by me in the office of the Secretary of State, with my objections.

"From the peculiar language of the last clause of the 16th section of the 5th Article of the Constitution, it is somewhat difficult to determine what is the actual status of the above mentioned bills. If they had been returned by the Governor, with his objections, to the Houses respectively in which they originated, the General Assembly being in session, then the course of procedure would have been plain; for, in that case, it is provided by the Constitution that the House in which the bill originated, shall proceed to reconsider the bill, and if two-thirds of the members elected agree to pass the same, it shall be sent, together with the objections, to the other House, by which it shall be likewise reconsidered; and if approved by two-thirds of the members elected to that House, it shall become a law, notwithstanding the objections of the Governor.

"The foregoing provision is substantially like that upon the same subject in the Constitution of 1847, but instead of being followed, as in the Constitution of 1847, by the further language that, 'If any bill shall not be returned by the Governor within ten days (Sundays excepted) after it shall be presented to him, the same shall be a law in like manner as if he had signed it, unless the General Assembly shall, by their adjournment, prevent its return; in which case the said bill shall be returned on the first day of the meeting of the General Assembly after the expiration of the said ten days, or be a law,' the last clause in the section of the present Constitution is: 'Any bill which shall not be returned by the Governor within ten days (Sundays excepted) after it has been presented to him, shall become a law in like manner as if he had signed it, unless the General Assembly shall, by their adjournment, prevent its return, in which case it shall be filed, with his objections, in the office of the Secretary of State, within ten days after such adjournment, or become a law.'

"The last quoted clause is unlike anything I have been able to find in the Constitution of any of the States, so that I know of no precedents that can be consulted to aid in its proper construction.

"The last clause of the 14th section of the 5th article of the Constitution of the State of Indiana, from which this provision of our Constitution was probably borrowed, is more complete; for, after providing for the filing of bills disapproved by the Governor, with his objections, in the office of the Secretary of State, within five days after the adjournment, it contains the additional requirement that the Secretary of State shall 'lay the bill and the objections of the Governor before the General Assembly at its next session, in like manner as if it had been returned by the Governor.'

"Whether the last clause of the 16th section of the 5th article of the Constitition is to be construed as if the words last quoted from the Constitution of Indiana were actually employed, or whether the Executive disapproval is to have the effect to defeat bills that have passed both Houses, as is the consequence in like cases under the Constitutions of most of the New England States, and New York, New Jersey and other States, is so uncertain, that I have thought it proper to call the special attention of the General Assembly to the matter, as one deserving most serious consideration." (*Id.* at 20-21.)

The matter was referred to committee in both houses, but nothing appears to have been reported back. There was a second special session convened on October 13, 1871, but it was devoted to consideration of problems caused by the Chicago fire of October 8th and 9th. At the Adjourned Regular Session in November, 1871, the Secretary of State wrote to the Speaker of the House in response to a request for two of the five vetoed bills and accompanying messages. The Secretary interpreted the statutes under which he operated to require him to retain the originals, but he attached certified copies to his letter. Again, nothing appears to have happened. No vote was taken on overriding any of the vetoes.

As noted in connection with Section 9 of Article IV (*supra,* p. 145), there were two other adjourned regular sessions after 1871 and before the 75th General Assembly's series of adjourned sessions in 1967, 1968, and a final session on January 8, 1969. The 27th General Assembly, the second under the 1870 Constitution, and the 45th General Assembly in 1907-1908, both had adjourned regular sessions, but in neither case were any post-adjournment vetoes considered.

Two important procedural decisions, one by the General Assembly, and one by the Governor, were made in connection with the 75th's adjourned regular sessions. At all times during the life of the 75th General Assembly, the offices of the Clerks of the House and the Senate remained open for business, a practice that obviously is not appropriate after adjournment *sine die.* Presumably because of this, the Governor addressed his veto message to the members of the appropriate house of origin and dispatched the messages to the proper Clerk. Thus, for example, the House Journal entry following the veto message of August 20, 1968, concerning House Bill 2633, reads:

"The foregoing message from the Governor, transmitting veto to House Bill No. 2633, having been received in the office of the Clerk of the House on Tuesday, August 20, 1968, at 10:46 a.m., was read by the Clerk and ordered placed on file." (Journal No. 106 for January 8, 1969 at 11.)

There were a number of veto messages so handled, but only the veto of House Bill No. 2633 was overridden. So far no lawsuit has been instituted contesting the validity of the legislative action in overriding the veto.

It is clear from the procedural decisions to keep open the Clerk's offices and to transmit messages to the Clerk's office, that everyone concerned has acted on the assumption that the key words in Section 16 are "prevent its return," and that "prevent" is to be read in the sense of physically preventing return because, so to speak, the door is locked. It is worth noting that the overriding of the veto of House Bill No. 2633 was only the fourth such since 1870, and the first since 1936. The system of minority representation in the House (see Sec. 7 of Art. IV, *supra*, p. 136) increases somewhat the difficulty of mustering a two-thirds' vote of the whole membership of the House of Representatives, but the more significant reason for the absence of overriding has been that so many bills are acted upon after the legislature adjourns *sine die*.

The message of Governor Palmer, quoted above, demonstrates that from the beginning there was a problem of bills passed at the last minute, but it was not until much later that the well-known "log jam" developed at the end of the session. By virtue of the July 1 effective date provision of Section 13 of Article IV (*supra*, pp. 160-1), there is a drive to finish business by June 30, and a great many bills are passed in the last few days of the session. In 1939, for example, 232 of the 474 bills passed during the regular session were passed on the last day. At the regular session in 1965, 429 bills were passed on the last day, and in the last three days of the session, 1,259 of the 2,211 total were passed. In 1967, the first year in which a schedule was adopted in an effort to control the log jam, there were 421 bills passed on the last day and 832 in the last three days out of a total of 2,603. In order to give the Governor adequate time to consider these last-minute bills, an informal practice has developed whereby bills are "'presented" to him in an orderly fashion over a period of several weeks following adjournment.

Unfortunately, the drafters in 1870 created an ambiguity in Section 16 which, when combined with this informal practice, finally required judicial resolution. (People *ex rel.* Petersen v. Hughes, 372 Ill. 602 (1939).) The ambiguity first arises because there are two ten-day periods referred to — from presentation of a bill and from day of adjournment. In passing, it may be noted that Sundays are specifically excepted in computing the ten days after presentation, but not the ten days from adjournment. The Supreme Court has excepted the day of rest from the adjournment ten-day computation also. (People *ex rel.* Akin v. Rose, 167 Ill. 147 (1897).) The Attorney General has told the Governor that he cannot approve or veto a bill on Sunday. (1917 Ill. Att'y Gen. Rep. 571.)

The initial problem of ambiguity arises when the legislature adjourns less than ten days after presentation of a bill. In the *Petersen* case, the

Supreme Court pointed out that for many years Governors had cautiously followed the practice of acting within ten days of presentation rather than to assume that a new ten days began to run upon adjournment. This is the course, familiar to every lawyer, of choosing the alternative that cannot be wrong.

What gave rise to litigation, however, was the practice of presenting bills to the Governor some time after adjournment. The two bills in question in the *Petersen* case were passed on the 30th of June, the day on which the legislature adjourned *sine die*. One bill was presented to the Governor on July 17 and the other on July 11. Both bills, with veto messages, were filed with the Secretary of State within ten days of presentation, but not within ten days after adjournment. The Court concluded that the Governor has ten days, Sundays excepted, from date of presentation regardless of how long after adjournment this may be. In reaching this conclusion, the Court relied upon and approved the practice mentioned above whereby the Governor always acts within ten days of presentation and does not permit adjournment to extend the period. The long and short of it is that a consistent and eminently satisfactory solution to a practical problem was found by the Court, but its reading of the veto provision in both instances of ambiguity is questionable, both as to the "plain meaning" of the words and the "intent" of the 1870 drafters. (One judge dissented without opinion.)

There are two minor rulings concerning the Governor's general veto power that should be noted. If, after adjournment *sine die,* the Governor formally approves or vetoes a bill and deposits it in the Secretary's office, he has lost all power over the bill even though his ten-day period for consideration has not expired. (People *ex rel.* Partello v. McCullough, 210 Ill. 488 (1904).) But if he deposits a bill without having approved or disapproved it, his power is not lost and he can recall it within his ten-day grace period. (See People *ex rel.* Akin v. Rose, 167 Ill. 147 (1897).)

Item Veto: There have been several straightforward Supreme Court decisions delineating the Governor's power to veto a line item in an appropriation. The principal ruling was that he could not reduce an item by, for example, striking "per annum," or saying "I approve in the sum of $3,500 and veto all in excess of said sum of $3,500." (Fergus v. Russel, 270 Ill. 304 (1915).) The Supreme Court has also held that a line item for a large sum followed by subsidiary lines stating how much of the sum is to be spent for each of several purposes permits the Governor to strike a subsidiary item even though, in a sense, this is reducing rather than striking the principal item. (People *ex rel.* State Bd. of Agr. v. Brady, 277 Ill. 124 (1917).) Finally, the Supreme Court has recognized that the Governor has the power to strike line items of appropriations for constitutional officers. (People *ex rel.* Millner v. Russel, 311 Ill. 96 (1924).) The thrust of this case is to underscore the point that the dispersion of executive power by the "long ballot" (see Section 1, *supra,* p. 253) can be undercut by the Governor if he wants to veto items for the operations of the offices of the elected constitutional offices.

Another line of decisions deals with the item veto portion of Section 16, but not all of them appear to be limited to the purpose of the provision. In *Peabody v. Russel* (302 Ill. 111 (1922)), the legislature attempted to create a general contingency fund of $500,000 which the Governor could allocate as he saw fit. The Supreme Court held that this was unconstitutional because the item did not "specify the objects and purposes" of the appropriation and did not appropriate "amounts in distinct items and sections." In dissent, Mr. Justice Cartwright pointed out that the purpose of the wording was to prevent the legislature from destroying the item veto power by appropriations in insufficient detail. Justice Cartwright was unable to construe the item veto amendment as an amendment of Section 17 of Article IV (*supra,* p. 181), which is the governing section on the "legality" of expenditure of public moneys. The irony of the *Peabody* case is that a provision designed to protect the Governor was used to deny to him a well-recognized budgeting tool. (The State Finance Act, Ill. Rev. Stat., ch. 127, §§ 149 (1967), does provide for contingency appropriations, but the "contingencies" are narrower than the appropriation involved in the *Peabody* case.)

A comparable, but not so devastating, construction of the item veto language was the ruling that an indefinite appropriation — *i.e.,* "such sums as may be necessary to refund taxes on real estate" — is unconstitutional. (Fergus v. Russel, 270 Ill. 304 (1915).) The case is comparable because the Governor's power is not protected by such a construction, but it is not devastating since the legislature, with executive help, can make an "educated guess" and put in a sum certain.

Although the Supreme Court was certain of its ground in the two cases just discussed, it has conceded that determining the required degree of specification of items is most difficult. (See People *ex rel.* State Bd. of Agr. v. Brady, 277 Ill. 124 (1917).) In many ways, the question of how far a breakdown must go is almost like the age-old question, "How long is a piece of string?" For example, an appropriation of $60,000,000 for the construction of roads was accepted. (Mitchell v. Lowden, 288 Ill. 327 (1919).) On another occasion, $400,000 for construction and maintenance of roads was accepted. (Martens v. Brady, 264 Ill. 178 (1914).) The Attorney General has said, however, that $500,000 for purchase of lands, machinery, supplies, salaries, wages, and materials will not do. (1912 Ill. Att'y Gen. Rep. 960.) It may be noted that the last appropriation includes many different *kinds* of expenditures, whereas the other two are comprised of large sums for many *units* of one kind of expenditure.

Comparative Analysis

General Veto: One state, North Carolina, has no gubernatorial veto of any kind. All other states require the Governor to return a bill within a specified number of days, usually excepting Sunday and sometimes excepting holidays. (Three days, nine states; five days, 21 states; six days, four states; ten days, 12 states; and 15 days, two states. Under the new Michigan Constitution, the Governor has "14 days measured in hours and minutes from time of presentation.") Overriding a veto requires a vote of two-thirds of elected members in 23 states and of those present in 15 states. A vote of three-fifths of elected members is required in four states and of those present in one state. A simple majority of elected members suffices in six states. In Alaska, the required two-thirds of elected members rises to three-fourths for revenue and appropriation bills, including item vetoes. The same step-up in vote is required in Arizona for emergency measures.

In 18 states, the intervention of adjournment permits a Governor to "veto" a bill by doing nothing. This, of course, is the pocket veto. In 31 states the Governor must specifically veto a bill. In New York, a pocket veto state, Governors have long followed a practice of acting on every post-adjournment bill even though it is not constitutionally required. This may very well be the practice elsewhere. In the light of the earlier discussion concerning the end-of-session log jam, it is to be expected that many states lengthen the time for gubernatorial action upon adjournment of the legislature. A total of 32 states give the Governor a longer time for consideration of bills following adjournment than during the session. In some cases, the increase may be only from three days to five, or from five to ten. In other cases, the period is quite long, frequently 30 days, and in a few cases 45 days.

The question of whether or not adjournment refers to *sine die* is not answered by the wording of most constitutional provisions. It seems likely that the more common assumption is that bills vetoed after any regular adjournment are permanently dead, if only because of some special provisions in a few of the states. For example, there are five states which convene in special session to consider post-adjournment vetoes. In three states, it is clearly stated that bills may be returned at the commencement of the next regular session. In a couple of states, the legislature as a matter of practice holds off adjourning until the Governor has acted on all bills.

Item Veto: There appear to be 42 states which give the Governor power to veto appropriation items, but in three of the states there is a limitation. In one case, Missouri, no reduction is permitted from appropriations for public schools or for debt interest payments. In Nebraska, appropriations in excess of the budget request require a three-fifths' majority, and any such items may not be vetoed. In West Virginia, the budget bill does not require the Governor's approval and his item veto covers only supplemental appropriations. (The legislature may not increase the executive portion of the budget.)

In five of the states, the Governor may reduce an item rather than strike it. The state of Washington has a unique provision which permits the Governor to object to "one or more sections or items while approving other portions of the bill." Thus, his "item" veto power is not limited to appropriations.

United States Constitution: The President has ten days, Sundays excepted, in which to act. A two-thirds' vote of members present in each house is required to override his veto. If Congress adjourns during the ten-day period, a bill dies unless signed by the President. The President has no item veto. On some occasions, the President has announced that he would not use certain funds which he did not want, a situation annoying to Congress but difficult for Congress to prevent. This sort of situation can exist, of course, only if no third-party rights are created. The President could refuse to build a battleship, for example, but he could not refuse to pay re-enlistment bonuses.

Model State Constitution: In view of the earlier discussion of the meaning of "adjournment" in the Illinois Constitution, it is appropriate to quote the Model's provision in full with certain words italicized:

"*Action by the Governor.*

"(a) When a bill has passed the legislature, it shall be presented to the governor and, if the legislature is in session, it shall become law if the governor either signs or fails to veto it within fifteen days of presentation. If the legislature is in *recess* or, if the session of the legislature has *expired* during such fifteen-day period, it shall become law if he signs it within thirty days after *such* [sic] *adjournment* or *expiration*. If the governor does not approve a bill, he shall veto it and return it to the legislature either within fifteen days of presentation if the legislature is in session or upon the reconvening of the legislature from its *recess*. Any bill so returned by the governor shall be reconsidered by the legislature and, if upon reconsideration two-thirds of all the members shall agree to pass the bill, it shall become law.

"(b) The governor may strike out or reduce items in appropriation bills passed by the legislature and the procedure in such cases shall be the same as in case of the disapproval of an entire bill by the governor." (art. IV, § 4.16 (emphasis added).)

Comment

General Veto: The extended *Explanation* above is indication enough that there is a need for a thoroughgoing reconsideration and redrafting of Section 16. It is necessary, of course, to mesh any such reconsideration with decisions concerning annual or biennial sessions, and concerning power of the General Assembly to call itself into session. (See *Comments* to Sec. 9 of Art. IV, *supra,* p. 151, and Sec. 8 of this Art., *supra,* p. 275.) But whatever is decided about these matters, it seems advisable to recognize the realities by giving the Governor a 30- or 45-day period in which to act after adjournment. (It should not be forgotten that the present system of staggered presentation is an informal one and that the legislature could change the system and dump several hundred bills on the Governor's desk all at once.) It would also be appropriate to give serious consideration to the relatively new policy of an automatic "veto session." The new Connecticut Constitution provides:

"If any bill passed by any regular or special session or any appropriation item described in Section 16 of Article Fourth has been disapproved by the governor prior to its adjournment, and has not been reconsidered by the assembly, or is so disapproved after such adjournment, the secretary of the state shall reconvene the general assembly on the second Monday after the last day on which the governor is authorized to transmit or has transmitted every bill to the secretary with his objections pursuant to Section 15 of Article Fourth of this constitution, whichever occurs first; provided if such Monday falls on a legal holiday the general assembly shall be reconvened on the next following day. The reconvened session shall be for the sole purpose of reconsidering and, if the assembly so desires, repassing such bills. The general assembly shall adjourn sine die not later than three days following its reconvening." (art. 3, § 2.)

Once all of the decisions on the veto process have been made, extreme care should be exercised in redrafting the veto section. In this connection, it should be noted that the veto section is in the Executive Article, but that the veto is part of the legislative process. (The veto provision in the United States Constitution and in some state constitutions is in the Legislative Article.) If, as is normal, the Convention has Committees on the Legislature and on the Executive, an effort should be made from the beginning to assure coordination of consideration of the veto problem. An alternative solution is to agree at the beginning that the Committee on the Legislature should have jurisdiction over Section 16 of Article V. As noted above, the 1920-1922 Convention moved the veto provision to the Legislative Article.

Item Veto: It would seem appropriate for the Convention to undertake a redrafting of the item veto language in a manner that wipes out the *Peabody* case discussed above. In these days of multibillion dollar budgets, covering an ever-increasing range of activities in a volatile economy, it seems unfortunate that the chief executive is not permitted to have a general contingency fund. Moreover, this is the day of program budgeting, or the even newer planning-programming-budgeting system (PPBS), and rigid line item constitutional language, though not an insurmountable hurdle, does inhibit experimentation.

If the Convention were to go the route of the strong executive budget with accompanying limitations on legislative power to alter it (compare the reference to the West Virginia item veto above), the restrictive item veto language would be of minimal significance. If the decision is to preserve legislative budgeting power, the way in which to protect the Governor's item veto is to use language of "strike out or reduce" as in the Model State Constitution section quoted above. With power to reduce, the Governor can defeat any legislative attempt to lump items together in order to protect an expenditure against an item veto. If this simple solution is unattractive, then some sort of "fuzzy" language should be substituted for the specific "objects and purposes" and "amounts in distinct items" language in order to insulate the item veto from a taxpayer's suit of the *Peabody* nature. Above all, it would seem most ill-advised to go the route of the 1920-1922 Convention of putting "objects and purposes" in a separate section, thereby killing any opportunity for the courts to change their minds and adopt Mr. Justice Cartwright's approach in his *Peabody* dissent.

Lieutenant Governor as Acting Governor

Sec. 17. In case of the death, conviction on impeachment, failure to qualify, resignation, absence from the State, or other disability of the Governor, the powers, duties and emoluments of the office for the residue of the term, or until the disability shall be removed, shall devolve upon the Lieutenant Governor.

History

There have been several twists and turns in the evolution of this section. The 1818 Constitution provided for the taking over by the Lieutenant Governor in the case of the Governor's impeachment, removal from office, death, "refusal" to qualify, resignation or absence. This would appear to cover impeachment, whether convicted or not. Such a disability as illness was not covered. The 1818 section also said that the Lieutenant Governor should serve "until the time pointed out by this Constitution for the election of governor shall arrive, unless the General Assembly shall provide by law for the election of a Governor to fill such vacancy." This literally would have meant that if the Governor were impeached but acquitted or left the state on a trip, he lost his office permanently. Such a meaning was undoubtedly not intended. In another section it was provided that while acting as Governor the Lieutenant Governor should receive a Governor's salary.

In the 1848 Constitution the provisions for succession were even more mixed up. The drafters divided the succession provision into two sections, one covering temporary succession and one covering permanent succession. In order to demonstrate the extent of the drafting confusion, the actual 1848 sections are set out, as follows:

Sec. 19. In case of the impeachment of the Governor, his absence from the State, or inability to discharge the duties of his office, the powers, duties and emoluments of the office shall devolve upon the Lieutenant-Governor; and in case of his death, resignation, or removal, then upon the Speaker of the Senate for the time being, until the Governor, absent or impeached, shall return or be acquitted; or until the disqualification or inability shall cease, or until a new Governor shall be elected and qualified.

Sec. 20. In case of a vacancy in the office of Governor, for any other cause than those herein enumerated, or in case of the death of the Governor elect before he is qualified, the powers, duties, and emoluments of the office shall devolve upon the Lieutenant-Governor, or Speaker of the Senate, as above provided, until a new Governor be elected and qualified.

The drafting error in the temporary succession section (19) was in inserting in the middle of the section the provision concerning the Speaker of the Senate. Without those words it would be clear that the Lieutenant-Governor ceased to serve as Governor if (1) the absent Governor returned, (2) the impeached Governor was acquitted, or (3) the disabled Governor recovered. (Even so, "disqualified" is left dangling.) But with the Speaker of the Senate tossed in, the section literally permitted the Governor to resume office only if during his absence, impeachment or disability the Lieutenant Governor happened to die, resign, or be removed. This is obviously not what was intended but it is what the section said. Moreover, in the section on election of Speaker of the Senate, provision was made for his succession to the duties of Lieutenant Governor and, if necessary, to the Governor. Thus, the interpolated language was utterly superfluous.

The permanent succession section (20) can be read in a straightforward manner if one assumes that "as above provided" refers to the relationship between the Lieutenant Governor and the Speaker of the Senate that the drafters meant to but did not clearly provide for. It is not clear in either section whether "until a new Governor (shall be) (be) elected and qualified" refers to the next regular election or implies that a special election may be provided for by law as was explicitly stated in the 1818 Constitution.

In a masterpiece of understatement, the Chairman of the Committee on the Executive Department reported to the 1870 Convention that Sections 17, 18 and 19 "are in substance the same as in the present Constitution, but they have been entirely recast and remodeled." (Debates 748. He was also inaccurate. See *History* of Sec. 19, *infra*, p. 310.)

The recasting of Section 17 certainly removed confusions from the earlier Constitutions. But a new ambiguity was created. The wording of Section 17 as it now stands either permits the Governor to serve following impeachment and until conviction or includes impeachment under "other disability." The proposed 1922 Constitution combined Sections 17 and 19. Succession rules were further clarified and the impeachment ambiguity was finessed by omitting the word and simply referring to "vacancy" which would be the case following conviction on impeachment, and to using "under disability" which may or may not have been intended to include the period from impeachment to the end of trial.

Explanation

Except for the possible ambiguity of whether or not the Governor is displaced during the period between impeachment and conclusion of his trial, this section is clear. There are problems that can arise, such as how long an absence from the state is necessary to justify temporary succession or how to determine whether in case of illness the Governor is disabled, but these are not problems of poor draftsmanship. They are practical problems that may or may· not justify additional constitutional coverage. (See *Comment* below.) Notwithstanding all of the confusion in rules of succession discussed above, there appears to have been no litigation, Attorney General opinion or other consideration of the problem of succession. The Attorney General has ruled that the Lieutenant Governor when occupying the Governor's chair, either temporarily or permanently, is the "Acting Governor." (1912 Ill. Att'y Gen. Rep. 162.)

Comparative Analysis

In all states (38) that have a constitutional lieutenant governor, he is, of course, the person who first assumes the office of governor in the line of succession. Among the remaining states, in seven the president of the senate first succeeds the governor; in four, the secretary of state; and in one state the legislature elects a successor, but if the legislature is in recess the president of the senate succeeds, pending a choice by the legislature. In general, the several states provide for succession under much the same circumstances set forth in Section 17. In a few states a special election is provided for in certain circumstances, but the more common practice is to permit the lieutenant governor or other first successor to serve out the unexpired term. There is also considerable variation in the provision concerning impeachment. The general rule is that upon impeachment the governor ceases to act until he is acquitted — *i.e.*, the disability removed; upon conviction, he would presumably be removed from office. Only a few states follow the Illinois ambiguity of succession upon conviction of impeachment.

With the adoption of the Twenty-fifth Amendment, the United States Constitution now has one of the more comprehensive provisions covering succession. It should be noted, however, that the President is not succeeded upon his absence from the United States and apparently not upon impeachment pending trial. Under the Twenty-fifth Amendment, the Vice President becomes President in case of removal, death, or resignation of the President. In case of inability of the President to act, two alternatives are provided for. The President may notify the President *pro tem* of the Senate and the Speaker of the House in writing that he is incapacitated, in which case the Vice President becomes Acting President until the President makes a contrary declaration in writing to the President *pro tem* and the Speaker. In the absence of a declaration from the President, the Vice President and a majority of either the cabinet or some other body created by law may make a written declaration of incapacity to the President *pro tem* and the Speaker, and the Vice President becomes Acting President. Thereafter, the President may make a contrary written declaration, but if there is disagreement, Congress by a two-thirds vote within a specified time may keep the Vice President in his capacity as Acting President; otherwise the President resumes his powers and duties.

The Model State Constitution also provides a comprehensive section on gubernatorial succession. The section first covers the problem at the beginning of the governor's term by providing that the presiding officer of the legislature — there being no lieutenant governor and the legislature being unicameral — serves until the governor-elect assumes office, but if this period exceeds six months, a special election is to be held and the presiding officer serves as acting governor until the newly elected governor assumes office. The section next covers temporary situations — impeachment, mental or physical disability, and continuous absence — in which case the presiding officer serves as acting governor in the interim, and if the disability exceeds six months the office becomes vacant. In the case of a vacancy, the presiding officer becomes governor for the remainder of the term or until a special election is held and a new governor assumes office. A special election is held unless the remainder of the term is less than a year. The legislature is given the duty to provide by law for special elections and the supreme court is given "original, exclusive and final jurisdiction" to settle any questions of absence, disability, existence of a vacancy or any other matter of succession.

Comment

In any major revision of a state constitution these days it is obvious that consideration should be given to the problem of succession, for only the more recent constitutions adequately provide for the rare but quite possible serious mental or physical incapacity of the chief executive. In a large industrial state, executive duties are much too important to be left in doubt for any extended period. It may be noted that it is not absolutely necessary to spell out the contingencies in such detail as in the Twenty-fifth Amendment and the Model State Constitution. The succession section could have a sentence saying in effect that the legislature shall provide by law for the manner of determining whether the governor is incapacitated.

In addition to the problem of incapacity, consideration should be given to whether the Governor continues to serve after impeachment. Rare as impeachment may be these days, it seems appropriate as a matter of principle to require the Governor to stop governing until the cloud is removed. An even more important consideration is whether to abandon the traditional "absence from the state" provision for temporary succession. With modern high-speed transportation and high-speed communication there is no reason for the Governor not to continue to govern from outside the state. After all, the President of the United States continues to govern when out of the country. The Model State Constitution solves this problem by providing for temporary succession after "continuous absence." It should be possible under such language to permit the Lieutenant Governor to take over at the request of the Governor when he expects to be absent for a considerable period of time or when, as in the case of a vacation, he wishes to be relieved of his duties.

Finally, it would be appropriate to clarify the distinction between Acting Governor on a temporary basis and succession as Governor on a permanent basis. The Model State Constitution, for example, puts it this way:

"When the presiding officer of the legislature succeeds to the office of governor, he shall have the title, powers, duties and emoluments of that office and, when he serves as acting governor, he shall have the powers and duties thereof and shall receive such compensation as the legislature shall provide by law." (art. V, §5.08 (c).)

By way of postscript to this *Comment,* it is perhaps appropriate to justify the extended discussion under *History* of the confusing language of the several succession provisions. In any constitution, there are provisions that should be broad and general to allow for accommodation to changes in the society. There are other provisions that should be as precise and clear as the ingenuity of draftsmen can make them. The former are exemplified by a bill of rights and other restrictions on government action, the latter by procedural provisions for the operation of the government. In the field of private law, by analogy, there are many instances when a judge should concentrate on finding the "right" or "good" decision, but other instances when it is more important to enunciate an unambiguous and precise rule than it is to worry about whether it is a "good" rule. The distinction lies principally in whether accommodation to the rule is easy or difficult. A rule of substance can cause great difficulty, but a rule of procedure, once known, can almost always be followed with ease. In constitution-drafting, the rules for the process of government should be clear and definite. There is little danger of injustice arising at some future time because changed conditions are inconsistent with the assumptions underlying the original formulation, but there is danger of confusion if there is procedural ambiguity. The moral is, of course, to let delegates to a convention make the policy decisions but to rely on professional draftsmen, particularly in the case of procedural matters, to translate the policies into constitutional language.

President of the Senate

Sec. 18. The Lieutenant Governor shall be President of the Senate, and shall vote only when the Senate is equally divided. The Senate shall choose a President, *pro tempore,* to preside in case of the absence or impeachment of the Lieutenant Governor, or when he shall hold the office of Governor.

History

In the 1818 Constitution, the substance of this section was spread among three sections. In one of them, the Lieutenant Governor was made Speaker of the Senate and given the right to debate and vote when the Senate sat as a Committee of the Whole, but otherwise could vote only to break a tie. In a second section, provision was made for election of a Speaker, from among the membership of the Senate, who was to preside in the absence of the Lieutenant Governor and was to succeed to the Governor's office if necessary. The third section called for the Secretary of State to convene the Senate to choose a Speaker if a necessity for succession to the Governor's office arose while the legislature was in recess. These three sections were carried over in substance to the 1848 Constitution. The 1870 changes consisted of boiling down the language, transferring the provision for succession to Section 19, dropping the Lieutenant Governor's participation in the Committee of the Whole, and adopting "President, *pro tempore*" in place of "Speaker." (In Section 19 of this Article the term used is "President of the Senate," in Section

9 of Article IV the term is "temporary President," and in Section 13 of Article IV the term "Speaker" is still used to designate the presiding officer of the Senate.) The proposed 1922 Constitution combined the substance of this section with the substance of Section 9 of Article IV concerning organization of the General Assembly.

Explanation

There appear to have been no problems concerning this section. Under Section 17, it was noted (*supra,* p. 303) that the Governor is apparently not succeeded even temporarily upon impeachment, but only upon conviction, whereas the President *pro tem* presides over the Senate from the moment of impeachment of the Lieutenant Governor. This is obviously necessary, for the trial on impeachment takes place in the Senate. Although the language is unclear, the fair import of the section is that the Lieutenant Governor would retake his seat as presiding officer if he were acquitted. (It may be noted that, in dealing with this technical matter of impeachment, the drafters of the proposed 1922 Constitution slipped up. They had the President *pro tem* preside "pending the impeachment of the Lieutenant Governor." Literally, this is the period of time from the filing of a motion of impeachment in the House of Representatives until it votes on the motion.)

Comparative Analysis

Lieutenant Governor: In 38 states the lieutenant governor is a constitutional officer and in 36 of those states he presides over the senate. In Massachusetts he presides over the governor's council and in Hawaii he has been given by law the duties normally held by a secretary of state. In Tennessee the title of lieutenant governor has been given by statute to the speaker of the senate who is a constitutional officer and succeeds to the governor's chair. In three states, the lieutenant governor has no vote and in the other 33 states, including Illinois, of course, he has only a casting vote in case of a tie. In a few states the lieutenant governor retains the right to debate and vote in committee of the whole as used to be the case in Illinois. The United States Constitution provides that the Vice President shall serve as President of the Senate and shall have a tie-breaking vote. No lieutenant governor is provided for in the Model State Constitution.

President pro tem: Twenty-eight states besides Illinois provide that the senate shall elect a president *pro tem* to preside in the absence of the lieutenant governor. In those states that have a lieutenant governor but do not provide specifically for a president *pro tem* there will still be such an officer elected pursuant to the usual provision that each

310Art. V, § 19

house of the legislature shall choose its own officers. The United States
Constitution provides that the Senate shall choose a President *pro tem*
to serve under the usual circumstances. The Model State Constitution
provides that the unicameral legislature choose a presiding officer from
among its members.

Comment

There has been considerable discussion in recent years about the need
for an elected lieutenant governor. On the one hand it seems appropriate that the person who may succeed to the governor's chair be elected
by all the voters of the state. On the other hand, it is difficult to find
enough for the lieutenant governor to do in that capacity, particularly
if the person chosen for the position is expected to be of sufficient
stature to become governor. Alaska chose to drop the lieutenant governor and to provide that the secretary of state be elected on a joint
ballot with the governor and to succeed the governor if necessary.
Hawaii did the reverse by leaving the lieutenant governor's duties to
be prescribed by law and then by statute making him, in effect, the
secretary of state. The 1964 Constitution of Michigan compromised by
continuing the lieutenant governor's traditional legislative function
of presiding over the senate but adding the following sentence: "He
may perform duties requested of him by the governor, but no power
vested in the governor shall be delegated." (Mich. Const. art. V, § 25.)
The Model State Constitution tries to avoid the difficulty by providing
that the presiding officer of the legislature, an official elected by one
segment of the state, can, in effect, serve as governor for only a relatively
short time, never more than a year, and by requiring a special election
for governor when a longer period is involved.

Acting Governor — Successions

Sec. 19. If there be no Lieutenant Governor, or if the Lieutenant Governor
shall, for any of the causes specified in section seventeen, of this article, become
incapable of performing the duties of the office, the President of the Senate shall
act as Governor until the vacancy is filled or the disability removed; and if the
President of the Senate, for any of the above named causes, shall become incapable of performing the duties of Governor, the same shall devolve upon
the Speaker of the House of Representatives.

History

In the discussion of the *Histories* of Sections 17 and 18 (*supra,* pp.
303 and 308), the matter of succession of the presiding officer of the
Senate as it appeared in the 1818 and 1848 Constitutions was covered.
The only significant substantive change made in 1870 was to provide for
succession by the Speaker of the House of Representatives if necessary.

The proposed 1922 Constitution combined this section with Section 17 and, in the course thereof, clarified the rules of succession.

Explanation

Although this section leaves much to be desired as a matter of drafting, its purpose is clear enough. Section 17 provides for the Lieutenant Governor to act as Governor under certain circumstances, and Section 18 provides for the President *pro tem* to act as presiding officer of the Senate in certain circumstances. Section 19 is designed to move the President *pro tem* into the Governor's chair when neither the Governor nor the Lieutenant Governor is available, and the Speaker of the House into the Governor's chair in the absence of the Governor, Lieutenant Governor and President *pro tem*. The drafting difficulty with Section 19 is that it literally fails to spell out an absence of the Governor in addition to that of the Lieutenant Governor as a condition for succession of the President *pro tem*. In the proposed 1922 Constitution, the drafters solved this drafting tangle by providing in effect that in the absence of the Governor, his duties and powers moved to the Lieutenant Governor; that in the absence of the Lieutenant Governor, his duties and powers moved to the President *pro tem*; and so on.

It is provided by statute that if the offices of Governor and Lieutenant Governor are both vacant, the person acting as Governor, or if there is none then the Secretary of State, shall issue a writ for a special election to fill the vacancies for the balance of the term. (Ill. Rev. Stat. ch. 46, § 25-4 (1967).) It is not at all clear what constitutional authority exists for such a law. Presumably, reliance would be placed on the words "until the vacancy is filled" on the theory that such words are superfluous if the "vacancy" is filled by the winner at the next regular election for a new term. But compare the language used in Section 20 to provide that a person appointed serves "until his successor shall be elected and qualified in such manner as may be provided by law." (See *Explanation, infra*, p. 314.) In any event, no occasion for a special election appears to have arisen and thus there has been no opportunity for a determination of the validity of the statute.

Comparative Analysis

There are a great many variations in the order of succession among the several states. Approximately 13 states join Illinois in moving from the lieutenant governor to the president *pro tem* to the speaker. A few of these states go on to list further successors or to authorize further succession as provided by law. In many of the states without a lieutenant governor the succession is from the president *pro tem* to the speaker. Among other variations, the commonest is to provide for

the succession of the secretary of state, either after the lieutenant governor if there is one or directly if there is none. Several states leave
succession after the lieutenant governor or other first successor to be
determined by law.

Prior to the adoption of the Twenty-fifth Amendment, the United
States Constitution left it to Congress to provide by law for succession
beyond the Vice President. Under the Twenty-fifth Amendment, the
President is to fill any vacancy in the office of Vice President by nomination with confirmation by "majority vote of both Houses of Congress."
In a case where the Vice President became President by virtue of the
President's removal from office, resignation or death, the new President
would nominate a successor Vice President. The amendment does not
cover the case of something happening to the Vice President while he
is Acting President. Presumably, the original language of the Constitution remains applicable, namely: "and the Congress may by Law provide for the Case of Removal, Death, Resignation or Inability, both of the
President and Vice President, declaring what Officer shall then act as
President, and such Officer shall act accordingly, until the Disability be
removed, or a President shall be elected." The statutory rules of succession enacted pursuant to the foregoing are still on the books and
their language is not inconsistent with the Twenty-fifth Amendment.
The line of succession runs from the Speaker of the House to the President *pro tem* of the Senate to the cabinet officers beginning with the
Secretary of State. (3 U.S.C., § 19 1964).)

The Commentary on the Model State Constitution notes that a virtually
unlimited line of succession is assured, for there will always be a presiding officer of the unicameral legislature and he is the named successor
to the governor. The implication is that either the legislature will have
provided by rule for a successor when its presiding officer has succeeded
to the governor's chair or that a special session will be called to elect
a new presiding officer.

Comment

It seems desirable to clear up the problem of succession by special
election. This could be done by language such as that quoted above
from Section 20 or by a separate sentence empowering the legislature
to provide by law for filling vacancies in the offices of both the Governor
and the Lieutenant Governor. Another solution is to empower the legislature to provide for further succession in much the manner quoted
above from the United States Constitution. Indeed, it may be that the
present statute calling for a special election was adopted because there
appeared to be no way to assure indefinite succession. But it may also

have been because of a belief that a person not elected by all the people should not serve for too long. This is the theory of the Model State Constitution's rules of succession. (See *Comparative Analysis* of Sec. 17, *supra*, p. 305.)

Financial Report of State Officers — Vacancies

Sec. 20. If the office of Auditor of Public Accounts, Treasurer, Secretary of State, Attorney General, or Superintendent of Public Instruction shall be vacated by death, resignation or otherwise, it shall be the duty of the Governor to fill the same by appointment, and the appointee shall hold his office until his successor shall be elected and qualified in such manner as may be provided by law. An account shall be kept by the officers of the Executive Department, and of all the public institutions of the State, of all moneys received or disbursed by them, severally, from all sources, and for every service performed, and a semi-annual report thereof be made to the Governor, under oath; and any officer who makes a false report shall be guilty of perjury, and punished accordingly.

History

Under the 1818 Constitution, none of the executive offices, other than Governor and Lieutenant Governor, was elective. The Governor's power to fill vacancies in appointive positions and his power, under the 1848 Constitution, in the case of both elective and appointive positions are described in the *History* of Section 11. (*Supra*, p. 283.) Neither Constitution had a requirement for financial reporting. In the 1870 Convention the Chairman of the Committee on the Executive Department described the first half of the section as "the ordinary section relating to vacancies . . . and . . . how they shall be filled." (Debates 749.) The second half was noted to be new. (*Id.*) There was no extended debate on this section. One delegate pointed out that the Governor is required to report to himself semiannually. The Chairman of the Committee on Revision and Adjustment retorted that it "mentions all the officers except the Governor." (Debates 1782.) The Chairman's reply was irrelevant, because the officers are mentioned in the first sentence, and incorrect, because the Lieutenant Governor who is an officer of the Executive Department is not mentioned. But the Chairman's explanation was accepted. The proposed 1922 Constitution made the substance of the first sentence of Section 20 into a separate section and combined most of the substance of the second sentence with Section 21. The official explanation stated that the first sentence was unchanged in substance (P.N.C. 37), but this is arguable, for the concluding clause, "in such manner as may be provided by law," was omitted. Presumably, this clause permits legislation providing for a special election for an unexpired term whereas its omission might not. The second sentence was changed

in substance only in omission of the perjury provision. The literal
requirement that the Governor report to himself was retained.

Explanation

Vacancies: The first sentence of Section 20 is straightforward and
unambiguous. As noted above, the final clause permits special elections
to be provided for by law. The implementing statute (Ill. Rev. Stat.
ch. 46, § 25-5 (1967)) provides, however, that the person appointed to
fill a vacancy serves out the remainder of the term.

Accounts: As noted above, this sentence of the section literally calls
for a semiannual financial report by the Governor in addition to the
other officers listed in Section 1 of this Article. In 1904, the Attorney
General dutifully ruled that the Governor, as an officer of the Executive
Department, was required to make a semiannual report which, for
obvious reasons, was to be filed with the Secretary of State. (1904 Ill.
Att'y Gen. Rep. 385.) In that same opinion, the Attorney General ruled
that this provision covers even officers who merely disburse appropriated
funds through warrants drawn by the Auditor of Public Accounts. (*Id.*)
He has also ruled that the State Board of Agriculture and the State
Horticultural Society are public institutions under this section. (1910
Ill. Att'y Gen. Rep. 163, 666.) The Supreme Court has held that acceptance of a financial report by the Governor does not relieve the reporting
officer of liability for errors. (People v. Whittemore, 253 Ill. 378
(1912).)

Comparative Analysis

Vacancies: The provisions for filling vacancies in the several named
offices vary greatly among those states that make such offices constitutional. In general, it appears that if the office is an elective one, the
governor normally fills the vacancy, sometimes on his own as in Illinois,
sometimes with the advice and consent of the senate. In some states,
it appears to be within the power of the legislature to provide for special
elections rather than to permit the person filling the vacancy to serve
out the unexpired term. Occasionally, a constitution specifically calls
for filling a vacancy only until the next general election. Neither the
United States Constitution nor the Model State Constitution has any
elected executives other than the chief executive and, of course, has no
provision for filling vacancies.

Accounts: Approximately a dozen states have a provision much like
that of Illinois. Eight of them require the account to be under oath,
but only three other states include perjury language. The absence of
an accounting provision in most states does not necessarily signify that

there is no constitutional requirement for accounting for public funds. (See *Comment* below.) The Model State Constitution has no comparable provision but the general reporting section (see *Comparative Analysis* of Sec. 21 *infra,* p. 317) could include financial reporting. There is no comparable provision in the United States Constitution.

Comment

Vacancies: If Illinois is to preserve the long ballot, a provision such as this is necessary. It is eminently satisfactory as it stands, for the legislature is given the flexibility to provide by law for special elections if at some future time there were a general feeling that the Governor ought not to have power to fill vacancies for a long period of time. It is a matter of choice whether to include the Senate in the appointing process as is done under Sections 10 and 11 of this Article for other offices and vacancies. Indeed, one can ponder why the delegates to the 1870 Convention made the choice the way they did. The debates throw no light on the matter. (See also discussions of Secs. 10 and 11, *supra,* pp. 280 and 283.)

Accounts: This is a curious requirement in the light of Section 17 of Article IV controlling expenditures through the Auditor. Moreover, in view of the magnitude of governmental expenditures in large industrial states, any assumption that requiring semiannual reports under oath from elective and appointive officials is the way to assure honest accounting is simplistic indeed. A comprehensive auditing process is the appropriate approach to the problem of control over public receipts and disbursements. (This may be the reason that so few states have a comparable financial reporting provision.). It would be appropriate for the Convention to look at the realities of modern-day accounting and auditing and provide constitutional responsibility therefor, but leave details to be spelled out by law.

Report of State Officers — Departments — Judges

Sec. 21. The officers of the Executive Department, and of all the public institutions of the State, shall, at least ten days preceding each regular session of the General Assembly, severally report to the Governor, who shall transmit such reports to the General Assembly, together with the reports of the Judges of the Supreme Court of defects in the Constitution and laws; and the Governor may at any time require information, in writing, under oath, from the officers of the Executive Department, and all officers and managers of State institutions, upon any subject relating to the condition, management and expenses of their respective offices.

History

The 1818 Constitution provided, in language much like that of the United States Constitution, that the Governor could require information in writing from the several executive officers upon any subject pertaining to their duties. Only changes in punctuation were made in 1848. In the 1870 Convention the Chairman of the Committee on the Executive Department explained the proposed expanded section in these words:

"This is a new feature, and is designed to give the executive such control over all the State officers and officers of the State institutions, that he can at least know what they are about, and have some check upon their administration. Heretofore the Governor of this State has been clothed with hardly any powers. He has been treated like a child under tutelage. He might complain, but he possessed no power to remedy any evil in the administration of public affairs." (Debates 747-48.)

This "new feature" did not include the reference to the reports of the judges on defects in the Constitution. That was added at a later session on motion of a member of the Committee on the Judiciary. The "reports of the judges" were reports called for by a section of the Judiciary Article. (Section 31 of Article VI prior to 1964.) That section required all judges of courts of record annually to report in writing to the Supreme Court on defects and omissions in the laws. In turn, the judges of the Supreme Court were to report annually to the Governor on the defects and omissions in both the Constitution and the laws and were to include appropriate bills to cure the defects and omissions in the laws. That section also originally included in parentheses an instruction to the Governor to send everything along to the legislature. In view of the addition of the instruction in Section 21, the Committee on Revision and Adjustment dropped the instruction from the section in the Judicial Article.

This judicial reporting requirement appears to have been an outgrowth of a device designed to increase the compensation of the judges, whose salaries had been frozen at a low level in the 1848 Constitution. In January, 1869, an act was passed requiring circuit court judges to report to the Supreme Court on "redundancies, omissions, inconsistencies and imperfections in the statutes, together with bills remedying these defects." For this service the judges were each to receive $1,000. A bare majority of the judges complied, but all were paid. The Supreme Court forwarded most of the reports to a Statutory Revision Commission which adopted some of them. (*See* Annotations 180.)

That this precedent of the year before was clearly in the minds of the delegates is evidenced by efforts on two occasions to have inserted in the section a prohibition on extra compensation for the reports. On both occasions, delegates were assured that extra compensation was prohibited by another section. (Debates 1185, 1495. The other section was 16 in the old Article VI.) One delegate objected that the reporting section was "special legislation, and rather inferior legislation at that," and moved to strike. In defense of the section, a member of the Committee on the Judiciary noted that all constitutions required the executive to make recommendations to the legislature but that judges, "who could be much more useful in this respect," were not required to make recommendations. He continued:

"This provision will be very useful if the judges do their duty. We would thus be enabled to make our laws plain, for judges like to have the laws plain after they get on the bench, however intricate they may desire them when they are off the bench. We will be enabled to abbreviate and simplify the law, and in fifteen years we will have the most perfect laws and rules of judicial procedure in America." (Debates 1495.)

The proposed 1922 Constitution removed that section from the Judiciary Article and the comparable language from the equivalent of Section 21. The proposed revision was a combination of the accounting sentence of Section 20 and the reporting requirements of Section 21. The end product was greatly simplified and the only changes of substance were the removal of the perjury words of Section 20 and the "under oath" words of Section 21. Section 19 of the present Article VI provides that the Judicial Conference report to the legislature on suggested improvements in the administration of justice. (See discussion of Sec. 19, Art. VI, *infra,* p. 376.)

Explanation

The first quotation set out above explains why such a detailed reporting requirement was inserted in the Constitution. Presumably, the executive departments have dutifully reported to the Governor. No one will ever know, however, whether they would have done the same under the customary short form of constitutional language.

The optimistic hopes expressed in the second quotation were never fulfilled. The judges apparently ignored the reporting requirement and in 1909 the Supreme Court formally declined to report. (See *Explanation* of Art. III, *supra,* p. 99.)

Comparative Analysis

Aproximately three-fourths of the states have the customary requirement that executive officers report to the governor at his request. Only a handful of states require such reports to be under oath. Almost as few states specify that periodic reports are to be made at the appropriate time for transmittal to the legislature at the beginning of its session. Only about seven states appear to join Illinois in expecting the judges to offer advice on what is defective in the constitution and laws. Eight states authorize the governor or the legislature to request advisory opinions, normally concerning the constitutionality of proposed legis-

lation, from the highest court of the state. (Two of the states authorizing advisory opinions are among those with judicial reporting requirements.) The United States Constitution simply states that the President
may "require the Opinion, in writing," of each executive officer. The
Model State Constitution says that the governor "may at any time
require information, in writing or otherwise," from any executive officer.

Comment

The interesting thing about the quotation from the 1870 Debates set
out above is that the Chairman may not have realized that he was con-
centrating on form and not substance in worrying about the Governor's
power as chief executive. Proponents of the short ballot (see *Comment*
on Sec. 1, *supra,* p. 258) are quick to point out that one of the advantages
thereof is that it enhances a governor's power. Appointed officials
are able to build a personal power base, of course, but it is much shakier
and weaker than that of the elected official. While the 1870 Convention
was readily accepting the Chairman's effort to increase the Governor's
power by means of this section, the Convention was also accepting an
increase in elected executive officers from three to five. Indeed, there
was an unsuccessful floor fight to add a sixth, a Superintendent of Public
Charities. (Debates 749-54.)

Even if the substance of executive power were to continue to be
denied by virtue of the preservation of the long ballot, the Convention
could still appropriately simplify this section. It should be sufficient
to state that the Governor may require information in writing or otherwise at any time from any executive officer. If the custom of requiring
formal reports for the use of the legislature is considered worth preserving, it would be preferable to provide that the legislature may by law
require such formal reports from such executive departments as it
deems necessary. Actually, we live in a society that thrives on reports
and our more serious problem is that there are too many of them. An
"information to the Governor" provision is more in the nature of an
attempt to spell out who is boss than it is a reporting device. Formal
reporting ought simply to be assumed as a normal element of the process
of government.

State Seal

Sec. 22. There shall be a seal of the State, which shall be called the "Great
Seal of the State of Illinois," which shall be kept by the Secretary of State, and
used by him, officially, as directed by law.

History

In the 1818 Constitution, the Schedule stated that the Governor should
use his private seal until a state seal was provided. The 1848 Consti-

tution provided that all grants and commissions be sealed with the great seal of state, signed by the Governor and countersigned by the Secretary of State. The section proposed to the 1870 Convention differed only in the last phrase which was originally worded "under the direction of the Governor." Upon objection, the phrase was changed to the present language. The proposed 1922 Constitution simplified the wording but made no change of substance.

Explanation

There is obviously no explanation required for this section, but it is worth noting that the nature of the duties of the Secretary of State is implied by this section.

Comparative Analysis

All but 11 of the states have some constitutional reference to a great seal. Over half of the references give custody of the seal to the secretary of state and another dozen give custody to the governor. Miscellaneous references are found in half a dozen states. Neither the United States Constitution nor the Model State Constitution has a reference to a great seal.

Comment

This section is obviously not essential, but neither is it obtrusive or capable of creating problems. If the Convention were to move to a short ballot (see *Comment* on Sec. 1, *supra*, p. 258), custody of the seal should be given to the Governor.

Fees and Salaries

Sec. 23. The officers named in this article shall receive for their services a salary, to be established by law, which shall not be increased or diminished during their official terms, and they shall not, after the expiration of the terms of those in office at the adoption of this constitution, receive to their own use any fees, costs, perquisites of office, or other compensation. And all fees that may hereafter be payable by law for any services performed by any officer provided for in this article of the constitution, shall be paid in advance into the State treasury.

History

Under the 1818 Constitution, the only references to executive compensation were a provision providing that the Governor receive a salary not subject to increase or decrease during his term and a provision that the Lieutenant Governor receive the same compensation as the Speaker of the House except that when serving as Governor he was to receive the Governor's salary. In the 1848 Constitution, fixed salaries were set out as follows:

Governor	$1,500.00
Secretary of State	800.00*
Auditor	1,000.00
Treasurer	800.00

*plus fees

In the 1870 Convention, a donnybrook broke out over the matter when the Committee on the Executive Department presented a proposal which in principle was the same as the section as finally adopted. Reading between the lines of the extended debate, one can see that the inadequate salaries provided for in the 1848 Constitution had caused various extralegal and perhaps even unconstitutional devices to be utilized to augment salaries. For example, one delegate observed that "for the last ten years, the Governor has had control of about $10,000 a year. His gardener has had $2,500 a year, and he has never had a gardener in fact that I know of." (Debates 801.)

It is also obvious from the strong language of prohibition of fees, that one popular device for getting around the constitutional limitations on salaries was to authorize the retention of fees. The view that prevailed among the delegates was that a fee system of compensation was susceptible of overcompensation and not the view that if one did not have to collect fees in order to get paid he would neglect his duties.

In the proposed 1922 Constitution, the substance of Section 23 was split up among several sections, some of which were applicable to other offices. In essence, the equivalent section in the proposed Executive Article simply said that officers of the executive department should be paid salaries and no other compensation. In a new article, "Public Servants," one section said that no legislative, executive, judicial, or county officer should receive any fees or other nonsalary compensation, another section said that no "public officer" should have his compensation increased or decreased during his term, and a third section said that every public officer should pay at least monthly to someone designated by law all public moneys received. In the Revenue and Finance Article a new section said that "[n]o payment of money belonging to or for the use of the state shall be held to be made to any officer of the executive department until evidenced by the receipt of the state treasurer." The official explanation simply said: "This section is new." (P.N.C. 52.) Except for the immediately preceding section, the work of the 1920-22 Convention was simply a matter of rearranging compensation provisions in terms of the principles involved rather than in terms of offices.

Explanation

This section does four things. It provides that officers of the executive department shall be paid salaries to be established by law. It reinforces the separation of powers principle by prohibiting increases or decreases in compensation of incumbents during their terms of office. It ends any fee system of compensation, and it reinforces that prohibition by making it clear that fee receipts go into the state treasury.

The only significant judicial gloss on this section is a ruling that appointed officers under Section 10 are also "officers named in this article," a construction that is not obvious. (Peabody v. Russel, 301 Ill. 439 (1922).) Several cases have held that the requirement to pay fees into the treasury means what it says and that no deductions are to be made before such payment. (People v. Sargent, 254 Ill. 514 (1912); Whittemore v. People, 227 Ill. 453 (1907).) One case relied upon the public policy behind this section to declare illegal an incredible scheme whereby the Treasurer had entered into an agreement with the sureties on his bond to deposit public moneys in the sureties' banks, the interest thereon to be divided personally among the sureties and the Treasurer. (Estate of Ramsay v. Whitbeck, 182 Ill. 550 (1900).)

Comparative Analysis

A large majority of the states either provide that salaries shall be set by law or stipulate a sum that is subject to change by law. It is customary to state that salaries cannot be changed during the incumbent's term of office. Some states specify salaries, most of which are unrealistically low. Only a small number of states appear to have specific prohibitions against fees and other emoluments. The United States Constitution states only that the President's compensation may not be changed during his term of office. The Model State Constitution has no provision on compensation.

Comment

Presumably, the battle over salaries which was won in 1870 will not have to be fought again. Presumably also, the involved language over fees could be dropped. That language was designed to end the abuses that had arisen under the ridiculously low salaries set out in the 1848 Constitution. It would seem obvious that omission of such language today would not lead to a revival of an old practice no longer necessary. It should also be noted that the fee language of this section is applicable only to this Article and any decision to drop the language would have no policy implications concerning fees for county and township officials. (See Art. X, Sec. 9, *infra*, p. 507.)

Definition of "Office"

Sec. 24. An office is a public position created by the constitution or law, continuing during the pleasure of the appointing power, or for a fixed time, with a successor elected or appointed. An employment is an agency, for a temporary purpose, which ceases when that purpose is accomplished.

History

This is a new section added in 1870. It appears to have grown out of the debate over Section 10 of this Article concerning appointments by the Governor with its accompanying prohibition against appointments by the legislature. Several amendments were proposed in an effort to clarify which appointments were to be covered by the section and which were not. The delegates were particularly exercised over the case of *Bunn v. People* ex rel. *Laflin* (45 Ill. 397 (1867)), where the Supreme Court held that commissioners who were to supervise construction of the state house were not "officers" and could, therefore, be chosen by the legislature. In the course of the debate, several members of the Committee on the Executive Department suggested that the proper way to solve the problem was not by amending Section 10, but by a separate definition of "officer" to be inserted at some appropriate place. Accordingly, the amendments were withdrawn and on the next day a resolution calling for a definition of "officer" was introduced. There was no further discussion of the matter and Section 24 appeared as part of the Executive Article upon final consideration by the Convention. Ironically, the section as adopted is essentially the definition worked out by the Supreme Court in the *Bunn* case and it would appear that the result of that case would be the same. Except for punctuation, the section was carried over unchanged into the proposed 1922 Constitution.

Explanation

There has been considerable litigation referring to this section, but in almost all cases the substantive issue involved another section of the Constitution or a statute. (See, for example, the discussion of the *Fergus* case under Sec. 16 of Art. IV, *supra*, p. 179.) This must be so since Section 24 is only a definition. The only significant effort to use this section as a substantive provision was in the attack on civil service wherein it was argued unsuccessfully that civil service tenure, being neither at the pleasure of the appointing power nor for a fixed term, was prohibited by Section 24. (People *ex rel.* Akin v. Loeffler, 175 Ill. 585 (1898).)

Comparative Analysis

No other state appears to have a definition of a public office. Both the United States Constitution and the Model State Constitution are silent on the subject.

Comment

The fact that no other state constitution defines a public office indicates at the very least that such a provision is not essential and at the most that such a provision is inappropriate. One should be chary about putting definitions in a constitution. A definition is designed to produce precision and in many areas of a constitution one needs imprecision in order to permit flexibility in coping with changing times. In a narrow procedural provision, a definition may be helpful, such as "ten days (Sundays excepted)" in the veto provision of Section 16 of this Article. (*supra,* p. 293.) But in something so pervasive as distinguishing "office" from "employment," a case-by-case method of developing the meaning of the word "office" in each context in which it appears is preferable. For example, "office" in the context of dual office holding need not necessarily have the same meaning as "office" for an oath or "office" for the purpose of determining whether salaries may be increased during incumbency. A single definition for all uses is likely either to thwart the purpose of some particular provision in some contexts or to result in judicial legerdemain in eroding the stated definition. (See discussion of the *Capuzi* case under Sec. 3 of Art. IV, *supra,* p. 122.)

In any event, it is doubtful that this definition should be preserved as is. As noted earlier, the definition is derived from the *Bunn* case and a careful reading of the majority and dissenting opinions of that case should convince one that the commissioners to supervise the construction of the state house were officers and not "agents." They were required to take an oath and to provide bond, and were to supervise the expenditure of $3,000,000, a princely sum in 1867. A definition tailored to exclude them from a constitutional provision referring to "office" inevitably focussed on the wrong attributes.

Oath of Office

Sec. 25. All civil officers, except members of the General Assembly and such inferior officers as may be by law exempted, shall, before they enter on the duties of their respective offices, take and subscribe the following oath or affirmation:

"I do solemnly swear (or affirm, as the case may be) that I will support the Constitution of the United States, and the Constitution of the State of Illinois, and that I will faithfully discharge the duties of the office of................ according to the best of my ability."

And no other oath, declaration or test shall be required as a qualification.

History

The 1818 Constitution simply required that all public officers take an oath to support the United States and Illinois Constitutions and an oath of office. The Schedule of that Constitution provided that justices of the peace could administer oaths until the legislature otherwise directed. Both provisions were repeated in the 1848 Constitution and a new oath was added: against dueling. The proposed 1922 Constitution left this section unchanged, but moved it to a new article called "Public Servants."

Explanation

No explanation of the oath itself is necessary. From time to time there has been litigation to determine whether a particular position was an office and to determine whether a particular "inferior" office had been exempted by law from the oath requirement. There has also been litigation over the word "test." It is clear that "test" is used in the traditional sense of "religious test" or "political test" and, for example, in no way precludes civil service examinations. (People ex rel. Akin v. Loeffler, 175 Ill. 585 (1898).) Similarly, the Attorney General ruled that a statute requiring an oath of ten years' residence before taking office was not a prohibited oath. (1913 Ill. Att'y Gen. Rep. 220.) Although the question has apparently never arisen, the "no other test" presumably applies equally to members of the General Assembly notwithstanding the opening exception. (Their oath is contained in Sec. 5, Art. IV, supra, p. 129.)

Comparative Analysis

The vast majority of the state constitutions require an oath to support the United States Constitution, the applicable state constitution, and to perform duties faithfully. A half dozen or so states permit some sort of exemption by law from the oath. Approximately ten states prohibit any other oath. The only constitutional oath in the United States Constitution is that required of the President. The United States Constitution states that "Members of the several State Legislatures, and all executive and judicial Officers, both of the United States and of the several States, shall be bound by Oath of Affirmation, to support this Constitution; but no religious Test shall ever be required as a Qualification to any Office or public Trust under the United States." (Art. VI.) The Model State Constitution provides for an oath through the back door. The Bill of Rights Article prohibits any oath except one as set forth therein. (It is much like Section 25.) But there is no literal requirement that any one take the oath.

Comment

In the *Comment* on Section 5 of Article IV (*supra,* p. 130), a question was raised as to the efficacy of that part of the oath requiring a detailed disclaimer of wrong-doing. If a decision is made to preserve the detailed disclaimer, the question arises, as it did in 1870, of why only legislators should so swear. In short, it would seem appropriate to treat all constitutional oath-takers — legislative, executive and judicial — alike. In other words, one constitutional oath section might well suffice.

Article VI

JUDICIAL DEPARTMENT

General Introductory History

Unlike other Articles of the 1870 Constitution, Article VI is a total revision of the Article as initially adopted. Except in minor respects, virtually nothing remains of the original 1870 Article. The amendment effecting this change was adopted by the voters in 1962 and became effective January 1, 1964.

The 1962 Amendment has a history more extensive, perhaps, than any other Article of, or amendment to, the 1870 Constitution. For this reason, as well as the comprehensive nature of its substantive changes, it may be helpful to the Convention members to have a brief organic development of that history, and the major revisions contained in the Article, in this introductory comment. This approach will not affect the established format of this publication under which each section will have its own *History, Explanation, Comparative Analysis* and *Comment,* all serving as a detailed supplement to this introduction. In respect to the detailed explanation for each section, it must be noted, however, that there is very little decisional law, since the Article has been in effect for only six years.

Pre-Gateway Amendment: Prior to the so-called 1950 Gateway Amendment which liberalized the constitutional amendment process (see *History* and *Explanation,* Art. XIV, Sec. 2), there had been few efforts to amend Article VI. The rigid electorate approval requirement virtually foreclosed any significant probability of successful amendment and eventually discouraged efforts to secure reform, notwithstanding a general professional consensus that Article VI of the 1870 Constitution (which itself made little changes in the 1848 Constitutional provisions relating to the State's Judicial Department) substantially hampered, in many respects, the objective of an efficient system for the administration of justice.

Post-Gateway Period: The passage of Gateway immediately inspired the movement for amendment. A Joint Committee of the Illinois State and Chicago Bar Associations, after extensive study, prepared a draft of a proposed new Article in 1952. In 1951 the Illinois General Assembly, conscious of the momentum for change motivated by the Gateway Amendment, created a legislative commission to study the needs for constitutional reform and to evaluate proposals and make recommendations with respect to these changes. The Joint Bar Committee and the Legislative Commission cooperated extensively in seeking to arrive at an agreed proposal for submission to the 1953 session of the General Assembly. Consensus was achieved for most of the suggested changes. An impasse developed, however, on the critical issue of the method of selecting judges. The Bar Committee insisted upon the American Bar Association proposal of 1938 (also popularly known as the Missouri Plan) which provided for the selection of a slate of nominees for judicial office by nonpartisan commissions and appointment by the Governor from the nominees so designated, followed, after a brief tenure, by submission to the electorate of the question of retaining the appointee in office for the full term. The purpose of this proposal was to eliminate or minimize the influence of political parties in the selection of judges. The Legislative Commission insisted upon the retention of the partisan adversary method of electing judges, urging that political involvement in the selection of judges had more to commend it in principle than the proposed nonpartisan nominating commission method. An important aspect of the Bar plan involved tenure of judges *after* initial selection. The Bar Committee insisted upon nonadversary, nonpartisan submission to the electorate of the question of retaining the incumbent in office for another term. This principle was also rejected by the Legislative Commission. The conflict on this issue was largely, though not solely, responsible for the failure of the Bar proposals to secure legislative adoption in 1953 and 1955. In 1957 the General Assembly adopted a substantially revised version of the Bar Committee draft which contained neither element of the selection and tenure plan endorsed by the Bar Associations. The proposal failed by a close margin to receive electorate approval in 1958. In 1962, the legislature accepted a variant of the 1957 compromise, retaining the political method of election of judges but adopting the nonadversary election on retention. (For a more detailed description of this compromise, see *Explanation,* Sec. 10, *infra,* pp. 356-7). Although selection and tenure of judges was a central issue in all of the proposals for constitutional amendment, it was by no means the only major concern of the legal profession and the public. The 1870 Constitution was deficient in a number of respects. Among the more important were the following:

(1) The absence of authority and responsibility in the Supreme Court for the administration of the judicial system.

(2) A proliferation of trial courts of general and limited jurisdiction,

including nonrecord justice of the peace and police magistrate courts.

(3) A hybrid intermediate appellate court structure, legislatively established, and manned by circuit judges temporarily assigned to the appellate courts.

(4) An allocation of mandated appellate jurisdiction to the Supreme Court which stifled it in a mass of comparatively unimportant litigation, effectively preventing it from considering many novel and important areas of procedural and substantive law.

The 1962 Amendment dealt with these and other matters in a significant manner. The method of treatment is contained in the *Explanation* under each of the sections. Suffice it to say in concluding this introductory comment that Article VI, on balance, is viewed in objective professional circles as one of the most far-reaching and constructive reforms in the history of state constitutional efforts to establish a modern and efficient system for the administration of justice. This is not to suggest that there is now a perfect and unanimous consensus as to its merits or that there is not responsible criticism of some of its features. These will be dealt with in the appropriate places in the materials which follow.

Courts

Sec. 1. The judicial power is vested in a Supreme Court, an Appellate Court and Circuit Courts.

History

The 1818 Constitution established only a Supreme Court but authorized the General Assembly to create inferior courts as it saw fit. The Constitution of 1848 gave constitutional status to a Supreme Court, circuit courts, county courts and justices of the peace. The General Assembly was authorized to establish additional inferior courts of uniform jurisdiction in cities. The 1870 Constitution added police magistrates, the Superior Court of Cook County, and the Criminal Court of Cook County to the 1848 category of constitutionally established courts. Authorization was given the legislature to establish an appellate court, probate courts in counties of a specified population, and courts in and for cities and incorporated towns. It should be noted that the Municipal Court of Chicago was established, not under the authority of Article VI of the 1870 Constitution, but under Article IV, Section 34. The consequence of the establishment of the Municipal Court of Chicago was the abolition of the offices of justices of the peace and police magistrates in the City of Chicago. (See *Explanation, Art. IV, Sec. 34, supra,* pp. 250-1.)

The 1922 Convention proposal provided for a Supreme Court, an independent appellate court, circuit and county courts and justices of the peace. No provision was made for the creation of additional inferior courts by the General Assembly, but the Municipal Court of Chicago was not affected.

Explanation

The present Section 1 has its greatest significance in (1) the simplicity of the constitutional judicial structure and (2) the withdrawal of power from the General Assembly to add courts to that structure. Of special importance also is the constitutional sanction and status given to the appellate court. Thus there is a streamlined three-tier structure of courts — a Supreme Court, the appellate courts, and circuit courts — which is not susceptible to legislative change.

The advantages which accrue from this simplified structure in the critical areas of allocation of jurisdiction to the Supreme and appellate courts and in the overall administration of the judicial system, should be very great. Moreover, the desirability of an independent constitutionally established appellate court for the first time in the state's history is generally, if not universally, recognized. But the truly significant reform effected by this section is in the establishment of a single unified and integrated trial court. There is and can be only one trial court, the circuit court. Of necessity, its jurisdiction is original and unlimited.

To fully appreciate the import of the integrated trial court concept, a look at the trial court structure which prevailed prior to the new Judicial Article will be helpful. The several circuit courts and the Superior Court of Cook County were the only trial courts of original and unlimited jurisdiction. The justice of the peace and police magistrate courts exercised a limited civil and quasi-criminal jurisdiction but their principal deficiency, aside from the generally low level of competence of their judges, most of whom were not lawyers, was the fact that they were not courts of record. Their decisions were re-triable de novo either in the county or circuit court at the instance of the losing party who frequently failed, quite deliberately, to defend in the justice or magistrate courts. The only other constitutionally created courts were Superior and Criminal Courts in Cook County and the county courts. These courts, as well as the legislatively established probate courts, municipal courts, and city, village and incorporated town courts, but excluding the Superior Court of Cook County, exercised only a limited jurisdiction. The appellate voidance of a judgment entered by one of these courts, sometimes after years of litigation, on the ground of lack of jurisdiction, was not an uncommon occurrence.

This hodgepodge of trial courts was wasteful and inefficient. City, village and town courts were legislatively authorized on occasion to satisfy a political rather than a public need. Many of these courts were virtually without business though manned by salaried judges and nonjudicial staff. The system of re-trials de novo from judgments of justice and magistrate courts was expensive, frustrating, and wasteful of judicial time and manpower.

The integrated circuit court eliminates multiple trials and vexatious questions of jurisdiction. A suit cannot be filed in the wrong trial court, since there is only one trial court. Problems of venue may remain but issues of trial court jurisdiction are eliminated. The problems of assignment of cases and control of the dockets are minimized in the integrated court with the aid of the administrative provisions established in the Article. In the last analysis, the concept of the single trial court is premised on the belief that every litigant is entitled to a single trial of his cause in a court of record and a guaranteed appellate review. This is what this section and related sections dealing wtih appellate jurisdiction seek to accomplish.

Comparative Analysis

While 46 other state constitutions provide for a highest court, only 12 provide for an intermediate appellate court — four of these having been authorized since 1960. Forty-two other states have constitutional provisions establishing general trial courts. Of these, ten also provide for separate county courts and 13 for separate probate courts. Twenty-one states still provide for justices of the peace, a reduction of five since 1961. At present, nearly all states authorize legislative creation of additional trial courts of limited jurisdiction. No state expressly authorizes legislative creation of a single general trial court of unlimited jurisdiction. No other state constitution provides for the single trial court structure established in Illinois.

The United States Constitution establishes only a Supreme Court and "such inferior Courts as the Congress [may provide]." The Model State Constitution vests the judicial power in a Supreme Court, an appellate court, a general court and inferior courts of limited jurisdiction as may be established by law.

Comment

There appears to be no reason to quarrel with the provisions establishing Supreme and appellate courts. The single integrated trial court has raised some sporadic criticism, largely because of the elimination of the small claims jurisdiction of former justice of the peace and magistrate courts. Despite the many failings of these courts, they provide an inexpensive and expeditious, if not necessarily a judicious, disposition of many small claims and litigation arising out of localized disputes. And notwithstanding the right to seek a re-trial de novo, many litigants, for reasons of economy, accepted the decisions of these courts as final. Under the new system, a small claims division of circuit courts is authorized by Supreme Court rule. If an appeal is desired, a record must be made. This expense factor irritates many small claim litigants who would prefer to avoid this expense. To overcome this objection, at least to some extent, provision is made in the rules of the Supreme Court for inexpensive small claims procedures and for records which need not be printed. Inexpensive typewritten or other methods of producing legible records are authorized, and other provisions permit further reduction in costs of appeal. The advantages of the integrated trial court system seem clearly to far outweigh the relatively minor criticisms which have been directed against it. Given the importance of the concept, its uniqueness, and its relationship to efficient judicial administration, it would appear that the single, integrated trial court concept should be retained.

Administration

Sec. 2.   General administrative authority over all courts in this State including the temporary assignment of any judge to a court other than that for which he was selected with the consent of the Chief Judge of the Circuit to which such assignment is made, is vested in the Supreme Court and shall be exercised by the Chief Justice in accordance with its rules. The Supreme Court shall appoint an administrative director and staff, who shall serve at its pleasure, to assist the Chief Justice in his administrative duties.

History

This section has no parallel in any of the prior Illinois Constitutions. Nor did the 1922 Convention proposal deal with this subject except for a provision authorizing temporary assignments of judges. Such administrative power as existed in the Supreme Court was of legislative origin. Primarily, the statutes granted limited powers of assignment of judges to serve in courts other than their own. In addition, the legislature in 1959 established the Office of Court Administrator under the administration of the Supreme Court. The powers of that office were largely routine and ministerial. The law granted no significant administrative control over the judicial system to the Supreme Court, but it did provide the rationale for the expression constitutionally of the principle of centralized administration of the entire judicial system by the Supreme Court.

Explanation

Under prior Constitutions, courts existed virtually as autonomous units. A degree of administrative control was exercised in several of the larger circuit courts, but for all practical purposes there was no administrative plan or purpose to guide a massive system of courts and its judicial and nonjudicial personnel. The absence of a centralized administrative authority over the judicial system was conceived by proponents of constitutional revision to be one of the major deficiencies of that system. Judicial manpower in many areas was largely wasted. In other parts of the state, courts were overburdened to the point of helplessness. Legislative palliatives authorizing transfer of judges were only partially satisfactory.

To rectify this gaping flaw in the judicial system, this section establishes general administrative authority over all courts in the Supreme Court to be exercised by its Chief Justice with the assistance of an administrative director and staff. These provisions, together with the provisions of Section 8 providing for administrative responsibility in the chief judge of each circuit court, subject to the authority of the Supreme Court, should provide the mechanism for a coordinated and efficient administration of the judicial system.

This section was not intended to deal with rule-making power respecting practice and procedure in the courts. Legislative history derived from prior drafts submitted to and considered by the legislature, as well as other contemporaneous history, make it clear that this section is not a general grant of authority to the Court to adopt rules of practice and procedure. Rule-making authority is granted to the Supreme Court in particular instances (see Sec. 5 — appellate jurisdiction of the Supreme Court, *infra*, pp. 338-9; Sec. 7 — rules for inexpensive and expeditious appeals and for appeal of nonfinal judgments of the circuit courts, *infra*, p. 345), but no general grant of rule-making power is made. Of interest in this connection was the recent assertion by the Supreme Court of an inherent rule-making power in the Court in a specific instance of a legislative rule conflicting with a Supreme Court rule. (People *ex rel.* Stamos v. Jones, 40 Ill. 2d 62 (1968).) The case does not, however, deny the existence of a concurrent or independent legislative rule-making power. (See *Explanation*, Art. III, *supra*, p. 102, for an additional discussion of the *Stamos* case.)

Comparative Analysis

Nearly one-third of the state constitutions provide for administrative control in some form by the state's highest court. Of these, however, only five have a constitutional office similar to the administrative director provided by Illinois, and four of these were established since 1959.

The Constitution of the United States has no comparable provision. The Model State Constitution contains basically the same administrative provision.

Comment

It would appear that a grant of administrative power to the Supreme Court deserves constitutional rather than legislative status. Given the unhappy history of the past and the critical importance of centralized administrative control, the case for retention of this section is strong.

Judicial Districts

Sec. 3. The State is divided into five Judicial Districts for the selection of judges of the Supreme and Appellate Courts. The First Judicial District consists of the county of Cook. The remainder of the State shall be divided by law into four Judicial Districts of substantially equal population, each of which shall be compact and composed of contiguous countries.

History

Geographic representation in state courts became a constitutional principle in the 1848 Constitution. Supreme Court representation was tied to three grand divisions, and circuit judges were elected from nine judicial districts. Under the 1818 Constitution, Supreme Court justices and the judges of inferior courts were appointed by joint ballot of the two houses of the General Assembly and commissioned by the Governor. Nothing in that Constitution suggested area representation as relevant to the selection of judges. The 1870 Constitution continued the 1848 precedent but mandated seven districts, from each of which one Supreme Court justice would be elected. The districts were defined in the Constitution but legislative alteration was authorized. Judicial circuits were also to be established by law for the election of circuit judges. The 1922 Convention proposal contained the 1870 provisions virtually unchanged. The 1870 Constitution authorized legislative establishment of appellate courts, with districts to be defined by law. The 1922 Convention proposal did not provide for appellate court election districts. It provided instead that appellate court judges would be appointed by the Supreme Court.

Explanation

The present Article adheres to the principle of geographic representation for the election of judges. Two major changes from the 1870 requirements were made. The first was the reduction from seven to five in the number of judicial districts for the selection of Supreme Court judges, and the second was the designation of Cook County as one of these districts. The four districts other than the Cook County district were to be legislatively adjusted to maintain substantial equality of population. With the creation of the new appellate court, the new section provided that the five districts would also be the area basis for the selection of appellate court judges.

The problem of area representation for judicial selection of judges serving in a state-wide capacity (as distinguished from judges elected for and serving defined political subdivisions such as circuits, counties and cities) is a troublesome one. It is difficult to see any rational relationship between Supreme and appellate court judicial service and the principle of limited geographic representation. The Constitution of the United States and the constitutions of those states which provide for the appointment of Supreme Court judges do not mandate area representation. It is difficult to equate the administration of justice with a particular constituency represented by a defined but impermanent set of county boundaries or other standard of area measurement. The Joint Committee of the Illinois State and Chicago Bar Associations, in its earlier deliberations and drafts, indeed proposed the selection of all or part of the Supreme and appellate court judges on a state-wide basis. Legislative resistance, based largely on tradition and considerations of political and public expediency, ultimately resulted in the decision to retain the principle of area representation for the selection of these judges, except for the changes in the 1870 provision already noted.

In connection with this issue it is important to note that the one man-one vote principle applicable to legislative representation has not been determined by the United States Supreme Court to be applicable to judicial elections. Such limited judicial precedent as exists suggests the contrary. Thus, in *Romiti v. Kerner* (256 F. Supp. 35 (N.D. Ill. 1966)), the federal district court rejected a taxpayer's challenge that the districting provisions of this section and the allocation of judges under Section 4 denied him the equal protection of the law, strongly hinting — though not deciding — that the one man-one vote principle was not applicable.

Comparative Analysis

Two-thirds of the states have a constitutional provision for the election of judges of the highest court. Of these, however, only nine, excluding Illinois, elect high court judges from districts. All other states provide for "at-large" elections.

In contrast, all seven states which provide for the election of appellate court judges create judicial election districts. Apparently only one state, Louisiana, provides for judicial election districts for both Supreme and appellate court judges.

Since the Model State Constitution provides for the appointment of judges to the Supreme, appellate, and general trial courts, there is no provision for election districts. Presumably, the legislature may establish districts. The Constitution of the United States, for like reason, has no provisions for election districts.

Comment.

Whatever the merits of area representation as applied to statewide judicial service, the principle is so deeply ingrained in constitutional

history and tradition that any attempt to repeal or alter it would, in all
probability, cause substantial political and public reverberations. It is
doubtful that there is any merit in provoking this kind of controversy.
As to the establishment of Cook County as a separate and single county
judicial district (as contrasted with the 1870 provision which grouped
Cook, Lake, Will, Kankakee and DuPage Counties into a single district),
it would seem that if area and population representation is the acceptable principle, the provision should be retained. It should be noted, however, that the 1870 districts were subject to legislative alteration, but that
the designation in the present section establishes Cook County permanently as a single judicial district. The judgment here was that in all
probability Cook County would continue to have approximately 50
per cent of the state's population for a considerable period into the
future.

Supreme Court — Organization

Sec. 4.   The Supreme Court shall consist of seven judges, three of whom
shall be selected from the First Judicial District and one each from the Second,
Third, Fourth and Fifth Judicial Districts. Four judges shall constitute a
quorum and the concurrence of four shall be necessary to a decision. The judges
of the Supreme Court shall select one of their number to serve as Chief Justice
for a term of three years.

History

The 1818 Constitution established a four-man Supreme Court with
legislative authorization to increase the number. The 1848 Constitution
reduced the membership to three and eliminated the legislative authorization to increase the number. The 1870 Constitution established the
number of Supreme Court justices as seven.

Quorum. The 1818 and 1848 Constitutions established a two-member-
ship quorum requirement. The 1870 Constitution increased this to four.

Districts. The 1818 Constitution had no district specifications. Supreme
Court justices were appointed by the General Assembly and commissioned by the Governor. As noted in the *History* of Section 3 (*supra,* p.
334), the 1848 Constitution introduced the district concept with provision
for the election of a judge from each of three districts. However, the legislature was authorized to provide for state-wide elections. The 1870
Constitution established seven election districts and eliminated the 1848
authorization for state-wide elections.

Chief Justice. The 1818 Constitution provided for a Chief Justice but
was silent as to the method of designation. The 1848 Constitution placed
this mantle upon the judge having the oldest commission. The 1870 Constitution provided for election of the Chief Justice by other members of
the Court with no period of service designated. The Court by rule pro-

vided for annual rotation of the position among the judges.

The 1922 Convention proposal dealt with these matters as follows:

Number of Judges: Nine, with three being elected from the district containing Cook County.

Quorum Requirement: Majority for a quorum; five for a decision.

Districts: Seven.

Chief Justice, Selection and Tenure: Selection by judges of Supreme Court; no provision for a term.

Explanation

The present Article changed the 1870 provisions in the following important respects:

(1) Reduction in the number of Supreme Court judicial districts from seven to five.

(2) Establishment of Cook County as one of the five districts.

(3) Reallocation of the seven judges so that three justices would be selected from Cook County and one justice from each of the other four districts.

(4) Establishment of a three-year term of service for the Chief Justice. Unchanged were the number of judges, the quorum requirement of four, and the requirement that the members of the Court elect the Chief Justice.

The *Explanation* of Section 3 above touched directly or indirectly upon points (1), (2) and (3) which deal with the districting principle. The increase to three in the number of Supreme Court judges to be selected from the Cook County district was a consequence of adherence to the district standard for the election of judges. With Cook County generating more than 50 per cent of the state's judicial business, and possessing approximately one-half the state's population, the political and professional pressures to equalize the representation of that district on the Court were substantial. Three-sevenths of the total was accepted as a reasonable adjustment.

With the provisions of the new Article vesting administrative authority in the Supreme Court to be exercised pursuant to its rules by the Chief Justice and Adiministrative Director and staff (Sections 1 and 2), it was thought desirable to mandate a minimum three-year term as Chief Justice. The absence of a specified term could have led to the continuation of the Supreme Court's annual rotation rule. A longer term of administrative responsibility was deemed necessary for administrative efficiency. The three-year term seeks to accomplish this objective. Nothing in this section precludes the reappointment of the Chief Justice for additional terms.

Comparative Analysis

As was noted in the *Comparative Analysis* of Section 3 above, two-thirds of the states elect high court judges, nine states with judicial districts and 24 at large. Eleven states appoint high court judges, normally by the governor or legislature or a combination of both. The Model State Constitution provides for the appointment of the justices by the governor with the advice and consent of the unicameral legislature.

About four-fifths of all state constitutions deal in some fashion with the size of the state's highest court. Twenty-four states, excluding Illinois, set a specific size. Of these, 15 set the size at seven judges. Delaware with three, provides the smallest membership, and Mississippi, with nine, the largest. The average is six to seven. Sixteen states, however, set either a maximum and minimum or a recommended size with provisions for increases and decreases, typically as directed by the legislature or the Court itself.

Only four states — Kansas, Nebraska, Maryland and Michigan — have provisions similar to those of Illinois with respect to both size and selection.

Thirty-two other states provide a quorum requirement. Of these, 24 require a majority, four more than a majority, and four less than a majority.

Only 28 other states set a voting or decision requirement, however. Twenty-one states require a majority for a decision, four require less than a majority of all judges, and three require more than a majority at times.

Only nine other states provide for the Court itself to select the Chief Justice. Four states provide for appointment by the governor or legislature. Nine states provide that the justice with the shortest term remaining becomes Chief Justice. Five make the justice with the oldest commission the Chief Justice.

Four other states set a term for the position of Chief Justice, ranging from two to six years.

The Constitution of the United States, of course, specifies the term of office to be "during good Behavior." Selection is by presidential appointment with the advice and consent of the Senate. No mention is made of the size of the Court or the selection and terms of the Chief Justice. The Model State Constitution is silent on the subjects of quorum, voting, and selection and term of the Chief Justice.

Comment

There is no evidence of professional or public dissatisfaction with the provisions of this section. The only potentially controversial provision is that which allocates three Supreme Court judges to Cook County. Yet it is difficult to argue against this allocation if area representation is retained as a constitutional principle. Moreover, a reduction in the number of judges for Cook County would surely engender a bitter political controversy. It is doubtful whether the issue is of such importance as to risk a sharp partisan fight.

Supreme Court — Jurisdiction

Sec. 5. The Supreme Court may exercise original jurisdiction in cases relating to the revenue, mandamus, prohibition and habeas corpus, such original jurisdiction as may be necessary to the complete determination of any cause on review, and only appellate jurisdiction in all other cases.

Appeals from the final judgments of circuit courts shall lie directly to the Supreme Court as a matter of right only (a) in cases involving revenue, (b) in cases involving a question arising under the Constitution of the United States or of this State, (c) in cases of habeas corpus, and (d) by the defendant from sentence in capital cases. Subject to law hereafter enacted, the Supreme Court has authority to provide by rule for appeal in other cases from the circuit courts directly to the Supreme Court.

Appeals from the Appellate Court shall lie to the Supreme Court as a matter of right only (a) in cases in which a question under the Constitution of the United States or of this State arises for the first time in and as a result of the action of the Appellate Court, and (b) upon the certification by a division of the Appellate Court that a case decided by it involves a question of such importance that it should be decided by the Supreme Court. Subject to rules, appeals from the Appellate Court to the Supreme Court in all other cases shall be by leave of the Supreme Court.

History

The 1818 Constitution gave original jurisdiction to the Supreme Court in cases relating to the revenue, in cases of mandamus, and in such cases of impeachment "as may be required to be tried before it," and appellate jurisdiction apparently without qualification. The impeachment provision is somewhat curious, as the Legislative Article granted the "sole power of impeaching" to the House of Representatives with the trial to be conducted by the Senate. The 1848 Constitution added habeas corpus to the category of original jurisdiction, and otherwise re-enacted the 1818 provision, including the impeachment reference. The 1870 Constitution re-enacted the 1848 provisions respecting original and appellate jurisdiction, eliminating, however, the impeachment reference. With the authorization in the 1870 Constitution for the establishment of appellate courts, the Supreme Court's mandatory appellate jurisdiction was extended to include judgments "in all criminal cases and cases in which a franchise or freehold or the validity of a statute is involved, and in such other cases as may be provided by law."

The proposed 1922 Constitution gave the Supreme Court original jurisdiction in cases relating to the revenue, in quo warranto, mandamus, habeas corpus, prohibition and other cases involving questions of great public importance, and appellate jurisdiction in all other cases. In a separate section entitled "Appeals and Writs of Error," it was also provided that appeals *may* be prosecuted "to or from the supreme court in all criminal cases where the punishment allowed by law may be death or imprisonment in the penitentiary and in cases where a franchise or a freehold or the validity of a statute is involved . . . and to or from the supreme court in all other cases."

Explanation

The present Article adds to the original jurisdiction of the Supreme Court the authority to entertain writs of prohibition, while retaining revenue, mandamus and habeas corpus. The grant of original jurisdiction is couched in language of discretion and not mandate. The 1870 grant had been construed to reach the same result, the Court holding that in the cases enumerated the circuit courts enjoyed concurrent jurisdiction. (People ex rel. Taylor v. Board of Educ., 197 Ill. 43 (1902).) Experience teaches that the Supreme Court will accept original jurisdiction in only the most pressing of circumstances, normally when time is of the essence in construing important legislative enactments.

The great significance of the present section is in its severe proscription of the mandatory appellate jurisdiction of the Supreme Court. Because of this mandated jurisdiction deriving from prior Constitutional provisions, the Court, as a practical matter, had little flexibility in the exercise of its discretion to control or limit appeals to it. In addition to appeals from different courts in common law actions, the legislature established review responsibility in the Supreme Court in almost all instances of administrative action. And, as noted, with the establishment by law of appellate courts pursuant to Section 11 of the 1870 Constitution, mandatory appellate jurisdiction from the judgments of those courts was constitutionally imposed "in all criminal cases and cases in which a franchise or freehold or the validity of a statute is involved, and in such other cases as may be provided by law."

The effect of this open-ended mandatory appellate responsibility was to enmesh the Court in a mass of relatively unimportant litigation, leaving it little room for exercising its discretionary appellate jurisdiction in important and novel issues. A major objective of the new Article was to make the Supreme Court, in fact as well as in name, the pinnacle of the state judicial system by assuring that it would be primarily concerned with issues of paramount importance. This was achieved by severely circumscribing appeals as of right from the circuit and appellate courts to the Supreme Court. Thus under the existing provisions, litigants may appeal a final judgment of the circuit court directly to the Supreme

Court only in the four types of cases enumerated in the second paragraph of this section. Appeals as of right from the appellate court to the Supreme Court are limited to the two situations designated in the last paragraph of this section. However, the Supreme Court is granted the authority to permit direct appeals from the circuit court and other appeals from the appellate court in cases other than those which it is required to take. By this combination of limited mandatory appellate jurisdiction and discretionary authority to accept other cases for review, the Supreme Court can now fulfill the function of resolving the litigation and issues of greatest importance to the state. Many of the cases formerly heard by it are now shifted to the jurisdiction of the appellate court, thus assuring the objective of a single trial and a single judicial review by a competent judicial tribunal in every case.

Several important decisions under this section deserve reference. In *First National Bank & Trust Co. v. City of Evanston* (30 Ill. 2d 479 1964)), the Court construed the provision that appeal as a matter of right from the circuit court lies "in cases involving a question arising under the Constitution of the United States or this State" and refused to give it an exact and literal interpretation. Instead, it adopted the "substantial question" test as employed by the United States Supreme Court in the exercise of its discretionary jurisdiction. Conceding the difficulty of applying that test, the Court nevertheless observed that the purpose of the Judicial Article "seems clearly to have been to relieve [the Supreme Court] of the bulk of its mandatory appellate jurisdiction and to establish instead a basic pattern of discretionary review of determinations of the Appellate Court," and that in the light of that purpose the Court could deny jurisdiction in a case raising a constitutional issue if in its judgment the issue did not meet the test of substantiality. The principle has been applied in a number of criminal cases wherein constitutional issues were raised and preserved and in each of which the cause was transferred to the appellate court because the issues were not "fairly debatable" or "substantial." (People v. Wolfson, 34 Ill. 2d 585 (1966); People v. Hale, 31 Ill. 2d 200 (1964); People v. Arbuckle, 31 Ill. 2d 163 (1964).) Nevertheless in *People v. Perry* (34 Ill. 2d 229 (1966)), the Court assumed jurisdiction of a cause in which a constitutional issue was raised though it did not find it necessary to rule on the issue, a not unlikely occurrence where the Rule of Substantiality is itself grounded in judicial discretion.

In *People v. Turner* (31 Ill. 2d 197 (1964)), the Court interpreted the provision for appeal as a matter of right "from sentences in capital cases" as excluding a case in which a life sentence and not a sentence of capital punishment had been imposed. In *People v. Nash* (36 Ill. 2d 275 (1966)), the Court held it had jurisdiction to review directly a sentence of imprisonment for a term of 99 years to 150 years in a case in which the defendant was tried for murder. Though obscurely developed, the appeal appears to raise issues of procedural due process.

The effect of these interpretations is to protect the Court from appellate jurisdiction in numerous cases in which a constitutional issue is raised spuriously for the purpose of securing a Supreme Court review or where indeed the issue is not "fairly debatable" or "substantial." Fairly administered, this approach by the Supreme Court would seem in accord with the spirit if not the literal language of the section.

Comparative Analysis

Although the *Comparative Analysis of the Michigan Constitution* (C.A.M.C., vii-8) cautions that "[i]t is quite difficult to compare state constitutions with respect to their provisions for the jurisdiction of the highest court," the *Index Digest of State Constitutions* (Index) indicates that some general observations can be made.

While nearly half of all states provide the high court with some original jurisdiction, only eight others give it original jurisdiction over cases relating to habeas corpus, seven to mandamus, five to prohibition, one to revenue, and three "as necessary." On the other hand, nearly three-fourths of the states provide some form of mandatory appellate jurisdiction in terms of a case description. All others providing mandatory appellate jurisdiction do so in terms of a combination of case description and court, or by court alone. While only about one-sixth of the states provide discretionary appellate jurisdiction, nearly half authorize the court to issue writs in aid of its jurisdiction.

The Constitution of the United States grants the Supreme Court original jurisdiction in "all Cases affecting Ambassadors, other public Ministers and Consuls" and those in which a state is a party. In all other justiciable matters enumerated in Article III, Section 2, the Supreme Court is given appellate jurisdiction, "both as to Law and Fact, with such Exceptions, and under such Regulations as the Congress shall make."

The Model State Constitution provides the high court with original jurisdiction in two particular areas, review of legislative redistricting and all matters concerning the governor, and "in all other cases as provided by law." Appellate jurisdiction is granted in all cases arising under the state and federal constitutions, and "in all other cases as provided by law."

Comment

The provisions of this section limiting the mandatory appellate jurisdiction of the Supreme Court are among the most important in the Judicial Article. It is a fair estimate that the limitation has thus far operated in a manner consistent with its purpose. The work load of the individual members of the Court has not been reduced; rather, their efforts are now expended in the important areas defined and in the additionally important areas which are brought within the Court's discretionary appellate jurisdiction. There appears to be no professional or other opinion which is critical of the substance or application of this section.

Appellate Court — Organization

Sec. 6. The Appellate Court shall be organized in the five Judicial Districts. Until otherwise provided by law, the court shall consist of twenty-four judges, twelve of whom shall be selected from the First Judicial District and three each from the Second, Third, Fourth and Fifth Judicial Districts. The Supreme Court shall have authority to assign additional judges to service in the Appellate Court from time to time as the business of the Court requires. There shall be such number of divisions, of not less than three judges each, as the Supreme Court shall prescribe. Assignments to divisions shall be made by the Supreme Court and a judge may be assigned to a division in a district other than the district in which such judge resides with the consent of a majority of the judges of the district to which such assignment is made. The majority of a division shall constitute a quorum and the concurrence of a majority of the division shall be necessary to a decision of the Appellate Court. There shall be at least one division in each Appellate District and each division shall sit at times and places prescribed by rules of the Supreme Court.

History

A constitutionally authorized appellate court, intermediate between the trial and Supreme courts, first appears in the 1870 Constitution (Art. VI, Sec. 1, *supra*, p. 329). Its origin and status were both constitutional and legislative but its establishment, and thus presumably its continuation, was left to the discretionary power of the legislature. The constitutional authorization did not include provision for a separate and distinct judiciary. Instead it was provided that the court would be manned by "such number of judges of the circuit courts" and sit in "such time and places and in such manner, as may be provided by law." By law, appointments were made by the Supreme Court.

Judges of the Superior Court of Cook County, being determined to have the same constitutional status as circuit judges, were qualified to sit on the appellate court established for Cook County. At the time of the adoption of the Judicial Article in 1962 there were four legislatively established district appellate courts. Cook County was designated as the First District and the remaining three districts sat respectively at Ottawa, Springfield and Mount Vernon. The Cook County District was organized into three divisions of three judges each. The Second District had two divisions and the Third and Fourth Districts had one division each. Each division had three judges assigned to it by the Supreme Court. The 1870 Constitution had no provision respecting quorum or the number of judges necessary for a decision. It prohibited additional compensation for circuit judges assigned to appellate court service.

The proposed 1922 Constitution established a constitutional appellate court consisting of four districts. The districts, or divisions if applicable, were to sit where provided "by law." No mention was made of a quorum or decisional requirement. In a remarkable departure from the 1870 provisions, the Supreme Court was given the power to appoint all appellate court judges, and no requirement was made that such judges be selected from judges sitting on a circuit or lower court.

Explanation

The appellate court (or courts) established pursuant to the 1870 Constitution was hybrid in character. Having neither a permanent constitutional status nor its own judiciary, it lacked the independence and prestige essential to a properly conceived judicial system. Though it served well, and often with distinction, there was little question among most proponents of judicial reform that a new and independent intermediate appellate court structure was a constitutional imperative.

This section establishes the essential structure of the appellate court. Its most important features are (not necessarily in order of priority or importance):

(1) A permanent constitutional status.

(2) The establishment of the court into the five judicial districts provided by Section 3, thus coordinating the districts for the selection of Supreme and appellate court judges.

(3) Providing for the selection of the courts' own judiciary.

(4) Designation of the number of judges, initially 24, divided equally between the Cook County district and the four remaining districts, which number is subject to legislative change.

(5) Administrative authority in the Supreme Court to
    (a) assign additional judges (presumably circuit and associate circuit judges, although assignment of a Supreme Court judge is not prohibited) to appellate court service as the business of the court demands;
    (b) assign, subject to majority consent of the appellate judges of the district, an appellate court justice to a district other than the district in which he resides;
    (c) establish such number of divisions in each judicial district, of not less than three judges each, as the Supreme Court determines to be necessary; and
    (d) prescribe the times and places where each division shall sit.

(6) Designation of a majority of a division as necessary to a quorum and a decision.

The detail embraced in this section may seem at first blush to establish too rigid a structure and too many substantive principles which might better be left to legislative determination. In fact the structure is most flexible, permitting a wide latitude of administrative authority in the Supreme Court, and an important measure of legislative discretion in determining the number of judges.

Judicial implementation of these provisions has been effective. The First District has been divided into four divisions; the other districts remain with one division each. A presiding judge of each division is also authorized by rule. The assignment power has been employed to good advantage by the Supreme Court to meet the substantially increased jurisdictional responsibilities of the appellate court.

Comparative Analysis

As stated in the *Comparative Analysis* of Article VI, Section 1 (*supra,* p 331), only 13 states, including Illinois, or slightly more than one-fourth of all states, have constitutional provisions for an intermediate appellate court. The organization of each system varies considerably from jurisdiction to jurisdiction.

The Constitution of the United States itself establishes no intermediate appellate court. The federal courts are established by Congress pursuant to the constitutional provision vesting the judicial power in a Supreme Court, "and in such inferior Courts as the Congress may from time to time ordain and establish."

The Model State Constitution establishes an intermediate appellate court, but does not define its organization in detail.

Comment

There appears to be much support for and little observable complaint about the concept of an independent intermediate appellate court. Nor is there any evidence that the section as structured is in need of revision in any significant respect. Such problems as have arisen have been quite manageable, thanks to the flexibility and scope of the administrative power of the Supreme Court.

Appellate Court — Jurisdiction

Sec. 7. In all cases, other than those appealable directly to the Supreme Court, appeals from final judgments of a Circuit Court lie as a matter of right to the Appellate Court in the district in which the Circuit Court is located, except that after a trial on the merits in a criminal case, no appeal shall lie from a judgment of acquittal. The Supreme Court shall provide by rule for expeditious and inexpensive appeals. The Appellate Court may exercise such original jurisdiction as may be necessary to the complete determination of any cause on review. The Supreme Court may provide by rule for appeals to the Appellate Court from other than final judgments of the Circuit Court. The Appellate Court shall have such powers of direct review of administrative action as may be provided by law.

History

The 1870 Constitution left the jurisdiction of the appellate court to the discretion of the General Assembly. The provision was quite simple and general and was utilized by the legislature to relieve the Supreme Court of some of its awesome burdens of constitutionally and legislatively mandated direct appellate responsibility.

The proposed 1922 Constitution provided simply that appeals from circuit and county courts to the appellate court could be had in all cases, other than those involving direct appeal to the Supreme Court, as prescribed by Supreme Court rules. No mention was made of the cost of appeals, original jurisdiction, nonfinal judgments, or direct review of administrative decisions.

Explanation

The appellate jurisdictional philosophy of the Judicial Article, partially explored in Section 5 dealing with the Supreme Court, is completed and fully disclosed in this section. An appeal lies as a matter of right to the appellate court from all final judgments of the circuit court except in those cases in which appeal as a matter of right lies directly to the Supreme Court. Thus an aggrieved litigant has a constitutional right of appeal either to the appellate or Supreme Court in respect to final judgments of the trial court. In addition, the Supreme Court may by rule authorize appeals to the appellate court from other than final judgments of the circuit court. This discretionary power, not normally to be expansively exercised, recognizes that substantial rights may be threatened or impaired by interlocutory or other nonfinal trial court orders, for which immediate appellate review should be available.

The effect of the jurisdictional allocation designated here and in Section 5 is to enhance the importance of the appellate court by making it the final arbiter in the vast majority of cases which it decides. The discretionary power of the Supreme Court to accept appeals from the appellate court in cases other than those which it is constitutionally required to take assures an additional final appellate review in cases determined by the Supreme Court to be of sufficient importance to justify such action.

The provision which precludes an appeal from a judgment of acquittal after a trial on the merits of a criminal case was inserted out of a sense of extreme caution, it having been urged that an otherwise unconditioned right of appeal would repeal the double jeopardy provision of Article II, Section 10.

The elimination of the non-record justice and magistrate courts and the consequent probability of increased appellate review of decisions formerly terminated by a re-trial de novo of decisions of such courts led to the inclusion of the provision that the Supreme Court shall provide by rule for expeditious and inexpensive appeals. The cost problem was equally troublesome in other appeals. The direction is at best a pious and unenforceable pronouncement. Indeed it may be largely meaningless, since "inexpensive" and "expeditious" are largely abstract and relative concepts. Yet the Supreme Court has responded to this direction and by rule has eliminated the need of abstracts and the requirement of printed briefs in cases assignable to magistrates, as well as permitting the preparation of abstracts and briefs by methods less expensive than printing in other cases.

Of special importance may be the provision authorizing the General Assembly to provide for direct review of administrative action by the appellate court. Presently, as well as in the past, most review proceedings were initiated in a trial court with appeal either to the appellate or Supreme Court. The Illinois Administrative Review Act (Ill. Rev. Stat. ch. 110, §§264-279 (1967)) provides for this pattern in all review actions which are covered by that law. The new provision allows for a technique of review, similar to that which prevails in several areas of federal practice, whereby the public interest is deemed to be best served by permitting direct appellate court review of administrative decisions. Though not as yet utilized by the legislature, the provision permits a desirable flexibility in methods of reviewing administrative action.

There have been fairly substantial amounts of litigation and appellate decisions interpreting provisions of this section. The most important cases deal with the power of the appellate court to determine constitutional issues when the Supreme Court has transferred a cause to the appellate court because the constitutional issues raised were not "fairly debatable" or "substantial" for purposes of direct appeal to the Supreme Court. (See *Explanation* of Sec. 5, *supra,* pp. 339-41.) In *People v. Valentine* (60 Ill. App. 2d 339 (1965)), the First District Appellate Court considered the effect of such a transfer. It rejected both the defendant-appellant's contention that its power to hear and determine constitutional questions was unlimited and the state's contention that it totally lacked power to decide constitutional issues. It then proceeded to review the entire case, including the constitutional issues.

In *Belden Manufacturing Co. v. Chicago Threaded Fasteners, Inc.* (84 Ill. App. 2d 336 (1967)), the appellate court assumed that a transfer of the cause to it after the Supreme Court had first denied a motion for transfer, heard oral argument, and then entered an order to the effect that it had no jurisdiction, constituted a rejection on the merits of the constitutional issues raised by the appellant. There appears to be no Supreme Court decision or rule definitely resolving this issue at this time.

Other litigation concerns the "final order" requirement for appellate review. Illustrative is *People v. Miller* (35 Ill. 2d 62 (1966)), wherein the order of the circuit court denying defendant's motions to dismiss rape counts in the indictment was held to be an interlocutory and not a final order, and that consequently the appellate court had no jurisdiction of an appeal from that order. Other decisions establish and affirm the constitutional requirement of final order for purposes of appellate court review. (*See* Smith v. Lewis, 85 Ill. App. 2d 246 (1967) order relative to master's fees held interlocutory); La Salle Nat'l Bank v. Little Bill "33" Flavors Stores, Inc., 80 Ill. App. 2d 298 (1967); Schoen v. Caterpillar Tractor Co., 77 Ill. App. 2d 315 (1966); Robinson v. City of Geneseo, 77 Ill. App. 2d 308 (1966).)

Several decisions interpreting the provision prohibiting appellate review of a judgment of acquittal in a criminal case after a trial on the merits are worth noting. In *People v. Blanchett* (33 Ill. 2d 527 (1965)), it was held that an unqualified reversal of a criminal verdict of guilty by the appellate court did not constitute a judgment of acquittal from which an appeal would not lie. In *Village of Park Forest v. Bragg* (38 Ill. 2d 225 (1967)), a municipality was held entitled to appeal a judgment acquitting the defendant of an ordinance violation on the ground that the proceeding, though quasi-criminal in character, was civil in form and thus not within the intent of the constitutional ban on appeals.

Comparative Analysis

Of the states providing for an intermediate court of appeals, nine provide for appeal in some areas as a matter of right. The other three establish appellate jurisdiction "as prescribed by law." Only two states provide for direct appeals of administrative decisions, and only one mentions appeal from nonfinal orders. Only one prohibits the state from appealing an acquittal in criminal cases, and only one mentions costs of appeal. The Constitution of the United States has no comparable provisions.

The Model State Constitution provides only that the appellate court will have such jurisdiction as is provided by law.

Comment

The constitutional plan of allocation of appellate responsibility between the Supreme and appellate courts and the experience thereunder to date seem to provide vindication for the underlying philosophy of the Article. Of course any alteration of the jurisdictional provisions of this section would of necessity involve reconsideration and amendment of Section 5 as well. The necessity for revision is not only not apparent; it would appear to be unwarranted.

Circuit Courts — Judicial Circuits

Sec. 8. The State shall be divided into judicial circuits each consisting of one or more counties. The county of Cook shall constitute a judicial circuit and the judicial circuits within the Second, Third, Fourth and Fifth Appellate Districts, respectively, shall be as established from time to time by law. Any judicial circuit composed of more than one county shall be compact and of contiguous counties.

There shall be one circuit court for each judicial circuit which shall have such number of circuit and associate judges and magistrates as may be prescribed by law; provided, that there shall be at least twelve associate judges elected from the area in Cook County outside the City of Chicago and at least thirty-six associate judges from the City of Chicago. In Cook County, the City of Chicago and the area outside the City of Chicago shall be separate units for the election or selection of associate judges. All associate judges from said area outside the City of Chicago shall run at large from said area, such area apportionment of associate judges shall continue until changed by law. There shall be at least one associate judge from each county. There shall be no masters in chancery or other fee officers in the judicial system.

The circuit judges and associate judges in each circuit shall select one of the circuit judges to serve at their pleasure as Chief Judge of such circuit. Subject to the authority of the Supreme Court, the Chief Judge shall have general administrative authority in the court, including authority to provide for divisions, general or specialized, and for appropriate times and places of holding court. The General Assembly shall limit or define the matters to be assigned to magistrates.

History

Circuit courts, in name, found their first constitutional identity in the 1848 Constitution. The 1818 Constitution established only a Supreme Court, delegating authority to create "inferior courts" to the General Assembly. The 1870 Constitution continued and built upon the circuit court concept, providing for their establishment in Cook County and generally on a multicounty basis for the remainder of the state. The 1848 and 1870 Constitutions also established or alternatively authorized the establishment by law of courts of lesser geographic and jurisdictional scope than the circuit court. The *General Introductory History* and the *Explanation* of Section 1 (*supra*, pp. 328-9) have treated such lesser constitutional and statutory courts.

The establishment of the district or circuit structure for circuit courts was also first established in the 1848 Constitution, wherein provision was made for the division of the state into nine judicial districts. The 1870 Constitution continued the concept, authorizing circuits (other than Cook County) formed of "contiguous counties in as nearly compact form and as nearly equal as circumstances will permit, having due regard to business territory and population," but with a maximum circuit population of 100,000. One circuit judge was authorized for each such circuit. Authority was granted, however, to establish larger circuits by law, with a maximum of four judges to be elected in each circuit.

None of the prior Constitutions dealt with the remaining provisions in the present Section 8.

The 1922 Convention proposal was substantially the same as the 1870 constitutional provisions.

Explanation

In this section (and in the jurisdictional grant in Section 9, *infra*, p. 353) we see the full flowering of the integrated trial court concept—one of several great objectives of the new Judicial Article. All trial courts, constitutional and statutory, established prior to the new Article, were abolished, and all their powers, functions, and jurisdiction vested in a single circuit court for each judicial circuit. The nonrecord justice and magistrate courts, and the courts of record of limited jurisdiction, *e.g.*, county, probate, city and village, municipal, and the specially established courts in Cook County, were merged into a single circuit court for each judicial circuit as established by law, with Cook County being constitutionally designated, as in the 1870 Constitution, a single and separate judicial circuit. To maintain a desired continuity in the trial and appellate relationship, all circuits were to be established within the newly created five judicial districts.

The central and important substantive aspects of this section, beyond those already mentioned, deal with the following matters:

(1) The classification of the circuit court judiciary into three levels, *e.g.*, circuit judges, associate judges, and magistrates.

(2) The requirement that there be at least one associate judge from each county in a circuit.

(3) The requirement of the selection of a chief judge for each circuit in whom general administrative authority is vested, subject to the paramount administrative authority of the Supreme Court.

(4) The administrative authority of the chief judge to establish general and specialized divisions within the circuit court.

(5) The abolition of masters in chancery and other fee officers in the judicial system.

(6) The allocation of judges in Cook County.

Extended explanation of each of these principles is not practical, but an attempt will be made to distill the essence of each.

(1) *Classification of Circuit Court Judiciary*

With the abolition of all pre-existing trial courts of a lesser jurisdiction than the circuit court and the absorption of the judges of those courts into the newly created integrated circuit court structure, it was thought desirable to maintain to some extent the difference in judicial status which had theretofore prevailed. Thus county judges, probate judges, city, village, and town court judges, and municipal court judges, and the judges of the Municipal Court of Chicago (other than its chief judge), all having exercised limited jurisdictional powers, were absorbed into the circuit court as associate circuit judges. Circuit judges, the judges of the Superior Court of Cook County (a court on a constitutional parity with the circuit court), the Cook County probate and county court judges, and the chief judge of the Municipal Court of Chicago, were all absorbed as circuit judges in their respective new circuits.

Presumed differences in judicial experience, as well as the desire to establish a structure which would result in progressive advancement to the highest level of trial court service, were among the factors which motivated this classification.

Several points must be noted with regard to this classification. First and foremost is that all levels of the circuit court judiciary, including magistrates, exercise the full jurisdiction of the circuit court. However, the section authorizes the General Assembly to limit or define the matters to be assigned to magistrates. This provision derives from the notion that magistrates, selected by the circuit judges to serve at their pleasure (Sec. 12, *infra,* p. 361), would be selected initially from personnel having little or no judicial experience and that their judicial responsibilities should be equated to those previously vested in the prior justice and magistrate courts. It must be emphasized, however, that the newly created magistracy is not and was not intended to be a mere reflection of the prior justices and magistrates. They are judicial officers in the circuit court structure as fully as circuit and associate judges and theoretically it would appear that they can exercise the full jurisdiction of the court, though by law, and for the reasons noted, particular kinds of cases are assigned to them.

(2) *One Associate Judge for Each County*

To assure that each county within a multi-county circuit has a full time judicial officer, the section requires that there be at least one associate judge for each county. All counties had had county judges as of constitutional right and many had had probate judges. The provision seeks to maintain this standard and to assure the constant availability in each county of a judge prepared and competent to handle the full jurisdictional range of the circuit court.

(3) *Chief Judge and Administrative Authority*

The problems incident to the administration of judicial business in each circuit are many. Indeed, in Cook County and in larger circuits they are enormous and complex. Prior Constitutions made no provision for administrative responsibility. The consequence, in most cases, was that each court and each judge exercised virtually independent and autonomous power. The results were frequently unfortunate. The provision seeks to give each circuit a responsible role in the administration of its business, subject to the overall, centralized administrative authority of the Supreme Court. The importance of this concept cannot be over-emphasized.

(4) *General and Specialized Divisions*

With the absorption of all pre-existing trial courts into a single circuit court, the level of its business correspondingly increased. A com-pensating factor was the absorption of the judicial manpower from the abolished courts. Levels of judicial maturity and experience quite naturally may vary among the judicial personnel. Also, particular subject matter may call for specialized treatment, handling and experience, establishing the need for specialized divisions. The specialized division within a court of general jurisdiction is not a novel concept. In Cook County, by assignment, designated judges handled only divorce and sepa-rate maintenance cases. Others handled only a chancery docket; still others dealt exclusively with personal injury litigation. These examples are not exhaustive of this practice.

The provision has special relevance to the objectives of an efficient administration of the judicial business of the court and the maximum effective utilization of the judicial manpower available to the court. Again it is emphasized that the divisional structure within a unified court does not affect the jurisdictional status of the court. Thus in *Coleman* v. *Scott* (38 Ill. 2d 387 (1967)), it was held that an error in assigning a particular claim to a magistrate did not affect the validity of the ultimate judgment rendered by that magistrate, since the error did not affect the jurisdictional power of the court. Although the decision rests on statutory grounds, the validity of the statute, under the constitutional concept of a unified trial court, is implicit in the decision.

(5) *Abolition of Masters in Chancery and Other Fee Officers*

One of the most troublesome and vexatious practices under the pre-existing Article was the employment, generally in chancery cases, of masters in chancery or other special hearing officers to take testimony and make advisory recommendations to the court. The costs to litigants in many of these cases were enormous. With the larger pool of available judicial manpower in the integrated trial court structure, it was felt that there was neither need nor justification for the continuation of this prac-tice. The elimination of the fee officer is a major achievement in minimiz-ing costs of litigation.

(6) *Allocation of Judges in Cook County*

The provisions in this section which provide for a numerical allocation of associate circuit judges in Cook County between the City of Chicago and the remaining area in Cook County were designed to assure equitable area representation. The provision reflects a natural concern in both the city and suburban areas of a county containing approximately one-half the state's population that the elective process could conceivably result in too large a concentration of judges from either area of the county.

Comparative Analysis

Better than three-fourths (38) of all state constitutions provide for judicial districts. All but four of these states have flexible provisions allowing the legislature to draw the boundaries of the districts. Only five states, however, require at least one judge from each county, while 27 states require at least one judge from each district. Four states provide that changes in judicial districts will not affect the term of office of any judge.

Only eight other states have a constitutional provision abolishing the fee system or prohibiting the use of fees. The states have done away with masters in chancery.

The Constitution of the United States, having no express provisions establishing trial courts, understandably has nothing comparable to this section. The Model State Constitution provides that judicial districts may be "provided by law" but fails to mention district representation, general or special divisions, masters in chancery or other fee officers, or other items provided for in this section of the Illinois Constitution.

Comment

This section, in the breadth and novelty of its concept, is one of the main nerve centers of the new Judicial Article. In detail it has been subject to some criticism. Thus associate circuit judges have expressed concern over a system of classification which they believe unfairly saddles them with the stigma of inferiority. Exercising the full jurisdiction of the court, just as circuit judges, they nevertheless receive smaller salary and a somewhat less prestigious title. It is difficult to assess the problem of classification of judges. Salary differentials may be eliminated by legislation, thus removing a primary irritant. In other respects the problem may be simply one of failure in human relations. A fair conclusion, perhaps, is that the criticism may be valid but that it may not, in these still-formative years of the new Article, justify an amendment. This, of course, may be a controversial judgment. Otherwise the section appears to be fulfilling, albeit slowly, the great objectives claimed for it.

Circuit Courts — Jurisdiction

Sec. 9. The Circuit Court shall have unlimited original jurisdiction of all justiciable matters, and such powers of review of administrative action as may be provided by law.

History

There is no parallel in prior Constitutions for the grant of unlimited original jurisdiction to a single trial court. No specific trial courts were created by the 1818 Constitution. Special authorization for the establishment of inferior courts by law was coupled with legislative power to determine the jurisdiction of such courts. The 1848 Constitution was the first charter to designate circuit courts and to define a virtually unlimited jurisdiction "in all cases at law and equity." However, that Constitution initiated county courts and also authorized justice of the peace courts, in recognition of the need for a continuously available judicial service in all counties — a service which could not be provided by a limited number of circuit judges required to sit in all the counties within the circuit. County courts were granted constitutional jurisdiction in probate matters and minor criminal offenses, and such other jurisdiction in civil cases as the legislature determined to confer. Justice of the peace jurisdiction was also left to legislative determination. With the expanded number of trial courts authorized by the 1870 Constitution (primarily city, village and incorporated town courts, and probate courts authorized to be established by law), the allocation of fragmented segments of trial court jurisdiction was enhanced. Circuit courts, however, in addition to the constitutionally conferred general original jurisdiction in all cases in law and equity, were to exercise such appellate jurisdiction as the legislature might prescribe. This appellate jurisdiction was implemented primarily in respect to cases originating in the county and probate courts. Re-trials de novo from judgments of the nonrecord justice and magistrate courts were not the exercise of appellate jurisdiction but rather the exercise of an original trial court jurisdiction.

The proposed 1922 Constitution drew liberally on the 1870 provisions, making only relatively unimportant changes.

Explanation

The grant of general unlimited and original jurisdiction in all justiciable matters is a natural and unavoidable consequence of the single unified trial court structure. With the abolition of all trial courts of limited jurisdiction, the investiture of original and unlimited jurisdiction in the integrated trial court follows as inevitably as night follows day. The *General Introductory History* and the *Explanation* of Section 1 (*supra,* pp 338-9) have given the rationale behind the integrated trial court structure, with particular emphasis upon the elimination of vexatious problems of jurisdiction. There is no need here to develop that theme.

Special mention should be made of the use of the term "justiciable matters" in lieu of the formal terminology of "cases in law and equity."

Old-line concepts which distinguished courts on the basis of the nature of the litigation as "law" or "equity" are largely passé in terms of jurisdictional principles. Where the distinction is retained, it is primarily for procedural purposes and not for jurisdictional reasons. If a matter is justiciable, it is within the court's jurisdiction without regard to whether it is a case in law or equity. Justiciability, however, is not a simple or readily definable concept. It involves determination of the existence of legally recognized and protected rights, standing to secure judicial relief, ripeness, timing, exhaustion of remedies, and other principles which concern the rights of persons and the role of the judicial branch of government. In the last analysis, justiciability will be defined by the courts, as has been the case in the past, and by the legislature under its power to create new rights and duties and to define them in justiciable terms.

Lastly, the grant of power to exercise such powers of review of administrative action as may be provided by law is the first constitutional recognition in Illinois that administrative agencies exercise power which is commonly the subject of judicial review. The provision reflects the long-standing practice and tradition in Illinois and other states. Its expression as a constitutional principle was deemed important to complete the concept of the totality of the circuit courts' jurisdictional powers.

Comparative Analysis

No other state has provided for a single trial court with unlimited original jurisdiction. All other states have varying numbers of trial courts of limited jurisdiction. There is nothing comparable in the Constitution of the United States. The Model State Constitution provides that the general trial court shall have original and appellate jurisdiction as provided by law but also authorizes the establishment by law of courts of limited jurisdiction.

Comment

The section cannot be considered apart from the provisions of Sections 1 and 8 establishing a single integrated trial court. If that concept is affirmed, then this section must also be retained. The operation of the integrated trial court to date has merited the enthusiastic approval of most responsible professional, public and political analysts. It represents what many believe to be the most important single advance in judicial administration effected by the 1962 Amendment.

Selection and Tenure — Election or Selection

Sec. 10. All of the judges provided for herein shall be nominated by party convention or primary and elected at general elections by the electors in the respective judicial districts, judicial circuits, counties, or units. Provided, however, the General Assembly may provide by law for the selection and tenure of all judges provided herein as distinguished from nomination and election by the electors, but no law establishing a method of selecting judges and providing their tenure shall be adopted or amended except by a vote of two-thirds of the members elected to each House, nor shall any method of selecting judges and providing their tenure become law until the question of the method of selection be first submitted to the electors at the next general election. If a majority of those voting upon the question shall favor the method of selection or tenure as submitted it shall then become law.

The office of any judge shall be deemed vacant upon his death, resignation, rejection, removal or retirement. Whenever a vacancy occurs in the office of judge, the vacancy shall be filled for the unexpired portion of the term by the voters at an election as above provided in this Section, or in such other manner as the General Assembly may provide by law as set out in this Section and approved by the electors. Whenever an additional judge is authorized by law, the office shall be filled in the same manner as in the case of a vacancy.

History

With the exception of the 1818 Constitution, which provided for the appointment of judges by a joint ballot of the General Assembly and the issuance of a commission by the Governor, the constitutional tradition in succeeding state charters, both 1848 and 1870, provided for the popular election of all judges. This developed into the uniform practice of adversary political elections with prior nominations either by party convention in the case of Supreme and circuit court judges and primary elections in the case of county, probate and other judges in the judicial system.

The 1818 Constitution was silent as to vacancies. The 1848 Constitution simply authorized the General Assembly to provide a method of filling vacancies. The 1870 Constitution elaborated upon this by requiring vacancies of more than one year to be filled by special election and vacancies of less than one year to be filled by appointment by the Governor.

The proposed 1922 Constitution differed in several respects from the Constitution of 1870. While all judges (except appellate court judges appointed by the Supreme Court) were to be elected, the proposal contained an important innovation, subject to referendum approval by the voters in Cook County, providing for gubernatorial appointments to fill all vacancies on the Cook County circuit court from a list of nominees submitted by the Supreme Court. All judges so appointed were to hold office "during good behavior" but could be removed by vote of the electorate at an election to be held in the sixth or seventh year after appointment. In addition, the Governor was vested with the power to "fill vacancies in elective judicial offices," with no special election limitation on this power. The referendum option for Cook County is remarkably similar to the so-called Missouri Plan which came almost 20 years later.

Explanation

In the long fight for constitutional reform there was no issue more controversial or more hotly debated than the method of selection of judges. Proponents of judicial reform insisted that the abolition of the political method of electing judges was absolutely central to any meaningful improvement in the structure and administration of the judicial system. They proposed the so-called Missouri Plan which provided for selection of a panel of nominees by a nonpartisan nominating commission, followed by appointment by the Governor from among such nominees. The appointee would serve a short probationary term and then submit his unopposed candidacy for a full term to the voters of the appropriate district or other geographic unit which he represented. If the voters approved his candidacy on a ballot which simply asked, "Shall Judge Jones be elected to (or retained in) the office of Supreme (or circuit, etc.) Court for a full term?" he would be so elected. If the vote was unfavorable, the nomination and selection process would be repeated until the office was filled.

Opponents of this proposal were equally vehement in their insistence that judges, no less than other constitutional officers, should submit to adversary elections in which the voters would have a choice of candidates. The existing method was extolled as a necessary concomitant of a truly free and democratic society.

It is a fair assessment that constitutional judicial reform in Illinois would at this time still be an unrealized objective if the contending forces had not agreed on the compromise contained in this Section 10. Under this compromise, partisan adversary elections are mandated for all judges (excluding magistrates) in every case of a vacancy, but the non-adversary retention mechanism (running unopposed against the record) is provided for incumbents who seek another term. (The retention principle is contained in Section 11 and not in this Section 10.)

The compromise further permits a change in the selection and tenure provisions by a law adopted by two-thirds of the members elected to each house of the General Assembly and approved by a majority of the electorate at a state-wide election who vote upon the question. Under this provision, a mechanism less rigorous than constitutional amendment permits the replacement of the present system of adversary partisan election of judges by the Missouri Plan, or some variation thereof, by a nonpartisan adversary elective process, by appointment by the Governor, or by some other plan conceived by the legislature. In like manner, the retention provision is subject to the same legislative-referendum method of change.

Unlike the 1848 and 1870 Constitutions, there is no authority for interim special elections or gubernatorial appointments to fill vacancies. All vacancies must be filled by the adversary partisan method of general elections (defined in Sec. 13 to mean the biennial election at which members of the General Assembly are elected, *infra,* p. 363), or if a method has been substituted by the combined legislative-referendum technique authorized in this section, by that method. Notwithstanding these explicit provisions for the filling of vacancies, the General Asssembly in 1967 enacted a law which authorized the Governor, when notified by the Supreme Court of the existence of a vacancy, to fill the vacancy until the next general election. An exercise of this power by the Governor in 1969, shortly before the expiration of his term, was invalidated in *People* ex rel. *Scott v. Powell* (42 Ill. 2d 132 (1969)), as violative of this section.

Comparative Analysis

Only Illinois has a single constitutional provision establishing a uniform method of electing all judges. At least five other states, through several different sections, however, establish a uniform method of selecting all judges. A comparison of the practices, not constitutions, of all states other than Illinois reveals that only 17 states use a uniform method of selecting *all* judges, 14 by election and three by appointment. (*See* Council of State Governments, The Book of the States, 1968-69 at 110-111 (1968).) Seven states appoint all judges, though the method varies from court to court within a state. (*Id.*) Similarly, 16 states elect all judges with different methods within the state. Twenty-six states use a combination of appointments and elections. (*Id.*)

Of the 42 states which use elections, wholly or in part, to select judges, 20 use partisan ballots, 17 nonpartisan, and five a combination of both. (*Id.*)

While 15 states, in variable measure as to particular courts, use features of the Missouri Plan of a nonpartisan nominating commission followed by appointment (*Id.*), only eight have constitutional provisions incorporating the plan. California, in addition, uses a variant of the plan. (Model State Constitution n. 1 at 79.)

The methods of filling vacancies also vary a great deal from state to state, and often within a state according to the court involved. Nine states have constitutional provisions authorizing an appointment to fill judicial vacancies until a successor is qualified. Four states provide for appointments to fill the vacancy for the remainder of the term. Three states provide for filling vacancies as provided by law. All federal judges are appointed by the President with the advice and consent of the Senate.

The Model State Constitution provides that all judges shall be appointed by the governor with the advice and consent of the legislature. As an alternative, the Model provides for appointment by the governor from a list of nominees presented to him by a judicial nominating commission made up of the Chief Justice of the Supreme Court, three elected members from the local bar, and three citizens appointed by the governor.

Comment

The controversial nature of the selection and tenure provisions of this section and Section 11 has not diminished. Proponents of the Missouri Plan, or a variation thereof, which eliminates the adversary political elective feature, may insist that this concept be mandated by the Constitution rather than being made a contingent alternative by legislative action and electorate referendum. On the other hand, opposition has manifested itself in some quarters to the retention features (Sec. 11) whereby the uncontested election or retention virtually assures, as it was intended to do, a more permanent, if not indeed an indefinite, tenure for incumbent judges.

The issue is volatile, politically explosive and emotionally charged. The advocacy in respect to both election and tenure will probably be intense and unyielding from both sides of the issue. It is impossible to suggest an appropriate Convention resolution without being charged with bias and other lack of objectivity. In the last analysis, therefore, the resolution of this issue will depend on the Convention's sense of logic and principle as it is fashioned by the contending forces. It is important to note, however, that most recent constitutional proposals have incorporated the so-called Missouri Plan of selection and tenure for all or part of their judiciary. As noted in the *Comparative Analysis,* there is a growing measure of acceptance of this principle.

In respect to the vacancy issue, it would appear desirable to authorize a method of interim appointments (assuming the elective method of selection is retained). The Bar Association proposals suggested emergency temporary appointments but, for reasons not clear, the final legislative draft in 1961 omitted any authorization for temporary vacancy appointments. It seems that the issue here should not be controversial and that logic and principle support the inclusion of such authorization.

Selection and Tenure — Retention in Office

Sec. 11. Not less than six months prior to the general election next preceding the expiration of his term in office, any judge previously elected may file in the office of Secretary of State a declaration of candidacy to succeed himself, and the Secretary of State, not less than 61 days prior to the election, shall certify such candidacy to the proper election officials. At the election the name of each judge who has filed such a declaration shall be submitted to the voters, on a special judicial ballot without party designation, on the sole question whether he shall be retained in office for another term. The elections shall be conducted in the appropriate judicial districts, circuits, counties and units. The affirmative votes of a majority of the voters voting on the question shall elect him to the office for another term commencing the first Monday in December following the election. Any judge who does not file a declaration within the time herein specified, or, having filed, fails of re-election, shall vacate his office at the expiration of his term, whether or not his successor, who shall be selected for a full term pursuant to Section 10 of this Article, shall yet have qualified.

Any law reducing the number of judges of the Appellate Court in any District or the number of Circuit or associate judges in any circuit shall be without prejudice to the right of judges in office at the time of its enactment to seek retention in office as hereinabove provided.

History

There is, of course, nothing in the Constitutions of 1818, 1848 or 1870 which parallels the retention features in the present Section 11. The 1922 Convention proposal contained a provision in some aspects comparable to the retention feature for circuit judges in Cook County. (See *History*, Sec. 10, *supra*, p. 356.) The history of selection, including election, and tenure, under those instruments is set forth under Section 10. The 1870 Constitution and the proposed 1922 Constitution both preserved the tenure of circuit judges where a change in circuit boundaries occurred.

Explanation

The *Explanation* under Section 10 is equally relevant here, since retention is the second phase of the so-called Missouri Plan of selection and tenure. However, some brief additional observation may be helpful. Proponents of the "running against the record" method of retention candidly concede that this virtually assures indefinite tenure. Experience in Illinois and in other states establishes that an incumbent is rarely voted out of office in an uncontested submission of his candidacy. As an alternative to the sometimes unhappy experience of tying a judge's expectancy for retention to the political process, and as a means of freeing judges from political influences and establishing their independence from political controls, the advocates of the retention plan are willing to accept the risk that an incompetent judge may not be subject to removal by the electorate. On the other hand, opponents of this plan cite this assured tenure as being productive of judicial "arrogance" in judges who no longer need curry the favor of political parties or the electorate. There is probably a modicum of truth in this latter charge, but to generalize and apply it to the judiciary as a whole or in significant part is assuredly inaccurate and unfair. Many judges seeking retention are indeed concerned with and apprehensive about voter approval and public and professional assessment of their competence in other unofficial appraisals. Thus the issue narrows to the priority to be given to the concept of judicial independence and freedom from political controls or restraints. Proponents of the retention provision give this the highest priority; they believe that the administration of justice absolutely demands a judiciary freed from traditional political controls. Opponents are equally certain that the political adversary process is an indispensable aspect of the democratic process.

Several important decisions have interpreted this section. *People* ex rel. *Barrett v. Barrett* (31 Ill. 2d 360 (1964)) held that the constitutional requirement of a "special judicial ballot" (without party designation) precluded the use of voting machines in retention elections as authorized by law. In *People* ex rel. *Nachman v. Carpentier* (30 Ill. 2d 475 (1964)), a statute which required a sitting judge to vacate his office if he sought election to another judicial office was invalidated as an unauthorized legislative addition to the constitutionally prescribed and limited qualifications and conditions for judicial office.

It is important to note that, though the new Judicial Article reserves to the legislature the authority to determine the number of appellate, circuit, and associate circuit judges, this section precludes a reduction which affects the status of incumbent judges or their right to seek retention in office. This provision was deemed necessary to assure incumbents that their tenure was not subject to unreasonable or whimsical legislative determinations to lessen the number of judges. It is a factor related to recruitment of competent candidates for judicial office, and to the necessity of providing assured tenure.

The Model State Constitution, which provides for the appointment of all judges, contains no similar provision.

Comparative Analysis

Four other states provide for general trial court judges to run for retention unopposed. Only two states, however, provide for such run-on-record elections of appellate court judges. Six states, other than Illinois, have similar constitutional provisions for re-election of incumbent high court judges. In practice, nine different states employ, at least in part, a run-on-record election at some level for judicial selection. The Constitution of the United States provides for tenure during "good Behavior after initial appointment."

Comment

The *Comment* under Section 10, as well as the *Explanation* under this section, leaves little room for additional treatment. Perhaps one yet unremarked point should be noted. Proponents of nonpolitical selection and tenure of judges believe that tenure (running against the record) is best related to an initial nonpolitical, nonelective method of selecting judges. They are not particularly happy with a system which virtually assures lifetime tenure for judges initially elected by the routine adversary political process. This factor must be considered in the overall evaluation of the selection and tenure provisions of Sections 10 and 11.

Selection and Tenure — Appointment of Magistrates

Sec. 12. Subject to law, the circuit judges in each circuit shall appoint magistrates to serve at their pleasure; provided, that in Cook County, until and unless changed by law, at least one-fourth of the magistrates shall be appointed from and reside in the area outside the corporate limits of the City of Chicago.

History

There is no prior constitutional history which is truly relevant to the present section. The magistrates authorized by Section 12 have no constitutional relationship to the justices of the peace and police magistrates of prior Constitutions. Those officers were elected for specified terms, exercised a very limited civil and quasi-criminal jurisdiction as established by law, were not judges of courts of record, and in the case of justices of the peace, administered justice by the much-condemned fee system which was finally legislatively abolished in 1961. Although there is a measure of similarity in respect to the kinds of cases tried, there is no other relationship.

The proposed 1922 Constitution dealt with justices of the peace and magistrates in the same manner as prior Constitutions.

Explanation

Section 8 contains the first reference in the Judicial Article to magistrates. As indicated in the *Explanation* of that section (*supra*, p. 350), the magistrates are a part of the three-tiered classification of trial judges which consists of circuit judges, associate circuit judges, and magistrates. The cases to be assigned to them are determined by the legislature. The legislature did act in 1963 and in subsequent sessions, and maintained, in general, the principle of assignability to magistrates of the kinds of cases theretofore handled by justice and magistrate courts. Significantly, however, there has been an expansion in several areas, as well as increases in the monetary maximum which had severely circumscribed the "jurisdiction" of old justice and magistrate courts.

Because magistrates are now an integal part of the circuit court judiciary, it is no longer proper to speak of their "jurisdiction." This Article, Section 8, carefully states that the matters "assigned to magistrates" shall be determined by law. Constitutionally, however, magistrates can exercise the full jurisdiction of the circuit court. (Coleman v. Scott, 38 Ill. 2d 387 (1967).) The judgments of magistrates, unlike those of prior justices of the peace and police magistrates, are judgments of record, carrying the full authority and official imprimatur of the circuit court. These judgments are thus reviewable directly by either the appellate or Supreme Court in accordance with the appellate jurisdictional principles already discussed.

Magistrates differ from their judicial brethren, however, in several major respects. They are appointed and serve at the pleasure of their circuit judges (this term does not include associate judges of the circuit court) instead of being elected to office for constitutionally specified terms, and they are not within the tenure provisions of Section 11, *e.g.*, running against their records. The "at pleasure" principle was introduced largely on the premise that magistrates would initially be drawn from lawyers of a lesser degree of experience and maturity than the other judges, and that their service should be subject to a continuing and closer critique and administrative supervision than other trial judges, with broader and more flexible powers of removal for incompetence or other good cause.

To assure an equitable distribution of magistrates between Chicago and the Cook County area outside of Chicago, this section, as in the case of associate circuit judges in Chicago and Cook County (Sec. 8, *supra,* pp. 348-9) allocates one-fourth of the magistrates to the county areas outside of Chicago. Unlike the associate judge allocation, however, the percentage division of magistrates between the two areas of Cook County is subject to legislative change.

Comparative Analysis

No other state constitution contains a similar provision. As noted earlier, no other state has established a single general trial court of unlimited jurisdiction as has Illinois. The Model State Constitution is silent on the subject.

Comment

The "at pleasure" provision of this section has caused considerable unhappiness, not without justification, among magistrates. With a tenure wholly subject to the judgment and discretion of the circuit judges, the magistrates understandably live in a climate of constant apprehension. In Cook County the circuit judges have somewhat alleviated the problem by an administrative designation of one-year appointments. In downstate circuits the "at pleasure" status remains. The problem is more than one of effective control over the least-experienced segment of the trial judiciary. It involves recruitment and retention of qualified personnel. In most cases, qualified lawyers who are interested in a judicial career will not give up their practice for an office whose tenure is so precarious.

Although there is no evidence of arbitrary exercise of the "at pleasure" principle through unwarranted dismissals from service, the problem nevertheless remains. The serious nature of this issue has led to the formation of a special committee of the Illinois Judicial Conference which is now studying possible legislative or judicial approaches to strengthening the tenure of magistrates. This issue deserves the serious consideration of the Convention.

Selection and Tenure — General Election

Sec. 13. As used in this Article, the term "general election" means the biennial election at which members of the General Assembly are elected.

History

There are no antecedents to this section in any prior Illinois Constitution or in the proposed 1922 Constitution. Prior provisions mandated elections of all classes of judges (beginning in 1848) but the time or nature of the election was not tied to any constitutional mandate. Legislative implementation was not consistent. Many judicial elections were held at the time of the general elections in November of even-numbered years. Others were held at different times.

Explanation

The requirement that judges be elected at general elections, defined as the biennial election for members of the General Assembly, has a purposeful relationship to the election and tenure provisions of Sections 10 and 11. Initial adversary political elections, when held previously at times other than the general November elections, produced little voter interest or participation. The apathy was oppressive and the percentage of voter participation alarmingly low. The result was a contest which was a poor reflection of the desirable concept of substantial electorate paticipation.

More importantly, however, with the adoption of the tenure provisions of Section 11, *e.g.*, a judge running uncontested against his record, the necessity for assuring a large measure of voter participation was thought to be of utmost importance for two reasons. The first was that the novel elective method, designed to assure a greater degree of tenure than was normally possible in contested elections, required larger voter participation to justify the judgment of retention in office or rejection of an incumbent. Secondly, since it was more than a remote possibility that an incumbent might be voted out of office by a small segment of the electorate determined, for reasons good or bad, to be rid of him, an election held at times other than the general election, with a minimum voter turnout, could unfairly accomplish the intended result. By requiring retention elections to be held with general elections as defined, this possibility is blunted without destroying the legitimacy of appropriate campaigns to remove an incumbent for a cause thought to be adequate by any segment of voters.

Comparative Analysis

No other state constitution contains a similar provision. The same is true also of the Model State Constitution.

Comment

The rationale behind this provision, whether or not elections continue initially to be adversary or the retention provision is maintained, seems sound. There is little in history or experience which commends a return to elections for judges at times other than general elections.

Selection and Tenure — Terms of Office

Sec. 14. The term of office of judges of the Supreme Court and of the Appellate Court shall be ten years and of the circuit judges and associate judges of the Circuit Courts six years.

History

All judges held office during "good behavior" under the 1818 Constitution. Fixed terms were constitutionally introduced in 1848 and continued in 1870. Under both latter Constitutions, Supreme Court judges held nine-year terms; circuit judges (and Superior Court judges in Cook County), six years; county and probate judges, and justices of the peace and magistrates, four years; and judges of the Municipal Court of Chicago and of other municipal, city, village and town courts authorized by law, six years.

The 1922 Convention proposal provided a ten-year term for Supreme Court judges; six years for appellate, circuit and county court judges; and two years for justices of the peace.

Explanation

It is generally conceded that judges, in order to assure the recruitment of competent men into service, and their independence from political ties and influences customarily present and acceptable for nonjudicial officers, should have a substantial measure of constitutionally prescribed tenure. This is reflected in the Federal Constitution and in the constitutions of several states which provide for tenure based on "good behavior." This, for all practical purposes, is the equivalent of life tenure. In several other states, the fixed tenure exceeds substantially the terms specified in this section. (See *Comparative Analysis* below.)

The contrary view holds that all elective officers exercising governmental power, including judges, should be subjected to periodic and relatively frequent voter evaluation, lest they be tempted to abuse the power exercised by them.

However one views the merits of these positions, the provisions of this section establishing ten-year terms for Supreme and appellate court judges, and six-year terms for circuit and associate judges of the circuit court, are hardly a significant departure from the long-established constitutional and statutory tradition in this state, as the *History* of this section attests. The terms designated, however, must be viewed in the light of the tenure provisions of Section 11 which provide for the nonadversary running against the record. This factor, for all practical purposes, gives added dimension and scope to the fixed terms specified in this Section 14. Also, it is again important to recall that neither the specified terms of this section nor the retention provisions of Section 11 apply to magistrates of the circuit court, all of whom serve at the pleasure of the circuit judges. The only significant decision to date respecting tenure is *People* ex rel. *Nachman v. Carpentier* (30 Ill. 2d 475 (1964)) which, as already noted, held invalid a legislative attempt to require an incumbent judge to relinquish his office if he sought election to another judicial office.

Comparative Analysis

While over three-fourths of the states have constitutional provisions respecting the terms of office of high court and general trial court judges, only one-fifth have provisions for appellate court terms. Only nine other states have provisions for terms of office for all three courts.

No other state sets a ten-year term for high court judges. Terms provided by the other state constitutions vary from two years in Vermont to 21 years in Pennsylvania. The most frequently established terms are six years (13 states) and eight years (eight states). Only one state provides a term of "during good behavior." Several states provide terms as established by law.

Only ten other states provide a term of office for appellate court judges. These terms vary, extending to a maximum of 12 years in several other states. One state provides that the term shall be set by law.

Thirty six states, other than Illinois, set a term of office for general trial court judges, ranging from two years in Vermont to 14 years in New York. Most popular are terms of four years, in 13 states, and six years, in 13 states. Three states provide terms as prescribed by law.

The Model State Constitution provides that all judges shall hold office for seven years and upon reappointment during good behavior. Only one state, New Jersey, follows the Model Constitution principle.

The Constitution of the United States provides for appointment and tenure during good behavior.

Comment

The terms specified in this section fall within generally accepted constitutional and statutory designations and agree substantially with the pre-existing standards in this state. Apart from the relevance of this section to the tenure provisions of Section 11, and the "at pleasure" tenure of magistrates (Section 12), in respect to which analysis and comment have already been made, there appears to be no quarrel with the tenure provisions of this section.

Selection and Tenure — Eligibilty for Office

Sec. 15. No person shall be eligible for the office of judge unless he shall be a citizen and licensed attorney-at-law of this State, and a resident of the judicial district, circuit, county or unit from which selected. However, any change made in the area of a district or circuit or the reapportionment of districts or circuits shall not affect the tenure in office of any judge incumbent at the time such change or reapportionment is made.

History

The Constitution of 1818 contained no provisions pertaining to eligibility for judges. The 1848 Constitution, in contrast, dealt with eligibility in detail, prescribing for all judges a United States citizenship status, a five-year state residency requirement, and a two-year residency requirement in the division, circuit or county in which elected for service in courts of limited geographic area. In addition, age requirements, 35 and 30 respectively, were established for Supreme and circuit court judges. The 1870 Constitution continued the 1848 requirements of citizenship and state residency, required geographic residency but without a minimum specified term, and reduced to 30 and 25 years, respectively, the age requirements for Supreme and circuit judges. In addition, all the foregoing requirements applicable to circuit judges were made applicable to the "judge of any inferior court." None of the prior Constitutions required a licensed-attorney status. The proposed 1922 Constitution contained no citizenship requirement, and judges were merely required to reside in the district, circuit or county for which they were selected. Judges of the Supreme, appellate and circuit courts were required to be at least 35 years of age and for ten years a licensed and practicing attorney or judicial officer. County court judges were required to be at least age 30 and to be licensed and practicing for five years.

It also contained a provision whereby alterations in circuits would have no effect upon the term of any judge.

Explanation

The first important observation is that the provisions of Section 15 have no application to magistrates of the circuit court. The careful restriction of the language to the "office of judge," here and in other provisions of the Article, clearly confirms this conclusion. The legislature, however, has enacted its own eligibility requirements for magistrates. (Ill. Rev. Stat. ch. 37, §§ 160.1-160.5 (1967).) A licensed-attorney status is required, subject to limited exceptions for justices of the peace and police magistrates in office on January 1, 1964, the effective date of the

Judicial Article Amendment, and for circuits which have ·no available resident attorneys. (Ill. Rev. Stat. ch. 37, § 160.3 (1967).)

The present constitutional section retains the citizenship and general current geographic residency requirements of prior Constitutions, eliminating the minimum age and five-year state residency requirements, but adding the licensed-attorney-at-law requirement. The attorney requirement assures, at the least, a minimum age geared to the degree and bar examination requirement, normally age 21. Pre-existing age and state residency requirements were thought to be unduly restrictive and practically dubious as constitutional standards. The normal process of selection or election of judges should reasonably assure a judiciary sufficiently mature in age and, hopefully, experience. Reference is again made to *People* ex rel. *Nachman v. Carpentier* (30 Ill. 2d 475 (1964)), which held that legislative attempts to add to eligibility requirements for judges under this section will not be tolerated.

The second sentence of this section is not new. The 1870 Constitution contained a similar provision. It is designed to protect incumbents in their tenure against legislative changes or reapportionment in district or circuit areas.

Comparative Analysis

No state has an identical provision. The constitutional requirements for judicial officers not only vary from state to state, but also vary from court to court in nearly all states.

Nearly half the states require that a general trial judge be an attorney. Aside from Illinois, only six states require him to be a citizen of the state. Eleven states provide that trial judges must be citizens of the United States. Eleven, including Illinois, require that he reside in the district from which he was selected.

Only one-fifth of the states, however, require that an appellate judge be an attorney. Five other states provide that he must be a citizen of the state and three require him to be a citizen of the United States. Only two other states require that an appellate judge reside in the district or circuit from which he is selected.

Seventeen states provide that all high court justices be attorneys. Nine require justices to be citizens of the state, while 13 require them to be United States citizens. Only five other states provide that a high court judge reside in the geographical unit from which he is selected.

While Illinois sets no age requirements, many states do. Nearly two-fifths of the states set a minimum age for both high court and general trial judges. These qualifications range from 25 to 35 for high court judges and from 25 to 38 for general trial court judges. The most common requirement for the high court is 30 (13 states) and the most common for general trial court judges are 25 (seven states) and 30 (six states). All five states setting a minimum age for appellate court judges require him to be at least 30. The Constitution of the United States established no age, citizenship or residency requirements. The Model State Constitution provides that all judges must have "been admitted to practice law before the supreme court for at least .... years."

Comment

It is difficult to quarrel with the eligibility provisions of this section other, perhaps, than in its inapplicability to magistrates. As to the latter, the gap, to some extent, has been filled by legislation, but the importance of the subject may deserve constitutional treatment. Professional or other criticism of this section is virtually nonexistent in its applicability to judges.

General — Prohibited Activities

Sec. 16. Judges shall devote full time to their judicial duties, shall not engage in the practice of law or hold any other office or position of profit under the United States or this State or any municipal corporation or political subdivision of this State, and shall not hold office in any political party. Compensation for service in the State Militia or the armed forces of the United States for such periods of time as may be determined by rule of the Supreme Court shall not be deemed "profit."

History

The 1848 Constitution first expressed a limitation upon judges in its provision which barred Supreme and circuit court judges from eligibility for any other state or federal office of public trust or profit during their elective terms and for one year thereafter. The 1870 Constitution, in its Legislative Article (Art. IV, Sec. 3), disqualified judges generally from having a seat in the General Assembly and, even more expansively, prohibited any person holding any office of honor or profit under any foreign government or the government of the United States (except postmasters earning less than $300 annually) from holding any office of honor or profit under the authority of the state. (See, however, interpretation of this provision in regard to eligibility of officers as members of the Constitutional Convention (Livingston v. Oglivie, – Ill. 2d – (1969)); also, *Explanation,* Art. IV, Sec. 3, *supra,* p. 123.) In its Judicial Article (Art. VI, Sec. 16), the 1870 Constitution provided that judges of the Supreme and circuit courts could neither receive "any other compensation, perquisite or benefit, in any form whatsoever, nor perform any other than judicial duties to which may belong any emoluments." Neither of the prior Constitutions contained a ban on the holding of office in any political party, but presumably such office could fall within the other general proscriptions. No judicial interpretations exist on this or other provisions or issues raised by the 1848 and 1870 provisions.

The proposed 1922 Constitution, in its specific application to judges, provided that "[n]o justice of the supreme court or judge of any court of record . . . shall receive any compensation, perquisite or benefit other than his salary or engage in the practice of law."

Explanation

The provisions of this section are not markedly different from the prior constitutional restraints noted in the *History*, with the single exception of the ban on holding office in a political party. This addition reflects and emphasizes the concern explicit or implicit throughout the Article and its history relative to the removal of judges as far as possible from political relationships and influences.

The provision excluding compensation for service in the State Militia or the armed forces of the United States from the definition of profit finds a partial parallel in Article IV, Section 3, of the 1870 Constitution already alluded to in the *History*.

This section has no application to magistrates. However, the General Assembly, in its 1963 law pertaining to magistrates (Ill. Rev. Stat. ch. 37, § 160.5 (1967)), enacts language identical to this section of the Constitution, thus applying the full thrust of the prohibitions to them.

Comparative Analysis

No other state prohibits all judges from engaging in all three activities: the practice of law, dual office holding, and holding an office in a political party. Nineteen other states, however, prohibit all judges from practicing law. One state places this restriction only on some judges. While 38 other states have a provision respecting dual office holding, only 30 prohibit all judges (with minor exceptions such as special judges and justices of the peace in some cases) from holding another office. Only three other states provide that all judges may not hold an office in a political party, though three others place such a restriction on some judges. Those states placing similar restrictions on some, but not all, judges typically place them on higher court judges only. The Constitution of the United States has no comparable provisions.

The Model State Constitution provides that Supreme, appellate and general trial court judges "shall [not] hold any other paid office, position of profit or employment under the state, its civil divisions or the United States."

Comment

The provisions of this section are relatively standard and no serious challenge to them has been made. Again it may be desirable, as in the case of the eligibility provisions of Section 15, to extend the constitutional sanctions to magistrates, rather than to rely upon legislative implementation. The Bar Association draft proposals in fact applied both Section 15 and Section 16 to magistrates but for reasons unknown, the legislature modified the sections to exclude magistrates.

General — Judicial Salaries and Expenses

Sec. 17. Judges and magistrates shall receive for their services salaries provided by law. The salaries of judges shall not be diminished during their respective terms of office. Judicial officers may be paid such actual and necessary expenses as may be provided by law. All salaries and expenses shall be paid by the State, except that judges of the Appellate Court for the First District and circuit and associate judges and magistrates of the Circuit Court of Cook County shall receive such additional compensation from the county as may be provided by law.

History

The constitutional history of judicial salaries has followed a curious pattern. The 1818 Constitution established a temporary fixed salary for Supreme Court judges, but established a permanent principle of salaries fixed by law for all judges, which could not be diminished (increase thus permitted) during their terms of office. The 1848 Constitution established fixed and unchangeable salaries of $1,200 and $1,000 per annum for Supreme and circuit court judges, respectively, while the salaries of county judges were to be set by law. The 1870 Constitution established annual salaries of $4,000 and $3,000 for such judges, respectively, but authorized legislative change, subject to the limitation that such salaries could not be increased or diminished during a term of office. That Constitution also authorized supplemental compensation to be provided by Cook County for its circuit and Superior Court judges. The county board was empowered to fix the salaries of all county offices. County judges, and, inferentially probate court judges, were within this category of county officers. All other courts being established by law, the General Assembly thus fixed the salaries of the judges of such courts. The 1870 Constitution was silent as to who assumed the obligation of judicial salaries. By law the state paid Supreme, appellate (temporarily assigned circuit and Cook County Superior Court judges), and circuit and Superior Court judges (with Cook County supplement as noted). Also the state paid the salaries of city, village and incorporated town judges; shared with counties the salaries of county and probate judges, and the judges of the Municipal Court of Chicago, but saddled the burden of other municipal court judges upon the cities and villages which established such courts. Until 1961, justice of the peace courts were fee offices, but thereafter and until January 1, 1964, the justices' salaries were fixed by law and paid by the counties.

The proposed 1922 Constitution provided for salaries to be paid by the state for Supreme, appellate, circuit and county court judges, and authorized Cook County supplementation for its appellate and circuit court judges. It omitted the provision of the 1870 Constitution barring increases or decreases in salary during terms of office.

Explanation

The significant provisions of the existing Article are (1) the assumption, as a state obligation, of the salaries and expenses of all judges and magistrates (retaining, however, the authorization for Cook County supplementation and extending its application to appellate judges elected from the Cook County judicial district, all circuit and associate circuit judges, and magistrates of that district), and (2) prohibiting decreases, but not increases, of salaries during terms of office. All salaries are left to legislative determination. (See also *Comment*, Art. IX, Sec. 11, *infra*, p. 476.)

The imposition upon the state of the obligation for all judicial salaries and expenses gives explicit constitutional sanction to the principle that judicial service, whatever may be the geographic areas from which judges are elected, is a state service. The administration of justice thus assumes coordinate status with constitutional state officers in Executive and Legislative Departments of government. This principle had in fact been long established under the State Judges Retirement Act, wherein the state alone was considered the governmental employer responsible for the employer contributions for the judges of all courts of record who had opted to become members of the system.

Comparative Analysis

Four-fifths of the state constitutions provide that judicial salaries may be fixed by law. Only one state sets a rigid salary, and only three set maximums or minimums. Seven other states expressly provide for payment of expenses. More than half the states place a constitutional restriction on increases or decreases during a judge's term. The pattern varies substantially as to the obligation for payment of salaries, with local governments assuming all or part of the salary obligation in the case of trial courts.

Comment

The principle of state responsibility for all judicial salaries is a constitutional extension of what had been for the most part a combined constitutional and legislative policy under the 1870 Constitution. It may be argued with justification that county or municipal responsibility in the first instance, for judicial salaries, whether or not shared by the state, demeans the nature of judicial service and even the judicial office. The provision regarding Cook County supplementation stands perhaps on a different plane because the primary responsibility is the state's. The tradition of Cook County supplementation goes back to the 1870 Constitution and is based on the premise that the cost of living in Cook County is, as a generality, higher than in the remainder of the state. There is some unhappiness with this authorization among some downstate judges who believe the provision is unjustifiably discriminatory. It is not known whether this concern has created a conviction that a change is necessary.

Perhaps of greater importance is the existing legislative classifications which establish differentials in salary between associate and circuit judges. Again, it is hard to gauge this problem from a constitutional point of view. Unlike the county supplementation authorization which is limited to Cook County, the other problems of salary differentials are wholly legislative. Since the legislature can rectify any differential it believes to be discriminatory, the necessity for constitutional consideration would appear to be less evident.

General — Retirement, Suspension and Removal

Sec. 18. Notwithstanding the provisions of this Article relating to terms of office, the General Assembly may provide by law for the retirement of judges automatically at a prescribed age; and, subject to rules of procedure to be established by the Supreme Court and after notice and hearing, any judge may be retired for disability or suspended without pay or removed for cause by a commission composed of one judge of the Supreme Court selected by that court, two judges of the Appellate Court selected by that court, and two circuit judges selected by the Supreme Court. Such commission shall be convened by the Chief Justice upon order of the Supreme Court or at the request of the Senate.

Any retired judge may, with his consent, be assigned by the Supreme Court to judicial service, and while so serving shall receive the compensation applicable to such service in lieu of retirement benefits, if any.

History

These provisions have no counterpart in prior Illinois constitutional history.

The 1818 Constitution provided in its Legislative Article (art. II, § 23) that the Governor "and all other civil officers under this state" could be impeached for any misdemeanor in office. That this applied to judges seems clear from that Constitution's provision in its Judicial Article (art. IV, § 5) that for any reasonable cause "which shall not be sufficient ground for impeachment" judges of the Supreme and inferior courts could be removed from office by a two-thirds vote of each house of the legislature. Substantially identical provisions appeared in the 1848 Constitution. The 1870 Constitution continued the general impeachment provision for the Governor and "all civil officers of this State," and in the Judicial Article (Art. VI, Sec. 30) authorized the General Assembly "for cause entered on the journals" and after "due notice and opportunity of defense" to remove any judge from office upon a three-fourths vote of the members of each house.

The proposed 1922 Constitution was the same with respect to judicial removal as the 1870 Constitution except the proposal also provided that appellate court judges (appointed by the Supreme Court) could be removed by the Supreme Court "for good cause shown of record."

Explanation

The relationship of the general impeachment provision in the 1870 Constitution to the special provision for legislative removal of judges is not clear. One decision, *Donahue v. County of Will* (100 Ill. 94, (1881)), treats the phrase "all civil officers of the state" in Article V, Section 15, and determines that it is inapplicable to all officers who by Article 10 of the Constitution are designated as county officers. This designation included county judges who were thus immunized from impeachment.

The question is important since Article V, Section 15, is still very much a part of the existing Constitution. Its relation to Section 18 of Article VI, now under discussion, which authorizes a judicial commission for the suspension or removal of any judge for cause is not spelled out in Article VI. The commission is to be convened by the Chief Justice upon order of the Supreme Court or at the request of the Senate. The question is as to the effect of this provision on the impeachment provision regarding civil offices of the state in Article V, Section 15. On the one hand, it may be argued that the removal provisions of the new section are exclusive and constitute an implied repeal of the impeachment provisions in Article V as applied to judges. Authority for such an interpretation can be found in *City of Chicago v. Reeves* (220 Ill. 274 (1906)), wherein the Court held that the adoption of Article IV, Section 34, of the Constitution pursuant to which the office of justice of the peace in Chicago was abolished upon the establishment of the Municipal Court of Chicago, though in fact an amendment of Article VI, was not thereby invalid, the amendment being incidental to the primary objective of Article IV, Section 34. On the other hand, an interpretation that the suspension and removal provision in this new Section 18 left intact the wholly independent power of impeachment for misdemeanor in office would not be unreasonable, especially since "cause" for removal or suspension is not defined in Section 18. The issue probably cannot be resolved short of litigation or constitutional clarification. It is noted here because in recent months the role of the Courts Commission established under Section 18, and the powers to be exercised thereunder, have been relevant in several instances of alleged dereliction in office by judges. In addition, the recommendation of a specially convened Joint Committee of the Illinois and Chicago Bar Associations for a revision of Supreme Court Rule 51 which established the Illinois Courts Commission to deal with cases of removal or suspension has been adopted by the Supreme Court. The issue may prove troublesome if at any time the General Assembly determines to invoke the impeachment provision in Section 15 of Article V. It is noted, however, that the explanatory statement of the Joint Committee on the Judicial Article of the Illinois State and Chicago Bar Associations, which provided an interpretation of the 1953 proposal, indicated that this section was not intended to disturb the legislative impeachment power.

Two additionally important constitutional principles introduced by this Section 18 are (1) authorization to the General Assembly to provide for the retirement of judges automatically at a prescribed age (implemented by law in Ill. Rev. Stat. ch. 37, §§ 23.71, 23.72 (1967)), providing an automatic retirement age of 70 subject to deferred retirements for present incumbents for certain periods), and (2) authorization to use the services of a retired judge with his consent. In addition, provision is made for retirement for disability by rule of the Supreme Court, in addition to suspension without pay or removal. Supreme Court Rule 51 covers this aspect through the Courts Commission authorized by that rule to implement Section 18. The composition of the Courts Commission authorized by this Section 18 includes Supreme, appellate and circuit court judges, and, by its terminology, inferentially excludes associate circuit court judges from appointment to the commission.

Comparative Analysis

About half the states have constitutional provisions concerning the retirement of judges. A little more than half of these, about one-third of all states, set a specific retirement age. The remainder provide for a retirement age as established by law. Fourteen states other than Illinois provide for the assignment of retired judges to judicial service.

All states provide a constitutional method of removal. Forty-six states, have an impeachment provision. Twenty other states provide for a judicial commission or similar court on the judiciary. Twenty-eight states provide for address, a formal request by the state legislature asking the governor to remove a judicial officer. Seven utilize the recall, typically a petition for a new election filed by the electorate. Only four states provide for a special board dealing with involuntary retirement of disabled judges.

The Constitution of the United States provides for legislative impeachment but is silent on suspension and removal for cause, or retirement for age and disability, by any judicial tribunal.

The Model State Constitution provides for a retirement age of 70 and the appointment of retired judges to special judicial assignments. The Model also provides that appellate and general court judges may be removed for cause by the Supreme Court. Under the Model State Constitution all judges are subject to impeachment.

Comment

Impeachment and the alternative removal authority by General Assembly action (see *History,* above) are apparently ineffective devices for the removal or suspension of judges for cause. The mechanism authorized by Section 18 was thought to provide a more effective device for such removal or retirement for disability. In fact, the existence of this device has, on several occasions, caused allegedly offending judges to resign rather than face the proceedings before the Courts Commission.

It is not possible to assess the effectiveness of this method. The revision of Rule 51 seeks to strengthen the concept. The principle of a judicial removal technique appears sound and is a device more and more utilized by other states. (See *Comparative Analysis.*) In the final analysis, the effectiveness of this mechanism will depend upon the vigilance of the public and the bar and the desire and dedication of the officers in the judicial system, in whom administrative power is vested, to make it work. The compulsory retirement provisions and the provision for voluntary service for retired judges make good sense and are not subject to serious criticism. It may be desirable to clarify the impeachment problem discussed above. If legislative impeachment of judges is to be assured, the Constitution should be amended to remove the existing uncertainty.

General — Judicial Conference

Sec. 19. The Supreme Court shall provide by rule for and shall convene an annual judicial conference to consider the business of the several courts and to suggest improvements in the administration of justice, and shall report thereon in writing to the General Assembly not later than January thirty-first in each legislative year.

History

The provision that the Supreme Court convene an annual judicial conference is novel in Illinois constitutional history. The requirement that the conference suggest improvements in the administration of justice and report thereon to the General Assembly appears to be a lineal descendant of Article VI, Section 31, of the 1870 Constitution, but in fact it is quite different in scope and purpose. The 1870 provision required (1) judges of inferior courts of record to report to the Supreme Court annually "such defects and omissions in the laws as their experience may suggest"; (2) judges of the Supreme Court to report annually to the Governor such "defects and omissions in the Constitution and laws as they may find to exist, together with appropriate forms of bills to cure such defects and omissions"; and (3) judges of the circuit courts to report to the General Assembly the number of days they held court in the respective counties of their circuit in the preceding two years.

These 1870 reporting requirements, including the Supreme Court's duty to study the Constitution and laws and prepare legislative bills for curing defects, were ignored after 1909, when, after an exchange of correspondence between the Governor and the Supreme Court, reported in 243 Ill. 9, the Court flatly rejected the notion that the Governor could compel reports from judges of the Supreme Court, asserting that advisory opinions and suggestions for constitutional and legislative changes, unrelated to specific litigation, was not an appropriate judicial function and could not, despite Section 31, be demanded of the courts by the Governor. The reporting requirements became a dead letter from nonuse. (See also *Explanation, Art. III.*)

The 1922 Convention proposal contained no similar provision.

Explanation

The annual judicial conference requirement and the requirement that "improvements in the administration of justice" be reported to the General Assembly are much more modest in scope and purpose than the repealed 1870 reporting requirements of Section 31. Annual judicial conferences, both federal and state, are relatively recent phenomena and reflect a laudable judicial involvement and concern in the business of the courts. Though it seems hardly necessary to mandate an annual judicial conference in the Constitution, the decision to do so was motivated by the belief that the importance of this mechanism was so great that it deserved constitutional status.

Comparative Analysis

Only two other states provide for a periodic judicial conference or council meeting similar to this. The Constitution of the United States and the Model State Constitution are silent on this subject.

Comment

The section establishes an important principle related to the general administrative authority vested in the Supreme Court. Annual judicial conferences have been held and are regarded as constructive and eminently worthwhile. Though we may argue with the constitutional status given this requirement, its overall importance would seem to justify its retention.

General — Clerks of Courts

Sec. 20. The General Assembly shall provide by law for the selection by the judges or election, terms of office, removal for cause and salaries of clerks and other non-judicial officers of the various courts; provided that a clerk shall be selected or elected for each Appellate Court District.

History

Constitutional designations of clerks of courts first appeared in 1848.

Popular elections were provided for clerks of each of the then-existing three grand divisions of the Supreme Court, circuit court clerks in each county of the circuit, and clerks of county courts. Supreme Court clerks were given six-year terms and the other clerks, four-year terms.

The 1870 Constitution provided for elections as in the 1848 Constitution, but added expressly the elective offices of the Criminal, Superior and circuit courts of Cook County. The legislature implemented the constitutional authorizations for the establishment of appellate courts, probate courts and municipal, city, village and incorporated town courts by providing for the election of clerks for each of such courts. In like manner, provision was made for the election of a clerk of the Municipal Court of Chicago.

The proposed 1922 Constitution provided that the Supreme Court and each appellate court should appoint a clerk for a term of six years subject to removal by the respective court. Clerks of the circuit and county courts were to be elected as provided in the 1870 Constitution.

Explanation

The present section departs significantly from the pattern of prior Constitutions by authorization to the General Assembly to provide either for the selection of clerks by judges or for the popular election of clerks as theretofore authorized. The General Assembly has not acted to accept the new alternative of selection of clerks by the judges, but the option remains when and if the legislature deems it advisable.

Also raised to the level of constitutional status, a consequence of the establishment of constitutional appellate courts, is the provision for the election or selection of one clerk for each appellate court district. The legislative authorization to establish grounds for removal of clerks for cause is new, as is the authorization to establish the terms of office. In other respects, the provisions of this section pertaining to clerks and other nonjudicial officers represent no significant changes in prior provisions or practice.

Comparative Analysis

Over three-fourths of the states have constitutional provisions dealing with clerks and other nonjudicial officers. Only two other states, however, leave the method of selection to the discretion of the legislature. The remaining states are split into three classes, approximately equal: those appointing clerks, those electing clerks, and those combining both methods. All but one of the 21 states mentioning compensation leave the amount to be set by the legislature. One allows the court to set the figure. Over half the states mention terms of office, but only two (excluding Illinois) leave the term to be set by the legislature. Nineteen states set a specific term, ranging from two to eight years. The rest leave the term to the court's discretion. Just over a fifth of the states specifically mention removal of clerks, but only two delegate this authority to the state legislature. The rest allow the court to remove, either for cause or at its pleasure.

Neither the Constitution of the United States nor the Model State Constitution deals with this subject.

Comment

The most important constitutional change effected by this section is the authorization to the legislature to provide for the selection of clerks by judges (instead of popular election) and other nonjudicial officers. This provision reflects a judgment that the offices in question, being largely ministerial, should be manned by administrators whose competence may more likely be assured by the selective rather than the elective method. The section also quite properly, it seems, delegates to the legislature the determination of terms of office, removal for cause and salaries for clerks and nonjudicial officers. The section seems soundly conceived as a matter of constitutional principle.

State's Attorneys — Selection — Salary

Sec. 21.   There shall be a state's attorney elected in each county in the year 1964 and every fourth year thereafter for a term of four years. No person shall be eligible for such office unless a citizen and licensed attorney-at-law of this State. His salary shall be prescribed by law.

History

The office of state's attorney was first constitutionally established in 1848. The framers of that Constitution evidenced an uncertainty as to the nature and scope of the office by providing for an election in each judicial circuit with authorization in the legislature to substitute for that office the office of county attorney in each county, an authority which was never exercised. The 1870 Constitution established the present pattern of the election of a state's attorney in each county with a four-year term. Neither prior constitutional provision established a licensed-attorney status as a qualification for office.

The proposed 1922 Constitution differed from the 1870 Constitution only in that the state's attorney was required to be licensed to practice law in this state.

Explanation

The only new aspects of the present section are the express requirements that the state's attorney be a citizen and licensed attorney-at-law of this state and that his salary be prescribed by law. In fact, the attorney requirement simply codified prior judicial interpretations that although

the 1870 Constitution established no such requirement, want of a license
was a bar to eligibility due to the nature of the office. (People *ex rel.*
Elliot v. Benefiel, 405 Ill. 500 (1950); People v. Munson, 319 Ill. 596
(1926).) In respect to salary, the Court has held that the state's attorney
was not a county officer within Article X, Section 10, of the 1870 Constitution, and thus his compensation could be fixed by the legislature.
(Hoyne v. Danisch, 264 Ill. 467 (1914).) For a period after the adoption
of the 1870 Constitution, state's attorneys were held entitled to certain
fees in addition to their salary paid by the state, but fee payments were
abolished by law in 1912, with the result that salaries are paid by the
state, with county supplementation.

Comparative Analysis

Over three-fourths of the states provide for state's attorneys. Of these,
25 set a specific term of office ranging from two to eight years; 19 states, including Illinois, provide a four-year term. Others apparently leave the
term of office to the legislature. Nearly half the states mention salary, but
all but three leave the amount to the legislature. Only two other states
require the state's attorney to be a state citizen, while seven other states
require him to be a practicing attorney. Of the 32 state constitutions
specifying a means of selection, 31 require the state's attorney to be
elected. Only one state specifies that he be appointed.

The Model State Constitution is silent on this subject.

Comment

There appears to be little or no basis for suggesting any substantive
changes in the present section, which, as noted, substantially reflects a
long-standing constitutional tradition.

Article VII

SUFFRAGE

Qualifications for Voting

Sec. 1. Every person having resided in this State one year, in the county ninety days, and in the election district thirty days next preceding any election therein, who was an elector in this State on the first day of April, in the year of our Lord one thousand eight hundred and forty-eight, or obtained a certificate of naturalization, before any court of record in this State prior to the first day of January, in the year of our Lord one thousand eight hundred and seventy, or who shall be a male citizen of the United States, above the age of twenty-one years, shall be entitled to vote at such election.

History

The 1818 Constitution gave the franchise to "white male inhabitants above the age of 21 years, having resided in the state six months next preceding the election." The Constitution also said that one could vote only in the "county or district" in which he resided on election day. In the 1848 Constitution, the foregoing qualifications were preserved as of the date of the Constitution, but for the future, citizenship was added to the qualifications. This, of course, covered people moving into the state thereafter and people reaching the age of 21 thereafter.

In the 1870 Convention, the principal controversy concerned the deletion of the word "white." The Committee on Right of Suffrage proposed to continue the 1848 arrangement. Four of the nine members of the committee filed a minority report supporting "impartial suffrage." They observed that the majority feared that the proposed Constitution would be rejected if the word "white" were omitted. The minority proposed to offer the voters alternative sections, one with the word "white," one without. The minority further proposed to permit the voters to decide whether or not to omit the word "male."

When these reports were first presented to the Convention, consideration was delayed several weeks, apparently to see whether or not the Fifteenth Amendment was ratified. (Illinois had been one of the first to ratify the amendment almost a year earlier.) A few days after the adoption of the amendment was certain, a delegate moved to recommit the committee report "because great changes have occurred in our country in reference to this matter, in the brief time that has elapsed since this report was made. . . ." (Debates 758.) The motion was agreed to. When the committee reported again, the word "white" had been deleted. A minority report was filed by the same four delegates who had been in the minority before, but this time they were proposing only that a separate vote be authorized on the question of woman suffrage. Three other members filed a second minority report in favor of retaining the word "white."

When Section 1 was taken up in Committee of the Whole, there was no debate and the section was accepted by a vote of 32 to 18. In the Convention proper, however, an extended debate developed around the question of whether to allow aliens to vote. In part, the debate involved doubt concerning the acceptability under federal law of certifications of naturalization issued by county courts. It was to meet this objection that the words "or obtained a certificate of naturalization before any court of record in this state" were added. The more significant argument for allowing aliens to vote was made by those who objected to allowing Negroes to vote. The pro-citizenship bloc prevailed and Section 1 was accepted.

On two occasions, votes were taken on woman suffrage. On a motion to strike the word "male," there were 12 in favor and 46 against. The vote was closer on a motion to submit the question to the voters as a separate question. Twenty-eight delegates favored the submission and 32 opposed it. There was also a motion to reduce the voting age to 18, but no vote appears to have been taken on the motion. The delegate who so moved had announced earlier that he would do so because under the militia article 18 year olds were subject to a draft. (Debates 861.)

The 1848 section had said that a person could vote only "in the district or county in which" he resided "at the time of" an election. Section 1, it should be noted, shifts the wording around to say that a resident for the requisite period "shall be entitled to vote at [an] election." When Section 4 (*infra*, p. 392) was under consideration, it was proposed to add to that section an authorization to the legislature to provide for absentee voting by military personnel. It was pointed out by one delegate that the "only in the district" language in the 1848 Constitution had prevented absentee voting and that a careful reading of the proposed Section 1 would show that the legislature could provide for absentee voting. Another delegate pressed the point as follows:

"The first section does not say one word as to the place of voting, but simply as to the necessity of residence in the election district.

"The [fourth] section says that the elector shall not be deemed to have lost his residence by reason of his absence, and the General Assembly are left free to fix where the party shall cast his vote. The only thing required is, that he shall have a particular residence. Having that residence he can cast his vote at the place prescribed by law." (Debates 1295.)

The proposed addition to Section 4 was rejected. It is not possible to say with certainty that the vote was a ratification of the foregoing interpretation of Section 1, but it seems the more likely understanding, for if the delegates were voting against the absentee ballot, they would have questioned the wording of Section 1. In fact, a delegate moved to reconsider Section 1 because he thought it was "left on dangerous ground." The Convention voted against him, 40 to 13. (*Id.*)

The proposed 1922 Constitution combined Sections 1 and 7 to read:

"Excepting only idiots and persons adjudged insane or convicted of infamous crime and not restored to civil rights, every citizen of the United States above the age of twenty-one years who has resided in the state one year and (unless naturalized because of military or naval service) in the United States five years shall be a qualified elector. He may vote only in the election district and county in which he has resided thirty and ninety days respectively next before such election." (art. VI, § 132.)

It is to be noted that the foregoing deleted the obsolete material concerning electors in 1848 and 1870, but other changes were made, the most significant of which was the reversion to the "only in the district" language of 1848. The Committee on Phraseology and Style reported that the revised section was intended to make absentee voting constitutional. (Journal 294-6.) In the light of the foregoing history, it would appear that the committee had in fact endangered absentee voting.

Explanation

Prior to the adoption of the Nineteenth Amendment, there was considerable litigation concerning whether or not there were any "elections" at which women could be permitted to vote. In general, the cases permitted extension of the franchise to women in any election for any office not named in the Constitution and in any referendum not required or specifically authorized by the Constitution. (*See* Scown v. Czarnecki, 264 Ill. 305 (1914).) The question can be raised whether that line of cases should be relied upon in all other contexts. The courts were sympathetic to woman suffrage and undoubtedly stretched a point in authorizing legislative inroads on the masculine ballot. Courts might not have the same attitude in the case of legislative extension of the franchise to aliens, or to people with only a few days' residence. Nevertheless, as recently as 1952, the Supreme Court *said* that the legislature could provide qualifications for voting in school elections differing from those required by Section 1, but the Court construed the School Code in a manner consistent with Section 1. (Scofield v. Board of Educ. 411 Ill. 11 (1952).)

The question could be presented squarely by Section 3-1 of the Election Code. (Ill. Rev. Stat. ch. 46 (1967).) As amended in 1963, that section permits an adult citizen to vote in a presidential election if he has resided in the election district for 60 days and would have been eligible to vote some place else had he not moved. It seems likely at this late date that the *Scown* case, which was a full-dress consideration of the issue with three dissenting opinions, would be followed at least in the case of presidential elections. (See *Comment* below for a further discussion of the judicial interpretation of Sec. 1.)

In the light of the earlier discussion of absentee voting, it is interesting to note that absentee voting has been authorized by law since 1917 without, apparently, any reported constitutional challenge. (Ill. Rev. Stat. ch. 46, §§ 19-1 to 19-44 (1967).) In 1912, the Attorney General expressed some doubt that an absentee voting law would be constitutional. He noted that the courts of other states were in conflict and that until the Supreme Court spoke, no one could be sure of the result in Illinois. (1912 Ill. Att'y Gen. Rep. 1266.) In 1917, the legislature passed a general absentee voting law and a special one which permitted military personnel to vote as a unit. On the assumption that National Guard units called into the federal service would remain intact, the necessary quantity of ballots would be sent to a unit commander, polling would take place, and the ballots would be bundled up and returned to the Secretary of State for distribution. On June 16, 1917, the Attorney General rendered an opinion that Section 4 (*infra,* p. 392) justified permitting military personnel to vote as a unit. (1917 Ill. Att'y Gen. Rep. 300.) On July 11, 1918, he rendered an opinion to the Governor, concluding rather cautiously that Section 1 would authorize absentee voting for military personnel not voting as a unit. The Attorney General noted that there were no Supreme Court opinions on the validity of either the military unit voting act or the general absentee voting law previously enacted. He relied on the difference in wording between the 1848 and 1870 sections, but he did not refer to the 1870 debates concerning that difference. (1918 Ill. Att'y Gen. Rep. 345.)

The first reported Supreme Court case construing the absentee voting law was decided in 1920. (McCreery v. Burnsmier, 293 Ill. 43 (1920).) The second case appears to have been in 1932 (Talbott v. Thompson, 350 Ill. 86 (1932)), with a good many more since then. No case appears to have involved an attack on the statute. In the recent case of *Craig v. Peterson* (39 Ill. 2d 1991 (1968)), however, there was an attack on the absentee voting law by absentee voters whose votes had not been counted because the election judges failed to initial the ballots. In that case, all voting for candidates, except for judges seeking retention, was by voting machine and only absentee ballots were capable of being initialed. The Supreme Court distinguished earlier cases, which had held initialing to be mandatory, by noting that in the case in litigation there was no allegation of fraud and initialing would have served no essential purpose. The Court concluded that to protect the right to vote, guaranteed by this Section 1 and Section 18 of Article II (*supra,* p. 83), uninitialed absentee ballots should be counted under the circumstances set forth. This case can reasonably be accepted as an affirmation of the validity of absentee voting, for a court can hardly be expected to invalidate part of a statute on the ground that that part is inconsistent with a constitutional provision if the constitutional provision in fact prohibits the entire statute.

There have been numerous decisions interpreting the residency requirements of Section 1. The courts have held that "residence" refers to a permanent abode (Coffey v. Board of Election Comm'rs, 375 Ill. 385 (1940)), but have noted that there is a large element of subjective intent in the permanence of a person's abode. (*See* Welsh v. Shumway, 232 Ill. 54 (1907).) In this respect, residence for voting purposes is somewhat like the elusive term "domicile." Because of the element of intent, someone once observed that the only truly accurate definition of domicile is that it is something a person has only one of. This is the case with voting residence, and it seems unlikely that any purpose is served in a constitution by trying to go beyond using the word "resident."

A problem arises under a time-of-residence provision when one becomes eligible to vote too late to comply with the administrative scheme of registration. One of the defects in one of the several invalidated primary election laws was a provision that in effect prevented voting by anyone reaching 21 or becoming a citizen within four months of the election. (People *ex rel.* Phillips v. Strassheim, 240 Ill. 279 (1909).) The Supreme Court did, however, uphold a provision that required registration within three weeks of election, thus disfranchising those who became 21 or were naturalized in the intervening period. (People *ex rel.* Grinnell v. Hoffman, 116 Ill. 587 (1886).) The present statutory provision permits registration in advance if a person will be qualified by the next election day. (Ill. Rev. Stat. ch. 46, § 4-2 (1967).)

The requirement of residence in the "election district" for 30 days preceding the election has also created some difficulty. The Supreme Court once noted that "election district" had no settled meaning and decided that a 30-day resident in a town, who was otherwise qualified, was a legal voter regardless of his length of residence in a particular election district within the town. The rationale was that any voter should be able to vote at a town meeting and that it was not consistent to deny him the right to vote for town officers. But the Supreme Court went on to say that in any other election, the 30-day residence requirement referred to the denominated election district. (People *ex rel.*

Delaney v. Markiewicz, 225 Ill. 563 (1907).) In a city, "election district" may be a precinct, but if the precinct is divided into districts, then it is the district. (Donovan v. Comerford, 332 Ill. 230 (1928).)

Section 1 limits qualifications to matters of age, residence, and citizenship. Nevertheless, the Supreme Court has said that idiots and insane persons cannot vote. (Welsh v. Shumway, 232 Ill. 54 (1907); Behrensmeyer v. Kreitz, 135 Ill. 591 (1891).) Literacy is not required, and the Supreme Court has said that a statute which prohibited voter assistance would be invalid, for it would deny the right to vote to an illiterate. (People ex rel. Drennan v. Williams, 298 Ill. 86 (1921).) Likewise, disabled people would be entitled to assistance. (*Id.*)

Comparative Analysis

Citizenship: There appear to be two states, New Hampshire and Texas, that have no constitutional citizenship requirement. Delaware and West Virginia require state citizenship, but the wording of the Delaware provision makes it clear that a voter must be a United States citizen. Massachusetts simply says that a voter must be a "citizen." (The Index Digest of State Constitutions is the primary source for checking comparable provisions in other state constitutions. There are errors in the Index Digest and for this reason references to other states are usually couched in terms of approximation. In the case of citizenship qualifications for voting, 44 states are listed, but Illinois is labeled "Ind VII I" instead of "Ill VII I." Four states with citizenship requirements are not entered at all. Moreover, the Council of State Governments, The Book of the States, 1968-69 (at 30 (1968)) notes that all states require United States citizenship. This notation would be based, of course, on constitutional *and* statutory provisions.)

Age: Forty-six states set the minimum voting age at 21, assuming, as is undoubtedly the case, that in West Virginia "minors" means "persons under 21." The minimum age is 20 in Hawaii, 19 in Alaska, and 18 in Georgia and Kentucky.

Residency:

State: According to the Book of the States, 1968-69, state residency requirements are as follows:

Two years	1 state
One year	32 states
Six months	15 states
Three months	1 state
90 days	1 state
	(*Id.* at 30.)

County: Only 36 states have a county residency requirement, distributed as follows:

Six months	10 states
Four months	1 state
Three months	4 states
90 days	7 states
Two months	1 state
60 days	5 states
40 days	3 states
30 days	5 states

(Id.)

Election District: Forty-one states have a residency requirement in an election district, as follows:

One year	1 state
Six months	5 states
Three months	7 states
60 days	3 states
54 days	1 state
40 days	1 state
One month	1 state
30 days	14 states
20 days	2 states
10 days	5 states
By fifth Friday preceding election	1 state

(Id.)

In the case of residency requirements for county and election districts, the information set out above includes both constitutional and statutory time periods and does not include various exceptions. It should also be noted that, over the past decade, residency requirements have been changed in several states. Invariably, the time has been shortened. In South Carolina, for example, the residence requirement which used to be two years (ministers, teachers and their spouses, six months) was shortened in 1963 to one year (same six-month exemption), and under a current proposed constitutional revision would be cut to six months.

Literacy: Not quite half of the states include a literacy requirement among the qualifications for voting. (But apparently only 14 states require a literacy *test*. Council of State Governments, The Book of the States, 1968-69 at 30 (1968).) Usually, the requirement is one of being able to read the English language; but in New Mexico, it is English or Spanish; in Hawaii, English or Hawaiian; and in Louisiana, English or mother tongue. In many cases, the requirement has been superseded in part by the Federal Voting Rights Act of 1965. (42 U.S.C. §§1971, 1973.)

Mental Condition: Almost half the states exclude idiots from voting, and almost three-fourths exclude the insane. About ten states exclude incompetents.

Other Qualifications: Many states have qualifications that are no longer effective. For example, six states besides Illinois have not removed "male" from their suffrage article, and a few states still retain a poll tax requirement. Nine states disqualify paupers, three states require good moral character, and one state requires "quiet and peaceable behavior."

The United States Constitution has no affirmative suffrage provisions but by the Fifteenth Amendment prohibits denial of suffrage "on account of race, color, or previous condition of servitude"; by the Nineteenth Amendment prohibits denial of suffrage "on account of sex"; and by the Twenty-Fourth Amendment prohibits denial of suffrage in federal elections "by reason of failure to pay any poll tax or other tax." Since adoption of the amendment, the United States Supreme Court has outlawed the poll tax in *all* elections. (Harper v. Virginia Bd. of Elections, 383 U.S. 663 (1966).)

The Model State Constitution's article on Suffrage and Elections reads as follows:

"Qualifications for Voting. Every citizen of the age of....years and a resident of the state for three months shall have the right to vote in the election of all officers that may be elected by the people and upon all questions that may be submitted to the voters; but the legislature may by law establish: (1) minimum periods of local residence not exceeding three months, (2) reasonable requirements to determine literacy in English or in another language predominantly used in the classrooms of any public or private school accredited by any state or territory of the United States, the District of Columbia, or the Commonwealth of Puerto Rico, and (3) disqualifications for voting for mental incompetency or conviction of felony." (art. III, § 3.01.)

"Legislature to Prescribe for Exercise of Suffrage. The legislature shall by law define residence for voting purposes, insure secrecy in voting and provide for the registration of voters, absentee voting, the administration of elections and the nomination of candidates." (art. III, § 3.02.)

Comment

The suffrage article of a constitution should do two things: it should provide for the qualifications for being allowed to vote and it should guarantee that those who have such qualifications can vote. With one exception, the Model State Constitution suffrage article succinctly covers all of the essentials. The exception is the problem of voting in presidential elections. The Model State Constitution has a short residence requirement, but even so, the Illinois statute for presidential voting, referred to *supra,* pp. 383-4, probably would not be valid. It may well be that, before long, Congress will set national standards for voting in presidential elections, but until then, a state suffrage provision ought to permit the waiver of state residence requirements for voting in presidential elections. This is especially significant if the minimum residence requirement is six months or a year. It should be noted that, under the Model

State Constitution, the legislature would be able to waive local residence requirements for voting for state officers.

Although the Model State Constitution's suffrage article contains all of the essentials, there is room for different policies on details. The Convention should consider whether to shorten the present state residence minimum, but it is certainly not unreasonable to consider three months too short. It is also questionable whether a literacy test should be inserted at this late date. In the light of the history of the misuse of literacy requirements in other parts of the country, a proposal to include even permission for one in Illinois would undoubtedly be misunderstood. The point is that the Model suffrage article has all the necessary constitutional guarantees and qualifications for voting and all the necessary flexibility for appropriate legislative regulation of the electoral process.

The old saying that "Hard cases make bad law" certainly applies to the cases in which the Supreme Court granted women the right to vote in "nonconstitutional" elections. It is clear from the debates of the 1870 Convention that the delegates intended Section 1 to cover all voting. Thus, if one follows the intent of the drafters, the decisions were wrong. If Section 1 is read strictly and literally, it says that the persons described shall be entitled to vote at "such" election, and "such" election is "any election" in the voting district. Thus, if one follows the rule of strict construction, the decisions were wrong. There is a theory that the legislature has all the sovereign powers of government except those withdrawn by the people through the Constitution. Under this theory, one could argue that Section 1 denies to the legislature the power to exclude from voting the persons described but does not deny the power to enlarge the franchise. Under this theory, the courts could have upheld an extension of voting rights to women, but could not have distinguished between constitutional elections and other elections. The moral, other than that one should never underestimate the power of women, is that no amount of careful draftsmanship can foreclose an erroneous interpretation, whether for a good cause or a bad cause.

A word is in order about a bit of inadvisable constitution-making in the proposed 1922 section quoted above. (*Supra*, p. 383.) That section provided that a naturalized citizen had to have been a resident in the United States for five years before he could vote. The debates of the Convention make it clear that the purpose of this language was to prevent wives of United States citizens from voting just because, under the law as it was then, they automatically acquired the citizenship of their husband. (State of Illinois, Proceedings of the Constitutional Convention 967 (1920) [hereinafter cited as Proceedings].) The five-year residence requirement would put wives on a par with any other alien who had to live in the

United States for five years before he could get his final papers. It presumably did not occur to any one in the Convention that the United States might make any number of changes in the Naturalization Act, and that it was not necessarily appropriate to enshrine in a semipermanent state constitution a special exception to cover a specific federal statutory rule. This is not to say that the provision was necessarily bad, though the actual wording raises the question of whether a citizen, naturalized or not, who had been out of the country had to be back for five years before he could vote. The point is that the reason for the provision was both ephemeral and beyond the control of Illinois. One of the most important attributes of good constitution decision-making is to take the long view, to remember that what is to be proposed should be good for at least a generation and preferably for longer.

Ballots Required

Sec. 2. All votes shall be by ballot.

History

The 1818 Constitution provided that voting should be *viva voce* until changed by the legislature. In 1848 it was provided that "[a]ll votes shall be given by ballot." The change in verb form was made by the Committee on Revision and Adjustment of the 1870 Convention. The proposed 1922 Constitution dropped the word "All."

Explanation

As the history above indicates, the purpose of this section is simply to avoid *viva voce* voting. At the time of adoption in 1870, the section did not insure secret voting. Nevertheless, in the debate on the floor, it was clear that the delegates assumed that the existing statutory system permitting a voter to demand a secret ballot would be preserved. In those days, the Australian ballot had not been generally accepted and a frequent practice was to have different colored paper for the different political parties. It was in this context that a delegate observed that it was "clearly the right of a voter, if he is offered a blue or red ticket, to procure a ticket on white paper of the kind usually employed." (Debates 1294.) In 1905, the Supreme Court upheld the use of voting machines, and in doing so announced that the real purpose of this section was to preserve secrecy in voting. (Lynch v. Malley, 215 Ill. 574 (1905).) Thus, to the three provided by Illinois, there are preservations of voting rights Court, so to speak, switched the meaning so that, in effect, Section 2 now reads: Secrecy in voting shall be insured.

Comparative Analysis

Approximately two-thirds of the states specify that voting shall be by ballot. About a third of the states specify that secrecy shall be preserved. A dozen or so states specifically authorize the use of voting machines. The United States Constitution provides that the "times, Places and Manner of holding Elections for Senators and Representatives, shall be prescribed in each State by the Legislature thereof; but the Congress may at any time by Law make or alter such Regulations...." (art. I, §4.) The Model State Constitution instructs the legislature by law to "insure secrecy in voting" and to provide for "the administration of elections."

Comment

Since the Supreme Court in 1905 produced the brilliant result both of making this section guarantee secrecy in voting and of permitting the use of voting machines, it would appear advisable to leave the section alone. It would be appropriate, of course, for the Convention to make a legislative record to the effect that the section was retained in the light of the judicial gloss. It might also be appropriate for the delegates to "assume" formally that "voting machine" includes whatever the electronic magic of computers may make possible so long as secrecy is preserved.

Freedom from Arrest — Military Duty

Sec. 3. Electors shall, in all cases except treason, felony, or breach of the peace, be privileged from arrest during their attendance at elections, and in going to and returning from the same. And no elector shall be obliged to do military duty on the days of election, except in time of war or public danger.

History

This first appeared in substance in the 1848 Constitution as two separate sections. In the 1870 Convention, the two sections were agreed to without discussion. The Committee on Revision and Adjustment produced the combined section. The proposed 1922 Constitution retained the substance of the provision.

Explanation

There does not appear to have been any interpretation of this section. The only question likely to arise is the meaning of the exception of "treason, felony, or breach of the peace." (See discussion of Sec. 14, Art. IV, *supra*, p. 174.)

Comparative Analysis

Freedom from Arrest: Approximately half the states have the same provision as the first sentence of this section. Another eight states or so have variations in the privilege, including five that limit it to civil process. Most of the newer constitutions omit the privilege. Michigan, for example, deleted it in its new constitution. Neither the United States Constitution nor the Model State Constitution has such a constitutional privilege.

Military Duty: Not quite a third of the state constitutions contain this privilege. The statements above concerning newer constitutions, Michigan, the United States Constitution and the Model State Constitution are applicable to this privilege, also.

Comment

These privileges are appropriate ones but not so fundamental as to require constitutional protection. Legislative extension of the privileges could be afforded without any specific constitutional authorization.

Losing Voting Residence

Sec. 4. No elector shall be deemed to have lost his residence in this State by reason of his absence on the business of the United States, or of this State, or in the military or naval service of the United States.

History

The civilian part of this section was first adopted in the 1848 Constitution. The military part was added in 1870. At that time there was a debate over whether specifically to provide for absentee voting by the military. The argument was made that legislation on absentee voting was permitted by the revised language of Section 1 (see *History* of Sec. 1, *supra,* pp. 382-3), and apparently on the basis of this representation a proposed addition to Section 4 concerning absentee voting was defeated. The proposed 1922 Constitution retained the substance of this section in combination with the substance of Section 5.

Explanation

Several cases have construed this section, but all of them have simply confirmed that the section means what it says. The Attorney General has expressed the opinion that this section may authorize absentee voting for military personnel. (1917 Ill. Att'y Gen. Rep. 300. See also, *Explanation* of Sec. 1, *supra,* p. 384.)

Comparative Analysis

A majority of the states spell out various circumstances when the privilege of voting is not lost by absence from one's residence. In addition to the three provided by Illinois, there are preservations of voting rights notwithstanding attendance at college; confinement in jail, an asylum, or an almshouse; and while navigating in state waters and the high seas.

Presumably, most states with no such provision permit appropriate determinations by law. Michigan, for example, deleted its comparable provision and a provision comparable to Section 5. The new Michigan Constitution has a general section on voting qualifications that ends with the sentence: "The legislature shall define residence for voting purposes." (art. II, § 1.) The United States and Model State Constitutions have no comparable provision.

Comment

In the Comment on Section 1 (*supra,* pp. 388-9), it was suggested that a suffrage article along the lines of the Model State Constitution would be appropriate. Such an article would eliminate the need, if there ever was any, for this section.

Military Service — Residence

Sec. 5. No soldier, seaman or marine in the army or navy of the United States, shall be deemed a resident of this State in consequence of being stationed therein.

History

This section, in a slightly expanded form, was first adopted in the 1848 Constitution. The 1870 Convention retained the section without debate, and the Committee on Revision and Adjustment shortened the section by substituting "therein" for "at any military or naval place within the State." (One wonders why not "herein.") The proposed 1922 Constitution retained the substance of this section in combination with the substance of Section 4.

Explanation

In 1848, this perfectly straightforward principle may have been deemed to be of constitutional status for some reason no longer apparent. In any event, there does not appear even to have been any occasion to interpret it.

Comparative Analysis

Just under half the states have a comparable provision. Some states simply work out a "gain and loss" reciprocal arrangement and thus such other circumstances as attendance at college, confinement in prison, and the like, do not create residence for voting. (See *Comparative Analysis* of Sec. 4, *supra,* pp. 392-3.) Again, it may be noted, Michigan deleted a comparable provision. (*Id.*) The United States and the Model State Constitutions have no comparable provisions.

Comment

It seems doubtful that this section was ever necessary. If, as suggested earlier (*supra*, pp. 388-9), a suffrage article along the lines of the Model State Constitution were used, this section would be unnecessary, for that article instructs the legislature to define residence for voting purposes.

Qualifications for Civil or Military Office

Sec. 6.   No person shall be elected or appointed to any office in this State, civil or military, who is not a citizen of the United States, and who shall not have resided in this State one year next preceding the election or appointment.

History

This section was first adopted in the 1848 Constitution with the word "before" instead of "preceding." In the 1870 Convention, the Committee on Right of Suffrage proposed a section reading: "No person shall be elected or appointed to any civil office, public position or place of trust, profit or emolument, in this State, who is not an elector of this State." This was accepted without debate, but when the section came back to the floor in final form from the Committee on Revision and Adjustment, the wording had reverted to the 1848 language with the one word change noted above. In the proposed 1922 Constitution, this parochial provision was moved to the article on Public Servants and made somewhat less restrictive in one respect but gratuitously more restrictive in another respect. It read: "To hold any office created by this constitution a person shall be a citizen of the United States, resident in this state one year and able to read and write the English language." The less restrictive language was presumably designed to conform to the *McCormick* case discussed below.

Explanation

In the leading case of *People* ex rel. *Hayne v. McCormick* (261 Ill. 413 (1913)), the Supreme Court limited the coverage of this restrictive section to offices, state and local, provided for by the Constitution. It further held that legislation could not make the restrictions on such offices more onerous as, for example, requiring five years' residence; but that in the case of offices created by statute, it was wholly within the power of the legislature to determine the qualifications of the office. The Attorney General has ruled, however, that statutory officers must meet the citizenship and residency requirements. (1900 Ill. Att'y Gen. Rep. 237 (Notary Public a citizen); 1915 Ill. Att'y Gen. Rep. 593 (overseer of the poor a resident); 1917 Ill. Att'y Gen. Rep. 108 (civil service applicant a citizen); 1926 Ill. Att'y Gen. Rep. 71 (probation officer a resident).)

In the 1917 opinion, the Attorney General was faced with construing the provision of the Civil Service Act that opened applications for "offices or places" to all citizens of the state. Since "offices" can be filled only by United States citizens, and since he doubted that the legislature intended to distinguish between "offices" and "places," he concluded that only United States citizens were eligible for civil service positions. That act was repealed in 1955 and replaced by the Personnel Code under which there appear to be no citizenship requirements and under which residence requirements may be waived under certain circumstances. (Ill. Rev. Stat. ch. 127, §63b108b.1 (1967).) In the light of the *McCormick* case, *supra,* and the *Wilson* case, *infra,* it seems likely that the courts will not follow the several opinions of the Attorney General.

In 1960, the Supreme Court utilized the distinction between "office" and "employment" (see Sec. 24 of Art. V, *supra,* p. 322) to permit Chicago to hire nonresidents as Administrator of the Police Board and Superintendent of Police. (People *ex rel.* Adamowski v. Wilson, 20 Ill. 2d 568 (1960).)

Comparative Analysis

A restrictive provision like Section 6 is relatively rare among the states. Only five or so require United States citizenship and two or three more require state citizenship. Approximately eight states require residency, but a few of them do not appear to require residency for as long as a year. Hawaii requires three years' residence for certain positions. (This may be simply an attempt to discourage "vacationland" immigration. California, Arizona and Florida, for example, make it difficult for retired professional men to get a local license to practice.) Some states have weird exclusions from public office. Several states prohibit duellers from holding public office. Idaho has perhaps, the weirdest provision. Excluded are polygamists, bigamists, persons who are idiotic or insane, Chinese and persons of Mongolian descent not born in the United States, and Indians not taxed who have not severed their tribal relations and adopted habits of civilization. The United States and Model State Constitutions exclude nobody from public office.

Comment

As indicated above, this is a parochial provision conceivably suited to the Jacksonian concept that anyone is competent to hold any government job, but not suited to today's requirements for high competence in specialized fields. It is, of course, possible to rely on the courts to exclude professional positions from the term "office," but it would seem more realistic simply to confine requirements of citizenship and residency to elective positions.

The *McCormick* case, discussed above, raises an interesting question in constitution-drafting. It seems doubtful that the drafters of this section, either in 1848 or 1870, meant to limit the section to offices created by the Constitution. As a matter of hindsight, it is easy to word the section to cover statutory offices. As a matter of foresight, it is not easy to anticipate a judicial refusal to read clear language to mean what it says. But in constitution-drafting, there is great danger in being too specific. For one thing, a constitution can quickly become too much like a statute. For another, the times may change and it may be a lot simpler to permit the courts to rewrite the language than it is to amend a constitution. The best way to avoid worrying over whether the courts will read sections properly is to concentrate on limiting constitutional provisions to principles that will hold good for at least two or three generations. But then even this exemplary outlook must be tempered by the political realities of getting a constitution adopted. The voter who reads as he runs rarely thinks in terms of two or three generations ahead. Fortunately, he is also likely to accept clear and simple language and not worry about whether it can be misread.

This section provides an opportunity to make a couple of "nuts and bolts" observations about constitution-drafting. The section states most explicitly that *no* person can be elected to *any* office in the state who is not a United States citizen. Section 3 of Article IV (*supra,* p. 120) states that a member of the legislature must be a United States citizen. Section 5 of Article V (*supra,* p. 267) states that the Governor and Lieutenant Governor must be United States citizens. Section 3 of the original Article VI required judges of the Supreme Court to be United States citizens and Section 17 of the same original article required circuit and inferior court judges and county commissioners to be United States citizens. (The present Judicial Article is another matter. It was put together as a self-contained package and any cautious draftsman would hesitate to rely on some other part of the Constitution to cover the judiciary. For the record, the present Sections 15 and 21 of Article VI (*supra,* pp. 366 and 379) require judges and state's attorneys, respectively, to be citizens "of this State." See *Comment* on Sec. 1 of Art. XII, *infra,* p. 538, concerning state citizenship.)

There are two obvious morals here. He who drafts a blanket provision ought to touch base with anyone who is affected by the provision. Presumably, no one on the 1870 suffrage committee checked with other committees concerning the duplication. The second moral is that the Committee on Style and Arrangement ought to add "and Consistency" to its title. In addition to the mammoth tasks of trying to impress a single writing style on the various draft sections and of trying to get everything arranged logically, the committee has to watch for inconsistencies and duplications. In the long run, the elimination of inconsistencies may be more important than style and arrangement. (Anyone interested in an even better story of drafting confusion can search out the variations in referendum wording in the Constitution. There are at least 15 references to a referendum by voters.)

Infamous Crime — Loss of Franchise

Sec. 7. The General Assembly shall pass laws excluding from the right of suffrage persons convicted of infamous crimes.

History

In the Legislative Article of the 1818 Constitution, the legislature was given "full power to exclude from the privilege of electing or being elected any person convicted of bribery, perjury or any other infamous crime." In 1848, this section was retained but a shortened version was added in the new article on Elections and Rights of Suffrage, giving the legislature "full power to pass laws excluding from the right of suffrage persons convicted of infamous crimes." This latter language was in the original proposal of the Committee on Right of Suffrage of the 1870 Convention. The original proposal was referred back to the committee for resolution of disputed matters concerning Section 1 (see *History* of Sec. 1, *supra,* pp. 381-2), and during this period of reconsideration the Convention, in debating what is now Section 4 of Article IV, decided to spell out the prohibition against office-holding rather than grant power to the legislature to prohibit certain classes of people from holding office. (See *History* of Sec. 4, Art. IV, *supra,* pp. 127-8.) When the committee resubmitted Article VII to the Convention, this principle showed up in a revised version of Section 7. This version was accepted without debate. (One may note, however, that the Convention did not go all the way, for instead of mandating legislation, it could have provided that no person convicted of an infamous crime could vote.) In the proposed 1922 Constitution this section was combined with Section 1 in a self-executing form. Excepted from the privilege of voting were persons "convicted of infamous crime and not restored to civil rights."

Explanation

It is clear from the historical development of this section and from the wording of Section 4 of Article IV (*supra,* p. 127) that bribery and perjury are infamous crimes. This was reinforced in 1903 when the Supreme Court upheld a long-standing statute that disfranchised for a period anyone convicted of bribery in an election. (Christie v. People, 206 Ill. 337 (1903).)

Under the current Election Code, no person legally convicted in Illinois, in any other state or in federal court, of any crime punishable by confinement in the penitentiary may vote unless rights of citizenship are restored by the Governor or by a court. (Ill. Rev. Stat. ch. 46, §3-5 (1967).)

Comparative Analysis

Almost every state has some constitutional restriction on voting by persons who have engaged in criminal activity. In some cases the restriction is spelled out on a self-executing basis, in others in the form of a command to the legislature as in Illinois, and in still others in the form of a permission to the legislature to act. Some 20 states use the adjective "infamous." The United States Constitution has no comparable provision. The Model State Constitution provides that the legislature may by law establish "disqualifications for voting for mental incompetency or conviction of felony."

Comment

There is no need to spell out in a constitution what criminal activity is cause for disfranchisement, but it is necessary to give the legislature power to provide for disqualification for certain criminal activity if that is desired. Once there is a suffrage provision that says "any person who, etc., can vote," there is no legislative power of exclusion unless authorized. (See also *Comment* on Sec. 1, *supra*, p. 388.)

Article VIII

EDUCATION

Free Schools

Sec. 1. The General Assembly shall provide a thorough and efficient system of free schools, whereby all children of this state may receive a good common school education.

History

This section of the Constitution was new in 1870; neither the 1818 nor the 1848 Constitution contained a mandate requiring the legislature to establish a state-wide school system, although as a matter of fact considerable effort had been made toward that goal before 1848. The first effective school code for a general school system in Illinois was passed in 1845.

In the 1870 Convention there was a much-debated amendment to strike out all the words following "schools," and insert the words "for all persons in the state." This amendment was opposed on two grounds. There was a considerable immigration of southern Negroes in the southern part of the state, and it was feared that the education of these adults at public expense would be unduly burdensome. It was also felt that retaining the requirement of "common school education" would indicate that "academic" and "collegiate" educations were not to be supported by taxation. The amendment failed. In the proposed 1922 Constitution the provision was retained unchanged. The Committee on Education proposed an additional provision that the state educate and care for defective, delinquent, and dependent children, but this was rejected on the grounds that it was not directly relevant to the subject of public education and was adequately covered by legislation.

Explanation

This section grants no new powers to the General Assembly, for in the event of constitutional silence on the subject, it would certainly be within the authority of the legislature to create a public school system, as in fact was done prior to 1870. Rather, this section requires the legislature to provide a system of "common school education" and establishes three standards by which that system is to be maintained — that it be (1) thorough and efficient, (2) available to all children of the state, and (3) free.

The question of what constitutes a "common school education" has not caused any difficulty in the courts, which have in general been content to acquiesce in whatever curriculum requirements have been established by the legislature. In an early case where a group of taxpayers challenged the teaching of German in the elementary schools because it was not on the list of subjects required for licensing teachers, the court held that any academic subject matter could be taught in the schools so long as it was not specifically prohibited by the General Assembly. The court suggested that the only constitutional limitation would be that the medium of instruction in the schools must be English. (Powell v. Board of Educ., 97 Ill. 375 (1881).) It is doubtful that such a limitation would be implied today. Legislative provisions for the establishment of high schools were earlier approved as a legitimate part of the common school system (Richards v. Raymond, 92 Ill. 612 (1879)), and indeed in later cases the courts said that it was the duty of the legislature to provide high schools. In carrying out this duty, it was proper for the legislature to organize those parts of the state which do not maintain high schools into "non-high school districts" and to authorize taxes on those districts for the payment of tuition of their qualified resident students to attend high school in neighboring districts. (People ex rel. Goodell v. Chicago & Nw. Ry., 286 Ill. 384 (1918); Cook v. Board of Directors, 266 Ill. 164 (1915)). In a recent decision, the Court held that the state schools for the mentally incompetent were charitable and hospital institutions, and were not part of the common school system; hence there was no obligation to provide free school training to the mentally incompetent. (Department of Pub. Welfare v. Haas, 15 Ill. 2d 204 (1958).)

The question of whether the school system is "thorough and efficient" has been raised in numerous cases. The trend in Illinois school system organization has been to simplify, consolidate and enlarge school districts as transportation and communication services improve. There has been a continuing legislative program which has resulted in substantial changes in school district boundaries, administrative structure and operation, and financing through property taxes. These changes are ordinarily effected by local referendum and have frequently been challenged in the courts. Often one of the grounds of challenge is that the new organization will render the schools less thorough and efficient for a variety of particular reasons. As a general matter, the Court has refused to intervene in school reorganizations on these grounds, if the reorganization conformed to statutory requirements. It has said that the "thorough and efficient" requirement was solely a matter for legislative discretion and the courts will not look into it. The most complete statement of this position can be found in *People v. Deatherage* (401 Ill. 26 (1948)).

This principle has been applied in one case to approve annexation proceedings in which the territory annexed to a new district included the only schoolhouse in the old district and it was alleged that there was insufficient property valuation in the remaining old district to build a new building. (Board of Educ. v. Board of Educ., 11 Ill. App. 2d 408 (1956).) However, one recent case has invalidated annexation proceedings which left the remaining district in three separate islands of territory on the grounds that this violated the constitutional requirement of efficiency. (People *ex rel.* Community School Dist. v. Decatur School Dist., 31 Ill. 2d 612 (1964).)

The language "all children of the state" has been interpreted to mean that the school system must operate uniformly throughout the state and that within a particular school district, the school system must not discriminate among students. There has been little controversy over the application of this principle. It was early established in Illinois that school boards could not separate white and nonwhite students, regardless of whether the facilities were equal. (People *ex rel.* Bibb v. Mayor of Alton, 193 Ill. 309 (1901); Chase v. Stephenson, 71 Ill. 383 (1874).) Children who live in orphanages or foster homes were held entitled by this provision to attend schools in the districts where the homes were located, even though their legal domiciles were elsewhere. (Dean v. Board of Educ., 386 Ill. 156 (1944).)

The provision that the schools must be free has caused little difficulty. It does not require that the schools provide free textbooks. (Segar v. Board of Educ., 317 Ill. 418 (1925).) A statute was held unconstitutional under this provision which granted all eighth-grade graduates of a school district not maintaining a high school the right to attend high school in another district, but required parents who were financially able to pay the transfer tuition. (People v. Moore, 240 Ill. 408 (1909).)

It is clear that under this section the powers of the General Assembly to operate the school system may be delegated to local school boards. (Smith v. Board of Educ., 405 Ill. 143 (1950).) There have been a number of cases in which the conduct of school affairs by the General Assembly, or its authorized agency, the local school board, has been challenged as violating other provisions of the Constitution. In general, the Court has held that the broad mandate of this Article supersedes particular proscriptions of other sections. For example, a tax required by the General Assembly to be levied by local school districts for contribution to the state teachers' pension fund was relevant to the general mandate of Article VIII, and therefore it was not a tax levied by the General Assembly for a purely "corporate purpose" which is prohibited by Article IX, Section 10. (People *ex rel* Nelson v. Jackson-Highland Bldg. Corp., 400 Ill. 533 (1948).) And Article IV, Section 20, prohibiting state aid to private corporations, was held not to prevent the General Assembly from making appropriations to Illinois State Normal School, a private corporation, since under Article VIII, Section 1, the state may maintain normal schools to supply teachers for the common school system. (Boehm v. Hertz, 182 Ill. 154, (1899). See also the discussion of special legislation under Art. IV, Sec. 22, *supra*, pp. 218-9.)

Comparative Analysis

Approximately 30 states have provisions substantially identical to this one. Many state constitutions go into considerably more detail than does Illinois on the structure of the public school system. It would seem that in the interests of flexibility the more general provisions are preferable. The Model State Constitution (art. IX) contains a similar provision in somewhat different language as its only provision on the subject of education. It provides:

"The legislature shall provide for the maintenance and support of a system of free public schools open to all children in the state and shall establish, organize and support such other public institutions, including public institutuions of higher learning, as may be desirable."

Comment

It is a common but not uniform practice for state constitutions to endorse public support for education. The language of the Illinois provision could be modernized, and perhaps there should be recognition of the state's function in providing college and university education, though it is hardly likely that a state would today refuse to assume this obligation if there were no constitutional directive.

School Property and Funds

Sec. 2. All lands, moneys, or other property, donated, granted or received for school, college, seminary, or university purposes, and the proceeds thereof, shall be faithfully applied to the objects for which such gifts or grants were made.

History

This new section was adopted without debate by the 1870 Convention. A similar but differently worded section was approved without significant debate by the 1920 Convention.

Explanation

As interpreted by the Supreme Court, the major effect of this section is to prohibit taxation or special assessment of public school property acquired by gift. Since the legislature is prevented by this section from directly appropriating public school lands and applying them to other purposes, it cannot accomplish the same purpose indirectly by taxing them. (People *ex rel*. Little v. Trustees of Schools, 118 Ill. 52 (1886).) The Court has held that this section applies only to property acquired prior to 1870, not subsequently; and that it refers primarily to Section 16 of every township (or property acquired with the proceeds of Section 16) which was reserved for school purposes in the original federal grant of land for statehood. It is the burden of the school trustees to trace property, and in the absence of a showing that it was purchased with funds from protected property, any property acquired subsequent to 1870 is subject to taxation or special assessment under a proper statute. (Grosse v. People *ex rel*. Ruch, 218 Ill. 342 (1905).) "Proceeds" in this section includes rents and profits from protected property, even if the property is not directly used for school purposes. (People *ex rel*. Hanberg v. City of Chicago, 216 Ill. 537 (1905).)

This section does not exempt the property of private educational institutions from taxation. (University of Chicago v. People *ex rel*. Seipp, 118 Ill. 565 (1886).) Where a public school board has leased protected school-owned property to a private person or corporation, the lessee's interest is subject to taxation and special assessment, regardless of who has title to the improvement. (People *ex rel*. Paschen v. Hendrickson-Pontiac, Inc., 9 Ill. 2d 250 (1956).)

Comparative Analysis

Approximately 20 states have similar provisions. No analogous section is found in the Model State Constitution.

Comment

This provision may have been desirable to provide a fund for educational purposes at a time when broad public support of schools by taxation was not as common as it is today. However, currently, the section is not applicable to the vast bulk of school property, and its main effect would appear to be the creation of bookkeeping difficulties. Article IX, Section 3 (*infra*, p. 435), authorizes the General Assembly to exempt school property from taxation and the exercise of this authority should accomplish whatever ends are thought to be desirable through such exemption. As noted in that discussion, Article IX, Section 3, applies to both public and private schools. Of course, leaving the matter of tax exemption to be covered only by that section would make it entirely a matter of legislative discretion. Because of the limited application of this Section 2, the delegation of discretion to the legislature under Article IX, Section 3, should cause little concern.

Public Funds for Sectarian Purposes Forbidden

Sec. 3. Neither the General Assembly nor any county, city, town, township, school district, or other public corporation, shall ever make any appropriation or pay from any public fund whatever, anything in aid of any church or sectarian purpose, or to help support or sustain any school, academy, seminary, college, university, or other literary or scientific institution, controlled by any church or sectarian denomination whatever; nor shall any grant or donation of land, money, or other personal property ever be made by the state or any such public corporation, to any church, or for any sectarian purpose.

History

This was a new section of the Constitution proposed by the Convention of 1870. As originally submitted, the section ended with the word "whatever." When the point was raised that only appropriations to sectarian institutions were prohibited, the last clause was added to prevent any form of aid. This proposal was apparently prompted in part by what was believed to be the New York experience, where it was alleged that one-half million dollars had been appropriated to convents and seminaries. One ground of opposition to the provision was that it injected such a note of controversy that the whole Constitution might be rejected by the public. In general, the debate centered on the pro's and con's of giving aid to parochial schools or of permitting the public schools to establish or maintain a sectarian influence if the majority of voters in a district so desired. One amendment was offered permitting the appropriation of public funds to sectarian schools to the extent of taxes paid by those members supporting the public schools. This was defeated primarily on the grounds that this would fragment and destroy the public school system, since it would not have a broad base of support and every denomination would demand equal rights.

This section generated great controversy in the 1920 Convention because of the *Dunn* decision, discussed in the *Explanation* below, which permitted the state to pay to sectarian institutions at least part of the cost of caring for dependent children committed to them by the state. The majority report of the Committee on Education reported out Section 3 as it now stands. Immediately, a minority report, the exact text of which is not available, was offered in substitution for the majority report. The gist of the minority report was to prohibit absolutely any payments to sectarian institutions, in effect reversing the *Dunn* decision, on the grounds that the rationale of that case went considerably beyond the limited problem of caring for dependent children and could permit a "partnership" of church and state in dealing with any social problem, including public education. Several supporters of the majority report pointed out that the rejected sentence, noted in the *History* of Section 1 above, amending Section 1 had been intended to remedy the problem of caring for dependent children, and for that reason no change was suggested for Section 3. In view of the Convention's rejection of the amendment to Section 1 (see *History* of Section 1, *supra*, p. 399), they now supported the minority report. Initial debate focussed on the issue that the state could not afford to build its own institutions for dependent children, and there would be no care for them if the minority report were approved. Much concern was voiced that the charities would no longer accept the children if state aid were not forthcoming and that large numbers would be turned out into the streets. In answer to this, one delegate pointed out that of the total cost of supporting the children, including both private donations and state aid, only 12 per cent consisted of state aid to sectarian institutions. The chief problem was in Cook County, where there were large numbers of dependent children; but downstate counties feared that their dependent children were so few in number that a public institution could not be economically supported. Eventually the debate shifted to the broader implications of the *Dunn* decision, namely, that it could be used to justify payments to general sectarian schools so long as the payments did not exceed the costs of educating the students. Ultimately there was a compromise and as the section was finally included in the proposed Constitution, it provided that public money could not be paid to sectarian institutions when public institutions were available, and that when it was paid it was not to exceed the cost of maintenance and care of persons "temporarily committed" to such institutions. Since this was obviously not limited to schools, but included, for example, hospitals, it was placed in the Revenue Article and Section 3 was eliminated from the Education Article altogether.

Explanation

This section of the Constitution, which relates to the authority of the state and other public corporations, is often construed in conjunction with Article II, Section 3, of the 1870 Constitution and the First Amendment to the Federal Constitution, which relate to individual religious freedom. Although only a few cases have arisen under this section, they have been exceptionally controversial. Basically, this section poses two issues: one, the problem of religion in the public schools, and the other, the problem of aid to parochial schools. Involved in both of these problems may be two questions: (1) to what extent is the challenged state activity an "establishment" of religion; (2) to what extent is the challenged state activity a violation of the personal freedom to worship. Although the terms of this section would seem to be primarily directed at the first question, often the two issues are inextricably intermingled.

The problem of religion in the public schools is most acutely demonstrated in the so-called "released-time" cases. Various forms of "released-time" programs had became popular across the United States. The essence of the plan involved the release of students from school attendance for one hour a week in order to attend religious education classes. In the first program to be litigated in Illinois, students who had their parent's permission were excused from classes for one hour per week to attend classes in religious instruction conducted in their own churches. The Illinois Supreme Court held that this violated neither Article II, Section 3, nor Article VIII, Section 3, because there was no discrimination among sects, attendance at the classes was not compulsory, and no significant public support in terms of monetary aid was shown. (People *ex rel.* Latimer v. Board of Educ., 394 Ill. 228 (1946).) A year later the Court upheld another released-time program whose features differed somewhat from the *Latimer* case. In this case, the religious education teachers from the various denominations were "approved" by the Superintendent of Schools and came into the school building at the end of the school day once a week to conduct the religious education classes in the school classrooms. Attendance was taken and reported during these classes. Those students desiring not to participate were assigned to a study hall. The Illinois Supreme Court held that this was not a violation of Article VIII, Section 3, because no significant public expenditures were shown. The United States Supreme Court reversed this decision on the ground that the program constituted an "establishment" of religion in violation of the First and Fourteenth Amendments of the Constitution of the United States. The establishment was found, not in any monetary support given to religion, but in the use of public facilities coupled with the coercive use of state power (in this case, the compulsory school attendance laws) to encourage cooperation with the religious enterprise. (People *ex rel.* McCollum v. Board of Education, 396 Ill. 14 (1947), *rev'd*, 333 U.S. 203 (1948).) A few years later, the United States Supreme Court sustained a released-time program whose features were essentially the same as those of the *Latimer* case, the religious instruction taking place away from the school premises. (Zorach v. Clauson, 343 U.S. 306 (1952).) Critics of the *Mc-Collum* decision viewed *Zorach* as a victory for their cause and a reversal of the Court's position. Probably this is unjustified optimism, although from a certain viewpoint the cases are difficult to reconcile. While attendance was taken in the *Zorach* program, the Court specifically noted that truancy laws did not appear to be enforced, and it clearly indicated that it believed the "coercive" features of *McCollum* were not present. Perhaps the *McCollum* case is more analogous to the school prayer cases (School Dist. v. Schempp, 374 U.S. 203 (1963); Engel v. Vitale, 370 U.S.

421 (1962).) In those two cases, the religious exercises were conducted on school property, they had the specific sponsorship of school authorities, and students not specifically requesting to be excused were required to participate. It should be noted here that the Illinois courts were considerably ahead of the federal Supreme Court on the issue of public school prayers and bible reading, having decided in 1910 that these practices were unconstitutional on essentially the same grounds as the later federal decisions. (People *ex rel.* Ring v. Board of Educ., 245 Ill. 334 (1910).)

The problem of public aid to parochial schools has prompted little litigation in Illinois, except for one significant series of decisions around 1917. The subject has, however, been receiving renewed national attention and the United States Supreme Court recently rendered its first decision on the subject in more than 20 years (Board of Educ. v. Allen, 392 U.S. 236 (1968)); so it seems reasonable to assume that Illinois may again face the issue soon. Despite what would appear at first reading to be a clear constitutional prohibition against public aid to sectarian schools in Section 3 of Article VIII, a decision of the Illinois Supreme Court has cast considerable doubt on this issue. That case has already been referred to in the *History* of this Section, but its importance justifies a more detailed analysis. The case is *Dunn v. Chicago Industrial School for Girls* (280 Ill. 613 (1917).) Pursuant to statute, the juvenile court of Cook County was authorized to commit dependent girls to various private institutions for their care. Many of these institutions were owned and run by religious organizations. The state paid $15 per month to these institutions for the support of each girl. In a taxpayer's suit to prevent the payment of this support, it was shown that the amount was considerably less than the actual cost of maintenance for the girls and that the cost for similar care in a state institution amounted to about $30. The Court upheld the validity of this arrangement on the ground that there was no "aid" to an institution where the value of services rendered exceeded the payment which was received for them. The decision was followed in a series of similar cases. This principle could well be applied to justify payments to parochial schools in proportion to the value of the educational services they perform in the community, and indeed at least one commentator has suggested that such a standard is completely consistent with the Federal Constitution. (Choper, "The Establishment Clause and Aid to Parochial Schools," 56 Cal. L. Rev. 260, 286-87 (1968).) The federal cases on this issue have not as yet drawn any definitive lines as to what, if any, may be the permissible extent of public support of parochial schools under the First Amendment. Two kinds of "indirect" aid have been sustained. In the first case on this issue the

United States Supreme Court held that free public bus transportation for children attending parochial schools was not unconstitutional because the statute had a general public purpose (safety of school children) and the "aid," if any, was for the benefit of the child, not the school (Everson v. Board of Educ., 330 U.S. 1 (1947)); Illinois provides such transportation. In a recent case, the Court upheld the furnishing of free textbooks at public expense to parochial school children as well as public school children. Again the Court pointed out that the aid was for a public purpose, namely the general education of the children, and the aid went to the child, not the school. (Board of Educ. v. Allen, 392 U.S. 236 (1968).) In this case, the Court specifically pointed out that the parochial schools perform a real secular service under state supervision in providing a general education to their students. It is certainly conceivable that this decision may clear the way, at least as far as federal constitutional impediments are concerned, for more aid to parochial schools than has been customary in the past, although the states are not bound by such holdings in interpreting their own constitutional provisions.

The latest experiment in Illinois in the field of cooperation between the public and parochial schools has been the "shared-time" arrangements which are becoming more common throughout the state. Under these arrangements, students take about half of their courses in the public school (usually so-called "nonvalue" courses such as mathematics, science, physical education) and the remainder (literature, humanities and social sciences) in the parochial schools. This system has been challenged only once in the upper courts of Illinois where it was upheld without any significant discussion of the constitutional issues. (Morton v. Board of Educ., 69 Ill. 2d 38 (1966).)

Comparative Analysis

Approximately 13 states have provisions similar to those of Illinois. The Model State Constitution has no similar provision, although the prohibition in its bill of rights against an "establishment" of religion would be applicable to some of the problems in the same way as the First Amendment of the Constitution of the United States has been applied through the Fourteenth Amendment.

Comment

This section of the Constitution will have to be given careful attention in conjunction with Article II, Section 3, and the First Amendment of the United States Constitution. At least three approaches can be taken. It could be eliminated altogether, leaving the restrictions of the First and Fourteenth Amendments of the Constitution of the United States applicable to needed restraints upon the legislature. If it is decided that the state as a matter of constitutional policy should impose, or have the authority to impose, more restrictive standards upon state aid to sectarian institutions than are imposed by the Federal Constitution, then some redrafting of this provision would be necessary, in the light of the *Dunn* decision. Or the provision may be retained in its present form. It seems that as a practical matter this last option would have no different legal effect from the first unless the Illinois Supreme Court were to modify the position taken in *Dunn*. As noted in other portions of this study, it is not thought to be desirable state constitutional policy to "abdicate" a field simply because of a holding that a comparable provision in the federal Bill of Rights has been held applicable to the states through incorporation into the Fourteenth Amendment of the Constitution of the United States. (See *Introductory and Preliminary Comment,* Art. II, *supra,* pp. 5-8.)

School Officers not to be Interested in School Contracts

Sec. 4. No teacher, State, county, township, or district school officer shall be interested in the sale, proceeds or profits of any book, apparatus or furniture, used or to be used, in any school in this State, with which such officer or teacher may be connected, under such penalties as may be provided by the General Assembly.

History

This section dates from 1870. When the section was first considered in Committee of the Whole, the debate, with the exception of the remarks of one delegate, was of the sort one would expect to find in a legislative session — namely, an extended exposition of the evil to be legislated against, argument as to the breadth of the proposed wording, and consideration of amendatory language to provide appropriate exceptions. One delegate addressed himself to the question of whether the section belonged in the Constitution, argued that the legislature could properly cope with the evil complained of, and moved to strike the section. His motion carried. But when the Convention voted on whether to confirm the Committee's action, a tie resulted and the proposed deletion was lost. On a subsequent vote to adopt the section following an amendment that added the words "with which such officer or teacher may be connected," the result was 33 to 19, with 31 not voting.

The proposed 1922 Constitution pulled together the conflict-of-interest provisions of Sections 15 and 25 of Article IV (*supra,* pp. 176 and 230) and, in part, this Section 4. The proposed section in the article on Public Servants stated that no officer should be beneficially interested in any contract with the government entity of which he was an officer. Notwithstanding this blanket prohibition, the proposed Constitution retained a section in the Education Article reading: "No school officer shall be financially

interested in any contract concerning any school with which he is connected or in any book, apparatus or furniture used in such school."

Explanation

No questions concerning this section appear to have arisen. The implementing statute is Section 22-5 of the School Code. (Ill. Rev. Stat.
ch. 122, § 22-5 (1967).) That section substantially repeats the constitutional language and provides penalties of fines from $25 to $500 and
jail terms from one to 12 months.

Comparative Analysis

Two states, Mississippi and South Dakota, have a comparable provision. West Virginia also has a comparable provision but adds a proviso
that allows an author to receive his royalties. (The words "with which
such officer or teacher may be connected" were added in the 1870 Convention to cover this problem in part. Under these words, a teacher could
receive royalties from books used in any school except the one in which
he taught.) The Model State Constitution has no comparable provision.

Comment

Prohibitions against conflicts of interest are legislative matters. As noted
elsewhere (see *Comment* on Sec. 15 of Art. IV, *supra,* pp. 177-8.), conflict-
of-interest coverage may be appropriate in the case of legislators, but if
that is done, it seems likely that the legislature will enact legislation
covering conflicts of interest of other government officials.

County Superintendent of Schools

Sec. 5.   There may be a County Superintendent of Schools in each county
whose qualifications, powers, duties, compensation, and time and manner of
election, and term of office, shall be prescribed by law.

History

This section dates from 1870. The section as originally proposed by
the Committee on Education said that there "shall be a county superintendent" and contained no words concerning election of superintendents. When the Convention first undertook consideration of the
section in the Committee of the Whole, the words concerning election
had been included. During the debate there was a proposal to change
"shall" to "may" in the interest of flexibility, but instead the Committee
voted to strike the section. In the Convention proper, the decision was to
retain the section but to substitute the word "may" for "shall." This
compromise solution was designed to preserve flexibility. On the one
hand, it would be constitutionally possible to dispense with county superintendents and on the other hand, there would be no danger that someone would argue that such an office could not be created by law. This

danger arose because the article on Counties created a number of offices (see Sec. 8 of Art. X, *infra,* p. 504.), and under the ancient maxim *expressio unius est exclusio alterius*—the expression of one is the exclusion of another— it could be argued that the legislature could not create a county office in addition to those listed in that article.

In the proposed 1922 Constitution, this section was moved to the county part of the proposed article on Local Governments. One important substantive change was made by adding the words "or appointment" after the word "election."

Explanation

There have been several cases interpreting this section, but all have been relatively obvious confirmations of the meaning of the words used. There has apparently been some question as to whether "manner of election" would permit the legislature to provide that the superintendent of schools be elected by the county board. There has been no definite answer to the question.

Comparative Analysis

There appear to be approximately 15 states besides Illinois that have constitutional references to county school superintendents. Half a dozen states or so mandate an elected superintendent. Some states authorize abolition of the office either by the legislature or by local vote. Several states provide flexibility in determining whether superintendents shall be elected or appointed. In general, the states with county superitendents provide that compensation, powers and duties, and qualifications shall be set by law. In most of these states, the term is fixed at either two or four years. The Model State Constitution has no comparable provision.

Comment

The tentative decision by the 1870 Convention not to make the county superintendent of schools a constitutional office at all was probably the better one. The compromise of permitting the legislature to create or not to create the office was the next-best solution. The additional flexibility of permitting appointment in place of election as proposed in 1922 was also an improvement. In reviewing the matter now, the position of county school superintendent should be considered as a part of the problems of county government and not of education.

Article IX

REVENUE

Taxation of Property — Occupations — Privileges

Sec. 1. The General Assembly shall provide such revenue as may be needful, by levying a tax, by valuation, so that every person and corporation shall pay a tax in proportion to the value of his, her, or its property—such value to be ascertained by some person or persons, to be elected or appointed in such manner as the General Assembly shall direct, and not otherwise; but the General Assembly shall have power to tax peddlers, auctioneers, brokers, hawkers, merchants, commission merchants, showmen, jugglers, inn-keepers, grocery-keepers, liquor-dealers, toll bridges, ferries, insurance, telegraph and express interests or business, vendors of patents, and persons or corporations owning or using franchises and privileges, in such manner as it shall, from time to time, direct by general law, uniform as to the class upon which it operates.

Enlarging Tax Base

Sec 2. The specification of the objects and subjects of taxation shall not deprive the General Assembly of the power to require other subjects to be taxed, in such manner as may be consistent with the principles of taxation fixed in this Constitution.

History

In the 1818 Constitution there was no Revenue Article, but Article VIII (the bill of rights), Section 20, provided: "[T]he mode of levying a tax shall be by valuation, so that every person shall pay a tax in proportion to the value of the property he or she has in his or her possession." It was very early decided that this provision did not impose any substantial restriction on the legislative power to tax. In *Sawyer v. City of Alton* (4 Ill. 126 (1841)), the city sued to collect a penalty of $3.00 for failure to perform required road labor. Sawyer argued that this was a tax and violated the 1818 Constitution because it was levied per capita and not by valuation. The Supreme Court agreed that it was a tax, but held that this constitutional provision merely prescribed the method of levying *property* taxes and did not prohibit the legislature from imposing other kinds of taxes. The next significant case under this provision was *Rhinehart v. Schuyler* (7 Ill. 473 (1845)). In this case the Court held that lands could be classified for purposes of tax

413

levies — *i.e.,* taxed at different rates — and that the General Assembly could assess land by statute without actual visitation of the property in question. The *Rhinehart* case is of particular importance because the revenue provisions of the 1848 Constitution were specifically intended to reverse both grounds of this decision.

Sections 2 and 6 of the 1848 Constitution are the direct antecedents of Sections 1 and 2 of the 1870 Constitution. (Because of the close relationship between Sections 1 and 2, they are considered together.) Since the state was in very bad financial circumstances in 1848, the matter of revenue consumed a great deal of the Convention's attention. It seems clear that the primary intent of Section 2 (which corresponds almost exactly to the present Section 1) was to prohibit the classification of property for the purposes of the property tax and to require individual assessment of specific parcels. Whether any further restrictions of the taxing power were intended is not clear. The author of the most thorough historical review of these provisions suggests that no other restrictions were contemplated. (*See* Lucas, "Nonproperty Taxes Under the Illinois Constitution," 25 U. of Chi. L. Rev. 63, 72-74 (1957).) Judicial decisions on the meaning of these sections, when examined with reference to their particular facts, are not particularly instructive. Some of the looser language used in these cases suggested that the property tax was intended as the primary system of taxation with only limited exceptions permitted. However, since there were no serious legislative experiments with other modes of taxation, such observations were gratuitous and the nature of any such restrictions, speculative.

When the Constitutional Convention of 1870 was called, the state's financial condition was relatively satisfactory and there was practically no pressure upon the Convention for reform of the 1848 general revenue sections. These sections were reported out of committee with the observation that they could not be improved upon. There was remarkably little debate over them. What debate there was indicated a difference of opinion among the delegates as to whether the last clause of Section 1 was intended to operate as an exclusive limitation. The substance of the debate did nothing to clarify the issue or to define any particular understanding of the Convention. The one substantial change in the section — the addition of the last phrase "by general law, uniform as to the class upon which it operates" — was not even commented upon. Presumably, the addition was simply another manifestation of the strong feelings of the delegates against special legislation. (See *History* of Art. IV, Sec. 22, *supra,* pp. 204-5.)

Since 1900, six unsuccessful attempts have been made to amend Sections 1 and 2. The most comprehensive revision was the entirely new

Article in the proposed 1922 Constitution. Among the more significant changes proposed, insofar as they related to Sections 1 and 2 of the 1870 Constitution, were the following: (1) all property, real and personal, was to remain unclassified, with the exception that forest lands could be classified; (2) in lieu of a property tax on intangibles, a uniform tax on income from intangibles could be levied; (3) in place of the long list of business activities, and other subjects designated in Section 1, it was simply provided that taxes could be imposed on "privileges, franchises, and occupations, uniform as to class"; (4) a graduated income tax was authorized, with the highest rate not to exceed three times the lowest; (5) an exemption from the property tax of up to $500 value for household goods was authorized.

Explanation

General Constitutional Principles of Taxation in Illinois. A broad outline of the constitutional structure of the tax system in Illinois may be helpful in understanding the more specific problems that have arisen. It is generally understood that Article IX, Section 1, limits the state to three kinds of taxes: (1) a general property tax; (2) occupation taxes; (3) franchise and privilege taxes. The broader language of Section 2 does not ameliorate this limitation, but merely permits the imposition of occupation, franchise and privilege taxes on subjects in addition to those listed in Section 1. It should be noted that the restrictions imposed on the state apply equally to the taxing powers of county and municipal corporations, since they are but subdivisions of the state. (See *Addendum, infra,* p. 435, for recent Supreme Court of Illinois decision overruling dicta establishing above three classifications as a limit on state's taxing power.)

The general property tax is governed by two important principles — the uniformity and *ad valorem* requirements. The Constitution requires that "every person or corporation shall pay a tax in proportion to the value of his, her or its property." This means that *all* property must be taxed, if any is taxed, and no property may be exempted (with certain very limited exceptions discussed in Section 3 but not relevant here). "Property" as used in this section means real and personal, tangible and intangible. The *ad valorem* principle is really just a specific application of the uniformity principle. The tax must be levied "by valuation." This means that all property must be taxed at the same rates. Property may not be classified for the purpose of taxing it at different rates nor, what amounts to the same thing, may it be assessed at different ratios when applying a tax rate. Thus, if urban residential real estate is taxed on the basis of 50 per cent of its full cash value, then rural agricultural real estate, as well as industrial real estate, must be similarly taxed; and correspondingly, all personal property, tangible and intangible, such as household goods, stocks and bonds, must be taxed at 50 per cent of full cash value. In the light of common knowledge of assessment practices in Illinois, the mere statement of these principles reveals the extent to which the general property tax, as a revenue measure in Illinois, epitomizes the avoidance of, rather than the compliance with, the Constitution's mandates.

In contrast to the rigid uniformity rules governing the property tax, occupation, franchise and privilege taxes must only be "uniform as to the class upon which they operate." Since classification of these taxes is expressly permitted by the Constitution, it is obvious that the requirement of uniformity means something quite different from its meaning in conjunction with the property tax. Essentially, it means that where the legislature defines and levies one of these taxes upon a class, the definition must be reasonable in relation to the purpose of the tax and in terms of the membership comprising the class; the class as defined must include only those properly within it and not exclude those reasonably a part of it. The legislature has broad discretionary powers in this respect, including the power to prescribe subclassifications, exclusions, exemptions, graduated rates, and the like, so long as they are reasonable. Occupation and franchise taxes are traditional methods of imposing taxes on business and commerce. A franchise tax is normally imposed as a condition to legally carrying on certain kinds of business, and may be imposed for purposes of regulation or revenue, or both. On the other hand, an occupation tax is imposed merely as an incident of doing business and is primarily a revenue measure. The use of privilege taxes as significant sources of revenue is a currently expanding fiscal development. What constitutes a taxable privilege is a complex and elastic concept, the limits of which have not yet been defined.

The General Property Tax. More than half of all revenue produced by taxation in Illinois comes from the property tax, nearly all of which goes to local governments. Approximately 90 per cent of local revenue is derived from the property tax. No general state property tax has been levied since 1932. Although it has been estimated that from one-half to two-thirds of all property in the state is in the form of personal property of various kinds, only 20 per cent of property tax revenue is produced by personal property taxes, of which only 3 per cent is from intangibles, and 80 per cent by real estate taxes. These percentages are, of course, variable annual approximations, but it is apparent, as an accurate generality, that the property tax in Illinois is the single most important revenue-producing tax in the state, that it is practically the sole support of local governments, and that it is primarily a real estate tax.

The administration of the property tax depends on two factors — valid tax levies and proper assessment procedures. The requirements for tax levies are dealt with in later sections of this Article. The procedures for assessment of property are dependent to a large extent upon this section. Initially, it is to be noted that assessed valuation is "to be ascertained by some person or persons, to be elected or appointed in such manner as the General Assembly shall direct, and not otherwise." The administrative machinery of the assessment procedure has not of itself been a subject of much constitutional controversy. The constitutional standards are very general and the authority of the legislature quite broad. (A notable exception to this generalization is the case of *Giebelhausen v. Daley* (407 Ill. 25 (1950)), which held that a newly prescribed method of selecting local assessors was an unconstitutional delegation of legislative power to the executive and an encroachment on the authority of local governments.) However, since the great bulk of constitutional decisions on the property tax arise out of a controversy over a particular assessment, it is necessary to understand the mechanics of assessment and the requirements for a successful challenge. Nearly all property assessments are made by local assessors, usually at the township level, selected in various ways. These local assessments are subject to supervision and review by administrative agencies at the county level. There are a few exceptions to this practice, the principal one relating to the property (both real and personal) of railroads and certain other corporations which is assessed at the state level by the Department of Revenue, with the appropriate proportion of property value being certified to county assessing offices for purposes of local taxes.

Since 1947, administrative machinery has existed at the state level designed to facilitate and assure uniformity of assessment practices among the counties throughout the state. The Department of Revenue is required to investigate the assessed valuations of each county, and if it finds that property is being assessed at less than its fair cash value, it must assign a "multiplier" to the county which when applied will raise the valuations to 100 per cent. For example, if a county assesses property at 50 per cent of its cash value, a multiplier of 2.0 will raise the assessment to 100 percent. There are several reasons for such a system. Most important, the Constitution requires statewide uniformity, but, as the cases discussed below reveal, the courts are unable to fashion suitable remedies, and administrative machinery is necessary to obtain the objective. This is particularly critical in the case of taxing authorities (close to 1,000 in number) whose boundaries cross county lines. Secondly, many state grant-in-aid programs, for schools, welfare and the like, are tied to the aggregate assessed valuation of the taxable property in the recipient governmental units. Third, the legal tax rate and indebtedness limits of local governments are expressed in terms of assessed property valuation. Finally, since some property is assessed by state procedures at 100 per cent of value, in order for this property to bear no more than its fair share of the tax burden, property must be assessed locally at 100 per cent. It should be emphasized that this state-wide administrative procedure equalizes assessments only among counties and does not affect uniformity within a county. This latter problem must be dealt with by appropriate procedures at the local level.

Since the great majority of cases establishing the constitutional principles of property taxation arise from challenges to individual assessments, it may be helpful to summarize the basic requirements for judicial review of property assessment. First of all, Illinois courts will review an assessment only when it is made fraudulently. If the assessment is erroneous because of an error of judgment or difference of opinion as to value, the only remedy is administrative. Secondly, even if a fraudulent assessment is made, a taxpayer must first exhaust his administrative remedies before a court will hear his challenge. Finally, even a fraudulent assessment, through undervaluation or omission of one kind of property, will not invalidate assessments on other kinds of property. The rationale for this last principle is that dereliction of duty of an individual tax assessor should not render the whole tax void and make it impossible to collect any taxes. (Bistor v. McDonough, 348 Ill. 624 (1932).)

It was the emergence of this last rule that finally led to the almost complete collapse of the collection of personal property taxes in Illinois, although the difficulties of collecting a flat *ad valorem* tax on personalty, especially intangibles, were apparent earlier. In one of the first cases on this issue, it was proved that the stock and securities of the protesting bank were valued at 75 per cent of their fair cash value, while real estate in that district was assessed at only 43 per cent. The Supreme Court held that this variation violated the constitutional requirement of uniformity and, further, that the magnitude of the discrepancy was itself proof of fraud. However, the Court held that the proper remedy was not to reduce the bank's assessment, but to compel the assessor to assess other property at the proper value; it said that the former remedy would be unfair to other taxpayers who had paid taxes on a high valuation without protest. (First Nat'l Bank v. Holmes, 246 Ill. 362 (1910).) While this case concerned overvaluation of intangible property in relation to real estate, the converse situation soon became a primary difficulty in collection of the property tax. Intangible property, although it accounts for well over half of the wealth of the state, contributes little to tax revenues. The inequity of this situation became especially severe during the economic depression of the late 1920's and early 1930's, and real estate owners sought relief in the courts by alleging that the omission of personal property from the tax rolls was unconstitutional. Although this challenge was indisputable, the courts were unable to fashion an effective remedy. Reluctant to jeopardize the whole tax structure, the Court reinforced its *First National Bank* rule by holding that owners of real property could not challenge the validity of the assessment and taxation of real property on the grounds that personal property was omitted or undervalued on the assessment rolls. (Koester v. McDonough, 351 Ill. 492 (1933).) In another attempt to secure relief, taxpayers of Cook County sought to mandamus the assessor to add omitted property to the tax rolls and to value it properly. The petition contained very detailed allegations of property which was not being taxed, such as seats on the Board of Trade, bank deposits, estates in the probate court, boats in the harbor, and the like. Nevertheless, the Court held that in order for mandamus to issue, the petitioner must show the name and residence of the owner of the property, its situs, character, and all facts necessary to prove that it was taxable. (People *ex rel.* Koester v. Board of Review, 351 Ill. 301 (1932).) Since as a practical matter these facts cannot be obtained by a private party, mandamus is an illusory remedy. Thus, although classification of property is unconstitutional, de facto classification established deliberately, even arbitrarily, by an assessor is immune from judicial attack.

There has been more success in achieving the uniformity standard in the assessment of real estate than with all property generally. Grossly excessive valuation of real property in relationship to assessments on like property has been sufficient in some cases to prove constructive fraud, and the courts will provide relief. More importantly, it was early established that the constitutional requirement of uniformity takes priority over legislative requirements of full valuation Thus, if property values are debased for purposes of assessment in violation of legislative standards, they must still be uniformly debased; and a taxpayer may challenge his assessment as being fraudulent when it is considerably in excess of the ratio of assessed value of other property in the district, even though it is not actual full value. (People *ex rel.* McDonough v. Illinois Cent. R.R., 355 Ill. 605 (1934); People *ex rel.* Wangelin v. Wiggins Ferry Co., 357 Ill. 173 (1934); People's Gas Light & Coke Co. v. Stuckart, 286 Ill. 164 (1918).) Despite these rules, which are often effective in providing relief from unequal real estate assessments, the principle of uniformity continues to create difficult problems. For one thing, the rule discussed above, that owners of one class of property cannot challenge the assessment of another class, seems to have worked its way into real estate taxation. In a case where plaintiffs urged the invalidity of assessments of 35 per cent of value on their agricultural property because urban property was assessed at only 25 per cent of value, the Court invoked this rule in denying relief. (Tuttle v. Bell, 377 Ill. 510 (1941).) Although not entirely clear, the decision appears to be based primarily on the premise that disparate classes of property are involved and that a differential in assessment of one class provides no basis for equitable relief of the "unassessed" class. The decision in no way suggests a departure from or modification of the rules theretofore determined.

A more critical problem, which led to the present system of state equalization of assessments, is that of inequality of assessment practices among counties. The unfairness of these practices was demonstrated in a case where three municipal taxing districts overlapped both Lake and Cook Counties. Property in Cook County was assessed at 75 per cent of value, whereas property in Lake County was assessed at 21 per cent. Thus, property owners in Cook County paid almost three times as large a tax as property owners in Lake County for identical services and under identical tax rates. The Court conceded this to be clear violation of the Constitution, but held that it was powerless to grant a remedy. The solution, if any, was legislative. (People *ex rel*. Schlaeger v. Allyn, 393 Ill. 154 (1946).) This situation and this decision led to the passage in 1947 of the so-called "Butler Bills," which required full value assessment and state equalization of assessments among counties. While these provisions contributed much toward achieving uniformity in real estate taxation (they have no effect on personalty), they have not been entirely successful, as the recent so-called "railroad strike" cases showed. In these cases, the railroads proved that their property was assessed by the state at 100 per cent of full value; proportionate values were certified to the counties for extension of taxes. However, local property, even after application of the equalizing multiplier, was still assessed at only 50 per cent of full value. The railroads were granted relief. (People *ex rel*. Kohorst v. Gulf & O. R.R., 22 Ill. 2d 104 (1961); People *ex rel*. Hillison v. Chicago, B. & Q. R.R., 22 Ill. 2d 88 (1961).) However, instead of ordering debasement of the assessment on railroad property, the Supreme Court held that the proper remedy was reimbursement of taxes paid in excess of what would have been extended had local property been assessed at full value. The application of this remedy is very complex and will require litigation in every county for the railroads to receive relief.

Bachrach v. Nelson — The Structure of Nonproperty Taxes in Illinois. It is impossible to understand the structure of nonproperty taxes in Illinois without considering the pervasive influence of *Bachrach v. Nelson,* (349

Ill. 579 (1932)), for this case has governed either directly or indirectly all subsequent tax legislation and litigation up to the present. (Note: The entire remaining analysis under this *Explanation* has been substantially affected by a recent decision of the Illinois Supreme Court sustaining the new Illinois Income Tax Act. See *Addendum, infra,* p. 435.) With the advent of the economic depression, the property tax ceased to be a viable source of state revenue, although it has continued to provide most local revenue. In searching for new means of support for the state government, the legislature passed a graduated income tax. This tax was immediately challenged under the limitations imposed by Section 1. The state contended that the tax was constitutional under the broader terms of Section 2. With the possible exception of the inheritance tax, this was the first time that the Court had been confronted with the validity of a tax which was not clearly of a kind specified in Section 1. Thus there were two significant new questions to be answered: (1) what were the exact limitations, if any, imposed on the taxing power by Sections 1 and 2? And (2) was the income tax within these limitations?

The answer to the first question was by far the most crucial for the future development of tax policy in Illinois. The Court held that Section 1 limited the legislature to three kinds of taxes — property, occupation, and franchise and privilege. The language of Section 2 that "other subjects or objects" might be taxed was held to mean, not that other kinds of taxes might be imposed, but only that the list of permissible occupation, franchise and privilege taxes in Section 1 was not exclusive. While nearly all other aspects of the *Bachrach* opinion have been subject to considerable erosion, both judicial and academic, this particular formula seems to have become accepted, if not necessarily welcomed, dogma. In reaching this conclusion, the Court considered a large amount of historical evidence which it said showed that the drafters of the Constitution intended the property tax to be mandatory and the main source of support for the government. The exceptions were limited and of a merely supplementary nature. Of course, this aspect of the Court's opinion is of no validity today, as there has been no state property tax since 1932, and the principal source of state tax revenue, since 1933, has been the retailers' occupation tax.

In considering whether the income tax met the formula required by Section 1, the Court did not have the benefit of a complete analysis by the state. Since the state's position had been that the tax was *sui generis* and hence justified under Section 2, it had not argued that the tax could be sustained under Section 1 as a privilege tax. Thus the Court did not consider this possibility. But it did conclude that an income tax was a property tax and that its graduated features violated the uniformity requirement.

The Court is open to criticism on a number of counts, several of which may be briefly noted. For one thing, the historical analysis was not entirely accurate, for there was a failure to perceive that alternatives to the property tax had not been seriously contemplated as constitutional issues in 1870; thus no real decision either for or against them had then been made. And of course, the conclusion that the property tax was mandatory as the primary source of revenue is decisively rejected today. Finally, the conclusion that an income tax is a property tax was unsound then and would certainly not be accepted in theory today. It was directly contrary to an earlier decision of the Court which held, in interpreting a lease, that an income tax was not a property tax for which a lessee could be held liable (Young v. Illinois Athletic Club, 310 Ill. 75 (1923)), and the principal case on which the Court relied (Pollock v. Farmer's Loan & Trust Co., 157 U.S. 429 (1895)) has since been in effect overruled. (See New York ex rel. Cohn v. Graves, 300 U.S. 308 (1937).) The fact that the Court explicitly failed to consider whether an income tax was a privilege tax, coupled with the presently expanding concept of what constitutes a taxable privilege, makes it an open question whether the Illinois Court would today validate an income tax; some constitutional law scholars believe it would. (For a complete discussion of this issue, see Cohn, "Constitutional Limitations on Income Taxation in Illinois," 1961 U. Ill. L. F. 586.) Perhaps it should also be noted that a corporate franchise tax measured by net income, as distinguished from a personal income tax, could probably be enacted under present provisions. (See Young, "Constitutional Problems," in Report of the Commission on Revenue 354, 380-82 (1963).)

Franchise, Occupation and Privilege Taxes. In considering these kinds of tax, it is important to keep in mind the distinction between the subject of a tax and the measure of the tax. The statutory definition of the subject of a tax, if the uniformity requirement of the last clause of Section 1 is met, will determine its constitutionality. For example, what is popularly known in Illinois as the "sales tax" is actually defined in the statute as a tax "on the business of selling tangible personal property at retail." So defined, it is clearly an occupation tax. At the time the statute was passed, it was believed that a tax on the sales transaction itself would not fall within the property-occupation-privilege formula required by the Constitution. The peculiar consequences of structuring the tax as an occupation tax will be discussed below. On the other hand, however, if the subject of the tax is constitutional, the measure of the tax — *i.e.,* the formula by which it is imposed — will not affect its constitutionality, so long as it is reasonable. With regard to occupation and privilege taxes, the test of reasonableness does not come so much from the uniformity clause of Article IX, Section 1, as from the due process clauses of the state and federal constitutions. (*See* Bode v. Barrett, 412 Ill. 204 (1952). *Compare* Fiorito v. Jones, 39 Ill. 2d 531 (1968).) Thus it was soon decided that an occupation tax on brokers could be imposed as a flat fee, even though it was objected that by failing to take into account the size of the business, the tax was not uniform as to property (Banta v. City of Chicago, 172 Ill. 204 (1898)); that graduated features of privilege taxes were valid (Metropolis Theater Co. v. City of Chicago, 246 Ill. 20 (1910); Kochersperger v. Drake, 167 Ill. 122 (1897)); and that even a combination of the two methods was proper (McGrath v. City of Chicago, 309 Ill. 515 (1923)).

In imposing an occupation tax, the crucial constitutional issue in terms of the uniformity requirement is the definition of the occupation to be taxed—which businesses are to be included and which are to be excluded? The case most clearly setting out standards for such a decision is *Peoples Gas Light & Coke Company v. City of Chicago* (9 Ill. 2d 348 (1956)). In this case, the city, under an appropriate state statute, passed ordinances taxing gas companies and electric companies at the rate of 5 per cent of gross receipts. The electric company was allowed a credit equal to its payment of street use taxes of 4 per cent of gross receipts so that the effective occupation tax was 1 per cent. The gas utility did not pay street use tax, so its rate was 5 per cent. The gas company challenged the tax on the ground that the tax violated the uniformity requirement of Section 1, because the distinction between the utility companies, which compete for much of the same business, was discriminatory. In rejecting this contention, the Court discussed three standards to be used in determining reasonableness. (1) Are the businesses competitive? Here it pointed out that there were many cases in which the utilities were not—*e.g.*, illumination. (2) Even if they are competitive, that is not conclusive if there are basic differences in the means of production, distribution and use of products—an obvious situation here. (3) Finally, classification of even similar objects may be justified under special circumstances. Here the different street taxes paid by the utilities were such a circumstance. The standards have not been referred to in all cases, but they are helpful in understanding the uniformity requirement.

Since 1933, the principal source of revenue for the state government has been the retailers' occupation tax (Ill. Rev. Stat. ch. 120, §§ 440-452 (1967)) and a small group of related taxes. The history of this legislation is revealing of the constitutional gauntlet through which tax legislation in Illinois must run. As originally passed, the tax was imposed on those "engaged in the business of selling tangible personal property at retail" and exempted from its coverage retailers of motor fuel (because that was already taxed) and agricultural producers who also sold their produce at retail. This act was held unconstitutional because the exemptions violated the uniformity requirement. (Winter v. Barrett, 352 Ill. 441 (1933).) The legislation was quickly passed again without the offending exemptions, and was sustained by the Court. (Reif v. Barrett, 355 Ill. 104 (1933).) In this case, special note was taken of the fact that the tax was measured by gross receipts of the business; it was contended that this was an income tax and hence invalid under the rule of *Bachrach v. Nelson*. But the Court held that the tax was in fact an occupation tax, that retail selling was a taxable occupation, and that gross receipts was a reasonable measure.

In 1961, the Retailers' Occupation Tax Act was amended to exempt retail sales to units of the state government and to charitable organizations. These exemptions were challenged as violating the uniformity provision because they made the amount of the tax dependent on the character of the purchaser rather than the occupation. Such a challenge would appear to be well founded on the basis of the *Winter* decision discussed above. But the Court held that this objection was not sufficient to invalidate the exemption. The purpose of the exemption was to mitigate certain economic effects of the tax—*i.e.*, that it was passed on to the purchasers—and as such the classification was not arbitrary or capricious. However, although the statute exempted sales to the state government, it did not provide a comparable exemption for sales to the federal government, and this difference was held to be discriminatory since there were no rational distinctions between them; therefore the state exemption was not allowed. With regard to the exemptions to charitable institutions, a substantial difference between governmental organizations, such as the public schools, and charitable organizations, such as private schools, was found in the ability of governments to tax in order to meet their budgets. Therefore the charitable exemptions were valid. (People *ex rel.* Holland Coal Co. v. Isaacs, 22 Ill. 2d 477 (1961).)

Since the "sales tax" was formulated as an occupation tax on the business of selling at retail, large amounts of personal property transfers at retail escaped taxation because they were made by businesses which were primarily of a service nature. For example, businesses which serviced automobiles and television sets were held not to be in the business of selling at retail, and therefore the incidental transfer of such items as tubes, batteries, and carburetors was not taxed as a sale at retail. In an effort to include these transfers in the tax, the General Assembly amended the Retailers' Occupation Tax Act by adding the following provision: "Persons who engage in the business of repairing, remodeling or reconditioning tangible personal property for others by adding or incorporating therein other tangible personal property for use or consumption shall be deemed to be engaged in the business of selling tangible personal property at retail within the meaning of this Act . . . ." The measure of the tax was the value of the personal property so transferred. The tax was challenged by a number of businesses primarily engaged in repair work. While both the plaintiffs and the Court conceded that these businesses and transactions could be taxed under a proper statute, it was held that the amendment violated the uniformity requirement because it attempted to include within a class persons not reasonably a part thereof. (Central Television Serv., Inc. v. Isaacs, 27 Ill. 2d 420 (1963).)

In direct response to this case, the General Assembly in 1963 passed the Service Occupation Tax Act. (*See* Ill. Rev. Stat. ch. 120, §§ 439,101—439,121 (1967), for present provisions.) The tax was on "persons engaged in the business of making sales of service" and taxed transfers of personal property in those occupations measured by the cost of the property to the serviceman. Under this statute, the transfer of ink, newsprint, paper, etc., by "job printers" (*e.g.,* for letterheads, advertising brochures, etc.) was taxable, but transfers of the same property "for the primary purpose of conveying news" were exempted. This was held to be valid classification, since even though the performance of the service might be the same, the finished products were for essentially different purposes. (Klein v. Hulman, 34 Ill. 2d 343 (1966).)

It is difficult to distill any consistent set of principles from these cases. The *Winter* case sets out a very strict rule of classification in not permitting exemptions from the defined class to be subjected to an occupation tax. But the exemptions which were permitted in the *Holland Coal Company* case and *Klein v. Hulman* were not significantly different from those invalidated in the *Winter* case. One might simply conclude that these later cases had in effect overruled the restrictive interpretation of *Winter* were it not for the fact that *Winter* was one of the cases relied upon in invalidating the first attempt to tax retail transfers in service occupations. That attempt, while admittedly a departure from customary drafting techniques, could hardly be said to have been capricious. Since the sales in question were indisputably retail transactions, it is not at all clear why it is arbitrary to classify the sellers as being in the business of selling at retail, even if they were engaged in another kind of business as well. The fact that these very transactions were made validly taxable by means of another statute suggests that there was nothing essentially unreasonable about the legislative action. It also suggests the difficulties inherent in structuring a sensible tax system under existing and uncertain constitutional standards.

It may be seriously questioned whether the uniformity principle in Article IX performs any useful function with regard to occupation and privilege taxes. It might appear that its main effect has been to serve as another impediment to a rational tax structure. In the cases discussed above, the legislative actions were based on plausible and reasonable assumptions. In the *Peoples Gas Light & Coke Company* case (9 Ill. 2d 348 (1956)), the effort was actually to equalize tax burdens. In the various attempts to formulate a "sales tax" under the artificial strictures of the property-occupation-privilege tax formula, care was being taken not to impose undue hardships—*e.g.,* double taxation in the case of motor fuel—while reaching transactions which should be legitimately taxed. In the one case in which the legislature could be said to have acted unreasonably—in discriminating between the state and federal governments—the same result could have been reached on other grounds, namely the due process clauses of the state and federal constitutions. (*See* United States v. Department of Revenue, 191 F. Supp. 723 (N.D. Ill. 1961).)

This last point is well illustrated in *Fiorito v. Jones* (39 Ill. 2d 531 (1968)). In 1967, the General Assembly passed a series of amendments which significantly altered the nature of the Service Occupation Tax Act. Although the tax still purported to be taxing retail transfers, instead of applying to all persons who engaged in "sales of service," it was applied to four restricted service categories; and instead of being measured by the value of the property transferred, it was measured by the gross receipts of the business. The Court concluded that there was no rational basis for this particular scheme. If the intent of the tax was really to reach the property transfers, which were analogous to the transfers taxed by the retailers' occupation tax, then the gross receipts measure was totally inappropriate because receipts from property sales were a very small amount of the gross receipts of these service businesses. On the other hand, if the purpose of the tax was to tax the value of services performed by these businesses, which was what the gross receipts measure suggested, then to discriminate among services to be taxed on the basis of whether an incidental transfer of personal property was involved was arguably unreasonable. The important point of emphasis in this decision is that, while the conclusion seems to be justified, it was founded on the due process clauses as well as the more particular uniformity requirement of Section 1. Thus, in the rare case in which the legislature does act arbitrarily, the Constitution can provide satisfactory protection without the uncertain and ambiguous hazards of the uniformity clause.

Privilege taxes comprise the third category of taxes which can constitutionally be imposed in Illinois. What constitutes a taxable privilege is critical to current revenue policy in Illinois, since "privilege" is the most expansive and ambiguous of the tax classifications designated in Section 1 of Article IX. Considering the date when this provision was included in the section (1848) and the context in which it was used, one could safely conclude that the privilege tax was intended in its classic sense as defined in these words — "[a] tax on the privilege of carrying on a business for which a license or franchise is required." (*See* Black's Law Dictionary 1360 (4th ed. rev. 1968).) However, the concept of a taxable privilege has been substantially expanded from its connotation of a commercial undertaking licensed by the state. The first significant development was the passage of the inheritance tax. Under this statute, each person who inherited all or part of a decedent's estate paid a tax according to the value of the inheritance; the tax was classified into six classes according to the relationship of the successor to the decedent, and different flat tax rates were imposed on each class. It was contended that this tax was a property tax — *i.e.*, a tax on the estate — and the graduated rates violated the uniformity required of a property tax. The Court held that the tax was not on the property itself, but on the right of succession to the property, a right which was created and controlled exclusively by the legislature. Such a right could be taxed as a privilege and, as the classifications were reasonable, the uniformity requirement was not violated. (Kochersperger v. Drake, 167 Ill. 122 (1897).)

The next significant decision came ten years later when the City of Chicago imposed a wheel tax on vehicles using the city streets. It was contended that the use of the public streets was a common right enjoyed by everyone, not a special privilege which could be bestowed or withheld by the legislature, and hence was not a proper subject of taxation. The Court disposed of this contention on two grounds. First, it held that even if this was not a taxable privilege, it was a subject or object of taxation which could be permitted under Section 2. In view of the restrictive interpretation of the taxing power which was thereafter adopted in the *Bachrach* case, this exceedingly liberal position must be discounted. The Court also held that since the construction and control of the public streets rested entirely with the legislature, a tax could be imposed on those who used this public benefit. (Harder's Fireproof Storage & Van Co. v. Chicago, 235 Ill. 58 (1908).) In 1931, the State Motor Fuel Tax was sustained against the challenge that it, combined with the vehicle license tax, constituted double taxation on the same privilege, on the grounds that the combination of the two taxes did not exceed a reasonable charge for the privilege of using the highways. The license tax was measured by the weight and capacity of the vehicle, while the fuel tax was measured by actual use of the vehicle. (People v. Deep Rock Oil Corp., 343 Ill. 388 (1931).)

The concept of taxable privilege has been most substantially expanded with the recent development of "use taxes." Use taxes are designed to prevent the avoidance of the retailers' occupation tax which occurs when personal property is purchased out of state and hence is not subject to that tax. The first use tax in Illinois was enacted in 1951, the statute imposing a tax on "the privilege of using cigarettes in this state." (See Ill. Rev. Stat. ch. 120, §§ 453.31-453.67 (1967).) This tax was equal to the cigarette "sales" tax which was framed as an occupation tax "on the business of distributing cigarettes in this State." To the extent that a dealer paid the occupation tax he was excused from paying the use tax, so that the effect of the tax was to reach only out-of-state purchasers. This tax was challenged in Johnson v. Halpin (413 Ill. 257 (1952)) on two grounds: (1) the use of cigarettes was not a right which derived exclusively from the authority of the state (as was the right to inherit property) nor was it a benefit conferred by the state (as was the use of the public highways) and therefore it was not a taxable privilege; and (2) no reasonable distinction could be drawn between persons who used cigarettes purchased within the state and those who used cigarettes purchased outside the state, and since the use tax fell only on the latter it violated the uniformity requirement. On the first issue, the Court could have premised its decision that use of cigarettes was a taxable privilege on a prior case regulating tobacco content which had said that the legislature could prohibit the use of cigarettes. However, the Court, after extensive analysis of the Illinois cases, defined taxable privilege as follows:

"[T]he concept of 'privilege' with reference to the taxing power has not been limited in Illinois...to conduct previously authorized by the legislature, or which the legislature could entirely abolish, or to benefits conferred by the State.... [A] taxable privilege may involve lawful rights and conduct enjoyed without previous legal authority, but over which the legislature has some power of control or classification." (Johnson v. Halpin, 413 Ill. 257, 270 (1952).)

While the exact limits of "some power of control or classification" are not yet certain, it is clear that there is considerable room for legislative action in this area. As to the second contention, non-uniformity of classification, the Court held that even though the use tax fell primarily on out-of-state purchasers, the offsetting provisions of the Cigarette Tax Act had the effect of distributing the tax burden uniformly. It is important to note here that two separate taxes — the privilege tax on cigarette use and the occupation tax on cigarette distributors — were combined to meet the uniformity requirement of the Constitution, rather than each tax having to meet that test individually.

The success of the cigarette use tax prompted the legislature to adopt the same device to prevent avoidance of the retailers' occupation tax in a significant segment of retail sales — automobile purchases out of state. The Motor Vehicle Use Tax Act was passed in 1953. The tax was imposed only on out-of-state purchases of automobiles, the amount of the tax was equal to the retailers' occupation tax, and proof of payment was required before the vehicle could be licensed. In the inevitable constitutional challenge which followed (People ex rel. Schoon v. Carpentier, 2 Ill. 2d 468 (1954)), the state sought to justify the tax on the ground that the tax was complementary to the retailers' occupation tax, just as the cigarette use tax was complementary to the cigarette distributors' occupation tax, and should be sustained on the authority of *Johnson v. Halpin.* However, the Supreme Court held that the tax was unconstitutional because it violated the uniformity requirement in three ways. First of all, the tax depended on the tacit assumption that Illinois car dealers would pass on the retailers' occupation tax to the customer in the purchase price, and would in fact remit the tax although no proof of this payment was required. The Court said this assumption was speculative and "wholly without legal sanction." Presumably it was warranted in the cigarette case because tax stamps were required to be affixed to the packages. (It must be pointed out that the very same assumption was the justification for the exemption of charitable purchases from the retailers' occupation tax which was permitted in the *Holland Coal Company* case discussed above.) Secondly, the tax was not uniformly applied to users, since if the retailers' occupation tax were repealed, in-state purchasers would not have to pay a tax while out-of-state purchasers would. This was not true in the cigarette case because the use tax applied to all purchases but was abated to the extent that the retailers' occupation tax was paid. Finally, the two acts were not coordinated to assure that one or the other tax would be paid. An in-state purchaser would not be prevented from getting a license if the occupation tax were not paid.

Following the failure of this act, the legislature attempted to prevent the erosion of the retailers' occupation tax base by enacting a comprehensive use tax drafted to avoid the objections in the *Schoon* case. (*See* Ill. Rev. Stat. ch. 120, §§ 439.1-439.22 (1967).) This tax was levied on "the privilege of using in this state tangible personal property purchased at retail," and applied to all retail purchases. The tax was at the same rate as the retailers' occupation tax and was basically coextensive with that act. The tax was collected on in-state purchases by the retailer, but to the extent of the occupation tax remitted, he retained the use tax. On out-of-state purchases, the out-of-state retailer could be licensed to collect and remit the tax; if he were not, the purchaser was required to remit it. The tax was upheld in *Turner v. Wright* (11 Ill. 2d 161 (1957)), a case which has very significant implications for the concept of privilege taxes in Illinois, the scope of Section 2, and the meaning of the uniformity requirement with respect to non-property taxes.

The first challenge was that using personal property was not a taxable privilege. Had the Court held squarely that such a subject was a tax-able privilege, it would have been tantamount to saying that an ordinary right or legal activity — such as the right to earn income — was a taxable privilege. However, the Court declined to base its ruling quite so broadly and instead held that a tax which was supplementary to an admittedly valid tax — in this case, the retailers' occupation tax — was constitutional under Section 2 of Article IX. To support this conclusion, the Court cited the cigarette use tax and an old case which had approved the application of the inheritance tax to *inter vivos* gifts in contempla-tion of death. (*In re* Estate of Benton, 234 Ill. 366 (1908); it probably should be noted that this case did not in fact involve a supplementary tax, such as a gift tax, but turned on what property could constitu-tionally be included in the estate for purposes of the inheritance tax.) The fundamental significance of this holding is that for the first time the Court read Section 2 as being broad enough to permit a form of tax which did not fit the property-occupation-privilege formula of Sec-tion 1. As the dissent points out, the basic proposition of *Schoon v. Carpentier* was that any tax, allegedly supplementary or not, had to meet the constitutional requirements of a basic tax permitted by Section 1. The Court completely ignored this case. It would not require too much effort to find other kinds of taxes which might be similarly justi-fied. For example, it could be argued that a tax on income from in-tangible property was supplementary to the general property tax.

Plaintiffs tried to avoid this justification for the tax by arguing that the use tax was not an actual supplementary tax, either in form or in its effect on the tax base. This argument was supported by three points: (1) the form of the tax was not complementary in that it was imposed, not alone on out-of-state purchases not reached by the retailers' occu-pation tax, but on domestic transactions as well; (2) the set-off provisions were an unconstitutional commutation of state taxes in violation of Sections 6 and 7 of Article IX; and (3) the tax bases were not identical because the use tax was collected on the basis of "selling price," includ-ing the value of trade-ins or other credits, while the retailers' occupation tax was collected on "gross receipts," which was defined by a 1955 amendment to exclude the value of trade-ins. The first two points were met by the answer that this had to be viewed as an integrated system by which only one tax was intended to reach the treasury. The Court observed, "it may be cumbersome, but it is not unconstitutional." (One cannot resist remarking that it is cumbersome because of the restrictions imposed by the *Schoon* case.) The last point was answered by nullifying, in effect, the 1955 amendment. The example was used of a $3,000 car purchased in part with a $1,000 trade-in; the retailers' occupation tax, which excluded the value of trade-ins, would be $50, while the use tax on selling price would be $75. Since the retailer was excused from paying the use tax only to the extent of the occupation tax, he would be required to remit $50 occupation tax plus $25 use tax. Thus, there was no discrimination between purchasers. But it seems impossible to avoid the point of the dissent that such a device has the effect of the "supplementary" use tax actually increasing the base of the primary occupation tax.

The final challenge to the use tax was that it violated the uniformity requirement because the exemptions were arbitrary and discriminated between purchasers of personal property. For purposes of the retailers' occupation tax, certain occupations were held to be more of a service than retail selling and were thus exempt — *e.g.*, a tailor selling tailor-made suits. These exemptions were carried over to the use tax. The Court admitted that considered as a use tax per se, such distinctions made no sense (a tailor-made suit is just as usable as a ready-made suit), but this flaw would not invalidate the tax because of its supplementary nature. It was held that such a classification attack should be directed at the main statute, not the supplementary one. This is a highly debatable holding. The plaintiff was subject to the use tax because he was an out-of-state purchaser; but he was not subject to the occupation tax because he was not a retailer. Consequently, he had no standing to challenge the classification scheme of the retailers' occupation tax. Therefore, even if his objection were valid, as the Court seems tacitly to concede, he had no remedy. This position is reminiscent of the Court's foreclosure of any effective remedy for the omission of personal property from the tax rolls. It may well be that the Constitution (as well as judicial decisions) substantially hampers legislative efforts to devise a rational tax scheme. It is an unfortunate consequence that the Court is virtually forced into strained and awkward avoidances of what appear to be valid constitutional challenges.

The uniformity requirement has caused as much confusion in the area of privilege taxes as it has with occupation taxes. In the case of the use tax, in the first hearing of *Turner v. Wright*, the Supreme

Court held the tax unconstitutional because of the classification scheme before reversing itself and sustaining the tax. As has been noted, that decision is itself unsatisfactory in several respects and is particularly difficult to reconcile with the standards of *Schoon v. Carpentier,* involving the motor vehicle use tax. In neither case was the legislature acting arbitrarily; it was merely trying to equalize the tax burden. The failure of the motor vehicle use tax did not result in any lessening of the tax burden but merely caused the enactment of an even more comprehensive tax. Thus the conclusion may be drawn that the uniformity rule, rather than providing a viable standard by which to formulate equitable tax legislation, actually serves as a somewhat crude weapon to impede tax reform.

Comparative Analysis

It is difficult to make exact comparisons of revenue articles among state constitutions, since these are probably the most variable provisions of all, and because judicial construction of these articles is critical. However, some very rough generalizations can be made. The following information is from the Illinois Legislative Council Research Department Publication 134, *Constitutional Mandates for Uniformity of Taxation* (1959). Although the information is ten years old, and there have been a few state constitutional changes in the interim, it is believed that the basic information is still adequate to give an overall perspective. (Another helpful source of comparative material is Young, "Constitutional Problems," in Report of the Commission on Revenue 354, 416-36 (1963), which analyzes the provisions of 14 states selected for geographical distribution and industrial development.)

On the issue of classification of real property, the states appear to be about evenly divided between those whose constitutions require uniform taxation of realty and those which permit some form of classification. Twenty-four states require uniformity, Illinois being included in this group. Four states permit a very limited classification, usually in the form of special treatment for forest and mineral lands, and small-homestead exemptions. Twenty-two states permit reasonable classification, although it appears that this power has not been used to any great extent.

As to personal property, the situation is quite different. Only Arkansas appears to be as rigid as Illinois in requiring the uniform taxation of personal property. Nineteen states allow a limited form of classification, primarily on intangibles, automobiles, and small amounts of household goods. Twenty-nine states permit general classification.

Constitutional mandates on the subject of non-property taxes vary considerably. About one-fourth to one-third of the states have a general rule of uniformity within classes specifically applicable to taxation. In the remaining states, general rules of classification are governed only by the due process clauses. However, there are numerous specific rules applicable to individual cases. For example, Ohio's Constitution specifically exempts food from the sales tax.

Since the issue of the income tax is particularly important in Illinois, it may be relevant to review the other state provisions in this area. The following summary is taken from Advisory Commission on Intergovernmental Relations, *Federal-State Coordination of Personal Income Taxes* 154-161 (1965). It should be pointed out that these provisions vary considerably from state to state in their details, and only a general overview is presented here. In 1965, thirty-four states levied personal income taxes. Of these, 20 state constitutions contained specific authority for such a levy; 14 contained no reference to an income tax. Thirty of these taxes were graduated, while only four were flat rate. Of the remaining 16 states which levied no income tax, 11 of them probably could, including four which have specific authority. In three states, including Illinois, authority for an income tax is debatable (see *Addendum,* infra p. 435, for change re Illinois status); and in two, Florida and Tennessee, an income tax is specifically prohibited.

The Model State Constitution has an exceptionally brief article on finance, containing only the following requirements: (1) that no state debt may be contracted except that authorized by law for specific objects; (2) that the governor must annually submit to the legislature a budget and an appropriation bill; (3) that no obligations may be incurred nor money withdrawn from the treasury except as authorized by law; and (4) that all expenditures, including salaries, shall be matters of public record. (See also *Comparative Analysis* of Art. IV, Sec. 18, *supra*, pp. 191-3.) The commentary accompanying the finance article of the Model State Constitution is reproduced here because of its relevance to the overall problem of constitutional revenue principles. Serious consideration should be given to the reasons expressed for avoiding constitutional restrictions on the revenue powers.

The *Model State Constitution* is based upon confidence in the system of representative democracy. The finance article reflects these beliefs by leaving to the legislature and the governor, the people's elected leaders, broad responsibility for the conduct of the state's fiscal affairs with ample power to adjust needs to the rapid changes characteristic of modern times.

Ideally, some authorities believe, a state constitution should be silent on matters of taxation and finance, thus giving the legislature and the governor complete freedom to develop fiscal policies to meet current and emerging requirements.... [T]he complex and lengthy fiscal articles found in many state constitutions...obviously are barriers to responsible government.

Despite elaborate constitutional limitations upon the legislature designed to insure fiscal prudence, state revenues, expenditures, and outstanding debt have grown enormously since World War II....Legislatures have been resourceful in circumventing tax and debt limitations. (Model State Constitution 91.)

Comment

The central problem confronting the Convention with respect to the necessary reform of the Revenue Article has been well stated by Professor Cohn:

Revenue reform has been impaled upon the horns of a policy and legal dilemma. On the one hand, the rigidity of the uniformity and ad valorem principles as applied to tangible and intangible personal property is almost uniformly recognized as the major obstacle to an equitable tax system. On the other hand, a relaxation of these principles to authorize classification of property for tax purposes risks the danger of permitting the levy of a graduated income tax, a prospect which is viewed with abhorrence in many quarters. Underlying these alternatives is the deeper issue of the appropriate scope and content of the taxing power generally.... (Cohn, "Constitutional Limitations on Income Taxation in Illinois," 1961 U. Ill. L. F. 586, 588.)

Of course, it is the fundamental task of the Convention to frame the constitutional principles by which legislative policies are to be formulated. It is critical to the successful completion of this task that basic, long-term constitutional decisions do not become enmeshed in and obscured by more immediate political problems. Illinois has already experienced serious problems arising from detailed and rigid constitutional standards. The lessons of this experience should be seriously considered by the Convention as it formulates constitutional revenue policies.

Some states have placed no direct limits on the taxing power of the legislature. (Of course, there are many indirect constitutional limits, the principal one being the due process clause.) The only requirement in the Alaska and Hawaii constitutions is that any tax imposed must be for a public purpose. The Vermont constitution has contained only one limitation on the taxing power since its adoption in 1793; it must appear that the pulic benefit is greater than it would be if the money were not collected. Connecticut has no reference to taxation in its constitution. Other examples could perhaps be found, but they are admittedly few in number.

If such an approach is rejected and a more restricted taxing power is desired, then the following problems must be considered. With respect to property taxes, it appears that there should be some provision for reasonable classification of tangible personal property. This could be by grant of general classification powers, or by giving special attention to household goods, motor vehicles, business and industrial equipment, inventories, and agricultural property. Intangible personal property should also be given special treatment, perhaps by tax alternatives other than of an *ad valorem* tax. Classification of real property is a more difficult problem, but one which will have to be faced in view of the de facto classification which already exists, particularly in Cook County. Also, some attention should probably be given to assessment and equalization standards. With respect to non-property taxes, the retention of the artificial formula of occupation and privilege and franchise taxes would appear to be questionable, since it would continue to force a strained and cumbersome tax structure. Also, the uniformity clause specifically applicable to non-property taxes could well be eliminated, since it has had little effective meaning and application. The reasonableness of such taxes would then be tested, as in fact is now the case, by due process principles.

Addendum

On August 14, 1969, after this document went to press, the Supreme Court of Illinois issued an opinion sustaining the newly enacted state income tax against constitutional objections. The Court overruled its decision in *Bachrach v. Nelson* (349 Ill. 579 (1932)) that an income tax was a property tax; and it also overruled the highly influential dictum in that case that the legislature was limited to three kinds of taxes — property, occupation, and franchise and privilege taxes. It sustained the income tax on the basis of Section 2 of Article IX. (Thorpe v. Mahin, — Ill. — (1969).)

It is not possible in this analysis to assess fully the implications of this decision. It is reasonably clear that it may open up new sources of revenue through the broadened concept of "privilege" and the more liberal interpretation of the authority in Section 2. The validation of different income tax rates for individuals and corporations is further indication of a relaxation of both the privilege and uniformity requirements.

The decision will apparently have no effect on clearly identifiable property taxes. Classification of property, whether real or personal, tangible or intangible, will remain beyond the authorizations of the Constitution; the *ad valorem* and uniformity requirements will still be applicable.

Tax Exemptions

Sec. 3. The property of the state, counties, and other municipal corporations, both real and personal, and such other property as may be used exclusively for agricultural and horticultural societies, for school, religious, cemetery and charitable purposes, may be exempted from taxation; but such exemption shall be only by general law. In the assessment of real estate encumbered by public easement, any depreciation occasioned by such easement may be deducted in the valuation of such property.

History

This section derives from Article IX, Section 3, of the 1848 Constitution which provided that "the property of the state and counties, both real and personal, and such other property as the general assembly may deem necessary for school, religious, and charitable purposes, may be exempt from taxation." Two important changes were made in this provision. The first required that any exemptions were to be only by general law. This was designed to correct the common abuse of including exemptions in special charters. Various schools, libraries, and religious groups would receive special corporate charters which, among other provisions, exempted their property from taxation. The United States Supreme Court held that such charters were contracts between the state and the organization which could not be modified subsequently by the state to remove the exemption, because that would constitute an impairment of the obligation of contracts in violation of Article I, Section 10, of the Federal Constitution. (See the discussion in Northwestern Univ. v. Hanberg, 237 Ill. 185 (1908).) Requiring exemptions to be granted only by general law would permit subsequent modification if that was deemed desirable. The other significant change was to substitute "used exclusively" for exempt purposes for "necessary." Although Supreme Court interpretations under the prior language had tended to be restrictive, it was felt that the limited nature of the exemption should be made explicit. Property used for business purposes should be subject to taxation, even though the income it produced was used for exempt purposes and could be deemed "necessary" for those purposes.

The new exemption of cemeteries was not commented on. The inclusion of the new exemption for "agricultural and horticultural societies" was primarily intended to exempt county fair grounds. There was considerable opposition to this exemption by members who felt that these operations were mainly for profit. The last sentence was included as a compromise over an attempted exemption of highways. Since in many instances the public highways are merely easements over private property, they are included in the assessments of that property. It became clear upon debate that any actual exemption would pose impossible survey and assessment problems, so the compromise was a concession to farmers who felt that their property containing highways was being overassessed. Since the highways are often as much of a benefit as a detriment to the farms themselves, the problem is mainly one of accurate assessment. This provision has caused no litigation.

There was considerable debate in the 1870 Convention over the propriety of exempting property used for religious purposes from taxation. Many members felt that "churches should bear their fair share" of the property tax burden for the benefits and protection they received from the community, while others felt that there should be no "tax on religion." This is very much a contemporary concern and the issue is explored in depth in the *Explanation* below.

This section received only minor changes in the 1922 Convention proposal. Parsonages and societies of war veterans were added to the exempt list, as well as household furniture to the extent of $500. The great part of the debate over exemptions was concerned with what should be done with the income of exempt properties from endowments in the event that an income tax was passed as authorized by the proposed Constitution. Some members argued that since property used for exempt purposes was exempt, so should be income used for exempt purposes. Opponents of such an exemption had several bases of opposition. First, there were members who opposed any exemptions at all, except for publicly owned property. There were others who approved the limited exemption of property directly used for exempt purposes but disapproved any extension of the exemption. Some members feared that exempting income could logically lead to exempting property producing that income which was not presently exempt — for example, school-owned property leased to businesses, where rents were applied to school purposes. Others simply felt that the burdens of taxation should be shared by these institutions to some extent. In the end, exemption from the income tax was not allowed.

Explanation

This section operates as a limitation on the power of the General Assembly to exempt property from taxation. The general principle established by Section 1 is that all property is to be taxed and the only exceptions to that rule are those permitted by this section. It is not self-executing, as are many similar provisions in other state constitutions, but requires legislation for any of the exemptions to take effect. A number of statutes providing exemptions from the property tax have been declared unconstitutional because the exemptions were not permitted by this section. Some of these attempted exemptions were for purposes not specifically mentioned in the section. (*See* Consolidated Coal Co. v. Miller, 236 Ill. 149 (1908) (coal companies and other corporations); International College of Surgeons v. Brenza, 8 Ill. 2d 141 (1956) ("philosophical" societies).) In other cases, the legislature was merely giving a broader interpretation to the constitutional language than the Court thought warranted. (People *ex rel.* Thompson v. First Congregational Church, 232 Ill. 158 (1907) (exemption of parsonages unconstitutional because such a use not for religious purposes); People

ex rel. McCullough v. Deutsche Gemeinde, etc., 249 Ill. 132 (1911)
(exemption of all school property not used for profit unconstitutional
because exemption limited to property actually in use as school premises). *See also* People *ex rel.* Lloyd v. University of Ill., 357 Ill. 369
(1934) (discussed below). For the current statutory exemptions, see
Ill. Rev. Stat. ch. 120, §§ 499-500, 22 (1967).)

For purposes of exemption from property taxes, this section establishes two general divisions of property. First is property which is
publicly owned. While the legislature has authority to exempt such
property solely on the basis of its ownership, and has in a few cases
exercised this authority, it has usually been more restrictive in granting
exemptions and has required use for a public purpose, as well as public
ownership, in order to qualify for exemption. The other authorized
division of exempt property is that which is used for certain specified
purposes, in which case it may be exempt regardless of its ownership.
Here again, the legislature has not always been as liberal as the Constitution permits. At one time, property used for religious purposes
had to be owned by a religious organization in order to be exempt;
this restriction was removed in 1909. (People *ex rel.* Bracher v. Salvation Army, 305 Ill. 545 (1922).)

In deciding whether specific property may be exempted, the Supreme
Court has adopted the general principle that it is the primary use to
which the property is put which determines its exempt status, not an
incidental or "secondary" use. (People *ex rel.* Fix v. Trustees of Nw.
College, 322 Ill. 120 (1926).) While this principle is somewhat more
liberal than the "exclusive use" required by the Constitution, still the
Court in general has been strict in validating exemptions, often denying
them in cases where other states have allowed them under comparable
constitutional language. Where property can be physically separated
into exempt and nonexempt uses, it may be partially taxed and partially
exempt. (City of Mattoon v. Graham, 386 Ill. 180 (1944).) Whether or
not the property produces income is irrelevant to the determination of
its exempt status. The fact that its revenue is applied exclusively to
exempt purposes will not confer exemption on property not itself used
for such purposes; nor will the fact that exempt property produces
revenue vitiate its exemption.

It should be noted that this section relates only to general property
taxation and does not authorize the legislature to exempt any property
from special assessments. (South Park Commr's v. Wood, 270 Ill. 263
(1915).)

The Court has developed working definitions of the exempt classes,
the most important of which are discussed below. However, the exemp-

tion of property in nearly all cases depends upon its actual use, which is primarily a factual determination, and the relationship of that use to the definition, which is a matter of judgment not readily controlled by definitive standards. Therefore, many of the "borderline" cases granting or denying exemptions are not easily reconcilable, and it is necessary to keep in mind that these cases cannot always be generalized to other situations.

The largest class of exempt property is that which is owned by the state, counties and other municipal corporations. So far as the statutory exemptions are concerned, this class can be divided into two sub-classes — that which is exempt solely by virtue of ownership and that which is exempt because of public ownership and use for public purposes. A notable example of the first sub-class is park districts, all of whose property is exempt, even if it is located outside municipal limits and is used for nonpark purposes. (People *ex rel.* Curry v. Decatur Park Dist., 27 Ill. 2d 434 (1963).) Property owned by the state is also exempt by the test of ownership, but in this case there has been some difficulty over what constitutes state ownership. The University of Illinois claimed that certain property, which because of its restricted use was not exempt as school property, was exempt as state property by virtue of its ownership by the University as trustee. The Court held that in order for property to be owned by the state for purposes of tax exemption, there must be a complete title free from any legal or equitable interest. In this case, the property was held in trust for the benefit of agriculture students. (People *ex rel.* Olmstead v. University of Ill., 328 Ill. 377 (1927).) Following this decision, the legislature amended the statute to provide that any property of a public educational institution held for educational purposes was property of the state. This amendment was held unconstitutional in a case involving the same property on the grounds that the question of state ownership was a matter of constitutional interpretation. (People *ex rel.* Lloyd v. University of Ill., 357 Ill. 369 (1934).)

In most cases, however, the legislature has required that publicly owned property be used for a public purpose before it is exempt from taxation. In *People* ex rel. *Lawless v. City of Quincy* (395 Ill. 190 (1946)), the Court defined "public purpose" as applied to municipal property. Where the property is located within municipal limits, it is used for a public purpose if it is open to residents of the municipality. If it is located outside the corporate limits, it must be open on equal terms to the public generally. A municipal airport located outside the city limits meets this test; and the fact that a fee is charged for its use does not disqualify it for exemption, since the use does not have to be free. However, where part of the airport property was rented for farming, that part was taxable even though the rents were necessary for airport operations. (City of Lawrenceville v. Maxwell, 6 Ill. 2d 42 (1955).) Property located outside a sanitary district (a drainage channel) has been held not to be exempt from taxation. In this case the property was not rented to private parties and the public had a right of easement over the channel (*i.e.,* boats could run on it). But the purpose of the sanitary district was to provide drainage and sewage treatment for the municipality, and the public outside its limits could not use its property for this puurpose. Therefore, the Court held that the property was not used for a public purpose. (Sanitary Dist. v. Gibbons, 293 Ill. 519 (1920).)

Property used exclusively for school purposes is also exempt from property taxation. For purposes of this section, there is no distinction between public and private schools. (People *ex rel.* Gill v. Trustees of Schools, 364 Ill. 131 (1936).) In this respect, the section should be contrasted with Section 2 of Article VIII. (*Supra,* p. 402). That section applied to school purposes is subject to taxation. (People *ex rel.* Gill v. to 1870, regardless of its use. Under Section 3 of Article IX, the property must be actually used for school purposes. Thus, property owned by a school but leased to business enterprises with the income being applied to school purposes is subject to taxation. (People *ex rel.* Gill v. Trustees of Schools, 364 Ill. 131 (1936).) Furthermore, this case held that so long as title is in the public school trustees, it is not property of the state for that exemption. What constitutes use for school purposes has generated considerable litigation. It has been held that residence halls, dining rooms, club houses and recreational facilities are proper to the function of a university and hence are exempt. The fact that these buildings produce income and are owned by a nonprofit corporation, rather than the educational institution itself, will not remove the exemption. (People *ex rel.* Goodman v. University of Ill. Foundation, 388 Ill. 363 (1944).) On the other hand, fraternity houses owned by the college but not open to the student body generally, the college president's home, and unimproved lots which were part of the general endowment, were held not exempt. (Knox College v. Board of Review, 308 Ill. 160 (1923).)

In the most recent decision involving private schools, the Court denied tax exemption to staff housing facilities, notwithstanding that the property was owned by the colleges and was contiguous to the campus. The basis of denial was that the primary use of the facilities was residential, and the absence of a showing that residence in the facilities was required of faculty and staff because of their professional duties, coupled with the fact that a majority of faculty and staff members resided in private non-college-owned housing of their own selection, precluded holding that a tax-exempt educational status existed for this property. (MacMurray College v. Wright, 38 Ill. 2d 272 (1967).)

Private schools which do not provide a general course of education as that is commonly understood have usually been held not to qualify for exempt status under this section, even though they may qualify for exemption as educational institutions for purposes of the federal income tax and may be recognized for purposes of veteran's education benefits. The stated basis for this rule is that exemption is granted the institution on the premise that it assumes responsibility for education which would otherwise be borne by the taxpayers. (Milward v. Paschen, 16 Ill. 2d 302 (1959) (mortuary school); People *ex rel.* Brenza v. Turnverein Lincoln, 8 Ill. 2d 198 (1956) (physical education school); Coyne Elec. School v. Paschen, 12 Ill. 2d 387 (1957) (electrical school).) However, property of the Association of American Medical Colleges was exempted as being used for public educational purposes, since the association and accredited medical schools conducted numerous activities designed to improve medical education. The Court held that these were educational purposes and the fact that the organization itself did not conduct classes did not affect its exempt status. (Association of Am. Medical Colleges v. Lorenz, 17 Ill. 2d 125 (1959).)

Cases involving exemptions for charitable uses are perhaps the most difficult to reconcile. The exempting statute requires that property be put to a charitable use and be owned by a charitable organization. While the Court has defined both tests, the application of the tests to the cases has not been uniform. A "charitable organization" is one which has no capital and makes no profits but derives its funds mainly from public or private charity and holds them in trust for the objects expressed in the instrument creating the organization. (Methodist Old Peoples Home v. Korzen, 39 Ill. 2d 149 (1968).) A charitable use of property is one which is applied for the benefit of an indefinite number of people, either by "bringing their hearts under the influence of education or religion"; by relieving their bodies from disease, suffering or constraint; by assisting them to establish themselves for life; by erecting or maintaining public buildings or works; or otherwise lessening the burdens of mankind. (Milward v. Paschen, 16 Ill. 2d 302 (1959).) As will be seen, there appear to have been peculiar discrepancies in the application of these tests.

A school of "domestic arts and sciences" taught cooking and sewing to girls. All girls who applied were accepted up to the seating capacity of the school. Those who were able paid tuition for the classes, while others were taught free. There were two other sources of income — donations from the public and a restaurant open to the public which served food cooked by the girls. The school did not make a profit. It was held to be tax exempt as a charitable institution. (School of Domestic Arts & Science v. Carr, 322 Ill. 562 (1926).) On the other hand, a school which conducted physical education, life-saving, and first-aid classes was denied exemption. Funds were derived primarily from membership dues and gifts from members, but anyone who was unable to pay was forgiven the dues and it appeared that only about half of the members actually paid dues. The Court apparently viewed the "school" as primarily a recreation club. (Turnverein "Lincoln" v. Board of Appeals, 358 Ill. 135 (1934).)

An interesting comparison can be made of two cases involving associations of surgeons, one of which was granted and the other denied exemption for its national headquarters building. The American College of Surgeons and the International College of Surgeons were both nonprofit corporations whose purpose was to advance the art of surgery. Both derived their income primarily from membership dues. Both maintained a library and museum, although it does not appear whether International's was open to the public. So far as the Court's opinions are concerned, the chief difference seems to be that the educational activities of the American College are set out in considerable detail, whereas the International College was merely said to have held "meetings." American was granted an exemption while International was denied one. (American College of Surgeons v. Korzen, 36 Ill. 2d 340 (1967); International College of Surgeons v. Brenza, 8 Ill. 2d 141 (1956).) Another interesting comparison is suggested by cases where a local chapter house of the D.A.R. which contained a "public rest room" was exempted, while the headquarters of the Rotary clubs was not. (People ex rel. Greer v. Thomas Walters Chapter D.A.R., 311 Ill. 304 (1924); Rotary Int'l v. Paschen, 14 Ill. 2d 480 (1958). See also Kiwanis Int'l v. Lorenz, 23 Ill. 2d 141 (1961).)

Recently tax exemption as a charity was denied to a church-affiliated old people's home. (Methodist Old Peoples Home v. Korzen, 39 Ill. 2d 149 (1968).) The statute designating exempt charitable uses had been expressly amended in 1967 to include "old people's home," but the Court held that the statute was not intended to deviate from the constitutional requirement that the property be used exclusively for charitable purposes. Reasserting its frequently stated rule that it is the province of the courts, and not the legislature, to determine whether or not property is used exclusively for charitable purposes within the meaning of this section, the Court denied exemption because of the practice of charging residents substantial fees determined by the type of accommodation, without guaranteeing that an individual resident, who by other rules had to meet certain health and financial requirements prior to admission as a resident, would be permanently cared for by the home. On similar grounds, tax exemption was denied another not-for-profit home for the aged in *People* ex rel. *Norlund v. Association of the Winnebago Home for the Aged* (40 Ill. 2d 91 (1968)).

On occasion the Court has gone considerably beyond its own definitions in granting charitable exemptions. Public housing authorities have been granted exemption as charities (not as publicly owned property), although it is obvious that they are not supported by charitable contributions, nor do they lessen the burdens of government. (Springfield Housing Authority v. Overaker, 390 Ill. 403 (1945).) And an arboretum established by a private trust and open to the public was exempted, the Court saying, "a charitable use may be applied to almost anything that promotes the well-doing and well-being of society." (People *ex rel.* Hellyer v. Morton, 373 Ill. 72, 78 (1940).) However, such broad interpretations are rare.

Special attention should be given to the exemption from taxation of property used for religious purposes. While such exemptions are permitted in all states, as well as exemptions for church income from federal income taxes, serious questions have been raised as to whether they violate the First Amendment of the Federal Constitution prohibiting an "establishment" of religion. Before this problem is explored in depth, the extent of the exemption in Illinois and its distinction from other kinds of exemptions should be examined. By the terms of Section 3, such property must be used exclusively for religious purposes. The Court has held that this relates primarily to church buildings actually used for public worship (People *ex rel.* Bracher v. Salvation Army, 305 Ill. 545 (1922)), and also includes funds used to pay the salaries of ministers and other church officials (Yates v. Board of Review 312 Ill. 367 (1924)). However, it does not apply to parsonages, even when they are supplied rent-free as part of the minister's compensation, because these are used for residential purposes and are indistinguishable from any other residence. (People *ex rel.* Thompson v. First Congregational Church, 232 Ill. 158 (1907).) By analogy, it has been held that a convent for nuns who have renounced all connection with the world is used primarily as a residence and hence is not exempt, even though the property contains a chapel open for public use. (People *ex rel.* Carson v. Muldoon, 306 Ill. 234 (1922).) Particular rules applicable to exemption of religious property vary widely from state to state, with Illinois being among the strictest in granting such exemptions. For example, many states exempt parsonages. (For a comprehensive review of state law in this area, see Van Alstyne, "Tax Exemption of Church Property," 20 Ohio St. L.J. 461 (1959).) The exemption of property used exclusively for religious purposes should be distinguished from the exemption of property used for educational or charitable purposes, such as parochial schools or hospitals, which might incidentally be owned by religious organizations. As noted above, the traditional justification for the latter exemptions is that they perform functions which would otherwise have to be born by the taxpayers, and the fact of ownership has no bearing on the grounds of the exemption. Indeed, to deny such exemptions solely on the basis of religious ownership when they are granted to others might itself be an unconstitutional discrimination. However, this justification clearly cannot be applied to property used for worship and other exclusively religious purposes, because this is not an activity in which the state could engage.

In debating the constitutionality of this exemption, opponents and proponents have managed to agree on only one point, but that is a very fundamental one. Tax exemption in its economic effect is indistinguishable from a direct state subsidy of religion, which is clearly unconstitutional. Taxes of all other taxpayers are raised in the exact amount that churches are exempt, and churches receive indirectly from the state an amount equal to an appropriation of the taxes they would otherwise pay. Even the most recent state court decision upholding the constitutionality of the exemption conceded this point. (Murray v. Comptroller of the Treasury, 241 Md. 383 (1965).) Yet despite this concession, the exemptions have consistently been upheld in the state courts, and for some time the United States Supreme Court refused to review these decisions. (*See* Murray v. Comptroller of Treasury, 241 Md. 385 (1965), *cert. denied,* 385 U.S. 816 (1966); General Fin. Corp. v. Archetto, 93 R.I. 392 (1961), *appeal dismissed,* 369 U.S. 423 (1962); Lundberg v. County of Alameda, 46 Cal. 2d 644 (1956), *appeal dismissed sub nom* Heisey v. County of Alameda, 352 U.S. 921 (1956).) Recently, however, the Court has agreed to take a case involving this issue and a definitive ruling hopefully may be expected within the year. (Walz v. Tax Comm'n, 24 N.Y. 2d 30 (1969), *prob. juris. noted,* 395 U.S. 957 (1969).)

Some proponents of religious exemptions have argued that the exemption is in fact required by the "free exercise" clause of the First Amendment. They assert that to tax church property is to tax the exercise of religion by its members. Support for this position is found in a Supreme Court decision which held that an occupational tax on booksellers could not be applied to Jehovah's Witnesses who sold books and pamphlets as a religious duty. It was held that such a tax violated the Witnesses' exercise of their religious beliefs. (Murdock v. Pennsylvania, 319 U.S. 105 (1943).) The *Murdock* case is not entirely persuasive in the recent instance for two reasons. The ownership of property by an organization is not the exercise of a duty compelled by a religious belief. And there was no issue raised in that case that the law, or exemption from it, constituted a forbidden establishment of religion.

Other proponents of the exemption argue that, while not necessarily required by the Constitution, it is a permissible form of accommodation to the religious needs of the community. Since it is admitted that churches perform many charitable and educational tasks beneficial to the state, it is argued that these functions cannot be entirely separated from the organization itself; and the exemption enables the churches to perform these functions without a partial diversion of their resources to the public treasury. Furthermore, churches contribute to the general welfare of the community by improving the moral climate of the public. The case of *Zorach v. Clauson* (343 U.S. 306 (1952)) discussed in Article VIII, Section 3 (*supra,* p. 406), which approved a form of released-time program for religious education classes, is frequently cited as illustrative of a principle that the state may adjust its own programs to accommodate religious preferences of the citizenry, so long as there is no discrimination among religions. Finally, and this argument is perhaps the strongest of all, the universal practice of the states and Congress since the inception of the Constitution in granting these exemptions is pointed to as evidence that they are not the kind of "establishment" referred to in the First Amendment. (*See* Kauper, "The Constitutionality of Tax Exemptions for Religious Activities," in The Wall Between Church and State (D. Oaks ed. 1963).)

In the face of these various arguments, opponents of the exemption make only one argument for its unconstitutionality, but it is a strong one theoretically. Churches receive all the benefits of organized government, without paying for them as does the general public. Tax exemptions are a substantial subsidy of religion by the state, and subsidies of any or all religions are forbidden by the First Amendment. *Illinois* ex rel. *McCollum v. Board of Education* (333 U.S. 203 (1948)), invalidating released-time programs conducted on school premises, is cited in support of this. Furthermore, the United States Supreme Court in that case based its decision in large part on language from *Everson v. Board of Education* (330 U.S. 1, 15-16 (1947)) which is particularly relevant here: "Neither a state nor the Federal Government can set up a church. Neither can pass laws which aid one religion [or] aid all religions . . . . No tax in any amount, large or small, can be levied to support any religious activities or institutions . . . ." Since the exemptions are indistinguishable, economically, from appropriations, it is argued that they are unconstitutional. (*See* Note, "The First Amendment and Financial Aid to Religion: Limits on the Government's Conduct," 61 NW.U.L. Rev. 777, 787-93 (1966); for similar arguments attacking the constitutionality of federal income tax exemptions, see Korbel, "Do the Federal Income Tax Laws Involve an Establishment of Religion?," 53 A.B.A.J. 1018 (1967).)

No satisfactory conclusion can be drawn on this issue. As a matter of pure logic, the arguments against the exemption are extremely persuasive. On the other hand, the historical evidence strongly indicates that these exemptions are not offensive under the First Amendment. While historical tradition is not decisive on questions of constitutional interpretation, in this case it is unusually explicit.

Comparative Analysis

Exemption provisions vary widely among the states. Ten state constitutions provide that the legislature may grant any exemptions so long as they are by general law. Another 11 states prohibit any exemptions other than those specifically permitted by the constitution. Thirty-five constitutions provide for the exemption of charities, 35 for property used for religious purposes, and 40 for educational institutions. In addition to these common exemptions, there is a long list of special exemptions in a few states. In some of these states, the constitutional exemptions are self-executing, while in others, as in Illinois, legislative action is necessary to make them effective.

The Model State Constitution, in keeping with its policy of allowing the widest possible freedom for legislative action in fiscal affairs, is silent on this subject.

Comment

What action is taken on this section depends in large part upon the Convention's decision on general taxing powers of the legislature. If it is decided to grant the legislature wide discretion in matters of taxing policy, then the need for a special section on exemption is minimal and it could well be dispensed with. On the other hand, if substantial restrictions are placed on the taxing power, and particularly if a uniformity requirement is imposed on property taxation, then it will be necessary to make some provision for exemptions if they are to be allowed. This provision could be in the form of a broad grant of power to allow such exemptions as are reasonable and promote the general welfare, or a more restricted limitation such as the present section. In any event, the last sentence of this section should be dropped, as it does not deal with a problem of constitutional dimensions.

Sale of Real Property for Tax Delinquency

Sec. 4. The General Assembly shall provide, in all cases where it may be necessary to sell real estate for the non-payment of taxes or special assessments, for State, county, municipal, or other purposes, that a return of such unpaid taxes or assessments shall be made to some general officer, of the county, having authority to receive State and county taxes; and there shall be no sale of said property for any of said taxes or assessments but by said officer, upon the order or judgment of some court of record.

History

This section of the Constitution and Section 5, discussed below, replaced Section 4 of the 1848 Constitution. That section contained extremely complex provisions relating to notice and affidavit procedures required in order to obtain tax deeds to property on which taxes were in default. While the requirements of the present Section 4 were new additions to the Constitution, there was no significant debate in the Convention proceedings revealing why the delegates felt it necessary to include them.

This section, together with Section 5, engendered considerable debate in the 1920-22 Convention, which ultimately proposed some significant changes. These changes are discussed below in the *History* of Section 5.

Explanation

This section imposes two limitations on the power of the General Assembly to direct a sale of property for nonpayment of taxes: (1) the sale must be conducted by the county officer in charge of collecting taxes and (2) it must be done only after a judicial proceeding. Except for these limitations, the General Assembly may enact any provisions it thinks desirable to encourage the collection of delinquent taxes. For example, it may authorize penalties for delinquency and provide for the sale of property for nonpayment of such penalties. (Chambers v. People *ex rel.* Fuller, 113 Ill. 509 (1885).)

The requirements of this section, as well as of Section 5, apply only to proceedings in rem against the property for collection of back taxes. They do not apply to executions on property enforcing in personam judgments, even where those judgments are based on delinquent taxes. In order to enforce an in personam judgment for delinquent taxes, the procedures applicable to ordinary judgment enforcement must be followed — *e.g.,* the sale is conducted by the sheriff, not the county collector, and there is a different period of redemption. (Langlois v. People, 212 Ill. 75 (1904).) Perhaps it should be noted that while general property taxes are a personal liability of the owner, special assessments are not. (Craw v. Village of Tolono, 96 Ill. 255 (1880).) Also, while public property is not exempt from special assessment, it cannot be sold for payment of delinquent assessments. The proper remedy in this case is mandamus to compel payment from the treasury. (County of McLean v. City of Bloomington, 106 Ill. 209 (1883).)

The provisions of Section 4 are self-executing and repeal all statutes in conflict. Thus, prior to 1870, sales for delinquent taxes in Chicago were made by the city collector, but following the adoption of the Constitution, a county officer was required to discharge this duty. (Garrick v. Chamberlain, 97 Ill. 620 (1880).) This section requires only that the sale be made by the county collector; the application for a judicial order of foreclosure and sale may be made by any interested taxing authority, such as a municipality. (Village of Downer's Grove v. Glos, 307 Ill. 293 (1923).)

The requirement that a sale of property for nonpayment of taxes can be held only after a court order reflected a very common practice prior to the adoption to the 1870 Constitution, but apparently it was not universal. There is one case suggesting that the 1861 charter of a board of water commissioners authorized sale of property for delinquent assessments in a summary manner. The Supreme Court held that this provision was invalidated by the 1870 Constitution. (Board of Water Comm'rs v. Conkling, 113 Ill. 340 (1885).) The authority of a court to supervise tax sales includes the power to disapprove a sale because of the inadequacy of the price; and a board of county commissioners cannot compromise taxes due so as to bind the court and force approval of the sale. (People v. Schwartz, 397 Ill. 279 (1947).)

The fact that there is a court order for a sale of property for nonpayment of taxes and a subsequent attempt to sell it does not mean that the property will actually be sold to the highest cash bidder. There may be no cash bidders at all, in which case the property is forfeited to the state; or where the cash bids are not sufficient to cover the taxes due, the county may acquire the property under certain circumstances by a noncash bid of the amount of taxes. In either case, there may be a subsequent sale of the land in order to pay the taxes, and the question has arisen whether the subsequent sale must also be under a court order. The Supreme Court held that it is not necessary, so long as there is proper notice of the sale to interested parties. (Keilty v. Chicago Real Estate Co., 25 Ill. 2d 581 (1962); People v. Wrage, 20 Ill. 2d 55 (1960).)

Comparative Analysis

This constitutional requirement is unique to Illinois. Most state constitutions are entirely silent on the subject of sales of property for nonpayment of taxes. Three states expressly permit sales without judicial proceedings, where certain notice requirements are followed.

Comment

While there is nothing fundamentally objectionable about this sec-

tion, it is primarily legislative in nature. There may well be more efficient ways of collecting taxes on delinquent property than requiring
judicial sales, and it might be desirable to permit the legislature more
flexibility. It is doubtful if the provisions of this section merit constitutional status.

Redemption from Tax Sale

Sec. 5. The right of redemption from all sales of real estate for the nonpayment of taxes or special assessments of any character whatever, shall exist
in favor of owners and persons interested in such real estate, for a period of not
less than two years from such sales thereof. And the General Assembly shall
provide by law for reasonable notice to be given to the owners or parties interested, by publication or otherwise, of the fact of the sale of the property for
such taxes or assessments, and when the time of redemption shall expire:
Provided: that occupants shall in all cases be served with personal notice before
the time of redemption expires.

History

As noted in the *History* of Section 4 *(supra,* p. 446), this section replaced
Section 4 of the 1848 Constitution which contained very complicated
notice requirements. Although several unsuccessful attempts were made in
the 1870 Convention to reinstate the former section, there was no substantial debate revealing why one section was preferred over the other. The
major substantive change introduced by this section was the fixing of the
redemption period at not less than two years. Several amendments were
introduced lengthening the period to as much as five years, presumably in
an effort to benefit economically destitute owners who lost their land for
unpaid taxes. These amendments failed because of determined opposition
which pointed out that the longer redemption period would not necessarily benefit the small landholder because the increased interest and
penalties over the longer period of time would result in a greater financial
burden to redeem, and that the longer period would encourage speculators to withhold taxes even more than was already the case and would
also discourage buyers at tax sales who would have an even more difficult
time obtaining a valid title. In both cases, loss of tax revenues would
increase.

The Committee on Revenue of the 1920-22 Convention was concerned
with the problem of delinquent taxes and proposed several substantial
changes in these sections. At that time, there was a large amount of delinquent property on the tax rolls which remained unsold for a number
of reasons. Decisions of the Illinois Supreme Court had made it almost
impossible to obtain a good tax title, so that a purchase at a tax sale was
a highly speculative investment. In addition, the General Assembly had
substantially reduced the amount of interest and penalties that could

be collected by the tax buyer. The lower rate of return on this investment, combined with the difficulty in obtaining a valid title, substantially
restricted the number of buyers who were willing to bid at a tax sale.
And the small number of tax buyers, combined with the invalidity of
tax titles, encouraged tax delinquency, so that collection of taxes became
more difficult.

In an effort to remedy this situation, the proposed 1922 Constitution
made two substantial changes in the requirements. For ordinary tax sales,
the provisions were retained that the sale be made by the county treasurer after a court order, with a two-year redemption period. However, the only notice required was "notice as provided by law." This
eliminated the compulsory notice to occupants which was cited as one
of the chief obstacles to obtaining good title under the Supreme Court's
strict requirements. It was argued that compulsory notice to occupants
served no essential purpose. Where the occupant was also the owner, his
interests were sufficiently protected by serving notice on the owner,
although there were cases in which the owner-occupier had been served
notice as owner which was constitutionally defective because it failed to
specify him as the occupant also. Where the occupant was merely a
tenant, it was argued that his interests in the tax sale were not substantial enough to mandate a constitutionally required notice. And where
the property contained a large number of tenants, as in the case of an
office building, or where the tenants were of a transient nature, the constitutional mandate was impossible to fulfill.

The other major change proposed in the 1922 Constitution was a
provision that the tax buyer could waive his title acquired at the tax sale,
be subrogated to the state's tax lien and foreclose the lien in equity. This
procedure would eliminate the two-year redemption period. It was believed, perhaps over-optimistically, that this would effectively assure the
acquisition of good title to the property.

A large number of members of the 1920-22 Convention recognized
that these provisions were essentially legislative in nature, and there was
considerable opposition to including anything at all on the subject of
tax sales in the proposed Constitution. At one point in the debate, a
motion to eliminate the section altogether failed by only one vote.

Explanation

In Illinois, there are three primary methods of selling land in order to
collect delinquent taxes. The requirements of Section 5, as well as Section
4, apply to all of them, and a brief explanation of these methods may be
helpful in understanding the cases. Taxes and special assessments become
a lien on the property as of April 1 in the year for which they are levied.
Proceedings by any of the three methods may be commenced only after

entry of a judgment for the delinquent taxes and an order of sale in accordance with the requirements of Section 4.

The most common procedure is the annual tax sale. All delinquent property is offered for sale annually at a public auction. The property must be sold for the full amount of taxes due, and the bidding is to determine the amount of penalty which will be charged for redemption. Thus, the successful purchaser at the tax sale is the bidder who is willing to accept the lowest penalty. Payment of taxes by the bidder extinguishes the lien. Redemption may be made within two years for the amount of taxes plus penalties. If there is no redemption in this period, the purchaser is entitled to a tax deed upon fulfilling certain notice requirements. If there are no bidders on the property at the annual tax sale, the property is forfeited to the state.

The second method is the tax foreclosure. Where taxes are delinquent on the property for two or more years and there has been a forfeiture to the state at the tax sale, proceedings may be instituted by the state to foreclose the tax lien. Under a decree ordering foreclosure of the lien, the property is sold to the highest bidder regardless of whether the amount is sufficient to pay all the taxes due. The lien is merged in the foreclosure decree and is extinguished by the sale. The right of redemption exists for two years from the time of the sale, and at the expiration of that period the purchaser is entitled to a deed, again after fulfilling certain notice requirements.

The third method of collecting taxes by a sale of property is a proceeding under the so-called "Scavenger Act." Where taxes have been unpaid for ten or more years, the county treasurer, upon approval by the court, may offer the delinquent property for sale at the annual tax sale. In this case, however, the property is sold to the highest bidder, whether or not that bid is for the full amount of taxes. As in the above proceedings, there is a two-year period of redemption, at the expiration of which the buyer is entitled to a tax deed if he fulfills the notice requirements. (For a thorough treatment of this subject, see Harbert, "Tax Foreclosures and Tax Titles," 1952 U. Ill. L. F. 209.)

It is extremely difficult to obtain a valid tax title to property in Illinois under any of the foregoing methods. The reason is that the Illinois Supreme Court has evidenced a consistently hostile attitude toward the sale of property for delinquent taxes and as a result has required very strict compliance with the mechanics of obtaining a tax deed. The chief obstacle to obtaining a valid deed has been the notice requirements prior to the expiration of the period of redemption. Under Section 5, only personal service of notice on occupants is constitutionally mandatory; otherwise the General Assembly is free to specify any kind of notice it likes. (Frew v. Taylor, 106 Ill. 159 (1883).) The service of notice must be on occupants at the time of the expiration of the period of redemption. In one case, the notice was served on Fred *Meyers,* owner and occupier of the land at the time it was sold. This was defective because it did not specify that Meyers was the occupier at the time of service of notice. The attorney's affidavit that Fred *Meyer* was the owner and occupier at time of service did not cure the defect because of the discrepancy between the two names. (Gonzalia v. Bartelsman, 143 Ill. 634 (1892).)

It has been held that a statute directing in the words of the Constitution that notice be served on owners, occupiers and "parties interested" in the property confers no right to notice on anyone other than the owners and occupiers, since it is impossible to determine who is meant by "parties interested." Thus a mortgagee has no right to notice of the expiration of the period of redemption under this statute. (Glos v. Evanston Bldg. & Loan Ass'n, 186 Ill. 586 (1900).)

In order to acquire a valid tax title, every statutory requirement must be strictly complied with, and it is irrelevant that the defects are neither harmful nor misleading. Numerous examples could be given of the extremes to which this proposition has been carried, but two will suffice for illustration. One tax deed was held invalid because of two defects in the notice. It stated that the period of redemption expired October 18, when in fact it expired September 8; obviously there was no harm here, since the owner was given an extra month in which to redeem. Another defect was that the owner was stated to be in possession on April 19 and served on May 20. The notice should have stated who was in possession on May 20, even though other evidence in the case showed that possession had not changed. (Wisner v. Chamberlain, 117 Ill. 568 (1886).) The notice must specify whether the property was sold for taxes or special assessments. A notice that the property was purchased at a "sale of lots and lands for taxes and special assessments" does not meet this requirement because the words refer to the sale and not to the property. This notice was also deficient in specifying the date for expiration as November 3, 1878, because that day fell on Sunday, and the owner could actually still redeem on Monday, November 4, even though there was no attempt to redeem. (Gage v. Davis, 129 Ill. 236 (1889).)

The economic depression of the 1930's caused a substantial increase in tax delinquency. And the difficulty of obtaining valid tax titles to delinquent property discouraged buyers at tax sales. Thus, in the decade beginning in 1940, there were large amounts of property in the state which produced no tax revenue because of chronic delinquency of the owners, and which the counties were unable to sell to buyers in order to return them to revenue-producing status. In an effort to mitigate this situation, the legislature in 1943 passed the so-called

"Scavenger Act" (Ill. Rev. Stat. ch. 120, § 716a (Supp. 1968)), which provided that property which was delinquent for as long as ten years or more should be sold at the annual tax sale to the highest bidder. The act specifically stated that it was to be given a liberal construction so as to enable conveyance of a merchantable title. Notice was to be provided under the statute applicable to other tax sales. There have been few cases decided under this act; but the first one construing the notice provisions held that since the same statute governed all tax sales, the requirements relative to the Scavenger Act would be applied in conformity with the rules governing other sales — *i.e.*, strict compliance would be required. (Gaither v. Lager, 2 Ill. 2d 293 (1954).) In that case, the owner of the land had continuously occupied the property and was delinquent in his taxes for more than 15 years. He was personally served with the notice of the correct expiration date of the period of redemption, but the notice was held defective because it failed to specify for what years' taxes the property was sold and whether it was for general taxes or special assessments. Again, it was clear from the other evidence that the owner had this information.

Section 5 secures the right of redemption to owners and gives a minimum of two years in which to exercise that right. The General Assembly has always observed this provision, and there have been no cases holding that the right of redemption has been violated. (*See, e.g.,* Ziccarelli v. Stuckart, 277 Ill. 26 (1917).) However, the right of redemption is favored over the rights of purchasers at tax sales, and the General Assembly may enlarge the right of redemption beyond the protection afforded by the Constitution. By this justification, a statute was sustained against due process objections which provided that if the tax buyer failed to take possession of property within one year from issuance of the tax deed, the prior owner could still redeem. (Elmhurst State Bank v. Stone, 346 Ill. 157 (1931).)

The right of redemption under Section 5 exists in favor of owners and "persons interested" in the property. In recent years there has been some confusion as to who has the right to redeem. The difficulty stems from a 1961 Illinois Supreme Court decision which held, four to three, that a stranger to the record title could not redeem from a tax sale. (Weiner v. Jobst, 22 Ill. 2d 11 (1961).) In that case, a bank claimed title to the property under a deed of trust and attempted to redeem by its agent-attorney. The bank's record title was incomplete because of a 1937 conveyance which was not recorded. As the dissent points out, the Court's decision denying redemption was not consistent with prior decisions (*see* Franzen v. Donichy, 9 Ill. 2d 382 (1956)), and resulted in no one being able to redeem from the sale. Later decisions of an Illinois appellate court have cast considerable doubt on the viability of the *Weiner* decision. In one case, the appellate court ignored the express language of the majority in *Weiner* and held that record title was not a prerequisite to the right to redeem, but that equitable owners could also redeem. In this case the defect in title consisted of a contract to convey which was recorded and marked paid in full, but with no deed having issued. (*In re* County Treasurer, 63 Ill. App. 2d 135 (1965).) In a later case, the executor of an estate was allowed to redeem, even though at the time of redemption he had not yet received his appointment as executor and hence was technically a stranger to the title. (*In re* County Collector, 72 Ill. App. 2d 272 (1966).) Neither of these cases was reviewed by the Supreme Court. While the question is still unsettled, one may infer that owners of equities in property and certainly equities of which there is some record notice, may redeem from tax sales.

Comparative Analysis

Four states besides Illinois guarantee the right of redemption in their constitutions; in three states the right is protected for two years and in one for three years. West Virginia's Constitution specifies that the right is not to extend beyond 20 years. Notice requirements are mentioned in only three other constitutions: in one, as in Illinois, notice must be given to occupants; in another, notice is required for owner; and in the third, notice is to be provided by law. The Model State Constitution is silent on the subject.

Comment

Like Section 4, this section deals with problems that are primarily of legislative concern, and very few states find it necessary to treat them in their constitutions. It is extremely difficult to suggest any compelling reasons which justify a continued constitutional status for this section.

Release from Taxation Forbidden

Sec. 6. The General Assembly shall have no power to release or discharge any county, city, township, town or district, whatever, or the inhabitants thereof, or the property therein, from their or its proportionate share of taxes to be levied for State purposes, nor shall commutation for such taxes be authorized in any form whatsoever.

History

This section of the Constitution was adopted in 1870 for the express purpose of forbidding legislation of questionable merit which had taken several forms. For example, acts had frequently been passed exempting communities from state taxes in order to permit them to construct levies and embankments for protection from river flooding. In 1869, an act had been passed partially exempting communities which had subscribed to railroad stock in order to facilitate their payment for the stock. (See discussion of Ramsey v. Hoeger, below.) There was widespread opposition to such legislation, and this section resulted.

The substance of this section was retained without significant debate in the 1922 Convention proposal. The language was considerably simplified to read, "Taxes levied for state purposes shall never be released, discharged, or commuted."

Explanation

There has been little significant litigation over this section, probably because its provisions are relatively clear and the legislature has apparently made no attempt to circumvent them. An 1875 case held that the section applied retroactively to repeal all inconsistent legislation. In that case, an 1869 act of the General Assembly attempted to ease the tax burden on communities which had incurred indebtedness by subscribing to railroad stock. The act required the State Auditor, before assessing state taxes, to deduct a certain proportion of the property valuation in those counties which had subscribed to railroad stock. This was held to be a partial release of state taxes and a violation of this section. (Ramsey v. Hoeger, 76 Ill. 432 (1875).)

In only one case has a law passed after 1870 been held unconstitutional because of this section. Under the school law as it stood in 1915, all eighth-grade graduates were entitled to attend a high school. In those school districts which did not maintain a high school (a non-high school district), the district was required to pay the tuition of its students attending school in other districts. The state school tax was distributed by the county superintendents of schools to the various township school districts in proportion to the number of school-age children residing in them. In 1915, the legislature passed a statute directing the superintendents first to pay the tuition of non-high school district students and then to distribute the tax as above. The effect of this mode of distribution was to increase that portion of the state school tax returned to the non-high school districts, while decreasing that returned to the high school districts. This was held to be the equivalent of the commutation of the state school tax and a violation of this section. (Board of Educ. v. Haworth, 274 Ill. 538 (1916).)

The Supreme Court's decision in the *Haworth* case seems questionable. It is extremely doubtful that this section should be applied to a dispersal of state funds, as distinguished from their initial collection.

Any time that state funds are dispersed to a community in an amount greater than that which is collected from them, there is a "commutation" of state taxes in the vague sense in which that concept was used in the *Haworth* case. Adherence to this view could jeopardize any program of state aid which is related to the taxable wealth of communities. Fortunately, *Haworth* has not proved to be a viable precedent, although it has not been overruled.

When the legislature drafted the Use Tax Act, in an effort to avoid constitutional problems under Article IX, Section 1 (see discussion, *supra,* pp. 327-31), it provided that the use tax must be collected on all sales, but did not have to be remitted to the extent that the retailers' occupation tax was paid. This was attacked as a release of the use tax in violation of this section. But the Court held that the two taxes were to be viewed as an integrated system, that only one tax was intended to reach the treasury, and that the purpose of the use tax was to reach only out-of-state sales. Viewed in this light, the method was cumbersome, but not a violation of Section 6. (Turner v. Wright, 11 Ill. 2d 161 (1957).)

Section 6 applies only to commutation of state taxes and does not prevent commutation of local taxes. Thus, a 1944 case held that it was not a violation of this section to sell land for less than the amount of delinquent taxes because state taxes were not involved. In addition, the purpose of the proceeding was remedial — to return the land to active tax-paying status. (Schreiber v. County of Cook, 388 Ill. 297 (1944).) However, Sections 9 and 10 (see discussion, *infra,* p. 462) have been construed to prohibit commutation of local taxes. (Raymond v. Hartford Fire Ins. Co., 196 Ill. 329 (1902).) It is not clear whether the remedial objective sustained in *Schreiber* is precluded under Sections 9 and 10 by virtue of the earlier *Hartford Fire Insurance Co.* case.

Comparative Analysis

Seven other states have constitutional provisions prohibiting commutation of taxes. The Model State Constitution has no similar provision.

Comment

While the principle of this section is certainly not objectionable, nor a serious impediment to fiscal operations, consideration might well be given to eliminating it from the Constitution. Forty-three states do without it. The chief evil at which the section was directed was the commutation of the state property tax. This, of course, is now and for the foreseeable future, a moot issue since a state property tax is not likely to be revived. The policy of this section can be assured, if deemed necessary in any given case, by legislative action. Finally, in this area, as in others, serious abuses of power could be controlled by the due process clause.

If this provision is to be retained, the language used in the proposed 1922 Constitution (see *History, supra,* p. 454) is much simpler in form.

State Taxes Paid into State Treasury

Sec. 7. All taxes levied for State purposes shall be paid into the State treasury.

History

This section dates from 1870. In explaining this section to the Convention, the Chairman of the Committee on Revenue said that it was "simply to carry the intent of the [sixth] section more fully into effect . . . ." The section was accepted without debate. The proposed 1922 Constitution left the section unchanged.

Explanation

Section 6 (*supra,* p. 454) forbids release by the legislature of any state taxes due from any political subdivision. Prior to 1870, the legislature sometimes would authorize the diversion of state taxes due from a particular subdivision in order to pay for some local improvement. Section 7 is designed to prevent this sort of diversion. (The background is set out in the dissenting opinion in Green v. Black, 352 Ill. 623 (1933).)

It is to be noted that this section requires taxes, but not all moneys, to be paid into the treasury. This is, of course, the other side of the coin referred to in the *Explanation* of Section 17 of Article IV (*supra,* pp. 182-3), where it was pointed out that under certain circumstances, operations may be carried on without the benefit of an appropriation.

There is, however, an exception to the requirement that *all* taxes be paid into the treasury. The tax that supports unemployment compensation is not paid into the treasury. The statute relative to the payment of state moneys into the state treasury provides that it is not applicable to the Unemployment Compensation Act. (Ill. Rev. Stat. ch. 127, § 176a (1967).) This is undoubtedly the case because of the interrelationship between the state tax and the federal tax. In any event, this aspect of the unemployment compensation system does not appear to have been attacked constitutionally.

Comparative Analysis

There appear to be six states besides Illinois with a comparable provision. The United States Constitution and the Model State Constitution have no comparable provision.

Comment

This section was probably not necessary when adopted. The type of

diversion referred to above is clearly prohibited by Section 22 of Article
IV. (*Supra,* pp. 203-4.) The unemployment compensation practice demonstrates the need for more flexibility than is permitted by the literal
wording of the section.

County Tax Limit

Sec. 8. County authorities shall never assess taxes, the aggregate of which
shall exceed seventy-five cents per one hundred dollars' valuation, except for
the payment of indebtedness existing at the adoption of this Constitution, unless
authorized by vote of the people of the county.

History

This was a new section in the 1870 Constitution and was adopted without debate. The lack of debate is particularly interesting in view of
the fact that an attempt to impose a similar limitation on the tax rate
of the state met with vigorous opposition and was ultimately defeated.
The principal argument of the opponents of the state limitation was
that it would be ineffective because it would only serve as an impetus
to increase the assessment ratio which was then 25 per cent.

The limitation was retained in the proposed 1922 Constitution, but
was included in the article on Counties and was phrased as ¾ of 1 per
cent of assessed valuation. A new provision of that section permitted
counties which were the unit for road taxation to levy up to an additional ¾ of 1 per cent. At that time, the townships, which are not
limited by this section, were the governmental units primarily responsible for roads, but it was felt that with the coming of the automobile
and hard roads it would be more efficient for the counties to control
road-building. If they were to assume that responsibility, however, they
would need considerably more taxes than the 75-cent limit provided.

There was considerable opposition to the inclusion of this limitation
in the 1922 Constitution on the ground that there were no constitutional
rate limits on other governmental units, and the counties should be
regulated only by statute just as the others were. There were three votes
taken on the issue, and the vote was against inclusion of the limit the
first two times, but on the third vote it was adopted.

Explanation

Counties derive their taxing powers from the legislature, and the
legislature is free to place any conditions on that power it likes; this
section only specifies the upper rate limit which may be levied without
a vote of the people. But the legislature may fix a county rate limit lower
than the constitutional limit. (People *ex rel.* Bothfuhr v. Chicago & E. Ill.
Ry., 305 Ill. 454 (1922).) This section in no way governs the assessment
of property against which the constitutional limit may be extended;

and the counties may be required to use the assessment value determined by the State Board of Equalization, instead of their own county board of review, even where this results in less revenue. (Chicago, B. & O.R. R. v. People *ex rel.* Sonnet, 213 Ill. 458 (1904).)

When a county tax is improperly levied in excess of the 75-cent limit, only the excess is invalid. (Mix v. People *ex rel.* Pierpont, 72 Ill. 241 (1874).).

The problem of what qualifies as a county tax for purposes of this section was settled by early decisions. Taxes levied by the county board for funds administered by the county are county taxes; and the legislature may not designate any such tax as not a county tax so as to exempt it from the 75-cent limit. (People *ex rel.* Lusk v. Cairo, V. & C. Ry., 266 Ill. 557 (1915).) On the other hand, taxes levied and administered by townships are township taxes, and they do not become county taxes merely because they are certified by the township trustees to the county board which directs the county collector to extend them. (Wabash, St. L. & P. Ry v. McCleave, 108 Ill. 368 (1884). *Compare* Wright v. Wabash, St. L. & P. Ry., 120 Ill. 541 (1887).) When an election is held to authorize a tax rate above the constitutional limit, either the statute, the notice of the election, or the ballot itself must specify that the tax to be voted on is above the constitutional limit. If such notice is not given, an affirmative vote on a particular tax referendum will be interpreted as authorizing the particular levy up to, but not over, the constitutional limit. (People *ex rel.* Hileman v. Missouri P.R.R., 319 Ill. 433 (1925); People *ex rel.* Flick v. Chicago, B. & Q. R.R., 291 Ill. 502 (1920); People *ex rel.* Graff v. Wabash Ry., 286 Ill. 15 (1918).) In order to authorize a rate above the constitutional limit, a majority of votes cast at the election (not a majority of electors voting on the proposition) must be recorded in favor of the proposition; where the vote is merely to exceed the statutory limit, a majority of votes on the proposition is sufficient. (People *ex rel.* Lawrence v. Cleveland, C. C. & St. L. Ry., 339 Ill. 169 (1930).)

This section of the Constitution is in no way a limitation on the power of counties to incur debt, and it is not a valid objection to the assumption of a county obligation that it will require a tax levy over the constitutional limit; the only limitation on debt incurrence is Section 12. (County of Coles v. Goehring, 209 Ill. 142 (1904).)

The exception to this section for debts existing prior to its adoption is, of course, obsolete now. (For interpretations, *see* County of Pope v. Sloan, 92 Ill. 177 (1879); Chiniquy v. People *ex rel.* Swigert, 78 Ill. 570 (1875).)

Comparative Analysis

There are 27 states, including Illinois, which have some sort of property tax rate limitations in their constitutions. These provisions vary so widely that only the most general comparisons can be made. It might be noted that many states have statutory limitations which have not been included in this analysis. Five states have overall limits on the rate of taxes which can be assessed against property for both state and local purposes. Another 18 states have specific limits on the rate of state property taxes; six of these states do not limit local taxes. Sixteen states limit the rates of local property taxes; but of these, four states do not limit state property taxes, while 13 limit both county and municipal rates, and three limit only the county rates.

Illinois is in the rather unique position of being one of only four states which limit county taxes but not state taxes, and one of only three states which limit county taxes but not municipal taxes.

The Model State Constitution is expressly opposed to such limitations.

Comment

Property tax rate limits have had a long statutory history in Illinois, in addition to this constitutional provision. There have been many attempts to establish overall limits to the property tax, most of which were notably unsuccessful for two reasons — the vicissitudes of the assessment procedure and the increasing demands for services. (For a general review, see Howards, "Property Tax Rate Limits," in Report of the Commission on Revenue 521 (1963).) Most authorities oppose these limits in any form and particularly oppose their inclusion in a constitution. Regardless of the general merits of the argument, this particular limit standing alone in the Illinois Constitution seems highly illogical.

Local Municipal Improvements

Sec. 9. The General Assembly may vest the corporate authorities of cities, towns and villages with power to make local improvements by special assessment, or by special taxation of contiguous property, or otherwise. For all other corporate purposes, all municipal corporations may be vested with authority to assess and collect taxes; but such taxes shall be uniform in respect to persons and property, within the jurisdiction of the body imposing the same.

History

This section of the Constitution derives from the Constitution of 1848, Article IX, Section 5, which provided in part:

The corporate authorities of counties, townships, school districts, cities, towns and villages may be vested with power to assess and collect taxes for corporate purposes; such taxes to be uniform in respect to persons and property within the jurisdiction of the body imposing the same.

The most significant decision of the Illinois Supreme Court under the 1848 Constitution, in respect to its effect on Section 9 of the 1870 Constitution, was *City of Chicago v. Larned* (34 Ill. 203 (1864)). That case held that municipalities had no powers of special taxation for making local improvements. These projects came under the power of eminent domain for which compensation had to be made. While such compensation could be made by benefits conferred, such benefits had to be specifically assessed against the individual properties benefitted, with the right of judicial review, and any excess cost of the improvements had to be paid for by general taxation. Although this position seemed sound in theory, as a practical matter it made the construction of many local improvements, particularly sidewalks, exceedingly complex and expensive. This case was the main concern of the 1870 Convention with regard to Section 9, and it was finally determined to grant cities, towns and villages the authority to make local improvements by special assessment, special taxation or otherwise. The distinction between these methods is discussed below.

The 1922 Convention proposal took the first sentence of Section 9 and made it a separate section of the Revenue Article and included park districts in the list of municipal authorities which could construct local improvements by special assessment. There was some discussion as to whether the provision restricting special taxation to contiguous property should be removed, but it was finally retained. Another change permitted municipalities to join together to make local improvements. The remainder of Section 9 was combined with Section 10 into one section with some change in wording, but the essential features were retained.

Explanation

This section and Sections 10 and 12 form the basis of the taxing powers of local governments for local purposes. In addition to these sections, local governments derive taxing powers from the General Assembly through a delegation of its authority under Sections 1 and 2. The authority of cities to prescribe license taxes, for example, is such a delegated power and is governed by principles already discussed in Sections 1 and 2; it is not affected by this section. (Harder's Fireproof Storage Van Co. v. City of Chicago, 235 Ill. 58 (1908); Banta v. City of Chicago 172 Ill. 204 (1898).) Of course, these powers are also governed by the limitations of the due process clause and the police power. (Condon v. Village of Forest Park, 278 Ill. 218 (1917).) Thus, the principles of this section relate only to property and can be analyzed under two main classifications, (1) special assessment and taxation for local improvements, and (2) general property taxation for corporate purposes.

Before these general problems are investigated, it would be well to delineate the relationship of these sections to the powers of the General Assembly. The authority to grant taxing powers to municipalities under this section is permissive only and not self-executing. Thus in creating municipal governments, the legislature has discretion in deciding whether or not to give them the power of taxation, and in fact often has not. (People *ex rel.* Tuohy v. City of Chicago, 399 Ill. 551 (1948).) But once it is decided to grant the power, certain restrictions must be observed. It has been held that this section, together with Section 10, prevents the legislature from commuting local taxes. Otherwise, taxes would not be uniform within the jurisdiction. Therefore, insurance companies could not be exempted from their local personal property taxes upon payment of a state tax on their premiums collected. (Raymond v. Hartford Fire Ins. Co., 196 Ill. 329 (1902). Note: Section 6 of Article IX prevents commutation of state taxes, but has no effect on local taxes. *Supra,* p. 454.) And when the power is granted, it must be granted to the proper authority. The power to levy special assessments and special taxes for local improvements is limited to a small list of municipalities, and the power of general taxation for corporate purposes is limited to "corporate authorities." The exact definition of authorities who can exercise each power is discussed below in the analysis of the respective taxing powers. Finally, it should be noted that the legislature's power to grant taxing authority under this section is often construed in conjunction with the restriction in Section 10 preventing the legislature itself from imposing local taxes on municipalities for corporate purposes. While the two questions are often involved in the same case, analytically they can be distinguished and the latter issue is discussed in the analysis of Section 10.

The power to make local improvements is authorized for cities, towns and villages, and the Supreme Court has held that this list is exclusive. Thus a statute which enabled drainage districts to make such improvements by special assessment (*i.e.*, to charge lands which are drained with the whole cost of draining) was held unconstitutional. (Updike v. Wright, 81 Ill. 49 (1876).) Article IV, Section 31, was amended specifically to overrule this decision for drainage districts. The general principle of *Updike* was followed later when it was held that counties could not be given this power. (People *ex rel.* Van Slooten v. Board of Comm'rs, 221 Ill. 493 (1906).) However, by an accident of constitutional history, park districts had also been given this power and had exercised it unchallenged for many years. When a case finally reached the Supreme Court, it held that because many rights had already become settled, the power would be upheld, but this was recognized as an exception to the general rule. (VanNada v. Goedde, 263 Ill. 105 (1914).) One further apparent deviation from this principle is worth noting. In 1925, the Supreme Court held that it was within the police power of the state to authorize sanitary districts to construct local improvements by means of special assessment. (Taylorville Sanitary Dist. v. Winslow, 317 Ill, 25 (1925).) While the opinion is rather unclear, the basis of this decision appears to be that the activities of sanitary districts are not local corporate purposes, but part of the general health and welfare of the state, and therefore not covered by the restrictions of this section. The broad implications of this decision have not been tested; it would appear to modify the *Updike* decision. One further very important restriction has been judicially grafted onto this provision of the Constitution. In order to be financed as a "local improvement," a project must be entirely under the control of one municipality. Chicago and Cicero attempted to construct one continuous sewer, with the outlet in Cicero because there was no suitable location in Chicago. Although the cost of the sewer construction in Chicago was only one-fifth of that in Cicero, two-thirds of the cost was apportioned to Chicago. This excess represented primarily the cost of the outlet, plus an administrative assessment that the property in Chicago would be more greatly benefitted than that in Cicero. Applying the rule of single municipal control, the Court held the project unconstitutional. (Loeffler v. City of Chicago, 246 Ill. 43 (1910).) Obviously, this restriction greatly hampers efforts of municipalities with contiguous boundaries to coordinate their municipal services.

The most recent decision limiting the authority to make local improvements to the municipalities designated in this section is *Committee of Local Improvements v. Objectors to the Assessment* (39 Ill. 2d 255 (1968)), wherein the Court interpreted "towns" to mean "incorporated towns" and not "townships," and in consequence held invalid a statute authorizing townships to levy special assessments for local improvements.

The definition of a project which constitutes a local improvement has not caused any difficulty, although it is important because it determines the method of financing which a municipality may utilize for its projects. It has been said that a local improvement implies a permanent benefit which will significantly enhance the market value of property affected by the improvement. This encompasses, for example, the construction of streets, sewers, and lighting; but it does not include the mere maintenance and repairs of existing streets (Crane v. West Chicago Park Comm'rs, 153 Ill. 348 (1894)); nor does it include the removal of noxious weeds (People *ex rel*. Van Slooten v. Board of Comm'rs, 221 Ill. 493 (1906)). The taking of land for a park is a local improvement which may be financed by special assessment. (Winnetka Park Dist. v. Hopkins, 371 Ill. 46 (1939).) Local improvements are to be distinguished from projects of general utility to the community. Thus, in constructing a city waterworks system, the reservoir, wells, pumping stations, etc., are general improvements which must be paid for by general taxation, while the laying of main lines along streets is a local improvement which may be financed by special assessment or taxation. (Hughes v. City of Momence, 163 Ill. 535 (1896).)

The most important constitutional questions with regard to local improvements lie in the area of financing. Three methods of financing are authorized by Section 9: (1) special assessment, (2) special taxation of contiguous property, and (3) general taxation within the "or otherwise" provision. General taxation needs no attention here, since the principles governing it in regard to local improvements are no different from those in any other taxing problem. Special assessment and special taxation must be distinguished. In either case, the city passes an ordinance describing the improvement to be made and specifying the method of financing. In the case of special assessment, each piece of affected property is individually assessed to determine the increase in market value conferred upon it by the improvement, and the cost of the improvement is apportioned among the properties in relation to these benefits. In no case may the charge on the property exceed the actual value of the benefits, and the determination of this value is subject to the right of trial by jury and judicial review. Where the method of financing is by special taxation, the municipality determines in advance and declares in the ordinance the method of apportioning the cost. The most common way of doing this is by foot frontage on the improvement. In this case, the determination of benefits and costs by the city is conclusive and there is no right of judicial review, except on due process grounds. (Kuehner v. City of Freeport, 143 Ill. 92 (1892).) It has been held that a statute passed in 1897 giving the right of review in cases of special taxation did not abolish the distinction between the two methods (*see* Ill. Rev. Stat. ch. 24, §9-2-41 (1967)); it merely required that the special tax not exceed the benefits actually conferred, which question is subject to review, but it does not require that the tax be in proportion to the benefit conferred, and the ordinance itself is prima facie evidence of the benefit. (City of Nokomis v. Zepp, 246 Ill. 159 (1910); Pfeiffer v. People *ex rel.* McCormick, 170 Ill. 347 (1897).) Special taxation is limited to property contiguous to the improvement, while special assessment is made of all property benefitted, whether or not contiguous. (Guild v. City of Chicago, 82 Ill. 472 (1876).)

In financing local improvements, municipalities may combine either special assessment or special taxation with general taxation for part of the costs, and indeed this combination is often necessary in the case of special assessments because the cost of the improvement may exceed the specific benefits to individual property. But special taxation and special assessment may not be combined, since this would be an unequal and unfair discrimination among taxpayers paying for the same improvement. (Kuehner v. City of Freeport, 143 Ill. 92 (1892).) However, while combination methods of financing are permitted, once the decision is made on how the improvement is to be financed and is prescribed by ordinance, the municipality cannot later change its mind and adopt another method, at least after the project has been completed. The City of Chicago issued local improvement bonds which were to be paid for out of the proceeds of a special assessment. When it subsequently appeared that delays in collection of the assessment would prevent payment of the bonds on time, the city purchased the bonds out of its general funds, making provisions to reimburse itself out of the final assessment collections. The city argued that this action was justified because it had the power to finance the improvement by combining both special assessment and general taxation. The Court held that the procedure was unconstitutional because it was unfair to the property owners who had already paid their assessments in full. (City of Chicago v. Brede, 218 Ill. 528 (1905).) The Court's reasoning in this case seems clearly erroneous. So far as property owners who pay their assessments in full are concerned, it is immaterial to their position of equality whether nonpaying owners default on the obligation to the bondholders or on an obligation to the general fund of the city; it is a default in either case, and this decision affords the paying owner no protection whatsoever in that regard. Furthermore, the collection remedy in the case of either obligation is the same — levy and execution on the assessed property in default. Thus the question resolves itself to whether the bonds will be paid on time, with the city ultimately reimbursing itself for costs and interest and a consequent saving of its financial rating, or whether they must be dishonored, with a consequent impairment of the city's borrowing power even though they would eventually be paid.

In addition to combining methods of financing a local improvement, it is within the power of a municipality to make local improvements, such as the laying of sewer lines, in one part of the city by general taxation and in another part by special assessment or special taxation. (Murphy v. People ex rel. Weiennett, 120 Ill. 234 (1887).) This is commonly done, for example, in street lighting where major traffic arteries are lit by general taxation while residential areas are lit by one of the special methods.

The other major division of municipal taxing powers is the authority to levy general property taxes for corporate purposes. Since this section requires that such power can be vested only in corporate authorities, the initial problem in this area is the definition of "corporate authorities." The general rule is that corporate authorities are those officers whom the people have elected or to whose manner of appointment they have assented. Thus where the original charter of a park district organized by election of the voters of the district specified the appointment of commissioners to be by the judge of the circuit court, the legislature could not later change the method of appointment without the consent of the voters. That would be vesting the taxing power in other than corporate authorities. (Cornell v. People ex rel. Walsh, 107 Ill. 372 (1883).) Officers can be corporate authorities only of territory under their jurisdiction; thus where territory is detached from the school district, the school board is no longer a corporate authority of that territory and cannot levy taxes on it even for indebtedness incurred while the territory was part of the corporation. (People ex rel. Bergan v. New York Cent. R.R., 390 Ill. 30 Ill. (1945).)

The difficult question is what constitutes an exercise of taxing power by a particular body. It is clear that the power to create a debt is the equivalent of the power to tax. A municipal corporation cannot be empowered to undertake projects for its own corporate purposes and then charge the cost of those projects to another municipality. For example, a drainage district had the authority to build bridges to connect adjacent land to public highways where they were separated by a drainage ditch. The cost of the bridges was to come from the road and bridge fund of the town. This was held unconstitutional because it vested taxing powers of the town in other than the corporate authorities. (Morgan v. Schusselle, 228 Ill. 106 (1907).) This situation should be distinguished from one in which municipal corporations jointly undertake projects where the participation of each is not compulsory. Projects of one municipal corporation may be entirely financed by the taxes of another, so long as the taxing municipality determines voluntarily the extent of its financial participation. For example, the Land Clearance Commission, a corporation which had the power to create its own debts and could be sued, was authorized to acquire land for slum clearance. It had no taxing power and its finances were obtained from taxes of the City of Chicago and state matching grants. This was held not to vest the taxing power of the city in other than corporate authorities, because the city itself determined the extent of its appropriations to the commission. (People ex rel. Tuohy v. City of Chicago, 339 Ill. 551 (1948). Compare People ex rel. Gallenbach v. Franklin, 338 Ill. 560 (1944) with McFarlane v. Hotz, 401 Ill. 506 (1948).)

Taxes levied by corporate authorities must be for corporate purposes.

With one significant exception, the Supreme Court has not interpreted this provision to impose any substantial restriction on municipalities. A tax for corporate purposes is one which promotes the general prosperity and welfare of the municipality which levies it; it must be germane to the objects of the creation of the municipal corporation. A tax levied by the city for civil defense purposes meets this test. (People v. City of Chicago, 413 Ill. 83 (1952).)

The two significant cases, in which the requirement that taxes must be for corporate purposes was held to invalidate municipal levies, both involved attempts to maintain credit ratings of Chicago. In order to understand the more important of these decisions, it is necessary to explain the use of tax anticipation warrants as a method of financing local governments prior to actual collection of a levied tax. A full discussion of this problem can be found in Section 12. (*Infra,* p. 484.) Here it is sufficient to note that the warrants are interest-bearing "i.o.u.'s" issued by the municipality following the levy of a tax and payable only from the receipts of that particular tax. These warrants have been held not to be a debt of the municipality and therefore not to be computed in determining debt limits under Section 12. However, it is obvious that if a city were to default on the warrants, its future ability to borrow, either by the issuance of warrants or bonds, would be substantially impaired. Such a situation occurred in 1929 when the City of Chicago issued warrants in the amount of 60 per cent of anticipated tax revenues. A reassessment of property in the interval between levy and collection, coupled with the effects of the economic depression, caused the actual tax receipts to be wholly inadequate for payment of the warrants. The resulting default on the 1929 warrants made it practically impossible to find buyers for warrants in ensuing years; and the city, especially in its school system, was virtually bankrupt. In an attempt to remedy the situation, the city issued bonds to redeem the outstanding warrants. However, the Supreme Court invalidated the bond issue, holding the enabling statute unconstitutional on the grounds that since the warrants were not a debt which could be enforced against the city, the issuance of bonds to pay them was not for a corporate purpose. (Berman v. Board of Education, 360 Ill. 535 (1935).). This position was reinforced a few years later when it was held that bonds could not be issued to pay outstanding judgments against the city, where the judgments represented actions on the warrants. (Leviton v. Board of Educ., 374 Ill. 594 (1940). *See* Comment "Judicial Treatment of Tax Anticipation Warrants in Illinois," 45 Ill. L. Rev. 653 (1950).) A similar situation occurred where Chicago attempted to pay local improvement bonds out of its general funds, when it appeared that the collection of the special assessment to pay the bonds would be delayed. It was held that since the bonds on their face specified liability only out of the special assessment, payment out of the general fund was not for a corporate purpose even if it would ultimately be reimbursed. (City of Chicago v. Brede, 218 Ill. 528 (1905).) In each of these cases, the Court seemed to be unconcerned with the financial facts of life. Maintenance of a municipality's credit rating should be a valid corporate purpose, and no protection whatsoever is offered to a taxpayer by preventing such transactions.

Comparative Analysis

Six other states have constitutional provisions similar to this section. Another 11 states have one section which combines the substance of Sections 9 and 10 of the Illinois Constitution. The Model State Constitution contains no similar provision.

Comment

What action is taken on this section depends, in large part, upon decisions made in two other areas of constitutional revision — home rule for local governments, and the taxing powers of the General Assembly. If significant reforms are adopted in the area of local self-government permitting extensive home rule, the taxing powers necessary to implement such government should be included in those provisions. Of course, to be consistent with the principles of home rule, such powers should be substantially independent of legislative control. If home rule is not incorporated into the new Constitution, then the taxing powers of local governments would rest on the same relationship to state government as exists now — i.e., they are derived solely from grants by the state legislature, subject to whatever restrictions are imposed on that body by the Constitution. If it is decided to leave the legislature substantially unrestricted in matters of fiscal policy, then the need for a section such as this would be minimal. But if substantial restrictions are imposed on the legislature, then consideration must be given to the relationship of these restrictions to the needs of local governments for taxing authority.

If a special provision relating to local taxation is included, several alternatives may be pursued. One would be simply to give the legislature broad authority to vest local governments with such taxing authority as may be needed. Another would be to adopt a more restrictive provision such as the present section, making some attempt to ameliorate the specific problems inherent in the present section. Still another would be the recommendation of the Chicago Home Rule Commission that authorization be requested of the legislature either for a permissive tax statute listing a series of tax powers, with authority in the city government to levy any or all of the taxes specified, or, alternatively, power to levy one or more, but less than all, of the taxes specified. (Chicago Home

Rule Commission, Modernizing A City Government 327-28 (1954).)

Among the more serious problems of this section, the most numerous are those pertaining to the making of local improvements. The restricted list of governments permitted to make local improvements should be changed to allow any municipality to undertake such projects so long as they are consistent with its governmental functions. Joint participation in the construction of local improvements by two or more municipalities should be permitted. Consideration could be given to removing the restriction that special taxation be limited to contiguous property, thereby allowing special taxation for projects benefitting more than contiguous property. Finally, attention should be given to the possibility of allowing methods of financing local improvements other than special assessment, special taxation, or general taxation — for example, user charges.

In the area of general property taxation, two questions are of primary concern. The uniformity requirement of this section is subject to all the problems and defects discussed above in relation to Section 1. Also, the maintenance of confidence in the financial integrity of local governments should be recognized as a valid "corporate purpose" for which taxes could be levied, thus avoiding, for example, the rigid treatment of tax anticipation warrants.

In the last analysis, consideration may well be given to the repeal of this section in its entirety, leaving the resolution of tax authority for local purposes to legislative judgment, where in fact it largely rests anyway.

Municipal Taxation

Sec. 10. The General Assembly shall not impose taxes upon muncipal corporations, or the inhabitants or property thereof, for corporate purposes, but shall require that all the taxable property within the limits of municipal corporations shall be taxed for the payment of debts contracted under authority of law, such taxes to be uniform in respect to persons and property, within the jurisdiction of the body imposing the same. Private property shall not be liable to be taken or sold for the payment of the corporate debt of a municipal corporation.

History

Section 5 of the 1848 Constitution contained the provision that property shall be taxed for the payment of debts contracted by municipalities under authority of law. Apart from this provision, this section is a product of the 1870 Constitution. Although the section was adopted without debate or explanation, it has generated considerable litigation.

The 1922 Convention proposal retained the essence of this section, with a minimum of debate.

Explanation

The two most important questions which arise under this section are what constitutes the imposition of a tax by the legislature and for what purposes a tax may be imposed without violating this section.

The concept of the imposition of a tax is not confined to the actual levy. It extends to the imposition of a debt which must be paid by taxation and to the specification of amounts and purposes which must be included in a municipal budget, such as the fixing of minimum wages. (See cases discussed below in regard to the purposes of a tax.) In exceptional cases, and where the levy of a tax is optional with the local government, the legislature may direct the disposition of receipts without violating this section. For example, in one case both cities and townships were authorized to levy library taxes. When both governments levied such taxes and the township was located within the city, it was required to pay over to the city a proportion of its tax collection relative to the amount of its territory in the city; the city was required to abate its library tax by that amount. The township contended that this was the imposition of a debt in violation of this section, but the Court held that the requirement was valid because it was in the township's discretion whether to levy the tax in the first instance. (Board of Library Directors v. City of Lake Forest, 17 Ill. 2d 277 (1959).) Also, the creation of a cause of action against a municipality, which may or may not materialize in the future, is not the imposition of a debt. An act of 1887, known as the Mob Law, gave a property owner the right to collect from the city damages to his property caused by a riot. In a suit to recover under this statute, the Court held that there was no imposition of a debt. (City of Chicago v. Manhattan Cement Co., 178 Ill. 372 (1899).) Furthermore, the Court said that even if it were conceded to be the imposition of a debt, it would not be prohibited by this section because it was an exercise of the general police power of the state to promote peace and tranquility rather than a tax for a corporate purpose of the municipality.

This last aspect of the Court's opinion raises the other important question under this section — what kinds of taxes fall within the proscription? This section prohibits the imposition of taxes for local corporate purposes; it does not prevent the imposition of taxes relating to general governmental functions of the state which may be delegated to and required of a municipality. Municipalities are subdivisions of the state and may be required to perform functions related to the administration of general public policy as well as their own local functions. Thus, for example, general elections are part of the welfare and security of the state, and municipalities may be required to bear the expense of them even if they are not directly benefitted by the elections. (People *ex rel.* Sanitary Dist. v. Schlaeger, 391 Ill. 314 (1945).) Even the special corporate purpose of a municipality may be so related to the public welfare that the state may require the municipality to perform its duties more thoroughly though this results in an increase in taxes. A sanitary district's obsolete facilities resulted in raw sewage being discharged into a river. A district referendum held in 1957 to authorize the issue of bonds for modernization was defeated. Thereupon, a private party sued the sanitary district, charging that the pollution was a nuisance and seeking an order of abatement. If such an order was issued, then a statute permitted the district to issue bonds without a referendum in order to comply. The district defended the suit on the grounds that this constituted the imposition of a debt by the state for a local corporate purpose. The Court held that the treatment of sewage was directly related to the health and welfare of the public, and that a municipal corporation could be required to perform that duty adequately, even when this resulted in additional taxes. (Ruth v. Aurora Sanitary Dist., 17 Ill. 2d 11 (1959).)

In nearly all cases which have challenged a statute under this section, the Court has upheld the law on this ground that it relates to the general welfare of the state rather than to a local corporate purpose. There are some cases, however, in which the application of the principle appears to be inconsistent. Usually these cases involve a construction of this section in conjunction with the provision of Section 9 prohibiting the granting of taxing powers to other than corporate authorities. *Heffner v. Cass & Morgan Counties* (193 Ill. 439 (1901)) concerned an action in trespass against a drainage district which had removed a bridge across a road while constructing a ditch. The complaining counties sought damages in the amount of the cost of replacing the bridge. The drainage district relied on a statutory provision which required the counties to replace the bridge at their own cost. The Court accepted this defense, holding that the statute was not a violation of this section because the construction and maintenance of bridges was a general public purpose of the state, and not a local corporate purpose. However, in a later case on the same issue, the Court overruled the *Heffner* case and held that such a procedure violated Section 9, vesting taxing power in other than corporate authorities, as well as Section 10 because it imposed a debt without consent. (People *ex rel.* Burow v. Block, 276 Ill. 286 (1916).) But in a still later case, the Court held that the legislature can compel counties to contribute to the cost of constructing bridges near the county line, even though the bridge is located wholly within the one county which undertakes the construction. The Court again adopted the rationale that this was for a general public purpose not prohibited by Section 10, and relied in part on the presumably overruled *Heffner* case. (County of Stark v. County of Henry, 326 Ill. 535 (1927).)

Another situation in which Section 9 has caused confusion in conjunction with Section 10 is the fixing of compensation for municipal employees. It has been clearly established that prescription of minimum wages, while it does impose a debt, does not violate Section 10 because it is for a general public purpose. (*See, e.g.,* People *ex rel.* Cannon v. City of Chicago, 351 Ill. 396 (1933) (minimum salary for probation officers); People *ex rel.* Moshier v. City of Springfield, 370 Ill. 541 (1939) (minimum salary for firemen).) There have also been a number of cases upholding, for the same reason, statutes requiring municipal contribution to retirement funds. (*See, e.g.,* Board of Trustees v. Commissioners of Lincoln Park, 282 Ill. 348 (1918) (pension fund for park policemen); People *ex rel.* Nelson v. Jackson-Highland Bldg. Corp., 400 Ill. 533 (1948) (teachers' retirement fund).) However, in one case the Court invalidated a system set up to administer a firemen's retirement fund on the ground that it violated Section 9. (People *ex rel.* Gallenbach v. Franklin, 388 Ill. 560 (1944).) Although the issue seems to correspond with the *Lincoln Park* case above, the Court simply dismissed that case as not being in point. In any event, the bridge cases, together with these retirement fund cases, illustrate the confusion which sometimes arises when Sections 9 and 10 are construed together.

In the area of curative tax legislation, this section has caused serious difficulties for municipal taxing authorities. In order to pass a valid tax ordinance, municipal authorities must comply with statutory requirements which are exceedingly complex. These requirements range from the very fundamental, such as what authorities may levy taxes, to the rather trivial, such as the manner of publication of an ordinance; and the statutory prescriptions are subject to constant change. Mistakes in this situation are inevitably made, most of them of a minor nature which do not affect the basic issues of the fairness of the tax or the important procedures employed in the levy. In most states, as well as in the federal government, such mistakes can be corrected by curative tax statutes so as to validate the tax. In Illinois, however, a number of such validation efforts have been held to violate this section, with the result that municipalities are often faced with serious losses of revenue. It is difficult, if not impossible, to reconcile all the cases, many of which have sustained curative legislation. The general rationale is that the legislature may validate a defective exercise of power but cannot remedy a total absence of power. For a statement of this position, see *People* ex rel. *Ward v. Chicago & E. Ill.*

Ry., (365 Ill. 202 (1936)). In that case, a county board was directed by statute to make its tax levy for the year in September. It did not make the levy until December, and the legislature attempted to validate the levy after it had been made. The Court held that the county board had no power to make the levy in December, and the curative act could not validate the levy without violating this section. It is again emphasized that the procedures under attack are not usually of a nature that go to the fundamental fairness of a tax; serious abuse of the taxing power can and should be prevented by the due process clause. What may be needed, perhaps, is greater power to pass curative tax statutes in those cases where the defect in the exercise of the taxing power is insubstantial and not prejudicial. The cases in the area are voluminous, and it would not be particularly helpful to detail the complexities of the litigation. Two good sources which deal with the problem in detail are Comment, "Curative Tax Legislation," 32 Ill. L. Rev. 456 (1937) and Blomquist, "Effect of Curative Statutes on Taxation in Illinois," 27 Chi.-Kent L. Rev. 211 (1949).

There are several minor points in this section which may be dealt with briefly. The last sentence specifying that private property may not be taken in payment of corporate debts has not been a cause of litigation; the principle is so well settled that it would seem not to necessitate an express constitutional statement. The clause in the first sentence requiring property to be taxed for the payment of debts was last construed in 1873; that case held that the General Assembly could require the State Auditor to levy taxes on property in towns which had subscribed to railroad stock in order to pay the bonds funding the subscription. (Decker v. Hughes, 68 Ill. 33 (1873).) The clause does not seem to be of much contemporary utility. There was a dictum in another early case that this Section 10 does not apply to counties and townships (Wetherell v. Devine, 116 Ill. 632 (1886)); and this point was commented on favorably in a more recent case (People *ex rel.* Lindheimer v. Gaylord Bldg. Corp., 369 Ill. 371 (1938)). However, that is contrary to a prior holding of the Supreme Court (Sleight v. People, 74 Ill. 47 (1874)); and in nearly all subsequent cases in which this issue could have been raised, the Court apparently preferred to rely on the general principles discussed above rather than on a distinction in the type of governmental unit.

Comparative Analysis

As noted above, nine states have constitutional provisions which combine the essential provisions of Sections 9 and 10. Only one state appears to have a separate section comparable to Section 10. The Model State Constitution contains no comparable section.

Comment

The usefulness of this section is doubtful and it could well be eliminated. To the extent that it merely reinforces the requirement of Section 9 (that taxing power for local corporate purposes is vested only in corporate authorities), it is superfluous; and there are many situations in which its relationship to Section 9 has caused considerable confusion. Given the nebulous, perhaps even nonexistent, distinction between a purely local corporate purpose and a purpose of general state concern, the section seems to deal with what is largely an anachronism. The one situation in which this section has exerted an independent influence — in curative tax statutes — has occasionally caused undesirable results and should be corrected. Two of its requirements, that the legislature require property to be taxed for the payment of debts and that private property not be taken for the payment of corporate debts, have not been the subject of significant litigation. They, surely, can be safely repealed.

Municipal Officers — Defaults — Compensation

Sec. 11. No person who is in default, as collector or custodian of money or property belonging to a municipal corporation shall be eligible to any office in or under such corporation. The fees, salary or compensation of no municipal officer who is elected or appointed for a definite term of office, shall be increased or diminished during such term.

History

The Schedule to the 1818 Constitution had a section comparable to but broader than the first sentence of Section 11. The 1818 section said that no sheriff or collector of public moneys in default was eligible "to any office in this State." This prohibition was moved to the Legislative Article of the 1848 Constitution and rephrased to cover a seat in the legislature and "any office of profit or trust in this State." (See Art. IV, Sec. 4, *supra*, p. 127.) Neither of the earlier Constitutions contained a provision comparable to the second sentence of Section 11.

Section 11 was offered to the 1870 Convention as two separate sections, each of which was modified slightly in the Committee of the Whole. Apart from a discussion of technical modifications, there was no debate. They were combined into one section by the Committee on Revision and Adjustment and placed in the Revenue Article, presumably because there was no other place to put it.

In the proposed 1922 Constitution, the section was split in two and placed in an article on Public Servants. In both cases, the section was an amalgam of several sections dealing with the same subject matter. In the one case, the section included matter from Sections 3 and 4 of Article IV and the first sentence of Section 11; in the other case, one section on increasing or diminishing compensation covered a principle expressed in some eight different sections of the 1870 Constitution. (Sections 21 and 22 of Article IV; Section 23 of Article 5; Sections 7, 16, and 25 of the original Article VI; Section 10 of Article X; and this Section 11.)

Explanation

Default: The first sentence of this section is probably redundant because it seems unlikely that any situation would arise that is not covered by the broader language of Section 4 of Article IV. (*Supra*, p. 127.) In any event, no question appears to have arisen under this sentence.

Compensation: The courts decided long ago that this section was to be the catchall for prohibiting salary increases and decreases. As noted above in the *History*, there were originally seven other sections in the Constitution that expressed the principle that those "officers" elected or appointed for a definite term should neither receive an increase in compensation nor suffer a decrease. (See *Comment* below for a discussion of the broad principle.) Whatever the meaning of "municipal officers" in the minds of the delegates to the 1870 Convention, the courts decided the words were "intended to include all officers not specifically mentioned in other provisions of the constitution, occupying offices created by the laws of the State in and for any of the political subdivisions of the State . . . ." (Wolf v. Hope, 210 Ill. 50, 61 (1904).) Consequently, all sorts of positions not normally thought of as "municipal officers" are covered by Section 11. (*See* People *ex rel.* Judge v. Board of Comm'rs, 260 Ill. 345 (1913) (board of election commissioners); People v. Williams, 232 Ill. 519 (1908) (state's attorneys); Wolf v. Hope, 210 Ill. 50 (1904) (city judge); Jimison v. Adams County, 130 Ill. 558 (1899) (county superintendent of schools); County of Cook v. Sennott, 136 Ill. 314 (1891) (probate court clerks).) On various occasions, the Attorney General has followed the catchall approach of the courts. (*See* 1926 Ill. Att'y Gen. Rep. 123 (county highway superintendent); 1915 Ill. Att'y Gen. Rep. 318 (county oil inspector); 1912 Ill. Att'y Gen. Rep. 447 (county commissioners); 1912 Ill. Att'y Gen. Rep. 564 (county commissioners); 1910 Ill. Att'y Gen. Rep. 900 (drainage commissioners).)

Apart from the all-inclusive construction given to this section, the courts have generally drawn routine lines within its bounds. Thus, reimbursement of expenses would not be an increase in compensation, but purporting to fix a sum in lieu of audited expenses would be. (Peabody v. Forest Preserve Dist., 320 Ill. 454 (1926).) An "officer" who holds his position at the pleasure of a superior can, of course, receive a salary increase or suffer a decrease. (Village of Forest Park v. Collis, 329 Ill. App. 273 (1946) (village attorney); Morgan v. County of DuPage, 371 Ill. 53 (1939) (assistant county superintendent of schools).) A statutory classification of salaries tied to federal census figures does not run afoul of Section 11 if, after a census, an officer's salary is cut because his county dropped in population. (Brissenden v. Howlett, 30 Ill. 2d 247 (1964).) The same rule would apply to a salary increase, but presumably no taxpayer has sued to prevent the increased payment. The pesky problem of pensions, discussed more fully in connection with Section 19 of Article IV (*supra,* pp. 195-6), has shown up here. Pensions are valid under this section. (DeWolf v. Bowley, 355 Ill. 530 (1934); People *ex rel.* Kroner v. Abbott, 274 Ill. 380 (1916).)

One problem has arisen under this section that should delight a law professor and anyone else interested in the finer weaving of judicial logic. The president of a village board, serving without compensation, was reelected, following which his board adopted an ordinance fixing his compensation at $2,000 per year retroactive a few months to the beginning of his new term. The Supreme Court said he could not be paid. (Baumrucker v. Brink, 373 Ill. 82 (1939).) One judge dissented on the ground that many years earlier the Supreme Court had held that to create a salary where none had existed before was not an increase. In reply, the majority opinion simply said that the earlier case arose under Section 10 of Article X (*infra,* p. 509), and this case arose under Section 11 of Article IX, a distinction which the dissenting judge could not comprehend.

Comparative Analysis

Default: See *Comparative Analysis* of Section 4 of Article IV. (*Supra,* p. 129.)

Compensation: Only a few states appear to have a comparable provision. Alabama prohibits increases or decreases during the term of an incumbent, Missouri prohibits an increase, Louisiana prohibits a decrease, and Kentucky and Washington say that compensation may not be changed. California says no increase, except (1) during wartime by two-thirds' vote of the legislature, or (2) in the case of a board or commission, the members of which are chosen for staggered terms, when one or more members becomes eligible for an increase at the beginning of his term. The Model State Constitution is silent on the subject of compensation.

Comment

There are two simple principles involved in this increase or decrease in salary business, but in the welter of litigation the principles sometimes seem to be forgotten. One principle is that the man who determines the amount of a salary should not be allowed to use that power to influence someone who is not responsible to him. Thus, it is appropriate — indeed, essential — to prohibit decreases in salaries of judges, for that could destroy the independence of the judiciary. If judges are appointed or elected for relatively short terms, a prohibition of an increase is acceptable, but, particularly today, if the terms are longer than four years, even a "normal" increase in the cost of living results in a salary cut. (Note that United States judges are appointed for life, and the United States Constitution prohibits only a salary cut for them, whereas the salary of the President may be neither increased nor decreased during his four-year term. Note also that under Section 17 of Article VI, salaries may be increased but not diminished during the judicial term of office, whereas under the 1870 Constitution, salaries could be neither increased nor diminished. See *History* and *Explanation* of Sec. 17 of Art. VI, *supra*, pp. 370-2.)

Where compensation is set by a legislative body for executive and administrative officials, the principle is applicable to any officials who are elected by the voters, for under the theory of separation of powers, the fact of election means that they are supposed to be independent of the legislature. The principle is not applicable in the case of appointed officials who are answerable to an elected official. Notwithstanding the theoretical possibility that, for example, the legislature might try to influence the Governor by decreasing the salaries of stenographers so low that he could find no one to type his letters, in general such pressure is sufficiently remote that the danger is outweighed by the need for flexibility in adjusting salaries. The close question of principle is the case of officials appointed for a term of years where the purpose of the term of years is to make them independent. If there were a policy that independence would be the only reason for having a set term for an appointive position, the inclusion of such appointive positions in a constitutional prohibition on increases and decreases in compensation would make sense. The very fact that the foregoing sentence is in the subjunctive suggests the weakness in the theory, for a constitutional prohibition ought not to rest on an assumption that people will follow a policy that is not mandatory.

The second principle is that a man ought not to be able to increase his own salary. Thus, it is appropriate to prohibit those people who make appropriations — legislators, supervisors, commissioners, councilmen, aldermen — from increasing their own salaries during the term for which they are elected.

The foregoing, by implication, rejects two other arguments in support of a no increase or decrease in pay provision. One is the argument that a man running for office, or accepting an appointment, ought to know definitely what his remuneration will be. The other is the argument — probably the one uppermost in the minds of the delegates to the 1870

Convention — that if left alone, government officials will raid the treasury. This may very well have been a problem in the middle of the Nineteenth Century. In today's complex world, there are problems galore in finding money enough in the treasury to do all the things people desire of their government. The amount of money saved by an unnecessarily broad constitutional prohibition on salary increases is a drop in the bucket.

Limitation of Municipal Indebtedness — Debt Retirement

Sec. 12. No county, city, township, school district or other municipal corporation, shall be allowed to become indebted in any manner or for any purpose, to an amount, including existing indebtedness, in the aggregate exceeding five per centum on the value of the taxable property therein, to be ascertained by the last assessment for state and county taxes, previous to the incurring of such indebtedness. Any county, city, school district, or other municipal corporation, incurring any indebtedness as aforesaid, shall before, or at the time of doing so, provide for the collection of a direct annual tax sufficient to pay the interest on such debt as it falls due, and also to pay and discharge the principal thereof within twenty years from the time of contracting the same.

This section shall not be construed to prevent any county, city, township, school district, or other municipal corporation, from issuing their bonds in compliance with any vote of the people which may have been had prior to the adoption of this constitution in pursuance of any law providing therefor.

History

This section limiting municipal indebtedness was new in the 1870 Constitution. The reasons for its adoption are not entirely clear from the debates, but apparently the main concern was over the large debts which had been incurred by counties and municipalities for subscriptions to railroad stock. The issue of railroad debts was a very heated one at this Convention and was reflected not only in the debates on this section, but also in those on Section 6 (see discussion, *supra,* pp. 454-5) and on the Separate Section on loaning municipal credit to private corporations see discussion, *infra,* p. 576). There was evidenced a considerable downstate feeling that Chicago was attempting to impose these restrictions to prevent those areas from getting railroads. In any event, the proponents of this section advocated the view that excessive indebtedness led to high taxes and that a restriction on debt-incurring power would serve as a means of limiting taxes. Opponents of the section argued that the people should have the right to determine their own indebtedness. Several amendments were offered changing the amount of the limit, but all were defeated. As originally proposed, the limitation for retirement of the debt was ten years; this was amended to 20 years with little debate. The saving clause for the existing debt was added to the committee report for purposes of clarity. Many Convention members felt that the section was so controversial that its inclusion would endanger the whole

Constitution. They unsuccessfully advocated that it be submitted as a separate section.

The proposed 1922 Constitution made several changes in this section. Counties, towns, and school districts retained the 5 per cent limit, but other municipal corporations had a 6 per cent debt limit. The mandatory tax to retire the debt in 20 years was to be levied in "substantially equal annual installments," except that provision could be made to retire it before maturity. The last sentence of the secction was omitted as obsolete. Also, because of the extensive special provisions which were made for Chicago and Cook County, the section did not apply to them. As to the special sections on Cook County and the municipalities within it, their debt limit was to be 7 per cent of assessed value. If the municipalities undertook consolidation as provided for, then the limit was to be 7 per cent of the full value of real property.

Most of the debate on debt limits in the 1920-1922 Convention was devoted to the problems of Chicago. Debate was minimal on the more general provisions. The requirement that the tax to retire the debt be levied in substantially equal annual installments was inserted to prevent the practice which had become prevalent of deferring payments on the principal until close to the bonds' maturity dates, and then refunding them upon maturity. It is entirely unclear from the Proceedings how or why the debt limit for "other municipal corporations" was raised to 6 per cent. The original committee report proposed the 5 per cent limit. Possibly the change represented a compromise resulting from the defeat of another proposal authorizing cities to issue utility bonds in the amount of 15 per cent of assessed value, the bonds to be paid for out of revenue from the utilities.

Explanation

The limitations of this section apply only to municipal corporations which are local governmental units; they do not apply to administrative units of the state government which have state-wide jurisdictions. (People v. Illinois Toll Highway Comm'n, 3 Ill. 2d 218 (1954).) This section limits the powers of the General Assembly in one respect — it cannot authorize a debt for a municipal corporation in excess of 5 per cent of assessed valuation. However, in creating those corporations, it may specify a limit under 5 per cent and may increase or decrease that limit without the consent of the voters of the municipality. (People ex rel. Adamowski v. Metropolitan Sanitary Dist., 14 Ill. 2d 271 (1958).) There is a further indirect limitation on the power of the General Assembly to control the taxing authority of municipal corporations. Since the section requires the levy of a tax sufficient to pay bonded indebtedness, the General Assembly may not restrict the taxing power so as to make this requirement impossible to meet. (See the discussion below in respect to the necessity to levy a tax.) This section in no way restricts the General Assembly in fixing the assessment ratio for purposes of taxation. In fact, it has been a not unusual practice for the General Assembly to increase assessment ratios while at the same time adjusting tax rates so that no more revenue is produced, the sole purpose of the change being to increase the borrowing power of municipalities. (People *ex rel.* Campe v. Board of Review, 290 Ill. 467 (1919).)

Although the language of this section is negative, it has been interpreted as conferring upon municipalities the power to borrow money, at least in the absence of any statutory restriction. The City of Chicago extended taxes to pay for general expenses up to the statutory limit. This left a budget deficit of $8,000,000, and the city issued bonds to cover this amount. The bond issue was attacked by taxpayers as being without statutory authority and merely a scheme to get around the tax rate limit. The Court held, however, that the city could borrow money under this section for whatever corporate purposes it desired so long as the constitutional limit was not exceeded. (People *ex rel.* Carr. v. Chicago & N.W. Ry., 308 Ill. 54 (1923).) This section does not restrict the power of municipalities to levy taxes. Where a school district issued bonds up to the constitutional limit and the proceeds were not sufficient to complete the building, it was proper for the district to levy taxes up to the statutory maximum in order to finish it. (People *ex rel.* Trobaugh v. Chicago & T.R.R., 223 Ill. 448 (1906).)

It was clearly understood by the 1870 Convention that this section was a limitation only on the indebtedness of municipal corporations, and was not a limitation of the amount of indebtedness as applied to particular property within those corporations. Thus it was frequently pointed out in the debates on this section that although municipalities had a 5 per cent debt limit, property itself might bear a municipal debt of 20 per cent if all of the enumerated governments incurred the maximum debt. What the Convention probably did not foresee was the extent to which this section would encourage the creation of numerous overlapping municipal corporations, each with a limited function, in order to evade the debt limitations. The Supreme Court sanctioned this trend in an early decision which held that functions which ordinarily were performed by the city (in this case, construction and maintenance of a sewer system) could be vested in an independent municipal corporation which would have its own taxing powers and debt limit. (Wilson v. Board of Trustees, 133 Ill. 443 (1890).) In many cases, the proliferation of overlapping municipalities, particularly of school districts, led to extremely inefficient administration. Efforts to effect consolidation were hampered by problems of distributing existing debt between the old and new districts and required continuous legislative supervision. (For a thorough treatment of this problem in relation to school consolidation, *see* McLain v. Phelps, 409 Ill. 393 (1951); People *ex rel.* Community High School Dist. v. Hupe, 2 Ill. 2d 434 (1954). *See also* Kocsis v. Chicago Park Dist., 363 Ill. 24 (1935).)

The problem of ascertaining the limit to which a municipality may become indebted has not created much difficulty. The Supreme Court originally held that the assessment value to be used as the basis for the 5 per cent limit was that of the county board of review, not the State Board of Equalization. (People *ex rel.* Standerfer v. Hamill, 134 Ill. 666 (1888).) However, four years later, without reference to the *Hamill* case, the Court held that the state's equalized value was the proper base, and this rule has since been followed. (Wabash R.R. v. People *ex rel.* Reed, 202 Ill. 9 (1903).) For purposes of determining the constitutionality of a debt, the limit is figured as of the time of the incurring of the debt; thus a subsequent drop in property assessment value does not cause a debt that was legal when incurred to become illegal. (Kocsis v. Chicago Park Dist., 362 Ill. 24 (1935).) Where there is an outstanding debt, a sinking fund which may by law be applied only to the reduction of that debt may be set off against that debt for purposes of determining the amount of additional debt which may be incurred. (People *ex rel.* Lindeheimer v. Hamilton, 373 Ill. 124 (1940).) But general funds in the treasury may not be set off against the debt limit, since the question is one of indebtedness, not insolvency. (City of Chicago v. McDonald, 176 Ill. 404 (1898).)

Municipal obligations may take a wide variety of forms and may be incurred in many ways. For purposes of analyzing the effect of this section, these obligations may be divided into three classifications. First are those obligations which are voluntarily assumed and for which the general credit of the municipality is pledged; such obligations are debts within the limits of this section and may not be incurred in excess of the constitutional limit. The second classification includes obligations for which the general credit of the municipality is liable, but which are not voluntarily assumed; these are debts for purposes of determining the limit to which further indebtedness may be voluntarily incurred, but this section is not a bar to their incurrence by the municipality. The final classification includes a group of obligations which are voluntarily incurred by the municipality, but the municipality's liability is substantially restricted; these obligations are not subject to any of the restrictions of this section. Each of these classifications will be discussed individually.

Voluntarily assumed obligations which fall within the restrictions of this section can be of many different types. The most obvious debt which this section sought to control is long-term, general-obligation bonded indebtedness, and the incurrence of such indebtedness is subject to the 5 per cent limit. In determining the amount of bonds which can be issued within this limit, the amount of interest which the bonds will carry is not to be included; the 5 per cent limit applies to the principal amount only. (Goodwine v. County of Vermilion, 271 Ill. 126 (1915).) Also, contracts which are to be paid for solely out of the proceeds of bond issues are not considered as debts; otherwise, the projects to be funded by the bonds could not be undertaken. (Hartmann v. Pesotum Community Consol. School Dist., 325 Ill. 268 (1927).) Other than this exception, long-term contracts and leases are debts within this section; and the total amount of the contractual liability must be included in determining the debt limit. (People *ex rel.* Adamowski v. Public Bldg. Comm'n, 11 Ill. 2d 125 (1957) (long-term lease of space for municipal offices); Wade v. East Side Levee & Sanitary Dist., 320 Ill. 396 (1926); Baltimore & O. Sw. R.R. v. People *ex rel.* Gaston, 200 Ill. 541 (1903) (13-year contract with private power company to furnish city lights culminating in purchase of power plant).) Mortgages of municipal property are debts within this section (City of Joliet v. Alexander, 194 Ill. 457 (1902)), and at one time it was thought that this rule applied to pledges of future income from revenue-producing municipal property (Schnell v. City of Rock Island, 232 Ill. 89 (1908)). However, this latter position has been overruled; see the discussion below of revenue-producing projects. The public benefits assessed against a city in a local improvement project are also debts under this section if they are to be financed by credit; however, if they can be paid for out of current taxes, they are not debts. (People *ex rel.* Toman v. Crane, 372 Ill. 228 (1939).)

One of the most difficult questions was whether the liabilities for current operating expenses of a municipality constitute debts within the meaning of this section. Tax levies and budget appropriations are made by the municipality at the beginning of the year, but taxes are not actually collected until the end of the year. To carry on normal operations in the interim, unless there is a huge surplus carried over from the prior year (a rare occurrence in municipal finance), the municipality must rely on temporary credit in some form, either contingent contracts or outright loans. In deciding whether such credit is a debt within this section, the Court faced a dilemma. On the one hand, to hold it a debt subject to the 5 per cent limit would mean that a very large number of municipalities already indebted to the limit would simply have to cease carrying on their governmental functions. On the other hand, if it were not considered a debt, the opportunity would arise to carry over such ostensibly "temporary" debt from year to year, possibly resulting in a total indebtedness greatly in excess of the 5 per cent limit. Most states with similar constitutional debt limits had decided that they applied only to long-term debts. While the 1870 Convention had not addressed itself to this question directly, there is considerable evidence in the debates that these long-term debts were what it had in mind. Furthermore, this position was buttressed by the provision requiring an annual tax sufficient to pay off the principal and interest of the debt within 20 years; obviously such a requirement could apply only to a long-term debt. However, after due consideration in a series of cases, a divided Court held that even current liabilities of a municipality were to be considered debts within the requirements of that section. (City of Springfield v. Edwards, 84 Ill. 626 (1877); Law v. People ex rel. Huck, 87 Ill. 385 (1877); Prince v. City of Quincy, 105 Ill. 138 (1882); Prince v. City of Quincy, 105, Ill. 215 (1883); City of Chicago v. McDonald, 176 Ill. 404 (1898).) The harsh results of this conclusion on municipalities which have reached their debt limit are mitigated to some extent by the Court's decisions permitting tax anticipation warrants, a restricted form of short-term borrowing. This subject is discussed below in relationship to obligations which do not fall within this section.

There is a large group of obligations which a municipality may incur and for which it is generally liable even though it is already indebted beyond the 5 per cent limit. These generally may be classified as "obligations imposed by law." It is not accurate to say that these obligations do not constitute debts within the meaning of this section, for they must be included in the amount of existing indebtedness when determining whether a municipality has reached its constitutional limit, and the requirement that an annual tax be levied to pay them is also applicable. However, they must be distinguished from the obligations discussed above in that this section cannot be invoked as a bar to their aquisition by a municipality, whereas with obligations voluntarily incurred, both the municipality and the taxpayer have numerous remedies based on this section by which to avoid them. (See the discussion of remedies below.)

Probably the most common kinds of obligations within this classification are funding and refunding bonds — general obligation bonds issued to finance unfunded debt or to refinance funded debt. Such bonds can be issued if the underlying debt was valid when incurred, even though at the time of issuance the debt limit has been reached. (Kocsis v. Chicago Park Dist., 362 Ill. 24 (1935).) The reasoning here is that since the underlying debts are valid and enforceable, a municipality should not be denied rational means of retiring them, and no additional new debt is created by the funding mechanism. For the same reason, bonds issued to fund valid judgments are not barred by this section. (Elmhurst Nat'l Bank v. Village of Bellwood, 372 Ill. 204 (1939).)

Judgments, of course, can represent a wide variety of obligations imposed by law, and the cases give numerous examples of these obligations.

Municipalities are responsible for their torts (City of Bloomington v. Perdue, 99 Ill. 329 (1881)); statutory liability may be imposed for failure to maintain the peace (City of Chicago v. Manhattan Cement Co., 178 Ill. 372 (1899) (property damage resulting from riot)); and general liability may result from a breach of fiduciary duty as trustee of a special fund (Indiana Harbor Belt R.R. v. City of Calumet City, 391 Ill. 280 (1945) (misappropriation of special assessment funds)). A municipality may not enter into voluntary contracts which are illegal because of this section and by collusion have them reduced to judgements to be funded by judgment bonds. (See the discussion of remedies below.) However, where valid contracts are made, they must be performed in good faith; and where the municipality by its own fault breaches those contracts, liability may still be imposed on a *quantum meruit* or contract theory, whichever is appropriate, without regard to this section. (City of Chicago v. Sexton, 115 Ill. 230 (1885); DeLeuw, Cather & Co. v. City of Joliet, 327 Ill. App. 453 (1945).)

There is finally to be considered a group of municipal obligations which, while they are debts in the ordinary sense of that term, are not debts within the meaning of this section; that is, they need not be included in determining the amount of municipal indebtedness, and there is no constitutional limit on the amount which may be incurred. In general, the liability of a municipality for these debts is very strictly limited, and the rationale for excluding them is that this section was designed to prevent property from being overburdened with taxes which would have to be raised in order to support excessive debt. But where the liability of the municipality is very strictly limited, so that creditors cannot force a resort to general taxation in order to collect the debt, then the reason for the restrictions of this section disappears and it should not apply.

One of this kind of indebtedness is local improvement bonds which are financed solely from special assessments on the property benefitted. The theory here is that there is no taxation in the general sense, but merely an equal exchange of values; and so long as the municipality is liable to the bondholders only from the special assessment fund, there is no debt. While there appear to be no direct holdings on this subject in Illinois, the doctrine was already established in 1870 and has been commented on favorably in a number of cases. Indeed, the 1870 Convention itself recognized that many projects which were then financed by general taxation, and hence subject to this section, could be financed by special assessment and escape its restrictions.

From the standpoint of municipal finances, probably the most important form of obligation in this classification is tax anticipation warrants.

As was noted above, taxes are levied early in the year but are not collected until much later, usually the following year. In the interim, some way must be found of paying for governmental operations. There may be a cash surplus, or there may be enough ordinary debt-incurring power to carry on credit transactions. But if neither of these situations obtains, resort is usually had to tax anticipation warrants. If these warrants conform to a strictly prescribed form, they will not be considered debts within this section. The taxes must already have been levied for the year in question, and the warrants must clearly state on their face that the only liability is out of the tax funds collected for that year. If the warrants do not follow this prescription, they are considered ordinary debts and are subject to the requirements of this section. (City of Springfield v. Edwards, 84 Ill. 626 (1877); Law v. People *ex rel.* Huck, 87 Ill. 385 (1877); Hodges v. Crowley, 186 Ill. 305 (1900); Holmgren v. City of Moline, 269 Ill. 248 (1915).)

Local improvements which are revenue-producing may be financed by long-term contracts which pledge only the revenue from the project in payment of the debt. At one time the Court held that only revenue from new projects could be so pledged; to pledge revenue (which was available to the general fund) from existing municipal property was thought to constitute a mortgage of existing property and thus a debt. Hence, a sewer extension could not be financed out of charges from the existing system plus the new one. (Schnell v. City of Rock Island, 232 Ill. 89 (1907).) However, in a later case involving the expansion of a water supply system, the city undertook a joint venture with a private company in which the revenue from the whole system was pledged as payment; and this was upheld without reference to the *Schnell* case. (Maffit v. City of Decatur, 322 Ill. 82 (1926).) *Maffit* has since been cited as "modifying" *Schnell,* and such projects are uniformly upheld as not being debts within this section. (Ward v. City of Chicago, 342 Ill. 167 (1930); Poole v. City of Kankakee, 406 Ill. 521 (1950).)

By the same token, bonds issued to fund revenue-producing projects, whose payment is to be solely from the revenue of the project, are not Section 12 debts. (City of Edwardsville v. Jenkins, 376 Ill. 327 (1941); see the discussion of state debt under Art. IV, Sec. 18, *supra,* pp. 189-91).)

The requirement of this section that an annual tax be levied to pay the interest and principal within 20 years is self-executing. However, it does not apply to every obligation which is a debt under this section. It applies only to debts whose payment is deferred to a *fixed* future date and whose amount is certain. (Town of Kankakee v. McGrew, 178 Ill. 74 (1899); County of Coles v. Goehring, 209 Ill. 142 (1904).) The levy should include an amount sufficient to cover loss and collection expenses. (People *ex rel.* Korzen v. Englemann, 32 Ill. 2d 196 (1965).) Because of its self-executing nature, the constitutional provision may override a statute. For example, sanitary districts were authorized to levy bond taxes for two years in advance. Because there had been considerable delays in tax collection for four years, a district levied for two and one-half years in order to be sure of a sufficient amount to pay maturities. The Court held that because of the Section 12 requirement, the district was justified in exceeding its statutory authority, and the tax was legal. (People *ex rel.* Gill v. 110 S. Dearborn St. Corp., 363 Ill. 286 (1936).) Where a statutory tax rate limit is too low to produce an amount sufficient to pay the bonds, the municipality may validly exceed the statutory limit. (People *ex rel.* Henry v. New York Cent. R.R. Lines, 381 Ill. 490 (1942).)

The question arises as to what remedies are available to enforce the provisions of this Section 12. In general, those who deal with a municipal government are bound to know its powers, and if it exceeds its powers in contracting indebtedness, the debt is void and there can be no recovery. This section may be pleaded by a municipality as a bar to collection of a debt. Thus, a city contracted with a plaintiff to construct a waterworks system which the city was then to lease for 30 years. After several years, the city broke its lease, and in the subsequent suit pleaded that the contract was void because it violated this section. This was held to be a complete defense to the claim, and in a later suit between the same parties on the same facts, the plaintiff was denied a recovery based on *quantum meruit*. (Prince v. City of Quincy, 128 Ill. 443 (1889); Prince v. City of Quincy, 105 Ill. 215 (1883).) Recovery on ordinary instruments of indebtedness may be denied where at the time of issuance the municipality was indebted over the limit. (East St. Louis Gas Light & Coke Co. v. City of East St. Louis, 45 Ill. App. 591 (1892).)

A more common situation is for a municipality to attempt voluntarily to exceed the constitutional debt limit, and in this situation the most effective means of enforcing this section is by taxpayers' remedies. An objection to the collection of a tax on an illegal debt will be sustained. (Baltimore & O. Sw. R.R. v. People *ex rel.* Allen, 195 Ill. 423 (1902).) The shortcoming of this method is that it gives relief only to the objecting taxpayer. Broader remedies are to enjoin the issuance of illegal bonds or the making of illegal contracts (Village of East Moline v. Pope, 224 Ill. 386 (1906), or to enjoin the extension and collection of taxes on illegal debts (Green v. Hutsonville Township High School Dist., 356 Ill. 216 (1934). *Compare* Austin v. Healy, 376 Ill. 633 (1941)).

Comparative Analysis

Constitutional limitations on municipal and county indebtedness are very common. For purposes of general analysis here, restrictions on municipal corporations may be divided into six categories, with several qualifications to be noted. (1) Twenty-nine states have no constitutional restrictions on debt of municipal corporations. (2) In three states, there is no limit to the amount of debt which can be incurred, but the debt must be approved by a referendum. (3) In five states, the authorities may incur debt up to a certain limit (usually low) without referendum approval; above that limit there must be a referendum, and in any event indebtedness cannot exceed a maximum upper limit. (4) In three states, there is a maximum upper limit, but any debt incurred within this limit must be submitted to a referendum. (5) In ten states, including Illinois, there is a maximum limit, but no referendum is required.

The above breakdown applies to municipal corporations generally. Many constitutions have provisions applicable only to specific municipalities, such as school districts or counties. For example, while only 21 states restrict municipalities generally, 31 restrict counties, with these provisions distributed generally among the categories discussed above. The details of these requirements, such as the amount of the limit and the vote required in the referendum, vary widely. In addition, it should probably be noted that many states having no specific constitutional debt limitations have enacted statutory limits.

The Model State Constitution is silent on this subject.

Comment

The merits of a constitutional debt limit can be questioned on three counts. First of all, its effect on holding down taxes is doubtful. To the extent that necessary (or even desired) municipal services cannot be financed by borrowing, they must be financed by higher taxes. Secondly, the limits can be evaded to a large extent. Despite a statutory requirement of full-value assessment, property is currently equalized at the state level at about 50 per cent of value. Thus municipal borrowing power could be administratively doubled. The large number of overlapping municipalities, often with resulting inefficiency of administration, is directly attributable in part to the need for evading the debt limit. And the many devices discussed above for limiting municipal liability and thus avoiding Section 12 altogether enable municipalities to conduct large amounts of credit transactions in excess of the 5 per cent limit. But this situation raises the third objection. To the extent that liability on borrowed funds is limited, the cost of that credit is much more expensive than with ordinary borrowing, thus increasing the net cost to a municipality.

There are at least three possible alternatives which the Convention may consider. First, the section may be eliminated entirely. This would not necessarily leave municipalities with unlimited borrowing power, for the legislature could still impose statutory limitations to the extent thought desirable. The second possibility would be to retain the limit, but allow it to be exceeded by referendum approval. Of course, the provision could simply be retained as is, with possible consideration being given to increasing the amount of the limit.

World's Columbian Exposition

Sec. 13. The corporate authorities of the city of Chicago are hereby authorized to issue interest-bearing bonds of said city to an amount not exceeding five million dollars, at a rate of interest not to exceed five per centum per annum, the principal payable within thirty years from the date of their issue, and the proceeds thereof shall be paid to the treasurer of the World's Columbian Exposition, and used and disbursed by him under the direction and control of the directors in aid of the World's Columbian Exposition, to be held in the city of Chicago in pursuance of an act of Congress of the United States: *Provided*, that if, at the election for the adoption of this amendment to the constitution, a majority of the votes cast within the limits of the city of Chicago shall be against its adoption, then no bonds shall be issued under this amendment. And said corporate authorities shall be repaid as large a proportionate amount of the aid given by them as is repaid to the stockholders on the sums subscribed and paid by them, and the money so received shall be used in the redemption of the bonds issued as aforesaid: *Provided,* that said authorities may take, in whole or in part of the sum coming to them, any permanent improvements placed on land held or controlled by them: *And provided further,* that no such indebtedness so created shall in any part thereof be paid by the State, or from any State revenue, tax or fund, but the same shall be paid by the said city of Chicago alone.

History

This section was added by the fifth amendment to the 1870 Constitution. The amendment was necessary because at the time the City of Chicago had reached its constitutional debt limit. The proposed 1922 Constitution omitted this section.

Explanation

The Supreme Court subsequently held that the Columbian Exposition bonds did not have to be counted in computing the city's debt for purposes of determining whether the constitutional limitation had been reached. (Stone v. City of Chicago, 207 Ill. 492 (1904).)

Comparative Analysis

Obviously, no other state has a provision just like this one. Presumably, other states with rigid debt limits have had to amend their constitutions to permit additional borrowing.

Comment

This section is obsolete and should be dropped.

Article X

COUNTIES

New Counties

Sec. 1. No new county shall be formed or established by the General Assembly, which will reduce the county or counties, or either of them, from which it shall be taken, to less contents than four hundred square miles; nor shall any county be formed of less contents; nor shall any line thereof pass within less than ten miles of any county seat of the county or counties proposed to be divided.

History

This section first appeared in the 1848 Constitution and only minor stylistic changes were made in 1870. At the Convention, however, there was extended debate on four occasions. The principal battle was over a proposal to include an exception permitting any city over 200,000 in population — i.e., Chicago — to form itself into a separate county. This was apparently objectionable to the delegates from that part of Cook County outside of Chicago and at almost the last moment the words were deleted under a suspension of the rules.

The proposed 1922 Constitution considerably shortened the section but retained its substance. The proposed section was part of a block of sections with a subheading "Counties other than the County of Cook." Another block of sections covered "County of Cook" and contained a specific authorization for legislation consolidating the city and the county subject to a referendum and approval by a majority of those voting on the question both within and outside the city.

Explanation

In 1851, the legislature combined two counties into one. In a case attacking the statute, the Supreme Court held that consolidation could not be effected without the concurrence of the people affected. Although the Court noted that the thrust of this section and Sections 2 and 3, all of which were substantially the same under the 1848 Constitution, was to prevent division of counties and shifting of parts from one county to another, it ruled that the legislature could not by indirection thwart the interests of county residents. (People ex rel. Stephenson v. Marshall, 12 Ill. 391 (1851) (A. Lincoln and R. Wingate for the winning party).)

The present statutory system for consolidating counties provides, first, for a petition by not fewer than 200 voters, "one-half of such members being freeholders," residing in a county desiring to be annexed; second, for a vote in each county at a county or state regular election; and, third, for ratification by a majority of the votes "polled" in each county "at such election." (Ill. Rev. Stat. ch. 34, §151 (1967).) No case appears to have arisen under this section, and it is not known whether this statutory scheme meets all constitutional requirements. The only serious question arises under the second half of the first sentence of Section 3. (*Infra*, p. 492.) That calls for ratification by a majority of the voters of any county to which territory is to be added. Section 151 of Chapter 34 requires only a majority "polled" in the election.

The Attorney General has stated that the ten-mile minimum distance from county line to county seat is measured from the municipal line and not from the county buildings in the county seat. But he went on to state that subsequent extension of a municipal boundary has no constitutional significance, that the critical boundary is that of the time of establishment as a county seat. (1908 Ill. Att'y Gen. Rep. 706.) In 1954, the Supreme Court held that the Chicago Regional Port District, a municipal corporation, is not a "county." (People *ex rel.* Gutknecht v. Chicago Regional Port District, 4 Ill. 2d 363 (1954).)

Comparative Analysis

Approximately 22 states have constitutional geographical limitations on making little counties out of big counties. Just over half of them use the magic number of 400 square miles. Except for Tennessee, the remaining states require larger areas, from 432 square miles (12 townships), to 900 square miles. Tennessee permits the formation of a county of not fewer than 275 square miles, but the old county's area may not be reduced below 500 square miles. Approximately ten states have provisions concerning proximity of the county seat to the county line. Virginia has an interesting exception to a 600 square mile minimum. It is provided that any county which is three times as long as its mean breadth or any county more than 50 miles long can be divided at the legislature's discretion. The Model State Constitution requires the legislature by general law to provide for "methods and procedures of . . . merging, consolidating and dissolving [counties] and of altering their boundaries . . . ."

Comment

There are only five states that have more than 102 counties. Originally, counties tended to be no larger than would require a one-day trip by horse and buggy to the county seat. With modern transportation, this traditional limitation has no meaning. Nevertheless, there are many factors inhibiting rational consolidaton of counties and it is not likely that great strides in reducing the number of counties would take place even were the Constitution silent on the subject. In the light of this practicality, it is arguable that a provision substantially as flexible as the Model State Constitution's requirement quoted above should suffice. The Convention must weigh, however, the desirability of flexibility for the future against the danger that the very interests that inhibit county consolidation might oppose any constitutional revision that even potentially makes consolidation easier. Nevertheless, the Convention should be able to combine this section and Sections 2 and 3 into one simple provision comparable to the 1922 proposal quoted in the *History* of Section 2 below. Such a provision could, of course, contain a minimum allowable area for new counties, but even though the foregoing argument indicates that the wave of the future is believed to be consolidation of counties, there is no necessary virtue in constitutionally foreclosing alternatives that could result in smaller counties or even more counties.

Division of Counties — Referendum

Sec. 2. No county shall be divided, or have any part stricken therefrom, without submitting the question to a vote of the people of the county, nor unless a majority of all the legal voters of the county, voting on the question, shall vote for the same.

History

This section was first adopted in the 1848 Constitution and carried over unchanged into the 1870 Convention. An unsuccessful effort was made on the floor to permit the legislature to switch one or two townships from one county to another without the affirmative vote called for by this section. The proposed 1922 Constitution combined this section and Section 3 into a concise section, the first sentence of which read:

"No county shall be changed in area unless the change is approved by a majority of those voting on the question in each county and each part affected." (art. VIII, §168.)

In most situations, this would appear to require four separate approvals: (1) by the group moving from one county to another; (2) by the entire old county; (3) by the people left in the old county; and (4) by the county to which the move is to be made. Under Sections 2 and 3 as they stand, approval (3) above is not required.

Explanation

No problems appear to have arisen under this section. There were 102 counties in 1870, and of these only 15 are large enough to permit division

into two counties, since Section 1 would require each county to contain
no fewer than 400 square miles. Moreover, 30 counties are already below
the minimum of 400 square miles, and under the restrictions of Section
1 no territory can be taken from them. Another 18 counties have more
than 400 square miles of territory but fewer than 500, and this limits the
feasibility of transfer of area. All in all, considering these geographical
limitations, the stringent petition requirement in Section 3 below, and
the traditional reluctance to change, it is no surprise to find over the past
century a lack of activity in altering county lines.

Comparative Analysis

Approximately 24 states have a constitutional provision limiting the
division of counties. In most instances, a referendum is required, usually
of the voters of the areas affected, but in some cases only the voters in
the area to be stricken have to approve. In some states, a majority of
those voting on the question is sufficient; in others, a majority of the
voters is required. In at least four states, the requirement is a two-thirds'
vote, of those voting (two states) or of the voters (two states). The Model
State Constitution has no referendum provision.

Comment

Although counties are theoretically only convenient administrative
subdivisions of the state and not necessarily to be frozen into the Constitution, it is consistent with democratic principles for county residents to
have some voice in their fate. It would seem appropriate to preserve this
principle by a simple referendum provision along the lines of the proposed 1922 Constitution quoted earlier. It does not seem appropriate
to put a premium on the preservation of the status quo, which is the
effect of a requirement that a majority "of all the legal voters of the
county" approve a geographic alteration. This assumes, of course, that
"voting on the question" means "at an election." The sentence can be
read to mean a "majority of those voting on the question at an election
open to all the legal voters of the county." At the very least, it is appropriate, if not imperative, to tidy up the referendum language.

Counties — Territory Added or Taken

Sec. 3. There shall be no territory stricken from any county, unless a majority of the voters living in such territory, shall petition for such division; and
no territory shall be added to any county without the consent of the majority
of the voters of the county to which it is proposed to be added. But the portion
so stricken off and added to another county, or formed in whole or in part into
a new county, shall be holden for, and obliged to pay its proportion of the indebtedness of the county from which it has been taken.

History

The first sentence of this section appeared in the 1848 Constitution in the same form. The second sentence is new. There was a related section in the 1848 Constitution, but it simply stated that if a new county did not organize within the prescribed period, the county remained a part of the old county until otherwise provided by law. In the 1870 Convention, the section proposed by the Committee on Counties consisted of the first sentence only. The second sentence was added by an amendment agreed to without debate. The proposed 1922 Constitution contained the sentence quoted in the *History* of Section 2. (*Supra*, p. 491.) A second sentence provided that "[a]ny territory taken from a county shall be liable for its proportion of the debt of such county."

Explanation

In an early case, the Supreme Court held in effect that Section 2 and this section could not be bypassed by legislation purporting to settle a boundary dispute but in reality taking land from one county and adding it to another. (Rock Island County v. Sage, 88 Ill. 582 (1878).) The Attorney General was asked whether in proposing to form a new county out of parts of two existing counties, the petition must be signed by a majority of the voters of each part. He suggested that it would be advisable so to do. (1908 Ill. Att'y Gen. Rep. 706.)

Comparative Analysis

The *Comparative Analysis* of Section 2 (*supra,* p. 492) is applicable to the underlying principle of this section. Only two states besides Illinois appear to require a petition by a majority of the voters of an area that wishes to move out of a county. Approximately 20 states have a provision for apportionment of debt. Three states optimistically provide for apportionment of assets. There is no comparable provision in the Model State Constitution.

Comment

The requirement that a petition contain the names of a majority of the voters of an area that wishes to move from one county to another seems unduly harsh. It would seem sufficient to provide in the Constitution for referenda along the lines of the provision quoted earlier. (*Supra,* p. 491.) It would seem unnecessary to include words giving the legislature authority to set up the ground rules, but in an abundance of caution, the words "in such manner as shall be provided by law" could be inserted at the appropriate place. The legislature could provide for an appropriate initiating petition and for such details as apportionment of debt. In short, it is suggested that Sections 1, 2 and 3 could easily be compressed into one simple sentence.

Removal of County Seats

Sec. 4. No county seat shall be removed until the point to which it is proposed to be removed shall be fixed in pursuance of law, and three-fifths of the voters of the county, to be ascertained in such manner as shall be provided by general law, shall have voted in favor of its removal to such point; and no person shall vote on such question who has not resided in the county six months, and in the election precinct ninety days next preceding such election. The question of the removal of a county seat shall not be oftener submitted than once in ten years, to a vote of the people. But when an attempt is made to remove a county seat to a point nearer to the center of the county, then a majority vote only shall be necessary.

History

The first half of the first sentence of this section appeared in the 1848 Constitution with two differences. The required vote was only a majority and the words "to be ascertained in such manner as shall be provided by general law" were not included. In the 1870 Convention this section produced extended debate. As one delegate remarked: "I have known of no more violent or lasting quarrels than those arising from attempts to remove county seats." (Debates 1331.)

The debate centered on two issues: how difficult should it be to make a county seat change and how frequently should an effort to change be permitted. After several alternatives were considered, the Convention agreed on frequency of efforts to change county seats. How difficult change should be was left up to the voters. The referendum on the Constitution included a separate vote on whether the required approval should be three-fifths or a majority. The voters chose three-fifths. (There were only 11 counties in which the vote was in favor of a majority for changing the county seat. *See* Debates 1894-95.)

The proposed 1922 Constitution changed the substance of the section only in regard to the required vote. The vote was increased to three-fourths, but of those voting on the question and not of the "voters of the county," and the exception for "nearer to the center of the county" was made a majority of those voting on the question.

Explanation

There are some fascinating wrinkles in the statute implementing this section. In order to start the ball rolling, a petition to remove the county seat must be filed with the clerk of the circuit court. One particularly significant requirement is that the petition must be signed by a number of voters equal to two-fifths of the votes cast in the county in the preceding presidential election, but no one who lives in the existing county seat may sign the petition. (Ill. Rev. Stat. ch. 34, §203 (1967).) As of the 1960 census, there would appear to be nine counties, including Cook, in which 60 per cent or more of the population lives in the existing county seat. Assuming equal distribution of voters between the county seat and the balance of the county, it would be mathematically impossible to change any of those county seats. In another eight counties, over 50 per cent of the population lives in the county seat. On the same assumption of distribution of voters, it would be impossible, as a practical matter, to produce a petition that would have to contain the names of at least 80 per cent of the voters living outside the county seat. It should be noted, however, that this stringent petition requirement is not constitutionally required, but is consistent with the stringent three-fifths' vote requirement.

The implementing statute provides that the number of legal votes cast at a county seat election, which by the tenor of the statute is expected to be a special election on the county seat issue alone, shall be taken as *prima facie* evidence of the number of legal voters of the county. The statute further provides that if the election is contested, the court "may ascertain the number of such voters by taking or causing to be taken, legal evidence tending to show the actual number of legal voters . . . ." (Ill. Rev. Stat. ch. 34, §213 (1967).) This provision is in accordance with the words, added in 1870 as noted above, "to be ascertained in such manner as shall be provided by general law." Those words were added because under the 1848 Constitution, the courts had had difficulty in determining how many voters there were in a county. Interestingly enough, the method used by the legislature is the same as that devised by the courts. (People *ex rel.* Mitchell v. Warfield, 20 Ill. 160 (1858).)

The Supreme Court has held that "county seat" means the county town of the seat of government and not the county buildings. (Dunne v. County of Rock Island, 283 Ill. 628 (1918).)

Comparative Analysis

Just under half of the states require a referendum on changing the county seat. Some states require a two-thirds' vote of all voters, and some only of those voting on the question. Three states use the three-fifths' rule, but only of those voting. One of the three states also requires a two-thirds' vote of those voting in the city or town to which the county seat would be moved. One state besides Illinois permits a lower vote if the new seat is nearer the center of the county; one state, if it is from more than five miles from the center to within five miles; and one, if from not on a railroad to a "railroad seat." Approximately 12 states limit the frequency of referenda, but only Oklahoma requires as long as a decade. There is no comparable provision in the Model State Constitution.

Comment

It can be argued that, if there is little reason in the last half of the Twentieth Century for constitutionally enshrining the existing county lines, there is even less reason to enshrine county seats. But as the quotation from the 1870 Convention illustrates, there may be a variant of Parkinson's Law of Triviality operating in the constitutional area: the less fundamental a constitutional issue, the more controversial it becomes. Whether or not this is the case with county seats today, a cautious disposition of the county seat issue would be a simple section along the following lines: No county seat shall be changed without the approval of a majority of those voters of the county voting on the question in such manner as shall be provided by law.

Counties under Township Organization

Sec. 5. The General Assembly shall provide, by general law, for township organization, under which any county may organize whenever a majority of the legal voters of such county, voting at any general election, shall so determine, and whenever any county shall adopt township organization, so much of this constitution as provides for the management of the fiscal concerns of the said county by the board of county commissioners, may be dispensed with, and the affairs of said county may be transacted in such manner as the General Assembly may provide. And in any county that shall have adopted a township organization, the question of continuing the same may be submitted to a vote of the electors of such county, at a general election, in the manner that now is or may be provided by law; and if a majority of all the votes cast upon that question shall be against township organization, then such organization shall cease in said county; and all laws in force in relation to counties not having township organization, shall immediately take effect and be in force in such county. No two townships shall have the same name, and the day of holding the annual township meeting shall be uniform throughout the State.

History

In order to understand the significance of this section and the next section, it is necessary to recall a little general history of the state. The county as the principal unit of local rural government developed in the South. In New England, the town was the principal unit. When the 1818 Constitution was adopted, the county form of rural government was in place and the Constitution reflected this system. By 1848, the northern part of the state had been largely settled by people from New England and other northern areas where town/township government was traditional. This northeastern influence resulted in a section substantially the same as the first sentence of Section 5. It is worth noting that today only 17 counties are not under township organization. Fourteen of these are in the southernmost portion of the state and the other three are south and west of Springfield.

In the 1870 Convention, there was considerable debate over whether to go beyond the 1848 provision and spell out the details of township government, but in the end the delegates were content to provide constitutional protection to the privilege of abandoning township government. The final sentence of the section was accepted without debate.

The proposed 1922 Constitution contained three new sections that, presumably, were to take the place of Sections 5 and 6, but to what extent the Convention intended to make substantive changes is not clear. The official explanation states as to each section, "This section is new." (P.N.C. 38.) One section provided that the board of supervisors in township counties, the Cook County commissioners, and the commissioners of non-township counties "shall constitute the county board of their respective counties." (art. VIII, § 163.) The second section authorized changes in organization "by law uniform as to classes of counties; but any such law shall become effective in a county only after approval by a majority of those voting on the question." (art. VIII, § 166.) The third section stated that no county could abandon or adopt any form of organization unless ratified by a majority of those voting on the question. (art. VIII, § 167.)

Explanation

It is to be noted that to adopt township organization requires a majority vote of the legal voters of a county, voting at a general election, but to abandon it requires only a majority vote of those voting on the question at a general election. Interestingly enough, the required majority was the same for both adoption and abandonment when the Convention referred the "Township Article" to the Committee on Revision and Adjustment, but the present language appeared when that Committee reported back the Article on Counties. There does not appear to be any explanation of the substantive change. (*See* Debates 882, 1835.)

The implementing statute for adoption and abandonment is Ill. Rev. Stat. ch. 139, §§ 1-24 (1967). Chapter 34 of the Revised Statutes (Ill. Rev. Stat. ch. 34 (1967)) covers the manner in which the "affairs of said county may be transacted" on the county level. The balance of Chapter 139 (§§ 25ff) covers the manner in which the "affairs of said county may be transacted" in the townships. One would assume that the legislature's power over the affairs of townships, like its power over cities, towns and villages, is an attribute of general state power, but the courts have held otherwise. The Supreme Court has said:

"A town organized under the township organization laws of the State is, as before said, a political or civil subdivision of a county. It is created as a subordinate agency to aid in the administration of the general State and local government. The distinction between such a town and other chartered municipal corporations proper, sometimes denominated towns, is, that a chartered town or village is given corporate existence at the request or by the consent of the inhabitants thereof for the interest, advantage or convenience of the locality and its people, and a town under township organization is created almost exclusively with a view to the policy of the State at large for purposes of political organization and as an agency of the State and county, to aid in the civil administration of affairs pertaining to the general administration of the State and county government, and is imposed upon the territory included within it without consulting the wishes of the inhabitants thereof." (People *ex rel.* Deneen v. Martin, 178 Ill. 611, 621 (1899).)

Accordingly, the quoted words from Section 5 are the constitutional basis for legislation concerning township government. Although the quoted words do not include the phrase "by general law," the legislature is required to provide for the government of townships by general law, but reasonable classifications are permitted. (*E.g.*, People *ex rel.* Hatfield v. Grover, 258 Ill. 124 (1913).)

Comparative Analysis

There appear to be three other states that specifically provide for the adoption of township organization with approval by referendum. Two states require the legislature to provide for township organization. Oklahoma provides for abolition of township organization by referendum and for re-establishment by referendum, the implication being that all counties were under such organization when the Constitution was first adopted. Several states call for a general law covering the government of townships. No other state appears to have a provision comparale to the last sentence of this section.

The Model State Constitution provides:

"Section 8.01. *Organization of Local Government.* The legislature shall provide by general law for the government of counties, cities and other civil divisions . . . including provisions:

(1) For such classification of civil divisions as may be necessary, on the basis of population or on any other reasonable basis related to the purpose of the classification;

(2) For optional plans of municipal organization and government so as to enable a county, city or other civil division to adopt or abandon an authorized optional charter by a majority vote of the qualified voters voting thereon;

(3) For the adoption or amendment of charters by any county or city for its own government, by a majority vote of the qualified voters of the city or county voting thereon, for methods and procedures for the selection of charter commissions, and for framing, publishing, disseminating and adopting such charters or charter amendments and for meeting the expenses connected therewith."

Comment

Notwithstanding the judicial theory that this section grants power to the legislature to legislate concerning township government, it seems likely that the delegates to the 1870 Convention meant only to cover the subject of *type* of county government. Otherwise, it would seem likely that there would have been some grant of power concerning organization of cities and incorporated villages. A section including such language was offered in a minority report of the Committee on Municipal Corporations in the 1870 Convention but was not accepted. (Debates 1672-74.) But whatever the constitutional theory accepted by the 1870 Convention, it is important that agreement be reached on the operative theory for the next Constitution. For purposes of the present discussion, it will be assumed that the Convention will proceed on the theory that there is no need to *grant* power to the legislature, but that there is a need to *limit* power. This is, of course, the purpose of a bill of rights and of limitations on taxation and indebtedness. It is also the purpose of the first four sections of Article X and of this section. In all of these sections, except Section 1, the limitation is in the nature of local home rule. It would be appropriate to consider all local governments together and to frame an article that includes the following:

(1) a requirement that applicable legislation be general, but with reasonable classifications;

(2) a general grant of power to local governments to govern themselves subject to legislative limitation by general law;

(3) a limitation on legislative power to impose forms of government without the consent of the local unit;

(4) a mandate to the legislature to provide suitable mechanisms by which alternate forms of government may be adopted by local units; and

(5) such constitutional limitations as may be desired — for example, debt limits, taxing power, and the like.

Such an approach — and this is *only* an approach, for under (5) above, the substance of power can be controlled — has two important advantages. First, it ends such conceptual distinctions as set forth by the Court in the *Martin* case; and second, it kills off the "Dillon rule" that, as creatures of the state, the powers of local governments should be strictly construed. The Dillon rule has been relied on as recently as 1967, when the Supreme Court said: "County boards may exercise only such powers as are expressly granted by the State or arise by implication from these granted powers or are indispensable to the purpose of their existence." (Crumpler v. County of Logan, 38 Ill. 2d 146, 149 (1967).) In this connection, it should be noted that the provision from the Model State Constitution quoted in the *Comparative Analysis* of Section 34 of Article IV (*supra,* p. 251) is specifically designed to kill off the Dillon rule.

Counties not under Township Organization

Sec. 6. At the first election of County Judges under this Constitution, there shall be elected in each of the counties in this State, not under township organization, three officers, who shall be styled "The Board of County Commissioners," who shall hold sessions for the transaction of county business as shall be provided by law. One of said commissioners shall hold his office for one year, one for

two years, and one for three years, to be determined by lot; and every year thereafter one such officer shall be elected in each of said counties for the term of
three years.

History

The Schedule of the 1818 Constitution provided that each county
should have three elected county commissioners to transact county business, with term of service, power and duties to be regulated and defined
by law. As noted in the *History* of Section 5 (*supra,* p. 496), the 1848
Constitution authorized township county government. For counties not
opting for such government, the management of the fiscal concern of
the county rested with the county court in accordance with a section of
the Judicial Article that provided: "The county judge, with such justices of the peace in each county as may be designated by law, shall hold
terms for the transaction of county business, and shall perform such
other duties as the General Assembly shall prescribe. . . ." (art. V, § 19.)
Both the Committee on Counties and the Committee on the Judiciary
of the 1870 Convention proposed to replace the county court with a
board of county commissioners in nontownship counties. The Convention adopted the language proposed for the Judicial Article, but the
Committee on Revision and Adjustment transferred the material to the
Article on Counties and rearranged it in the manner now appearing in
Section 6. The Schedule, Section 4, continued the county court system
until boards of county commissioners could come into existence.

Since the original language was proposed by the Committee on the
Judiciary, it is not surprising to find that county commissioners were included in the eligibility section that required judges of lower courts to
be at least 25 years old, a United States citizen, and a resident of the
state for the preceding five years. Commissioners are not included in the
new Judicial Article and presumably the only existing eligibility requirement is that contained in Section 6 of Article VII. (*Supra,* p. 394.)
The proposed 1922 Constitution continued the staggered three-year
terms of commissioners. (See also, *History* of Sec. 5, *supra,* p. 497).)

Explanation

Seventeen counties continue to operate under boards elected pursuant
to this section, but there do not appear to have been any problems in
construing the section. The implementing statute required by this section
is contained in Sections 801-804 and 806 of Chapter 34 of the Revised
Statutes (1967).

Comparative Analysis

There appear to be about 17 states besides Illinois that refer to a
board of county commissioners. Approximately seven states have refer-

ences to a board of supervisors, but not all of those states appear to operate exclusively by such boards in all counties. Six states appear to continue to operate under the traditional county court system, but one of them combines the county court and the commissioners for the transaction of county business. Another five states appear to authorize the legislature to determine the form of county government. The balance of the states presumably do not specify in their constitutions the form of county government. For the Model State Constitution, see *Comparative Analysis* of Section 5. (*Supra,* p. 498.)

Comment

In a sense this section is an historical anachronism. In the 1870 Convention, the delegates decided to end the county court system of administration in counties not under township organization and did so by this section. It would seem appropriate today, at the very least, to permit the legislature to have the same power for the 17 counties not under township organization that it has for the 84 counties under township organization. At most, the comments above on Section 5 are in part applicable here. (See discussion, *supra,* p. 499.)

Cook County Government

Sec. 7. The county affairs of Cook county shall be managed by a Board of Commissioners of fifteen persons, ten of whom shall be elected from the city of Chicago, and five from towns outside of said city, in such manner as may be provided by law.

History

At the time of the 1870 Convention, Cook County was organized as a township county. It was pointed out to the Convention that the Board of Supervisors of Cook County was almost as large as the Convention, which consisted of 88 delegates. It was also pointed out that Chicago contained seven-eighths of the population of the county, but a majority of the Board of Supervisors came from outside of the city. The delegate who pointed out the foregoing noted that he came from an agricultural area of the county and had no hesitation in saying that the limited representation of Chicago was unfair and unjust. He proposed to add what is now Section 7 to the Article on Counties which, he hoped, would be adopted unanimously and without debate. Upon completion of his explanation, the Convention, sitting in Committee of the Whole, adopted the proposal by voice vote. (Debates 1366-67.) The proposed 1922 Constitution retained the substance of this section.

Explanation

Very early, the Supreme Court held that this section did not remove Cook County from the class of counties under township organization.

(People *ex rel.* Miller v. Brislin, 80 Ill. 423 (1875).) But the Supreme Court has also held that by virtue of the words "in such manner as may be provided by law," the legislature could adopt special legislation concerning the management of Cook County, notwithstanding the prohibition on special legislation contained in Article IV, Section 22, *supra,* pp. 203-4. (People *ex rel.* Stuckart v. Day, 277 Ill. 543 (1917).) The legislature cannot, however, change the size of the board or its ten and five apportionment. (See *Comment* below concerning the drafting problem exemplified by this case.)

Although the legislature can legislate for Cook County alone, the Supreme Court has assured the Board of Commissioners that it has some implied powers. In *Nye v. Foreman* (215 Ill. 285 (1905)), the Court permitted the board to appropriate money for assistant state's attorneys in the absence of legislative authorization therefor. Almost 40 years later, however, the Court denied the board the power to engage private attorneys to collect delinquent taxes even though the state's attorney and his assistants were too busy to do so. (Ashton v. County of Cook, 384 Ill. 287 (1943).) Moreover, notwithstanding legislative authorization to manage county property, including such powers as were deemed necessary for the proper maintenance and operation of all buildings, the Court held that because the common law duties of a sheriff include those of custodian of courthouses and because he is a constitutional officer, he cannot be deprived of the power to select and appoint the janitorial force for the courthouses. (People *ex rel.* Walsh v. Board of Comm'rs, 397 Ill. 293 (1947.) *See also* Dahnke v. People, 168 Ill. 102 (1897).)

The implementing statute provides for four-year terms, no staggering of terms, election of the ten from the city and the five from the towns at large, respectively, and filling vacancies in either group by appointment by the remaining members of the group. (Ill. Rev. Stat. ch. 34, §901 (1967).) Prior to 1914, terms were for two years.

Comparative Analysis

Obviously, there is no comparable provision in any other state. In New York there is a "county" exception for New York City because there are five counties wholly inside the City. In Washington there is a county exception for counties that are a combination of city and county. In Missouri, St. Louis is an independent city and not part of St. Louis County. The same is true of Baltimore, Maryland. For the Model State Constitution, see *Comparative Analysis* of Section 5. (*Supra,* p. 498.)

Comment

No matter how it is looked at, Cook County is a difficult problem. As noted in connection with Section 1 (*supra,* p. 489), there was an abortive effort in the 1870 Convention to permit Chicago to be a separate county. The adoption of Section 34 of Article IV (*supra,* pp. 246-7) reinforces the complex status of the city. The comments concerning home rule (*supra,* p. 499) must be tailored to the Cook County problem, for so long as Cook County includes a city containing an estimated 65 per cent of the population of the county, it is not feasible to grant total home rule to the county. The "one man-one vote" rule would, of course, preclude a home rule charter that gave the city more representation in county government than its share of the population warranted. Indeed, it is remarkable that, a century later, the mandated distribution of seats on the county board is still fair. Remarkable though that may be, it is arguable whether a specific form of government for Cook County should be frozen in the Constitution. It should be sufficient to permit the legislature to set the ground rules for Cook County government subject to a veto power by referendum of the people of the city and the county.

It has been observed from time to time in comments on various sections that the principles of good constitution-writing must be tempered with political realities. "Tempered" is, perhaps, an understatement so far as Chicago, Cook County, and the remainder of the state are concerned. There are formidable political difficulties facing any Convention that has to deal with Chicago and its relation to the rest of the state. This was true in 1870 and 1920, and will be true in 1970. In advance of a Convention, there are just two comments to be made, one by way of caution, one by way of principle laced with caution. Everyone concerned with the Convention should be alert to the danger that uncompromising rigidity on any proposed constitutional solution to the Chicago-Cook County-downstate problem can spell disaster for the Convention's product or its acceptability to the people, or both. But whatever the compromises demanded by the political realities, they should be flexible. That is, they should be limited to determinations of who shares in the decision-making process on forms of government through time. If at all politically possible, the structure of government for Chicago and Cook County should not be frozen in the Constitution. And in no event should compromises be in terms of the substance of government. For example, it would be most unfortunate to have a constitutional requirement either that state aid to public schools must be on the basis of average daily attendance or must be on the basis of initial enrollment. That sort of compromise, even if in trade for something of constitutional significance, is mixing apples with oranges. The result is to give constitutional status to a legislative compromise on an ephemeral problem.

It is worthwhile to comment on an interesting drafting ambiguity in Section 7. As noted earlier, the Supreme Court held that the final clause, "in such manner as may be provided by law," permits special legislation for Cook County. This is based on the premise that the clause modifies both "managed by a Board of Commissioners" and "elected." The Court explicitly rejected the equally, perhaps more, appropriate reading of the clause to modify only "elected." No great harm has come from this ambiguity. Indeed, the ambiguity was useful, for special legislation for Cook County makes good sense, and if the 1870 Convention had meant otherwise and expressed itself clearly, the courts might not have been able to get around the language. Nevertheless, as a general rule, this sort of drafting imprecision is to be avoided.

County Officers — Term of Office

Sec. 8. In each county there shall be elected the following County Officers at the general election to be held on the Tuesday after the first Monday in November A.D. 1882, a County Judge, County Clerk, Sheriff and Treasurer, and at the election to be held on the Tuesday after the first Monday in November A.D. 1884, a Coroner and Clerk of the Circuit Court (who may be *ex-officio* recorder of deeds, except in Counties having 60,000 and more inhabitants, in which Counties a Recorder of deeds shall be elected at the general election in 1884) each of said officers shall enter upon the duties of his office, respectively on the first Monday of December, after his election, and they shall hold their respective offices for the term of four years, and until their successors are elected and qualified. *Provided* that no person having once been elected to the office of Sheriff or Treasurer shall be eligible to reelection to said office for four years after the expiration of the term for which he shall have been elected.

History

The only elected county officials provided for in the 1818 Constitution were the sheriff and coroner, both of whom had two-year terms. The 1818 Constitution also provided that circuit court judges were to appoint their own clerks. The 1848 Constitution continued the election of a sheriff every two years, but provided that no person could be eligible to serve more than once in any four years. The coroner was dropped as a constitutional officer. County judges and clerks of the circuit court were to be elected in each county for four-year terms.

In the 1870 Convention, the Committee on Counties proposed a section not differing greatly from Section 8. Considerable debate and many amendments occurred before the section reached its final form which, of course, differed from the present amended section. In that form it provided for the election of all the officers now listed in Section 8 plus a surveyor. The sheriff, treasurer and coroner were elected for two years and the rest for four years. There were no prohibitions on re-election. The significant changes made by the amendment adopted in 1880 were to drop the surveyor, to extend all terms to four years, and to make the treasurer and sheriff ineligible for re-election.

Several changes were proposed in the 1922 Constitution. All of the elective county offices were continued as elective for four-year terms except for the county judge, whose term was extended to six years. (Actually, the county judge was covered in the Judicial Article, and other changes were made concerning the county court but are not pertinent here.) The task of collecting taxes was shifted from the sheriff to the treasurer, and the sheriff, but not the treasurer, was allowed to succeed himself. In counties other than Cook, the proposed Constitution mandated an assessor but left details up to the legislature. Likewise, in counties over 50,000 population, an auditor was authorized but not mandated. (An auditor is a statutory elected official in all counties over 75,000 population except Cook County. (Ill. Rev. Stat. ch. 34, § 1501 (1967).)

Beginning in 1944, four amendments to this section were put to the voters. All received a favorable plurality, but all failed to receive a constitutional majority. The first three efforts, voted upon in 1944, 1952 and 1958, simply omitted the proviso against re-election of the sheriff and treasurer. The fourth try, voted upon in 1966, left the proviso in as to the sheriff, but omitted the treasurer.

The new Judicial Article adopted in 1962 abolished the office of county judge. A county clerk and a clerk of the circuit court continue to be elected in each county. (For some strange reason, the amendment voted upon in 1966, which was after the abolition of the office of county judge, still called for his election.)

Explanation

The most important judicial gloss put upon this section is the proposition that duties of a constitutional officer may be added to by statute, but traditional duties, especially those known at the common law, may not be taken away. (People ex rel. Walsh v. Board of Comm'rs (379 Ill. 293 (1947)), discussed supra, p. 502. See also People ex rel. Nelson v. West Englewood Trust & Sav. Bank, 353 Ill. 451 (1933) (county treasurer).)

The Attorney General has had occasion to make many rulings concerning the prohibition against succession in office. He has ruled that a sheriff can run for treasurer where the treasurer's term begins at the expiration of the sheriff's term (1925 Ill. Att'y Gen. Rep. 408); that the wife of a treasurer may succeed him (1925 Ill. Att'y Gen. Rep. 184); that a person appointed to fill out an unexpired term as treasurer until the election could succeed himself (1928 Ill. Att'y Gen. Rep. 51; 1912 Ill. Att'y Gen. Rep. 696); that a change from commission form to township organization does not permit succession in office (1926 Ill. Att'y Gen. Rep. 85); and that a person elected to fill out an unexpired term as sheriff or treasurer is not eligible to succeed himself. (1925 Ill. Att'y Gen. Rep. 187; 1918 Ill. Att'y Gen. Rep. 778, 798.)

Comparative Analysis

The following table approximates the constitutional county officers in the several states. Many other states may elect one or more of these county officers, but pursuant to statute or home rule charter.

	Number of States	
Office	*Elected*	*Appointed*
County judge	11	2
County clerk	14	—
Sheriff	32	—
Treasurer	17	—
Circuit court clerk	19	1
Coroner	14	7
Recorder of deeds	15	—
Assessor	10	1
Auditor	5	—
Surveyor	12	2
Tax collector	2	—

In some nine states there are limitations on how long one can be a sheriff, but in only five of them is the prohibition one of immediate succession. West Virginia is one of those five, and it also prohibits a deputy sheriff from becoming the next sheriff and prohibits the sheriff from serving as a deputy to his successor. Two states join Illinois in prohibiting a treasurer from succeeding himself and three other states limit terms to two. There are no constitutional county officers under the Model State Constitution.

Comment

There are many good reasons for not freezing in the Constitution a collection of mandated local offices. Among the reasons are the disadvantages of a long ballot, the dispersal of administrative authority, the inability to try out new governmental forms, and the Procrustean nature of the administrative structure. This last was recognized in 1870 by the limitation on a mandated recorder of deeds to counties of 60,000 and more inhabitants. The Supreme Court has added a new reason by virtue of its decision in the *Walsh* case *(supra,* p. 502) that constitutional officers retain their common law duties and that no such duty can be given to another governmental unit.

Notwithstanding the good arguments against preservation of a section like this one, the utmost caution is in order. There are a great many strong political interests behind these several county positions and any disturbance of the status quo may raise considerable opposition. Preservation of a few outmoded offices may be a small price to pay for a successful campaign for adoption of a new constitution. One possibility would be to preserve the constitutional offices but authorize a county to adopt a county charter under which any or all of the constitutional offices could be abolished. In any event, it would seem most desirable to include language that would blunt the thrust of the *Walsh* case. It is one thing to preserve some historical offices; it is another to preserve almost the entire county system of the Eighteenth Century.

Salaries of Officers — Cook County

Sec. 9. The clerks of all the courts of record, the Treasurer, Sheriff, Coroner and Recorder of Deeds of Cook county, shall receive as their only compensation for their services, salaries to be fixed by law, which shall in no case be as much as the lawful compensation of a Judge of the Circuit Court of said county, and shall be paid, respectively, only out of the fees of the office actually collected. All fees, perquisites and emoluments (above the amount of said salaries) shall be paid into the county treasury. The number of the deputies and assistants of such officers shall be determined by rule of the Circuit Court, to be entered of record, and their compensation shall be determined by the County Board.

History

This section, in a slightly different form, was presented to the 1870 Convention as part of the Article on the judiciary. The only significant debate was over whether excess fees should be paid into the county treasury. Delegates from downstate, relying on the complaints of Cook County delegates that county officers were earning fantastic sums, asserted that once compensation was cut back to reasonable amounts, a large surplus would be paid into the county treasury and that this would benefit the taxpayers of Cook County at the expense of the many nonresidents who paid fees. Debate became fairly acrimonious in the Committee of the Whole and the matter was referred back to the Convention without recommendation. At a later date, a substitute section in substantially the present form was offered and accepted with a minimum of debate. (Debates 1172-78; 1480-81.) The Committee on Revision and Adjustment transferred the section to the Article on Counties. The proposed 1922 Constitution retained much of the substance of this section, but removed the fee limitation as to the source of compensation and made the section applicable to all county officers.

Explanation

This is the first of five consecutive sections which the 1870 Convention developed to end the abuses of the fee system of compensation for county officials. For the purpose of the discussion of this and the next four sections, it is essential to consider the ambiguity of "fee." One meaning of fee is that charge made directly to the person for whom a service is rendered as, for example, the fee charged for recording a deed. A second meaning is that of a compensation based on a percentage of some value related to the service performed, as, for example, paying a tax collector a fee of 2 per cent of the amount of his collections. A third meaning is analogous to salary, as in the case of paying part-time officials a *per diem* for each day worked. It is not crystal clear, but it would appear that "fee" is used only in the first two senses in this section and Section 10, but in all three senses in Sections 11, 12 and 13.

This separate and potentially more flexible section for Cook County presumably was adopted in recognition of the development of Chicago as an urban center which would require a larger and costlier governmental structure than the rest of the local governmental units. Nevertheless, the section both retains state control over compensation and constitutionally preserves some indirect control over what the state can permit. Compensation for the named officers is set by law but the amount cannot equal or exceed that of circuit court judges, and it seems unlikely that the legislature would raise judicial salaries solely to raise the ceiling on county salaries. It would appear that the delegates to the 1870 Convention were also worried about overstaffing, presumably either for patronage purposes or to permit a county officer to delegate all work and collect pay for doing nothing. Thus, the section gives the staffing authority to the circuit court judges.

As might be expected, disputes arose over this administrative tangle and the courts had to resolve them. The Supreme Court has pointed out that the Board of County Commissioners must appropriate the funds necessary to pay deputies and assistants and must set a reasonable level of compensation. (People *ex rel.* Meyering v. Whealan, 356 Ill. 402 (1934).) The Court also held that the Cook County sheriff was entitled to a writ of mandamus commanding the circuit court to determine the number of assistants required by the sheriff, but such writ could only command some action, not what action. (People *ex rel.* Walsh v. Board of Comm'rs, 397 Ill. 293 (1947).)

It is also to be noted that the rules of compensation under this section apply only to the named officers and their deputies and assistants. Section 10 sets forth the rules for all other county employees. Thus, the legislature cannot set the compensation of the Board of Commissioners of Cook County. (Wulff v. Aldrich, 124 Ill. 591 (1888).)

A great many other cases have involved questions arising under this section, but only one of them need be cited here. The Supreme Court has noted that the limitation on payment of compensation out of fees actually collected applies only to the named officials and not to their deputies and assistants and that, by virtue of the "except" clause of Section 10, the limitation therein is inapplicable to Cook County. (County of Cook v. Hartney, 169 Ill. 566 (1897).)

Comparative Analysis

Although no other state has a section like this, there are some states that have a provision that singles out a specific county for special rules of compensation. Alabama, for example, requires laws regulating fees, commissions, or allowances to be applicable to all counties, but there are 22 amendments with detailed exceptions for named counties. Florida added a section in 1956 requiring all fees of county officers of Escambia County to be paid into the treasury and calling for special legislation to compensate such officers. There does not appear to be any other state that puts the control over the number of assistants and deputies in the hands of the general trial court judges. In Idaho, the control is in the hands of the county commissioners. In West Virginia, the assessor must get the approval of the county court when appointing assistants.

Comment

It would seem that the time has come to drop most of what is contained in this and the next four sections. As the *History* of the several sections demonstrates, they constitute a quasi-statute to end or regulate an evil in the system. That purpose has been served. The most that could be worth saving is a prohibition on local legislation as to fees, a requirement that fees be paid into the treasury, a statement concerning who sets compensation levels, and, in the case of elected officials, a prohibition against salary increases or decreases during the term. As for a prohibition on local legislation, it is more appropriately covered in the Legislative Article. Details on compensation levels depend on the extent to which the principle of home rule is accepted. Fees and salary changes can be adequately covered in two simple sentences. (See also *Comment* on Sec. 11 of Art. IX, *supra,* pp. 476-7.)

It almost goes without saying that the last sentence of Section 9 should be dropped. Under all sound principles — separation of powers, independence of the judiciary, professional personnel management — circuit court judges should not be given any power over county nonjudicial personnel matters.

Salaries of Officers — Other Counties

Sec. 10. The county board, except as provided in Section 9 of this article, shall fix the compensation of all county officers, with the amount of their necessary clerk hire, stationery, fuel and other expenses in such manner and subject to such limitations as may be prescribed by law, and in all cases where fees are provided for, said compensation shall be paid only out of, and shall in no instance exceed, the fees actually collected; Provided, that the compensation of no officer shall be increased or diminished during his term of office. All fees or allowances by them received, in excess of their said compensation, shall be paid into the County Treasury.

History

This section dates in part from an amendment adopted in 1952. That amendment added the words "in such manner and subject to such limitations as may be prescribed by law," and deleted the following maximum compensation limitations, shown in tabular form:

County Population	Maximum Compensation
Up to 20,000	$1,500.00
20,000 to 30,000	2,000.00
30,000 to 50,000	2,500.00
50,000 to 70,000	3,000.00
70,000 to 100,000	3,500.00
100,000 to 250,000	4,000.00
For each 100,000	For an additional
over 250,000	1,000.00

The original section was "dreamed up" by the 1870 Convention as a device to eliminate the evils of the fee system of compensation. As proposed by the Committee on Counties, the section, so far as is pertinent here, differed from the section as finally adopted only in omitting the limitation on compensation to fees actually collected and the incremental compensation scale for counties over a quarter of a million. Notwithstanding the limited nature of the changes made, there was a prolonged debate on this section. It is clear that the delegates were deeply incensed over the existing system. One evil of the system was that, in the more populous counties, officials drew down excessive sums. This section was aimed at that problem. Sections 11, 12 and 13 dealt with other evils that will be discussed in connection with those sections. The drafters of the proposed 1922 Constitution disposed of this entire problem by simply ending fees on the county level. In one section, county officers were forbidden to receive to their own use any fees, fines, costs, and the like; and in another section, the county board in all counties other than Cook was empowered to set the compensation of all officers, other than school superintendents, and the number and compensation of their employees.

Long overdue relief from the stringencies of Section 10 came, of course, with the adoption of the Ninth Amendment in 1952.

Explanation

This is the second of the five consecutive sections dealing with abuse of the fee system. Prior to amendment in 1952, it was obviously the most obnoxious of the stringent controls devised by the 1870 Convention. The error was in setting up a scale of maximum salaries in absolute dollars. (Today, with a large number of elderly people living on fixed incomes and watching the inexorable increase in the cost of living, it seems unlikely that such a mistake will be made again.) Presumably, the section as amended in 1952 is tolerably workable. At least, there does not appear to have been any litigation involving construction of the amended section.

Prior to 1952 there was an incredible amount of litigation concerning this section. Reading between the lines, one can easily discern various devices adopted in an effort to get around the unreasonably low maximum salaries allowed under the original section. With the underlying causes eliminated, it seems pointless to review these cases. It is worth noting, however, that the constitutional power of the county board to fix the compensation of all county officers is limited to the constitutional county officers provided for in Section 8. (*See* McFarlane v. Hotz, 401 Ill. 506 (1948).) The foregoing was not applicable to the county judge. Evidently, the courts put him under Article VI to get away from the salary limitations of the unamended Section 10. But this is all academic, since there is no longer a county judge. Likewise, the "no change in compensation" proviso applies only to constitutional county officers, but it must be recalled that statutory county officers, in effect, have been brought under the proviso by judicial gloss on Section 11 of Article IX. (See *supra*, pp. 474-5.)

Comparative Analysis

Among those states providing for constitutional county officers there is a profusion of provisions concerning compensation, running from a flat maximum of $5,000 in one state to a simple "shall be fixed by law." A few states have a "no change during term of office" provision. Some seven states require all fees to be paid into the treasury and another three states modify this with some legislative authority. A few states limit payment of compensation to the amount collected in fees. In Kentucky, the sheriff in any county with a population over 75,000 is to be paid a salary, but his salary, that of his deputies, and office expenses may not exceed 75 per cent of all fees collected. Several states call for classification of counties for purposes of setting salary levels. At least two states specifically permit special or local legislation for fixing compensation. A few states provide for local determination of salaries, usually for counties that have adopted a home rule charter. There is no comparable provision in the Model State Constitution.

Comment

See the *Comment* for Section 9. (*Supra,* p. 509.)

Fees of County and Township Officers

Sec. 11. The fees of township officers, and of each class of county officers, shall be uniform in the class of counties to which they respectively belong. The compensation herein provided for shall apply only to officers hereafter elected, but all fees established by special laws shall cease at the adoption of this Constitution, and such officers shall receive only such fees as are provided by general law.

History

One of the abuses of the fee system that appears to have been particularly galling to the delegates in 1870 was the practice of local officials lobbying for special acts that increased the fees to be charged for services in their county. There was apparently general agreement that the new Constitution should forever end this abuse, but devising a method proved difficult. Since the effort in this section and the next section was to destroy a body of statute law, the delegates got tangled up in all sorts of legislative problems, such as repeal by implication, uncertainty as to whether their new "statute" covered all existing legislative schemes, and the like. There was also, apparently, a recognition of the need for some flexibility in the limited authority to be granted to the legislature. The end result of the deliberations was the adoption of Sections 11 and 12, which together comprise a constitutional scheme for legislating fee schedules and a quasi-statute repealing existing laws and providing for a transition to new laws to be enacted.

The proposed 1922 Constitution discarded the obsolete matter in the two sections and substituted one simple sentence reading:

"Fees of county and town officers, as provided by law, shall be uniform as to classes of counties or towns and for this purpose there shall not be more than three classes of counties." (art. VIII, § 165.)

Explanation

It appears from the litigation involving this section and Section 12 that "fees" refers to any system of compensation other than a salary for a full-time employee. (*See, e.g.,* People *ex rel.* Olson v. Atchison, T. & S.F. Ry., 389 Ill. 204 (1945). *But see* Board of Supervisors v. Johnson, 64 Ill. 149 (1872) (per diem for days worked was compensation, not "fees.").) "Fees" presumably also refers to the fees that are charged to the public. (See the discussion of the meaning of "fee" in the *Explanation* of Sec. 9, *supra,* p. 507.)

Comparative Analysis

No other state has a comparable provision. Several states prohibit special legislation concerning fees.

Comment

See the *Comment* for Section 9. (*Supra,* p. 507.)

Regulation of Fees by General Laws

Sec. 12. All laws fixing the fees of State, County and Township officers shall terminate with the terms, respectively, of those who may be in office at the meeting of the first General Assembly after the adoption of this constitution; and the General Assembly shall, by general law, uniform in its operation, provide for and regulate the fees of said officers and their successors, so as to reduce the same to a reasonable compensation for services actually rendered. But the General Assembly may, by general law, classify the counties by population into not more than three classes, and regulate the fees according to class.

This article shall not be construed as depriving the General Assembly of the power to reduce the fees of existing officers.

History

This is the fourth of the five consecutive sections aimed at ending the abuse of the fee system of compensating government officials. As noted in the *History* of Section 11 (*supra,* p. 512), these two sections must be read together. Except for limiting classes to three, this section speaks solely to the immediate transition after adoption of the Constitution. This is reflected in the comparable section of the proposed 1922 Constitution. (*Supra,* p. 512.)

Explanation

In view of the limited purpose of this section, it is hardly worthwhile to trace its judicial gloss. Nevertheless, it is worthy of note that the 1870 Convention left a loophole in the section, for the Supreme Court upheld a statute granting the City Council of Chicago the authority to fix municipal court fees. The Court pointed out that the clerk of the municipal court is not included in "State, County and Township officers." (People *ex rel.* Soble v. Gill, 358 Ill. 261 (1934).)

There has, of course, been litigation over whether more than three classes of counties have been created. (*See e.g.,* People *ex rel.* City of Peoria v. Weston, 358 Ill. 610 (1934).)

Comparative Analysis

No other state has a comparable provision. Several states authorize classification of counties, and, in one instance, of townships, for the purpose of setting compensation levels.

Comment

See the *Comment* for Section 9. (*Supra,* p. 509.)

Reports by Fee Officers

Sec. 13. Every person who is elected or appointed to any office in this State, who shall be paid in whole or in part by fees, shall be required by law to make a semi-annual report, under oath, to some officer to be designated by law, of all his fees and emoluments.

History

This is the last of the sections designed to end abuses in the fee system.

In the manner of good statute-drafting, it simply calls for reports to assure proper supervision of the constitutional policy. The section was offered on the floor of the Convention, was quickly amended to add "under oath," and accepted without debate. In contrast to the simplification of Sections 11 and 12 (see *History* of Sec. 11, *supra,* p. 512), the proposed 1922 Constitution not only preserved this section in substance but added a requirement that every such officer pay over "at least monthly to some official designated by law all public moneys and interest thereon received by or for him."

Explanation

The Supreme Court has held that this section applies to constituitonal officers and not statutory officers. (People *ex rel.* North Am. Restaurant v. Chetlain, 219 Ill. 248 (1905) (statute need not require official court reporter to report his fees).)

Comparative Analysis

Approximately nine states provide for accounting by county officers, either in detail or by mandating appropriate legislation. Three states require accounting by township officers.

Comment

See the *Comment* for Section 9. (*Supra,* p. 509.)

Article XI

CORPORATIONS

Organization of Corporations

Sec. 1. No corporation shall be created by special laws, or its charter extended, changed, or amended, except those for charitable, educational, penal or reformatory purposes, which are to be and remain under the patronage and control of the State, but the General Assembly shall provide by general laws, for the organization of all corporations hereafter to be created.

History

The first section of the Corporations Article of the 1848 Constitution provided that corporations, not possessing banking powers or privileges, could be formed under general laws, and in the last section of the Article instructed the legislature to "encourage internal improvements, by passing liberal general laws of incorporation for that purpose." The first section also prohibited creation of corporations by special acts, except for municipal purposes, but ended with a glorious loophole in the form of an exception "in cases where, in the judgment of the general assembly, the objects of the corporation cannot be attained under general laws."

From the fact that, in the 1870 Convention, the Committee on the Legislative Department included corporate charters in its section prohibiting special acts on various subjects (see *History* of Sec. 22 of Art. IV, *supra,* p. 205), and the Committee on Miscellaneous Corporations included a like prohibition, it is evident that the practice under the 1848 Constitution was to grant corporate charters by special act. There was no debate on either of the proposals, and although the Convention chose the Legislative Article wording, the Committee on Revision and Adjustment placed the section in Article XI.

In the proposed 1922 Constitution, the prohibition on special acts of incorporation and the exceptions thereto were placed in the section prohibiting local and special legislation and the mandate to the legislature to provide for corporations by general law was dropped.

Explanation

Judicial interpretation pertinent to this analysis consists of (1) cases concerning reasonableness of classifications as a factor in distinguishing

between general and special legislation, a subject discussed in the analysis
of Section 22 of Article IV (*supra,* pp. 212-15); (2) a determination that
only private corporations are covered, thus permitting special legislation,
not otherwise prohibited, chartering public corporations other than those
specifically exempted in this section (Owners of Lands v. People *ex rel.*
Stookey, 113 Ill. 296 (1885) (Drainage District)); and (3) cases holding
that corporations chartered by special acts under the 1848 Constitution
continued in existence, and were subject to applicable provisions of that
Constitution (Chicago Home for Girls v. Carr, 300 Ill. 478 (1921)).

Comparative Analysis

Approximately three-fourths of the states authorize the formation of
corporations by general law and almost as many forbid formation by
special acts. About ten states have a "charitable, educational, penal or
reformatory" exception to the general law requirement. The Model
State Constitution is silent as to corporations but has a general prohibition on special legislation. (See *Comparative Analysis* of Sec. 22,
Art. IV, *supra,* p. 224.)

Comment

There is no need for any affirmative statement about legislative power
to authorize the creation of corporations. Nor is there any need for a
specific section prohibiting the creation of corporations by special act.
(For that matter, there really is no need for an Article on Corporations
at all. This argument will be developed in the *Comments* to the various
sections of Art. XI.) The problem of special legislation is generic, and
such limitations as are appropriate should appear in a comprehensive
section in the Legislative Article. (See *Comment* to Sec. 22 of Art. IV,
supra, p. 226.)

Revocation of Certain Special Charters

Sec. 2. All existing charters or grants of special or exclusive privileges, under
which organization shall not have taken place, or which shall not have been in
operation within ten days from the time this constitution takes effect, shall
thereafter have no validity or effect whatever.

History

This section is the result of a protracted debate in the 1870 Convention
over a section designed to undo what the delegates evidently thought
was the damage previously done through the granting of corporate charters by special acts. The section as originally proposed included, in addition to a slightly different version of Section 2, a provision that no
existing special act could thereafter be changed except by a two-thirds'
vote of the legislature. A learned discussion on constitutional principles

ensued and it was eventually agreed that the United States Constitution's prohibition on states' impairing the obligation of contracts, as well as the general uncertainty of the effect of such a limitation on legislative power of amendment of special charters, made it advisable to be content with killing off special charters that existed only on paper. The proposed 1922 Constitution omitted the section.

Explanation

Since this section is now obsolete, it serves no purpose to discuss the judicial interpretations in the early years following adoption of the 1870 Constitution.

Comparative Analysis

There are apparently about 15 other states that had the same need to kill off unused special act charters as did Illinois in 1870. There are three states with a continuing provision covering revocation of unused charters, but this would cover charters issued under a general corporation act.

Comment

This section is obsolete and should be dropped.

Election of Directors

Sec. 3. The General Assembly shall provide, by law, that in all elections for Directors or managers of incorporated companies every stockholder shall have the right to vote, in person or by proxy, for the number of shares of stock owned by him, for as many persons as there are directors or managers to be elected, or to cumulate said shares, and give one candidate as many votes as the number of directors multiplied by the number of his shares of stock, shall equal, or to distribute them on the same principle among as many candidates as he shall think fit; and such directors or managers shall not be elected in any other manner.

History

When this section was brought up for consideration in the Committee of the Whole in the 1870 Convention, the delegate from Greene County said: "As this is a matter for the Legislature to dispose of, I move to strike it out." Joseph Medill, who, it will be recalled, was the principal architect of cumulative voting in the House of Representatives (see *supra,* pp. 136-8) immediately arose and said, in part:

"Mr. Chairman: I hope the committee will consider and reflect a little on this section, before striking it out. My friend from Sangamon [Mr. Hay] suggests to me that it is 'legislation.' Well, we have been doing a good deal of that, all along, and this is not the first, nor will it be the last 'legislation.' A very large portion of our work is 'legislative.' In one sense, it is all legislative in character.

"The object of this section is simply to protect the rights of stockholders in incorporated companies — to protect the right of every stockholder, and to prevent the formation of rings to control absolutely, to abuse and plunder the property of the minority of every incorporated company. The object of this section is not to take away any rights of the majority of the company, but to protect the minority."

Another delegate from Cook County spoke vigorously in favor of the section, ending with these comments:

"I admit that it is a new principle sought to be incorporated in our Constitution, in the management of corporations. But with the reflection I have given it, and the thought I have bestowed upon it, I believe that it is the assertion of a principle of right, the insertion of which in the fundamental law can wrong nobody. . . .

"I hope it will not be stricken out, but that we will give honest minorities protection against the rapacity and dishonesty of reckless majorities in the management and control of all corporations within the limits of our authority.

"Mr. ENGLISH. Mr. Chairman: I withdraw my motion to strike out the section. Having no interest in the matter myself, and supposing it was a matter the General Assembly could provide for and control, I made the motion. But inasmuch as gentlemen interested in it desire to have it adopted, I, having no other objection to it than I have stated, withdraw the motion to strike out." (Debates 1666-67.)

No one spoke against the section and it was agreed to by voice vote. The proposed 1922 Constitution preserved cumulative voting for banks *only*.

Explanation

Since, as Mr. Medill conceded, this section is legislation, it is not surprising that there has been considerable litigation arising out of the section. The landmark case is *Wolfson v. Avery* (6 Ill. 2d. 64 (1955)) involving the battle for control of Montgomery Ward. There the Supreme Court outlawed staggered terms for directors. The Court has also outlawed nonvoting (for directors) preferred stock (People *ex rel.* Watseka Tel. Co. v. Emmerson, 302 Ill. 300 (1922)); a bylaw allowing bondholders to vote for directors (Durkee v. People *ex rel.* Askren, 155 Ill. 354 (1895)); a contract among stockholders giving one stockholder a long-term irrevocable power to vote all their stock (Luthy v. Ream, 270 Ill. 170 (1915) (but the Court probably would have held the contract contrary to public policy even without Section 3)); and a statute permitting directors to fill vacancies on the board (People *ex rel.* Weber v. Cohn, 339 Ill. 121 (1930)). The Court has, however, upheld irrevocable voting trusts created as part of a reorganization under the Bankruptcy Act. (Rittenberg v. Murnighan, 381 Ill. 267 (1942).) The section is not applicable to not-for-profit corporations. (Westlake Hosp. Ass'n v. Blix, 13 Ill. 2d. 183 (1958).) The Court has even stated that a corporation may vote its stockholding in another corporation notwithstanding a statute prohibiting such voting where the effect might be to lessen competition. (Hall v. Woods, 325 ·Ill. 114 (1927) (but the Court noted that if the result was to lessen competition, such result would be unlawful under Illinois laws).)

Comparative Analysis

There appear to be another ten states with comparable cumulative voting requirements. It would appear at first glance that these are all in constitutions adopted after 1870 and are presumably copied after the Illinois provision. At least two states have adopted amendments cutting back the blanket coverage of the section. In one of those cases, West Virginia, the cutback did not include banking institutions.

Comment

Notwithstanding the fact that a few states appear to have copied this unusual constitutional brain-child of Joseph Medill, it seems inadvisable to preserve it. The intricacies of corporation law call for the flexibility available only to the legislature. Moreover, the competitive nature of state corporation laws tends to put a state with unusual restrictions at a disadvantage. There may very well be good arguments for cumulative voting — several "professional" stockholder gadflies constantly recommend it — but at the very least it seems to be a matter for legislative, not constitutional, consideration.

Street Railroads

Sec. 4. No law shall be passed by the General Assembly, granting the right to construct and operate a Street Railroad within any city, town, or incorporated village, without requiring the consent of the local authorities having the control of the street or highway proposed to be occupied by such street Railroad.

History

This was one of the sections proposed by the Committee on Miscellaneous Corporations. It was accepted without explanation or debate. The proposed 1922 Constitution broadened the provision to read: "The general assembly shall not grant the right to occupy the streets or public grounds of any municipal corporation without its consent." (art. III, § 61.)

Explanation

It is to be noted that this section is not a referendum provision. The operable words are "local authorities." These are the officials chosen by the community to act for them in a formal manner, as, for example, by ordinance duly adopted in accordance with the city charter. (See Potter v. Calumet Elec. St. Ry., 158 F. 521 (7th Cir. 1908).) This requirement for local consent gives the local authorities power to impose reasonable conditions on the street railway company, but these conditions can be superseded by the state. (*See* City of Chicago v. O'Connell, 278 Ill. 591 (1917).) The section confers absolute power only to determine whether or not the railway may operate and if so, upon which streets. (*Id.*) It is also to be noted that the section is limited to street railways. Elevated lines, for example, are not covered. (Hoyne v. Chicago & O.P. Elev. R.R., 294 Ill. 413 (1920).)

Comparative Analysis

There appear to be only a couple of states with comparable requirements for local authority consent. (Strangely enough, the Index, the source for comparable provisions, does not list Section 4 under the appropriate heading.)

Comment

The underlying principle of this provision is home rule. If home rule is to be given any significant status, it should be by some general statement, not by such limited, specific protections as evidenced by this section. (Compare the 1922 proposal quoted above.) In any event, street railroads are a thing of the past and this section as such can be considered obsolete.

State Banks Forbidden — Bank Laws — Referendum

Sec. 5. No State Bank shall hereafter be created, nor shall the State own or be liable for any stock in any corporation or joint stock company or association for banking purposes, now created, or to be hereafter created. No act of the General Assembly authorizing or creating corporations or associations, with banking powers, whether of issue, deposit or discount, nor amendments thereto, shall go into effect or in any manner be in force, unless the same shall be submitted to a vote of the people at the general election next succeeding the passage of the same, and be approved by a majority of all the votes cast at such election for or against such law.

History

A section of the bill of rights of the 1818 Constitution provided that there should be "no other banks or moneyed institutions in this state than those already provided by law, except a state bank and its branches." This was followed by a grant of power to the legislature to establish and regulate the state bank. The 1848 Convention stomped on the state bank with a vengeance. In the Legislative Article, as noted earlier (*supra*, p. 234), the section prohibiting lotteries also denied to the legislature the power "to revive or extend the charter of the state bank, or the charter of any other bank heretofore existing in the state." In the 1848 Article on Corporations, one section was the same as the first sentence of Section 5 except for the omission of the words "now created, or." A second section was the same in substance as the second sentence of Section 5 except for the omission of the words "whether of issue, deposit or discount, nor amendments thereto." The Committee on Banks and Currency of the 1870 Convention proposed as two sections what is now Section 5, that is, including the words noted above as omitted from the 1848 Constitution. When the two sections and the other sections on banking were taken up in Committee of the Whole, the Chairman of the Banknig and Currency Committee did not discuss the several sections, which he said were "plain and simple," but contented himself with the observation that the United States was providing currency and would presumably continue to do so, but just in case the United States might change its mind, his Committee thought it best to place "a necessary amount of limitation on the Legislature, that they might not at any time inaugurate a State banking system that might prove as disastrous as the banking law under which we organized our banks in 1851 — for fear that the disastrous results might follow that we experienced in 1857 and 1861, when our banks broke." (Debates 1678).

The proposed 1922 Constitution indicated total confidence in the continued issuance of currency by the United States. In place of the first sentence was the following:

"No law shall be passed authorizing any bank of issue or authorizing the state to conduct, own any interest in or incur any liability for any banking business." (art. III, § 49.)

The referendum sentence was omitted. That sentence, of course, permits the legislature to authorize banks with powers of "issue." Not long after national banks were authorized, Congress enacted a tax on state bank notes. That killed off all state currency "issue." This was the state of affairs in 1870, equally so in 1922, and continues to be so.

Explanation

There has been no occasion for an interpretation or ruling on the first sentence of the section. As can be imagined, a lot of problems have arisen under the second sentence, but they have substantially all concerned the one question — Is the legislation at issue of the type required to be submitted to referendum? There seems to be little point in reviewing the many cases. Assuming a general consistency over the years, the essence of the judicial gloss is that a referendum is required only for those legislative acts that affect "banking powers" as commonly understood. Thus, on the one hand, a statute regulating corporations generally might have to be read as not covering banks because the regulation would affect corporate banking powers, whereas, on the other hand, legislation specifically regulating banks might not be subject to referendum because the regulations did not affect banking powers. (Representative cases include Gorham v. Hodge, 6 Ill. 2d 31 (1955); American Legion Post No. 279 v. Barrett, 371 Ill. 78 (1939); People v. Gould, 345 Ill. 288 (1931); Boor v. Tolman, 113 Ill. App. 322 (1904).)

Comparative Analysis

State Bank: Two states, Missouri and Oregon, specifically prohibit a state bank. Four more states prohibit state ownership of bank stock. Iowa specifically authorizes a state bank, but only on an actual specie basis.

Referenda: Three other states, Iowa, Kansas and Ohio, also require a popular referendum on banking laws. Three states require a two-thirds vote for legislative passage of banking bills.

Comment

It would seem appropriate to take a leaf from the proposed 1922 Constitution and have confidence that the United States will continue to provide a monetary system. It hardly seems necessary to go so far as to prohibit banks of issue, but the restriction, being so obviously unnecessary, is certainly harmless. It would also seem unnecessary these days to prohibit the state from buying bank stock, but retention of the prohibition would be relatively harmless. It is possible to imagine a crisis situation when the state might have to rescue state banks, and in such a situation the state ought to have the power to secure any loans by such a device as a pledge of the bank's stock, or the like. But the realities of banking today are national in scope, and in any crisis only the Federal Government will be able to cope with the situation.

It would also seem appropriate to take a second leaf from the proposed 1922 Constitution and drop the referendum requirement. The voters have enough to worry about without getting snarled up in the intricacies of banking, a subject about which precious few people have even a little knowledge. Moreover, with two coexisting banking systems, national and state, it ill serves the state system to make it less flexible than the national system.

A word about the ambiguity at the end of the section is appropriate. The required majority appears to be of those voting on the question — *i.e.,* "votes cast at such election for or against such Laws." The Index, page 51, states that the majority required is that of all votes cast at the election. Professor Garvey, in his treatise on Illinois government, makes the same statement. (N. Garvey, The Government and Administration of Illinois 438 (1958).) The Banking Act of 1965 requires only a majority of those voting on the question. (Law of July 23, 1965, §82, [1965] Ill. Laws 2071.)

Liability of Bank Stockholders

Sec. 6. No stockholder of a banking corporation or institution shall be individually responsible or liable to its creditors for the liabilities of such banking corporation or institution under any constitutional or statutory provisions heretofore creating or declaring such stockholder responsibility or liability, provided, however, that any rights of creditors existing at the date of the adoption hereof shall not be impaired hereby, provided that action to enforce such stockholder responsibility or liability with respect to any existing bank liability which is payable on demand or for which a cause of action has already accrued shall be commenced within one year from the date of the adoption hereof, and with respect to any other existing bank liability shall be commenced within one year from the time when the cause of action therefor first hereafter accrues against such banking corporation or institution, or could so accrue by demand. No law creating or declaring any such stockholder responsibility or liability shall be passed.

History

The original section as adopted in 1870 provided for the traditional double liability of stockholders in banking institutions. The section was a modification of a section in the 1848 Constitution which provided for double liability if the banking institution issued bank notes, "or any kind of paper credits to circulate as money." On the floor of the 1870 Convention, three delegates proposed to make stockholders' liability unlimited, but it was quickly pointed out that double liability was the usual requirement and that unlimited liability would totally destroy the possibility of corporate banking. Indeed, the Chairman of the Committee on Banks and Currency said that the entire Article as proposed by his Committee "is almost a prohibition against starting banks in Illinois." Unlimited liability was rejected by voice vote. (Debates 1679.) When the Convention considered the action of the Committee of the Whole, unlimited liability was again proposed and under the rules a roll call vote was taken. The proposed change was defeated 44 to 11, with 28 absent or not voting.

The proposed 1922 Constitution retained the principle of double liability, but a change was made to permit the legislature to regulate the manner in which bank creditors could enforce their rights.

The 1952 amendment was designed simply to kill double liability, but the amended section contains the detail necessary to avoid any impairment of creditors' rights as of the time of adoption of the amendment.

Explanation

In view of the fact that the 1952 amendment ended double liability, there is no point in discussing the voluminous litigation produced by the original section. No problems of interpretation appear to have arisen under the amendment.

Comparative Analysis

There is, of course, no constitutional provision concerning banking as such in the United States Constitution, but it is worth recalling that the original Section 6 was modeled on the original National Bank Act, and that the double liability provision thereof was dropped as to new stock in 1933, permissibly as to old stock in 1937, and fully in 1953. (See 12 U.S.C. Sec. 64a (1964).) Six states appear to continue double liability, but in four of them double liability is lifted so long as the bank is insured through the Federal Deposit Insurance Corporation. A seventh state empowers the legislature to impose double liability.

Comment

This section, and the resulting amendment, are an object lesson in the dangers implicit in putting statutory material into a constitution.

Specie Payment — Bank Reports

Sec. 7. The suspension of specie payments by banking institutions, on their circulation, created by the laws of this State, shall never be permitted or sanctioned. Every banking association now, or which may hereafter be, organized under the laws of this State, shall make and publish a full and accurate quarterly statement of its affairs, (which shall be certified to, under oath, by one or more of its officers) as may be provided by law.

History

This section is a combination of two sections proposed to the 1870 Convention. The first sentence, which was one of the sections, was, as a practical matter, inoperative when adopted because the federal tax on state bank notes made state currency uneconomical. The delegates were aware of this, but as noted earlier (*supra,* p. 521), the restriction was included just in case the United States Government changed its mind. In presenting the second sentence, which was the other section, the Chairman of the Committee on Banks and Currency pointed out that in Illinois there were a lot of banking institutions, "in regard to the financial condition of which nobody, except the parties engaged in them, know anything." He went on to say: "A *law* requiring a publication of the business affairs of the institution will give the people some idea of their soundness and of their financial condition, which I regard as very important." (Debates 1678. Emphasis added.) The two sentences were accepted without debate. (Actually, when the Convention considered the action of the Committee of the Whole, a previous amendment to correct a grammatical error was ratified. This means that there is an omission in the Debates as printed. *See* 1679 and 1685.)

The proposed 1922 Constitution omitted this section. In the light of that Constitution's prohibition of banks of issue (*supra,* p. 521), the first sentence would have been meaningless. The second sentence is not limited to publication of data concerning note issues, and it is not immediately obvious why this sentence was also dropped. (The Official Explanation makes no reference to omitted sections.)

Explanation

The only judicial interpretation of this section appears to be an ancient case in which the Supreme Court said that the opening phrase of the second sentence did not legalize all banks in business in 1870, that is, did not include those not legally constituted prior to 1870. (People *ex rel.* Badger v. Loewenthal, 93 Ill. 191 (1879).)

The implementing statute for the second sentence is Section 147 of Chapter 16½ of the Revised Statutes.

Comparative Analysis

Specie Payments: Four other states have a comparable provision.

Quarterly Report: Only one other state, Alabama, appears to require a report, and that is a semi-annual report not specified to be under oath.

Comment

The first half of this section is clearly unnecessary in today's world, and the second half is hardly earth-shaking in its fundamental nature. Indeed, it is perhaps appropriate to point out that in any case where, as here, there is an implementing statute on the books, the need for continuing a constitutional reporting requirement seems nonexistent. Surely, no legislator would seriously entertain a request from Illinois bankers to repeal the reporting requirement once the constitutional command was removed. It is inconceivable that legislators would put themselves in the position of saying, in effect, "There is no need for quarterly banking reports; the only reason we used to require them was that the 1870 Constitution forced us to."

Requirements of General Banking Law

Sec. 8. If a general banking law shall be enacted, it shall provide for the registry and countersigning, by an officer of State, of all bills or paper credit, designed to circulate as money, and require security, to the full amount thereof, to be deposited with the State Treasurer, in United States or Illinois State Stocks, to be rated at ten per cent below their par value; and in case of a depreciation of said stocks to the amount of ten per cent below par, the bank or banks owning said stocks shall be required to make up said deficiency, by depositing additional stocks. And said law shall also provide for the recording of the names of all stockholders in such corporations, the amount of stock held by each, the time of any transfer thereof, and to whom such transfer is made.

History

This section, modeled after the requirements of the National Bank Act, was proposed in the 1870 Convention as a contingency in case the national banking system was ever disbanded. (As noted earlier, *supra,* p. 521, it was not feasible under the national system for state banks to issue paper currency.) There was an impassioned debate on the floor over this section, but the argument was between the Populists and the sound money people. The latter won, which is to say that so far as Illinois was concerned, locally issued currency would have to be backed 100 per cent plus by United States or Illinois bonds.

Since the proposed 1922 Constitution forbade local currency, this section was necessarily omitted.

Explanation

No occasion has ever arisen for the first sentence of this section to come into operation and there has been no interpretation of it. It is not clear whether the requirement for recording the names of all stockholders "in such corporations" is operative since there are no banks of issue. (See *Comment* below.) The fact is that Section 115 (8) of Chapter 16½ of the Revised Statutes (1967) requires such recording, including all transfers "not later than thirty days after such transfer."

Comparative Analysis

Money: Several states specifically prohibit the circulation of state currency. Approximately eight states have provisions comparable to Illinois, but these are, of course, also inoperable.

Stockholder Records: No other state appears to have a comparable constitutional requirement.

Comment

The first sentence of this section is fairly obviously obsolete. The *Comment* under Section 7 concerning reporting (*supra,* p. 525) is equally applicable here.

It is appropriate to note a bit of careless draftmanship in the second sentence of this section. The reference is to "such corporations." (At least in this sentence, the grating word "said" was not used as in the first sentence.) The problem is that "such" is a referent and there are no "corporations" mentioned in the first sentence. If one is to go back to Section 7, an improper assumption, the only references are to banking "institutions" and "association." If one is to go all the way back to the original Section 6, the reference is "banking corporation or institution." Although this is an equally improper assumption, Section 6 is probably the correct reference because there is an obvious need to have an accurate list of stockholders for purposes of imposing double liability.

Railroad Corporations

Sec. 9. Every railroad corporation organized or doing business in this State, under the laws or authority thereof, shall have and maintain a public office or place in this State for the transaction of its business, where transfers of stock shall be made and in which shall be kept, for public inspection, books, in which shall be recorded the amount of capital stock subscribed, and by whom; the names of the owners of its stock, and the amounts owned by them respectively; the amount of stock paid in and by whom; the transfers of said stock; the amount of its assets and liabilities, and the names and place of residence of its officers. The directors of every railroad corporation shall, annually, make a report, under oath, to the Auditor of Public Accounts, or some officer to be designated by law, of all their acts and doings, which report shall include such matters relating to railroads as may be prescribed by law. And the General Assembly shall pass laws enforcing by suitable penalties the provisions of this section.

History

This section, as offered, was the first section of the Article proposed by the Committee on Railroad Corporations of the 1870 Convention. When the Committee of the Whole took up the Article, the first words after the reading of the section by the Clerk were:

"Mr. HAINES, of Lake. Mr. Chairman: The word 'railroad' seems to have been omitted before 'corporations.' I move to insert it."

"Mr. ALLEN, of Crawford. The section was intended to embrace all corporations." (Debates 1637.)

After a short debate, Mr. Haines' motion was agreed to. Three other changes were made before the section reached its present form. One added the requirement for a transfer office in Illinois, one added the sentence requiring an annual report under oath, and the third removed a command that the legislature pass the penalty laws referred to "at its first regular session after the adoption of this Constitution." In connection with the last-mentioned change, Mr. Fox, a delegate from Schuyler County, moved to strike the whole sentence, saying:

"I think the provision is merely mandatory, and will amount to nothing, as there is no power to enforce a mandatory constitutional provision. I am certain it will amount to nothing, if the Legislature has no more respect for this Convention, than the Convention has shown for the Legislature." (*Id.*)

There was some parliamentary by-play, but no one responded to Mr. Fox. By voice vote, they rejected his motion. (*Id.* at 1638).

The section was omitted from the proposed 1922 Constitution.

Explanation

The Supreme Court has noted that this section, and the remaining sections of Article XI, are aimed at "steam trunk line" railroads and not commuter lines. (People v. City of Chicago, 349 Ill. 304 (1932).)

The requirements of the first sentence of this section are implemented by Sections 7 and 30 of Chapter 114 of the Revised Statutes (1967) in substantially the language of the Constitution. Section 31 provides for a fine of not less than $ 4,000 for failure to carry out the statutory requirements. The reporting requirement of the second sentence, including appropriate penalties, is now covered by Section 19 of Chapter 114⅔ of the Revised Statutes (1967) which calls for annual reports to the Commerce Commission from all public utilities. Prior to 1939, there were provisions in Chapter 114 specifically implementing the second sentence of this section, including suitable penalties.

Comparative Analysis

Approximately six states have some or all of the several requirements contained in the first sentence of this section. About eight states require reports to be made to an appropriate state office.

Comment

Inasmuch as all of the requirements of this section are embodied in existing statutes, it seems appropriate, for the reasons set forth earlier (*supra,* p. 525), to drop this section.

Railroads — Personal Property

Sec. 10. The rolling stock, and all other movable property belonging to any railroad company or corporation in this State, shall be considered personal property, and shall be liable to execution and sale in the same manner as the personal property of individuals, and the General Assembly shall pass no law exempting any such property from execution and sale.

History

This was the second section of the Article proposed by the Committee on Railroad Corporations of the 1870 Convention. The section was accepted unchanged, without debate, and without a recorded vote.

The proposed 1922 Constitution shortened the section to read:

"Rolling stock and other movable property of common carriers shall be subject to execution sale." (art. XII, § 227.)

Explanation

Prior to 1870, the Supreme Court had held that rolling stock was realty, at least for the purpose of coverage by railroad mortgages. (Titus v. Mabee, 25 Ill. 232 (1851).) Apparently, the sole purpose of this section was to overrule the Court. The United States Supreme Court did not so read the section, however, and went right ahead and included rolling stock under an equity decree of foreclosure and sale under a mortgage of an entire railroad. (Hammock v. Farmers' Loan & Trust Co., 105 U.S. 77 (1881).) Presumably, this section has had no significant effect on the body of private law governing creditors' rights.

Comparative Analysis

Apparently, some ten states besides Illinois have a comparable provision.

Comment

Whatever value this section may have had in 1870, it surely has long since outlived its usefulness. In the high finance of railroad operations, including the practice of mortgaging rolling stock by equipment trusts, a provision like Section 10 is probably no more than an inconvenience to the financial lawyers who arrange for and draft the many papers involved in railroad financing.

Railroad Consolidation

Sec. 11. No railroad corporation shall consolidate its stock, property or franchises with any other railroad corporation owning a parallel or competing line; and in no case shall any consolidation take place except upon public notice given, of at least 60 days, to all stockholders, in such manner as may be provided by law. A majority of the directors of any railroad corporation, now incorporated or hereafter to be incorporated by the laws of this State, shall be citizens and residents of this State.

History

Early in the deliberations of the 1870 Convention, it was evident that there were unusually strong feelings about the power of railroads. Several resolutions were offered, one of which included the concept of preservation of competition. This was, of course, more than a decade before the passage of the Interstate Commerce Act and more than two decades before passage on the Sherman Act. The Article submitted by the Committee on Railroads included a section consisting of the first sentence of what is now Section 11. In Committee of the Whole, the proposal was accepted without debate.

When the section was taken up by the Convention proper, proposals were made to prohibit all consolidations. After much debate, in the course of which several delegates, particularly Joseph Medill — "It is a mere sieve, through which everything can run, without any trouble at all. . . ." —, pointed out that there was no real way to prevent consolidations, the Convention accepted the original section with the addition of the sentence concerning Illinois directors. (Debates 1718-20.)

The section was omitted from the proposed 1922 Convention.

Explanation

Notwithstanding Mr. Medill's pessimistic observation quoted above, the first half of the first sentence operated to prevent a merger of two competing belt line railroads in the East St. Louis area. (East St. Louis Connecting Ry. v. Jarvis, 92 F. 735 (7th Cir. 1899).)

No other significant case appears to have arisen, but since the railroad world is essentially interstate and regulated by the United States Government, this is not surprising.

Comparative Analysis

Competing Lines: About a dozen states join Illinois in prohibiting the consolidation of "parallel or competing" lines. A few states have other restrictions on consolidation, particularly with foreign corporations. Kentucky and Washington also prohibit a railroad's combining with another common carrier whereby the earnings of the one doing the carrying are shared with the one not doing the carrying.

Public Notice: Four other states require at least 60 days' public notice of a proposed consolidation.

Residence of Directors: No other state has a comparable provision.

Comment

In the light of the wave of railroad mergers, as well as every other kind, which the orthodox anti-trusters have been unable to stem, it seems unlikely that this little local prohibition will have much effect. In any event, it seems unlikely that in the foreseeable future the railroads of Illinois will have such political power that the legislature would fail to protect the public against monopolistic practices. As was proposed in 1922, this section could safely be omitted.

Railways as Public Highways — Regulation of Rates

Sec. 12. Railways heretofore constructed or that may hereafter be constructed in this State, are hereby declared public highways, and shall be free to all persons, for the transportation of their persons and property thereon, under such regulations as may be prescribed by law. And the General Assembly shall, from time to time, pass laws establishing reasonable maximum rates of charges for the transportations of passengers and freight on the different railroads in this State.

History

The essence of this section was accepted by the 1870 Convention, sitting in Committee of the Whole, as a substitute for a section proposed by the Committee on Railroads. (That proposed section eventually was adopted as Sec. 15. See *infra,* p. 534.) When the proposed Article on Railroads was considered by the Convention proper, there was a learned debate that, paradoxically, ran in opposite directions. Some delegates thought the section added nothing, that it really only was declarative of the common law rules for common carriers. Other delegates were worried that the section went too far, that it purported to give the legislature power that, under the United States Constitution, would be invalid. At the conclusion of the debate, the section was accepted and referred to the Committee on Revision and Adjustment, including a final clause for forfeiture of charters. (See the final clause of Sec. 15, *infra,* p. 534.) For some unexplained reason, that clause was omitted when the Corporation Article was reported back for final action.

The proposed 1922 Constitution retained the substance of this section.

Explanation

Judicial interpretation of this section has, in the main, dealt with technical matters. The first sentence, of course, adds up to the declaration that railroads are common carriers and as such, to use the honored term, are "affected with the public interest." That term became distorted in the decades of judicial interference with economic regulation and is now of little significance. But the concept that some businesses are not privileged to pick and choose their customers is still valid, and the first sentence of this section is one way of expressing that concept in the area of transportation. The foregoing comment reinforces the remarks of some delegates in 1870 that the sentence did not in fact add anything to the traditional common law.

The only important case dealing with the second sentence held that the legislature could both set a maximum rate for transportation and authorize an administrative agency to fix a rate lower than the legislated rate. (State Pub. Util. Comm'n ex rel. Mitchell v. Chicago & W. T. Ry., 275 Ill. 555 (1916).) Judicial review of the reasonableness of any rate set has traditionally been a matter of due process of law. (See discussion of Sec. 2 of Art. II, *supra*, pp. 9-14.)

Comparative Analysis

Public Highway: Some 17 states declare railroads to be public highways. Thirteen of the states pile Pelion on Ossa by also declaring railroads to be common carriers. Two states are content to declare them common carriers.

Maximum Rates: Four states have comparable provisions. Oklahoma sets a maximum rate of two cents per mile for "first class" passenger fares, "unless otherwise provided by law," with a proviso that the Corporation Commission can exempt any railroad that offers satisfactory proof that it cannot earn a "just compensation" unless it charges more than two cents per mile.

Comment

In the light of the comprehensive statutory system for the regulation of all public utilities provided in Chapter 111⅔ of the Revised Statutes (1967), this section seems unnecessary.

Railroads — Stock — Bonds

Sec. 13. No railroad corporation shall issue any stock or bonds, except for money, labor or property, actually received, and applied to the purposes for which such corporation was created; and all stock dividends, and other fictitious increases of the capital stock or indebtedness of any such corporation, shall be void. The capital stock of no railroad corporation shall be increased for any purpose, except upon giving sixty days public notice, in such manner as may be provided by law.

History

The essence of the first sentence of this section was proposed by the Committee on Railroads of the 1870 Convention and was initially accepted with a minor change to make it applicable only to railroads. The second sentence was proposed from the floor as an additional section and was accepted without debate. The two sentences were accepted by the Convention proper after one minor technical correction. The Committee on Revision and Adjustment combined the sentences to make Section 13 of the Corporations Article. The section was omitted from the proposed 1922 Constitution.

Explanation

There have been some important cases construing this section, but, interestingly enough, they probably say no more than would have been said without the section. For example, the Court held that a *prima facie* case under the section is not made out by an allegation that more securities had been issued than "money, labor or property actually received." Fraud must be alleged. (People v. Union Consol. Elev. Ry., 263 Ill. 32 (1914). Fraud was alleged the next time around. People v. Union Elev. R.R., 269 Ill. 212 (1915).) It is not possible to be certain what courts would have done in the absence of Section 13, but it seems fairly clear that the law would have developed as it did had the Constitution been silent. The foregoing comments do not, of course, apply to the second sentence of the section.

Comparative Analysis

This provision appears to be unique to Illinois.

Comment

Except for the honor of having a unique provision, there seems to be no reason for keeping this section.

Railroads — Eminent Domain

Sec. 14. The exercise of the power, and the right of eminent domain shall never be so construed or abridged as to prevent the taking by the General Assembly, of the property and franchises of incorporated companies already organized, and subjecting them to the public necessity the same as of individuals. The right of trial by jury shall be held inviolate in all trials of claims for compensation, when, in the exercise of the said right of eminent domain, any incorporated company shall be interested either for or against the exercise of said right.

History

At the conclusion of the consideration of the proposal of the Committee on Railroads in the 1870 Convention, a report was received from the Committee on the Judiciary proposing the addition of three sections, the first two of which are the two sentences of Section 14. The third proposed section purported to preserve the right of users of railroads to have a jury trial in cases where the railroads denied service. There was considerable confusion among the delegates concerning this third proposal and some disposition to feel that the bill of rights would provide adequate protection to the public. In the end, the proposal was rejected. The other parts were accepted with little opposition.

With a minor reservation, this section was dropped from the proposed 1922 Constitution. In one of the sections concerning the powers of the City of Chicago, the proposed Constitution made it clear that the City's power of eminent domain covered "public utilities and the privileges or licenses held in connection therewith."

Explanation

The Constitution as printed at the end of the proceedings of the 1870 Convention did not have headings for each section. The print did have the word "Railroads" inserted at the end of Section 8 and before Section 9. (The word "Banks" appears between Sections 4 and 5, and the word "Corporations" heads the Article.) (Debates 1877.) The interesting thing about this is that of the seven sections following the word "Railroads," all except Section 14 are by their terms clearly limited to railroads. Section 14 refers in the first sentence to "incorporated companies already organized" and in the second sentence to "any incorporated company." It is clear from the debates that, at least as to the first sentence, the delegates were thinking only of railroads. For example:

"Mr. ROSS. I would ask the gentleman whether that refers to railroads hereafter to be built, as well as those now built?

"Mr. CHURCH. In the case of railroads established under this Constitution, there will be no necessity to apply the provision, as the whole power of regulation will be reserved by the clause in the bill of rights, 'No irrevocable franchise or privilege shall be granted.' Also, by the reservation in the legislative article, which provides for full control in the General Assembly of all charters hereafter granted." (Debates 1656.)

There was no clear indication of the delegates' understanding of the words "any incorporated company." The Supreme Court has spoken as if the second sentence is not limited to railroads. (*See e.g.*, Wabash R.R. v. Coon Run Drainage & Levee Dist., 194 Ill. 310 (1901).) The difficulty with that case, and others, is that the complainant was, in fact, a railroad. Moreover, the statute in question was held defective in its jury trial

provisions under both Section 14 and Section 13 of Article II (*supra,*
pp. 56, 65), which also call for trial by jury in condemnation cases.

Comparative Analysis

Some 20 states authorize the taking of the property of corporations.
Only Illinois limits such power to corporations "already organized." The
foregoing reads as if the Illinois power of eminent domain is less extensive
than that of the other states. This is not true. Just as Section 14 was undoubtedly unnecessary when adopted, so the reservation of power over
corporations in the other states was probably unnecessary. Approximately
ten states provide for trial by jury in condemnation cases. Another five
states limit the privilege of jury trial to cases other than a taking by the
state. Two states limit the privilege to cases of the taking of private roads.

Comment

An eminent domain provision is essential, but it belongs in the bill
of rights. There are important policy questions in the determination of
both the substance and procedure of the provision, but these have already
been considered. (See Sec. 13 of Art. II, *supra,* p. 56.) There is no earthly
need for a separate section concerning "any corporation," already organized or not.

In all fairness to the 1870 Convention, the foregoing categorical dismissal of this section would not have been an appropriate comment at
that time. As the quoted explanation by Mr. Church indicates, the delegates were worried about the status of then-existing corporations that
might have received special privileges by special acts. The thrust of the
section was to try to kill off any claim that such an existing corporation's
property could not be taken by the state. Under the provision of the
United States Constitution forbidding the impairment of the obligation
of contracts (art. I, § 10.), Section 14 probably did not in fact add anything, but the delegates were certainly justified in trying.

Regulation of Freight and Passenger Rates

Sec. 15. The General Assembly shall pass laws to correct abuses and prevent
unjust discrimination and extortion in the rates of freight and passenger tariffs
on the different railroads in this State, and enforce such laws by adequate penalties, to the extent, if necessary for that purpose, of forfeiture of their property
and franchises.

History

As noted earlier (*supra,* p. 530), this was one of the sections proposed
by the Committee on Railroads of the 1870 Convention. What is now
Section 12 was substituted on the floor, but, as the Convention was com-
pleting action on the railroad provisions, this section was proposed again,

The argument was that the courts might decide that the legislature had no power to set maximum rates, as provided for in Section 12, and that this Section 15 would give the legislature something to fall back on. The argument was convincing enough to lead to adoption of the section by a vote of 32 to 27, with 24 not voting or absent.

The substance of this section was retained in the proposed 1922 Constitution.

Explanation

In an early case, the Supreme Court substantially emasculated this section. First, the Court noted that under the legislature's inherent "police power," it could enact laws prohibiting unjust and unreasonable discrimination in rates. Second, the Court noted that, at common law, common carriers had to charge reasonable rates and could not unjustly discriminate. Third, the Court said that all this section did was to tell the legislature to carry out the traditional policy. Fourth, the Court said that the common law prohibited only unjust and unreasonable discriminations and by implication, therefore, the legislature could not prohibit discriminations not unjust and unreasonable by common law. Finally, the Court held that a statutory provision requiring the forfeiture of all franchises for a first offense violated this section since the penalty of forfeiture should be invoked only in cases of extreme necessity, after more lenient penalties, such as graduated fines, had proved to be ineffectual. (Chicago & A. R.R. v. People *ex rel.* Koerner, 67 Ill. 11 (1873).)

Comparative Analysis

Approximately 14 states have a comparable provision concerning unjust discrimination.

Comment

Since the Supreme Court made it clear over a century ago that this section was both unnecessary and substantially ineffective, no harm can come from omitting it.

Article XII

MILITIA

Membership

Sec. 1. The militia of the State of Illinois shall consist of all able-bodied male persons, resident in the State, between the ages of eighteen and forty-five, except such persons as now are, or hereafter may be, exempted by laws of the United States, or of this State.

History

The substance of this section first appeared in the 1818 Constitution and was carried over into the 1848 Constitution unchanged. There was one significant difference between that section and the present one: only "free" persons were in the militia and "negroes, mulattoes and Indians" were specifically excluded. The Committee on Military Affairs of the 1870 Convention proposed the section in substantially its present form, but a minority report was filed which specifically preserved the old provision limiting militia service to white men. There was a short, sharp debate in the Committee of the Whole and upon a division, the committee voted 23 to 18 against the white only proposal. There was also a motion to change the minimum age from 18 to 21. The delegate so moving observed that "while we will not permit a young man to vote, we should not compel him to do military service." The motion was defeated by voice vote. (Debates 861.) The proposed 1922 Constitution retained the section unchanged except for the removal of some of the commas.

Explanation

No problems appear to have arisen under this section. In the early case of *Dunne v. People* (94 Ill. 120 (1879)), the Supreme Court upheld the constitutionality of the section against the claim that Congress had exclusive power over militias.

The present statutory scheme, as provided for in Chapter 129 of the Revised Statutes (§ 220.01 (1967)), first defines those subject to military duty in the Illinois State Militia as "[a]ll able-bodied citizens of this State and all other able-bodied residents in this State who have declared their intention to become citizens of the United States, between the ages of 18 and 45, except such as are expressly exempted by the laws of the United States and the State of Illinois...." The Illinois State Militia is then divided into the Organized and the Unorganized Militia. The former is the National Guard and the Naval Militia; the latter are all others within the definition. When the Organized Militia is called into federal service, the Governor by proclamation may call into existence the State Guard to serve until the emergency is over. The State Guard would be formed out of the Unorganized Militia and other volunteers. The State Guard is strictly a war-time expedient.

Comparative Analysis

Approximately 19 states have a provision much like that of Illinois. A couple of states have different age limits, and a few states leave details up to the legislature. The new Michigan Constitution omits the detailed article on the militia, one section of which was similar to Section 1, and substitutes the following: "The militia shall be organized, equipped and disciplined as provided by law." (art. III, § 4.) New York had a detailed article on the militia which was removed by an amendment in 1962 that states that everyone has an obligation to defend the state, and provides for statutory implementation as in the new Michigan Constitution. The Model State Constitution is silent on the subject except for the "Commander-in-Chief" provision of the Executive Article. (See *Comparative Analysis* of Sec. 14, Art. V, *supra*, pp. 291-2.).

Comment

In the *Comparative Analysis of the Michigan Constitution,* prepared in 1961, the chapter on the Militia Article was written by Brigadier General (Retired) Philip C. Pack, a former Judge Advocate General of Michigan. After discussing the several federal laws on the subject, he concluded that "to all practical intents annd [sic] purposes, the United States has taken over the organized militia" and that the United States "has placed such an inclusive priority label upon the unorganized, inchoate militia by [the Universal Military Training and Service Act of 1951] as to leave the states virtually without any manpower pool potentially responsive to state military draft." (C.A.M.C. at xv-3.)

In his study, *State Constitutions: The Shape of the Document* (1968), Professor Robert B. Dishman concludes a discussion of the militia with this recommendation:

"Even if the militia provisions in our state constitutions were not so archaic, it would be well to drop them altogether. If this were done, only two references to the militia would be needed in the constitution. One would simply declare the governor to be the commander-in-chief of the National Guard (or organized militia), except when called into the service of the United States. . . . The other would simply empower the legislature to provide for the organization, equipment and regulation of an adequate militia in conformity with federal laws governing the armed forces of the United States. This has already been done in Missouri and a few other states." (*Id.* at 47.)

A comment is in order concerning the statutory definition. It differs from the constitutional definition in two respects: the word "male" is omitted, and "persons" has become citizens or aliens who have taken out first papers. From the context of the definition, one can conclude that "citizen of the State" means "citizen of the United States who resides in this State." This meaning grows out of the Fourteenth Amendment which provides that all "persons born or naturalized in the United States, and subject to the juridiction thereof, are citizens of the United States and of the State wherein they reside." It is a logical fallacy, however, to conclude that citizens of Illinois can *only* be United States citizens resident therein. All that the Fourteenth Amendment commands is that a state's definition of "citizen" must include United States citizens resident therein. To be sure, the distinction is technical, but, as always, it is appropriate to be accurate, and unless Illinois specifically defines and limits state citizenship to United States citizenship and residency in Illinois, it is better to avoid the undefined term "citizen of this State."

Organization — Equipment — Discipline

Sec. 2. The General Assembly, in providing for the organization, equipment and discipline of the militia, shall conform as nearly as practicable to the regulations for the government of the armies of the United States.

History

At the end of the section that is now Section 1, the 1818 and 1848 Constitutions added the words "and shall be armed, equipped and trained as the general assembly may provide by law." Section 2 as proposed to the 1870 Convention purported to give the legislature power to act in connection with the militia, but only in conformance with federal regulations. A delegate protested that it was unnecessary to grant such power and moved to strike the section. The Committtee Chairman argued that the section was important because of the conformance limitation on the legislature's power, but when the protesting delegate then proposed a substitute not essentially different from Section 2, he was voted down. In some unexplained way, the Committee on Revision and Adjustment changed the section to meet the original objection. (As a general rule, a Committee on Revision and Adjustment, or Style and Arrangement, is not permitted to make substantive changes in the Articles referred to it by the Convention. The change made in this instance was not a change in substance in constitutional fact, but it was a change that the Convention sitting in Committee of the Whole had specifically rejected.)

The race question came up again in the consideration of this section. An amendment was proposed that would have required segregated troop units. This was voted down. A proposal was also made to add a section prohibiting a Negro from ever commanding white militia. This was also voted down. (Debates 865. There is an error of some sort in the transcript, for the roll call vote shows the proposal passing. The vote may have been on a motion to table.)

The proposed 1922 Constitution omitted this section.

Explanation

No questions appear to have arisen under this section. The statute governing the militia contains a similar section. (Ill. Rev. Stat. ch. 129, § 220.41 (1967).)

Comparative Analysis

Five states substantially duplicate the Illinois section. Another nine states have minor variations in wording, and four states use the negative formulation of providing that the legislature shall act in a manner not inconsistent with federal requirements.

Comment

The very fact that a section like this one is included in an Article on the Militia reinforces the recommendation quoted earlier, *supra*, pp. 538-9, that the rest of the Article be dropped.

Officers

Sec. 3. All militia officers shall be commissioned by the Governor, and may hold their commissions for such time as the General Assembly may provide.

History

The 1818 Constitution provided that officers should hold their commissions "during good behavior, or until they reach the age of 60 years." The 1848 Constitution read "for such time as the legislature may provide." The section as originally offered to the 1870 Convention combined the two earlier ideas by providing that commissions be held "during good behavior, or for such time as the General Assembly may provide." A proposal to strike "during good behavior, or" was immediately accepted by the Chairman of the Committee on Military Affairs, and the section sailed through without debate. The proposed 1922 Constitution removed the comma from the sentence.

Explanation

The implementing statute, Section 220.40 of Chapter 129 of the Revised Statutes, provides that officers in the Organized Militia must have United States Commissions. (*See also* Ill. Rev. Stat. ch. 129, §§ 220.37, 237, 240-242 (1967).)

Comparative Analysis

Eleven states provide that all officers are commissioned by the governor. Some states make distinctions between low-ranking and certain high-ranking officers, requiring the latter to be confirmed by the legislature, or the senate. In a few states, certain officers are to be elected by their men. In at least one state, the adjutant- and inspector-general are elected by the voters for four-year terms. Three states join Illinois in leaving the term of commissions to the legislature. One state provides that the term shall not be longer than six years.

Comment

Since the Organized Militia is effectively controlled by the United States, the many state provisions are not significant. Presumably, most of those states have a comparable statutory provision making a federal commission a condition precedent to a state commission. Except for the very highest ranks, particularly the adjutant-general, the Governor's commissioning act is probably *pro forma*.

Freedom from Arrest

Sec. 4. The militia shall, in all cases, except treason, felony or breach of the peace, be privileged from arrest during their attendance at musters and elections, and in going and returning from the same.

History

This section is in substance the same as the section originally adopted in 1818 and carried unchanged into the 1848 Constitution except for the omission of two words. Under the earlier Constitutions, the words "of officers" followed "elections." Under those Constitutions, commanding officers from captains through major generals were elected to their positions by the members of the units from companies through divisions, respectively. The committee report in the 1870 Convention omitted these provisions. In order to make Section 4 consistent with the omission, the committee dropped the words "of officers." No one mentioned the fact that this change turns the section in part into a suffrage section duplicating Section 3 of Article VII. (*Supra*, p. 391.) The proposed 1922 Constitution retained the section, but inserted the word "military" in front of "elections." Interestingly enough, the Official Explanation states that the "section is the same as Sec. 4, Art. XII, constitution of 1870." (P.N.C. 45.)

Explanation

The only interpretation of this section appears to have been the opinion of the Attorney General discussed earlier in connection with Section 14 of Article IV. (See *Explanation, supra*, p. 174.)

Comparative Analysis

Seven other states have a privilege from arrest section. Only one other state refers to "elections," but three states refer to "elections of officers."

Comment

Apart from the meaningless inclusion of "elections," there is nothing wrong with the provision except that it is unnecessary and probably ineffective in any real sense. (See discussion of the "treason, felony or breach of the peace" exception, *supra*, p. 174.)

Preservation of Records

Sec. 5. The military records, banners and relics of the State, shall be preserved as an enduring memorial of the patriotism and valor of Illinois, and it shall be the duty of the General Assembly to provide by law for the safe-keeping of the same.

History

This hortatory salute to the men in blue was offered by the Committee upon Military Affairs to the 1870 Convention without explanation or justification. Upon the reading of the section by the Clerk, the following "debate" took place:

"Mr. FOX. Mr. Chairman: I object to that section because it is a species of special legislation. I am opposed to all legislation in the organic law.

"The question being upon the adoption of section five, it was agreed to." (Debates 863.)

The proposed 1922 Constitution, coming on the heels of World War I, preserved the sentiment in an appropriately plural wording:

"The military records, banners and relics of the state shall be preserved as enduring memorials of the patriotism and valor of the men of Illinois." (art. XI, § 215)

Explanation

Obviously, there have been no problems in interpreting the section. In accordance with the constitutional command, the legislature has provided for the "safe-keeping of the same" in Section 220.25 of Chapter 129 of the Revised Statutes (1967).

Comparative Analysis

Seven states join Illinois in directing the legislature to provide for preservation of records, banners and relics.

Comment

This section is both unnecessary and harmless. Since no one wishes to appear to be opposed to patriotism and valor, it may not be possible to drop the section.

Conscientious Objectors

Sec. 6. No person having conscientious scruples against bearing arms, shall be compelled to do militia duty in time of peace: *Provided,* such person shall pay an equivalent for such exemption.

History

The substance of this section appeared in both the 1818 and 1848 Constitutions. In the 1870 Convention, the Committee on Military Affairs omitted the section from its proposed Article. The delegate who had objected to the inclusion of Section 5 (*supra,* p. 542) offered the conscientious objector section as it had appeared in the 1818 and 1848 Constitutions. According to the transcript there were shouts of "That's right" when the Clerk read the section, and it was accepted by voice vote without debate. The final wording came from the Committee on Revision and Adjustment.

The proposed 1922 Constitution added this section to Section 1 and changed the thrust from the positive to the negative, thus: "No person, because of conscientious scruples against bearing arms, shall be exempted by the laws of this state from any military service declared by the governor to be noncombatant." (art. XI, § 212)

Explanation

There has been no direct interpretation of this section, but there was an ironic case involving a conscientious objector who was denied admission to the bar because he could not conscientiously swear to uphold Section 1 of this Article. (*In re* Summers, 325 U.S. 561 (1945).)

Comparative Analysis

Some 19 states provide for conscientious objectors, either by a self-executing provision or by providing for mandatory or permissive legislative action. Eleven of those states include a requirement for payment of an equivalent. Only four other states appear to limit the exemption to peacetime.

Comment

In the light of the comprehensive federal system concerning conscientious objectors, it seems pointless to preserve a constitutional provision such as this one, particularly one with a "payment of equivalent" anachronism.

Article XIII

WAREHOUSES

Public Warehouses

Sec. 1. All elevators or storehouses where grain or other property is stored for a compensation, whether the property stored be kept separate or not, are declared to be public warehouses.

History

In the 1870 Convention, the Chairman of the Committee on Miscellaneous Corporations offered an Article on Warehouses consisting of seven sections, each of which was somewhat different from the section as finally adopted, but all of which covered the same ground as the final product. In order to understand the occasion for the adoption of an Article like this one, it is appropriate to quote at some length from the opening debate, beginning with the remarks of the committee chairman:

"Mr. CARY: Mr. Chairman: This is a matter of very great importance to every grain producer, grain dealer and farmer in the State of Illinois, who has anything to do with selling or shipping grain. Elevators and warehouses have got to be great monopolies. The elevator men control the whole grain trade of the northwest, and control it in such a manner that it becomes necessary, for the welfare of the people of this State, and of all who do business with the grain dealers of the State, that they should have some protection.

"It has been said, sir, that there is too much legislation in this article. But, sir, there is no more legislation here than in many other articles that we have passed. And if there is legislation in it, it is legislation for the great mass of the people of the State." (Debates 1622.)

"Mr. BROWNING: Mr. Chairman: This is a subject of difficulty, and one that I think the Convention ought to enter upon with very great circumspection, if it touches it at all. In my opinion, we ought not to touch this subject. There are very few of us who know anything of these complications of trade. There has been no investigation here, and I am sure that I am not so informed as to be able to give a vote that will satisfy myself. It is a subject that is completely under the control of the General Assembly. Why not leave it to the General Assembly?

". . . It is not a matter for a Constitution; it is not elemental or fundamental law. It is mere police regulations, that has (sic) no more place in the Constitution than the provision of penalties for selling liquor.

". . . The General Assembly will possess one advantage that we have not, as they can appoint committees, and enter upon an investigation. They can send for worehousemen (sic), for members of the board of trade, for grain-brokers, for farmers, elicit all the information that can be elicited upon this complicated subject, and then be prepared to prescribe just and proper remedies for the evils that exist." (*Id.* at 1624-25.)

"Mr. COOLBAUGH. Mr. Chairman: . . .

"Gentlemen may say this is a species of legislation. Well, if it is, I am glad we are legislating for once in the interest of the people against the extortions of corporations. Whenever we do that, and raise that issue, I desire to put myself on the side of the people. But I deny that it is any more legislation than the people of the State require." (*Id.* at 1626.)

"MR. UNDERWOOD. Mr. Chairman: . . .

"The misfortune, in undertaking by constitutional provision to regulate warehouses, is that we may go too far or not far enough. A Constitution is not flexible, but the Legislature may change the law from time to time so as to meet the dishonesty of men in any kind of business. It is one of those subjects over which the General Assembly should, with the greatest care and circumspection, legislate. I do not believe we have time enough to fully examine the subject in all its aspects so as to legislate wisely on the subject." (*Id.* at 1628.)

Section 1, at least, is a statement of general principle, and even if not of constitutional stature, is, one would assume, not particularly controversial. Nevertheless, there was considerable debate over the wording. Apparently, a statute passed in 1867 had made a distinction between private and public warehousemen in terms of whether grain was kept in separate bins or was mixed in a common bin. Although the section as proposed appeared to cover both types, an amendment was proposed and accepted that added the words "whether the property stored be kept separate or not."

Warehouses and grain elevators were still a touchy item in 1920, and the proposed 1922 Constitution preserved the Article on Warehouses notwithstanding a general recognition that it was purely legislative. (*See* Proceedings 3862-63.) In the case of Section 1, the statement of principle was shortened, principally by removing the clause which had been added on the floor of the 1870 Convention.

Explanation

In some respects, the courts have recognized the legislative nature of this Article and treated it as if it were a statute. For example, the Supreme Court has said that the legislature's power to regulate warehouses is not derived from this Article, but is part of what is commonly called the "police power." (State Pub. Util. Comm'n v. Monarch Refrig. Co., 267 Ill. 528 (1915).) Moreover, the declaration of what constitutes a public warehouse is not necessarily accepted by the courts. For example, one may occasionally store property for compensation and not become a public warehouseman. (*See* Mayer v. Springer, 192 Ill. 270 (1901).)

But to the extent that this "statute" sets forth a policy, the legislature has no power to change it. In *Central Elevator Company v. People* ex rel. *Moloney* (174 Ill. 203 (1898)), the Supreme Court had decided as a matter of equity that the owner of a public warehouse could not store his own grain in his own warehouse. While the *Central Elevator* case was in the Supreme Court, the General Assembly authorized the practice in a carefully worded amendment to the implementing statute. The amendment provided in effect that there should be additional assistant grain inspectors in any warehouse where the owner commingled grain with that of others, that the Railroad and Warehouse Commission had full power to issue regulations governing such commingling to the end that the warehouse owner should have no benefit or advantage over others, and that the assistant inspectors should take care to assure compliance with such regulations. When the case came back up, the Supreme Court held the act void as in conflict with the policy of Article XIII. (Hannah v. People *ex rel.* Attorney General, 198 Ill. 77 (1902).) In 1965, the legislature again opened the door to permitting warehousemen to commingle their own grain with depositors' grain, but the new statute has not yet been tested. (*See* Eaton, "Present Problems of Article XIII," 17 De Paul L. Rev. 545, 551 (1968).)

As with banks, there is a national system of warehouse regulation, and the United States Supreme Court has held that a warehouseman who complies with the requirements of the United States Warehouse Act cannot be regulated by the state in any area covered by the federal statute. (Rice v. Santa Fe Elevator Corp., 331 U.S. 218 (1947).)

Comparative Analysis

California has a comprehensive provision concerning the regulation of public utilities. Any private corporation, individual or association directly or indirectly furnishing storage or wharfage facilities to or for the public is declared to be a public utility. Kentucky has a definition substantially the same as Section 1. Except for a provision in North Dakota empowering the legislature to create state-owned or -operated grain elevators and an Oklahoma provision concerning railroad connections to grain elevators, no other state appears to have any constitutional provision specifically covering warehouses. The Model State Constitution has no substantive provision in the area of economic regulation.

Comment

Mr. Eaton concludes his article on warehouses with this observation:
"In conclusion, Article XIII has caused serious problems making it more difficult for a large industry to function as it should. Experience under the "United States Warehouse Act" which does authorize grain warehouses to mix their own grain with depositors' grain should alleviate concern over authorizing elevators

licensed by the State of Illinois to engage in the same practice. Article XIII is an excellent example of detailed constitutional provisions which have outlived conditions which existed at the time they were written. If the provisions of Article XIII had been written into statutory law, the legislature could have corrected the problem. As a part of our Constitution, even if obsolete, the legislature and the grain industry are without power to correct the problem. (Eaton, *supra* at 553.)

Warehouses — Grain — Reports

Sec. 2. The owner, lessee or manager of each and every public warehouse situated in any town or city of not less than one hundred thousand inhabitants, shall make weekly statements under oath, before some officer to be designated by law, and keep the same posted in some conspicuous place in the office of such warehouse, and shall also file a copy for public examination in such place as shall be designated by law, which statement shall correctly set forth the amount and grade of each and every kind of grain in such warehouse, together with such other property as may be stored therein, and what warehouse receipts have been issued, and are, at the time of making such statement, outstanding therefor; and shall, on the copy posted in the warehouse, note daily such changes as may be made in the quantity and grade of grain in such warehouse; and the different grades of grain shipped in separate lots, shall not be mixed with inferior or superior grades, without the consent of the owner or consignee thereof.

History

This, the first of the detailed, substantive, self-executing provisions in this Article, was offered to the 1870 Convention without the 100,000 population limitation. A delegate from Warren County expressed the fear that the Convention, "by assuming to this extent legislative functions," might put into the organic law provisions "which may prove stumbling blocks and embarrassments in all future legislation." (Debates 1697.) He indicated that he understood the principal evils to be in the operation of the large grain elevators, and to protect the small-town warehouseman from complicated paper work, he offered the limitation, but with the population figure left blank. He stated that he left the figure out because he was not sufficiently knowledgeable to choose a minimum population. After the Convention settled on 100,000, an effort was made to substitute a section that simply commanded the legislature to pass appropriate regulatory legislation and a motion was made to strike the entire section, not only because it was legislative in nature, but because it was a species of special legislation by virtue of the population limitation. The motion to strike was defeated 39 to 11 on a roll call, and the substitute was rejected by voice vote. The section as originally proposed did not contain the final provision for consent before mixing different grades of grain. This addition was proposed by Mr. Medill of Cook County and after an explanation by him, was accepted by voice vote.

The proposed 1922 Constitution retained the substance of the section and made one significant change. In connection with the 100,000 population limitation, the words "or such population as may be provided by law" were added. (See *Comment, infra,* p. 550, for a discussion of this change.)

Explanation

It is fairly clear from the 1870 debates that the delegates believed that the 100,000 population figure was a dividing line between the constitutional self-executing regulation and the legislature's power to enact the same, or similar, regulations for other parts of the state. Unfortunately, in the early case of *People v. Harper* (91 Ill. 357 (1878)), the Supreme Court read the section otherwise. The Court said that Section 2 "discriminates between public warehouses in cities of not less than 100,000 inhabitants, and those in cities of less population, and recognizes that there is a necessity for regulations in respect to the former, not necessary to the latter." (*Id.* at 370.) But since the Court was answering an argument that it was unconstitutional to put the big city warehouses in a separate class in the implementing statute, too much should not be read into the quoted sentence.

Prior to 1955, the statutory scheme for regulating warehouses was an amended version of the original act passed in 1871 pursuant to the requirements of Article XIII. The first section of the 1871 statute divided public warehouses into three classes, and the second section defined those classes in a manner that was unchanged until 1935, when warehouses for the storage of personal property were excluded from the definition. Under that definition, Class A and Class B warehouses were those in which grain was stored in bulk and commingled; and for A, located in cities of 100,000 and up; and for B, located somewhere else. Class C embraced all other public warehouses. (Act of April 25, 1871, ch. 114, §2, [1871] Ill. Laws 762 (repealed 1955).)

Under the 1955 scheme, the Public Grain Warehouse and Warehouse Receipts Act, the class distinctions are abolished, and in all respects except one, the 100,000 limitation has disappeared. In order to comply literally with Section 2, the act requires a warehouseman with a warehouse in a city of not less than 100,000 inhabitants to make the required weekly statements under oath. (Ill. Rev. Stat. ch. 114, §214.15 (1967). The act begins with Section 214.1. In 1961, Illinois adopted the Uniform Commercial Code and in connection therewith repealed the warehouse receipts' portion, Sections 233-292 of Chapter 114.)

Comparative Analysis

No other state has such a provision.

Comment

In the 1920-22 Convention, efforts were made to take out the 100,000 limitation or to substitute 50,000. In the course of the debate, there was a learned discussion on implied limitations — the judicial doctrine that a grant of detailed power to the legislature implies a denial of power to go beyond the detailed grant. No reference was made to the *Harper* case quoted from above. The compromise solution was the addition of the words quoted above, "or such population as may be provided by law." (*See* Proceedings 3863-64.) It should be noted that this solution did not get around the implied limitations problem, if there is one. The solution would have permitted the legislature to extend the coverage of the stated requirement, but not to set up a different requirement. If anything, the added words increased the likelihood that a court would be tempted to invoke the doctrine of implied limitations.

Whether there is any need for weekly postings under oath ought to be a question of legislative determination. And if there is a need, the legislature ought to be able to decide the appropriate classification of warehouses to which it should apply. Population of the community in which the warehouse is located is not necessarily the most appropriate classification.

Right to Examine Property

Sec. 3. The owners of property stored in any warehouse, or holder of a receipt for the same, shall always be at liberty to examine such property stored, and all the books and records of the warehouse in regard to such property.

History

This section, as originally proposed by the Committee on Miscellaneous Corporations, was somewhat more detailed than it is now, but the additional details were dropped almost before debate began, and it seems unnecessary to discuss the earlier wording. It should be noted, however, that the usual complaint was made that the section, in any event, was "special legislation," and was unnecessary. The proposed 1922 Constitution retained the substance of the section in a still further simplified version.

Explanation

The section seems self-evident and, indeed, appears never to have been litigated. Actually, the privilege accorded the receipt holder is a normal one, and it is not far-fetched to say that all the section really does is prevent the legislature from depriving the receipt holder of his normal privilege. (Ill. Rev. Stat. ch. 114, § 214.16 (1967) provides for examination.)

Comparative Analysis
No other state has such a provision.

Comment
Since there is a statutory protection for examination that is not likely to be taken away, this insignificant section could certainly be dropped.

Grain Shipments — Weighing — Liability of Carrier
Sec. 4. All railroad companies and other common carriers on railroads shall weigh or measure grain at points where it is shipped, and receipt for the full amount, and shall be responsible for the delivery of such amount to the owner or consignee thereof, at the place of destination.

History
The section as originally proposed in the 1870 Convention read as follows:

"All railroad companies and other common carriers shall be required to weigh grain into the cars at points where it is shipped, and receipt for the amount, and be held responsible for the delivery of the amount received, at the place of destination."

The changes made by the Convention can be demonstrated by the following composite in which omitted words are in brackets and added words are italicized.

All railroad companies an other common carriers *on railroads* shall [be required to] weigh *or measure* grain [into the cars] at points where it is shipped, and receipt for the *full* amount, and shall be [held] responsible for the delivery of [the] *such* amount [received,] *to the owner or consignee thereof,* at the place of destination.

Of the several changes, only two were made by the Committee on Revision and Adjustment. These were the grammatical shifts to direct commands to "weigh" and "be responsible" from the third party method of wording the commands. All other changes were made by the delegates in the course of debating the proposal. In almost all cases, the delegate proposing the change was either aiming at removing a specific evil or was seeking to grant an exemption to someone. For example, "or measure" was added because, a delegate pointed out, some shipments, particularly by steamboat, were by the bag rather than by weight. At the second round of debate, a delegate argued that the river carriers ought to be excluded because they could not afford to maintain the necessary weighing equipment, and so the words "on railroads" were added. (For the full flavor of the "legislative process" in operation, see Debates 1632-33, 1700-01.)

The proposed 1922 Constitution made a substantive change by removing the words "on railroads," and otherwise greatly simplified the wording.

Explanation

The courts appear to have heeded the strong feelings against railroads exhibited by the 1870 delegates. Although the Supreme Court observed that the carrier is not an absolute insurer of the grain, it did rule out any limitation of liability for leakage, shrinkage or discrepancies in elevator weights. In so ruling, the Court made inapplicable in Illinois a limitation apparently permitted by the Uniform Bills of Lading Act. (Shellabarger Elevator Co. v. Illinois Cent. R. R., 278 Ill. 333 (1917).)

Comparative Analysis

No other state has such a provision.

Comment

In the last half of the Twentieth Century, one would assume that most people in business, including most farmers, are sufficiently knowlegeable to require appropriate determination of the quantity of a product involved in a transaction and to know the significance of who bears the risk of loss. On this assumption, it seems unnecessary to have a constitutional command to weigh grain or a constitutional allocation of risk of loss. It should be sufficient for the legislature to provide for regulation of the accuracy of weighing devices and to forbid unconscionable shifts in risks.

Railroads — Delivery of Grain

Sec. 5. All railroad companies receiving and transporting grain in bulk or otherwise, shall deliver the same to any consignee thereof, or any elevator or public warehouse to which it may be consigned, provided such consignee or the elevator or public warehouse can be reached by any track owned, leased or used, or which can be used, by such railroad companies, and all railroad companies shall permit connections to be made with their track, so that any such consignee, and any public warehouse, coal bank or coal yard may be reached by the cars on said railroad.

History

This section appears to have been aimed at one specific evil as explained by the Committee Chairman to the delegates at the 1870 Convention:

"Many of the elevators are built along the sides of that public track, and I was shown, when there, an elevator that was built on the supposition that all the railroads running on that track would deliver grain at this warehouse or elevator, but the owner of that elevator could not get the grain he had purchased in the country, shipped in the cars, and sent to Chicago to his own elevator, without having it shipped to other elevators, and first paying tribute to them, as I understand." (Debates 1634.)

There were several amendments from the floor of the Convention, but none of them represented any substantial change. The one significant alteration was a proposal to extend the section to cover coal yards. The extension was defeated on a roll call vote. Coal yards were presumably added by the Committee on Revision and Adjustment.

The proposed 1922 Constitution made one change of substance by limiting the privilege of spur connection to public warehouses, coal banks and coal yards. The present section allows "any such consignee," that is, any consignee of grain, to demand a spur connection.

Explanation

It is interesting to find that half the reported cases arising under this section concerned those coal yards that were slipped into the section at the last moment. But the several coal cases, as well as those involving warehousemen and elevators, are of such limited technical nature that no purpose is served in digesting them here.

Comparative Analysis

Oklahoma has a provision that, with the approval of the Corporation Commission, any owner or operator of a grain elevator, a coal, lead, iron, or zinc mine, or sawmill, or other industry, may connect a spur with a railroad provided that the railroad is reimbursed for the cost of the connection.

Comment

In these days of ubiquitous concrete ribbons all over the landscape with mammoth tractor-trailers whizzing by, it is inconceivable that any railroad would turn away a proposed spur connection or refuse to deliver grain to the consignee.

Warehouse Receipts

Sec. 6. It shall be the duty of the General Assembly to pass all necessary laws to prevent the issue of false and fraudulent warehouse receipts, and to give full effect to this article of the constitution, which shall be liberally construed so as to protect producers and shippers. And the enumeration of the remedies herein named shall not be construed to deny to the General Assembly the power to prescribe by law such other and further remedies as may be found expedient, or to deprive any person of existing common law remedies.

History

The original proposal offered to the 1870 Convention simply said that the legislature should pass all necessary laws to give full effect to the Article, which, of course, was to be liberally construed. In a bewildering series of rapidly accepted amendments, the section evolved to its present wording. (The Committee on Revision and Adjustment made no changes in the wording.) One delegate rather timidly suggested that the liberal construction clause could just as well be stricken. It "means nothing in law," he observed, "and is at the most but a stump speech." (Debates 1635.) The delegates did not agree with him.

This section caused a great deal of trouble in the 1920-22 Convention. When the section was under consideration in Committee of the Whole, an amendment was offered and accepted to include "consumers and other interests" under the "liberally construed" clause. (Proceedings 1765.) When the Article came back from the Committee on Phraseology and Style in the customary greatly shortened wording, the Chairman of the Agricultural Committee asked to have "consumers and other interests" removed. He explained that under the existing Warehouse Article, warehousemen could not mingle their own grain in their own warehouse. (See *Explanation* for Sec. 1, *supra,* p. 547.) He further explained that inclusion of "consumers and other interests" might open the door to a change in the Supreme Court's ruling. The chairman was unsuccessful in his argument and after losing, served notice that he would move to reconsider. (Proceedings 3876-79.) On a subsequent day, he was successful in his motion to reconsider. (*Id.* at 4035.) He then moved to retain Sections 6 and 7 exactly as they appeared in the 1870 Constitution rather than in the shortened, combined wording of the Committee on Phraseology and Style. After much debate, the Convention accepted Section 6. (*Id.* at 4039.) When Section 7 was taken up, an effort was made to include consumers in the list of people to be protected, but the effort failed and Section 7 went back in unchanged. (*Id.* at 4045.)

Explanation

Since the entire section is not much more than a "stump speech," the appellation suggested for one portion of it, it is not surprising to find that, with one exception, the section has had no life of its own. That exception was a case in 1945 wherein it was argued that the section precluded a local licensing ordinance designed to prevent spontaneous combustion or dust explosions in grain elevators. The argument was unsuccessful. (Edward R. Bacon Grain Co. v. City of Chicago, 325 Ill. App. 245 (1945).)

Comparative Analysis

No other state has such a provision.

Comment

The hassle in 1920 over including "consumers or others interested" is instructive on two scores. It demonstrates the inadvisability of tampering with constitutional language with an accepted meaning. This was not a case where someone wanted to improve on the wording for its own sake, but the proposal to add consumers was almost as irrelevant, and certainly was not sufficiently significant to jeopardize an accepted and settled interpretation of the entire Article. (For purposes of this discussion, it is not pertinent whether that interpretation was a good one then or now.) It was presumably in recognition of the importance of not changing language that the Chairman of the Agricultural Committee used the gambit of trying to restore the original language of Sections 6 and 7.

The other point to be made is that a group that has a vested interest in a particular constitutional doctrine, whether spelled out in the document or the result of judicial decisions and whether appropriately in the Constitution or not, can be expected to exert great pressure to preserve their interest. One can read between the lines of the debates in 1922 and see that there was great pressure from shippers and dealers to preserve the policy of prohibiting commingling of warehousemen's grain with depositors' grain. But having said all this, the moral is only partly helpful. One should not put into constitutions provisions that give rise to such vested interests. Once in a constitution, the damage is done and it may be next to impossible to remove the provision.

Inspection of Grain

Sec. 7. The General Assembly shall pass laws for the inspection of grain, for the protection of producers, shippers and receivers of grain and produce.

History

The essence of this section was offered on the floor of the 1870 Convention by a delegate who explained: "Having caught the animal and built a pen to keep him, this section is needed to tie him." (Debates 1636.) Another delegate observed that there were serious complaints about inadequate grain inspection and that the legislature ought to be charged with doing something about the complaints. The section was agreed to.

The foregoing occurred while the Convention was sitting in Committee of the Whole. Just before the Committee rose, a delegate offered an additional section, as follows:

"This act shall be deemed a public act and shall be in force from and after its passage." (Debates 1637.)

The proposal was voted down. As the Convention proper was subsequently about to refer the Warehouse Article to the Committee on Revision and Adjustment, another delegate offered an additional section, reading: "Be it enacted by the people of the State of Illinois, in Convention assembled." The proposal was ruled out of order.

The proposed 1922 Constitution inserted the word "and" after "inspection of grain" and before "for the protection." The Official Explanation states that the section is the same as Section 7, but this is arguable. (P.N.C. 47.) Incidentally, the same assertion is made concerning Sections 4 and 5 (*Id.*), but these were clearly changed. (See *supra*, pp. 551 and 553.)

Explanation

This section appears to tell the legislature to pass laws for the inspection of grain, the purpose of which inspection is to protect producers, shippers and receivers of grain and produce. This is the way the section was paraphrased in the *Bacon* case. (*Supra,* p. 554.) The addition of the word "and" as proposed in the 1922 Constitution would have told the legislature to pass laws for the inspection of grain and to pass other laws for the protection of producers, shippers and receivers. This is the way Chief Justice Waite paraphrased the sentence in the famous case of *Munn v. Illinois* (94 U.S. 113, 132 (1876)). Actually, the difference is academic since there is no way to force the legislature to act. Moreover, the Supreme Court noted that the legislature under its police power could pass grain inspection laws without this section. (People v. Harper, 91 Ill. 357 (1878).)

As noted above, it is not possible to force the legislature to act under one of these mandatory instructions. It is also not possible to knock out the legislature's effort on the ground that it has not done a good enough job. See *Board of Trade v. Cowen* (252 Ill. 554 (1911)), where the Supreme Court turned aside an argument that the inspection law was unconstitutional because the legislature did not appropriate enough money for adequate inspections.

Comparative Analysis

No other state has such a provision.

Comment

In addition to the ambiguity caused by the absence of the word "and," there is the curious inclusion of the word "produce." It may be that the two ambiguities make a clear sentence. If the sentence has the meaning suggested at the beginning of the *Explanation,* then "produce" is meaningless. But if the sentence should be read as if "and" were included, then "produce" makes sense.

Article XIV

AMENDMENTS TO THE CONSTITUTION

Constitutional Convention

Sec. 1. Whenever two-thirds of the members of each house of the General Assembly shall, by a vote entered upon the journals thereof, concur that a Convention is necessary to revise, alter or amend the constitution, the question shall be submitted to the electors at the next election. If a majority voting at the election vote for a convention, the General Assembly shall, at the next session provide for a convention, to consist of double the number of members of the Senate, to be elected in the same manner, at the same places, and in the same districts. The General Assembly shall, in the act calling the Convention, designate the day, hour and place of its meeting, fix the pay of its members and officers, and provide for the payment of the same, together with the expenses necessarily incurred by the Convention in the performance of its duties. Before proceeding the members shall take an oath to support the Constitution of the United States, and of the State of Illinois, and to faithfully discharge their duties as members of the Convention. The qualification of members shall be the same as that of members of the Senate, and vacancies occurring shall be filled in the manner provided for filling vacancies in the General Assembly. Said Convention shall meet within three months after such election, and prepare such revision, alteration or amendments of the Constitution as shall be deemed necessary, which shall be submitted to the electors for their ratification or rejection, at an election appointed by the Convention for that purpose, not less than two nor more than six months after the adjournment thereof; and unless so submitted and approved, by a majority of the electors voting at the election, no such revision, alterations or amendments shall take effect.

-History

The 1818 Constitution provided that, upon the initiative of "two-thirds of the General Assembly," the question of calling a convention should go to the voters. If a "majority of all the citizens of the state, voting for representatives," voted for a convention, the General Assembly at its next session was to provide for one. There were to be as many delegates as members of the General Assembly, "to be chosen in the same manner, at the same place, and by the same electors that choose the General Assembly." There was no provision for a referendum on the product of the Convention.

The 1848 Constitution made three changes. First, it was specified that two-thirds of the members elected to each house had to vote for a convention. Second, the word "electors" was substituted for "citizens" in defining the majority required to approve the calling of a convention. Third, the number of delegates was to equal the number of representatives.

In the 1870 Convention, the Committee on Future Amendments split three ways over the issue of an oath to be taken by delegates to a convention, and three versions of a convention section were placed before the Committee of the Whole. The majority proposal was silent as to oaths, one minority proposal empowered the delegates by majority vote to prescribe an oath to be taken, and the other minority proprosal contained the oath sentence now appearing in Section 1.

This problem of an oath was taken most seriously by the delegates. In fact, three of the first four days of the Convention were spent in what Joseph Medill described as "one of the ablest debates . . . which it has been my pleasure ever to have heard." (Debates 37.) The immediate subject of debate was whether or not a delegate could swear to support the Illinois Constitution, but the substance of the debate was over the philosophical question of how delegates chosen to "revise, alter or amend" the Illinois Constitution could properly take an oath to support it. A subsidiary question was whether the legislature, which had mandated the oath in the Enabling Act, could exercise such control over delegates. The debate concluded with the adoption of an oath to support the Illinois Constitution, "so far as its provisions are compatible with, and applicable to my position and duties as a member of the Convention." Following the taking of this oath, consent was given to permit any delegates so desiring to rise and take a second oath in the words of the Enabling Act.

Both in Committee of the Whole and in the Convention proper, the various proposals on oaths were brought up, but there was no debate to speak of. The arguments had been amply aired at the outset of the Convention. It is interesting to note, however, that most delegates had refused to take an oath in the form which they subsequently put into Section 1.

One of the other changes made in 1870 also grew out of the experience of the delegates. This was the addition of the words "and vacancies occurring shall be filled in the manner provided for filling vacancies in the General Assembly." In the course of the Convention, several delegates died and there was considerable debate over whether the Convention should "order" an election, "invite" an election, recommend to the Governor that he order an election, or simply announce that if the voters of the deceased delegate's district elected someone, the Convention would seat him. The decision was to invite the district to hold an election on a stated date.

The 1870 Convention made two other additions to the 1848 provision. One was instructions to the General Assembly concerning material to be included in the Enabling Act. The other, which was the subject of debate, was the size of the Convention — whether, in effect, there should be approximately 50, 100, or 150 or more delegates. The choice was "double the number of members of the Senate." The only change made in the proposed 1922 Constitution was to add seven members at large from Cook County to "double the number" of Senators. This addition is related, of course, to the 1922 permanent apportionment of 19 senate seats to Cook County and 38 seats to the rest of the state. (See *History* of Sec. 6 of Art. IV, *supra*, p. 132.) Under the 1922 proposal, Cook County would have had 45 delegates and the rest of the state would have had 76.

Explanation

Prior to July 10, 1969, there were no definitive rulings concerning Section 1. At the time of the 1920-1922 Convention, there was a belief that delegates could not be elected on a nonpartisan basis and the Attorney General is reputed to have issued an opinion to that effect. (The opinion is cited in Annotation 284, but no one has been able to find the actual opinion.) The same Attorney General is reported to have issued an opinion to the effect that a member of the General Assembly could run as a delegate but if elected, he would vacate his legislative seat when he qualified as a delegate. (Annotations 283. This opinion has never been found, either.) Apparently, some legislators were elected and qualified as delegates, but retained their legislative seats. No objections appear to have been raised and no lawsuit appears to have contested the dual office holding.

The crucial words in Section 1 that raise the two problems discussed at the time of the 1920-1922 Convention are the reference to election of delegates "in the same manner" as senators are elected, and the statement that the "qualification of members shall be the same as members of the Senate." In the first case, the question is whether "in the same manner" covers party primaries, since senators are so nominated. In the second case, the question is whether a legislator serving as a delegate would be holding a "lucrative office" contrary to the prohibition in Section 3 of Article IV. (*Supra*, p. 120.)

The Enabling Act for the forthcoming Convention provides for nonpartisan primaries and elections, and also provides that "legislators and other public officials, so long as they retain their elected or appointed offices and serve as members of the Convention, shall receive no compensation for their Convention services other than [expenses]." (Act 76-40, Laws 1969.) A test case, *Livingston v. Ogilvie* (— Ill. — 2d (1969)),

was brought to determine the constitutionality of these two parts of
the Enabling Act. The test case also included questions concerning
the recent one man-one vote cases handed down by the United States
Supreme Court, discussed in connection with Section 7 of Article IV
(*supra,* pp. 138-9); the requirement that a delegate be a qualified voter; the
non-Communist affidavit required of a candidate; and the provision
purporting to terminate the authority of the Convention on June 30,
1971.

The Supreme Court handed down an opinion in *Livingston v. Ogilvie*
on July 10, 1969, upholding the Enabling Act in almost all respects.
The decision was unanimous as to all decided issues except eligibility
to be members of the Convention, and on that the Court split five to
two. Two of the original issues in the suit — voter status and termination
date — are not mentioned in the opinion of the Court, but the dissenting
judges make use of the fact that the Enabling Act has a termination date
without addressing themselves to its constitutionality.

Even though these two issues were not discussed, a word about them
is in order. Actually, even in a declaratory judgment action, which this
suit was, it is appropriate to avoid issues that are, so to speak, speculative, and both voter status and date of termination are speculative. As
a practical matter, no one who is not a voter is likely to run for delegate,
but if such a person does, he alone has sufficient interest to litigate the
issue of his qualification. Were such litigation to arise, the decision
should be that the requirement is invalid. Voter status is not a qualification under Section 3 of Article IV, and the Supreme Court has said
that the constitutional qualifications for membership in the legislature
cannot be added to. (See *Explanation* of Sec. 3, *supra,* p. 122.) The effort
to set a termination date for the work of the Convention — a laudable
effort, to be sure — will not be significant legally unless the Convention
in fact continues to work past June 30, 1971. (See *Comment* below for
the theoretical issue involved.)

The Court came down with all four feet on the issue of the non-
Communist affidavit. The Court first observed that Section 1 provides
for the oath to be taken by the members of the Convention, and held
that the Enabling Act was unconstitutional because it went beyond Section 1 in including loyalty provisions other than that of supporting the
United States and Illinois Constitutions. The Court went on to say that
the loyalty oath was also unconstitutional under the Fourteenth Amendment of the United States Constitution.

The Court disposed of the other minor issue — one man-one vote — in
a straightforward but not wholly convincing manner. Relying upon
cases from other states, the Court concluded that the one man-one vote

principle is not relevant to a constitutional convention because a convention can do no more than propose something to the voters. This is an example of disposing of a difficult problem by a too-simple answer. If, as an extreme example, the Constitution had been silent on apportionment of delegates and the legislature had provided for a convention with no delegates from Chicago, the Court's argument would not fly.

In all fairness to the Court, one must concede that it was in a box. The present senatorial districts were court-created and it is a little difficult for the Court to condemn its own handiwork. There is a way around the recent one man-one vote cases, but it is a sophisticated argument that is not particularly becoming for a court to spell out. The recent United States Supreme Court cases are designed to close avenues by which legislatures can give the appearance of honoring the one man-one vote rule but simultaneously subvert it. Courts are not likely to engage in the same devious maneuvers, and this alone should protect the existing judicially determined senatorial districts in Illinois. But, as suggested above, this is not an argument that a court would find it easy to make. The end result in the *Livingston* case is undoubtedly a good one, and, as a matter of practicality, it is unlikely that the Court's reasoning will ever return to haunt it.

On the major question of nonpartisan elections of convention members, the Court discussed the intricate arguments that revolve around "manner" — that is, convention members are to be elected in the same "manner" as senators — but came up with the simple, straightforward conclusion that the word means no more than "elected by the people" in "free and equal" elections by "ballot." The Court brushed aside all invocations to political parties, party primaries, and legislative implementation of the party system. These, the Court implied, are simply not essential parts of the Constitution.

On the remaining major issue, that of eligibility to serve as a member of the Convention while holding another state office, the Court reached a conclusion that is clear enough but by a route that is most confusing. The conclusion, in short form, is that legislators can be members of the Convention without giving up their seats in the legislature, that judges may be members if they give up their judgeships, that the Governor and the other executive officers listed in Section 5 of Article V (*supra,* p. 267) cannot be members, and that any other office-holder may be a member of the Convention. For present purposes, nothing is gained by explaining the way in which the Court reached its conclusion, or the way in which the dissenting judges said the Court should have reached a different conclusion.

Comparative Analysis

It may come as a surprise to many to learn that the constitutions of a fifth of the states have no provision for the calling of a constitutional convention. It may be equally surprising to know that two of these states, Pennsylvania and Rhode Island, recently had constitutional conventions, and that one of them, Arkansas, has a convention underway now. (The Commentary to the Model State Constitution (p. 109) states that all except one of these "no convention" states have held at least two conventions.) As a matter of constitutional theory, it is generally accepted that the absence of specific authority for a convention is no insurmountable obstacle. Indeed, it can be argued that if a legislature adopts an entirely new constitution and submits it to the people and they ratify it, the new constitution becomes the organic law of the state. The argument is particularly appropriate if no machinery for a convention is provided in the existing constitution. The theory is, of course, that the people have the inherent power to change their government. When, however, the people have provided the machinery for a convention, the theoretical argument is "stickier," and in any event hypothetical.

All other states provide for constitutional conventions, usually on the initiative of the legislature but subject to a referendum by the electorate. In approximately a dozen states there is a mandatory requirement that every so often, usually either every 20 years or every ten years, the question of whether or not to hold a convention goes on the ballot automatically. In Maryland, this is the only road to a convention; in the other states, the method is in addition to legislative initiative. Two states, Georgia and Maine, permit the legislature to call a convention without a referendum. Legislative initiative for calling a convention usually requires a two-thirds' vote, but a half dozen states require only a simple majority. In Kentucky, the simple majority is required of two successive legislatures. In a number of states, the size of the legislative majority is not specified.

In most states, the referendum on whether or not to hold a convention must take place at a general election. The states are about equally divided between those requiring approval by a majority of those voting on the question and those requiring a majority of those voting at the election. In Kentucky, the simple majority must be at least 25 per cent of the vote cast at the preceding gubernatorial election, and in Nebraska the majority must be at least 35 per cent of the votes cast in the election.

There are so many variations among the several states in the details concerning a constitutional convention that only a few generalizations can be made. There is, for example, a great range in the quantity of detail provided. The new Connecticut Constitution simply says that the legislature, by a two-thirds' vote, shall prescribe by law the manner of selecting delegates, the date of convening a convention and the date of final adjournment. The New York Constitution goes to the other extreme and provides such abundant detail that an Enabling Act is almost unnecessary. A good many states specify the size of a convention, or a maximum or minimum number of delegates, but only a few join Illinois in predetermining the districts from which the delegates are to be chosen. Two states, Missouri and New York, provide for election of 15 delegates at large, a number that is 18 per cent of the total size of a Missouri convention but only 8 per cent of the New York membership.

The requirements for ratification of the results of a convention's work are spelled out in detail in some states, left up to the convention in other states, and in still other states, including Illinois, are spelled out in part and in part left up to the convention.

The United States Constitution provides that "on the Application of the Legislatures of two thirds of the several States," Congress shall call a convention for proposing amendments. Recently, this mode of amendment has been much in the news, for there is a proposal for a convention going the rounds of the several states. Since an "application" has never before been made, there is a great deal of controversy concerning what happens if two-thirds of the states do act.

There are several interesting suggestions in the Model State Constitution. The Model provides, as would be expected, for legislative initiative of a referendum for a convention and for automatic submission of the question, but only if 15 years have passed since the last referendum. Then appears this sub-section:

"The legislature, prior to a popular vote on the holding of a convention, shall provide for a preparatory commission to assemble information on constitutional questions to assist the voters and, if a convention is authorized, the commission shall be continued for the assistance of the delegates. If a majority of the qualified voters voting on the question of holding a convention approves it, delegates shall be chosen at the next regular election not less than three months thereafter unless the legislature shall by law have provided for election of the delegates at the same time that the question is voted on or at a special election." (art. XII, § 12.03.)

The Model continues with provisions for any qualified voter to be eligible as a delegate and for a single delegate from each district of the unicameral legislature. The Model also sets forth a limited number of convention rules, such as that proposals must be upon the desks of delegates three days before final passage, and a self-executing provision for adoption of convention proposals.

The Model's article on constitutional revision ends with the following section:

"If conflicting constitutional amendments or revisions submitted to the voters at the same election are approved, the amendment or revision receiving the highest number of affirmative votes shall prevail to the extent of such conflict." (art. XII, §12.04.)

One state, New York, has an analogous section to the effect that a convention proposal submitted at the same election as an amendment proposed by the legislature shall, if adopted, supersede the legislative proposal. In the unsuccessful proposed 1967 Constitution, this provision would have been altered to be operative only if the proposals were "inconsistent" and then only to the "extent of such inconsistency" would one supersede the other.

Comment

As pointed out above in connection with the oath debate in 1870, there is a nice, but rather theoretical, question concerning the extent to which a constitutional convention is a "sovereign" body, a free agent, not subject to any limitation imposed by the legislature or by a preceding constitution. But, as noted, the question is mainly theoretical. For one thing, the supposed restrictions on the "sovereign" convention usually are not too burdensome to live with. For another thing, a convention would be a bit rash and insensitive to the needs of its constituency to jeopardize its work product solely to flaunt its "sovereign" power. Finally, most restrictions are likely to be sensible ones. For example, the section of the Enabling Act that repeals it on June 30, 1971, is a sensible nudge to make sure that the Convention proceeds with all deliberate speed. It would be foolhardy, to say the least, for the Convention to set out on a deliberate plan to sit past June 30, 1971. But if unforeseen events forced the Convention past that day, the theoretical argument that a constituent assembly is "sovereign" would probably serve to validate the work of the Convention.

One minor point about a constitutional convention provision is that delegates should hesitate before spelling out details for the next constitutional convention. As noted above in connection with the 1870 Convention, two changes in the convention provision arose out of problems confronting that Convention. This propensity to insert solutions to known problems for the benefit of a future generation has two drawbacks: it is likely to clutter up a constitution, probably producing an unbalanced provision; and it projects a problem of the past into the relatively distant future when things may be so changed that the provision ends up including nonsolutions to nonproblems. By far the best route is to tell the legislature to set up a convention and stop. The legislature in, say, 1990 or 2010, is likely to be better qualified to anticipate convention problems of that day than are the most prescient convention delegates of 1970.

It was noted above that the Model State Constitution covers the unlikely event of duplicate constitutional proposals facing the voter at a single election. The Model Commentary concedes that this is "not common," but "may happen." (Model State Constitution 111.) The fact that the New York 1967 Convention fussed around "perfecting" the New York provision is evidence enough that this is the sort of constitutional provision that is dreamed up by a perfectionist overly anxious to anticipate every possibility.

Constitutional Amendments Proposed by Legislature

Sec. 2. Amendments to this Constitution may be proposed in either House of the General Assembly, and if the same shall be voted for by two-thirds of all the members elected to each of the two houses, such proposed amendments, together with the yeas and nays of each house thereon, shall be entered in full on their respective journals, and said amendments shall be submitted to the electors of this State for adoption or rejection, at the next election of members of the General Assembly, in such manner as may be prescribed by law. Each proposed amendment shall be published in full at least three months preceding the election, and if either a majority of the electors voting at said election or two-thirds of the electors voting on any such proposed amendment shall vote for the proposed amendment, it shall become a part of this Constitution. But the General Assembly shall have no power to propose amendments to more than three articles of this Constitution at the same session, nor to the same article oftener than once in four years. The proposition for the adoption or rejection of the proposed amendment or amendments shall be printed on a separate ballot or in a separate column on the ballot as the General Assembly by law may provide and the votes thereon shall be cast by voting upon such separate ballot or in such separate column as the case may be.

History

The 1818 Constitution did not provide for amendment by legislative proposal. With two major exceptions, the section in the 1848 Constitution was substantially as Section 2 appeared before adoption of the Gateway Amendment in 1950. One major difference was a requirement that a proposed amendment be passed a second time after an intervening general election. The second vote was to be by a majority of the elected members of each house. The second major difference was that, in the 1848 Constitution, there was a prohibition against proposing amendments to more than one article at a time, but there was no requirement for a four-year gap between submissions. In the 1870 Convention, the principal debate was on whether the "one article every four years" limitation was too restrictive. Notwithstanding the assertion that no other constitution in the United States had such a limitation, the Convention upheld it. The section as adopted in 1870 differed from the present Section 2 in the omission of the "two-thirds of the electors voting" on the amendment, in the limitation of amendments to a single article, and in the omission of the last sentence.

After five failures, a Gateway Amendment was finally adopted in 1950 following an unusually vigorous campaign. The "majority of those voting at the election" problem did not even exist until after 1890. In fact, the first five amendments proposed were all adopted. The turning point was the adoption of the Australian ballot in 1891. Prior thereto, each political party printed its own ballot and a voter who used a party ballot and marked the party circle was counted as voting for any amendment that was on the ballot. With the adoption of an official ballot, the amendment question was separately stated and separately counted.

A Gateway Amendment was the first amendment to appear on the ballot following adoption of the Australian ballot. Almost 80 per cent of the voters failed to vote, but the 20 per cent who did vote rejected the amendment. It would have permitted amendments to two articles at a time, but otherwise made no change. Four years later another effort was made, this time to authorize amendments to three articles at a time and resubmission every two years. This one was favored two to one, but again, almost 80 per cent failed to vote.

In the midst of the Gateway Amendment efforts came the proposed 1922 Constitution. It included a proposal to permit amendments to two articles at a time and the four-year-gap requirement was changed from amending an article to amending a section. The majority required to adopt was changed from those voting at the election to those voting for members of the House of Representatives. (This was designed to "overrule" the *Stevenson* case discussed below.) After defeat of the proposed Constitution, a third Gateway Amendment was proposed. This one increased coverage of permitted simultaneous amendments from one to two articles and left the four-year gap unchanged, but provided that no constitutional amendments could be "proposed or voted on during the time that the United States is engaged in war or within one year following the declaration of peace." The favorable vote was almost two to one, but 57.3 per cent failed to vote on the amendment.

The fourth Gateway Amendment was submitted in 1932. It increased coverage of simultaneous submission from amendment of one to amendment of three articles, but made no other change. This was favored almost four to one, but 60.9 per cent did not vote. The fifth effort was in 1946. For the first time, other than the minor 1922 proposed change, attention was given to the required majority problem. The proposal was to drop the majority voting at the election and substitute two-thirds of those voting on the question. Amendment of three articles simultaneously was also proposed. Again, the favorable vote approached four to one, but 55 per cent failed to vote. The sixth and successful Gateway Amendment is the current Section 2 with its alternative required majorities. The favorable vote was better than three to one, and the absolute majority was better than 67 per cent. Only 13 percent of those voting failed to mark their blue ballot.

Explanation

The Gateway Amendment is clear and explicit and few questions appear to have been raised about it. The Supreme Court did rule that a direction by statute that a voter must mark his ballot with a cross required the voiding of ballots marked with a check or the word "Yes." (Scribner v. Sachs, 18 Ill. 2d 400 (1960).) Presumably, the legislature could revise the direction and permit alternative markings.

The most important case under the earlier Section 2 was *People v. Stevenson* (281 Ill. 17 (1917)), where the Supreme Court held that "electors voting at said election" must include those who did not vote for members of the General Assembly. As noted above, the proposed 1922 Constitution would have changed this. In the light of this history, it would be normal for a court to construe the Gateway Amendment wording the same way as the Court did in the *Stevenson* case.

In *City of Chicago v. Reeves* (220 Ill. 274 (1906)), the Supreme Court ruled that the original limitation of amendment of a single article at a single session was not violated because an amendment explicitly amending one article amended other articles by implication. (Compare the discussion of "Revival and Amendment" under Sec. 13 of Art. IV, *supra,* p. 165-6.) The rule of the *Reeves* case has recently been reaffirmed. (People ex rel. Engle v. Kerner, 32 Ill. 2d 212 (1965).) The Attorney General once ruled that the limitation could not be evaded by proposing additional amendments at special sessions. ('1912 Ill. Att'y Gen. Rep. 1102.)

An amendment becomes a part of the Constitution upon approval by the voters. In an early case, the Supreme Court said that an amendment is operative at least from the moment it is proclaimed operative by the proper canvassing authorities and, in theory, from the moment the polls close. (People ex rel. Lynch v. Board of Supervisors, 100 Ill. 495 (1881).)

For the record, the fate of amendments since the adoption of Gateway in 1950 can be summarized as follows: Fifteen amendments have been submitted to the voters. Six carried and nine failed, but only one of the nine had more votes cast against it than for it. Five of the six that carried received a two-thirds' vote of those voting on the question, but three of them also received a majority vote of those voting in the election. One,

the Judicial Article, received a majority vote of those voting in the
election but failed to receive two-thirds of the votes cast on the amendment. So far, at least, the two-thirds' alternative has facilitated the
adoption of only two out of 15 proposed amendments. (See Kitsos, Constitutional Amendments and the Voter, 1952-1966 at 4 (1968).)

Comparative Analysis

Initiating the Amendment: Illinois is one of 35 states that permit an
amendment to be submitted to the voters after one passage through the
legislature. Eleven states require passage twice, almost invariably with
the requirement that a general election for the legislature intervene.
Three states have alternatives of two passages by simple majority or one
passage by an extraordinary majority, as follows: Connecticut (three-
fourths); Hawaii (two-thirds); and New Jersey (three-fifths). Delaware
requires passage by two-thirds' vote by two consecutive legislatures, but
no ratification by the voters.

The 35 states requiring only one passage of a proposed amendment
divide, as to size of vote, thus: two-thirds — 18, including Illinois; three-
fifths — eight; simple majority — nine, but in at least two of the states
there are certain circumstances when an extraordinary majority is required. All except three of the states requiring double passage call for
only a simple majority vote each time around. (The three exceptions
have combinations of majority and two-thirds as between houses of the
legislature and between first and second passage.)

Restrictions on Initiation: Only three states join Illinois in limiting
the frequency with which the same article may be amended: Kentucky
(every five years); Pennsylvania (same); New Jersey (every three general
elections). Five states join Illinois in limiting the number of amendments to be submitted at any one election: Arkansas, Kansas and Montana
(three); Colorado (six); Kentucky (two). Three states, Florida, Missouri,
and Oklahoma, have an equivalent of the "one subject to a bill" rule —
i.e., a single amendment may apply to only one article or one general
subject. (This restriction is different from the claim in the *Reeves* case
discussed above, for Section 2 used to allow only one article to be amended
at a time. Today, presumably, a single amendment could amend three
articles at once.) Vermont permits the legislature to propose amendments
only every tenth year. Prior to 1964, New Hampshire did not authorize
initiation of amendments by the legislature.

Voter Ratification: About 30 states call for approval by a majority of
the voters voting on the amendment and 11 appear to require a majority of those voting at the election. Rhode Island requires a 60 per cent
majority of those voting on the question, and Hawaii and Nebraska

require that the majority on the question be at least 35 per cent of the total vote cast. (A 35 per cent requirement would have constituted approval of all but one of the amendments that have failed since the Gateway Amendment was adopted and that one, in 1956, had more votes against it than in favor of it.) New Mexico allows approval by a majority of those voting on any amendment except one applying to or affecting either the Suffrage or the Education Article, in which case three-fourths of those voting in the election and two-thirds of those voting in each county must ratify. No other state appears to have the precise requirements of the Gateway Amendment.

United States Constitution: Article V provides that Congress by two-thirds' vote of each house may propose amendments subject to ratification by the legislatures or conventions of three-fourths of the states, "as the one or the other Mode of Ratification may be proposed by the Congress . . . ." There is also a proviso "that no State, without its Consent, shall be deprived of its equal Suffrage in the Senate." The only amendment ever proposed for ratification by convention was the Twenty-first, repealing prohibition.

Model State Constitution: The Model provides for legislative initiation of amendments by a simple majority of all the members and approval in a referendum by a majority of those voting on the question.

Amendment by Initiative: A third method of amendment is by initiative petition. Fourteen states authorize this method. There are, of course, a great many possible details involved in an initiative system, but for present purposes, it seems sufficient to quote the language of the Model State Constitution:

"*Amending Procedure: Proposals.*

" (a) Amendments to this constitution may be proposed by the legislature or by the initiative.

" (b) An amendment proposed by the legislature shall be agreed to by record vote of a majority of all of the members, which shall be entered on the journal.

" (c) An amendment by the initiative shall be incorporated by its sponsors in an initiative petition which shall contain the full text of the amendment proposed and which shall be signed by qualified voters equal in number to at least . . . . per cent of the total votes cast for governor in the last preceding gubernatorial election. Initiative petitions shall be filed with the secretary of the legislature.

" (d) An amendment proposed by the initiative shall be presented to the legislature if it is in session and, if it is not in session, when it convenes or reconvenes. If the proposal is agreed to by a majority vote of all the members, such vote shall be entered on the journal and the proposed amendment shall be submitted for adoption in the same manner as amendments proposed by the legislature.

" (e) The legislature may provide by law for a procedure for the withdrawal by its sponsors of an initiative petition at any time prior to its submission to the voters." (art. XII, § 12.01.)

"Amendment Procedure: Adoption.

" (a) The question of the adoption of a constitutional amendment shall be submitted to the voters at the first regular or special statewide election held no less than two months after it has been agreed to by the vote of the legislature and, in the case of amendments proposed by the initiative which have failed to receive such legislative approval, not less than two months after the end of the legislative session." (art. XII, § 12.02)

Comment

It has been argued that a decision on whether to make amendment difficult or easy depends upon whether a constitution is limited to truly fundamental matters or includes statutory details. It has also been said, in effect, that the foregoing argument confuses cause and effect, that constitutions with statutory detail get amended frequently whether or not the amending process is difficult and that true constitutions do not get amended frequently no matter how easy amendment is. It is not necessary to choose between these propositions, and it is probably not possible to settle the matter, anyway. The important thing to do is to keep one's eye on the ball by keeping statutory detail out of the constitutions.

A less controversial argument in constitutional theory is that, since a constitution is the people's fundamental law, they ought to retain the power to change it. Such a power exists, of course, in those states that mandate a periodic question on the ballot: Should there be a constitutional convention? But some would argue that this "all or nothing" power is not sufficient and that selective amendment by initiative petition is a proper supplement to the power to call a convention.

At the turn of the century, "initiative, referendum and recall" was all the rage as the latest thing for bringing democracy to the people. Over the years, the bloom has worn off and there is much less interest in initiative, referendum and recall as the answer to the ills of society. Indeed, it is ironical that the proponents of 70 years ago were the Populists and the radicals whereas today one is likely to find ultra-conservatives advocating initiative. This is simply to say, perhaps, that legislatures tend to be less unrepresentative of majority opinion than many critics claim.

Some may say, however, that the initiative's "black eye" has come from ill-advised legislation and that it remains appropriate to preserve initiative for constitutional amendments. This argument had a great deal more appeal before the one man-one vote cases came down, for it did seem difficult to induce legislators to commit political suicide by redistricting in a manner that the voters would undoubtedly prefer. But today, with that problem taken care of, the dangers of initiative seem to outweigh the claimed advantage of a bypass around an insensitive legislature. For the danger of the initiative route to constitutional amendment is that it will be used to adopt ill-advised legislation. In short, if you close the door to "crack-pot" laws but leave the constitutional window open, they will get in anyway. (By way of analogy, a behind-the-scenes development at the 1967 New York Constitutional Convention is instructive. New York is a "two session" amendment state, and it was proposed in committee to adopt the Connecticut approach of permitting submission after one session upon a three-fourths' vote of the total membership of each house. At the last minute, some legislative leaders suggested that such a change was ill-advised on the ground that frequently the first vote was taken under such pressure that an almost unanimous vote could be obtained for a "bad" amendment, whereas two years later things would have quieted down and there would be no difficulty in killing the proposal. It is this sort of high-pressure, emotional situation that creates problems in a state permitting initiative.)

In the discussion of Section 18 of Article IV (*supra,* p. 190), it was pointed out that a pending lawsuit attacks the "majority voting in the election" requirement for bond issues. If that lawsuit is successful, it does not necessarily follow that Section 2 would fall by the wayside since, under the Gateway Amendment, there is an alternative vote count for adoption under which failure to vote on the question is not a vote against the amendment. Nevertheless, consideration should be given to changing the rule here so that under no circumstance does a failure to vote necessarily count as a vote against the amendment. If a simple majority voting on the question is not deemed a high enough hurdle, then the requirement could be an extraordinary majority or an affirmative vote that was also equal to or in excess of some percentage, less than 50, of course, of those voting in the election. (As noted above, the percentage in Hawaii and Nebraska is 35.) In neither case, does a failure to vote necessarily count as a vote against the amendment.

SECTIONS SEPARATELY SUBMITTED

Illinois Central Railroad

No contract, obligation or liability whatever of the Illinois Central Railroad Company, to pay any money into the State treasury, nor any lien of the State upon, or right to tax property of said Company, in accordance with the provisions of the charter of said company, approved February tenth, in the year of our Lord one thousand eight hundred and fifty-one, shall ever be released, suspended, modified, altered, remitted or in any manner diminished or impaired by legislative or other authority; and all monies derived from said company, after payment of the State debt, shall be appropriated and set apart for the payment of the ordinary expenses of the state government, and for no other purposes whatever.

History

For several years prior to 1851, Illinois had attempted without success to get a railroad built in the state. Because of its unhappy financial condition it was unable to finance such a project. Finally in 1851, with the aid of the federal government, the Illinois Central Railroad project was undertaken. Over two and one-half million acres of lands were granted from the federal government to the state for railroad purposes. The state chartered the Illinois Central Railroad to build two lines totaling approximately 700 miles across the state. The charter gave to the company the lands received from the federal government plus a right of way across state lands. In return for these grants, Section 18 of the charter required the company to pay 5 per cent of its gross receipts to the state treasury. Section 22 of the charter fixed the tax liability of the company. All lands of the company were exempted from taxation until they were sold. Stock and other property of the company was exempted for six years, and after that was to be listed with the State Auditor and taxed for state purposes. If the state tax exceeded three-fourths of 1 per cent, the excess was to be deducted from gross receipts. The total of payments under Sections 18 and 22 was to be at least seven per cent of gross receipts. Section 22 expressly provided: "The said corporation is hereby exempted from all taxation of every kind, except as herein provided for." The revenue from the railroad was to be applied to the payment of the state

This section was included in the 1870 Constitution for two The state debt had by then largely been retired and there w that political pressure from the railroad might persuade to amend the charter and reduce the payments requir

Secondly, and more importantly, there was considerable agitation from the counties through which the railroad passed to have some of the railroad revenue returned to them since it was exempt from local taxes. But the majority of delegates felt that the fund should be applied solely to state purposes.

The section was retained in identical form in the proposed 1922 Constitution, although the question was again debated in that Convention as to whether the counties should receive part of the revenue.

Explanation

This section of the Constitution has not been judicially interpreted, since there has never been any legislative attempt to depart from its provisions. However, the charter provisions of the railroad have been litigated several times. The issues have concerned the method of accounting and the formula for the assessment of the tax. (*See* People v. Illinois Cent. R.R., 273 Ill. 220 (1916); State v. Illinois Cent. R.R., 246 Ill. 188 (1910).) It should be pointed out that the 1851 charter applies only to the so-called "charter lines" of the original grant. They do not apply to the lines and property acquired subsequently to the original charter, which of course constitute the bulk of the company's holdings and revenues. This property is subject to ordinary taxation.

The most recent decision of the Supreme Court in regard to the tax status of the railroad was in 1921 and is worthy of attention here because of its implications should it be determined not to retain the present section in the proposed new Constitution. (Illinois Cent. R.R. v. Emmerson, 299 Ill, 328 (1921).) In 1919 the legislature passed a comprehensive corporate franchise tax. With respect to railroads, the tax was measured by the percentage of its lines within the state in relation to its total length, averaged with the percentage of its business within the state to its total business. The C_____ held that while the tax could be applied to the Illin___ _____ _____ rter lines (about 1400 miles) it could not _____ (about 700 miles). Four reasons were given _____ ise tax was a property tax from which the _____ terms of its charter. (2) Even if it were _____ "taxation of every kind" would exempt _____ was a contract between the state and the _____ II, Section 14, which forbids impair- _____ g a legislative change in the tax pro- _____ n the authority of *Citizen's Bank v.* _____ arter and its tax provisions were pro- _____ he Constitution of the United States _____ f the obligations of contract.

Two questions of current interest arise in connection with the tax status of the Illinois Central Railroad. The more immediate one is whether the newly enacted state income tax is applicable to the charter lines. If the *Emmerson* case is to be taken literally, namely, that taxation of any kind other than as specified in the charter is forbidden, one would have to conclude that it is not. However, it might be argued that all of the Illinois Central litigation, including the *Emmerson* case if read narrowly, established only that the railroad was exempt from property taxes; and that property taxation was the only form of tax exemption which the legislature intended in its charter grant, as this was the only common form of taxation in 1851. Of course, the broad language of the Article II, Section 22, exemption militates against this interpretation. If the charter lines are exempt from the income tax, substantial accounting and legal problems will arise.

The other question posed by *Emmerson* is what the powers of the state would be with respect to the charter in the absence of this section of the Constitution. Here the Court was probably correct in its conclusion that the provisions of the state and federal constitutions protecting the obligations of contract would prevent the state from taking any unilateral action to amend the charter.

Comparative Analysis

There are no comparable provisions in other state constitutions.

Comment

This section could be retained as is.

It might be thought desirable now to amend the section so as to permit distribution of the revenue from the railroad tax to the counties through which it passes. At the time this section was adopted, the railroad tax represented as much as 15 per cent of the state revenue. However, in 1961, the tax was only 3.6 million dollars out of total state revenue, not including federal grants, of over one billion dollars. Today the percentage is unquestionably lower. Thus, it is currently a much less important item in state finances than formerly. The revenues would be of considerable value to the counties. Such an amendment would be permissible, since no contractual obligations under the charter would be impaired.

Finally, the section might be eliminated altogether. This would open the way for renegotiation of the charter between the state and the railroad if mutually agreeable terms could be found, or for unilateral action by the state to the extent permitted by the contract clauses of the state and federal constitutions. The elimination of the section would probably be vigorously opposed by the railroad.

Municipal Subscriptions to Railroads or Private Corporations

No county, city, town, township, or other municipality, shall ever become subscriber to the capital stock of any railroad or private corporation, or make donation to or loan its credit in aid of, such corporation: *Provided, however,* that the adoption of this article shall not be construed as affecting the right of any such municipality to make such subscriptions where the same have been authorized, under existing laws, by a vote of the people of such municipalities prior to such adoption.

History

Under the Constitution of 1848, Article III, Section 38, the state was prohibited from aiding private corporations. (See Art. IV, Sec. 20, *supra,* p. 197.) But this did not prevent counties and other municipalities from such undertakings, the principal form of which was subsidies to railroads. (Prettyman v. Supervisors of Tazewell County, 19 Ill. 406 (1858).) The competition among communities for railroads reached such proportions that many projects were very unsound financially and many municipalities were on the verge of bankruptcy. This section was proposed by the 1870 Convention to put an end to such practices, but was submitted separately so as not to endanger the rest of the Constitution. Although it engendered considerable controversy in the Convention debates, it was adopted by a large majority in the election.

This section was omitted in the proposed 1922 Constitution and the Proceedings of the Convention do not reveal why.

Explanation

This section is largely self-explanatory and was effective in stopping the practices complained of. For many years, the only litigation under this section involved the question of what subscriptions were valid under the saving clause. (*See* Louisville v. Savings Bank, 104 U.S. 469 (1881); Williams v. People *ex rel.* Wilson, 132 Ill. 574 (1890); Richeson v. People *ex rel.* Jones, 115 Ill. 450 (1886); People *ex. rel.* Springfield, E. & S. R.R. v. Town of Bishop, 111 Ill. 124 (1884).)

Since 1900, the section has been used sporadically to attack various public projects undertaken by municipalities, but these attacks have uniformly failed for one or more of three reasons. First, the section does not prohibit all dealings between municipalities and private corporations. If there is a fair exchange of values between the municipality and the corporation — *i.e.,* if the corporation gives consideration for the benefits it receives — then there is no violation of this section. (People *ex rel.* Gutknecht v. City of Chicago, 414 Ill. 600 (1953); City of Chicago v. Pittsburg, C.C. & St. L. Ry., 244 Ill. 220 (1910). *Compare* Schuler v. Board of Educ., 370 Ill. 107 (1938), where there was no consideration; this is the only modern case finding a violation of this section.) Secondly, it does not violate this section for municipalities to allow private corporations to use public facilities to carry on their business, where a reasonable charge is made for that use. (People *ex rel.* Curren v. Wood, 391 Ill. 237 (1945) (airports); People v. City of Chicago, 349 Ill. 304 (1932) (subways).) Finally, the section prohibits municipal aid only to corporations having a capital stock or being organized for profit; it does not apply to *nonprofit* organizations or municipal corporations. (People *ex rel.* Adamowski v. Chicago R.R. Terminal Authority, 14 Ill. 2d 230 (1958) (municipal services made available to municipal corporation); People *ex rel.* Adamowski v. Public Bldg. Comm'n, 11 Ill. 2d 125 (1957) (loan of municipal personnel and grant of property to public corporation); People *ex rel.* Royal v. Cain, 410 Ill. 39 (1951) (public hospital districts not within section); Cremer v. Peoria Housing Authority, 399 Ill. 579 (1948) (subsidy to nonprofit housing development)).

Comparative Analysis

Eighteen state constitutions have provisions similar to the Illinois provision. In two states, municipal aid to corporations is prohibited unless approved by referendum. In one state only aid to railroads is prohibited, while another state prohibits aid to all private corporations except railroads. The Model State Constitution does not consider the subject.

Comment

This section seems harmless, although its contemporary utility might be doubted. Consideration could be given to eliminating it for the sake of simplicity. The subject could, of course, be covered by legislation.

Canal

The Illinois and Michigan canal or other canal or waterway owned by the State may be sold or leased upon such terms as may be prescribed by law. The General Assembly may appropriate for the operation and maintenance of canals and waterways owned by the State.

History

This section was amended in 1954, replacing the separate section on canals as originally adopted in 1870 and amended in 1908.

The Illinois and Michgian Canal, connecting the Illinois River with Lake Michigan, was open for navigation in 1848. Its operation was highly successful, and in 1871 its original cost was paid off. The original section on canals prevented the General Assembly from leasing or selling the canal, unless approved by a referendum. This was designed to prevent the railroads from obtaining control over the canal and drying it up to suppress competition. The original section also prohibited the General

Assembly from appropriating funds or lending credit in aid of railroads or canals. This was intended to make the canal self-supporting. The 1908 Amendment allowed a bond issue for the construction of a deep waterway from Utica to Lockport.

The 1922 Convention proposal dealt extensively with canals and waterways, providing, among other things, for an additional $10,000,000 appropriation, payable by a bond issue, for deepening the waterway; prohibiting sale or lease of a state-owned waterway or canal without referendum approval, except as a lease of all or part of the Illinois and Michigan Canal was permitted to provide terminals with the Illinois Waterway or other navigable channels.

Explanation

This section as it now stands has never been the subject of litigation. Decisions interpreting the prior provisions were few and have no current relevance. By its terms, the present section gives the General Assembly full control over the subject.

Comparative Analysis

Eleven other states have constitutional provisions regulating canals in some way, none of which is comparable to the Illinois provision.

Comment

As it now stands, this section is entirely legislative in nature and can be safely eliminated.

Convict Labor

Hereafter it shall be unlawful for the Commissioners of any Penitentiary, or other reformatory institution in the State of Illinois, to let by contract to any person, or persons, or corporations, the labor of any convict confined within said institution.

History

There seems to have been some confusion in the 1870 Convention about convict labor. A Stonecutters' Association sent in a petition protesting the use of convict labor on public works. The petition was referred to the Committee on Penitentiary and Reformatory Institutions. A petition from another Stonecutters' Association endorsing the first petition was referred to the Committee on Mines and Mining. A delegate's resolution on the same subject was referred to the Committee on State Institutions and Public Buildings. There were two other resolutions objecting to the use of convict labor, both of which were referred to the Committee on Penitentiary and Reformatory Institutions. Nobody appears to have taken any action on any of the petitions and resolutions.

The separate section was proposed by the General Assembly in 1885 and ratified by the voters at the general election in November, 1886. In the proposed 1922 Constitution the wording was simplified and the section was placed in the Legislative Article.

Explanation
No questions appear to have arisen over this section.

Comparative Analysis
About eight states have constitutional prohibitions against contracting out convict labor. The Model State Constitution is silent on the subject.

Comment
Although this sort of provision should never have gone into the Constitution and is clearly unnecessary now, it is just the sort of provision that probably cannot safely be taken out. Although it is poorly drafted as a constitutional provision, it is probably not advisable to tamper with the wording. If it does seem safe to fix up the language, the proposed 1922 provision is a good one to start with. It read:

No law shall be passed authorizing the labor of any convict confined within any penitentiary or other reformatory institution to be let to any corporation, association or person. (art. III, § 50.)

SCHEDULES

SCHEDULE — Year 1870

That no inconvenience may arise from the alterations and amendments made in the constitution of this State, and to carry the same into complete effect, it is hereby ordained and declared:

Existing Laws Continued

Section 1. That all laws in force at the adoption of this Constitution, not inconsistent therewith, and all rights, actions, prosecutions, claims, and contracts of this State, individuals, or bodies corporate, shall continue to be as valid as if this Constitution had not been adopted.

Accrued Items Due State Preserved

Section 2. That all fines, taxes, penalties and forfeitures, due and owing to the State of Illinois under the present Constitution and laws, shall inure to the use of the people of the State of Illinois, under this Constitution.

Existing Recognizances and Bonds Preserved — Prosecutions Continued

Section 3. Recognizances, bonds, obligations, and all other instruments entered into or executed before the adoption of this constitution, to the people of the State of Illinois, to any State or County officer or public body, shall remain binding and valid; and rights and liabilities upon the same shall continue, and all crimes and misdemeanors shall be tried and punished as though no change had been made in the Constitution of this State.

Existing County Courts Continued

Section 4. County courts for the transaction of county business in counties not having adopted township organization, shall continue in existence, and exercise their present jurisdiction until the board of county commissioners provided in this Constitution, is organized in pursuance of an Act of the General Assembly; and the county courts in all other counties shall have the same power and jurisdiction they now possess until otherwise provided by general law.

Other Courts Continued

Section 5. All existing courts which are not in this Constitution specifically enumerated, shall continue in existence and exercise their present jurisdiction until otherwise provided by law.

Existing Offices Continued

Section 6. All persons now filling any office or appointment shall continue in the exercise of the duties thereof, according to their respective commissions or appointments, unless by this Constitution it is otherwise directed.

Election of Judges

Section 7. On the day this Constitution is submitted to the people for ratification, an election shall be held for judges of the Supreme Court in the second, third, sixth and seventh judicial election districts designated in this Constitution, and for the election of three judges of the Circuit Court in the County of Cook as provided for in the article of this Constitution relating to the Judiciary, at which election every person entitled to vote, according to the terms of this Constitution, shall be allowed to vote, and the election shall be otherwise conducted, returns made and certificates issued, in accordance with existing laws, except that no registry shall be required at said election: *Provided*, that at said election in the county of Cook no elector shall vote for more than two candidates for circuit judge. If, upon canvassing the votes for and against the adoption of this Constitution, it shall appear that there has been polled a greater number of votes against than for it, then no certificates of election shall be issued for any of said Supreme or Circuit Judges.

Date and Method of Submission

Section 8. This Constitution shall be submitted to the people of the State of Illinois for adoption or rejection, at an election to be held on the first Saturday in July in the year of our Lord one thousand eight hundred and seventy, and there shall be separately submitted at the same time for adoption or rejection, sections nine, ten, eleven, twelve, thirteen, fourteen and fifteen, relating to railroads, in the article entitled "Corporations;" the article entitled "Counties;" the article entitled "Warehouses;" the question of requiring a three-fifths vote to remove a county seat; the section relating to the Illinois Central Railroad; the section in relation to minority representation; the section relating to Municipal subscriptions to railroads or private corporations; and the section relating to the Canal. Every person entitled to vote under the provisions of this Constitution, as defined in the article in relation to "Suffrage," shall be entitled to vote for the adoption or rejection of this Constitution, and for or against the articles, sections and question aforesaid, separately submitted; and the said qualified electors shall vote at the usual places of voting, unless otherwise provided; and the said election shall be conducted, and returns thereof made according to the laws now in force regulating general elections, except that no registry shall be required at said election: *Provided, however,* that the polls shall be kept open for the reception of ballots until sunset of said day of election.

Ballots and Election Supplies

Section 9. The Secretary of State shall, at least twenty days before said election, cause to be delivered to the County Clerk of each county blank pollbooks, tally lists and forms of return, and twice the number of properly prepared printed ballots for the said election that there are voters in such county, the expense whereof shall be audited and paid as other public printing ordered by the Secretary of State is, by law, required to be audited and paid; and the several county clerks shall, at least five days before said election, cause to be distributed to the board of election, in each election district in their respective counties, said blank poll-books, tally-lists, forms of return, and tickets.

Form of Ballot

Section 10. At the said election the ballots shall be in the following form:

For all the propositions on this ticket which are not cancelled with ink or pencil; and against all propositions which are so cancelled.

For the New Constitution.

For the sections relating to railroads in the article entitled "Corporations."

For the article entitled "Counties."

For the article entitled "Warehouses."

For a three-fifths vote to remove County Seats.

For the section to the Illinois Central Railroad.

For the section relating to Minority Representation.

For the section relating to Municipal Subscriptions to Railroads or Private Corporations.

For the section relating to the Canal.

Each of said tickets shall be counted as a vote cast for each proposition thereon not cancelled with ink or pencil, and against each proposition so cancelled, and returns thereof shall be made accordingly by the judges of election.

Canvass of Election Returns

Section 11. The returns of the whole vote cast, and of the votes for the adoption or rejection of this Constitution, and for or against the article and sections respectively submitted, shall be made by the several County Clerks, as is now provided by law, to the Secretary of State, within twenty days after the election, and the returns of the said votes shall, within five days thereafter, be examined and canvassed by the Auditor, Treasurer and Secretary of State, or any two of them, in the presence of the Governor, and proclamation shall be made by the Governor, forthwith, of the result of the canvass.

Effective Date

Section 12. If it shall appear that a majority of the votes polled are "For the New Constitution," then so much of this Constitution as was not separately submitted to be voted on by articles and sections, shall be the supreme law of the State of Illinois, on and after Monday the eighth day of August, in the year of our Lord one thousand eight hundred and seventy; but if it shall appear that a majority of the votes polled were "Against the New Constitution," then so much thereof as was not separately submitted to be voted on by articles and sections, shall be null and void.

If it shall appear that a majority of the votes polled, are "for the sections relating to Railroads in the article entitled 'Corporations';" sections nine, ten, eleven, twelve, thirteen, fourteen and fifteen, relating to Railroads in the said article, shall be a part of the Constitution of this State; but if a majority of said votes are against such sections, they shall be null and void. If a majority of the votes polled are "for the article entitled "Counties," such article shall be a part of the Constitution of this State and shall be substituted for article seven in the present constitution entitled "counties;" but if a majority of said votes are against such article, the same shall be null and void. If a majority of the votes polled are for the article entitled "Warehouses," such article shall be a part of the Constitution of this State, but if a majority of the votes are against said article, the same shall be null and void. If a majority of the votes polled are for either of the sections separately submitted, relating, respectively, to the "Illinois Central Railroad," "Minority Representation," "Municipal Subscriptions to Railroads or Private Corporations," and the "Canal," then such of said sections as shall receive such majority shall be a part of the Constitution of this State; but each of said sections so separately submitted against which, respectively, there shall be a majority of the votes polled, shall be null and void: *Provided*, that the section relating to "Minority Representation," shall not be declared adopted unless the portion of the Constitution not separately submitted to be voted on by articles and sections shall be adopted, and in case said section relating to "Minority Representation" shall become a portion of the Constitution, it shall be substituted for sections seven and eight of the Legislative Article. If a majority of the votes cast at such election shall be for a three-fifths vote to remove a

County seat, then the words "a majority" shall be stricken out of section four of the Article on Counties, and the words "three-fifths" shall be inserted in lieu thereof; and the following words shall be added to said section, to-wit: "But when an attempt is made to remove a county seat to a point nearer to the center of a county, then a majority vote only shall be necessary." If the foregoing proposition shall not receive a majority of the votes, as aforesaid, then the same shall have no effect whatever.

First Apportionment of House of Representatives

Section 13. Immediately after the adoption of this Constitution, the Governor and Secretary of State shall proceed to ascertain and fix the apportionment of the State for members of the first House of Representatives under this Constitution. The apportionment shall be based upon the Federal census of the year of our Lord one thousand eight hundred and seventy of the State of Illinois, and shall be made strictly in accordance with the rules and principles announced in the article on the Legislative Department of this Constitution: *Provided,* That in case the Federal census aforesaid can not be ascertained prior to Friday, the twenty-third day of September, in the year of our Lord one thousand eight hundred and seventy, then the said apportionment shall be based on the State census of the year of our Lord one thousand eight hundred and sixty-five, in accordance with the rules and principles aforesaid. The Governor shall, on or before Wednesday, the twenty-eighth day of September, in the year of our Lord one thousand eight hundred and seventy, make official announcement of the said apportionment, under the great Seal of the State; and one hundred copies thereof, duly certified, shall be forthwith transmitted by the Secretary of State to each county clerk for distribution.

Districts on First Apportionment

Section 14. The districts shall be regularly numbered, by the Secretary of State, commencing with Alexander County as Number one, and proceeding then northwardly through the State, and terminating with the county of Cook; but no county shall be numbered as more than one district, except the county of Cook, which shall constitute three districts, each embracing the territory contained in the now existing representative districts of said county. And on the Tuesday after the first Monday in November, in the year of our Lord one thousand eight hundred and [and] seventy, the members of the first House of Representatives under this Constitution shall be elected according to the apportionment fixed and announced as aforesaid, and shall hold their offices for two years, and until their successors shall be elected and qualified.

Senate at First Session

Section 15.   The Senate, at its first session under this Constitution, shall consist of fifty members, to be chosen as follows: At the General Election held on the first Tuesday after the first Monday of November, in the year of our Lord one thousand eight hundred and seventy, two Senators shall be elected in districts where the term of Senators expire on the first Monday of January, in the year of our Lord one thousand eight hundred and seventy-one, or where there shall be a vacancy, and in the remaining districts one Senator shall be elected. Senators so elected shall hold their office two years.

Apportionment by New General Assembly

Section 16.   The General Assembly, at its first session held after the adoption of this Constitution, shall proceed to apportion the State for members of the Senate and House of Representatives, in accordance with the provisions of the article on the Legislative Department.

First Election Under New Constitution

Section 17.   When this constitution shall be ratified by the people, the Governor shall forthwith, after having ascertained the fact, issue writs of election to the sheriffs of the several counties of this State, or in case of vacancies, to the coroners, for the election of all the officers, the time of whose election is fixed by this Constitution or schedule, and it shall be the duty of said sheriffs or coroners to give such notice of the time and place of said election as is now prescribed by law.

English to be Official Language

Section 18.   All laws of the State of Illinois, and all official writings, and the Executive, Legislative and Judicial proceedings, shall be conducted, preserved and published in no other than the English language.

Laws to Make Constitution Effective

Section 19.   The General Assembly shall pass all laws necessary to carry into effect the provisions of this Constitution.

Circuit Clerk as Recorders

Section 20.   The circuit clerks of the different counties having a population over sixty thousand, shall continue to be Recorders (ex-officio) for their respective counties, under this Constitution, until the expiration of their respective terms.

Judges' Salaries — Cook County

Section 21.   The judges of all courts of record in Cook county shall, in lieu of any salary provided for in this Constitution, receive the compensation now provided by law until the adjournment of the first session of the General Assembly after the adoption of this Constitution.

Circuit Court — Lake County

Section 22. The present judge of the circuit court of Cook county shall continue to hold the circuit court of Lake county until otherwise provided by law.

Certain Tax Discontinued

Section 23. When this constitution shall be adopted, and take effect as the supreme law of the State of Illinois, the two-mill tax provided to be annually assessed and collected upon each dollar's worth of taxable property, in addition to all other taxes, as set forth in article fifteen of the now existing constitution, shall cease to be assessed after the year of our Lord one thousand eight hundred and seventy.

City of Quincy — Provision Concerning

Section 24. Nothing contained in this Constitution shall be so construed as to deprive the General Assembly of power to authorize the city of Quincy to create any indebtedness for railroad or municipal purposes for which the people of said city shall have voted and to which they shall have given by such vote, their consent, prior to the thirteenth day of December, in the year of our Lord one thousand eight hundred and sixty-nine; *Provided*, that no such indebtedness, so created, shall, in any part thereof be paid by the State, or from any State revenue tax or fund, but the same shall be paid, if at all, by the said City of Quincy alone, and by taxes to be levied upon the taxable property thereof: *and provided, further,* that the General Assembly shall have no power in the premises, that it could not exercise under the present Constitution of this State.

Prior Constitution to Cease

Section 25. In case this Constitution, and the articles and sections submitted separately, be adopted, the existing Constitution shall cease in all its provisions, and in case this Constitution be adopted and any one or more of the articles or sections submitted separately be defeated, the provisions of the existing Constitution, if any, on the same subject shall remain in force.

Temporary Provisions to Take Effect

Section 26. The provisions of this Constitution required to be executed prior to the adoption or rejection thereof, shall take effect and be in force immediately.

* * *

SCHEDULE — Year 1954
(Reapportionment)
(Article IV, Sections 6, 7 and 8)

While this amendment of Sections 6, 7 and 8 of Article IV, if adopted, shall be effective upon its adoption, nevertheless the General Assembly meeting in 1955 or 1956 shall consist of fifty-one Senators and one hundred and fifty-three representatives as provided in Sections 6, 7 and 8 of Article IV of the 1870 constitution of Illinois before the adoption of this amendment.

If the 1955 General Assembly in its regular session redistricts and re-apportions, as required, or if upon its failure the commission does so, then those senators, who are still residents in odd numbered districts and who were elected in 1954, will retain their offices until the expiration of their terms. But in those odd numbered districts, as created in 1955, where no senator elected in 1954 has been a resident for one year next preceding the election in 1956, a vacancy in the office of senator for such districts exists. Likewise, a vacancy exists in the office of senator in such odd numbered districts where two or more senators elected in 1954 are residents of the district. In either case, a senator in such an odd-numbered district shall be elected in 1956 for a term expiring in 1958. The main purpose of this schedule is to provide for a senate with a full quota of members in 1957-1958.

Any senator elected in 1954, who is eliminated from his office by the redistricting, and who is not re-elected in 1956 for the two-year term, shall be paid the salary for 1957-1958, that he would have received if he had been able to serve the full term of his office and shall receive such other benefits as would have accrued if he had served such term.

SCHEDULE — Year 1954
(State Treasurer)
(Article V, Sections 1, 2 and 3)

This amendment shall first apply to the office of the treasurer elected in November, 1958.

SCHEDULE — YEAR 1962
(Judiciary)
(Article VI)

Paragraph 1. This Article and Schedule, with the exception of Schedule provisions expressly authorizing or directing earlier action, shall become effective on January 1, 1964, hereinafter called the "Effective Date." After the adoption of this Article the General Assembly shall enact such laws and make such appropriations and the Supreme Court shall make such rules as may be necessary or proper to give effect to its provisions.

Paragraph 2. Except to the extent inconsistent with the provisions of this Article, all provisions of law and rules of court in force on the Effective Date of this Article shall continue in effect until superseded in a manner authorized by the Constitution.

Paragraph 3. Until changed by law, (a) The Second Judicial District consists of the Counties of Jo Daviess, Stephenson, Carroll, Ogle, Lee, Winnebago, Boone, McHenry, Lake, DeKalb, Kane, Kendall, and DuPage; the Third Judicial District consists of the Counties of Mercer, Rock Island, Whiteside, Henry, Bureau, LaSalle, Grundy, Stark, Putnam, Marshall, Peoria, Tazewell, Will, Kankakee, Iroquois, Henderson, Warren, Knox, Fulton, McDonough, and Hancock; the Fourth Judicial District consists of the Counties of Adams, Pike, Calhoun, Schuyler, Brown, Cass, Mason, Menard, Morgan, Scott, Greene, Jersey, Macoupin, Sangamon, Logan, McLean, Woodford, Livingston, Ford, DeWitt, Macon, Piatt, Moultrie, Champaign, Douglas, Vermilion, Edgar, Coles, Cumberland, and Clark; and the Fifth Judicial District consists of all the counties south of the Fourth District; and

(b) the existing judicial circuits shall be continued.

Paragraph 4. Each supreme court judge, circuit judge, superior court judge, county judge, probate judge, judge of any city, village or incorporated town court, chief justice and judge of any municipal court, justice of the peace and police magistrate, in office on the Effective Date of this Article, shall continue to hold office until the expiration of his term, as follows:

(a) Judges of the Supreme Court shall continue as judges of said court.

(b) Circuit judges shall continue as circuit judges of the several circuit courts.

(c) In Cook County, the judges of the Superior Court, the Probate Court, the County Court, and the Chief Justice of the Municipal Court of Chicago shall be circuit judges; the judges of the Municipal Court of Chicago, and the judges of the several municipal, city, village and incorporated town courts shall be associate judges of the Circuit Court.

(d) In counties other than the county of Cook, the county judges, probate judges, and the judges of municipal, city, village and incorporated town courts shall be associate judges of the Circuit Court.

(e) Police magistrates and justices of the peace shall be magistrates of the several circuit courts, and unless otherwise provided by law shall continue to perform their non-judicial functions for the remainder of their respective terms.

(f) The provisions of this Article governing eligibility for office shall not affect the right of any incumbent to continue in office for the remainder of his existing term pursuant to the provisions of this paragraph. For the remainder of such existing term, the provisions of this Article concerning prohibited activities shall not apply to a judge of a county, probate, city, village or incorporated town court, a justice of the peace or police magistrate.

Paragraph 5.   On the Effective Date of this Article,

(a) All justice of the peace courts, police magistrate courts, city, village and incorporated town courts, municipal courts, county courts, probate courts, the Superior Court of Cook County, the Criminal Court of Cook County and the Municipal Court of Chicago are abolished and all their jurisdiction, judicial functions, powers and duties are transferred to the respective circuit courts, and until otherwise provided by law non-judicial functions vested by law in county courts or the judges thereof are transferred to the circuit courts;

(b) All the jurisdiction, functions, powers and duties of the several appellate courts shall be transferred to the Appellate Court provided for in this Article, in the appropriate district.

(c) Each court into which jurisdiction of other courts is transferred shall succeed to and assume jurisdiction of all causes, matters and proceedings then pending, with full power and authority to dispose of them and to carry into execution or otherwise to give effect to all orders, judgments and decrees theretofore entered by the predecessor courts.

(d) The files, books, papers, records, documents, moneys, securities, and other property in the possession, custody or under the control of the courts hereby abolished, or any officer thereof, are transferred to the Circuit Court; and thereafter all proceedings in all courts shall be matters of record.

Paragraph 6.   Each clerk of court in office on the Effective Date of this Article shall continue to hold office, until the expiration of his existing term as follows:

(a) The clerk of the Supreme Court shall continue in such office.

(b) The clerks of the several appellate courts shall continue as clerks of the Appellate Court and shall perform such services as may be prescribed by order of the Supreme Court.

(c) In Cook County, the Circuit Court shall by rule designate one of the clerks as clerk and the others as associate clerks to perform such services as may be prescribed by rule of the Circuit Court.

(d) In judicial circuits outside Cook County, the clerks of the circuit courts in their respective counties shall continue in said offices, and the clerks of the other courts of record shall be associate clerks of the circuit court in their respective counties, shall perform such services as may be prescribed by rule of the Circuit Court and shall continue to perform other duties prescribed by law.

Paragraph 7. On the Effective Date of this Article, the bailiff of the Municipal Court of Chicago shall continue in office for the remainder of his term, and he, his deputies and assistants shall perform such services as may be prescribed by rule of the Circuit Court.

Paragraph 8. Notwithstanding the provisions of Section 8 of this Article, masters in chancery and referees in office in any court on the Effective Date of this Article shall be continued as masters in chancery or referees, respectively, until the expiration of their terms, and may thereafter by order of court, wherever justice requires, conclude matters in which testimony has been received.

Paragraph 9. Until otherwise prescribed by the General Assembly, the cases assigned to magistrates shall be those within the jurisdiction of justices of the peace and police magistrates immediately prior to the Effective Date of this Article.

Paragraph 10. Notwithstanding the terms of office provided in this Schedule and unless otherwise provided by law, of the twelve judges of the Appellate Court initially elected from the first Appellate Court district pursuant to Section 10 of this Article, four shall be elected for a term of ten years, four for a term of eight years and four for a term of six years; and of the three judges of the Appellate Court so initially elected for the Second, Third, Fourth and Fifth Judicial districts respectively one shall be elected for a term of ten years, one for a term of eight years and one for a term of six years.

Paragraph 11. The Supreme Court shall assign judges of the circuit courts and of the Superior Court of Cook County to serve on the Appellate Court, in the Appellate Court Districts in which they respectively reside, from the Effective Date of this Article until the commencement of the terms of judges of the Appellate Court selected pursuant to Section 10 of this Article.

Paragraph 12.

(a) Those elected judges in offce on January 1, 1963 shall be entitled to seek retention in office under Section 11 of this Article.

(b) The terms of all judges in office on January 1, 1963 expiring otherwise than on the first Monday in December in an even numbered year are extended to the first Monday in December after the general election following the date at which such terms would otherwise expire. For the purpose of application of any laws providing for an increase in judicial salaries, every judge whose term is thus extended shall be regarded as commencing a new term on the date prescribed by prior law for the election of his successor.

(c) Judges in office on the Effective Date shall not be subject to compulsory retirement at a prescribed age until after expiration of their then current terms.

Paragraph 13.

(a) Notwithstanding the provisions of Section 4 of this Article, elections on declarations of candidacy of judges of the Supreme Court in office on the Effective Date shall be held in the Judicial Districts established under Section 3 as follows:

   (i) For incumbents from the former First and Second Supreme Court Districts, in the Fifth Judicial District;

   (ii) For incumbent from the former Third Supreme Court District, in the Fourth Judicial District;

   (iii) For incumbents from the former Fourth and Fifth Supreme Court Districts, in the Third Judicial District;

   (iv) For incumbent from the former Sixth Supreme Court District, in the Second Judicial District;

   (v) For incumbent from the former Seventh Supreme Court District, in the First Judicial District.

(b) The first vacancy in the office of judge of the Supreme Court which occurs in the former First and Second Supreme Court Districts, and the first vacancy which occurs in the former Fourth and Fifth Supreme Court Districts, and the vacancy which occurs in the former Seventh Supreme Court District shall be filled by the selection of residents of the First Judicial District created under Section 3 of this Article.

(c) The office of any judge shall be deemed vacant upon his death, resignation, removal, retirement, or failure to be retained in office pursuant to Section 11 of this Article.

TABLE OF CASES

LIST OF SECONDARY SOURCES CITED

Advisory Commission on Intergovernmental Relations, Federal-State Coordination of Personal Income Taxes (1965), 433

E. Anthony, The Constitutional History of Illinois (1891), 262

Banzhaf, "Multi-Member Electoral Districts — Do They Violate the 'One Man, One Vote' Principle?" 75 Yale L.J. 1309 (1966), 140

Black's Law Dictionary (4th ed. rev. 1968), 427

Blomquist, "Effect of Curative Statutes on Taxation in Illinois," 27 Chi.-Kent L. Rev. 211 (1949), 473

Chicago Home Rule Commission, Modernizing A City Government (1954), 469

Choper, "The Establishment Clause and Aid to Parochial Schools," 56 Cal. L. Rev. 260 (1968), 407

Citizens Conference on State Legislatures, State Constitutional Provisions Affecting Legislatures (May 1967), 126, 224

Cohn, "Constitutional Limitations on Income Taxation in Illinois," 1961 U. Ill. L.F. 586; 422, 434

Cohn, "The Process of Legislation," 1963 U. Ill. L.F. 27; 154, 163

Cohn, "Public Employee Retirement Plans — The Nature of the Employees' Rights," 1968 U. Ill. L. F. 32; 197

Comment, "Curative Tax Legislation," 32 Ill. L. Rev. 456 (1937), 473

Comment, "Judicial Treatment of Tax Anticipation Warrants in Illinois," 45 Ill. L. Rev. 653 (1950), 467

Council of State Governments, The Book of the States, 1968-69 (1968), 258, 358, 386, 387

J. Dillon, Municipal Corporations (5th ed. 1911), 195

R. Dishman, State Constitutions: The Shape of the Document (1968), 97, 538

Dolan, "Consequential Damages in Federal Condemnation," 35 Va. L. Rev. 1059 (1949), 63

Eaton, "Present Problems of Article XIII," 17 De Paul L. Rev. 545 (1968), 547

Elson, "Constitutional Revision and Reorganization of the General Assembly," 33 Ill. L. Rev. 15 (1938), 154

N. Garvey, The Government and Administration of Illinois (1958), 522, 274

Gove, "The Business of the Legislature," 1963 U. Ill. L. F. 52; 166

Harbert, "Tax Foreclosures and Tax Titles," 1952 U. Ill. L. F. 209; 451

Howards, "Property Tax Rate Limits," in Report of the Commission on Revenue 521 (1963), 460

Hubbard, "Special Legislation for Municipalities," 18 Harv. L. Rev. 588 (1905), 210

Illinois Legislative Council, Research Department, Publication 134, Constitutional Mandates for Uniformity of Taxation (1959), 432

Kales, "Special Legislation as Defined in the Illinois Cases," 1 Ill. L. Rev. 63 (1906), 209, 210

Kauper, "The Constitutionality of Tax Exemptions for Religious Activities," in The Wall Between Church and State (D. Oaks ed. 1963), 445

Kalven, "Invoking the Fifth Amendment: Some Legal and Practical Considerations," 9 Bull. Atom Sciences 181, 182 (1953), 44

T. Kitsos, Constitutional Amendments and the Voter, 1952-1966 (1968), 568

Korbel, "Do the Federal Income Tax Laws Involve an 'Establishment of Religion?'" 53 A.B.A.J. 1018 (1967), 446

Lavery, "The Boundaries Article of the Illinois Constitution," 16 Ill. L. Rev. 361 (1922), 3, 4

Lucas, "Nonproperty Taxes Under the Illinois Constitution," 25 U. Chi. L. Rev. 63 (1957), 414

"Methods of Establishing 'Just Compensation' in Eminent Domain Proceedings in Illinois: A Symposium," 1957 U. Ill. L. F. 289; 63

Nichols, "Bill-Drafting in Illinois," 41 Ill. Bar J. 136 (1952), 166

Note, "The First Amendment and Financial Aid to Religion: Limits on the Government's Conduct," 61 Nw. U. L. Rev. 777 (1966), 446

P. Pack, Comparative Analysis of the Michigan Constitution (1961), 538

Righeimer, "The Law of Eminent Domain," 43 Ill. Bar. J. 206 (1954), 57

Schaefer, "Police Interrogation and the Privilege Against Self-Incrimination," 61 NW. L. Rev. 506 (1966), 50

G. Schmutz, Condemnation Appraisal Handbook (1963), 63

J. Scurlock, Retroactive Legislation Affecting Interest in Land (1953), 67

Smith, "Retroactive Laws and Vested Rights," 5 Tex. L. Rev. 231 (1927), 67

Smith-Hurd, Illinois Annotated Statutes, Constitution, Articles I-V (1964), 214

G. Steiner and S. Gove, Legislative Politics in Illinois (1960), 143

Van Alstyne, "Tax Exemption of Church Property," 20 Ohio St. L. J. 461 (1959), 444

J. Wigmore, VIII Wigmore on Evidence §§ 2250-2284 (1961), 50

Young, "Constitutional Problems," in Report of the Commission on Revenue 354 (1963), 422, 434

(A list of extensively used sources, without page references, is at p. viii in the Preface.)

INDEX